Los Angeles in the 1930s

The publisher gratefully acknowledges the generous support of the Lisa See Endowment Fund in Southern California History of the University of California Press Foundation.

LOS ANGELES IN THE 1930s

The WPA Guide to the City of Angels

Federal Writers Project of the
Works Progress Administration

INTRODUCTION BY DAVID KIPEN

University of California Press
Berkeley   Los Angeles   London

The publisher gratefully acknowledges the generous support of the Lisa See Endowment Fund in Southern California History of the University of California Press Foundation.

University of California Press, one of the most distinguished university presses in the United States, enriches lives around the world by advancing scholarship in the humanities, social sciences, and natural sciences. Its activities are supported by the UC Press Foundation and by philanthropic contributions from individuals and institutions. For more information, visit www.ucpress.edu.

University of California Press
Berkeley and Los Angeles, California

University of California Press, Ltd.
London, England

ISBN 978-0-520-26883-8 (paper : alk. paper)
Library of Congress Control Number: 2010940089

19 18 17 16 15 14 13 12 11
10 9 8 7 6 5 4 3 2 1

Manufactured in the United States of America

This book is printed on Cascades Enviro 100, a 100% post consumer waste, recycled, de-inked fiber. FSC recycled certified and processed chlorine free. It is acid free, Ecologo certified, and manufactured by BioGas energy.

Contents

	Page
LIST OF ILLUSTRATIONS	ix
LIST OF MAPS	xiii
THE WPA GUIDE TO RENAISSANCE FLORENCE, OR A WRITER'S PARADISE. BY DAVID KIPEN	xix
PREFACE 1941	xxxi
GENERAL INFORMATION	xxxiii
HOTEL AND OTHER ACCOMMODATIONS	xli
RESTAURANTS	xliii
NIGHT CLUBS	xlvii
RECREATIONAL FACILITIES	li
CALENDAR OF ANNUAL EVENTS	lvii

Part I. Los Angeles: A General Survey

THE CONTEMPORARY SCENE	3
NATURAL SETTING	10
PUEBLO TO METROPOLIS	24
EDUCATION	61
RELIGION	67
THE MOVIES	73
RADIO	98
THE ARTS	103
THE BUSINESS OF PLEASURE	134

Part II. Los Angeles Points of Interest

DOWNTOWN LOS ANGELES	145
THE INDUSTRIAL SECTION	161
THE NORTH AND EAST SECTIONS	169

Page

THE NORTHWEST SECTION 176
THE WILSHIRE AND WEST SECTIONS 181
THE SOUTHWEST SECTION 187

Part III. Neighboring Cities

BEVERLY HILLS 197
GLENDALE 206
THE HARBOR: SAN PEDRO AND WILMINGTON 214
HOLLYWOOD 227
LONG BEACH AND SIGNAL HILL 238
PASADENA 254
SANTA MONICA 265

Part IV. The Country Around Los Angeles

TOUR 1 Los Angeles—San Marino—Arcadia—Monrovia—Azusa—
Claremont—Upland—San Bernardino—Arrowhead Hot
Springs—Lake Arrowhead—Big Bear Lake—Pine Knot
Village [N. Main St., Macy St., Mission Rd., Hunting-
ton Dr., N., US 66, State 18] 277

TOUR 1A South Pasadena — Pasadena — Flintridge — La Canada —
Mount Wilson Observatory [Fair Oaks Ave., Atlanta St., Arroyo Dr., La Canada—Verdugo Rd., State
118, Foothill Blvd., Haskell St., Angeles Crest Highway,
State 2, Mount Wilson Rd.] 295

TOUR 1B Azusa—Angeles National Forest—Pine Flats—Crystal Lake
[State 39, Crystal Lake Rd.]. 301

TOUR 2 Los Angeles—Monterey Park—Pomona—Ontario—Colton
— Redlands — Beaumont — Banning — Palm Springs —
Cathedral City—Indio [N. Main St., Aliso St., Ramona
Blvd., US 99, State 111] 305

TOUR 3 Los Angeles — Alhambra — El Monte — Puente — Pomona
—Ontario—Riverside—Perris—Elsinore—Corona—Anaheim — Norwalk — Downey — Southgate — Los Angeles
[Valley Blvd., US 60, US 395, State 71, State 18, State
10, Alameda St.] 321

TOUR 4 Los Angeles — Belvedere — Montebello — Whittier — Fullerton—Anaheim—Santa Ana—Tustin—Irvine—Capis-
trano—Doheny Park [US 101] 339

Page

TOUR 5   Los Angeles—Culver City—Venice—Redondo—Wilmington
—Long Beach—Seal Beach—Huntington Beach—New-
port—Balboa—Laguna Beach—Doheny Park [Wash-
ington Blvd., Venice Speedway, Vista del Mar, US
101A]   351

TOUR 5A   Wilmington—Santa Catalina Island [By Boat]   . . .   367

TOUR 6   Los Angeles — Hollywood — Sherman Oaks — Tarzana —
Girard—Topanga Canyon—Topanga Beach—Castellammare—Santa Monica [US 101, Sunset Blvd., Cahuenga Ave., Ventura Blvd., Topanga Canyon Rd.,
US 101A]   379

TOUR 7   Los Angeles — Burbank — San Fernando — Palmdale — Big
Pines—San Bernardino [US 6, State 138, Big Pines
Rd., US 66]   387

Part V. Appendices

CHRONOLOGY   405

SELECTIVE BIBLIOGRAPHY   413

INDEX   421

Illustrations

METROPOLITAN ASPECTS
Detail of Mural in Federal Build-
ing and Post Office
*Mural by Edward Biberman
Section of Fine Arts, Treas-
ury Department*
Seventh Street
Fred William Carter
Airview of Downtown Los An-
geles, looking South
*Los Angeles County Develop-
ment Committee*
Main Street
Fred William Carter
City Hall
Fred William Carter

ARCHITECTURE
Los Angeles County General Hos-
pital
Viktor von Pribosic
Los Angeles Public Library
*Bertram Goodhue, Architect
Burton O. Burt*
Mudd Memorial Hall of Philoso-
phy, University of Southern
California
*University of Southern Cali-
fornia*
McAlmon Residence, Los Angeles
*R. M. Schindler, Architect
Julius Shulman*
"Blue and Silver House," the resi-
dence of Jobyna Howland—
Beverly Hills
*Lloyd Wright, Architect
Julius Shulman*
A Palm Springs Residence
*Honnold and Russell, Architects
Thomas & Kitchel*

Page
Between 10 *and* 11
Los Angeles Stock Exchange
"Dick" Whittington
Lotus Pool in Echo Park
Frank L. Rollins
Duckpond, Westlake Park
Fred William Carter
Residential District
Burton O. Burt
Lafayette Park and the First Con-
gregational Church
Fred William Carter
First Sketch of Los Angeles
(1852), from Fort Moore Hill
Security First National Bank
Sixth and Spring Streets (1904)
Security First National Bank

Between 72 *and* 73
V. D. L. Research House, Los
Angeles
*Home of Richard J. Neutra,
Architect*
Luckhaus Studio
Federal Building and Post Office,
Los Angeles
*G. Stanley Underwood, Archi-
tect*
*F. E. Dunham: U. S. Forest
Service*
Columbia Broadcasting System
Studios, Hollywood
*William Lescaze, Architect
Columbia Broadcasting Sys-
tem*
Edison Building, Los Angeles
*Allison and Allison, Architects
Edison Company*

ARCHITECTURE—continued

A Sierra Madre Residence of Batten Construction
Graham Latta, Architect
George D. Haight

Page
Between 72 and 73

An Altadena Residence (Monterey Style) *H. Roy Kelley, Architect*
George D. Haight

MOVIES IN THE MAKING

The Main Studio at Burbank of Warner Brothers First National Pictures
Warner Brothers
The Samuel Goldwyn Lot, Smallest of the Major Studios
Samuel Goldwyn
Whenever there's a question there's a conference
Robert Coburn
Shooting a scene on a sound stage set
Samuel Goldwyn
Completed set
Samuel Goldwyn
Shooting a scene with a Technicolor camera
Samuel Goldwyn
Lunch Time on the Set
Samuel Goldwyn
Men's Wardrobe Department
Metro-Goldwyn-Mayer
Expert seamstresses are employed
Metro-Goldwyn-Mayer

Between 134 and 135

A Corner of the Property Room
Metro-Goldwyn-Mayer
Makeup
Samuel Goldwyn
Fog made to order
Samuel Goldwyn
A Hand-made Tree
Samuel Goldwyn
Waves are produced by motor-driven eccentric cylinders
Samuel Goldwyn
Vegetables are shellacked to prevent wilting under heat of lights
Samuel Goldwyn
A modern moviola is used in the process of editing, or "cutting," the film
Samuel Goldwyn
Music is synchronized on records which are played back later and recorded on film.
Robert Coburn

ART AND EDUCATION

A Station of the Cross, Mission San Gabriel Arcangel
Index of American Design
Prometheus, Mural by Jose Orozco in Fray Hall, Pomona College, Claremont
Boyd Cooper
Loggia, Mission San Juan Capistrano
Index of American Design
Belfry, Mission San Gabriel Arcangel
Burton O. Burt
Mission San Fernando
Fred William Carter

Between 164 and 165

Detail from Painting, *Rancho La Brea Pitch Pools*
Field Museum of Natural History, Chicago
Imperial Elephant, Los Angeles Museum of History, Science, and Art
Theodore Baron
In the Planetarium, Griffith Observatory, Los Angeles
Fred William Carter
Young Public School Artist
Board of Education, Los Angeles

Page

ART AND EDUCATION—*continued*
Experimental Public School, Los
Angeles
Richard J. Neutra, Architect
Luckhaus Studio
Thomas Jefferson High School,
Los Angeles
Stiles O. Clement, Architect
Board of Education, Los An-
geles

Between 164 *and* 165
Hollywood Bowl
Hollywood Chamber of Com-
merce
Mt. Wilson Observatory
Fairchild Aerial Survey

INDUSTRY AND COMMERCE
Unloading tuna fish, Fish Harbor,
Terminal Island
Burton O. Burt
Loading ship, Terminal Island
Burton O. Burt
Grain Elevator
Bret Weston
Natural Gas Tanks
Bret Weston
Oil Fields, Montebello
Fred William Carter
Airview of Industrial Section, Los
Angeles
Spense Air Photos
Wine Storage Vats
Los Angeles County Chamber
of Commerce

Between 226 *and* 227
Wine Experts Taste and Classify
California Vintages
In a Walnut Packing Plant
Art Streib
Lemon Sizing Machine
California Fruit Growers'
Exchange
Body Assembly Line, Automobile
Factory
Studebaker-Pacific Corpora-
tion
Assembly Room, Aircraft Factory
Douglas Aircraft Company,
Inc.

RECREATION
Tournament of Roses Parade,
Pasadena
Bathing Beauty Parade, Venice
Mardi Gras
Surf Board Riding, Hermosa
Beach
Los Angeles County Chamber
of Commerce
Bathing Scene at Long Beach
Inman Company
Sailing, Alamitos Bay
Los Angeles County Chamber
of Commerce
Marlin Swordfish (570 lbs.), Ca-
talina
Santa Catalina Island

Between 256 *and* 257
Ice Hockey on Jackson Lake, Big
Pines Park
Los Angeles County Chamber
of Commerce
Tobogganing in Big Pines Park
Los Angeles County Chamber
of Commerce
Skiing at Big Pines Park
Los Angeles County Chamber
of Commerce
Dog Sled, Arrowhead Lake
Lake Arrowhead Company
Fishing off the Pier, Santa Monica
Fred William Carter
Card Players in the Park
Burton O. Burt

Page

RECREATION—*continued*

Bowling on the Green, Exposition Park, Los Angeles
Burton O. Burt
Tennis Courts, La Cienega Playground, Beverly Hills
City of Beverly Hills

Between 256 *and* 257

Hollywood Park Race Track, Inglewood
Carroll Photo Service
Airview, Rose Bowl, Pasadena
Kopec Photo Company

STREET SCENES

In the Old Plaza
Burton O. Burt
Debate in Pershing Square
Burton O. Burt
Unpacking "huacales" (Mexican packing cases), Olvera Street
Viroque Baker
"La Vieja" (The Old Lady), Olvera Street
Viroque Baker
Mexican Blacksmith, Olvera Street
Burton O. Burt
Mexican Potters' "Priesto," Olvera Street
Burton O. Burt
Chinese Market
Burton O. Burt
Mexican Market
Burton O. Burt

Between 318 *and* 319

Mexican News Stand, North Main Street
Burton O. Burt
Japanese News Stand, East First Street
Burton O. Burt
Angelus Temple
Burton O. Burt
Flop House and "Nickel Show," Main Street
Burton O. Burt
A Rushing Business
Burton O. Burt
The Record of the Stars, Grauman's Chinese Theater
Burton O. Burt
The Brown Derby (Wilshire Boulevard)
Fred William Carter
Parasol Library in Pershing Square
Fred William Carter

ALONG THE HIGHWAY

North Shore, Santa Monica Bay
Fred William Carter
Palm Canyon, Palm Springs
Fred William Carter
Joshua Tree
Burton O. Burt
San Fernando Valley from Mulholland Drive
Burton O. Burt
Mt. San Jacinto
Fred William Carter
Grapefruit Grove
California Fruit Growers' Exchange
Roping Cattle
Theodore Baron

Between 380 *and* 381

Sheep
Horace Bristol
Casa Verdugo, Glendale
Burton O. Burt
Shinto Temple in Japanese Fishing Village, Terminal Island
Burton O. Burt
Lasky's Barn, Hollywood—First Home of Paramount Pictures
Theodore Baron
Old Lugo House on the Plaza, Los Angeles
Viroque Baker
Portuguese mending nets, Terminal Island
Viroque Baker

Maps

	Page
LOS ANGELES AND VICINITY	xiv–xv
TOUR KEY MAP	xvi–xvii
LOS ANGELES (with downtown insert)	146, 147
BEVERLY HILLS AND VICINITY	202, 203
GLENDALE	211
LOS ANGELES HARBOR	221
HOLLYWOOD	234, 235
PASADENA	246, 247
SANTA MONICA	259
THE CONTEMPORARY SCENE	268, 269

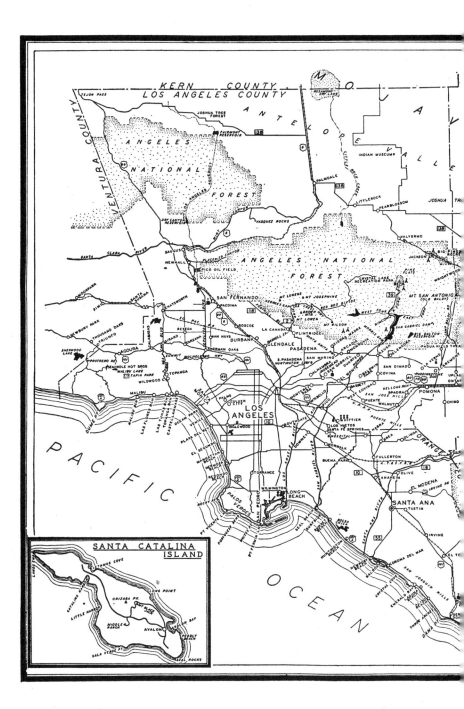

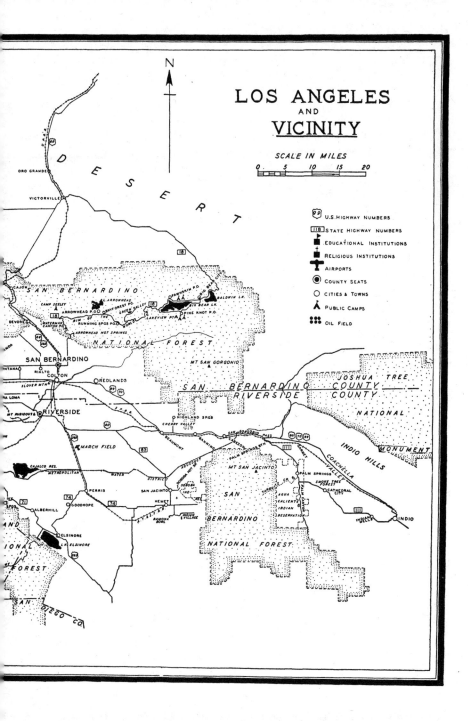

LOS ANGELES
AND
VICINITY

SCALE IN MILES

0   5   10   15   20

99 U.S. HIGHWAY NUMBERS
118 STATE HIGHWAY NUMBERS
EDUCATIONAL INSTITUTIONS
RELIGIOUS INSTITUTIONS
AIRPORTS
COUNTY SEATS
CITIES & TOWNS
PUBLIC CAMPS
OIL FIELD

D E S E R T

ORO GRANDE

VICTORVILLE

SAN BERNARDINO

CAMP SEELEY

EL ARROWHEAD P.O.
ARROWHEAD P.O.O.   CRESTFOREST PO.   18   18   BIG BEAR LK.   BALDWIN LK.
CEDAR GLEN VALLEY
RIM OF THE   LAKEVIEW PT.   PINE KNOT P.O.
WATERMAN CANYON RD.   RUNNING SPGS P.O.
ARROWHEAD HOT SPRINGS

N A T I O N A L   F O R E S T

MT SAN GORGONIO

SAN BERNARDINO

RIALTO
SLOVER MTN.
COLTON

MT DUBIOUS &   REDLANDS

RIVERSIDE

JOSHUA TREE
SAN BERNARDINO COUNTY
RIVERSIDE COUNTY

NATIONAL

INDIO HILLS

MONUMENT

CHERRY VALLEY

HIGHLAND SPGS

MARCH FIELD   63

BEAUMONT   BANNING

SAN GORGONIO PASS

PALM SPRINGS

COACHELLA VALLEY

CAJALCO RES.

METROPOLITAN   WATER   DISTRICT

MT SAN JACINTO

SNAKE TREE FOREST   CATHEDRAL CITY

71   74   PERRIS

GOODHOPE   74

SAN JACINTO

HEMET

RAMONA BOWL   INDIAN VILLAGE

S A N

B E R N A R D I N O

AGUA CALIENTE INDIAN RESERVATION

INDIO

ALBERHILL

ELSINORE   LK. ELSINORE

N A T I O N A L   F O R E S T

I O N A L

F O R E S T

SAN DIEGO CO.

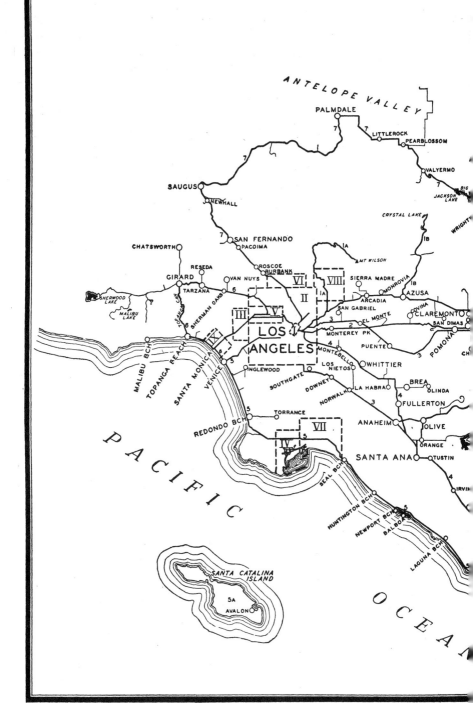

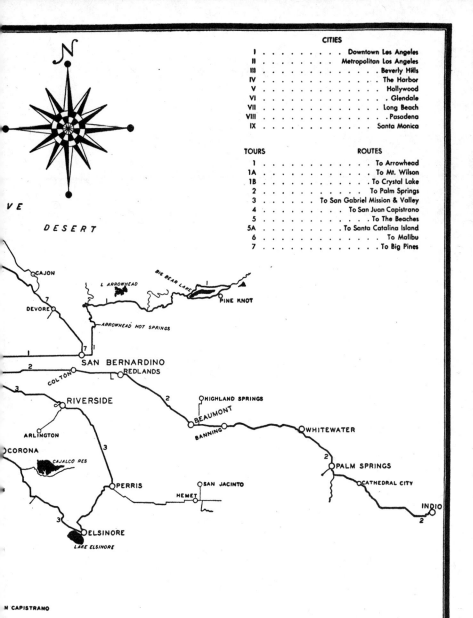

CITIES

I	. . . .	Downtown Los Angeles
II	. . . .	Metropolitan Los Angeles
III	. . . .	Beverly Hills
IV	. . . .	The Harbor
V	. . . .	Hollywood
VI	. . . .	Glendale
VII	. . . .	Long Beach
VIII	. . . .	Pasadena
IX	. . . .	Santa Monica

TOURS		ROUTES
1	. . . .	To Arrowhead
1A	. . . .	To Mt. Wilson
1B	. . . .	To Crystal Lake
2	. . . .	To Palm Springs
3	. . . . . .	To San Gabriel Mission & Valley
4	. . . .	To San Juan Capistrano
5	. . . .	To The Beaches
5A	. . . .	To Santa Catalina Island
6	. . . .	To Malibu
7	. . . .	To Big Pines

N

VE

DESERT

CAJON

L ARROWHEAD

BIG BEAR LAKE

PINE KNOT

DEVORE

ARROWHEAD HOT SPRINGS

SAN BERNARDINO

COLTON REDLANDS

RIVERSIDE

HIGHLAND SPRINGS

BEAUMONT

BANNING

WHITEWATER

ARLINGTON

CORONA CAJALCO RES

PALM SPRINGS

CATHEDRAL CITY

PERRIS

SAN JACINTO

HEMET

INDIO

ELSINORE

LAKE ELSINORE

N CAPISTRANO

TOUR KEY MAP
LOS ANGELES

NUMBERED TOURS ———4———

UNNUMBERED TOURS ————————

CITY & CITY SECTION MAPS ⌐‾‾III‾‾⌐

The WPA Guide to Renaissance Florence,
or
A Writer's Paradise

Los Angeles has usually needed water far too much to worry about what was in it. In 1939, though, the question becomes impossible to avoid: What *was* in the water? Raymond Chandler was stripping his pulp stories for parts to build his first novel, *The Big Sleep.* John Fante was mining his misery for *Ask the Dust.* F. Scott Fitzgerald was trying to stay on the wagon in Encino and mapping out *The Last Tycoon.* And Nathanael West was inventing film noir by day—hacking away at RKO B pictures like *The Stranger on the Third Floor*—and writing his masterpiece, *The Day of the Locust,* at night.

On the studio lot, Victor Fleming was cleaning up his betters' messes on both *Gone With the Wind* and *The Wizard of Oz.* Dalton Trumbo was working just as hard, climbing to the top of the screenwriter's pay scale and tossing off the great antiwar novel *Johnny Got His Gun* between assignments. And Orson Welles, like Los Angeles, was about to peak and didn't know it.

If only there were some record, some almanac of what it was like to walk those laughably walkable boulevards, to breathe that ludicrously perfumed air. If only some benevolent patron had stepped in and commissioned a panorama of prewar Los Angeles, so that future generations could enjoy it vicariously—maybe even try to replicate the freakish atmospheric conditions that made those masterworks possible. In other words, if only there existed the book that you, like a sleeper hoping vainly to drag some treasure back from dreamland, now hold in your hand.

On July 27, 1935, President Roosevelt had signed legislation authorizing the Federal Writers Project. The Project recognized that scribblers, no less than stonemasons and bridge builders, needed work. For any reader, the crowning glory of the New Deal will always be this and the other American Guides, a series of travel companions to 48 states, many cities, and any number of deserts, rivers, and other wonders—all created to "hold up a mirror to America." John Steinbeck navigated by the guides to write *Travels With Charley*, in which he called them "the most comprehensive account of the United States ever got together, and nothing since has even approached it."

The American Guide Series, in turn, was only one endeavor of the larger Federal Writers Project (FWP), which also turned out a raft of invaluable studies, including oral histories of freed slaves. The FWP, meanwhile, was but a single arm of Federal One, which also included the music, art, and theater projects that gave Orson Welles, among other artists, their biggest sandbox to date. And Federal One—stay with me here—was part of the Works Progress Administration (WPA), which belonged to a whole Scrabble rack of acronyms that came out of the New Deal. Finally, the New Deal was shorthand for all the programs devised to fight the Depression under the leadership of the most effective monogram of them all: FDR. He wrote this guide or nobody did.

To compile a well-organized guidebook to Los Angeles would be, of course, to misrepresent the city completely. Even a well-organized essay on the subject invites trouble. Neither attempt has been made here. The WPA guide to Los Angeles proceeds, sensibly enough, from I. Los Angeles: A General Survey, to II. Los Angeles Points of Interest, through III. Neighboring Cities, to, finally, IV. The Country Around Los Angeles. This has logic in its favor, but occasions a fair amount of unobjectionable repetition. The book develops more or less concentrically, like ripples in a tarn—or, to pick a more homegrown metaphor, like an earthquake.

This facsimile edition, *Los Angeles in the 1930s*, is many books in one. (Not surprising, since it had dozens of contributors.) It's a guidebook, of course, complete with still-enjoyable walking and driving tours, restaurant and hotel recommendations, even species-specific hunting laws. (Perhaps atoning for 1920s extermination of the state animal, the California grizzly, the California Department of Fish and Game apparently set a strict taking limit on the state bird: a mere ten California valley quail a day.)

The guide also qualifies as addictively readable history, with vivid accounts of L.A. under the flags of colonial Spain, Mexico, the fleeting California Republic, and, at last, the United States. And finally, no one thinks of it this way, but the WPA guide to Los Angeles is a compact coffee-table book of dazzling monochrome photography, with mostly (unlike the text) attributed contributions from the likes of Julius Shulman, Bret Weston, and the sadly unremembered Fred William Carter, about whom a bit more later.

But the guide may mesmerize most today as a set of elusive preconditions for a writer's paradise, a lost map to Shangri-La—an Eden kit. (The creator of Shangri-La himself, *Lost Horizon* author James Hilton, was even living in the vicinity, alternating underrated novels with overrated screenplays.) Against all reason, I can't help thinking that some-where within my first-edition copy must lurk the necessary recipe for this fleeting cocktail of genius, if we could only look closely enough to find it. Did the juice of a windfall orange drip off the original owner's chin, causing the fateful page to stick to its neighbor?

HINDSIGHT

Whatever the secret, it sure wasn't general prosperity. In the late '30s, plenty of people still lacked even a room to go to bed hungry in. The Depression plays an oddly recessive role in these pages, usually referred to in the past tense but occasionally in the imperfect, as if not quite safely behind us. And an auto tour to Crystal Lake includes a fascinat-ing if less than scenic side trip past "HOOVERVILLE, I m., now only a scattering of tattered tents and crude log shacks along the banks of the river between Susanna and Graveyard Canyons, but in the depression years 1930–33 a collection of 500-odd shacks, tents, and dugouts occu-pied by gold-seeking unemployed male transients" (p. 303).

When all else failed, this reflex to scratch a livelihood from the earth beat deep in the veins of Depression-era Angelenos—some of whom, even by 1938, were still a few years older than the state in which they lived. The lazy production designer's temptation to think of the period as a sleek metropolis of '30s Packards tooling endlessly past Art Deco showplaces is even more absurd than expecting everyone in 2010 to carry an iPad. On the contrary, Angelenos of the 1930s had ample reason to try and wring an extra few years' wear out of their pre-Depression hand-me-downs. One explanation for the crazy-quilt qual-ity of the built environment was that, for want of money, few teardowns ever got torn down. Capital improvements would have to wait for more capital gains. For better and worse, 1939 was the year in which a newly arrived Christopher Isherwood could miraculously confide to his diary, "We had an hour to spare, and we spent it finding an apartment."

So if material comfort wasn't the enzyme that catalyzed the class of 1939, what was it? We can safely rule out good government, too. A brief entry in the guide's chronology for Sept. 16 of that year, reading "Special recall election ousts Mayor Frank L. Shaw, electing in his stead Fletcher Bowron," doesn't begin to plumb the depths of corrupt executive cluelessness into which the city had descended. "The sun is shining in Southern California and all is well," Shaw had proclaimed a few months earlier in a national radio address, as more than a hundred of his constituents lay freshly drowned around him.

A shaky case might be made that bad government inspires better storytelling than good. Shaw's kleptocracy and his police department's strong-arm tactics certainly kept both Raymond Chandler and *Los Angeles*

Times publisher Harry Chandler (no relation, damn it) well provisioned with material—by no means all of which made it into the paper. Pervasive amorality has never exactly discouraged the production of great creative work, especially dark work, or what's a Borgia for? Fun though it may be to imagine Shaw and his cronies in the dock pleading, "I did it for art," this alibi ultimately doesn't wash. There are just too many counterexamples in history, too many badly governed regimes that generated little of lasting value beyond the cautionary. It's far likelier that Chandler and company variously rose above, hid out below, or plowed implacably along beside the petty distractions of municipal affairs. One hopes that they voted, though not necessarily that their candidates won.

If any single shared force impelled them, it may well have been rivalry—a mutual awareness of what good stuff the competition was turning out. The WPA guide lists no shortage of watering holes for the class of '39 to gather and goad each other in. Some of these establishments survive today, if not all at the same address or with remotely the same menu. Musso & Frank endures, but Lucey's Cafe on Melrose has long since thrown over "Italian food in an atmosphere of quiet conservatism" in favor of Mexican cuisine with a picture of Jerry Brown in the window.

Still, any image of Chandler, Fitzgerald, and the rest knocking back postprandial highballs at Musso's, then adjourning to Stanley Rose's Bookshop for bouts of poker and one-upmanship, probably owes less to history than to their idolaters' forgivable wishful thinking. These were loners, most of them, asocial bordering on anti-. Fante and the great California historian Carey McWilliams genuinely loved each other, bonding over their shared Colorado origins. But little proof exists that their fellow Coloradoan Trumbo, for instance, ever shared a conversation, let alone a bottle, with his *Five Came Back* co-screenwriter Nathanael West.

The titans of prewar L.A. literature likelier coexisted as discretely as they do now on our bookshelves, rubbing shoulders then as glancingly as they do spines today. Had they been joiners, the hungrier among them might have found work in the Southern California Writers Project office, but only *High Noon* screenwriter Carl Foreman, among writers remembered today, ever answered the project's call. Look no further than Foreman for the author of this heartfelt, regrettably evergreen passage: "Strangely enough, despite their power and the lavish salaries that many of them receive, screen and radio scribes remain virtually anonymous to the general public, their names being overshadowed by those of the stars, producers, and directors." Glad that's all behind us.

For their solitude, the geography of Southern California met these writers more than halfway. Maybe we should be grateful that so many of them lived a ways apart, since more benders of opportunity might have cost us too much good work. At the publication of the WPA guide in 1941, perhaps the most ubiquitous symbol of Los Angeles mobility had only just extended its first, modest tendril from downtown to Pasadena—the Arroyo Seco Parkway, whose more common synonym *freeway* appears not once in its pages.

On the subject of absent landmarks, you could look in vain here for any mention of the region's most beautiful edifice, though it was already nearing its 50th birthday. Designed by a correspondence-school architect who never again created anything approaching such weightlessly perfect loveliness, the Bradbury Building still hovers above the intersection of 3rd and Broadway downtown today—just across the street from its cherished sidekick, the Grand Central Market, which the guide writes off a bit breezily as "the city's largest retail dispensary of perishable foodstuffs." For perishability, these editorial judgments have it all over any Grand Central Market produce.

On the subject of brand new architecture, strangely, the guide does a bit better. The year 1939 in Los Angeles wasn't just a great year for writers and books. It also marked the grand opening of the city's greatest-ever gift to itself, enacted 13 years earlier in a landslide over the ironically unified opposition of the Union and Southern Pacific and Santa Fe railroads. The Union Passenger Terminal, aka Union Station, opened its doors over a giddy three-day weekend in May of 1939, rating three thorough—if maddeningly underimpressed—paragraphs from the guide. Yes, it's "huge," but isn't it also exaltingly graceful? Yes, "the South Patio, with pepper, palm, and olive trees and trumpet and cup-of-gold vines, is intended to represent California planting and garden design at its best," but what else? Are those intentions, just maybe, spectacularly met and surpassed? And Union Station may actually consist of "30 low stuccoed, tile-roofed buildings," as the guide helpfully notes, but how do those components manage to convey the impression of one enormous, thrilling cathedral to the twin gods of luxury and motion? The reader moves on, informed if not quite edified.

Union stations, of course, are ten a penny. Chicago has one. So does St. Louis. California has another one just down the coast, in San Diego. All a "union station" means is a train station serving more than one railroad company. And in 1930s Los Angeles, the name most certainly did not refer to the labor that created it.

Like the WPA guide to L.A., Los Angeles's Union Station is the work of many unremembered Depression-era hands. Also like the guide, this "Last of the Great Railway Stations" eclipsed expectations at first, only to lapse into disuse later. The shock of World War II became the guide's undoing, in part because few had the time or gasoline anymore for its sightseeing tours, yet the war proved the making of Union Station, through whose portals GIs poured in their hundreds of thousands.

By midcentury, red-baiting and tailfins had knocked both the Federal Writers Project and Union Station flat. Maybe only now, with the WPA guide to Los Angeles poised for republication, and Union Station the hub for a new multimodal, post-Hummer L.A., do both stand revealed as the quintessence of any great public works project: a bet on the future.

FORESIGHT

Did they know it wouldn't last? Could the artists we revere from L.A. circa 1940 have any inkling that the renaissance they were enjoying had less than a year to live? The question seems absurd, yet look at the masterpieces we cherish from those years. Forget, for a moment, the biographical quirks and crotchets that conspired to bring their creators to this idyllic, Edenic place and time. Imagine instead *Gone With the Wind, Citizen Kane, The Wizard of Oz,* and the great novels of '39 as the work of a single undifferentiated imagination—a Los Angeles oversoul. What do they have in common?

Pretty plainly, they're all, to varying but unmistakable degrees, parables of a paradise gone to rot. In *Gone With the Wind,* what is Tara but Scarlett's ideal of how the world used to work, before that nasty war had to come along and spoil everything? What is Xanadu in *Citizen Kane* but Charlie Kane's grossly overscaled vision of his place in the world, before the unappeasability of his own appetites finally hollowed it out from under him? And what might Oz be, if not the emerald embodiment of Dorothy's fantasy life until her fever broke, collapsing it in an eyeblink like one vast iridescent soap bubble?

A plantation house. A pleasure dome. A literal dream city. Los Angeles circa 1940 was all of these—a precarious crystal palace, poised on a historical fault line between depression and war.

Solitary arts like fiction or painting may provide the best window into a singular artist's soul. (Marlowe *is* Chandler, or who Chandler fancied himself to be.) But sometimes it takes a communal art form to achieve a window on the world beyond the frame, even a premonition of that world's future. Movies can be one such collaborative art; guidebooks, at their best, are another. The WPA guide to Los Angeles doesn't make too many explicit predictions about the city, but when it does, an interesting thing happens: Its usually reliable fetish for detail falters, but its crystal ball sharpens into near clairvoyance.

Just look at the guide's entry on Los Angeles literature. None of the writers who made 1939 such an annus mirabilis gets so much as a look-in. In their place we hear about Zane Grey, Edgar Rice Burroughs, Hamlin Garland, and Will Rogers, about the creators of Philo Vance and

Charlie Chan, and about Upton Sinclair, whose internationally best-selling Lanny Budd series began in 1940—in some cases underestimated writers, but none of them grew up in L.A. or, more important, ever set a good book here. Nonetheless, the guide has matters almost exactly right when it says, "The outlook for the emergence of a distinctive regional literature seems favorable." The reasons cited, too, are right on the money: "unusual themes and varied natural settings; a stimulating and romantic history as well as a dynamic contemporary life; and endlessly varied people in process of amalgamation; a wealth of curious customs, peculiar religions, bizarre political movements, and changing social modes."

Blithely flanking those semicolons are, in fact, the exact four reasons L.A. soon became—was already becoming, if only they'd noticed—home to a literature so rich that only a guide edited on the East Coast would dare call it regional:

"Unusual themes and varied natural settings." First position here, as in any discussion of L.A. writing outside the pages of the guide, goes to Chandler. Theme dictated setting for him, nowhere more so than in his first book, the most exquisitely *location-managed* novel the city had yet seen. To chart the hereditary corruption of the Sternwood fortune from first chapter to last, *The Big Sleep* burrows inexorably downhill from General Sternwood's mountaintop mansion to the sulfurous wrecked oilfield that underwrote it. When some anonymous WPA hand pauses to explain a diagonal oil drilling technique with the evocative name of "whipstocking"—"whereby wells are drilled at an acute angle to reach under the beach and sea"—any Chandler buff would recognize just the vector he means.

"A stimulating and romantic history as well as a dynamic contemporary life." It's hard to read a line like this today and not think immediately of historian Carey McWilliams. In 1939's *Factories in the Field,* and in the earlier *Southern California: An Island on the Land*—still the definitive resource on L.A. history up through the '30s, and not a half-bad bellwether for everything that came after—McWilliams combined scrupulous history with bracing outrage at the injustices around him. The acknowledgment to McWilliams in the guide's preface among "the many individuals who volunteered their assistance in special fields" goes a long way toward explaining how the work of so many hands can feel suffused by a singular intelligence. Too many L.A. novelists haven't read him, but, know it or not, everybody in town they admire probably has.

"Endlessly varied people in process of amalgamation." A half century before overuse debased *multiculturalism* into a cliché, the WPA guide recognized L.A.'s potential as a seedbed for fine first- and second-generation immigrant literature. By no means immune from the odd blithe racist

anachronism—Boyle Heights is described as "a section teeming with Jews and Mexicans"—the guide remains far too valuable to throw overboard for one or two linguistic indelicacies. It saw Oscar Zeta Acosta coming, even if it missed the likes of Carlos Bulosan under its very nose. For my part, as a descendant of those teeming Boyle Heights Jews and now one myself, I can live with it.

"A wealth of curious customs, peculiar religions, bizarre political movements, and changing social modes." This is Nathanael West's surreal side of the street. There's a whiff of carpetbagging condescension about L.A. here, but rueful Angelenos say as much and worse to themselves daily. There's no point in denying the carnivalesque side of L.A. life just because outsiders see little else. That's like avoiding the beach on a sunny December day, just so the folks back East won't think you shallow. The folks back East don't care. Half of them are down at the beach waiting for you.

To their credit as well, the guide's editors make room for *The Day of the Locust* in a brief bibliography of L.A. fiction, alongside the variously drier ink of P. G. Wodehouse's *Laughing Gas,* John O'Hara's *Hope of Heaven,* Helen Hunt Jackson's *Ramona,* Horace McCoy's *I Should Have Stayed Home,* and a dozen more books that make even those relative rarities look overexposed. Of pre-1939 literature, only Upton Sinclair's *Oil!,* which describes the process of wildcatting in Long Beach so lovingly that a reader gets to feeling he could almost bring in a well himself, is sadly absent from the guide's list.

Ultimately, then, it's a split decision. The guide rightly envisions a robust future for L.A. writing, but barely notices that it's already begun. "The emergence of a distinctive regional literature" is not only likely, as the guide predicts, it's emphatically under way—and the WPA guide to Los Angeles is a prime exemplar of it.

One more precondition exists for a writer's paradise, and Fred William Carter's picture of it can be found opposite page 319. Centered in direct sunlight stands what looks like a waist-high black metal sign reading, in white letters, LOS ANGELES PUBLIC LIBRARY: BORROW A BOOK TO READ IN THE PARK. Standing to the left is a giant fringed umbrella, the kind you might buy at a patio furniture store. Under it looks to be a checkout station, although, inspiringly, you can't see a librarian for all the patrons.

I like at least three other things about this picture. First, the seven or eight readers in it almost all have their backs to the photographer— maybe because he's just holding a camera instead of something important, like a book. Second, the only man whose face you can almost see, you can't, because he's wearing a natty fedora. And finally, looming up behind them all is what has to be described as a jungle. Several sturdy trunks stretch up out of frame, and the lush, dark, impenetrable foliage reaches back down almost to the brick footpath. A toucan would not feel out of place. The caption reads, in its entirety, "PARASOL LIBRARY IN PERSHING SQUARE."

I don't say a parasol library is necessary to transform Los Angeles back into a writer's paradise. I merely say that at one time Los Angeles had a parasol library—three of them, in fact—and it *was* a writer's paradise. Today it has none and, despite many fine points, it is not a writer's paradise. As Chris Isherwood might have said, do the maths.

YAHRZEIT

What took the class of 1939 so long to arrive, and where did it race off to in such a hurry? Periclean Athens lasted a good 30 years, after all. The Pax Romana reigned for two centuries. The Italian Renaissance hung in for three. We've seen that it wasn't generalized easy living or enlightened public officialdom that enabled the greatest flowering of creative production that American storytelling has ever seen. What, then? Factoring out the inevitable contributions of happenstance, the smart money is on three time-honored sources of artistic inspiration: beauty, depression, and guilt.

We shouldn't forget that Southern California in the 1930s was, to an even greater extent than it remains today, among the most beautiful natural settings on earth. The buttery sunlight, fragrant air, and crystalline vistas all conspired to make any curmudgeon doubly miserable. Essentially loving romantic relationships for Chandler, West, and Fitzgerald could only have added to their frustration. How else to exorcise this queasy sense of unearned happiness, if not in art?

To make matters worse, since 1929 the rest of America had been experiencing the desperation that should, in a just world, have been theirs to enjoy. Thanks in part to Hollywood, whose diversions the world now needed more than ever, Los Angeles claimed a higher standard of living than any American city had a right to. (L.A. had annexed Hollywood on Feb. 7, 1910, just seven months before motion-picture production began there. This looks almost as suspicious as if the United States had annexed California the very week after the discovery of gold—which, incidentally, also happened.)

For writers lately arrived from colder climes, all those actors' pretty mouths needed words, and the great literary steeplechase was on. Either the industry wrote you checks directly, or its ravenous story-hunger helped underwrite the publishers who wrote you the checks instead. Los Angeles was a relative boomtown in the middle of a depression, and it drew writers like moths to a night shoot.

The guilt must have been delicious. While the folks back home scrimped and shivered, writers like West got paid handsomely to slum.

And if family guilt didn't get you, your old muse was surely casting reproachful looks your way. What to do but buckle down and write some good fiction on the side, at least until the war—or liquor, or luxury, or some other saboteur—blew it all sky high? If the war hadn't come along and melted down the gravy train for scrap, could that golden year or two have dug in for the duration? Could Los Angeles literature, like Jack Benny, have stayed '39 forever? Unlikely. The sudden, successive deaths of Scott Fitzgerald and Nat West on December 21 and 22, 1940, came as a hammer blow from which L.A. writing would take years to recover. Was West just a constitutionally calamitous driver, or was he actually hurrying back from Mexico toward his friend and mentor's funeral? Nobody could ever agree. Either way, I picture him getting the news over his car radio— Motorola's recent gift to Californians everywhere. "Obscure Jazz Age chronicler dead," the announcer reads. West just locks eyes with his bride beside him in the passenger seat and floors it. After that bleak December, not until the heyday of Joan Didion would Southern California regain the kind of cultural moment that inspires nostalgia, or guidebooks worth savoring.

Los Angeles courts nostalgia, and punishes it. If there's a WPA guide to a more vanished American city, beats me what it is. L.A. is such a city of immigrants that most of its own name disappeared on the way here. My family lost an -owitz or two, but Los Angeles mislaid the whole rest of "El Pueblo de Nuestra Señora la Reina de Los Angeles de Porciuncula," and it's been traveling light ever since. If you don't like the weather in San Francisco, they say, just wait five minutes. If you don't like the architecture in Los Angeles, maybe give it ten. And if you love Los Angeles—love it to distraction, abjectly, like the sultriest of femme fatales—then you're begging for heartbreak.

There's a useful Yiddish word in this connection, one with no real English equivalent: *yahrzeit*. Atypically, it's not even a put-down. *Yahrzeit*—pronounced, more or less, *"yart-site"*—literally means "time of year," but it's come to signify any anniversary of a loved one's death. In our anniversary-happy society, when every news-crawl requires a roster of the day's trivial birthdays, without recourse to *yahrzeit* we still have no word for death's anniversary, let alone a ritual for it. But if we did, for L.A. writers it might entail the lighting of a *yahrzeit* candle every December for the lost promise of a sustained literary golden age.

We could second-guess the guide all day, of course. That's partly what it's good for. If all the American Guides did were to confirm our own opinions 70 years ahead of time, they might flatter us for a while, but pretty soon that would get old. *Los Angeles in the 1930s* exists to preserve not just the memory of a great city, but also the attitudes round and about it—the received wisdom of the time, regardless of whether anyone in their right mind would receive that wisdom in anything like the same way today. Had the guide gotten Los Angeles inarguably right, we might as well have padlocked L.A. in 1941 and all headed south. There's a WPA guide to San Diego, too. Instead we're here, clinging to this gerrymandered, strangely bridle-shaped metropolis despite its best periodic efforts to fling us clear. For fine company, now we have the WPA guide to Los Angeles back. Idea bin for historical novelists, iffy crib sheet for fact-checkers, God's gift to narrative historians, *Los Angeles in the 1930s* is a wayback machine for retrophile Angelenos everywhere. If the past really is another country, this book is our passport to it. Leave a forwarding address, and turn the page.

David Kipen
Los Angeles, 2010

Preface 1941

A guide book to Los Angeles could not logically be limited to the corporate city, far-flung as it is. So limited it would cover San Fernando Mission and omit Mission San Gabriel, godmother of Los Angeles Pueblo; it would also eliminate the beaches and the mountain and desert resorts associated with the city's recreational life. For this reason, and because greater Los Angeles is pretty much a unit—economically as well as geographically—the area bounded by Malibu, Palm Springs, the beaches, and the mountain resorts has been described in this book.

From the gathering of the first field notes to the last mark of a blue pencil, the guide was constructed by a staff working under a co-operative arrangement. With few exceptions, no one person is responsible for the accuracy or mode of expression of any single page. One staff of workers has painstakingly poured over research material in libraries, interviewed many persons of various interests and occupations, covered hundreds of miles of highway and set down what was learned by personal observation. Another staff has checked and rechecked the work of the research staff. A third has written and rewritten the field material, shaping it into the final pattern.

The aim has been to present Los Angeles truthfully and objectively, neither glorifying it nor vilifying it. For many decades the city has suffered from journalistic superficiality; it has been lashed as a city of sin and cranks; it has also been strangled beneath a damp blanket of unrestrained eulogy. The book shows Los Angeles as a composite, a significant city, the fifth largest in the United States.

For their generous aid and co-operation in the making of this book the editors wish to express their appreciation to the staffs of the Los Angeles Public Library, the Los Angeles County Library, the Los Angeles Museum of History, Science and Art, the Southwest Museum, the Los Angeles Chamber of Commerce, the California Institute of Technology, and the Scripps Institute of Oceanography.

Among the many individuals who volunteered their assistance in special fields the editors wish particularly to acknowledge their gratitude to Margaret Carhart, John Caughey, John P. Commons, Alexander S. Cowie, R. B. Cowles, L. H. Daingerfield, Rabbi Maxwell H. Dubin, Geraldine Espe, E. C. Farnham, Paul Hunter, Arthur M. Johnson, H. Roy Kelley, Mary Louise Lacy, Robert H. Lane, Carey McWilliams, John Peere Miles, Arthur Millier, Richard J. Neutra, Ernest H. Quayle, Hal B. Rorke, Bruno David Ussher, Robert H. Webb, and Lloyd Wright.

JOHN D. KEYES, *State Supervisor*
Southern California Writers' Project

General Information

Railroad Stations: Los Angeles Union Passenger Terminal, 800 N. Alameda St. (between Aliso and Macy Sts.), for Union Pacific R.R., Southern Pacific Lines, and Atchison, Topeka & Santa Fe Ry. Main Street Station, 610 S. Main St., for Pacific Electric Railway interurban and local street car lines; Subway Terminal, 423 S. Hill St., for Pacific Electric Railway interurban and local street car lines, and motor coach lines.

Bus Stations: Motor Transit District Lines of Pacific Electric Ry., 202 E. 5th St.; Pacific Electric Ry., 423 S. Hill St. (interurban bus service to Redondo Beach, Glendale, etc.); Pasadena-Ocean Park Stage Line, Inc. (Hollywood to Pasadena only), 1625 N. Cahuenga Blvd. (all interurban). Santa Fe-Burlington Bus Depot, 603 S. Main St., for Santa Fe Trailways and Burlington Trailways (National Trailways System), and Airline Bus Co.; Union Pacific Stage Depot, 451 S. Main St., for Union Pacific-Chicago & Northwestern Stages and Interstate Transit Lines; Union Stage Depot, 202 E. 5th St., for Original Stage Lines, Mt. Wilson Stages, and Inland Stages; Greyhound Terminal, 560 S. Los Angeles St., for Pacific Greyhound Lines and Inland Stages; Independent Bus Depot, 218 E. 7th St., for Dollar Lines and Independent Stages; All-American Bus Depot, 629 S. Main St., for All-American Bus Lines and Overland Stages; 809 E. 5th St., for Los Angeles-Trona Stages.

Bus Service: (Local and interurban) Pacific Electric busses, Subway Terminal Bldg., 423 S. Hill St.; Motor Transit Lines (interurban), 202 E. 5th St.; Los Angeles Motor Coach Co. (local); Los Angeles Railway (local and interurban); Asbury Rapid Transit System (local and interurban), 202 E. 5th St.

Bus Tours: Tanner-Gray Line (sightseeing), 544 S. Hill St., and Rosslyn Hotel, 111 W. 5th St.; California Parlor Car Tours, Inc. (to San Francisco and Yosemite), Pacific Electric Bldg., 610 S. Main St., and Biltmore Hotel, 515 S. Olive St.; Mac's Auto Tours, 518 S. Hill St.

Streetcars: Los Angeles Railway (yellow cars, local); Pacific Electric Railway (red cars, local and interurban), terminals at Pacific Electric Bldg., 610 S. Main St., and Subway Terminal Bldg., 423 S. Hill St.; interurban trains, Pacific Electric Railway (red cars), address above.

Airports: Grand Central Air Terminal, 1224 Airway, Glendale, for Pan American Airways, time from Los Angeles about 45 minutes; Union Air Terminal, 2627 Hollywood Way, Burbank, for American Airlines, United Air Lines, TWA, Western Air Express, time from Los Angeles approximately 55 minutes; from Hollywood, 30 minutes.

Taxis: Yellow Cab Co. of Los Angeles, 1408 W. 3rd St., five can ride for price of one; above company owns California Cab Co., Red Top Cab Co., Sunshine Cab Co. (confined to Hollywood), and Black and White Cab Co. (confined to Negro district).

Piers: Ships berth in Los Angeles Harbor, San Pedro, Wilmington, West Basin, and Terminal Island (*see The Harbor*). Coastwise passage on occasional freighters only. For travel to east coast, outlying possessions, and foreign countries consult classified telephone directory or travel bureaus.

Transportation to Santa Catalina Island (see Tour 5A): Leave Catalina Terminal (berths 184-185) foot of Avalon Blvd., Wilmington, 10 a.m. daily; automobile storage at pier. Boat train leaves Pacific Electric Station, Los Angeles, daily 9 a.m. Catalina Airport, Wilmington, near Catalina Terminal, to Catalina (Avalon) only, by Pacific Electric Railway to Wilmington, free fare to airport, 46 minutes from Los Angeles via Pacific Electric Railway, 5 minutes to airport.

Climate: Widely diversified in Los Angeles area where arid desert spaces and snow-blanketed mountains are easily accessible. Average seasonal rainfall in the city for 62 years, 15.22 in.; average yearly wind velocity, 6.1 m.p.h.; average annual temperature, 62.4°. Light clothing can be worn most of the year, but wraps are desirable in the rainy season and for general evening wear.

Information Bureaus: All-Year Club, official tourists' information bureau, 505 W. 6th St.; Chamber of Commerce, 1151 S. Broadway; Automobile Club of Southern California, 2601 S. Figueroa St.; Pacific Electric Ry. Information Bureau, 610 S. Main St.; Thomas Cook & Sons, 520 W. 6th St.; Los Angeles Times Information Bureau, 202 W. 1st St.; Southern Californians, Inc., 411 W. 5th St.; Better Business Bureau of Los Angeles, 742 S. Hill St.; Los Angeles Examiner Information Bureau, 1111 S. Broadway; Peck-Judah Co., 409 W. 5th St.; Randall Motor Club, Inc., 5901 Sunset Blvd., Hollywood.

Auto Clubs: Automobile Club of Southern California (47 branches), main office 2601 S. Figueroa St.; National Automobile Club (Southern California Division Office), 618 W. Olympic Blvd.; Randall Motor Club, Inc., 5901 Sunset Blvd., Hollywood.

Streets and Numbers: Owing to annexation of various areas by the city of Los Angeles, there are (1940) approximately 800 duplications in street names and designations. Strangers are advised to use street maps, obtainable free at information bureaus. The numbered streets run approximately E. and W. with Main St. as a base line. Streets running approximately N. and S. have 1st St. as a base. Numbers are assigned 100 to the block beginning at 100 E. and W. from Main St. and N. and S. from 1st St. Even numbers appear on the E. and S. sides of streets. This basic system is carried through most sections with as much continuity as varying terrain permits.

Traffic Regulations: Speed limit 25 m.p.h. in business districts, and in residential districts. Right turn against red signal permitted from right-hand lane after full stop, except in Central Traffic District (Central Traffic District is roughly bounded by Pico Blvd., Sunset Blvd., Figueroa St., and Los Angeles St.), but pedestrians and vehicles proceeding with signal have right of way. *Parking:* No standing or stopping at red curbs; loading zones (20 minutes, mdse.; 3 minutes, passenger) at yellow curbs; passenger loading zones (3 min.) at white curbs; parking (15 min.) at green curbs; otherwise 45 minutes in Central Traffic District 7 a.m.-4:30 p.m.; no parking 4:30-6 p.m. Unlimited parking 6 p.m.-7 a.m. (City traffic laws available at Police Stations.)

Liquor Regulations: No alcoholic beverages sold between 2 a.m. and 6 a.m. The law forbids automobile driving while under the influence of alcohol.

Public Buildings: Los Angeles Chamber of Commerce, 1151 S. Broadway; City Hall, 200 N. Spring St.; Hall of Justice, 211 W. Temple St.; Federal Bldg. (U.S. Post Office and Court House), 312 N. Spring St.; Hall of Records, 220 N. Broadway; Los Angeles Stock Exchange Bldg., 639 S. Spring St.; California State Bldg., 217 W. 1st St.; Y.M.C.A., 715 S. Hope St.; Y.W.C.A., 941 S. Figueroa St.; Los Angeles Public Library, 530 S. Hope St.; Department of Water & Power, 207 S. Broadway; Southern California Gas Co., 810 S. Flower St.; Department of Motor Vehicles, 3500 S. Hope St.

Art Galleries: Los Angeles Museum of History, Science and Art, Exposition Blvd., Exposition Park; California Art Club, 1645 N. Vermont Ave.; Henry E. Huntington Library and Art Gallery, 1151 Oxford Rd., San Marino; Biltmore Salon, Biltmore Hotel, 515 S. Olive St.; Stendahl Art Galleries, 3006 Wilshire Blvd.; Price Tone, 9045 Sunset Blvd., Hollywood.

Concert Halls: Philharmonic Auditorium, 427 W. 5th St.; Embassy Auditorium, 843 S. Grand Ave.; Shrine Civic Auditorium, 665 W. Jefferson Blvd.

Museums: Los Angeles Museum of History, Science and Art, Exposition Park, open 10-4:30 Tuesday to Friday; Sun. 1-9; Mon. 1-4:30; holidays 2-5; closed Thanksgiving and Christmas; free. Southwest Museum, Marmion Way and Museum Dr., open 1-5 daily except Mon.; closed July 4, Christmas, and during August; free. Marine Museum, Cabrillo Beach, 9-5 daily; closed Christmas; free.

Newspapers: Los Angeles *Times,* 202 W. 1st St., morn. and Sun.; Los Angeles *Examiner,* 1111 S. Broadway, morn. and Sun.; Los Angeles *Herald-Express,* 1243 Trenton St., eve., daily except Sun.; *The News,* 1257 S. Los Angeles St., morn. and eve., daily except Sun.; *Citizen-News,* 1545 N. Wilcox St., Hollywood, eve. only, daily except Sunday.

Radio Stations: KFI (640 kc.), National Broadcasting Co., 141 S. Vermont Ave.; KHJ (900 kc.), Mutual Broadcasting System, 1076 W. 7th St.; XEMO (860 kc.), Tijuana, Mex., Los Angeles address 643 S. Olive St.; Chamber of Commerce Bldg., 1151 S. Broadway; KFVD (1000 kc.), 338 S. Western Ave.; KFSG (1120 kc.), Angelus Temple, 1100 Glendale Blvd.; KRKD (1120 kc.), 541 S. Spring St.; KGFJ (1200 kc.), 1417 S. Figueroa St.; KFOX (1250 kc.), 542 S. Broadway; KFAC (1300 kc.), 645 S. Mariposa Ave.; KGER (1360 kc.), 643 S. Olive St.; KECA (780 kc.), 141 S. Vermont Ave.; KMTR (570 kc.), 1000 Cahuenga Blvd., Hollywood; KFWB (950 kc.), 5833 Fernwood Ave., Hollywood; KNX (1050 kc.), 6121 Sunset Blvd.; KMPC (710 kc.), 9631 Wilshire Blvd., Beverly Hills.

Shopping Districts: The downtown shopping area is bounded roughly by 1st (N) and 9th Sts. (S), and by Main (E) and Figueroa Sts. (W). Most of the department stores and specialty shops are along Broadway and Hill Sts. S. of 4th, and on W. 6th, 7th, and 8th Sts. to Figueroa; the larger ones on 7th. For the most part the stores N. of 4th on Hill, Broadway, and Spring Sts. deal in low-priced merchandise.

Just off the Plaza, near Main St., is gay Olvera St., one block long, a fragment of old Mexico. On Main St. itself, extending several blocks S. of the Plaza, Mexican establishments predominate. Then the street becomes a conglomeration of low-priced shops, cheap restaurants, cheap movie and burlesque houses, shooting galleries, pawnshops, and honky-tonks.

Downtown department stores and some shops maintain branches in many of the outlying communities and cities, including Hollywood, Beverly Hills, Santa Monica, and Westwood. Many groups of shops in both the moderate and higher price brackets may be found along Wilshire Blvd. from downtown Los Angeles through Beverly Hills and Santa Monica.

In and beyond Hollywood to Beverly Hills, Sunset Blvd. is dotted with specialty shops, restaurants and night clubs. This section is locally called The Sunset Strip.

Many of the communities that have been annexed to Los Angeles have their own shopping areas.

The financial district is centered in Spring St. between 4th and 7th Sts.

Theaters and Motion Picture Houses: More than a dozen legitimate theaters, many little theaters, 181 motion-picture houses and three amphitheaters (September 1940) are in the city. Most of the leading motion-picture houses in the downtown section are on Broadway and Hill Sts.; in Hollywood, on Hollywood Blvd. Among the more important theaters are:

Downtown Theaters

Biltmore, 530 W. 5th St., major road shows; Belasco, 1050 S. Hill St. (not leased) ; Mayan, 1040 S. Hill St., stock; Musart, 1320 S. Figueroa St., stock; Theater Mart, 605 N. Juanita Ave., *The Drunkard* now in eighth year (Dec. 1940).

Hollywood Theaters

El Capitan, 6838 Hollywood Blvd., road shows; Hollywood Playhouse, 1735 N. Vine St. (not leased).

Downtown Picture Houses

Hillstreet RKO, 801 S. Hill St.; Loew's State, 705 S. Broadway; Million Dollar, 307 S. Broadway, pictures and stage shows; Newsreel, 744 S. Broadway, first-run newsreels and shorts; Orpheum, 842 S. Broadway, pictures and road vaudeville; Paramount, 323 W. 6th St., pictures and stage show; Warner Bros. Downtown, 7th and Hill Sts.

Wilshire District Picture Houses

Four Star, 5112 Wilshire Blvd.

Hollywood Picture Houses

Grauman's Chinese, 6925 Hollywood Blvd.; Pantages Hollywood, 6233 Hollywood Blvd.; Tele-View, 6262 Hollywood Blvd., first-run news-reels and shorts; Warner Bros. Hollywood, 6433 Hollywood Blvd.

Amphitheaters

Greek Theater, N. Vermont Ave., Canyon Dr. in Griffith Park; Hollywood Bowl, 1711 N. Highland Ave., Hollywood, symphony programs and operas; Pilgrimage Play Theater, 2580 N. Highland Ave., Hollywood; Pilgrimage Play opened its 17th season, July 1940.

National Forest Regulations: Public use of forests is encouraged; free. Visitors to the forests are required to observe these rules:

1. A campfire permit must be obtained before any fire, including fire in stoves burning wood, kerosene, or gasoline, can be started on national forest land. All forest officers issue permits without charge.

2. Each camping party must bring into the forests a shovel and an ax for each vehicle or pack train. Shovel must have blade at least 8-in. wide and an over-all length of 36-in.; ax, not less than 26-in. long over all with head weighing 2-lbs. or more. Both tools must be in serviceable condition.

3. During the dangerous fire season, smoking is prohibited except in improved camps, places of habitation, and specially posted areas; smokers must extinguish lighted matches, cigars, cigarettes, and pipe heels. Watch carefully for "No Smoking" and "Smoke Here" signs.

4. In periods of high fire hazard, camping and camp or picnic fires are restricted to posted campgrounds, and part or all of the forests may be closed to public use and travel. Watch for "Closed Area" signs.

5. Build small fires. Clear an area not less than 10-ft. in diameter before starting a fire.

6. Never leave a fire without totally extinguishing it with water.

7. Keep camp clean. Where garbage pits and incinerators are not provided, burn or bury all garbage and refuse.

8. Do not pollute the springs, streams, or lakes.

9. Observe the state fish and game laws.

Wild Flower Protection: Picking and destroying wild flowers, ferns, shrubs, or trees, is prohibited by law and punishable by a fine not exceeding $200, or not more than 6 months in jail, or both. Permits for picking wild flowers for scientific purposes can be obtained free from the County Forest Service, 312 N. Spring St. Only one of each species may be picked. When wild flowers are growing on private property there is no restriction about picking them if owner's consent is obtained.

Hotel and Other Accommodations

Although Los Angeles possesses more than 800 hotels, ample normally to care for the heavy and continuous year-around stream of visitors, to prevent possible inconvenience or disappointment it is suggested that visitors write or wire in advance for accommodations desired.

Los Angeles rates are moderate in comparison with other large cities. The following list, alphabetically arranged, contains a few of the better-known hotels in both the moderate and higher brackets.

DOWNTOWN

Alexandria, 210 W. 5th St.; *Biltmore,* 515 S. Olive St.; *Clark,* 426 S. Hill St.; *Hayward,* 206 W. 6th St.; *Lankershim,* 230 W. 7th St.; *Mayfair,* 1256 W. 7th St.; *Mayflower,* 535 S. Grand Ave.; *Rosslyn,* 111 W. 5th St.

WILSHIRE DISTRICT

Ambassador, 3400 Wilshire Blvd.; *Chapman Park,* 615 S. Alexandria Ave.; *Town House,* 639 S. Commonwealth Ave.

BEVERLY HILLS

Beverly Hills, 1201 Sunset Blvd.; *Beverly-Wilshire,* 9514 Wilshire Blvd.

HOLLYWOOD

Christie, 6724 Hollywood Blvd.; *Hollywood,* 6811 Hollywood Blvd.; *Hollywood Plaza,* 1637 N. Vine St.; *Hollywood Knickerbocker,* 1714 Ivar Ave.; *Mark Twain,* 1622 N. Wilcox Ave.; *Roosevelt,* 7000 Hollywood Blvd.; *Wilcox,* 6504 Selma Ave.

APARTMENTS

More than 3,000 apartment houses, apartment hotels, and flats with a wide range of rates.

AUTO AND TRAILER CAMPS

Eighty-five trailer campsites within the city limits have been zoned by the City Planning Commission. Trailer and auto camps are also along all major highways leading into city.

Restaurants

Los Angeles is more noted for its drive-in sandwich stands than for venerable restaurants. Yet there are numerous first-class cafes, dining rooms, and restaurants scattered throughout the city and its environs, a remarkably large share of them being outside the downtown district. Among the better-known places (alphabetically arranged) are:

DOWNTOWN

Bernstein's Fish Grotto, 424 W. 6th St. Excellent sea food; Coo-Coo clams a specialty. See the aquarium windows.

Casa La Golondrina Mexican Cafe, 35 Olvera St. Mexican food, entertainment, and dancing in Los Angeles' oldest brick house.

Cook's Steak and Chop House, 633 S. Olive St. Popular with business people; leather lounges and pull-up tables.

Jee Gong Law, 739 N. Alameda St. Good a la carte menu; Suey Gow a specialty; reasonable prices. One of the better places in Old Chinatown.

Jerry's Joynt, 211 Ferguson Alley (near the Plaza). Prices moderate. Food good. A jade lounge with carved woodwork and handsome figurines make it an interesting spot to see, even if you're not hungry or thirsty.

Levy's Grill, 617 S. Spring St. One of the oldest restaurants in town. Noted for sea food and steaks.

Little Joe's, 900 N. Broadway. Lunches a la carte. Dinners. Good Italian food.

Mike Lyman's Grill, 751 S. Hill St. Especially popular with sportsmen, show people, and Spring Street quarterbacks.

McDonnell's, a dozen or more branches in various parts of the city. Prices are slightly higher at McDonnell's drive-in stands.

Normandie French Restaurant, 108 W. Olympic Blvd. First-class French food served in a quiet, conservative atmosphere.

Old Hickory Brick Kitchen, branches in various parts of the city. A la carte only; specialty: barbecued spareribs, chicken served with hot biscuits, honey, shoestring potatoes, a pail of water, and a washcloth.

Pig'n Whistle, branches in various parts of the city. Candy and confectionery counters in connection with cafes. Food and cocktails served in pleasant surroundings.

Rene & Jean French Table d'Hote, 639 S. Olive St. Soup and salad served family style.

Taix French Restaurant, 321 Commercial St. Sun. and Thurs. chicken dinner. Excellent food served family style. The atmosphere is congenial and informal.

Yee Hung Guey, 956 Castelar St. One of several good restaurants in New Chinatown. Open kitchen is an interesting feature.

WILSHIRE DISTRICT

Brown Derby Cafe, 3377 Wilshire Blvd. A la carte and table d'hote. Signs admonish passers-by to "Eat in the Hat." Popular with those who like to look for the movie stars. Excellent food served by waitresses in derby-shaped skirts.

Eaton's Chicken House, 3550 Wilshire Blvd. (Branches in other parts of city.) Superb chicken—all you want.

El Cholo Spanish Cafe, 1121 S. Western Ave. Enchiladas, tamales, and tacos in a Mexican atmosphere.

Lindy's Restaurant, 3656 Wilshire Blvd. Dinner a la carte only. Popular with late diners-out. Steaks, chops, and roast beef are specialties.

Lucca Restaurant, 501 S. Western Ave. Ample servings of everything from antipasto to spumone in a florid setting with strolling singers.

Mona Lisa, 3343 Wilshire Blvd. French-Italian restaurant favored by gourmets. Continental atmosphere. Vintage wines.

Perino's Restaurant, 3927 Wilshire Blvd. Table d'hote and a la carte. Specialties include scallopini of veal, chicken curry, crepes suzette, and strawberry Italienne.

HOLLYWOOD

Brown Derby Cafe, 1628 N. Vine St. A la carte only. Frequented by movie stars, especially Friday nights after the American Legion prize fights. Excellent cuisine.

Carolina Pines, 7315 Melrose Ave. Good Southern cooking. Reasonable.

Carpenter's Drive-In Sandwich Stand, 6290 Sunset Blvd. (Branches in various parts of city.) A la carte only. Barbecued sandwiches and fried chicken with honey and potatoes are featured.

Covey's Sardi's, 6315 Hollywood Blvd. Features are the amply laden hors d'oeuvres cart, the Kansas City roast beef and steaks, and the boneless squab chicken with wild rice.

Fred Harvey Hollywood Restaurant, 1743 N. Cahuenga Blvd. The usual standards of the Harvey Houses carried out here in modern dress.

Gotham Cafe, 7050 Hollywood Blvd. Combination delicatessen and restaurant. Paprika chicken is a dinner specialty; the Gotham Special Sandwich, big enough for two, is an all-day specialty; and for midnight supper, small hot cakes served with sour cream are featured.

Gourmet Hollywood, 6534 Sunset Blvd. Outdoor tables in patio. Good food.

The Hollywood Tropics, 1525 N. Vine St. So atmospheric you feel the rainy season coming on.

Al Levy's Tavern, 1623 N. Vine St. A Hollywood standby for luncheon, dinner, late supper, and cocktails. Steaks and roastbeef are features.

Lucey's Cafe, 5444 Melrose Ave. Italian food in an atmosphere of quiet conservatism.

Melody Lane of Hollywood, Vine St. at Hollywood Blvd., world famous street intersection. (Branches downtown and in Wilshire district.) Open all night. Concert music, afternoons. Moderate prices.

Musso and Frank Grill, 6667 Hollywood Blvd. Dinner a la carte only. Steaks, and salad mixed at your table, are favorites.

Palm's Grill, 5931 Hollywood Blvd. One of the few good outdoor restaurants in Los Angeles. Indoor dining room also.

BEVERLY HILLS AND THE SUNSET STRIP

Armstrong & Schroder, 9766 Wilshire Blvd. Salads are exceptional, cheese bread rolls notable. Booths and counter. No entertainment.

Bit of Sweden, 9051 Sunset Blvd. Smorgasbord with more than 75 delicacies. The dinner is excellent; for dessert Swedish apple pie is featured.

Bublichki Russian Cafe, 8846 Sunset Blvd. Dinner only. Superb Russian food with atmosphere. Russian orchestra. Bar.

House of Murphy, 4th St. at La Cienega Blvd. The a la carte entree is a complete meal. Cornbeef and cabbage cooked in old-fashioned dish style. Master of ceremonies Bob Murphy provides impromptu entertainment and the crowd chimes in.

Lawry's, Inc., 150 N. La Cienega Blvd. Dinner only. A huge, succulent beef roast is wheeled to the table, and cut to individual order.

The Marcus Daly, 314 N. Camden Dr. Lunch (winter only) ; dinner from 5 p.m. ; no couvert. A novel decorative feature is the Zodiac Bar, where time is shown on an overhead dome. The food is good, the atmosphere pleasant.

Perino's Roof, 9600 Wilshire Blvd. (Saks Fifth Ave.). Luncheon, tea, dinner. A la carte only. Elegant atmosphere, notable cuisine.

The Victor Hugo, 233 N. Beverly Dr. Couvert after 9 p.m. The continental lunch is a gourmet's favorite. First-rate French cuisine. Advance reservation necessary for the movie stars' impromptu Sunday night shows with dancing to name-bands.

CAFETERIAS

For those who wish to pick and choose, a few cafeterias are named :

Clifton's Brookdale, 648 S. Broadway, and *Clifton's Cafeteria of the Golden Rule,* 618 S. Olive St. Organ music and singing attendants. A novel feature at both places is the bulletin board just outside the entrance, where listings are displayed for employment, barter, sightseeing, and appeals for congenial friendship. At Brookdale a "country" atmosphere has been created with artificial trees, vines, brook, and waterfall. Inexpensive.

Fern, 665 S. La Brea Ave. Exceptionally good food, moderate prices.

Ontra, 757 S. Vermont Ave. in midtown Los Angeles, and 1719 N. Vine St. in Hollywood. Brighter and cheerier than most cafeterias. Also more expensive.

Schaber, 620 S. Broadway. Quiet and conservative in appearance and clientele ; on the expensive side.

Night Clubs

As in all large cities, the quality of Los Angeles after-dark entertainment varies. There is the honky-tonk area of Main Street and East Fifth Street, where semi-nude "B-girls" have brought Los Angeles nationwide notoriety by way of national magazine articles. There is also the fabulously chic Sunset Strip and Hollywood area, even more widely publicized.

These are the extremes, and most visitors will find a peek at both interesting. However, the heavy volume of Los Angeles night life pours through the relatively insignificant neighborhood bars, cocktail lounges, dine-and-dance establishments. Hundreds of thousands of Angelenos are acquainted with neither Main Street nor The Strip.

Following is a list, alphabetically arranged, of a few of the more widely-known clubs. Policies and times of events are those in effect in the Fall of 1940, and are of course subject to change.

DOWNTOWN

Biltmore Bowl, Biltmore Hotel, 515 S. Olive St. Dinner from 7:30 p.m.; no couvert. Orchestra; dancing. Two floor revues nightly. Bar. Much frequented by "visiting firemen" and the football crowd during the season.

Cafe Casino, 425 S. Main St. Prices reasonable. You can use your own judgment where to stop. Very ripe entertainment. Oldtime burlesque with seminude girls.

Paris Inn, 210 East Market St. Dinner from 5:30 p.m. Orchestra. Dancing. Floor shows 8 p.m. and 11 p.m. Separate bar. A rather unusual bar and singing waiters. Closed Sundays.

WILSHIRE DISTRICT

Cocoanut Grove, Ambassador Hotel, 3400 Wilshire Blvd. Dinner from 7 p.m.; couvert charge. Orchestra; dancing. Floor show 11 p.m. Bar. Very popular; consistently good entertainment.

Town House, 639 S. Commonwealth Ave. The Zebra Room is frequented by the young set. A more conservative atmosphere in the Wedgewood Room.

Wilshire Bowl, Inc., 5665 Wilshire Blvd. Dinner 6 p.m. to 2 a.m., no couvert.

HOLLYWOOD

Beachcomber Cafe, 1727 N. McCadden Pl. Prices are slightly stiff. Specializes in Oriental food and drinks. Frequented by the many lesser Hollywood actors.

Earl Carroll's Theater-Restaurant, 6230 Sunset Blvd. Dinner from 7:30 to 11 p.m., no couvert; without dinner, admission charge. Two acts with 30 principals and 60-girl revue. Shows, 9 and 12 p.m. For those who like girl shows and revolving stages.

Florentine Gardens, 5955 Hollywood Blvd. Dinner from 6:30 p.m., no couvert. Without dinner, a small admission charge. Orchestra. Dancing. Cocktail lounge. Three floor shows nightly. Girl revues. Situated in the heart of Hollywood.

Grace Hayes Lodge, 11345 Ventura Blvd. (north of town). Dinner, no couvert. Minimum charge. A gay informality. Celebs, if in the mood, usually put on impromptu acts—quality varies.

"It" Cafe, 1637 N. Vine St. Dinner 5 to 10 p.m. Supper 10 p.m. to 2 a.m. No couvert. Dancing. No floor show. Bar.

La Conga Club, Inc., 1551 N. Vine St. Dinner from 7 p.m. No couvert. Two orchestras; two revolving orchestra stages; continuous dancing. No floor show. Bar.

Slapsy Maxie Rosenbloom's Cafe, 7165 Beverly Blvd. Dinner from 6 p.m. No couvert. Orchestra, but no dancing by patrons. Three or four funny floor shows nightly, with Deadpan Maxie in the middle of things.

Seven Seas Cafe, 6904 Hollywood Blvd. Dinner from 6 p.m. No couvert. Hawaiian orchestra and entertainers, dressed in native costumes. Floor shows 11 and 12 p.m. and 2 a.m. Bar. Dancing from 8:30 p.m. Hawaiian Island atmosphere, complete with "rain on the roof."

BEVERLY HILLS AND THE SUNSET STRIP

Bali Restaurant, 8804 Sunset Blvd. Dinner; no couvert, no minimum. Atmosphere in keeping with the name. Light, risque entertainment. East Indian curry a specialty.

Beverly-Wilshire, 9514 Wilshire Blvd. Dinner. Separate bar. Dancing.

Cafe LaMaze, 9039 Sunset Blvd. Dinner. Dancing to name-bands. Special entertainment. Separate bar.

Ciro's, 8433 Sunset Blvd. Dinner 7 to 10 p.m.; couvert charge. Orchestra. Dancing to 2 a.m. A favorite spot with movie folks. Patrons are requested to dress formally on Saturday. Somewhat expensive.

Victor Hugo. (*See Restaurants.*)

SOUTHGATE

Topsy's Cafe, 2800 Firestone Blvd. Dinner from 6 p.m. No couvert. Floor shows, 9:30 p.m. and 12:30 a.m. Bar. Orchestra. Dancing. Closed Mon.

Recreational Facilities

Following is a partial list of facilities available:

Aquaplaning: Manhattan, Hermosa, and Newport-Balboa Beaches.

Baseball: Wrigley Field, 435 E. 42nd Pl., used by Los Angeles "Angels"; Hollywood Baseball Park (Gilmore Field), 7700 Beverly Blvd., used by Hollywood "Stars." Both teams are members of the Pacific Coast League. Girl's professional softball leagues play at Los Angeles Softball Park, 1650 W. Slauson Ave., Mon. to Fri. nights, inclusive, and at Fiedler Field, 470 So. Fairfax Ave., as scheduled.

Basketball: Collegiate basketball is played during the season, November to March, at Pan-Pacific Auditorium, 7600 Beverly Blvd., on scheduled dates, by southern section of Pacific Coast Conference, comprising U.S.C. and U.C.L.A.

Beaches: Following is a list of the more important beaches in the area and approximate distance in miles from downtown Los Angeles; those marked (M) or (C) are municipal or county-owned respectively: Malibu, 31; Santa Monica (C), 15-18; Ocean Park (M), 15-18; Venice (M), 13-14; Playa del Rey (M), 15-16; El Segundo, 18; Manhattan (C), 18-19; Hermosa (M), 19-20; Redondo (M), 20-21; Palos Verdes, 22-23; Cabrillo (M), 24-26; Long Beach (M), 20-23; Seal, 26-29; Huntington, 32-35; Newport, 38-41; Balboa, 39-42.

Boating and Yachting: Small boats available at most of the mountain lake resorts. At most of the major beaches, sailboats, speedboats and powerboats can be chartered with operators. Rowboats, electric motorboats, and canoes can be rented at Echo, Hollenbeck, Lincoln, and Westlake Parks. Collegiate rowing contests held on Marine Rowing Course at Long Beach and Ballona Creek. Prominent yacht clubs are: Balboa Yacht Club, Los Angeles Yacht Club, California Yacht Club, Newport Harbor Yacht Club, Long Beach Yacht Club, and others.

lii RECREATIONAL FACILITIES

Bowling: Arlington Bowl, 2225 W. Washington Blvd., 8 lanes; open
10 a.m.-2 a.m. Beverly Hills Bowling Courts, 9244 Wilshire Blvd.,
16 lanes; open 11 a.m.-12 p.m. Boulevard Bowl, 5766 Hollywood
Blvd., Hollywood, 8 lanes; open 10 a.m.-2 a.m. Bowling shoes free.
Hollywood Recreations, Inc., 1539 N. Vine St., Hollywood, 22 lanes;
open 10 a.m.-2 a.m. Pico Palace-Columbia Recreation Center, 6081
W. Pico Blvd., 19 lanes; open 10 a.m.-2 a.m. Southwest Bowling
Center, 7023 Pacific Blvd., Huntington Park, 16 lanes; open 10 a.m.-
2 a.m. (Sun. 9 a.m.-3 p.m.). Studio Bowling Academy, 1053 S. Vermont Ave., 14 lanes; open 9 a.m.-2 a.m. Sunset Center, 5842 Sunset
Blvd., Hollywood, 52 lanes; open 10 a.m.-2 a.m. Wilshire Recreations, 737 S. La Brea Ave., 28 lanes; open 9 a.m.-2 a.m.

Boxing: Hollywood Legion Stadium, 1628 N. El Centro Ave. (pro-
fessional), Fri., 8:30 p.m.; Ocean Park Arena, Pico and Main, Santa
Monica (professional), Mon. 8:30 p.m.; Wilmington Bowl, Anaheim
Blvd. at Mahar, Wilmington (professional), Wed., 8:30 p.m.; Jeffries
Barn, 2422 Victory Blvd., Burbank (amateur), Thurs. 8:30 p.m.;
South End Athletic Club, Main and 97th Sts. (amateur), Thurs.,
8:30 p.m.

Fishing (ocean): Surf fishing at most beaches. Pier fishing from
Santa Monica Municipal Pier, end of Colorado Ave., Santa Monica;
Lick Pier, end of Navy St., Ocean Park; Sunset Municipal Pier, Venice
Blvd. and Ocean Front, Venice; Hyperion Pier, El Segundo; Manhat-
tan Municipal Pier, Manhattan Beach; Hermosa Beach Municipal
pier, Hermosa Beach; Redondo Municipal Pier, Redondo Beach; San
Pedro Sport Fishing Dock, end of 22nd St., San Pedro; Belmont Pier,
Termino Ave. and Beach, Long Beach. Barge fishing. Shore boats to
barges leave from piers. Larger fishing boats accommodating 16 to 40
persons at most fishing piers. Boats for deep-sea fishing may be chartered. Regarding fresh water fishing, consult Department of Natural
Resources, California State Bldg., or sporting goods stores.

Fishing Licenses: Licenses and latest information obtainable at most
sporting goods stores. Fishing, inland or ocean, requires a license for
all except non-game marine fish. License year Jan. 1 to Dec. 31.
Resident citizens, $2; nonresident citizens, $3; aliens, $5; under 18
no license required.

Football: The University of Southern California and the University of California at Los Angeles, both participating in the Pacific
Coast Conference, play home games in Memorial Coliseum, 3911 S.

Figueroa St.; adm. is set by Conference and depends upon game's importance. Loyola University, and Los Angeles Bulldogs (professionals), usually play their home games at Gilmore Stadium, 100 N. Fairfax Ave.; Occidental College, at college field, 1600 Campus Road, Eagle Rock (Southern California Conference); the Annual Rose Bowl Game, at Pasadena Rose Bowl, on New Year's Day.

Golf: Municipal courses in Griffith Park; two 18-hole; one 9-hole. Other public courses: Sunset Fields, 3701 Stocker Ave., two 18-hole; Western Ave. Golf Course, 121st St. and Western Ave., 18 holes; Rancho Public Golf Course, 10100 W. Pico Blvd., 18 holes. Many other public and private courses throughout city and county.

Hockey: Collegiate games at Tropical Ice Gardens, Jan. to middle of March, every Sat., 7:30 p.m.

Horseback Riding: Municipal bridle trails in Griffith Park and Arroyo Seco. Many private stables where horses can be rented.

Horse Racing: Santa Anita (*see Tour 5*), Arcadia, approximately 14 miles from downtown Los Angeles; 1941 Season: Dec. 28 (1940)-Nov. 9 (1941); mutuels. Hollywood Park (*see Tour 1*), Inglewood, about 11 miles from downtown Los Angeles; 1940 Season: June 8-Aug. 10; mutuels. Del Mar, in San Diego County, is popular with Los Angeles residents and visitors; distance 105 miles; mutuels. Harness and running races at Los Angeles County Fair, Pomona, Sept.

Hunting: Deer, Aug. 10 to Sept. 9. No does, fawns or spike bucks. No sale of venison or skins. Two bucks per season. Quail (Valley, Desert, Mountain), Nov. 15 to Dec. 31, 1940; 10 per day, 10 in possession, 20 per week all species. Pheasant, Nov. 15 to 20, 1940-41; 2 male birds a day, 2 in possession; hens prohibited. Doves, Sept. 1 to Oct. 15; 12 a day, 12 in possession, 30 a week. Pigeons, Dec. 1 to 15, 1940; 10 a day, 10 in possession, 20 a week. Ducks, Oct. 16 to Dec. 14, 1940; 10 a day, 20 in possession, 30 a week. Geese, Oct. 16 to Dec. 14, 1940; 3 a day, 4 in possession, 8 a week. State regulations may be changed biennially; federal regulations, annually.

Hunting Licenses: License year July 1 to June 30. Residents under 18, $1; resident citizens, $2; nonresident citizens, $10; declarant aliens, $10; other aliens, $25. Deer tags, $1.

Midget Auto Racing: Atlantic Stadium, Atlantic Ave. and Bandini Blvd., Tues. nights from Apr. or May until Oct. Gilmore Stadium,

100 N. Fairfax Ave., from Apr. until Thanksgiving, Thurs. nights. Occasional racing at Southern Ascot Speedway, Southgate; no fixed dates.

Mountain Camps: (County supervised) Big Pines Recreation Camp (*see Tour 7*), in Angeles National Forest, 85 miles from Los Angeles; 6,864 ft. elevation; summer and winter sports. Crystal Lake Recreation Camp (*see Tour 1B*), in Angeles National Forest; 50 miles from Los Angeles; 5,717 ft. elevation; summer and winter sports. (City supervised) Camp Seeley (*see Tour 1*), in San Bernardino Mountains, near Lake Arrowhead; 75 miles from Los Angeles; 4,700 ft. elevation; summer and winter sports. Camp High Sierra in the High Sierras; 335 miles from Los Angeles; 8,400 ft. elevation; open summer only. Camp Radford in San Bernardino Mountains; 90 miles from Los Angeles; 6,000 ft. elevation; available only for large organized groups. Rates: for county camps apply 524 N. Spring St.; city camps apply 200 N. Spring St.

Parks and Playgrounds: There are 87 municipal parks totaling 5,486 acres. Griffith Park (*see Tour B*), the largest, contains 3,761 acres. Forty-nine playgrounds are municipally controlled. They offer almost every recreational facility. The following list of the more important playgrounds has been keyed for convenience and brevity and provides a comprehensive directory of playground facilities. Among the activities, horseshoe pitching, volleyball, basketball, paddle tennis, ping-pong, and croquet can be played at most playgrounds and are not keyed in the directory.

Key:

A—Archery Ranges
B—Baseball Diamonds
C—Community Clubhouse Bldgs.
F—Football and Soccer Fields
S—Softball Diamonds

SL—Softball Diamonds Lighted
    for Night Use
SP—Swimming Pool
T—Tennis Courts
TL—Tennis Courts Lighted
    for Night Use

Playgrounds: Anderson Memorial, 828 S. Mesa, San Pedro (C-SL-T-SP); Banning, 1331 Eubank St., Wilmington (C-SL-T); Benedict, 1811 Ripple St. (C-SL); Cabrillo, 38th St. and Bluff Pl., San Pedro (C-S); Central, 1357 E. 22nd St. (C-SP); Daniels Field, 845 12th St., San Pedro (B-C-F-S); Downey, 1772 N. Spring St. (C-B-SL-SP-T-F); Echo, 1632 Bellevue Ave. (C-SL-TL); El Sereno, 2501 Eastern Ave. (C-S-SP-T); Elysian, 1900 Bishop Rd. (SL-T); Evergreen, 2839 E. 4th St. (C-B-SL-SP-T-F); Exposition, 3981 S. Hoover St. (C-S-SP-TL); Fernangeles, 8851 Laurel Canyon Blvd. (C-B-S-

SP-F); Fresno, 1016 S. Fresno St. (C-B-SL-F); Griffith, Riverside
Dr. and Los Feliz Blvd. (C-B-SL-SP-TL-F); Harvard, 6120 Denker
Ave. (C-B-SL-F-TL); Hazard, 2230 Norfolk St. (C-B-SL-T-F);
Highland Park, 6150 Piedmont Ave. (C-B-SL-SP-TL); Lincoln
Heights, 2605 Manitou Ave. (B-C-F-S); Manchester, 8800 S. Hoover
St. (C-B-SL-SO-TL-F-A); Mayberry, 2408 Mayberry (S-F); North
Hollywood, 5301 Tujunga Blvd. (C-B-SL-TL-F); Oakwood, 767
California St., Venice (C-TL); 109th St., 1500 E. 109th St. (S-F);
Pecan, 127 S. Pecan St. (C-SL); Queen Anne, 1245 Queen Anne Pl.
(C-SL-T); Poinsettia, 7341 Willoughby Ave. (C-SL-TL); Poplar,
2630 Pepper St. (S); Rancho Cienega, 5000 Exposition Blvd. (A-B-
S-T-F); Reseda, 18411 Victory Blvd. (C-B-SL-SP-F); Roscoe, 8133
Vineland Ave. (C-SL-SP-TL); Ross Snyder, 1501 E. 41st St. (C-B-
SL-TL-F-A); James Slauson, 1244 E. 61st St. (C-B-S-T-F); South
Park, 345 E. 51st St. (SL); State Street, 716 N. State St. (C-SL);
Stonehurst, 11101 Wicks Ave. (A-B); Sunland, 8700 Foothill Blvd.
Tujunga (BB); Van Nuys, 14301 Van Owen Blvd. (SL-T); Ver-
dugo, 3580 Verdugo Rd. (C-B-SL-SP-TL-F); Vineyard, 2942 Vine-
yard St. (C-S); West Los Angeles, 1831 Stoner Ave. (C-B-SL-SP-
T-F); Yosemite, 1840 Yosemite Dr., Eagle Rock (C-B-SL-SP-T-F).

Polo: Riviera Country Club, Sunset Blvd. and Capri Dr., Pacific
Palisades, games nearly every Sun., 2:30 p.m.; Will Rogers Memorial
Field, Sunset and Chautauqua Blvds., Pacific Palisades, games nearly
every Sun., 2:30 p.m.; Midwick Country Club, Ramona and Atlantic
Blvds., Monterey Park, Sun., 2:30 p.m. (Note: Special adm. prices
at all tournament games.)

Skating, Ice: Pan Pacific Ice Arena, 7600 Beverly Blvd. Largest
indoor rink in the United States (22,000 sq. ft.). Polar Palace, 615
N. Vine St., Hollywood. (Season, June to Sept.). Aft. 2-5 p.m.;
eve., 8-11 p.m.; Sat. and Sun. 9:30-12 a.m.; skates may be rented.
Special price session for children under 16 yrs. Sat. morning and afternoon. Tropical Ice Gardens, Community Park, Westwood Village.
(Open all year) Morn. 8:30-12 a.m.; aft. 1:30-4 p.m.; skates may be
rented.

Skating, Roller: Lincoln Park Roller Rink, 2037 Lincoln Park Ave.
Aft. 2:30-5 p.m.; eve. 7:30-10:15 p.m. (Fri. 7-10 p.m.). Shrine
Roller Rink, 700 W. 32nd St. Aft. 2-5 p.m.; eve. 8-11 p.m. Roller-
drome, 11105 W. Washington Blvd., Culver City. Eve. 8-11 p.m.;
Sat. and Sun. aft. 2-5 p.m. Hollywood Rollerbowl, 1452 N. Bron-
son Ave., Hollywood. Aft. 2-5 p.m.; eve. 7:45-11 p.m.

Skiing, Tobogganing, Winter Sports: Municipal Camp Seeley and the two county camps, Crystal Lake and Big Pines (*see Mountain Camps*). Equipment for rent.

Soccer: Los Angeles Soccer League, comprising best teams in this section, play at Loyola Stadium, 1901 Venice Blvd., Los Angeles, Sunday afternoons, almost the year around.

Swimming (see Parks and Playgrounds):   All municipal pools are outdoor pools, open only during summer. Fernangeles, Downey, and Verdugo are shallow children's pools. (*See also Beaches*). Municipal recreation department, A.A.U., and collegiate swimming meets often are held at Los Angeles Swimming Stadium, among largest swim centers in U. S., at Exposition Park.

Tennis (see Parks and Playgrounds):   No permit needed for individual play on municipal courts. For special group use or tournaments, permit must be obtained. Fee is charged for use of night-lighted courts. Top-ranking tournament tennis played at Los Angeles Tennis Stadium, 5851 Clinton St., each summer.

Wrestling: Olympic Auditorium, 1801 S. Grand Ave., Weds., 8:30 p.m.; Hollywood Legion Stadium, 1628 N. El Centro Ave., Hollywood, Mons., 8:30 p.m.; Eastside Arena Club, 3400 E. Pico Blvd., Thurs., 8:30 p.m.; Huntington Park Coliseum, 2010 E. Gage Ave., Huntington Park, Fri., 8:30 p.m.; Pasadena Arena, Fair Oaks Ave. and Olive St. (professional), Mons., 8:30 p.m.; Wilmington Bowl, Anaheim Blvd. at Mahar St., Wilmington (professional), Tues., 8:30 p.m.; Ocean Park Arena, Pico and Main Sts., Santa Monica (professional), Fri., 8:30 p.m.

Calendar of Annual Events

Note: nfd means no fixed date.

JANUARY

1	Pasadena	Tournament of Roses
1	Pasadena	Intersectional Football Game
1	Los Angeles	Chinese Independence Day
1st week, nfd	Los Angeles country clubs	Los Angeles $10,000 Open Golf Tournament
5 days nfd (in Jan., Feb., Mar., Apr., May)	Location shifts	Southern California Skeet Association Inter-Club Team and Three-man Team Matches
1st week and successive Sundays	Los Angeles Griffith Park	Los Angeles Metropolitan Tennis Championships
Jan. through Apr. Sundays	Monterey Park Midwick Country Club	Annual Pacific Coast Elimination Championship Polo Matches
nfd	Los Angeles various courses	Southern California Open Golf Tournaments
nfd	Arcadia (Santa Anita Race Track)	Santa Anita Derby
1st week 2 days nfd	Big Bear Lake San Bernardino Mountains	Winter Sports Carnival and Ski Jumping Championships (Junior Chamber of Commerce sponsor)
nfd	Los Angeles Shrine Auditorium	Coast Conference Basketball Season opening
nfd	Wilmington, California Yacht Club	Sunkist Dinghy Sailing Championship Series
nfd	Pasadena	Pasadena Open Golf Tournament

JANUARY—Continued

17	Los Angeles, Olvera Street and Plaza Church	*El Día de San Anton* (Sp., Saint Anthony's Day). Anton, patron saint of animals, is revered by the annual procession and *Benedición de los*
	Hollywood, Plummer Park	*Animales* (Sp., blessing of the animals). Domestic pets are welcomed
24 or nfd, 8-day celebration includes Chinese New Year	Los Angeles, China City	*Trao Chun* (Festival of the Kitchen God.) Chinese ceremonials preparatory to the New Year, which is about the 28th of month
nfd	Long Beach Marine Stadium	Grand Prix Pacific Coast Inboard Regatta

FEBRUARY

3 days first part of month	Santa Catalina Island	Catalina Open Golf Tournament
nfd	Los Angeles	Boat and Aircraft Show
4 days approx. nfd	Catalina Channel	Midwinter Sailing Regatta
nfd	Arcadia (Santa Anita Race Track)	Santa Anita Derby
nfd	Pasadena Civic Auditorium	Annual Pasadena Dog Show
nfd	Los Angeles China City	*Teng Chieh* (Chinese: Feast of the Lanterns)
nfd	Los Angeles Harbor	Inter-Club Racing Series (Los Angeles Yacht Club)
nfd	Pasadena Badminton Club	Southern California Badminton Championships (all champions)
nfd	Los Angeles, Arroyo Seco Parkway	Southern California Annual Open Lawn Bowling Tournament
nfd	Los Angeles Municipal Playgrounds	Playground Kite Tourney (about 2500 contestants)

FEBRUARY—continued

| 3rd week to Apr. nfd | Sierra Madre | Wistaria Fete, celebrating blossoming of world's largest wistaria vine |
| 22 | Los Angeles Harbor | Southern California Yacht Association Midwinter Regatta. Cal. Yacht Club |

MARCH

First Saturday	Long Beach	Southern Pacific Association Amateur Athletic Union Relay and Field Meet (properly named the Long Beach Relays)
Easter Sunday	Hollywood (Bowl)	Easter Sunrise Service
Easter Sunday	Glendale (Forest Lawn), and many other places	Easter Sunrise Service
nfd	Los Angeles	Girls' Doll Festival (Japanese)
nfd	Los Angeles	International Tennis Matches
nfd	Los Angeles Harbor	San Clemente 130-mile Yacht Race
nfd	El Segundo	Kite Day
nfd	Arcadia (Santa Anita Race Track)	Santa Anita Handicap Race
All 2nd week	State-wide	California Conservation (of natural resources) Week
nfd	Los Angeles	Blooming Tulip and Hyacinth Season (35,000 bulbs) in Griffith and Exposition Parks
nfd 2 days	Arcadia, Rancho Santa Anita	All-breed Santa Anita Kennel Club Charity Show
nfd	San Pedro	Guadalupe Island Yacht Race (from San Pedro to Guadalupe Island and return)
nfd	Los Angeles Riviera Country Club	Horse Show, Easter Parade, and All-Star Polo Matches

MARCH—continued

nfd	Los Angeles	West Side Tennis Club invitational Tournament
nfd	Los Angeles, various courses	Professional Golf Association Open Meeting
nfd through Thanksgiving	Los Angeles, Atlantic Speedway and Gilmore Stadium	Midget Auto Races
nfd	Los Angeles	Ice Hockey Championship Play-off Games
nfd	Santa Monica	Dudley Cup Tennis Tournament (high school contestants)

APRIL

nfd	Los Angeles	Southern California Golf Tournament
2 days nfd	Pasadena	Pasadena Spring Flower Show
3 days nfd	Santa Catalina Island	Bobby Jones Trophy Tournament
1st week 5 days	Pasadena	California Institute of Technology Exhibit and Open House
Through Apr. and May	Los Angeles County Museum, Exposition Park	Annual Exhibition of Painting and Sculpture
nfd	Pasadena	Pasadena Dog Show
nfd	Long Beach Marine Stadium	Pacific Southwest Spring Motorboat Sweepstakes
nfd	Pasadena Brookside Park	Southern California Spring Flower Show
nfd	Beverly Hills	Beverly Hills Dog Show
nfd	Los Angeles	Southern California Band and Music Festival
nfd	Newhall vicinity	Newhall-Saugus Rodeo
1st and 2nd weeks, nfd	Los Angeles Harbor	Gold Cup Yachting, California Yacht Club
nfd	Beverly Hills	Beverly Hills Tennis Championships
Late April through May	Los Angeles Exposition Park	Los Angeles County Museum Wild Flower Show

MAY

5	Los Angeles	Boys' Festival (Japanese)
5	Los Angeles (Olvera Street)	Mexican Celebration of *Cinco de Mayo* and *Fiesta de las Cruces* (Sp., fifth of May and Feast of the Crosses)
1 week, early in month	Los Angeles	Southern California Festival of Allied Arts (presentations)
nfd	Los Angeles	Southern California Women's Golf Championship Matches
nfd	Los Angeles	Southern California Tennis Association Team Championship Matches
nfd	Los Angeles	Los Angeles Kennel Club Show
nfd	Los Angeles	Eisteddfod (Welsh Musical Celebration)
nfd	Compton	Invitation Track and Field Meet (West and Middle West)
nfd	Location shifts	Invitation Amateur Golf Championship of Southern California Golf Association
nfd	Los Angeles	Los Angeles Country Club Invitation Tournament
3 weeks nfd	Los Angeles Exposition Park	Giant Trade Exhibit
nfd	Los Angeles	Women's International Bowling Congress Tournaments
nfd	Santa Monica Bay	Annual Salt Water Carnival and Rough Water Swimming Competition (auspices of Santa Monica Junior College)
nfd	San Pedro, Cabrillo Beach	Harbor Day Aquatics (auspices Junior Chamber of Commerce)
3rd week 2 days	Los Angeles Harbor	San Clemente Island Yacht Race
10 days nfd	Pasadena, Civic Auditorium	Pasadena Music Festival
25	Harbor cities	Harbor Day
Late May	Los Angeles Harbor	Annual Predicted Yacht Races
30	All communities	Memorial Day Observance

JUNE

1 through Sept.	Santa · Catalina Island	Opening of Santa Catalina Island Fishing Tournament
1st week through summer	Hollywood (Bowl)	"Symphonies Under the Stars"
1st week 3 days	Altadena	Festival of the Mountains
nfd	Flintridge Riding Club	Children's Horse Show
nfd	Los Angeles Memorial Coliseum	Southern California Music Festival
nfd	Los Angeles various courts	Southern California College Tennis Championships
nfd 3 days	Los Angeles	Riviera Horse Show
nfd	Arcadia, Santa Anita Park	Sheriff's Relief Association Barbecue Picnic
nfd	Redondo	Covered Wagon Days
nfd	Los Angeles Griffith Park	Men's Public Links City Golf Championships
nfd	Long Beach Marine Stadium	Southern Outboard Association Regatta
nfd	San Fernando	San Fernando Fiesta and Pageant
nfd	From San Pedro	Tri-Island Sailing Race of 250 miles — San Pedro, around San Clemente, Santa Barbara and Santa Catalina Islands
3 or 4 days	Santa Catalina Island	Catalina Women's Invitation Golf Tournament
nfd	Los Angeles	Los Angeles City Golf Tournament Matches
nfd	Hollywood	Hollywood Golf and Country Club Invitation Tournament
nfd	Around Santa Catalina Island	Yacht Race around Santa Catalina Island, Los Angeles Yacht Club sponsor
nfd	Inglewood	Hollywood Turf Club Horse Races
June or July nfd	Ocean Park, Venice	Children's Floral Pageant
2nd week through Oct.	From San Diego to Santa Barbara	Southern California Salt Water Fishing Tournament (Los Angeles Junior Chamber of Commerce sponsor)

JULY

4	Los Angeles, Pasadena	Fourth of July Celebrations in Los Angeles Coliseum and Pasadena Rose Bowl
4 biennially	Location shifts	California to Honolulu Yacht Races
4 biennially	San Pedro	All Channel Islands Yacht Race
4	Long Beach	Craig Trophy Race (for big sloops)
1 week nfd	Los Angeles	Riviera Country Club Invitation Golf Tournament
July and Aug. nfd	Hollywood Bowl	"Symphonies Under the Stars"
July and Aug. nfd	Hollywood	Pilgrimage Play (Life of Christ)
nfd	Los Angeles Harbor	*Times* Trophy Race
nfd	Around Santa Catalina Island	Stewart Bros. Auxiliary Handicap Race
nfd	Avalon to Hermosa Beach	Santa Catalina Island-Manhattan-Hermosa Beach Aquaplane Race
nfd	Del Mar	Del Mar Turf Club Race Meeting
nfd (both month and day vary from year to year)	Long Beach (Long Beach Stadium usually)	The Hearst Regatta
nfd (both month and day vary from year to year)	Long Beach (Long Beach Stadium usually)	Model Yacht Races
nfd (both month and day vary from year to year)	Long Beach (Long Beach Stadium usually)	Outboard Races
nfd (both month and day vary from year to year)	Long Beach (Long Beach Stadium usually)	Sailing Races
nfd	Los Angeles	Riviera Horse Show

JULY—continued

nfd	Pasadena	Vista del Arroyo Tennis Tournament
nfd	Inglewood	Centinela Garden Clubs' Flower Show
nfd	Los Angeles Harbor	Nordlinger Trophy Yacht Race
nfd	Los Angeles various parks	Metropolitan Junior Tennis Championships
nfd	Los Angeles Swim Stadium	Aquatic Pentathlon
nfd	Los Angeles	Soapbox Derby

AUGUST

1st and 2nd week	Long Beach	Southern California Yachting Association Regatta
nfd 3 days	Venice	Mardi Gras
nfd	Los Angeles Griffith Park	Metropolitan Junior Tennis Championship Finals
nfd	Los Angeles Hotel Ambassador	Ambassador Tennis Club Tournament
nfd	Santa Monica	Santa Monica Tennis Championships
nfd	Los Angeles	Pacific Coast Public Parks Tennis Championships
nfd	Santa Monica Canyon	Five-mile Swim (to Venice) and Water Carnival
nfd	Avalon	Paddleboard Race (from Avalon to Cabrillo Beach)
nfd	Los Angeles Swim Stadium	Aquatic Show (Junior Chamber of Commerce sponsor)
nfd	Long Beach Marine Stadium	Southern California Outboard Regatta Championships
nfd	Santa Catalina Island	Commodore's Yacht Race (to the Island Isthmus)
Aug. or Sept. nfd	Newport Harbor	Tournament of Lights
nfd	Los Angeles	Nisei Festival (celebration week of Second Generation of local Japanese-Americans)

SEPTEMBER

1st Monday	Los Angeles	Labor Day Parade
8 and 9	San Gabriel	*La Fiesta de San Gabriel* (Sp., The Feast of St. Gabriel)
4	Los Angeles	Los Angeles Birthday Celebrations, Pageant from San Gabriel Mission to City Hall
nfd	Los Angeles Swim Stadium	Metropolitan Swim and Dive Championships
8 days nfd	Los Angeles	Pacific Southwest Tennis Championships
nfd	Los Angeles Griffith Park	Women's Public Links City Golf Championships
nfd	Long Beach Bixby Park	"Biggest Picnic in the World" (estimated attendance 150,000)
nfd	Los Angeles Riviera	Children's Country Club Horse Show and Pet Parade
nfd	Los Angeles	*La Fiesta de las Flores* (Sp., the feast of the flowers)
nfd	Los Angeles	Pacific Southwest Tennis Championship Matches
nfd	San Pedro	Opening Gold Cup Sloop Sailing Series
2 weeks Sept. and Oct. nfd	Pomona	Los Angeles County Fair (Running and Harness Races)

OCTOBER

10	Los Angeles (Chinatown)	Anniversary of Founding of the Chinese Republic
27	Los Angeles Harbor	Navy Day
9 days in early winter, nfd	Los Angeles	Los Angeles Annual Automobile Show
nfd	Pasadena Carmelita Gardens	Pasadena Fall Flower Show
2 days, nfd	Los Angeles	Riviera Country Club Horse Show
nfd	Long Beach Marine Stadium	Annual Pacific Coast Inboard Regatta
nfd	Pasadena	Annual Pasadena Weed Show
nfd	Los Angeles	Great Western Live Stock Show, Union Stock Yards

NOVEMBER

11	All communities	Armistice Day Celebration
nfd	Los Angeles Union Stockyards	Great Western Livestock Show and Rodeo
nfd	Los Angeles	Grand Prix Midget Auto Races
1 week nfd	Los Angeles	San Francisco Opera Company presentation
Nov. and Dec. nfd	Los Angeles	Golden Gloves Championship Matches
2nd week	Sierra Madre	Cascade Chrysanthemum Flower Show
nfd	Pasadena	Pasadena City Amateur Badminton Championship Tournament
nfd	Arcadia, Rancho Santa Anita	California Horsemen's Western Horse Show
nfd	Los Angeles Memorial Coliseum	Football Carnival Charity Game
Late Nov. to Christmas	Hollywood Hollywood Blvd.	Santa Claus Lane's Nightly Parades (except Sunday)

DECEMBER

12	Los Angeles (Olvera Street)	Mexican celebration of *Nuestra Senora de Guadalupe* (Sp., Our Lady of Guadalupe)
16-24	Los Angeles (Olvera Street)	Mexican celebration of *Las Posadas* (Sp., the lodgings). A unique observance of Mary and Joseph's journey to Bethlehem
nfd	Location shifts	Pacific Coast Intracircuit Polo Championship Matches
nfd	Inglewood Hollywood Turf Club	"Bridge Tournament Under the Stars" (world's largest bridge tournament, attracts more than 1000 players)
nfd	Long Beach	Southern California midwinter Championship Tennis Tournaments
nfd	Alhambra	All-States Barbecue

DECEMBER—continued

Late Dec. to March, nfd	Arcadia, Santa Anita Track	Pari-mutuel Horse Racing
Last 2 weeks	Altadena	The Parade of the Deodars— Christmas Tree Lane (one mile of lighted living Christmas trees)

HOME-STATE PICNICS

All State picnics are held in Sycamore Grove Park with the exception of the Iowa picnics, which are held in Lincoln Park, Los Angeles, in the winter, and Bixby Park, Long Beach, in the summer.

For further information call Federation of State Societies, Stowell Hotel, 416 S. Spring St., MUtual 1981, Los Angeles.

Alabama	Aug., 3rd Sat.
Arizona	Mar., 2nd Sat.
Arkansas	May, 1st Sat.
Colorado	Feb. and Aug., 2nd Sun.
Connecticut	May, 3rd Sat.; Oct., 1st Sat.
Delaware	May, 2nd Sat.
Florida	Aug., 3rd Sat.
Georgia	June, 2nd Sat.
Idaho	No fixed month or day
Illinois	Jan., next to last Sat.; Apr., July and Oct., 3rd Sat.
Indiana	Feb. and July, last Sun.
Iowa	Feb., last Sat.; Aug., 2nd Sat.
Kansas	Jan. 29; Apr., 1st Sat.; Sept., 2nd Sat.
Kentucky	May, 1st Sat.
Louisiana	Aug., 3rd Sat.
Maine	May, 3rd Sat.; Oct., 1st Sat.
Massachusetts	May, 3rd Sat.; Oct., 1st Sat.
Michigan	Jan., 1st Sat.; Mch. and Sept., 3rd Sat.
Minnesota	Feb., 3rd Sat.; Sept., 4th Sat.
Mississippi	Aug., 3rd Sat.
Missouri	Jan., 2nd Sat.; Mch., last Sun.; Aug., 3rd Sun.
Montana	Feb. 22
Nebraska	Mar., 4th Sat.; July, last Sat.
Nevada	Mar., 2nd Sat.
New Hampshire	May, 3rd Sat.; Oct., 1st Sat.
New Jersey	May, 2nd Sat.

HOME-STATE PICNICS—continued

New Mexico	Mar., 2nd Sat.
New York	Apr. and Oct., 2nd Sat.
North Carolina	June, 2nd Sat.
North Dakota	Feb., 1st Sat.
Ohio	Jan., last Sat.; Aug., 1st Sat.
Oklahoma	May 30; Sept., 1st Mon.
Oregon	Apr. and Oct., 2nd Sat.
Pennsylvania	Mar. and Nov., 1st Sat.
Rhode Island	May, 3rd Sat.; Oct., 1st Sat.
South Carolina	June, 1st Sat.
South Dakota	Jan. and Aug., last Sun.
Tennessee	May, 1st Sat.
Texas	Apr., about the 21st
Utah	Mar., 2nd Sat.
Vermont	May, 3rd Sat.; Oct., 1st Sat.
Virginia	June, 2nd Sat.
Washington	Apr. and Oct., 2nd Sat.
West Virginia	June, 3rd Sat.; Oct., 4th Sat.
Wisconsin	Feb., 2nd Sat.; Aug., 4th Sat.
Wyoming	Mar. and Aug., 1st Sun.

PART I

Los Angeles: A General Survey

The Contemporary Scene

LOS ANGELES, the metropolis of southern California and of a
vast adjoining area, is frequently regarded as one of the newer
American cities, as an outgrowth of the motion-picture industry
and as a creation of the real estate promoter. Actually, however, it
is almost as old as the nation itself, having been formally founded and
"subdivided" in the year the Revolutionary War ended—more than
half a century before Chicago was incorporated. Over Los Angeles
have waved the banners of royal Spain, imperial and republican Mexico,
of the Bear Flag Republic, and, since 1847, the stars and stripes of the
United States.

That the city seems perennially young and new despite its long,
picturesque history is not surprising, for the bulk of its population *is*
new. Only a handful of the inhabitants are descended from pioneer
Mexican and American families. Only a small number of adult
Angelenos were born in the city. The majority of the inhabitants
have come here in recent years, mostly from the Middle West. Since
1870 the population has either doubled, tripled, or quadrupled in every
decade except two. In addition to American settlers, Los Angeles has
attracted immigrants of many races. The distribution of population
among racial groups not characteristic of other large American communities in 1930 included Mexicans (97,116); Japanese (21,081);
Chinese (3,009); Filipinos (3,245). Other racial groups are of much
the same proportions that characterize the average cosmopolitan city.
The Negro population is estimated at about 45,000.

Los Angeles' population (1,496,792 by the 1940 census) is still
increasing rapidly. The normal influx has been accelerated in recent
years by droughts and dust storms, mortgage foreclosures, and factory
shut-downs in central, southern, and eastern states. In addition there
is a large transient population of tourists, job-hunters, climate-seekers,
elderly retired persons, and Hollywood hopefuls. It has been estimated
by the All-Year Club of Southern California that winter visitors increase the population by about one-half between November 1 and
April 30.

People who have lived here a dozen years are likely to regard themselves as old-timers; and in a way they are justified, for even in that
relatively brief time they have witnessed one of the city's most spectacular eras of expansion. Length of residence in Los Angeles often

3

replaces the weather as a conversation-starter. When strangers meet, one of them is likely to remark: "I came out in '26. How long have *you* been here?"

With these comparative newcomers, who form the majority of the population, ties with the home state remain strong. Angelenos dearly love to reminisce about "back East"—and "back East" may be anywhere east of the Rocky Mountains. Former residents of other states gather periodically at huge picnics, usually held in the public parks.

This attachment for the old home furnishes a clue to the character of the City of the Angels and its people. It suggests that the transplanted settler has never quite grown used to living here, has never quite been able to regard Los Angeles as his true home. Coming largely from the prairie regions, of rigorous climate and even more rigorous conventions, he suddenly finds himself in an exotic land of lofty purple mountains, azure ocean, and mild, seductive climate, where the romance of old Spain is nurtured and blends with the gaudiness of Hollywood, where rigid conventions are relaxed and comparative tolerance is the rule. To many a newcomer, Los Angeles is a modern Promised Land. It amazes and delights him, and thaws him out physically and spiritually. There is a heady fragrance in the air, and a spaciousness of sky and land and sea that give him a new sense of freedom and tempt him to taste new pleasures, new habits of living, new religions. Finding himself in the amusement capital of the West and at the hub of a vast natural playground offering every variety of sport from surfboarding to skijoring, he proceeds to have more fun than he ever dreamed was possible. He is fascinated by strange new industries and new agricultural products: movie studios, oil fields, almond orchards, vineyards, olive and orange groves. He encounters new and exotic types of people: movie actors and sombreroed Mexicans, kimonoed Japanese and turbaned Hindus. He develops an urge to try things that are novel and exciting, from Chinese herb doctors to Indian medicine men, from social credit to nudism, from a wine-colored stucco dwelling to a restaurant shaped like a hat. And because the array of things to do and see is so dazzlingly different from everything he has known, his curiosity is always whetted, his appetite never sated. He feels a certain strangeness in this place he now calls his home, a strangeness that is at once exhilarating and disturbing, and that he had not known in his native place "back East."

The environmental restlessness and novelty-seeking tendency provide a key to the city's distinctive character. They help to explain why new fads, strange cults, wildly mixed styles of architecture, and unusual political and religious movements blossom and flourish so profusely here, making Los Angeles a metropolis of "isms."

Even in their everyday attire, Angelenos sport the brightly-colored and the bizarre. Girls wear flapping, pastel-tinted slacks. Housewives go to market with furs thrown over cotton dresses. Boys blaze forth in multihued silk shirts. Beach costumes are seen on urban streets thirty miles from the sea. Schoolgirls wear gaily colored kerchiefs tied peasant-style over their heads. Men go hatless, women stockingless. Summer outfits are worn in winter, and vice versa.

On Main Street an occasional cowboy swaggers along in 10-gallon hat and high-heeled boots. Fringed leather jackets, Buffalo Bill style, are sometimes seen, and youngsters from the mountains or desert, in town for a spree, often wear Indian beadwork vests and belts studded with bright glass "jewels." Frequently a "messiah" of one of the dozens of bizarre local religious cults, garbed in biblical robes made of flour sacks, pads barefoot along a crowded sidewalk, apparently oblivious to the stares of the curious. And the curious are apt to be the newcomers, for seasoned Angelenos have long since become used to living in an open-air circus.

On occasion the variety of dress is even more striking. American business men parade in ball-fringed sombreros and dashing Spanish serapes during such celebrations as San Pedro's Cabrillo Day and Pasadena's Tournament of Roses. Japanese don flowered kimonos on Boys' Day, when huge paper fish flutter atop bamboo poles before their homes. Mexicans wear bright sashes and serapes on their numerous saints' days and fiestas. While these manifestations are exceptional, they vividly color the community's life and give it its character.

To the Easterner, descending the Pacific slope after the long trip across deserts and mountains, southern California is like a new world, a world set off by itself, with definite geographic boundaries of mountain ranges and sea. Los Angeles, sprawling across the slope, is like the capital of an empire in miniature; a land that has its own Riviera, its Alps, and its Sahara; a domain that is richer and more diversified than many an American state or foreign country. Los Angeles County alone is nearly as large as Connecticut.

The visual impression of this capital of the Pacific Southwest can be summed up in three words: whiteness, flatness, and spread. Bathed in relentless sunshine most of the year, Our Lady the Queen of the Angels is one of the "whitest" cities in the United States. Its newer office buildings gleam with concrete. Its miles of homes are bright with stucco. Glaring viaducts over the stony bed of the Los Angeles River and a maze of unshaded concrete roads add their shining whiteness to a sun-bleached setting that culminates in the tower of the City Hall, a long, tapering, chalk-like finger dominating the cubistic plain.

The flatness of the city is emphasized by its mighty backdrop of mountains. Along its northern and western edges, Los Angeles approaches these barrier ranges, breaking like a surf over the foothills and dashing up against the base of fire-scarred hills. Up gullies and draws and dry gulches it creeps and swirls in a tide of plaster and of palms. Yet for the most part the city stretches spaciously over a wide plain descending gently from the peaks to the Pacific. In many places, particularly in the level coastal areas, it is sometimes difficult to discern the dark-blue or snow-covered crests of the distant, semicircling mountains. The spread of Los Angeles arises from the fact that it is a vast agglomerate of suburbs, loosely strung together. In area it is the largest single municipality in the world, with 451 square miles of territory between the mountains and the Pacific. Curiously enough, when the pueblo was named, the Spanish founders seemed to have had a premonition of its ultimate expanse, for its full Spanish title is perhaps the most prodigious place name in American geography: El Pueblo de Nuestra Senora la Reina de Los Angeles de Porciuncula (The Town of Our Lady the Queen of the Angels of Porciuncula). Properly pronounced "Lóce Ahng-hay-lace," the abbreviated name is variously mispronounced "Lawss Angless," "Lawss Anjeless," and even further abbreviated to "Los" or "L.A."

Puzzling to the uninitiate is the fact that the city on the map and the city as it is, often do not correspond. On maps an inland town, some 15 miles from the coast, it dangles southward a "shoestring district" nine miles long and half a mile wide, to include within its corporate limits the two seaport towns of San Pedro and Wilmington, which form Los Angeles Harbor. To the west and north the city reaches out over quiet valleys where solitary ranch houses display street numbers running up into five figures. It penetrates brush-covered canyons inhabited chiefly by forest rangers and wild animals. On the other hand, many a street lined solidly with homes and other buildings extends far outside the city boundaries. Even more confusing are the independent towns which Los Angeles completely or partially surrounds: Beverly Hills, San Fernando, Culver City, Universal City, Santa Monica, Inglewood, and Burbank. One reason for this extensive urban expansion has been the widespread use of the automobile. Many people in these scattered areas motor in to work in Downtown Los Angeles. Others work in their own communities, but drive to town for shopping and amusement.

Each outlying municipality or community usually has its own important industrial resources: Culver City has motion pictures; Long Beach has oil wells and seaside resort facilities; Pasadena and Beverly Hills offer retreats to the financially secure; Inglewood has airplane factories and a race track; Glendale and Burbank have airports and various factories; San Pedro and Wilmington are supported by shipping, fisheries, and the Navy's Pacific Fleet; the San Fernando Valley communities depend mainly on farming. Not without reason, perhaps, has Los Angeles been dubbed "nineteen suburbs in search of a city."

The Los Angeles of the future is likely to evolve along highways. Already there is a vast network of superb roads. In other rapid transit facilities, however, Los Angeles is outranked by many a smaller town. Cumbersome, old-fashioned trolleys still rattle through the streets. The interurban service is incredibly slow and antiquated. Busses and a few lightweight streamlined trolleys have been introduced, but the inadequacy of the city's transportation as a whole has hardly been mitigated by these measures. Travel on public conveyances is often a distinct inconvenience because of long waits and overcrowding. In some instances the city has left outlying districts devoid of any method of travel except by automobile or on foot.

Though its tendency to spread and sprawl has been more or less unrestrained, the city has strangely enough denied itself the right to soar. Since 1906 a municipal ordinance has limited buildings to 13 stories and 150 feet in height. This restriction, sponsored by architects, fire underwriters, and others, was adopted for several reasons. Since Los Angeles had virtually unlimited space in which to expand, and since the city was becoming known as a health and resort center famed for fresh air and sunshine, it was felt that it would be a mistake to erect tall buildings that would create traffic congestion and turn the streets into dark, narrow canyons—conditions which people from the East were trying to escape. It was believed, further, that tall buildings were not a paying investment. With a few exceptions, such as the 32-story City Hall, the restriction has been rigidly enforced; and as a result, Los Angeles' sky line presents a series of long, low lines instead of the rearing, jagged contours of most large American cities. Another effect of limiting the height of buildings has been to decentralize the city. One of the distinctive aspects of Los Angeles is its number of community shopping centers, each virtually self-sufficient. The stranger, driving in what appears to be a residential section, may suddenly find himself in a highly concentrated area of shops and offices of every description. In these business districts, where buildings are frequently of the most bizarre architectural design, practically every service is represented. However, the tendency toward decentralization has not alleviated congested conditions downtown, since downtown streets are narrow, elevated railways are lacking, the single subway is short, and office buildings, large department stores, and a number of theatres are concentrated in a relatively small area.

Architecturally, Los Angeles has somewhat matured. Seldom perpetrated today are the monstrosities of a few years ago, the Moorish minarets sprouting from a Swiss chalet, the Tudor mansion with chromatic Byzantine arches. In many streets, these older homes survive, continuing the tradition of a florid era when the builder was the architect, and his bad taste was exceeded only by the vigor of his unrestrained imagination.   Contrasts between the Victorian and the contemporary structure are often ludicrous, as when a constructivist garage rubs rooftops with a grotesque gingerbread castle.   But in general the present-day designs are simple, pleasing, and well-adapted to the climate.   Much of it is in harmony with the city's Latin heritage.   Reminders of the days of the dons are becoming more and more numerous: in the municipal coat of arms, which embellishes such public works as the new Figueroa Street tunnels; and in the bright tile roofs and shady patios of private homes.   Here and there are buildings that are portents of the city-to-be: the dignified but striking edifice of the Public Library, the towering City Hall, the functional modern residences.

A lavish variety of flowers and trees bedecks the city.   Curious and exotic species offer the nature lover a surprising new world of colors, odors, and flavors.   Three kinds of trees—palm, eucalyptus, and pepper —against stucco walls and red tiles, are as characteristic of Los Angeles as are the elms and maples above the white frame farmhouse of New England.

The character of the city is also reflected in the facilities for openair living.   Angelenos not only enjoy sports the year round, but also patronize outdoor libraries—"parasol stations"—three of which are maintained by the Public Library in downtown plazas and parks.   They listen to "symphonies under the stars" in the Hollywood Bowl.   They patronize drive-in movie theatres and watch the show from their automobiles.   They park in front of restaurants shaped like zeppelins, icecream cones, or shoes, and dine within their own cars.   Multitudes go shopping in open-air markets, where displays of bright fruits, vegetables, and flowers remind easterners of the lavish exhibits at a state fair.

Other institutions that have either originated or been perfected in Los Angeles are cafeterias, supermarkets, and "motels" (auto camps). Cafeterias, especially, are in full glory, one of which treats its patrons to pipe-organ concerts, singing waiters and waitresses, and free fruit-ades.

Much of the foregoing has catalogued the more sensational manifestations of the character of Los Angeles.   However, the majority of the people live as conventionally and tamely as citizens of other large American cities, and many are inclined to frown on their less restrained brethren.   The average Angeleno, be he business man, professional man, tradesman, or artisan, is generally so busy with humdrum affairs that he has little time or inclination to indulge in the vagaries that delight his more leisured neighbors.

The city's cultural life, also, provides a contrast to its circus-day aspect.   In Los Angeles are educational and scientific institutions of a type characteristic of every modern American metropolis: public and private libraries, museums, and art galleries; colleges, universities, and technical schools, some of them with high reputations. The popular concerts, the numerous book stores and art shops, the writers' and artists' clubs, and the little theatres attest to the presence of a cultural awareness on the part of a considerable part of the population. Cultural Los Angeles, however, is not so much the outgrowth of native movements and traditions as it is the product of a recent influx of talent of all kinds, attracted chiefly by the motion pictures. The work produced by the hundreds of writers, musicians, and other artists who have come to Hollywood does not reflect the native scene. Los Angeles, as a locale, has inspired few outstanding works of literature or art; nor has the city developed a creative school of thought or—outside the motion-picture industry—had notable influence on culture in other parts of the country. It is possible, however, that in time a distinctive native philosophy and cultural cohesiveness may develop among the great numbers of gifted persons gathered together in this area; and if such a development occurs, Los Angeles may well become one of the world's most influential centers of culture.

Natural Setting

I N VARIETY of scene, southern California is richer than many vastly larger areas of the globe. It is a region where rugged mountains, cleft by deep gorges, tower in peaks 10,000 feet above sea level; a region of forests and wide deserts, of rolling foothills, fertile valleys, and seasonal rivers that sweep to the sea; a region with craggy shores, strands, capes, bays, and verdant islands washed by the Pacific Ocean. So diversified is the terrain that motion-picture studios film stories laid in African deserts, Alpine peaks, the South Seas, and a dozen other "foreign" places, without going more than 100 miles from Los Angeles.

Los Angeles County, measuring approximately 75 miles from north to south and 70 miles from east to west, covers 4,083 square miles, about half of it mountainous. Roughly, the northern part of the county is made up of desert and mountains, and the smaller southern part lies on a broad plain that slopes gently from the mountains to the Pacific. Most of the 451 square miles of the city of Los Angeles is spread over the plain, the city's downtown district lying midway between the mountains and the sea.

Ranges north of the city separate the urban area from the Mojave Desert. In the San Gabriel Mountains, rising from the coastal plain, and less than 40 miles from the sea, are nine peaks more than 8,000 feet in height. Loftiest of these are Mount San Antonio (Old Baldy) 10,080 feet, and Mount Baden-Powell, 9,389, whose crests are sometimes snowcapped. To the north, nearer Los Angeles, the San Gabriel Mountains rise more than 7,000 feet, and are gashed by numerous canyons down which streams tumble seaward during the spring.

West and northwest of Los Angeles are two smaller ranges, the Santa Monica and the Santa Susana Mountains. The Santa Susana, the more northern of the two, reach a maximum elevation of 3,956 feet and with the San Gabriel Mountains, form the northern boundary of the San Fernando Valley. In this wide, fertile valley, approximately twenty-two miles long, are three towns, several smaller communities, and a part of Los Angeles. The Santa Monica Mountains form the southern boundary of San Fernando Valley, while still farther west, their embayed southern slopes mark the north shore line of Santa Monica Bay. Their highest point is Sandstone Peak, 3,059 feet high. On the lower southern slopes of this range sprawl Hollywood and

Metropolitan Aspects

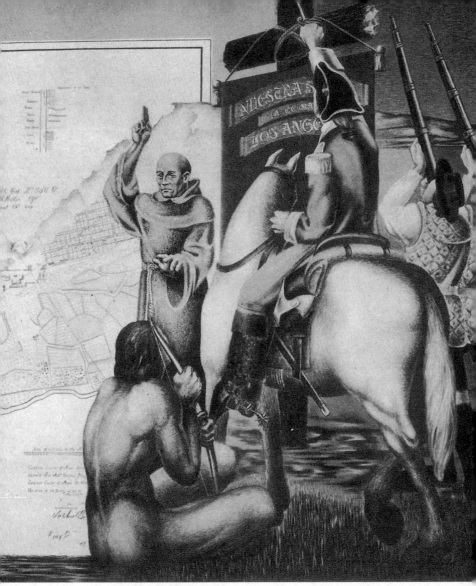

DETAIL OF MURAL BY EDWARD BIBERMAN
IN FEDERAL BUILDING AND POST OFFICE

F. W. Carter

SEVENTH STREET

AIRVIEW OF DOWNTOWN LOS ANGELES, LOOKING SOUTH

MAIN STREET

F. W. Carter

CITY HALL

LOS ANGELES STOCK EXCHANGE

LOTUS POOL IN ECHO PARK

Frank L. Rollins

DUCKPOND, WESTLAKE PARK

F. W. Carter

Burton O. Burt

RESIDENTIAL DISTRICT

LAFAYETTE PARK AND THE FIRST CONGREGATIONAL CHURCH
F. W. Carter

FIRST SKETCH OF LOS ANGELES (1852), FROM FORT MOORE HILL

SIXTH AND SPRING STREETS (1904

Beverly Hills. Between the Santa Monica and Santa Susana Ranges and the mightier San Gabriel are the Elysian, San Rafael, and Verdugo Hills, averaging 1,000 feet in height.

The ranges so converge and interlock north of the city that there is access to the northern part of the state only through well-defined mountain passes. Among these are the Cahuenga Pass, Mint Canyon, Newhall (the old Fremont Pass), and Tejon Pass. Nearer the coast are Topanga and Triunfo Passes.

Southeast of Los Angeles, and a few miles from the ocean, are the Dominguez Hills, only a few hundred feet high. Farther east of the city are the Montebello, Puente, and San Jose Hills.

The Los Angeles Plain, broken here and there by hills and mountains, descends to the sea from an elevation of about 900 feet at the base of the San Gabriel Mountains. On the plain are almost all of the county's forty-four incorporated cities, the orange groves, truck farms, and oil fields.

Two rivers, the San Gabriel and the Los Angeles, flow across the plain to the sea. Dry virtually throughout the summer, these rivers become turbulent in winter from heavy rains and melting snows. The San Gabriel River, the more important, drains approximately 700 square miles. It rises at the head of San Gabriel Canyon, receives the waters from a dozen small tributaries, and flows into the sea at Alamitos Bay, near the southwestern county line. The Los Angeles River has its source in the mountains adjacent to the San Fernando Valley, flows through San Fernando Valley, and is joined by numerous mountain creeks before it empties into the sea at Long Beach.

There are relatively few natural lakes in the county. Among the more accessible are Elizabeth, Crystal, Jackson, and Quail.

The county's coast line, nearly seventy-five miles long, is roughly divided into two crescent-shaped bays: Santa Monica Bay, facing west, and San Pedro Bay, facing south. At the northern end of Santa Monica Bay, canyons gape seaward and bold cliffs are broken intermittently by sandy beaches. From these headlands the coast line makes a wide curve southeasterly along several beaches until broken by the San Pedro Hills. These hills, also called the Palos Verdes, form one of the most decorative promontories on the southern California coast. From Point Fermin, where the crescent of San Pedro Bay begins, the shore line as far as Long Beach is indented by the channels of Los Angeles Harbor. At Long Beach it becomes once again a smooth strand.

Off the San Pedro Hills lies Santa Catalina, nearest of the Channel Islands. These islands are the projecting tops of a submerged mountain range running parallel to the coast. The famed resort island of Santa Catalina is dominated by Mount Orizaba and Black Jack Peak, each rising more than 2,000 feet. On the seaward side of the island are sheer cliffs; on the land side, the bay and town of Avalon. Thirty miles beyond is the island of San Clemente, now a United States Navy base and training ground. Most of the other islands are uninhabited; some, such as San Nicolas, are desolate; others are fertile and green. Some have natural harbors and some unapproachable shores; others are mere rocks rising from the sea, homes of gulls, pelicans, and cormorants.

Geology: Southern California geology is characterized by the extreme youthfulness of most of its exposed deposits. Strata laid down in the two most recent geological periods, the Quaternary and the Tertiary, are overwhelmingly predominant. Earlier strata are exposed in only a few places in the county, and no rocks definitely known to belong to the earliest period, the Archean, have been found.

Layers of marine deposits alternating with terrestrial sediment prove that the Los Angeles area has several times sunk beneath the ocean, and in almost every locality the strata have been folded, twisted, and broken by crustal movements. It is generally agreed that much of southern California lay beneath a sea during ancient geological time, and that thousands of feet of marine deposits accumulated on an ocean floor. Millions of years later, during the Jurassic period, long after some of the high mountains of the eastern states had been worn down to a low, old-age stage, this area entered an active and formative geological period. The great Sierra Nevada and lesser ranges arose, and the sea retreated to a new shore line along the western base of the Sierra.

Wind and water eroded the rock until much of California, including what is now the Los Angeles area, was a low plain. Geologists depict the southern California of the early Tertiary period as a jungle-covered lowland, bordered by a broad, shallow, island-spotted sea. There is evidence of volcanic action during these times. Lava rocks of this period are widely exposed in some sections of Los Angeles County.

Then came resubmergence of parts of the Los Angeles Plain. Marine life was deposited along with sands and muds, and when the rocks thus formed were uplifted, oil from the organisms was impounded at the apexes of folded strata. The rich petroleum deposits that constitute the county's chief natural resource are pumped or flow from such folds in the Baldwin, Puente, and San Jose Hills, and elsewhere in the county.

Southern California mountain ranges, worn down to relatively low relief at the beginning of the present geological period, were later converted by a rising movement of the land into great sheer-sided, angular masses of even greater bulk than they are today. Deeply depressed areas between the ranges may have held remnants of inland seas. The Great Ice Age followed, and some evidence of glaciation has been found as far south as Mount San Gorgonio (Old Grayback). The glacier nearest to Los Angeles today is the Palisades, approximately 250 miles north, in the Sierra Nevada Mountains. Though scientists disagree as to whether the present post-glacial period is one of increasing or diminishing crustal movement of the earth, seismic activity continues. Several times a day the seismograph at the California Institute of Technology records movement of the earth's crust. Sometimes the movement is far out on the floor of the Pacific; again it may be in Hawaii or Alaska; or, when sudden slippage occurs along one of southern California's many faults (fractures in the earth's crust), it is within the Los Angeles area.

These sudden displacements occur whenever the strain grows too great along a fault line, and the intensity of an earthquake depends upon the nature and extent of the movement. At least three of the several major quakes that have occurred in California since 1857 were caused by displacements along the San Andreas Fault, which runs the length of the state and is nearest to Los Angeles at a point about fifty miles east of the city. Movement along an ocean segment of the Newport-Inglewood structural belt or fault, about three and one-half miles offshore, southwest of Newport Beach, produced the Long Beach earthquake in 1933. This is the only earthquake in the last eighty years causing severe damage in Los Angeles.

Most geologists believe that the effective force of earthwaves resulting from sudden movements along faults is dissipated at a distance of from five to fifteen miles from the fault; hence it is probable that only movements along the Inglewood Fault and associated minor faults can seriously disturb the city of Los Angeles. Although other large faults run through the area, no recent movements have been recorded upon them, and geologists consider dangerous activity along them unlikely.

Fossils: Southern California's abundant plant and animal fossils, which belong predominantly to the three most recent geological epochs— the Pleistocene, the Pliocene, and the Miocene—furnish a picture of the flora and fauna that flourished here in prehistoric times.

One of the world's most important collections of Pleistocene animal remains has been taken from the asphalt pits at Rancho La Brea (*see Tour C*), about six miles west of the center of Los Angeles, where thousands of mammals, birds, reptiles, and insects were caught in the sticky seepage. Bones of several thousand creatures, including those of extinct animals such as the saber-toothed cat or tiger, the dire wolf, the imperial elephant, and the American mastodon have been removed from the pits. Altogether more than one hundred different kinds of animals and plants are represented. Many of the bones have been assembled and the skeletons are exhibited at the Los Angeles Museum (*see Tour D*).

The thick beds of Miocene and Pliocene fossiliferous deposits covering parts of southern California contain exceedingly valuable oil deposits. These were formed from marine life impounded in the rocks at a time when the Los Angeles area lay beneath an ocean. The strata are also remarkable for the abundance of fossil mollusks. Miocene shellfish are plentiful in the Santa Monica Mountains, where also are found the bones of extinct marine fish and mammals. Fossilized roots and branches of Miocene trees have been unearthed in Topanga Canyon and elsewhere in the Santa Monica Mountains, and are on display at local institutions.

Climate: Los Angeles' climate is Mediterranean. It has been called "a cool climate with a warm sun." The temperature seldom rises above 85° or falls below 40°; the annual mean is 62.4°. The weather is temperate all year, with a relatively slight variation between summer and winter, and few extremes of heat or cold. But it is never quite the same any two years in succession; hence the city's reputation for "unusual weather."

During the summer months, rainfall is exceedingly rare because of the subtropical high pressure belt off the coast. The northwest migration of the wind system greatly weakens the westerlies, so that the temperature in spring and summer seldom rises above 85° at noon, and then without high humidity. There are generally hazy or cloudy sunrises, with cool breezes drifting in from the ocean in the forenoon. Even in July, August, and September, which are usually the warmest months, the nights are occasionally so cool that wraps are necessary.

By November the first important rains have fallen; the mornings are clear, the San Gabriel Mountains possibly snowcapped and outlined against hazeless blue skies. During winter, as the city comes under the influence of more southerly winds and warm ocean rains, the daytime temperature even on the coldest days is rarely below 55°, and usually ranges around 65° at noon. The nights are chilly and the thermometer may occasionally drop to the freezing point in nearby valleys.

With the coming of spring, the morning coast fogs return, breezes blow in from the Pacific, and the maximum temperature hovers around 70° to 75°. In May or June there may be a warm spell for a few days, lifting the temperature to 85° or possibly 90°.

Rainstorms usually occur only in the cooler months of the year. Mild and warm, they rarely last more than two days or precipitate more than two inches of rain. The average yearly rainfall is 15.23 inches; the average number of rainy days is thirty-seven. The winter rains occasionally bring freakish thunderstorms. In the nearby mountains, beginning at elevations of 4,000 feet, three or more feet of snow may fall during the winter.

In summer, ocean breezes keep the beach cities from 5° to 10°

cooler than metropolitan Los Angeles, and correspondingly warmer in winter. There is less variation between day and night temperatures in the coast towns than in the city. The California current, flowing offshore, exerts a cooling effect that tempers the climate of the entire Los Angeles area.

No generalizations about weather give the story, for each year there are many departures from the normal. The rainy season may begin as early as September or as late as January; the winter may be relatively cold or warm; snow may fall on rare occasions within the city limits; there may be an extended dry spell, or rainfall so heavy that disastrous floods result. Meteorologists, long accustomed to questions concerning Los Angeles weather, remark that "unusual weather" is not unusual for southern California.

Fauna: The widely divergent temperatures and altitudes in the mountains, deserts, and valleys of the Los Angeles region enable it to support exceptionally varied and numerous forms of animal life. Small fauna is overwhelmingly predominant; nearly all the larger animals here at the time of the early Spanish explorers have disappeared. The California grizzly bear, foe of the early rancher and traveler, is believed to be extinct; the bighorn sheep is gone except for a bare dozen that range on the slopes of Mount Baldy; and there are only three or four prong-horned antelopes in sparsely settled areas of the county. The puma or mountain lion, is becoming rare. Together with the bobcat, it is often the object of government biological surveys. The California mule deer, despite the slaughter of hundreds during each annual hunting season, has been holding its own since the inception of the State Game Conservation Program.

Among the most numerous of the small animals in the foothill and valley regions of Los Angeles County are the coyote, the striped and spotted skunks, the jack rabbit, brush rabbits, cottontails, and one variety of hare. These animals often invade the residential sections of Altadena, Monrovia, and other foothill cities. California weasels are plentiful, and raccoon are common throughout southern California in timbered creek bottoms. Both of these animals were once believed to be a nuisance to chicken ranchers, but evidence now shows that they more than compensate for their "depredations" by destroying mice. The gray fox is abundant in the foothill areas, and the small, long-eared kit fox is common in Antelope Valley. California badger are less numerous that they were in the past, but the opossum, brought here from the eastern states many years ago, is increasing.

Rodents, including several varieties of chipmunk and squirrel, are plentiful. The desert slope of the San Gabriel Mountains and Antelope Valley harbor grasshopper mice, desert pack rats, kangaroo rats, and parasitic mice. The shrew and mole are not common, but gophers are plentiful everywhere on the Pacific slope—in the foothills, valleys, and even on city lawns. The many varieties of southern California bats include the very rare spotted, the pale lump-nosed grinnell, California mastiff, California leaf-nosed, Mexican free-tailed, and brown bat. The only poisonous reptiles in the county are four varieties of rattlesnake: the Pacific, largest and most common, found in foothill and mountain regions; the Mojave, the white, and the sidewinder, found in the northwestern part of the desert area. Other snakes common in the mountains, valleys, and foothills near Los Angeles are the small California boa, the coral king snake, red racer, gopher snake, and two varieties of water snake. The only turtle found in nearby streams is the Pacific mud turtle; the desert tortoise, capable of storing water, is confined to the desert slope. Several of the many varieties of lizards common to the arid and semiarid regions of the Southwest are found in Los Angeles County. The western skink, Blainville horned toad, brown-shouldered lizard, and whip-tailed lizard are found on the Pacific slope. Lizards of the desert slope and Antelope Valley include the desert horned toad, and the desert rough-scaled, desert whip-tailed, leopard, and night lizards. The iguana and the abundant chuckwalla, two of the largest North American lizards, have been seen in that part of the Mojave Desert that lies within the county.

Beside the rattlesnake, three other poisonous creatures inhabit the county: the black widow spider, the mildly poisonous scorpion, and the relatively harmless tarantula. The black widow spider, distinguished by the red, hourglass-shaped spot on its shiny black abdomen, is the most dangerous of the three, but its bite is seldom fatal. In cities it is found most frequently in garages, closets, and under rubbish. About half a dozen kinds of scorpion have been found in the desert sections of Los Angeles County. Their bite is painful, but rarely fatal. The large California tarantula is the most common of several members of the family. Although the tarantula possesses well-developed poison glands, its bite is seldom, if ever, serious, probably no more so than that of the trap-door spider, which can be found in almost any vacant lot.

Southern California is the home of some 220 species of birds, and attracts about the same number of bird visitors and migrants. Those of the perching order are most numerous, and include the California jay, Brewer's blackbird, the western mockingbird, that disturbs sleep by singing at night (*see Tour 3*), the western bluebird, the western lark sparrow, the San Diego red-winged blackbird, the western meadowlark, the California horned lark, the western raven, the western crow, Cassin's purple finch, the house finch, the willow goldfinch, the green-backed goldfinch, the San Diego towhee, the California shrike, Hutton's vireo, the Pacific yellowthroat, the cactus wren, the dotted canon wren, the San Diego wren, the sierra creeper, the slender-billed nuthatch, the pygmy nuthatch, the plain titmouse, the mountain chickadee, the wren tit, the California bush tit, and the western gnatcatcher.

Among the visiting perching birds are the Arkansas kingbird, the ash-throated flycatcher, the Say's phoebe, olive-sided flycatcher, the western peewee, the western flycatcher, the yellow-headed blackbird, the Arizona hooded oriole, the Bullock's oriole, the western savanna sparrow, the Gambel's sparrow, the black-chinned sparrow, the fox sparrow, the black-headed grosbeak, the cliff swallow, the cedar waxwing, the Cassin's vireo, the least vireo, the black-throated gray warbler, the ruby-crowned kinglet, the russet-backed thrush, and the dwarf hermit thrush. The road runner, a cuckoo whose leg muscles have greatly developed though it still retains the power of flight, is fairly common on the cactus-covered washes and mesas. It belongs to the same order as the California cuckoo and kingfisher, found sparingly in the Los Angeles area. The county has eight resident and four visitant woodpeckers, also the sapsucker and flicker. The visitant Texas and Pacific nighthawks and the resident dusky whippoorwill belong to the same order as the numerous swifts and hummingbirds seen here at various times of the year. The Anna hummingbird, largest of the species, sings, which puts him in a class by himself, so far as hummingbirds are concerned. It is greenish in color and remains here during the winter; the black-chinned and Costa hummingbirds migrate to lower regions during cold weather; the fairly common calliope is a summer visitor to the mountains; the rufous, distinguished by its reddish hue, migrates through Los Angeles County twice a year, and there are also the Island and Allen hummingbirds.

Among the most interesting of the resident birds of prey are the rarely seen California vulture or condor, Cooper's hawk, western redtail, pigeon hawk, desert sparrow hawk, prairie falcon, American barn owl, spotted owl, and California screech owl. Visiting birds of prey include the Swainson hawk, western sharp-shinned hawk, marsh hawk, and short-eared owl. The bald eagle is rare on the mainland, but a common resident of the Santa Barbara Islands. The golden eagle is common in mountainous regions. The California condor is still resident in small numbers in mountainous sections of Santa Barbara and Ventura counties, and has also been seen occasionally in the Santa Monica and Tehachapi Mountains, as well as in Mount Pinos, Kern County. It is protected by law to prevent extinction; it is estimated there are approximately fifty of the birds in California.

Gulls, including the glaucous-winged, western, herring, California, and ring-billed varieties, are common shore birds. Most of them migrate inland, sometimes hundreds of miles, during the rainy season. The pied-billed grebe and black-nosed stilt are fairly common in the few tule-margined ponds between Los Angeles and the seacoast, and the western grebe visits the salt lagoons along the coast in winter. Loons are winter visitors to large reservoirs and to the shore. The California brown pelican is a resident along the beaches, while the white pelican is a visitant to lakes, sloughs, and marshlands from fall to spring. Until most of Los Angeles County's marshland was filled in a few years ago, ducks were fairly plentiful during the winter on the marshes between Los Angeles and the beach cities. Mallards and ruddy ducks are still seen on reservoirs and privately owned artificial lakes; and the green-winged teal is a frequent winter visitor.

Quail and doves are the most numerous game birds, and are increasing under the State Game Conservation Program. Attempts to stock the county with pheasants have been unsuccessful.

Seals, whales, porpoises, and dolphins are the marine mammals of southern California waters. Of the seals, the sea lion is the most numerous and is present at all seasons in the Catalina Channel. Before the days of the Russian seal hunters the California sea elephant was common along the southern California coast, but continual slaughter has thinned the herds until only a few of them remain.

The once-plentiful whales have been almost totally exterminated. In the early days of California whaling the finback, sulphur-bottom, and California gray whales, all fast, hard-fighting animals, destroyed so much of the whalers' gear that they were seldom molested, but after the invention of the explosive harpoon their numbers dwindled rapidly. The humpback, low in oil content and therefore unprofitable, is the most numerous of the remaining whales, though the California gray and the sulphur-bottom, largest of living animals, are sometimes seen.

In the teeming waters of the southern California coast there are more than 120 varieties of commercial fish and game. Several varieties of mollusks, including mussels, clams, squid and octopi are found on either the rocky or sandy beaches; other varieties including abalone and rock mussels are common on rocky sections of the coast. Other forms of marine fauna found on such rocky beaches as Palos Verdes and Laguna include sea anemones, starfish, sponges, hydroids, and various crustaceans.

Grunion, small fish of the smelt family, sweep up onto the beach to spawn during high tides on moonlit nights during the spring and summer months. Crowds of people gather on the beach, particularly along the stretch between Long Beach and Huntington Beach where the grunion runs are most frequent and of greatest magnitude, to gather quantities of the small silvery fish by the light of the moon, or of bonfires, or of flashlights.

The grunion appear the second, third, and fourth nights after the full of the moon, very shortly after the tide's peak. It takes the grunion only about thirty seconds to dig a hole in the sand with her tail and extrude her eggs. One wave tosses her ashore and the next returns her to the sea. When the moon is well up a run may last for an hour or more, and where there is a slight run-off or curve in the beach, which produces a swirl in the wash of the waves, the sand becomes alive with their glittering bodies.

Flora: The history of southern California floriculture and agriculture has been linked with an unending quest for more water—from the time the Franciscan padres dug irrigation ditches from the San Gabriel River to their newly planted fields until the building of the Colorado River Aqueduct. Potentially fruitful because of its unusually wide variety of soils, its mild, equable climate, and its varied terrain, southern California has needed only water to enable it to support a diversified and an abundant plant life. Where water is plentiful, southern California is a region of orange groves, palm trees, and flower gardens; where water is lacking, it is a harsh and comparatively sterile land of chamise, cacti, and scrub oak.

Of the three main types of native vegetation found in Los Angeles County—hard-leaved shrubs and dwarf trees on the foothills, coniferous forests on the ranges, and desert plant life in Antelope Valley and the Mojave Desert—the chaparral is by far the most characteristic. Chaparral, from the Spanish *chaparro* (scrub oak), was the name given by the Spanish settlers to the expanse of brush covering a large section of the upper foothill and mountainous region. This tangle of shrubs and dwarf trees appears to be worthless, as compared with the tall conifers and spreading deciduous trees of moister climates, yet it is so valuable as watershed covering that the expanse where it grows has been made a part of the Angeles National Forest.

In the canyons of the San Gabriel Mountains, above the chaparral belt and often blending with it, lie the coniferous forests. At 2,500 feet, and even below this level, are Douglas firs. Growing at higher elevations, from 2,500 to 6,000 feet, are white firs; beautiful Coulter pines; and the handsome Digger pines with long, deep, blue-needled branches. The huge cones of the Digger pines provide "piñon" nuts. Various other varieties of pines are seen from elevations of 5,000 feet to the summits of the San Gabriel Mountains—the Murray, the yellow, and the Jeffrey pines predominating—and stands of incense-cedar, tall pyramidal trees with deep green and compact foliage. The great sugar pine grows only on the highest mountains of the county.

Along the slopes of the San Gabriel Mountains, in Antelope Valley, and in the Mojave Desert, characteristic desert vegetation prevails. The brush-covered slopes of the canyons descending into the desert are spotted with juniper, cacti, and yucca, with its dazzling masses of white blossoms, while along the dry water courses and washes appear various shrubs. Farther north and east the area is grayish-green with creosotebush, locoweed, saltbush, and mesquite, broken occasionally by the silhouette of a smoke tree (also called chittamwood). Near Palmdale is one of the extensive growths of Joshua trees, stretching grotesquely twisted arms upward. Until recently the wood of the Joshua tree was used for "breakaway" furniture in motion pictures and for surgical splints, but the plant is now protected by law.

Although the cactus is popularly associated with the desert, many varieties of it are found in the foothills, along the seacoast, in parts of the Los Angeles Basin, and even in the high mountains, where they are covered with snow during the winter months. Yellow- or green-flowered chollas (Opuntia) are plentiful on the flats and in washes and canyons. Common species of the prickly pear (Opuntia) grow in the San Fernando Valley and on the San Pedro Hills, while Mojave prickly pear appears in the canyons on the desert side of the San Gabriels. In some rocky areas of the Mojave Desert are barrel cactus (the desert's water reservoirs), hedgehog cactus, and the purple-flowered fishhook cactus.

Best known of the wild flowers is the California poppy, official state flower, called by the Spaniards Dormidera (drowsy one) whose golden-hued petals unfold to the sunshine during the day and close at night as though in sleep. During the spring, near Fairmont and Del Sur in the Antelope Valley, the countryside is bright with the yellow and gold of the poppies, interspersed with the purples, pinks, and violets of thistle sage and lupine.

Opening late in the afternoon among the sand dunes of the desert are the large white flowers of evening primroses. They bloom but once. The day-old flowers turn pink, and the withered plants become tumbleweeds, or are buried by drifting sands. Covering acres of sandy or gravelly flats, blossoming from February to May, are the long prostrate stems of purple-flowered sand verbena.

From early March until late June, the curious leather-like mahogany-red flowers of the western peony and the great clusters of white or pink blossoms of a shrubby kind of poppy appear along the banks of mountain streams and among the rocky hills. Two vine-like plants growing among the low shrubs in this area are the scarlet-flowered climbing Pentstemon, and the cucumber-plant (sometimes called manroot because its root is frequently as large as a man's body), which bears peculiar pulpy fruit covered with spines.

Fields along coastal highways are brilliant during April and May with yellow-flowered Coreopsis and the purple-flowered dwarf lupine softens the usually somber-colored cliffs facing the sea. Deep green mats of bright yellow- and purple-flowered Mesembryanthemum cover beach dunes and sandy slopes.

Among the plants introduced into the county, the commonest are the yellow-flowered wild mustard and the white-flowered wild radish, both brought in by the mission padres. Two other widely distributed plants are the native yellow-flowered California buttercups, and blue-flowered Phacelias (baby-blue-eyes), which blossom from February until late July.

The flowers that brighten the gardens, parkways, and driveways are too numerous to list. A few of those most commonly planted are geraniums, cosmos, sweet peas, asters and marigolds, petunias, zinnias, dahlias, daisies, pansies, violets, roses, hydrangea and chrysanthemums, snapdragons, gladioli, stocks, nasturtiums, hollyhocks, cyclamen, camellias and lantanas.

Southern California's hospitality to immigrant herbs, trees, and shrubs is great, and Los Angeles' floral display is drawn from the entire world. The early Spaniards brought many seeds from their native land, and the later Mexicans imported numerous forms. Many pioneers became agriculturists and horticulturists, and sent back home for seeds and plants.

In late fall the spectacular Poinsettia flares with red. A native of Mexico, where it is called Flor de Noche Buena (flower of the good night—Christmas Eve), it was introduced here about 1830 and named in honor of Joel R. Poinsett, one of the earliest American diplomatic representatives to that country. From Mexico have also come the Copa de Oro (cup of gold), with yellow funnel-shaped flowers nearly a foot long; the flaming scarlet-petaled sticky mallow or *monacillo* (altar box); and numerous forms of the showy flowered Hibiscus.

Many of the beautiful plants in parks and gardens of southern California have come from China, Japan, and other Oriental countries. Cotoneasters, firethorns, bamboos, and the Cherokee rose came from China; the Japanese rose or globe-flower, the gold-dust plant, and the Kud-zu vine came from Japan; and from Formosa came the large-leaved ricepaper-plant.

Perhaps the most spectacular of the introduced vines is the wisteria of the Orient, whose purple and white blossoms appear in spring and summer. At Sierra Madre a wistaria vine covers more than an acre of ground and during its flowering season in March it shelters an annual fete.

Some eucalypti, the first seeds of which were brought to the West Coast from Australia about 1850, vie in height with the native Sequoias. The blue-gum is the largest, most useful, and the one most widely planted in the county. During blossom-time, the abundance of white flowers in its swaying crown makes it seem dusted with drifted snow. In contrast to the tall blue-gum is a species of dwarf eucalyptus. Along North Rexford Drive in Beverly Hills, is a fine display of these dwarf trees. In August and September they riot with color; great clusters of brilliant scarlet, pink, and orange flowers appear against the large, dark, glossy leaves.   Belonging in the same botanical family, are the myrtle and its cousins, the Eugenias, beautiful ornamental trees and shrubs, and the odd Callistemons and Melaleucas, both called "bottle brush" and bearing very showy flowers.

More than a score of varieties of the acacia have come from Australia.   From early January until late summer these trees are enveloped with great sprays of yellow flowers, some also with beautiful fernlike, silvery blue-green foliage.   Also from Australia comes the silk-oak (Grevillea), a tall, slender tree with fernlike leaves, covered in summer with comblike golden-yellow flowers.   Another native of Australia is the flametree.   In early spring it presents a startling sight with its large, shining, maple-like leaves, and masses of small cup-shaped flowers of rich red on scarlet stems.

Blending into this subtropical growth is the pepper tree from the Andean valleys of Peru; the first seeds were brought to North America by sailors more than 100 years ago.   This tree, beautiful with drooping branches and red berries that remain throughout the winter, has almost become a symbol of California.   Other imported plants are the jasmine from Chile; the gorgeous bird-of-paradise flower and the colletia, from Argentina; and two plants from Brazil, the red- or magenta-colored bougainvillea, and the jacaranda tree bearing a mass of light violet-blue tubular flowers during June and July.

From the Indian slopes of the Himalayas has come the deodar, a magnificent coniferous tree of pyramidal form, silvery blue-green foliage, and great sweeping branches.   Two others of the same genus, the Atlas and the Cedar of Lebanon, are equally handsome ornamental trees, and have been planted in lawns and avenues in the Los Angeles district. More striking in appearance, however, are three curious imported conifers (Araucarias): the monkey-puzzle tree from Chile; the bunya-bunya from Australia; and the Norfolk Island Pine, a tree that was imported from a small island in the South Pacific where it was discovered by the early English navigator, Captain James Cook.

Besides these exotic woody forms widely represented in the county, there are, conspicuously planted, numerous kinds of palms.   The tall, graceful Washingtonia is a fan palm indigenous to the canyons along the southern fringe of the Colorado Desert.   Some streets in the older residential sections of Los Angeles are lined with it.   Rivaling the Washingtonia in popularity are two feathery-leaved palms—the Canary Island, which grows to a tremendous size, and the wine or honey palm of Chile.   A noteworthy growth of palms is in Pershing Square in downtown Los Angeles, but the Huntington Gardens in San Marino contain the largest collection of palms in southern California.   Huntington Gardens also has many varieties of cacti and succulents.

Oranges were first brought to California by the missionaries in 1769. It is believed that the San Gabriel Mission developed the first large California orange orchard, an area of six acres in which about 400 seedling trees were planted about 1805. Today, flanking the foothills and filling the valleys, stretch evenly planted rows of orange, lemon, and grapefruit trees. During the blossoming season, from March until early May, they bear waxy white, pungent flowers. In April, the deciduous trees of the county are in bloom—pink and white apple blossoms, white apricot blossoms, pink peach blossoms, and the white flowers of the pear trees. Blending with these are the white flowers of walnut trees, white and pink flowers of almond trees, and the pale yellow or green blossoms of the avocado.

Pueblo to Metropolis

THE history of the Los Angeles area abounds with the gargantuan, the fantastic. Settled more than sixteen miles inland from a shallow, unprotected bay, it has made itself into one of the great port cities of the world; lying far off the normal axes of transportation and isolated by high mountains, it has become one of the great railroad centers of the country; lacking a water supply adequate for a large city, it has brought in a supply from rivers and mountain streams hundreds of miles away. In little more than half a century lots listed at a tax sale at a price of 63 cents apiece have increased in value to the point where they are worth more than that price to the square inch. It is not surprising that a city of such incredible achievements should become the home of fantasy; the film industry could not have found a more stimulating environment.

When Los Angeles became an incorporated city under American rule in 1850, there was little evidence remaining even at that time to show that North Broadway, near the Los Angeles River viaduct, once had been the center of an Indian village, and that this entire area had at one time been the exclusive province of the Gabrielino Indians. And yet it was that primitive village which became the nucleus for twentieth-century Los Angeles.

The predominating linguistic stock was Shoshonean, the great Uto-Aztecan family which spread across North America from what is now Idaho southward to Central America. No less than twenty-eight Indian villages existed in what now constitutes Los Angeles County. One of these, Yang-na, was situated near the heart of modern Los Angeles.

These Indians, although primitive, were much more peaceful than many North American tribes. They seldom warred with other groups. Robbery was unknown and murder was punishable by death, as was incest. From chief and medicine man to squaw and child they lived according to strict ritual and taboos. They believed in only one deity, called Qua-o-ar, whose name never passed their lips except during important ceremonies, and then only in a whisper. The men seldom wore clothing, and women usually had only a deerskin about the waist. Along the coast women clad themselves in the fur of the sea otter. The homes, of woven tule mats, resembled gigantic beehives. Agriculture and domestication of animals were unknown to these aborigines;

24

they lived on what was at hand—edible roots, acorns, wild sage, and berries. Snakes, rodents, and grasshoppers supplemented the supply of such wild game as fell to their crude weapons. They knew little of basket weaving and nothing of pottery making. Cooking utensils and ceremonial vessels were made by the simple process of rubbing out a hollow place in a slab, or block of soapstone. Bows were unknown. Stone-tipped sticks and clubs were their only weapons. It is not recorded that these primitive people possessed boats of any character.

SPAIN SENDS THE MISSION FATHERS

Meanwhile, as the fifteenth century ended, adventurers from Spain and Portugal made their way to the New World. Cortez conquered Mexico in 1519. Twenty-three years later, in 1542, the age-long isolation of Yang-na and its fellow villages ended. In that year Juan Rodriguez Cabrillo, a Portuguese navigator in Spanish service, cruised northward along the Pacific and discovered what is now San Pedro Bay, naming it Bahia de los Fumos (bay of the smokes) because of the many Indian campfires he saw along its shore. Sixty years passed before another ship, captained by Sebastian Vizcaíno, entered the bay in 1602. During the remainder of the seventeenth century, occasional heavily laden Spanish galleons, returning to Mexico from the Philippines, touched the shores of California to repair their leaking ships and rest their thirsty, half-famished, scurvy-stricken crews. Tales of these great canoes and their pale-face sailors circulated among the natives for decades before white civilization was introduced.

In most sections of America, European colonists launched their settlements despite the Indians. In California, on the contrary, it was the presence of Indians that attracted pioneers and led to colonization and development of the region. Spain long had carried on missionary work among tribes in Mexico proper; as the eighteenth century drew to a close, the Spanish determined to bring Christianity to the natives along the Pacific slope. Conquest of California was to be achieved "not by force of arms, but rather by the gentle means of persuasion and evangical preaching."

But if the padres thought only in terms of spiritual conversion of the natives, government officials were prompted by more worldly consideration to promote colonization of the California slope. Spain spurred on the effort because other nations were casting covetous eyes on the section. Sir Francis Drake had visited its shores and had claimed it for Queen Elizabeth. Imperial Russia was reaching out across the Bering Sea to the American mainland. And France, with her newly acquired American empire between the Mississippi and the Rocky

Mountains, was already contemplating a move to extend her domain to the Pacific.

Frail, crippled, fifty-five-year-old Franciscan Father Junipero Serra and bluff, sturdy Captain Gaspar de Portolá were chosen to lead the expedition into hitherto unexplored Upper California and to select sites for missions. Father Juan Crespi, diarist of the expedition, was to give posterity its first description of the now famous route, El Camino Real (the King's Highway), which extends between San Diego and San Francisco. The expedition divided its forces, one group proceeding overland and the other by sea. After suffering great hardships, both parties arrived at San Diego Bay in 1769, and a few days later, on July 16, Father Serra founded the Mission San Diego de Alcalá, first link in the chain of twenty-one Franciscan missions in California.

Without waiting to witness the founding, Captain Portola and Father Crespi, with a force of sixty-seven men, had begun the long overland trek northward to Monterey, breaking the trail for El Camino Real. After more than a fortnight of arduous travel, they made camp near the southern declivity of what now is Elysian Park, not far north of what was to become the very hub of Los Angeles. Crespi's entry in his diary for this day on which white men first saw the site of Los Angeles read:

> After traveling about a league and a half through a pass between low hills we entered a very spacious valley, well grown with cottonwoods and alders, among which ran a beautiful river from north-northwest, and then, doubling the point of a steep hill (now Elysian Park), it went on afterward to the south. . . . This plain where the river runs is very extensive. It has good land for planting all kinds of grain and seeds, and is the most suitable site of all we have seen for a mission, for it has all the requisites for a large settlement. As soon as we arrived, about eight heathen from a good village came to visit us; they live in this delightful place among the trees on the river. They presented us with some baskets of pinole made from seeds of sage and other grasses. Their chief brought some strings of beads made of shells, and they threw us three handfuls of them. Some of the old men were smoking pipes well made of baked clay, and they puffed at us three mouthfuls of smoke. We gave them a little tobacco and some glass beads and they went away pleased.

Crespi's diary for the next day reported: "After crossing the river, we entered a large vineyard of wild grapes and an infinity of rosebushes in full bloom. All the soil is black and loamy and is capable of producing every kind of grain and fruit which may be planted." That day he also reported that members of the expedition "saw some large marshes of a certain substance like pitch; they were boiling and bubbling, and the pitch came out mixed with an abundance of water." Thus were discovered the La Brea tar pits (bordering on present-day Wilshire Boulevard); and thus was recorded the first indication of petroleum in western America.

Two years later, Father Serra's associates founded the Mission San Gabriel Arcangel near the recommended site. It was yet another decade before some two score settlers, at the command of Governor Felipe de Neve, founded the town of Los Angeles at Crespi's "delightful place among the trees on the river."

"This place," wrote Father Serra proudly to the Mexican viceroy in describing the site of San Gabriel Mission, "is beyond dispute the most excellent discovered. Without doubt, this one alone, if well cultivated, would be sufficient to maintain itself and all the rest of the missions."

San Gabriel, founded September 8, 1771, more than fulfilled Serra's high expectations. The natives were converted easily to the new faith under the benignant but rigorous mission system. The Indians were trained in agriculture, stock raising, gilding, brickmaking, and other trades. They were clothed, housed, and fed at the mission they erected under the padres' tutelage. Their children were taught to speak Spanish. As early mission records eloquently attest, the natives quickly learned tasks assigned to them. They labored long and diligently. A few decades later, hundreds of natives were tending thousands of head of cattle, on a million and a half acres of land surrounding San Gabriel Arcangel, from San Bernardino Mountains to the Pacific Ocean.

FOUNDING OF LOS ANGELES

A cornerstone in Spanish colonial policy was the principle that active colonization must begin once the spiritual mission center and the military presidios were established. The new governor of California, Felipe de Neve, acted in conformity with this policy when he recommended to the viceroy of Mexico that a *pueblo* be established at the place which Father Crespi in 1769 had suggested as an ideal spot for a mission. Thus was conceived the settlement that was to become Los Angeles. The town was ordained by royal decree, and Governor de Neve worked out every detail well in advance of actual settlement. Settlers were to be recruited and conducted to the site by government agents. Each was to be told where to live, what to build, what crops to grow, and how much of his time must be given to community undertakings.

De Neve staked out four square leagues—a small plaza surrounded by seven-acre fields for cultivation; pastures and royal lands for leasing to citizens. To plan a town was one thing; to get settlers for it was another, as the governor soon learned. Despite inducements of land, money, livestock, and implements, he was unable to obtain settlers from Lower California, and it was months before a group was recruited in Mexico, chiefly Sonora. On August 18, 1781, they reached San Gabriel

Mission, a small and sorry-looking group of eleven men, eleven women, and twenty-two children.   Only two of the adults were of Spanish origin, the remainder including one *mestizo* (half-breed), eight mulattoes, nine Indians, and two Negroes.   Despite misgivings of the mission fathers over the venture, De Neve was determined to push his scheme to realization.

Early in the morning of September 4, 1781, the expedition left the mission for the official founding of Los Angeles.   Governor de Neve himself led the procession, followed by soldiers, the forty-four settlers, mission priests and some of their Indian acolytes.   The Yang-na Indians gathered en masse to witness the strange spectacle as the procession marched slowly around the spot selected for the pueblo, and the padres invoked a blessing upon the new community.   Governor de Neve made a formal speech, followed by prayers and benedictions from the clergy.   Thus came into being *El Pueblo de Nuestra Señora la Reina de Los Angeles de Porciúncula* (Sp., the town of Our Lady the Queen of the Angels de Porciúncula), one of the few cities on earth which has been deliberately planned in advance and ceremoniously inaugurated.

Governor Pedro Fages, successor to De Neve, inaugurated the policy of giving huge grants of land to his old friends and comrades-in-arms. One of the first of these grants, a rancho of approximately forty-three thousand acres, went to Juan José Dominguez in 1785, and embraced the territory now included in Wilmington, Torrance, Redondo Beach, and several smaller communities.   It is the only one of the many Spanish grants of which a considerable part still remains in the possession of heirs of the original grantees.

The Spanish, and later the Mexican, governors were lavish in their distribution of vast tracts, each of tens of thousands of acres.   Except for the mission tract and that property directly assigned to the pueblo, nearly the whole of what now constitutes the coastal area of Los Angeles County passed into the hands of a score or more Spanish and Mexican hidalgos.   When the eighteenth century ended, the region was already divided into mission, pueblo, and rancho domain, and for both the first and last of these the outlook was promising.   Huge expanses covered with ever-increasing herds of cattle, fields of grain, vineyards, and orchards, all added to the prosperity and prestige of their owners.

But the pueblo homes remained small, mud-colored, square-walled, flat-roofed, one-story structures with rawhide doors and glassless windows.   Lawns, trees, and sidewalks were nonexistent, and the narrow streets were seas of mud in winter and clouds of dust in summer. The civic pride and courage of Corporal Vincent Felix, commander of the tiny garrison, held this uncomfortable community together.   He not only took his military duties seriously but, unofficially, assumed every administrative, legislative, and judicial task. Respected, feared, and loved, the little corporal remained the real power in the pueblo long after the election of the first of the alcaldes.

By 1790 Los Angeles numbered 28 householders and a population of 139. By 1800, the population was 315, and there were 30 adobe houses for the 70 families, as well as a town hall, guardhouse, army barracks, and granaries.

In this remote outpost, social gradations were unknown. No school existed to train the young in deportment and letters. Mail was carried to and from Mexico once a month—a distance of 3,000 miles—over the Camino Real. Few took advantage of these postal facilities, since the ability to read and write was rare among the first settlers. There was little trade or commerce of any kind. Such as there was remained largely in the hands of the padres and was carried on through the port of San Pedro.

There were certain compensations, however, for the primitive life of that period. No one paid taxes or rent. Each man lived in his own house and cultivated his own land. As the nineteenth century descended upon Los Angeles, its citizens were completely oblivious to that trio of modern civilization: the real-estate agent, the tax gatherer, and the instalment collector.

Cut off from the rest of civilization, these people neither knew nor cared for the issues and problems of the world at large. Most were unaware even of the fact that a young and lusty republic had been born on the other side of the continent—a new nation to which their fortunes soon would be irrevocably tied. Nor did they realize that a short, bow-legged Corsican was already at work yanking out the props from under the three-century-old world power of Spain; that the European turmoil would soon wipe out Spain's American empire; that in its wake would follow half a century of strife, culminating in destruction of Spanish control, and disintegration of Spanish missions and Spanish customs in California.

It was a principle of the early colonial powers that those regions they obtained by discovery or conquest were theirs alone to exploit. The produce of their colonies must be sold to their merchants alone, and transported in their ships. Likewise the people of the colonies were permitted to buy only goods produced in the home country or transported on its ships. Such was the relationship of England to its American colonies. Such, too, was the relationship of Spain to California. To Mexico and to Spain went the rapidly accumulating stores of hides and tallow from the California ranches; from them came the necessities and occasional luxuries of the Californians.

Yankee traders knew nothing of this forbidden market in California

until Captain William Shaler, of Boston, wrote enthusiastically about
it in 1808. Returning from the Orient in 1805, he spent several months
on the California coast trading with Indians and whites, in defiance
of Spanish laws. He saw huge vats of tallow and untold thousands of
hides, obtainable for next to nothing, for which New England shoe-
and-harness makers would pay well. Even more important in the eyes
of this shrewd Yankee were the vast quantities of valuable sea otter
pelts. Realizing that the laws of Spain did not count heavily so long
as local authorities could not enforce them, Shaler, when he reached
home, spoke out freely in the Boston press:

"The conquest of this country would be absolutely nothing; it
would fall without an effort to the most inconsiderable force. The
Spaniards have few ships or seamen in this part of the world . . . it
would be as easy to keep California in spite of the Spaniards, as it
would be to wrest it from them in the first instance."

Inspired by Shaler's report, more and more New England sea
captains put in at California ports, commencing an American economic
penetration on which mission fathers and hidalgos alike looked askance,
though some welcomed and abetted it. As for the Yankees, they
found the trade extremely profitable. Robert Glass Cleland, in his
History of California, tells how one trader obtained 300 sea otter skins
for 2 yards of cotton cloth apiece. Another obtained $8,000 worth of
furs for a rusty iron chisel, and a Captain Strugis purchased 560 skins,
worth $40 apiece, with goods that cost $1.50 in Boston.

By 1820 the sea otters had been almost exterminated, and the trade
in them was replaced by commerce in hides and tallow, also valuable
to the Yankee traders who had brought an end to California's isolation. Through the hides Los Angeles helped give New England a
monopoly of the early boot-and-shoe industry. Thus, too, New England
found a virgin market for her manufactured products, developed a
growing interest in southern California, and paved the way for the rise
of Yankee dons to power and prominence.

Companion to the highly successful Mission San Gabriel was Mission San Fernando, founded twenty-two miles northwest of Los Angeles on September 8, 1797. For years the new mission played an important part in the life of the Los Angeles area, supplying vast quantities
of foodstuffs to the pueblo and also to the presidio of Santa Barbara.
By 1819 it had a neophyte population of 1,080; its cattle numbered
21,745. Olives and dates were cultivated extensively; wheat, barley,
and corn were raised in abundance; and the products of the mission's
vineyards were second in fame only to those of San Gabriel. Wool
from more than 7,000 sheep was worked on looms in the great mission
quadrangle and woven into blankets and cloth. Indian artisans tanned

hides and made shoes, saddles, and fashionable equestrian trappings of the day.

Lean days began with the revolution in Mexico, which began in 1810 and continued for more than a decade. California revenues declined almost immediately. Spain's yearly contributions of $100,000 or more for soldiers, civil government, and missions ceased after 1811. Spanish trading vessels avoided the coast for fear of capture by South American rebel privateers. The governor forced the missions to supply his soldiers and staff with food, wine, clothing, and other goods, despite the padres' strenuous objections. Paid with drafts drawn on Spain— "to be presented whenever this war with the rebels is over"—the missions were eventually left holding more than $400,000 in worthless paper.

Meanwhile the pueblo, the City of the Queen of the Angels, spreading amoeba-like in all directions, without plan or purpose, poured out beyond the original protective walls. The population grew to 650 in 1820. Food was plentiful, especially meat. The Indians provided a cheap and plentiful supply of labor. By 1817, there were more than a hundred acres of vineyards under cultivation near the pueblo, and the making of wine and brandy attained considerable proportions.

MEXICAN RULE

The Mexican War of Independence, except for its economic consequences, scarcely touched the life of the Californians. They lived in a world apart. And when at last, in March, 1822, news reached Los Angeles that Spain had relinquished her western possessions, the citizens accepted the news without objection. At the Plaza, the barracks, and other public buildings, the flag of Spain was hauled down; that of Mexico was raised. On March 26, 1825, California officially became a territory of the Republic of Mexico.

The quarter century of Mexican rule (1822-1847) has been viewed variously. To some it represents the period of full flowering of the missions, followed by general industrial and moral disintegration as the missions were secularized; to others it represents the Golden Age of California, when life was easy and picturesque, when crimes were few, food plentiful, and hospitable dons held sway over lordly ranches; and to yet others it is the period of revolutions and rise of the spirit of home rule among the Angelenos, the period of American penetration and of the rise to power and influence of the Yankee dons. And each of these interpretations has a measure of truth as a base.

The simple social organism planted by De Neve a half century earlier had grown both large and complex. Large, in the sense that Los Angeles was now the most populous community in California, with an estimated twelve hundred inhabitants in 1830. Complex, because of the influx of new settlers from Mexico and Spain; because of the growing pains of the pueblo as it took its first halting steps in the direction of self-government; because of the secularization of the missions, the oldest, most stable, and economically successful institution hitherto known to the Californians; and finally, because of the slow but steady influx of foreigners—Germans, Scots, Englishmen, Frenchmen, and above all Yankees—bringing with them new ways of life.

The land and its inhabitants made a strong appeal to occasional American hunters, trappers, and traders who stumbled upon it, but they were quick to see the comparative somnolence of the Californians. James O. Pattie, a trapper who made the overland trip to southern California in 1828, wrote on his return to the East:

"The people live apparently unconscious of the paradise around them. They sleep and smoke and hum Castilian tunes while nature is inviting them to the noblest and richest rewards of honorable toil."

An outward semblance of peace camouflaged the conflicting forces already at work in the region. First and foremost was the issue of secularization. The mission system had not been adopted originally by Spanish authorities as permanent; rather, it was considered a practical method of civilizing the natives and making them amenable to government. When the first missions were established, it was believed that after about ten years of tutelage under the padres the Indians would be ready for citizenship entitling each to a small allotment of land, implements, and supplies. Under the patriarchal system of the padres, the Indians became docile neophytes, but did not develop the capacity of self-reliant citizenship, and the missions continued to hold the land in trust for the neophytes after the ten-year period was over. The first attempt at secularization was made by the Spanish *cortes* (congress) in 1813, by a decree never enforced because of the Mexican revolution begun in 1810, which occupied the full attention of the Spanish authorities.

The new Mexican government, established in 1824, took up the issue where Spain had left it. By 1834, a plan of secularization had been formulated by the *diputación* under Governor José Figueroa of California. Approved by the Mexican congress, enforcement was begun in 1835. Many approved the act in principle, others looked longingly at the missions' rich fields, fine pasture lands, well-kept orchards, and profitable vineyards; to them secularization meant a chance to take for themselves what the padres and neophytes had made productive.

The Mexican congress appointed commissioners to take inventory of the mission properties and to distribute shares of land, seed, implements, and cattle among the Indians. But the Indians were unable to shift for themselves when the advice and guidance of the padres were removed. Their religious and occupational training was soon forgotten. Thousands ran away to the mountains and returned to native habits. Others wandered helplessly from mission to mission. Only a few retained and cultivated the land given them; and the attempt to establish them in pueblos was a failure.

Foreseeing the inevitable ruin of the mission properties, the padres hastened to salvage what they and their thousands of neophytes had accumulated during more than half a century. Cattle, hitherto killed only as their meat was needed, were now slaughtered in herds by contract on equal shares. There was no market for the meat, only for tallow and hides. The discarded carcasses became carrion for the buzzards until the Los Angeles *ayuntamiento* passed an ordinance compelling all persons slaying cattle for hides and tallow to burn the remains.

Thus the mission system of California, to whose establishment Father Serra and many others had given their efforts, was destroyed almost overnight. These centers of culture and Christianity, of comfort and industry, with their beauty, wealth, spacious buildings, gardens, and chapels, had been the marvel of Spanish America. At the beginning of 1834 California's 21 missions had been directing the labor of 15,000 Indians; were producing 123,000 bushels of grain; tending 779,500 head of cattle, horses, sheep, goats, and swine, and cultivating orchards, vineyards, and well-kept vegetable gardens. Only eight years later scarcely one-eighth of the Indians were living in or near the missions; livestock had been reduced to 64,440 head; the mission buildings were already falling in ruin. Orchards, vineyards, and fields had succumbed to weeds and inroads of hungry cattle. Groves of olive trees were being chopped down for firewood.

"I am one of the great mass of laymen," said George Wharton James, "who love the old missions for their own sake, for their history, for the noble deeds they have enshrined, for the good their builders did—and more . . . what they sought to do—for the Indians, whom the later comers, my own race, have treated so abominably."

In the early 1840's the population of Los Angeles and the region immediately surrounding it had increased to nearly 1,250—forming the largest settlement in the territory. For this reason the Angelenos felt that the pueblo, rather than Monterey, should become the capital of California. The Mexican government agreed to the change, but the seat of government never was transferred.

During the second quarter of the century a handful of foreigners, who by accident or choice had landed in California, were gradually taking over control of commerce and industry. These newcomers, mostly Americans, gave their oath of loyalty to the Mexican government, joined the Catholic church, married into leading native families, and in many cases even took Spanish names and assumed the title of "don."

First of the Yankees to settle in California was Joseph Chapman of Massachusetts, who, arriving in 1818 as the unwilling member of a South American privateer crew, was captured near Santa Barbara by an irate posse of Californians. He not only talked his captors out of hanging him, but before long had married into the family whose rancho the crew had been on the point of plundering. He became the owner of a large ranch and built the first gristmill in California. In 1827, another son of Massachusetts, John Temple, arrived to become "Don Juan," and within the next four years came Jesse Ferguson and Nathaniel Pryor, "Don Abel" Stearns, and Jonathan (Don Juan José) Warner.

There came, too, in 1828, an influx of twenty-eight other foreigners, most of them being survivors of the American brig *Danube,* which had been wrecked at San Pedro on Christmas Day. These men and their immediate successors were received with all warmth and hospitality characteristic of the Californians. But most of these newcomers were hardworking, frugal Yankees, and they were unable to understand the easy-going, *mañana* existence of the Angelenos; to them, as to Richard Henry Dana, they were "an idle, thriftless people, and [could] make nothing for themselves."

Within a few years, these Yankees had become great landholders and monopolized local commerce. By 1840 they were so powerful as to be considered a threat to the peace and security of Mexico and were denounced as "foreign agitators." Within a score of years after the arrival of Joseph Chapman, Governor Juan Bautista Alvardo issued orders for the banishment of all unnaturalized interlopers. Half a hundred Americans and several Englishmen were rounded up, tried, convicted of activities hostile to Mexico, and shipped off in chains to a prison in Mexico. The English government promptly interfered in behalf of its subjects, with the result that all the exiles were freed, most of them making their way back to Alta California, where they remained to challenge the rule of the Mexican governors in California. In one of the many provincial revolutions—that led by Pío Pico against Governor Manuel Micheltorena—both sides appealed to the despised Yankees for aid, and the Yankees, with more humor than bellicosity, helped both sides.

Pío Pico placed his forces in command of José Castro during the one battle of this revolution. At the battleground in San Fernando Valley, Benjamin D. Wilson, William Workman, and James Mc-Kinley, of Castro's forces, slipped up a ravine and by the use of a white flag succeeded in attracting the attention of John Gant, Samuel J. Hensley, and John Bidwell, of Micheltorena's army, who joined their friends. They discussed the situation, and it was agreed that all the Americans with Micheltorena would desert and join Pico if Pico would agree to protect them in their land grants. Wilson found Pico and informed him of the agreement.

"Gentlemen," declaimed Pico, ". . . if you will abandon his cause I will give you my word of honor as a gentleman . . . that I will protect each one of you in the land that you now hold, and when you become citizens of Mexico I will issue you the proper titles."

The two forces, each numbering about four hundred men, met on February 20, 1845. Micheltorena had three pieces of artillery and Castro two. They opened fire on each other at long range, and after the burning of the gunpowder and much shouting of orders and waving of swords (there had been one casualty—a dead horse), Micheltorena marched away toward San Fernando. The following morning, Castro overtook him, fired a few rounds from his two guns, and Micheltorena hoisted a white flag. It was at this surrender that John Sutter was taken prisoner. He and his company of Indians were kept in a corral for a time, then were sent back to Sacramento.

Within two years after this deal with the Americans, Governor Pío Pico remorsefully declared in a speech before the Departmental Assembly:

"We find ourselves suddenly threatened by hordes of Yankee immigrants . . . whose progress we cannot arrest. . . . They are cultivating farms, establishing vineyards, erecting mills, sawing up lumber, building workshops, and doing a thousand other things which seem natural to them."

The Americans became so rich and powerful, and their numbers multiplied so fast that many of the native California leaders advocated a British protectorate for the Pacific slope, since they knew that Mexico was too weak to resist successfully any move by the United States to acquire the territory.

There had long been agitation in Washington for conquest and annexation of California. The watchword "manifest destiny" was expounded by orators and editors throughout the United States. The phrase meant, at least to the fervid expansionists, that the obvious and inevitable destiny of the United States was to expand, particularly to the westward, until it should comprise one unbroken empire from the Atlantic to the Pacific. Southern leaders, moreover, demanded annexation of California to the Union as an additional slave state. The agitation came to a head in 1846 with the outbreak of the Mexican War, which was brought about ostensibly by the fact that Mexico had refused to recognize the annexation of the Republic of Texas to the United States in 1845. At the time of the declaration of war against Mexico, Captain John C. Frémont, either fortuitously or by a most remarkable foresight, was in the heart of California with a force of Americans. Already, before being apprised of a state of war, he had inspired the Bear Flag Revolt and had spiked the guns of the old Spanish fort at the Golden Gate. Under orders from Commodore Robert Field Stockton, Frémont loaded his California battalion on the U.S.S. *Cyane* and sailed for San Diego, where he raised the American flag. He then marched northward and joined Commodore Stockton's force of sailors and marines, and they entered Los Angeles together, meeting no resistance, on August 13, 1846. The conquest had been accomplished without firing a gun.

Stockton and Frémont then marched northward, leaving Lieutenant Archibald H. Gillespie, U.S.M.C., with fifty men in command of the city of Los Angeles. This was one of the many mistakes made by both Stockton and Frémont. On several other occasions Gillespie had proved himself an excellent subaltern, but he was not an executive. He attempted to govern Los Angeles in the same manner he controlled a marine guard aboard a man-of-war, and the rambunctious Angeleno of that day was not accustomed to such discipline. Serbulo Varela, a wild young man of the town, started what was at first more like a personal feud with Gillespie than a rebellion; very quickly, however, dozens of kindred spirits joined with Varela, and he feinted an attack on the adobe building in which the Americans were garrisoned. The attack was repulsed, but overnight more than three hundred Californians joined Varela, and Captain José Maria Flores was chosen to command this new army. José Antonio Carrillo was second in command with the rank of major general, and Captain Andrés Pico was commander of a squadron.

On September 24th, Gillespie, harassed by the Fabian tactics of the rebels, sent a courier, John Brown—known as Juan Flaco, or Lean John—to Stockton to ask for reinforcements. Lean John carried a package of cigarettes, the paper of each bearing the inscription: "Believe the bearer" and Gillespie's seal. Brown started at eight o'clock in the evening of the 24th, closely pursued by fifteen Mexicans. His horse was shot through the body, but leaped across a ravine thirteen feet wide and ran for two miles before falling dead. Lean John then carried his spurs for twenty-seven miles and secured a second mount at Las Vírgenes. He rode night and day, and arrived in San Francisco at sunrise on the 29th, having traveled almost five hundred miles in five days.

Meanwhile, in Los Angeles, Gillespie had left his barracks to fortify a strong position on Fort Hill—now called Fort Moore Place. His force outnumbered at least ten to one, Gillespie called on Benito Wilson at Jarupa Ranch for aid. Wilson had been placed in that section to protect the inhabitants and their property from Indian raids.

But Wilson was having his troubles, too. Threatened by the forces of Serbulo Varela, Diego Sepulveda, and Ramon Carrillo, he had retired to the Chino Rancho of Isaac Williams, where the second battle of the rebellion was fought on September 26th-27th. The Californians surrounded the adobe ranch house in which Wilson had retreated with twenty Americans. In the assault one Californian, Carlos Ballestros, was killed and several of the Americans were wounded seriously. The American force surrendered and was taken to Los Angeles, where most of the more important men of the company were imprisoned in a small adobe house until released in January, 1847.

Learning of the capture of Wilson and his force, Gillespie surrendered on the 29th of September, 1846, the same day that Lean John delivered his message to Stockton in San Francisco. Flores and Pico gallantly permitted Gillespie to march his men to San Pedro, where, on October 4th, he embarked his men on the merchant ship *Vandalia,* but, anticipating aid from Stockton, did not leave the harbor.

In response to Lean John's message from Gillespie, Stockton ordered Captain William Mervine, U. S. Navy, to sail for San Pedro on the U.S.S. *Savannah.* He set out from Sausalito and arrived at San Pedro on the 6th to land 350 men.

Lieutenant Gillespie and his men at once joined with Mervine's force, and on the 7th they began the march to Los Angeles. They took no artillery from the ship, and the Californians had stampeded all the horses in the district—which resulted in one of the strangest defeats of a command in American military history. That afternoon the American advance guard met some of the Mexicans who had been sent out under command of Carrillo. Mervine halted and made camp in Dominguez rancho buildings. On the morning of the 8th, Mervine divided his force in three columns, two parties of skirmishers covering the flanks while his main body marched in the form of a square along the road. Carrillo also divided his mounted troops and worried the flanks and even the rear of the columns, but his shrewd use of his one small cannon was what defeated the sailors and marines. Carrillo mounted this gun on wagon wheels and set it in the middle of the road. When the Americans came within range, the gun was fired into the mass of men, then immediately was dragged away by *reatas* attached to the horsemen's saddles to be reloaded at a safe distance. This operation was repeated six times in less than a half hour. Six Americans were killed and as many wounded. According to Gillespie, in an article published in the *Sacramento Statesman* on May 6, 1858, Mervine lost thirteen men. Mervine ordered the retreat to San Pedro where the entire force re-embarked. The dead were buried on the little island which before and since then has been known as *Isla de los Muertos* (isle of the dead, or Deadman's Island).

The army of the Californians increased rapidly after this victory, and swarmed between San Pedro and Los Angeles, making it impossible for the Americans to land troops. Commodore Stockton arrived with 800 men on the U.S.S. *Congress,* and after making an erroneous estimate of the situation he decided to attack Los Angeles by way of San Diego. He arrived at that port with his entire force early in November.

On December 2nd, General Stephen W. Kearny entered California from Santa Fe, New Mexico, and on December 5th was joined by Lieutenant Gillespie and thirty-five men. On December 6th, near the small village of San Pasqual, a leading element of Kearny's force met a troop of mounted Californians under General Andrés Pico, and there ensued the bloodiest battle in California history.

The conflict was brief but furious. Because of the heavy rain and the time necessary for reloading, the American firearms were practically useless. The battle resolved itself into a hand-to-hand struggle of clubbed guns and sabers against the lances of the Californians. The Californians were ultimately put to rout by the arrival of Kearny's main body with two howitzers. Kearny's forces, exhausted, did not pursue. The exact number of casualties on each side is moot. A careful estimate, however, places American dead at eighteen, including three regular army captains, and wounded, fifteen. Kearny himself was wounded twice and Gillespie was for awhile left as dead on the field. Only one death resulted from gunfire, all the others being caused by lance thrusts. An estimate places the Californian wounded at twelve and, some accounts say, one killed.

On the following morning Kearny started his ragged detachment on its way to San Diego with the threatening Californians disputing his advance. Just past San Bernardo rancho, where the contingent had stopped for water, another skirmish occurred at the crest of a hill. Thirty or forty Californians had obtained possession of the hill, while the remainder threatened the Americans in the rear. The Americans were successful in driving off their opponents without any serious casualties, but it was apparent that an attempt to advance farther would result in additional disaster.

Three members of the party, Lieutenant E. F. Beale of the Navy, Kit Carson the scout, and an Indian, volunteered to attempt the perilous journey through the enemy country to Stockton at San Diego. Through the skill of Kit Carson the men eluded the besiegers and separately made their way to San Diego during the second night.

Kearny's call for aid was answered by the arrival of 80 marines and 100 sailors from Stockton's force. On December 12th the combined forces without further opposition from the Californians arrived in San Diego. The Americans marched from that southern port on

December 29th, and on January 8th, 1847, fought the Battle of San Gabriel at Paso de Bartolo just north of the present town of Whittier, Stockton's sailors and marines driving Flores' army from a strong position on the bluffs. The next morning Stockton and Kearny resumed the march into Los Angeles and again met the forces of Flores in the Battle of the Mesa in the southeastern outskirts of the city. One man and several animals were killed on each side; but as a result of this last battle of the campaign the Californians ceased to exist as a military unit. Neither Stockton nor Kearny would negotiate with Flores because he had broken his parole given at the first surrender of the city, and they would not accept the surrender of the city from Pico or Carrillo because neither of these officers would agree to give up their comrades-in-arms to certain execution. Flores assembled a small force of armed men, escaped from the city, and made his way to Mexico.

Frémont with his recruited battalion had been advancing toward Los Angeles from Santa Barbara since January 3rd, and on the 12th he was in the vicinity of Cahuenga. There, after a day and night of negotiations and the signing of an armistice, formal capitulation of Los Angeles was made to Frémont by Andrés Pico on January 13th, 1847. Frémont marched into the city on January 14th. Frémont's action is remarkable in American martial annals from the fact that he accepted the surrender of an enemy army and the enemy's most important city, though within a few hours' march of two American officers, both of whom were his superiors. (Frémont had left the United States as a captain but had taken the title of major in California; in 1846 he had been made a lieutenant colonel in the American Army, but did not know it.) Because of his irregular activities Frémont was later tried by court-martial in Washington and was convicted of mutiny, disobedience, and conduct to the prejudice of military discipline. He was sentenced to dismissal, but President James K. Polk commuted the sentence, and Frémont resigned. The immediate result of Frémont's armistice treaty, however, was his appointment by Stockton as the first American civil governor of California under the occupation—which office he assumed on January 19th and conducted from headquarters in Los Angeles until March 1st, when he was deposed by Stephen Kearny upon orders from Washington.

On July 4th, 1847, the American troops in Los Angeles celebrated the first American Independence Day by dedicating the newly completed Fort Moore, designed to accommodate two hundred soldiers and furnish protection to the pueblo. It was named Moore for Captain Benjamin D. Moore who was killed in the Battle of San Pasqual. It was abandoned in 1848.

UNDER AMERICAN RULE

Discovery of gold in northern California in 1848 at first had an adverse effect on the southern area. Many Angelenos left the pueblo to join the gold rush. Forty-niners, arriving by the southern transcontinental route, passed up Los Angeles in their haste to reach the gold fields. For a time the town's population decreased at an alarming rate, but it was not long before the rapidly increasing number of inhabitants in the north sent a wave of prosperity southward. The meat supply in the San Francisco and Sacramento areas was soon exhausted, and Los Angeles began to find a profitable market for its cattle. For many years hides and tallow had been virtually the only marketable products of the ranches. Now the handling of meat—shipped north on the hoof —became the principal local industry. Money, which had been scarce in Mexican times, began to circulate freely.

On April 4, 1850, the city of Los Angeles was incorporated and became the county seat. The first United States census gave the county of Los Angeles a population of 8,329, which included 4,091 native white Mexicans, 4,193 domesticated Indians and 295 Americans. The first newspaper, *La Estrella de los Angeles* or *The Los Angeles Star,* was issued on May 17, 1851, and was printed in both Spanish and English.

In the fifties and sixties, when tough frontier towns were common in the West, Los Angeles probably had the largest array, per capita, of gambling dens, saloons, and bordels, and the greatest collection of thieves, murderers, and assorted desperadoes. It was known as a "bad" town. Homicides averaged about one per day, and murdered Indians were not counted. Criminals who were too violent to be tolerated even in the mining towns or San Francisco found refuge in Los Angeles. Most degraded of all classes were the Indians who had survived long after their old village of Yang-na had disappeared.

An important development of this period was the gradual transfer of large tracts of land from the original Mexican owners to the Yankee newcomers. Often the procedures were of doubtful honesty, but more often when a Mexican owner cried out that he had been cheated of his property, the real cause was that he himself had no idea of the value of money, never having had need for its use before the American occupation. By various means, but usually through loan of money on a mortgage at an exorbitant rate of weekly interest, more than four-fifths of the great ranches around Los Angeles were soon in American hands.

Well before the Civil War new industries were being organized. A flour mill and a brick kiln were built. Vineyards were becoming so extensive that wine was one of the most important exports. Citrus trees had been planted on a small scale. In 1863 a water-supply system consisting of wooden pipes was installed.

Sentiment in Los Angeles during the early months of the Civil War was greatly in favor of the South. General Albert Sidney Johnston, commander of the Pacific Department of the Army, marched away with 100 volunteers, to join the Confederacy. On May 17, 1861, the California legislature unanimously adopted a resolution pledging the State's allegiance to the Union. Shortly thereafter a detachment of Union troops was stationed in the city, and the Southern sympathizers were forced to content themselves with denunciation of Abraham Lincoln, which appeared at intervals in the *Star*.

Of far more importance to Los Angeles than the Civil War was the great drought of 1862-64, when the grazing lands became so parched that cattle starved to death by thousands. In some cases farmers set patrols of armed men around gardens and vineyards to keep out famished animals. About thirty thousand head are said to have perished on a single rancho. It was decades before the once-prosperous southern California cattle industry recovered from effects of this drought. Times were so hard that in 1864 no county taxes were collected in Los Angeles, and when four downtown business lots (now worth several million dollars) were offered at a tax sale for sixty-three cents each, no buyers appeared. Several lean years followed before vineyard and orchard industries became profitable enough to replace cattle raising as a major source of income.

After the Civil War, Los Angeles gradually settled down, lost its wild frontier character, and began to take its place as an American community. There was a small but steady influx of population. Some of the old ranchos near town were subdivided and sold as home and farm sites. Iron water mains and gaslights were introduced in 1867. The erstwhile pueblo's first railway was built in 1869, to the harbor at Wilmington, and over it went increasingly large shipments of wheat, wine, fruit, and other agricultural products of the region. The first newspaper, the old *Star,* soon had lively competition. By 1870 Los Angeles' population had increased to 5,614. There was a saloon for every fifty persons. Larger buildings, including hotels, were erected from time to time.

In 1871 occurred the last lynching; and also in that year the town staged the Chinese Massacre, in which a mob of hoodlums hanged nineteen Orientals on the charge that one of them had shot an American.

In the same period, however, cultural innovations—a book store, a library association, a dancing academy, and amateur dramatic performances—were introduced; saloons were licensed and regulated for the first time; horsecars appeared on the streets; the first navel oranges were planted at Riverside; the suburb of Pasadena was founded (as the Indiana Colony); and the Federal government made small improvements at the harbor. Angelenos began to feel civic pride, to talk of their city's destiny. An editorial in the *Express* proclaimed: "Here is our beautiful city . . . set like a rich gem in one of the most picturesque, fruitful and luxuriant valleys in the world . . . with everything that man could desire to make him contented and happy."

Only one thing was believed lacking—a transcontinental railway connection.

Until 1876 Los Angeles had communication with the rest of the world only by stagecoach and freight-wagon and by sea. In that year the Southern Pacific Railroad, encouraged by cash and land subsidies, extended its line southward from San Francisco to Los Angeles, giving the latter a link with the transcontinental system. But at the same time, Los Angeles was hard hit by a local bank failure and by another severe drought, which wiped out the newly established sheep industry, so that even for several years after the coming of the railroad, the town suffered from business stagnation and general hard times.

In the mid-eighties the City of the Angels, despite its growth and slow Americanization, still presented many of the aspects of a Mexican pueblo. Drab, weatherbeaten adobes contrasted with the ornate General Grant-style houses of the Americanos. The streets were often ankle-deep with dust or mud. Loafers dozed in the scanty shade at the Plaza. Indeed, the town had such a reputation for being backward that the *Los Angeles Times* assured the rest of the country that "Los Angeles people do not carry arms, Indians are a curiosity, the gee string is not a common article of apparel here, and Los Angeles has three good hotels, twenty-seven churches, and 350 telephone subscribers."

Upon this sleepy little Spanish-American town there suddenly burst, in 1885-87, the most spectacular real-estate boom the world ever had seen.

The causes of this phenomenal land craze were many and diverse, its effects drastic and far-reaching. Probably no other boom ever more surprised the inhabitants of any region. For a decade or more Southern California had been attracting some settlers from the East—solid people, mainly, who were drawn by the mild climate and beautiful surroundings. On land made available by the breaking up of the huge cattle and sheep ranches these newcomers planted orchards, vineyards, and gardens, using irrigation and modern agricultural methods. As a result, southern California's fruit and other produce began to improve. Its oranges and lemons took first prize at the New Orleans International Exposition in 1884-85 and helped to make Southern California known as a sort of Garden of Eden. The idea of migrating to California for profit as well as for climate began to take hold in the East. The spirit of the gold rush began to revive.

Completion of the Santa Fe Railway to Los Angeles late in 1885 brought matters to a head. The Southern Pacific was at last faced with a competitor, and the two roads started a rate war almost immediately. It has been said they colluded in luring a new population—and hence a new market—to the West. In any event, they reduced fares to the point of absurdity until, on one day in the spring of 1886, a ticket from Kansas City to Los Angeles cost only $1.00.

Throngs descended on Los Angeles. As many as five trainloads of people arrived daily in the astonished city. At first, the majority of the new arrivals were homeseekers and investors, with only an occasional speculator. This phase of the boom was spontaneous and healthy.

"Property in all directions was changing hands, and prices were slowly rising," wrote Theodore S. Van Dyke, a contemporary observer. "But it was all good property; prices were not extravagant; and in only a few places were they at all ahead of what the stage of settlement would justify." Then, in midsummer of 1886, when about a thousand people a month were pouring into the city, the boom entered its fantastic phase. A wave of frenzied speculation began; prices skyrocketed overnight.

Even the natives themselves began to speculate, and the fever was fanned by professional "boomers" who had had experience in Eastern and Midwestern land rushes.

After Los Angeles city lots had been snapped up, promoters began to lay out new "cities"—in farming regions, on barren hillsides, in the desert, and even on mountaintops. These subdivisions were surveyed, marked with stakes and flags, and thrown on the market; almost overnight people flocked to the site, stood in line for hours to buy. Some paid as much as $1,000 for a place near the head of the line. By the end of 1887 there were twenty-five mushroom towns along the Santa Fe Railway between Los Angeles and San Bernardino, and still others were springing up all over the Los Angeles area. One speculator sold about four thousand lots in the Mojave Desert for as much as $250 apiece, the cost to him having been about ten cents each. Another, after advertising that a railroad would serve this tract, laid down fence posts to look like ties. A typical advertisement read:

THIS IS PURE GOLD!!
SANTA ANA,
The Metropolis of Southern California's Fairest Valley!
Chief Among Ten Thousand, or the One
Altogether Lovely!
Beautiful! Busy! Bustling! Booming! It
Can't be Beat!
The town now has the biggest kind of a
big, big boom.
A Great Big Boom! And you
Can Accumulate Ducats by Investing!

In 1887, in Los Angeles County alone, recorded transactions totaled about $100,000,000—and many, perhaps most, of the sales were not recorded. Land prices soared in a few months from $100 to $1,500 an acre. In all, approximately sixty new "cities" were laid out in Los Angeles County, principally by unscrupulous "town jobbers"—professional real-estate manipulators who had moved westward from one boom to another. By the end of the boom these "cities" had acquired a total population of less than 3,500. According to the historian Newmark: "There were enough subdivisions to accommodate ten million people; enough syndicates to manage the affairs of a nation." The frantic piling up of fictitious values began to subside toward the end of 1887. Land owners who sensed that the boom had reached its peak decided to cash in while prices were still inflated. Finding no takers, they reduced their prices—and the panic was on. By the summer of 1888, about two and a half years after it had begun, the boom collapsed entirely. Most of the new "townsites" were soon obliterated by sagebrush. Assessment figures dropped below their pre-boom levels, and banks loaned only on downtown property.

A MODERN METROPOLIS IS BORN

When the city recovered from the immediate after-effects, and took stock of its remaining assets, the situation was seen to be far less discouraging than might have been expected. Many of the more substantial newcomers had stayed in Los Angeles, determined to make a living. Not a bank had failed during the crisis. The climate, moreover, and the fertile soil, were still there to be enjoyed and exploited.

Local leaders not only began at once to publish prophecies concerning the magnificent future still awaiting the region, but they also almost immediately began to try to lure a new and different kind of immigration to southern California. This time the appeal was not to be addressed to get-rich-quick investors but to respectable, hard-working farmers of the Middle West. Businessmen, railroads, and editors co-operated to launch an intensive campaign of propaganda, and to carry out their plan they formed, in the autumn of 1888, the organization that has since then become the Los Angeles Chamber of Commerce. In the next two years, more than a million pieces of persuasive "literature" were broadcast in the corn and wheat belts. Exhibits of prize agricultural produce from southern California were established in Chicago and at fairs and expositions, and later a special train, "California on Wheels," made a two-year tour with prize fruits and vegetables, a brass band, tons of pamphlets, and a squad of high-powered Los Angeles salesmen.

These and similar tactics, carried out with increasing energy over a period of years, soon began to achieve the Chamber's prime object— "to induce immigration" of men and money. The boom had lifted the city's population from about 11,000 in 1880 to more than 50,000 in 1890, despite the fact that whole trainloads of people had fled after the collapse. As a result of the extraordinary campaign of the Chamber of Commerce, the population more than doubled in the next decade, exceeding 100,000 by 1900; and the newcomers, this time, were thrifty, industrious, God-fearing folk, many of whom possessed means and almost all of whom were anxious to work and progress with the country.

Los Angeles as a modern American metropolis may be said to date from the end of the boom and the founding of the Chamber of Commerce. The boom made a permanent change in the city's character. The hybrid Mexican-American pueblo was no more. It was now American-dominated not only in numbers but also in spirit. Its face had been lifted—streets had been paved, larger buildings erected, and modern urban facilities (electric car lines, electric lights, water mains, and sewers) had been introduced and swiftly expanded. Even the city's politics had changed. Until 1880 the Democratic party had ruled supreme. After that time, owing largely to immigration from the Middle West, the Republicans gained increasing majorities and reigned unchallenged for approximately half a century.

"The major part of our present population," editorialized the *Herald* in 1895, "hardly knew there was such a town as Los Angeles on the Pacific end of the United States ten years ago."

The tremendous commercial expansion throughout the county in the nineties amazed old-timers. There was, for instance, the discovery of petroleum near the heart of the Los Angeles business district. Exploration for oil in Los Angeles County had begun in the Newhall-Ventura district in 1860, and all production in California had been from that section. But in 1892 Edward L. Doheny and Charles A. Canfield brought to the man in the street the idea that boundless wealth might be in his own backyard. Their first oil well, flowing forty-five barrels a day, stirred the town as nothing else had before or since.

In less than five years, 200 companies were organized and 2,500 wells were drilled within the city limits. Houses were torn down to make room for oil rigs, and derricks and wells, as close together as holes in a pepperbox, were soon pumping oil over a wide residential area. The city council was forced to curtail the drilling operations after the derricks had ruined the district for residential purposes, but today, shut from public view behind stores, homes, and board fences, some of these early wells are still producing oil.

The town-lot drilling in Los Angeles stimulated exploration for oil in other sections of the state, until in the succeeding years California was producing a quarter of the world's supply, the greater part coming from the Los Angeles basin. In 1939 Los Angeles County alone produced 95,000,000 barrels.

The organization of the California Fruit Growers Exchange was another significant event, leading as it did to the development of the citrus industry as Los Angeles' most valuable agricultural asset.

But probably one of the most important events of the nineties— and one whose potentialities were most clearly recognized at the time —was the successful conclusion of Los Angeles' long fight to obtain an appropriation for the construction of a deep-water harbor at San Pedro.

Los Angeles Harbor, now the largest man-made port in the world, was a dismal mud flat when Juan Rodriguez Cabrillo marked it down on his crude discovery map in 1542. Subsequent explorers—Sebástian Vizcáino, who christened the bay San Pedro in 1602, Gaspar de Portolá, Captain George Vancouver of the English Navy, and numerous Spain-bound galleon commanders from Manila—noted the bay's existence but not its potential value. Its use increased steadily after the Yankee ship, *Leila Byrd,* out of Boston, home-bound from the Sandwich Islands, dropped anchor off San Pedro in 1805. Its captain, William Shaler, traded sugar, clothing, and household goods for sea-otter pelts, and mission-produced hides and tallow. He opened such a lucrative market that east-coast skippers flocked to the port despite attempts to enforce a foreign-trade ban imposed by the King of Spain. Mexico gained her independence, eased trade restrictions, and by 1820 a fleet of Yankee ships was sailing around the Horn to load California hides and tallow at San Pedro.

Little was done to improve port facilities. Cargoes were lightered from ship to shore. Describing the harbor in *Two Years Before the Mast* (1840), Richard Henry Dana wrote: "the desolate place . . . the worst we had seen yet."

Don Abel Stearns (*see The Harbor: San Pedro and Wilmington*), a Yankee whose itching feet carried him to Los Angeles before the American occupation, held the first port concession. Securing permission from the Los Angeles *Ayuntamiento* (city council), he erected a warehouse at San Pedro, and urged the annexation of that tiny pueblo by the inland city. Aging letters in museums show his efforts to get a road built and the landing place improved at public expense. Stearns operated a stage route connecting San Pedro and Los Angeles; one-way tickets from San Francisco to San Pedro were $55 for a tedious ride on puffing paddlewheelers and to this was added $10 for a buckboard trip inland to Los Angeles. Freight was approximately $10 a ton.

Congressional attention was drawn to the port when James Collier,

Commissioner of Customs at San Francisco, investigating rumors, reported: "More goods are landed at San Pedro than at any other port except San Francisco . . . a large amount of smuggling is carried on." Discovery of gold and the rush to the fields somewhat increased traffic through San Pedro. After California was admitted to the Union, efforts to cut freight rates began. A memorial presented to Congress by Thomas H. Benton, United States Senator from Missouri, showed it cost "as high as $10.25 to move a barrel of flour from a warehouse in San Francisco to San Pedro." Augustus W. Timms and Phineas Banning each opened a stage route from San Pedro to Los Angeles.

Senator Benton always had shown interest in California. He was the father-in-law of John C. Frémont, who received the surrender of the Pueblo de Los Angeles.

Next, Phineas Banning (see *The Harbor: San Pedro and Wilmington*), obtained permission to build a landing in the slough created by the floodwaters of the Los Angeles and San Gabriel rivers. He contrived a lighterage and ferry system, and shortened the route to Los Angeles four miles. In 1858, with Benjamin D. Wilson, another pioneer, Banning laid out the present town of Wilmington, the inner harbor.

Banning was one of the leaders in the movement that completed the Los Angeles and San Pedro Railroad in 1869 with its water terminal at Wilmington. In 1872 the road was incorporated in the Southern Pacific system and four years later the Southern Pacific completed its link from Oakland to Los Angeles, making Wilmington a terminal of this feeder to a transcontinental line. The Southern Pacific extended its tracks to San Pedro and spent $3,000,000 dredging and, thrusting a long wharf into what is now known as the outer harbor.

Fearing a monopoly, public sentiment demanded a "free port." That was the beginning of a long, stubborn fight. When the Southern Pacific extended its tracks to San Pedro, the little town of Wilmington, neglected, was left dozing in the sun. The government entered the fight indirectly when in 1871 it spent $200,000 on a breakwater between Deadman's Island and Rattlesnake Island, in an effort to force the main channel tides to scour out a sandbar. The Southern Pacific, sensing possibilities of large-scale government development and to forestall competition, began to acquire control of the oceanside. It purchased a railroad that Senator John P. Jones of Nevada and associates had built between Santa Monica and Los Angeles. Then Collis P. Huntington, Southern Pacific president, abandoned the San Pedro-Wilmington area and centered all development at Santa Monica (see *The Harbor: San Pedro and Wilmington*). The company built the Long Wharf, 4,600 feet long to deep water, devised a buoy system, and waited for the government to build a breakwater. The railroad leaders christened their site the "Port of Los Angeles."

San Pedro had been approved by one board of army engineers, but there was demand for a resurvey to include Santa Monica. A second board approved San Pedro, but pressure in Congress delayed action. Stephen M. White, United States Senator from Los Angeles, and affectionately known as the "Father of Los Angeles harbor," persuaded President Grover Cleveland to appoint a third board, a mixed commission later known as the Walker Board. This committee approved San Pedro in its report in 1897, but the Long Wharf backers refused to admit defeat. Senator White and Collis P. Huntington engaged in a bitter fight that echoed throughout the United States. Through Senator White's efforts, appropriations were earmarked for the "free port" plan. On April 26, 1899, President William McKinley pressed an electric button in Washington that dumped the first carload of rock into San Pedro Bay for the breakwater of the present outer harbor, which was completed in 1910.

While the breakwater was under construction, Los Angeles edged out toward her port. In 1906 the city annexed the "shoestring strip," a quarter-of-a-mile-wide path to the ocean, and in 1909 San Pedro and Wilmington were consolidated with Los Angeles. The beach area became officially the Port of Los Angeles on February 13, 1910.

Opening of the Panama Canal and the agricultural and commercial development of the Los Angeles area, with an increase in the import and export trade, continually taxed the harbor's facilities despite consistent development including construction of a second breakwater. The city of Los Angeles has spent more than $42,000,000 and the Federal government more than $17,000,000, in addition to what was spent on government buildings at the port.

While Los Angeles in the closing years of the century battled with her harbor and transportation problems, the Spanish-American War excited high and at times bitter interest.

A great proportion of the residents were of Spanish extraction, and although they proclaimed their loyalty to the United States before the outbreak of hostilities, some unpleasant events resulted from what today is known as "war hysteria."

When the actual declaration of war came, fears that the southern California coast would be raided by the enemy were expressed. Steps were taken immediately to mobilize this region's quota of volunteers, and the Seventh Regiment of the State Militia went into camp at the Presidio, San Francisco. Harrison Gray Otis, publisher of the *Times,* was named brigadier general of the volunteers, and was sent to the Philippines for service.

The Seventh Regiment was held at the Presidio during the entire period of the war despite the fact that regiments from elsewhere reporting later were successful in being sent to the front where they saw active service. Conditions at the Presidio camp were bad and as the members of the regiment impatiently awaited call, fevers developed and many soldiers died.

An oil boom marked the closing years of the nineteenth century. When oil had been discovered within the city limits several years before, feverish drilling in residential sections had resulted in over-production, waste, and low prices. Now, however, new uses were found for crude oil, and the industry began to flourish. A Los Angeles man invented a crude-oil burner for steam generation. Another discovered a way to fire brick with oil; and many of the refining processes were developed that increased its use in hundreds of ways. Another important innovation was the use of large tanks in which to store the product instead of allowing it to flood the market. Natural gas, which had formerly been allowed to escape from the wells, was piped and sold; its presence in large quantities became a powerful factor in drawing certain industries to Los Angeles. As a result of the boom, the oil fields were extended far beyond the original area, and the next few years saw the development of Southern California as one of the world's leading petroleum centers.

Los Angeles entered the twentieth century as a dynamic American city of 102,479 persons. In the fifty years since it had come under United States sovereignty, the one-time pueblo had weathered two severe droughts and an hysterical land boom. The successful struggle against these hardships had developed a civic pride and cohesiveness and had made Los Angeles a city in spirit as well as in name. True, it did not yet *look* like a metropolis. Many of the streets were still unpaved, and the increasing numbers of automobiles kicked dust or mud on passers-by; most of the downtown buildings were small and the houses drab frame structures. There was a definite "Old West" atmosphere. But despite its appearance the town was coming of age, acquiring cultural institutions, new industries and types of agriculture, a growing commerce—and receiving a never-ending stream of new-comers, who brought capital to invest and needs to be supplied by the local market.

The Chamber of Commerce campaign "to induce immigration" had proved fruitful, and was continued with varying intensity. Another kind of campaign was launched in 1907 by the Southern Pacific Railroad and the California Fruit Growers Exchange, formed ten years earlier by citrus growers to provide a nonprofit, co-operative marketing agency for their oranges, lemons, and grapefruit. Formerly they had had to depend on commission brokers, whose chaotic marketing methods left little profit for the growers. The Exchange's marketing system proved so effective that by 1907 it was shipping about half of the California citrus crop.   In this year the Southern Pacific offered to join the Exchange in an eastern advertising campaign, each organization to put up $10,000.   Iowa was chosen as the test ground.   Fruit was shipped in special trains.   The slogan "Oranges for Health—California for Wealth" was advertised throughout Iowa.   Other promotional activities were energetically undertaken, and the trademark "Sunkist" was adopted to identify Exchange oranges.

This combined effort to increase citrus consumption and lure population had sensational results.   The Exchange's business increased 17.7 per cent nationally, but consumption of California citrus fruits in Iowa went up 50 per cent.   At the same time, immigration from Iowa to California swelled markedly.

The delighted Exchange voted in the following year to expand the territory covered by its advertising, and to spend $25,000.   Since then the annual advertising appropriation has risen to many times that figure; oranges have been "sold" as a staple article of diet to a nation that formerly regarded them as a luxury, and the California Fruit Growers Exchange has served as the model for scores of co-operative marketing organizations throughout the world.   Though the appeal for immigration was dropped later by the Exchange, it was carried on by the Chamber of Commerce and other groups, with the result that Los Angeles' population more than tripled in the decade 1900-1910.

QUEST FOR WATER

Water—both fresh and salt—has been a vital factor in shaping Los Angeles' destiny.   It was the man-made harbor that enabled the city to spurt ahead of other Pacific Coast cities.   Similarly, it was the city's success in obtaining an ample water supply that made it possible to support a large population.   The story of how this vital water supply was created is as dramatic as that of the struggle for a harbor; in addition, it is the story of feats that are the pride of the engineering world.

Discovery of the Los Angeles River helped determine the site for establishment of Los Angeles in 1781 by Governor Felipe de Neve. The padres of San Fernando Mission, in 1799, two years after the mission's founding, dammed up the river and found themselves in the first local litigation over water rights, with the pueblo as complainant. The pueblo won the initial victory in a series of water-supply disputes that were to high light the history of the city.

Early in the nineteenth century, enterprising residents constructed a dam across the Los Angeles River, and installed the pueblo's first water wheel, with buckets attached to the paddles.   As the wheel was revolved by the force of the flowing stream, water was lifted from the river and spilled into a canal. Thus townspeople were able to irrigate land at an elevation considerably above that of the river.

For 133 years the river was the sole source of water for Los Angeles. From the beginning until 1865 the town's water-distributing system was publicly owned. Eventually the town council decided to lease the municipal system to a private operator, and three years later, in 1868, turned over the city's waterworks for a period of thirty years to a privately owned corporation, later known as the City Water Company. In 1898 the city sought to regain its water system and after four years of negotiation and litigation, purchased the distributing lines and equipment for $2,000,000. It immediately made a 63 per cent reduction in domestic rates.

The Los Angeles River, under normal conditions, was capable of supplying the needs of 250,000 people. By 1905 the city's population was more than 160,000, and increasing at an amazing rate. Then, during a series of dry years the river was barely able to meet the city's requirements, and it became clear that it would not be able to serve a larger community.

Seeking a solution, civic leaders conceived the plan of getting water rights in the valley of the Owens River, a stream 250 miles to the northeast, fed by the snow waters of the High Sierras. William Mulholland, chief engineer of the Municipal Water Bureau, was sent to investigate. When he returned, he formulated plans for construction of an aqueduct capable of delivering enough water to meet the needs of 2,000,000 persons.

The first bond issue of $1,500,000, needed to purchase rights-of-way and start preliminary work, was submitted to the people in 1905. The vote in favor of the issue was in the ratio of 14 to 1.

Work on the aqueduct was begun in the fall of 1907, and completed in 1913. When finished it included 142 separate tunnels aggregating 53 miles in length, 12 miles of inverted steel siphons, 24 miles of open unlined conduit, 39 miles of open cement-lined conduit, and 97 miles of covered conduit. Additional miles were taken up by three large reservoirs, the largest of which, the Haiwee Reservoir, was capable of storing more than 19,000,000 gallons of water.

Present length of the Los Angeles Aqueduct from the intake in Owens River Valley to the San Fernando Reservoir is 233.3 miles.

But the water was not brought to Los Angeles. The aqueduct ended at San Fernando—and Los Angeles went to the aqueduct; almost the whole of San Fernando Valley was annexed by the city. In the beginning, the bulk of the water was distributed to San Fernando farms, but by 1939, the amount furnished to Los Angeles amounted to 80 per cent of the city's supply.

In 1917, the first hydroelectric generating plant along the Los Angeles Aqueduct was completed at St. Francis Dam in San Francisquito Canyon. Power from this plant, distributed to consumers at low rates, opened the way to industrial expansion. Factory wheels began to hum, production of goods to multiply. New jobs were created for the ever-increasing population; the value of manufactured products increased. Success of this venture stimulated further power development; a second plant was proposed and a bond issue for it was approved by an overwhelming majority of the voters. Construction was started in August, 1919, and was rushed to completion with an installed capacity of 41,000 horsepower in July, 1920.

The necessity for the Los Angeles Aqueduct was more than justified by 1923, when it was apparent that an additional supply of water would soon be needed: the population was climbing toward the second million with 100,000 new residents a year.

Realizing that the city must begin to prepare for the future, Chief Engineer Mulholland began to survey a route for an adequate supply to bring water to the city from the Colorado River. Special problems were presented by the erratic flow of the river. Enormous floods threatened destruction of lower river areas but in some places flow was too low to meet needs of lands already under cultivation.

Possibilities of controlling the flow of the river had been under study by the Federal government. At the time the early aqueduct plans were made by the city of Los Angeles, the United States Reclamation Service was studying the problem of storing the water of the Lower Colorado. Earlier plans contemplated storage for flood control and irrigation only, but potential returns and benefits from these sources were inadequate to justify the cost of the project; but, when it developed that southern California offered a market for power that could be produced incidentally, the problem of financing was simplified.

A tangle of legal, diplomatic, and political complications preceded passage of the Boulder Canyon Project Act in December, 1928. Construction of Boulder Dam, rising 727 feet, has created the world's largest artificial lake, with a storage capacity of 30,500,000 acre-feet. This reservoir controls and conserves the flood waters of the river; and, in addition, makes possible development of from four billion to six billion kilowatt-hours of electrical energy a year.

With storage of the Colorado waters assured, and the quality of its water established, plans for an aqueduct went forward. The principal cities of Southern California became interested and the Metropolitan Water District of Southern California was incorporated on December 6, 1928, to embrace Los Angeles, Anaheim, Beverly Hills, Burbank, Compton, Fullerton, Glendale, Long Beach, Pasadena, San Marino, Santa Ana, Santa Monica, and Torrance.

A major problem was selection of a general route for the aqueduct, since all presented serious difficulties. With much of the area unsurveyed, the first task was contour mapping of approximately 25,000 square miles of desert and rugged terrain where roads were practically nonexistent. In many places the surveyors had to build trails. The survey showed that bringing water to the Metropolitan District by gravity was impossible, both physically and financially. Boulder Dam, however, provided the means for diversion of water by pumping, since power would be available, and construction of another dam, downstream, would enable diversion into an aqueduct to be built over a more advantageous route. The site selected was about sixteen miles upstream from Parker, Arizona. The aqueduct with a pump lift of 1,617 feet, reaches the coastal plain through a thirteen-mile tunnel in the San Gorgonio Pass of the San Jacinto Mountains, south of Beaumont. Five pumping plants, powered by a transmission line built by the Metropolitan Water District from Boulder Dam, lift water from Parker Dam to the coastal plain.

From the intake at Parker Dam to Los Angeles, the Colorado River Aqueduct covers a distance of 392 miles.

Although a total of forty-three tunnels was necessary to carry the water through mountainous territory, construction of the one through the San Jacinto Mountains was the most difficult. At the outset, a heavy inflow of water was encountered, submerging tunnel, shaft, and all equipment. Further boring encountered heavy, wet ground and large flows of water on all sides. Despite the hardships, determined men with modern machines went steadily forward through the mud and water to the final "holing through" on November 19, 1938.

A year later, to the day, the aqueduct from Parker Dam reached Lake Mathews, the storage basin at the upper end of the area to be served. This reservoir permits gravity delivery to the entire area. Under construction in 1940 near La Verne is a softening plant, which will treat all water serving the thirteen cities of the Metropolitan Water District. Also under construction are the various feeder lines that will carry water from Lake Mathews to the cities early in 1941.

While construction of Boulder Dam was precipitated by Southern California's need for water, of major interest to the city is the Boulder Dam power, first transmitted to Los Angeles in October, 1936. These mighty power generators are enabling fulfillment of prophecies of vast industrial growth for the region.

LOS ANGELES PARTICIPATES IN THE WORLD WAR

The first Sunday in April, 1917, at the time the star of the old German Empire seemed at its greatest ascendancy, and with the United

States nursing the wounds to its dignity and pride caused by a series of provocations by sea and land, a leading morning newspaper described the citizens of Los Angeles as "indifferent to the growing war cloud." Wednesday of the same week, the *Los Angeles Times* reported that President Woodrow Wilson was ready to present his war plans to the Congress, and, on the historic sixth of April 1917, stated:

"Los Angeles waited calmly for the fateful flash from Washington that spells war. The streets were very quiet."

This quiet, natural in view of the remoteness of Los Angeles from Europe, was a prelude to intense activity following promptly upon the declaration of war, and increasing for the ensuing two years. Before the month of April had passed, 375 local applications had been accepted "for entrance to the officers' training camp at the Presidio." The San Francisco army post, the old Spanish Presidio, was to receive a steady flow of Los Angeles' applicants until, by the time the camp opened on May 8th, approximately eight hundred Los Angeles men were enrolled for training.

Before this exciting April had passed, Mayor Frederick T. Woodman was setting an example—to increase food production—by converting his flower borders into vegetable gardens and the city was checking supplies available for immediate national use as prices for food soared; William Gibbs McAdoo, then Secretary of the Treasury and later United States Senator for California, coined the phrase "Liberty Loan"; social events assumed a patriotic air, with the Stars and Stripes as the prevailing decorative motif, and the first of the giant "community sings" of the war era was held in what is now the Philharmonic Auditorium.

A report, early in the war days, that the plot to blow up the Welland Canal had originated in Los Angeles tightened the nerves of citizens. Alleged enemy operations south of the Mexican border multiplied rumor and heightened public tension. Thousands of dollars began to pour into Red Cross and war-relief agencies. Registered nurses were organized in great numbers for home and foreign service. The "bluejackets" vanished from San Pedro streets and their ships disappeared from anchor off the breakwater. The Chamber of Commerce warned citizens against food hoarding. Film celebrities came forward to help in recruiting and war-aid activities. The large Mexican population and all foreign groups threw themselves in the war picture without reservation. Streets began to resound with fanfares, parades marched, flags waved in the doorways of recruiting offices, and the "quiet" that had received editorial notice at the beginning of April was no more. All processes of the city's life began to operate at high speed.

Enlistments from Los Angeles city and county totaled more than 75,000 men, most of whom were incorporated into the famous 91st and

40th Divisions. Other local men were found in practically every division of the American Expeditionary Forces and fought on the bloodiest battlefields during the closing year of the war.

Los Angeles was represented in the section of the American Expeditionary Force sent to Vladivostok to aid the Allies in maintaining order while the vast Russian Empire was torn by internal struggle, and to consolidate Czech forces operating in Siberia.

Among the training services in Los Angeles were an observation balloon school, at Arcadia, and the training base for naval recruits, at San Pedro.

Los Angeles underwent diverse changes while action was raging abroad. Food production in Los Angeles County attained immense proportions. Parties were turned into benefits to foster war aims. The city continuously entertained foreign representatives. Knitting for the soldiers became a public activity, with women purling on cars and busses and in theaters or on street corners. On September 1, 1917, the whole city joined in a monster rally to honor the fighting forces.

After the armistice Los Angeles sponsored numerous postwar developments. Local posts of the Veterans of Foreign Wars and the American Legion were organized. A little-known veteran organization, the A. E. F., Siberia, had its origin in Los Angeles, at the Del Mar Club, and has become a national institution, with members engaged in the study of Oriental politics as their objective. Patriotic women promoted the erection of the ornamental War Memorial statue in Pershing Square. A huge coliseum was built in Exposition Park as a war memorial.

The war was followed by the great southern California boom of the twenties—less spectacular than that of the eighties, but far more substantial and long-lived. The census of 1920 gave Los Angeles a population of 576,673, an increase of a quarter of a million since 1910; during the next decade, the total reached 1,238,048. Building operations in the county to provide housing for the newcomers and quarters for industrial expansion rose in value from $88,000,000 in 1920 to $177,000,000 in 1939, with a peak of more than $297,000,000 in 1923. In recent years Los Angeles has ranked second to New York in the amount spent in building construction. School enrollment in the county reached 693,000 in 1939, and the assessed valuation of county property trebled between 1920 and that year, to $2,551,000,000.

The growth of Los Angeles following the World War was equalled only by that of Chicago immediately after the Civil War. The Chamber of Commerce intensified its activities of previous years, advertising the city at fairs and expositions in the East, bringing conventions to the city, and persuading eastern manufacturers to establish branch plants in Los Angeles. Unlike the Chamber of Commerce, the All-Year Club, founded in 1921, had only one well-defined objective—to persuade tourists to come to southern California, in the hope they would spend money in summer as well as winter, and eventually decide to remain permanently. The hopes, thanks to advertising campaigns in eastern newspapers and magazines, were realized to a spectacular degree. According to All-Year Club reports, the annual tourist volume jumped from 200,000 in 1921 to 1,703,167 in 1939, and the visitors were estimated to have spent $193,834,763 in the latter year alone. Summer travel has surpassed that of winter, about one million tourists visiting the region in the summer of 1939. The All-Year Club estimates that one out of every ten tourists returns here to live, and that the largest part of southern California income belongs to retired persons living on private means. Even if these estimates are discounted, they show how successfully southern California has been sold to the Nation.

As new residents poured into Los Angeles during the early twenties it became, in population, area, and industry, the fastest-growing major city in the United States. There was a real-estate boom as spectacular as that of the eighties. Office buildings sprang up throughout the downtown section, and over the ever-expanding area of the city, residences of every architectural style were hastily put up. The peak of the building boom came in 1923 with the construction of 800 mercantile buildings, 400 industrial buildings, 60 hotels, 130 schools, 130 warehouses, 700 apartment houses and 25,000 single- and double-dwellings. As the boom reached its dizziest heights, foot frontage prices doubled, tripled and quadrupled. In 1923 alone, 1,057 tracts were put on the market and 11,608 acres were subdivided in the city. Similar booms hit surrounding communities. Thousands of people became quickly—and often only temporarily—wealthy.

With its population doubled in a little more than five years, the city annexed one community after the other, most of them induced to come in through their need of the water Los Angeles could supply. The original twenty-eight square miles of the town, multiplied thirteenfold by 1920, when the city stretched over a vast area from the Harbor to San Fernando Valley, now was to leap forward to its present area of 450 square miles. In 1923, twelve annexations brought in 19,000 acres of new city territory.

Accompanying the advertising campaigns of the booster organizations, the rapid influx of population and the building boom, industry on a large scale began to come to Los Angeles after 1919. The county had entered the manufacturing market with a $25,000,000 output in 1899, but by 1919 the annual production of $417,000,000 entitled it to twenty-seventh rank among the Nation's industrial counties. The only large industry had been motion pictures, already producing 80 per cent of the world supply. Now new and larger industries entered the city, attracted by the cheap and abundant water, power, and natural gas and oil, the excellent transportation facilities, the harbor, and the large growing local market. One of the first large industries to come was the Goodyear Tire and Rubber Company, which built a $6,000,000 plant in 1919. Throughout the twenties others followed, and in 1922 the Central Manufacturing District was formed in the city of Vernon, previously incorporated for industrial purposes exclusively. In 1924, the growth of new industry fell off, yet 700 new industries were established in that year. With the coming of the Firestone and Goodrich Tire companies in 1927, Los Angeles became the country's second rubber center. Later came the aircraft and automobile assembly plants. Established industries expanded enormously. Oil production in the county rose from 38,000,000 barrels in 1922 to 176,000,000 barrels in 1929. Numerous new oil refineries were built, including Pan-American Petroleum's $18,000,000 tank farm and refinery near the harbor, and the Shell Oil Company's $10,000,000 plant. The Santa Fe Springs oil field was developed successfully in 1919; the Huntington Beach section was discovered in 1920, and the Signal Hill bonanza the following year.

Los Angeles also became not only the richest agricultural county in the United States, but one of the most diversified agricultural regions as well. By 1935 every twenty-four hours saw at least one of the county's 150 commercial crops being harvested and shipped. This agricultural diversity gave the region a large degree of economic stability, despite heavy citrus losses in 1937. The agricultural wealth for that year was divided as follows: fruits and nuts, $39,927,207, livestock, $35,195,895, truck crops, $10,398,035, and field crops, $7,055,215. The total of all crops in Los Angeles county in 1939 was $76,074,000.

Citrus crops account for nearly one-third of the county's agricultural income; there are nearly 45,000 acres of oranges, 12,000 acres of lemons, and a smaller grapefruit acreage. In addition, Los Angeles County is a leading producer of walnuts and avocados. There are 130,000 acres of field crops—chiefly hay, grain, and beans—and 50,000 acres producing twenty-four different truck crops, mainly green beans, cabbage, cauliflower, celery, lettuce, and tomatoes.

Although Los Angeles has a success story that makes it the envy of other aspiring communities, it has not entirely escaped misfortunes. Development and growth of the region have been slowed down several times by disaster, but in each case the interruptions have been only temporary.

The region has been affected by earthquakes, some of which have resulted in loss of life and damage to property. The average Angeleno regards an earth tremor with less apprehension than persons elsewhere regard a severe electrical storm or a tornado. Of the quakes that have visited southern California during recent years, three have been severe enough to result in loss of life and in property damage. In 1920 a tremor struck Inglewood, and part of the business district was damaged. Probably the most severe quakes experienced in this region were those of 1925, in Santa Barbara, and 1933 in Long Beach, Compton, and the surrounding cities.

The Long Beach-Compton tremor, in which 118 people were killed, resulted in changes in the Los Angeles County building code; even more drastic restrictions now govern construction throughout the area. Other southern California counties adopted similar measures. Laws enforcing a height limit of 150 feet for buildings in Los Angeles proper have long been in effect and represent an added safeguard against earthquake damage.

The Los Angeles area has also had serious floods. Three of them, separated by long periods of years, came after exceptionally heavy rainfall in the semiarid region and resulted in great damage. In 1914, when precipitation reached record figures, the flood waters confined themselves in most cases to the natural stream beds and damage was small except to bridges and territory along stream beds. Damage was much greater in 1934, when the waters rushing down the mountain canyons swept over the La Crescenta Valley and the Montrose territory. Forty-five persons were drowned at this time. Four years later heavy rains again fell in the region and the storm waters backed into San Fernando Valley, causing heavy losses.

Perhaps the district's greatest disaster—at least that in which the largest loss of life was recorded—occurred when the St. Francis Dam, a unit of the Los Angeles Aqueduct, broke in 1928, and released a wall of water that swept down the Santa Clara River through Los Angeles and Ventura counties, leaving 451 dead and $12,000,000 worth of damage in its wake.

TROUBLE AHEAD

Los Angeles rushed through the decade of 1920-30 as a lushly prosperous, spectacular city. It was enjoying not only the nation-wide prosperity of the Harding-Coolidge-Hoover era, but the prosperity of a boom within a boom. Its prodigious motion-picture industry, the rise of industry and building, its sensational real estate values, and the rush of tourists and new residents, made it a mecca to workingmen and businessmen alike. Los Angeles not only had an assessed valuation of $2,000,000,000, bank debits of $14,000,000,000, and a harbor commerce of approximately $1,000,000,000 in 1929; it was also gifted with a prosperity which touched most of its citizens. Investments with high returns were available to all; nearly everyone had an automobile (there were more motor vehicles per capita than in any other American city) ; everybody was able to enjoy the sun, the climate, and the scenery.

As the prosperity wave reached its peak there were unrecognized hints that Los Angeles, in common with the rest of the United States, was to face bad times. Stock exchange transactions jumped from 27,000,000 shares in 1927 to 67,000,000 shares in 1928, and a series of financial crashes began.

The first phase of the depression after the 1929 stock crash affected Los Angeles much as it did other cities. Business slumped disastrously and thousands lost their livelihood. Economic discussion came to the fore. Public and private charities were swamped under demands for help. By the spring of 1932, with relief utterly inadequate, the unemployed in southern California began to respond to the depression in an unusual manner.

The first development was the self-help movement, which began in Compton when the unemployed went to the fields to harvest crops the farmers could not sell. Within a few weeks a self-help association had been formed to give farmers labor in exchange for surplus crops, and to swap labor with businessmen for surplus goods. The co-op members gathered and distributed among themselves surplus vegetables, milk, bread, gasoline, household goods, old clothing, and services. The movement spread with astonishing speed, and by the spring of 1933 it was enabling more than 200,000 persons to maintain themselves. Their central organization operated fishing boats, lumber yards, canneries, bakeries, repair plants, and other facilities. When Federal work relief started, the jobless largely abandoned the co-operatives though some small-scale production co-operatives, receiving state aid, survived for a few years. By 1939 most of them had died out.

Los Angeles' next reaction to the depression was to originate panaceas and movements, and turn to them with a zeal that astonished the country. Late in 1933 Upton Sinclair, the author-Socialist, announced his candidacy for governor in his EPIC (End Poverty in California) platform, which proposed liberal pensions for the needy, high taxes on wealth, and a "production for use" plan of putting the unemployed to work on idle land and in idle factories "to take the unemployed off the backs of the taxpayers." By August there were 2,000 EPIC clubs and a weekly paper averaging 500,000 copies; more than a million copies of Sinclair's leaflets were in circulation. After Sinclair was nominated on the Democratic ticket, there broke forth one of the most furious attacks ever leveled at an American political candidate. Sinclair was defeated and the EPIC movement soon disintegrated.

Simultaneously with EPIC there sprang up the Utopian Society, a secret organization whose members were initiated by "cycles." After Sinclair's defeat the Utopian movement also died out. Technocrats flourished at about the same time, but never enlisted the wide support of the other panacea promoters. In Long Beach Dr. Francis E. Townsend started his transactions-tax pension scheme, and it, unlike the other local movements, soon spread throughout the country.

THE FIFTH CITY

By 1935 Los Angeles was recovering economically. The county had risen to fifth rank among industrial counties in the United States. More than 140,000 workers were producing 2,300 classified products with an annual value of more than $1,000,000,000. Los Angeles County led the Nation in motion-picture production, oil refining, airplane manufacture, and secondary automobile assembly. It was second in the production of tires, fourth in furniture, and fourth in women's apparel. As in agriculture, industry was highly diversified; there were thirty types of industrial plants, each with an annual production volume valued at more than $5,000,000. Production of motion pictures remained the chief industry. All of the "big four" rubber companies—Goodyear, Goodrich, Firestone, and United States Rubber—operated plants in Los Angeles, and assembly plants were operated by General Motors, Ford, Chrysler, Studebaker, and Willys-Overland. Los Angeles aircraft plants, newest of the industries and next to motion pictures the largest employers of labor, turned out more than half the total value of the Nation's airplane construction.

Education

UNTIL after the American Occupation in 1847, the Los Angeles area had few schools. Education had no part in the colonization policies of the Spanish or Mexican governments. The purpose in establishing the first missions was twofold. The Spanish Crown, customary with its policy throughout New Spain, sought to elevate the native Indians of California from a state of savagery to that of peaceful, law-abiding, and, more particularly, tax-paying and revenue-producing subjects. The Franciscan fathers, while in accord with this program, were interested primarily "in saving the souls of the unfortunate benighted heathen."

At no time during the occupancy of the Province by the Spaniards, nor to the end of the Mexican reign in 1847, and the first period of American occupancy, was there a well-established system of schools. Such instruction, other than teaching the Indians to tan hides, make soap, weave, and harvest grain, was given by orders of succeeding governors, only a few of whom were sincere in their efforts to educate the inhabitants. But even this was spasmodic and short-lived. Not only were the colonists, mostly of mixed blood and drawn from the humbler ranks of Spanish colonial society, unable to read or write, but a similar condition existed among those of the highest rank in officialdom down to the noncommissioned officers and privates in the various presidios. The sole school of mission days in the pueblo of Los Angeles, which had been opened for a short time in 1817-18 by the last of the Spanish governors but had fallen into disuse, was reopened in 1828. Governor Echeandia, at the same time, ordered a similar school started at nearby San Gabriel Mission. Governor Figueroa, his successor, inaugurated the first normal school, and levied a tax to finance it. Governor Micheltorena instituted compulsory school attendance for young children, also a school for girls.

With the American Occupation local public education really began. Wherever he settled, the American pioneer installed "the little red schoolhouse" and the cradle wherein modern California had its birth. He had a full appreciation of the value bound between the covers of the primer, grammar, and arithmetic, as the majority of his predecessors had stressed the worth of spiritual development, contained in the *doctrina cristiana,* to the exclusion of almost any intellectual advancement beyond its crudely bound and well-worn pages. The first schoolmaster was an army hospital steward, Dr. William B. Osborn, but the school was soon closed by the gold rush exodus. When the new state constitution made provision for a public school term of three months, Los Angeles undertook to establish one even before the state was able to assist financially. Francisco Bustamente, the first teacher employed by the city council, taught reading, writing and "morals" in Spanish; and as other teachers arrived, English, along with supplementary subjects for which the parents paid, was added. Schools taught by private tutors, subsidized by the city, gave way to schools financed entirely by the city. The first of the public schools opened in 1855, and had separate classrooms for boys and girls. At first, the term was occasionally shortened by lack of money. Later, the system of fees payment by parents was gradually eliminated by the increase in state aid for city schools.

After state law ended public support of parochial schools, the Catholic clergy opened a collegiate school that was the first of many denominational institutions of higher education to be established locally within the next few years. St. Vincent's College, the nucleus of the present Loyola University, was opened in 1865 and received a state charter in 1869, the year in which the University of California was opened. A public high school was established in 1873 and the Methodist University of Southern California in 1879. With the waves of immigration in the eighties and the growth of large private fortunes, sectarianism in education receded and new institutions of higher learning were established with private aid and few denominational ties. In 1887 men of wealth but no particular religious bias aided Presbyterians to found Occidental College and Congregationalists to establish Pomona College. In 1891 Whittier College was founded by Quakers, La Verne College by the Church of the German Baptist Brethren and the Immaculate Heart College by the Sisters of the Immaculate Heart.

The depression of the nineties hit these and other private institutions severely, and caused them either to shut down or sharply to curtail their operations. The state, which had been assisting the city schools to make reasonable if less lavish progress, stepped into the breach. A Los Angeles branch of the state normal school had been opened in 1883. Laws were now revised to permit communities to open high schools.

At the beginning of the twentieth century the Los Angeles school system was not only adequate but well financed. Commercial and industrial activity, moreover, steadily increased the demand for semiprofessional training. By 1911 post-high school courses—precursors to the junior college—were offered in at least one secondary school. In 1919 a Los Angeles branch of the University of California was opened, to offer a two-year liberal curriculum in addition to courses previously given at the local normal school. Since the end of the nineteenth century few private institutions of higher learning have been established, though in numerous communities of the county academies and other private schools of various types have been opened. The general public school system has expanded rapidly in the last decade. In 1929 the first junior college was opened on the old campus of the local branch of the University of California, which in that year became the University of California at Los Angeles with a campus at Westwood.

In 1938 there were approximately 400 public schools in the Los Angeles school district, ranging from kindergartens to a city college. State laws requiring minors to attend school have resulted in high school education for nearly all the city's youth to the age of eighteen. In 1938 there were 23,047 children in kindergarten, 198,976 in 293 elementary schools, 79,988 in 27 junior and senior high schools, and 5,197 in the Los Angeles City College. The school plant in 1938 consisted of 931 permanent buildings and 1,647 tents, wooden bungalows, and other temporary structures. During the period 1905-1937 inclusive, $94,-213,000 in bonds was voted for new school buildings. In the county there were a total of 739 public schools with an approximate enrollment of 675,000.

The public schools of the Los Angeles school district are controlled by a Board of Education composed of seven elected, unsalaried members. The district today embraces a score or so of neighboring communities and includes the western part of the county, with a population of approximately 2,000,000.

The Board of Education is entirely separate from the city government, the school district being a governmental subdivision of the state. The board has the power to levy taxes for financing the system and manages all administrative and curricular matters, subject to state laws and supervised by the State Superintendent of Education. A superintendent of schools, appointed by the board, in 1939 directed the 17,000 employees, which include 11,000 class-room teachers. The 1938 annual budget was approximately $41,000,000, of which about $17,000,-000 came from the State.

The county Board of Education administers schools in incorporated and unincorporated areas outside the Los Angeles school district. The members are named by the county Board of Supervisors, which also must approve the county school budget.

The Los Angeles school system is yet in a transition stage and suffers from various handicaps: the conservatism of some officials and of teachers long in the service, lack of equipment, and large classes resulting from very rapid increases in population. But the foundations of a sound system have been laid. The schools have been largely freed from political control and many of the sounder principles of modern education have been adopted. Serious efforts are being made to replace the tents used in more congested districts with permanent buildings, despite the diversion of funds for replacing and repairing buildings damaged by the 1933 earthquake. The economic depression has also slowed up progress; funds which would have been available for plant expansion and salaries have been used to some extent to supplement philanthropic donations for meals, and medical and dental care for pupils whose parents were unable adequately to provide for them. In spite of these impediments, the ideal of the system is to train children according to their economic and social needs and their physical and mental abilities.

Contemporary education "seeks to be as informal as living and to achieve a successful foundation for living." Serious attempts are made to interest children in learning and to adapt instruction methods to their interests; in place of the old-fashioned competitive system has been substituted one that grades the pupil on whether his ability and talents are developing satisfactorily. Los Angeles schools also teach much that was formerly acquired at home—home-making, physical development, and social responsibilities and relations.

Public education in Los Angeles now begins very early. Starting in nursery schools and kindergartens, in the early grades there is directed play and the children are made acquainted with such everyday subjects as printing and gardening; at an early stage girls have the same opportunities as boys to learn about the world. In early grades girls may design dresses, but in later grades they join the boys in discussing current civic problems and local politics, and in visiting tire, airplane, and other factories to learn industrial problems and processes. In junior and senior high schools education is adapted to the needs of the students; a school in a district where few go on to college offers trade and agricultural training in place of the classics, dramatics, or highly specialized "majors" taught in a Hollywood school. There are also special vocational schools and schools for the mentally and physically handicapped.

Adult education in Los Angeles is not based on general theory but upon local needs and desires. Except among those seeking high school or junior college diplomas, there is little attention to terms and credits. That these educational facilities are appreciated is attested by the enrollment in 1938 of around 200,000 persons in adult classes at the 24 evening schools maintained by the Board of Education and in 12 similar schools maintained with Federal aid. Day classes are attended by 15,000 persons, mostly women.

The courses are highly diversified: elementary subjects are offered for those who desire them. Americanization courses for aliens seeking citizenship, college preparatory and other high school work, and numerous special courses ranging from those teaching short story writing to those giving the theory and practice in automobile repairing. The courses in the evening schools are adapted to the needs of the communities where they are held; the schools in Van Nuys, Gardena, Bell, and other rural areas stress agricultural training; Huntington Park and San Pedro emphasize mechanical and trade subjects; Hollywood and Los Angeles offer a general educational program, including art, literature, public speaking, commercial subjects, trade instruction, and college preparatory work. Vocational training, the largest field, is particularly stressed in such places as the Frank Wiggins Trade School.

The Adult Education Program employs several hundred teachers under WPA in conjunction with the Adult Evening College at City College. In 1938, 150 courses were offered, as well as classes in numerous evening schools and in nearly 50 welfare and community and church centers. The curriculum is similar to that of the regular evening schools.

The number of private schools has greatly increased since 1910; there were at least fifty in the Los Angeles area in 1939. Their curricula are similar to that of the public schools, except for specialization in subjects such as music, arts and crafts, languages, or physical education emphasized by the founders. The private institutions range from elementary to college preparatory schools and most of them, excluding a few boys' military academies and girls' preparatory schools, are coeducational. The private schools in Los Angeles, like those in other parts of the country, have the advantages of greater financial resources. Their affluence enables them to maintain more instructors for smaller student bodies, a ratio often as low as one teacher for every three students. The high fees tend to draw only children from well-to-do families, and most of the schools are relatively exclusive.

Despite the fact that many of the private schools were semi-religious in origin, almost the only ones now identified with denominations other than Catholic are the Berkeley Hall School, which since 1911 has conducted its education in line with Christian Science beliefs; Pasadena College, operated by the Church of the Nazarene since 1902, Los Angeles Pacific College, founded in 1903 by the Free Methodist Church, Whittier College, founded (1891) by the Society of Friends, and the Harvard School, an Episcopal institution. Educators have established the John Dewey School, the Sherwood Progressive School, and the Progressive School of Los Angeles, the last of which has a co-operative management and provides scholarships for needier pupils. These progressive schools, incorporating the progressive educational ideas of John Dewey of Columbia University, are rather similar to the Ethical Culture School of New York. Among the larger private schools, the Chouinard Art Institute offers training in painting and allied subjects. The Otis Art Institute offers a two- to four-year course in drawing, painting, sculpture, illustrative and commercial design, and stagecraft. It also offers, with county aid, a free museum education for 500 children.

In the foreign districts are a few schools offering instruction in the language, religion, and culture of their homelands; these are usually maintained by the residents of the districts or by their religious groups. Segregation of Negroes and Orientals was officially abolished in the 1880's by the public school system. In 1939 Los Angeles voters elected a Negro music teacher to the Board of Education.

The Roman Catholic Church today conducts nearly 100 schools, with 20,000 students, in the Archdiocese of Los Angeles and San Diego. Besides elementary schools, there are about a dozen secondary schools— including Cathedral, Loyola and the Catholic Girls high schools—and Loyola University. Protestants conduct only the traditional Sunday school, but many Jewish synagogues conduct schools where children, after finishing their day at public school, are taught Hebrew and racial history and tradition.

The increase of higher education in southern California, because of the length of schooling required by law and the proximity of tax-supported institutions for advanced education, was intensified during the depression. Many parents preferred to keep their children in school rather than have them sitting about jobless or seeking in vain for employment. More than 14,000 were enrolled in 1937-38 in a dozen junior colleges in the vicinity. In 1938 the number of freshmen enrolling at the city's junior college alone was nearly a third of the number graduated from city high schools at the end of the preceding term. In the colleges and universities near Los Angeles were approximately 30,000 students in 1938-39.

Ranking high in scholastic standards is the University of California at Los Angeles, with a 1939 enrollment of 7,729. The university also has a large extension division. The University of Southern California, second oldest institution of higher learning in the city, has 24 colleges and schools whose enrollment, including that in extension courses, was 16,929 for the 1939-40 sessions, second largest in the West.

The group of colleges at Claremont has adopted the English system of co-ordinate colleges, federated for common purposes but autonomous in their unit life. Included in the group are Pomona College, Scripps College for Women, and the Claremont Colleges of graduate study. The California Institute of Technology at Pasadena is a scientific and technical school. Occidental, Redlands, Whittier and a dozen other smaller colleges offer standard college work.

Religion

THE multiplicity and diversity of faiths that flourish in the aptly
named City of the Angels probably cannot be duplicated in any
other city on earth. With churches and meeting houses of all
the major Christian denominations and many of the minor ones, with
Jewish and non-Christian temples and shrines, Los Angeles is also the
birthplace and headquarters of several denominations of her own. These
include such denominations as Aimee Semple McPherson's International
Foursquare Gospel Evangelism, the Church of the Nazarene, the
Hebrew Evangelization Society, the Christian Fundamentals league,
and others which have come into being here.

This profusion of denominations is particularly striking in view of
the fact that not only was Los Angeles founded on and by Catholicism,
but that faith prevailed all through the Spanish and Mexican periods
of the city's history when all beliefs except those of the Roman Catholic
Church were discouraged. Even after the Yankee influx in the mid-
nineteenth century when the field was thrown open to all denominations, other religious groups appeared slowly.

The Franciscan missionaries directed by Father Junipero Serra, who
arrived in 1769 to Christianize the California Indians, found that the
natives of this region already worshiped only one God, Quao-ar (sometimes spelled Kwawar). So feared was this deity by the natives that
the tribesmen spoke his name only during religious ceremonies, which
consisted of songs and dances conducted by medicine men in special
open-air enclosures. For the conversion of these aborigines, the padres
established a chain of missions extending northward from San Diego.

When Los Angeles was founded by the Spanish government as a
colonizing venture in 1781, priests from near-by San Gabriel Mission
blessed the site. It was not until three years later, however, that a
house of worship was provided for the pueblo and in the interim it
was necessary for the citizens of the newly born Los Angeles to journey
to San Gabriel, a distance of nine miles, in order to attend Mass. In
1784, a tiny adobe, predecessor to the present Church of Our Lady the
Queen of the Angels, was erected to the northwest of the present structure, and a padre came from San Gabriel to officiate. Today more
than a thousand houses of worship are supported by groups of almost
every shade of religious belief.

From the first the Roman Catholic Church played an important part in the life of the growing community, since all the white inhabitants were of Latin descent and had been brought up in it. For years civic life revolved around the church on the Plaza. The supremacy of the beliefs and teachings of the padres survived the revolution which freed Mexico and her California possessions from Spain, and continued to a large extent even after secularization of the missions in 1834.

Among the few of other faiths who persisted in efforts to introduce a new order in the Los Angeles early-day religious scene was William Money. It was Money who founded the Reformed New Testament Church of the Faith of Jesus Christ, the first of Los Angeles metaphysical cults. His preaching attracted not only a few Yankees but some native Californians as well, and while he never endangered Catholic supremacy, his group remained active for a number of years.

Catholic activities continued to center around the Plaza Church, its affairs being directed by the California Mission System as a part of the territory of the Diocese of Sonora, Mexico, until the year 1840 when the Diocese of both "Californias" was established. Early in the 1870's, the magnificent Cathedral of St. Vibiana was projected, and the fine structure at Second and Main Streets was completed in 1876, whereupon Catholic headquarters were installed in the new cathedral, the first to be built in Los Angeles. In 1936, an archbishopric was created comprising the counties of Los Angeles, Orange, Santa Barbara, and Ventura, a territory of 9,508 square miles. Today there are 90 Catholic churches within the Los Angeles city limits, and 57 additional houses of worship of that faith spread over the county. Communicants in the city number 225,000 and in the entire county 317,000.

Protestantism made a poor start in Southern California and it was late in the 1850's before any appreciable foothold was gained. Its rise was rapid during the latter part of the century, and startling gains have been registered during the present century. Even though American rule granted religious freedom, few in Los Angeles took advantage of the new rule for almost twenty years. This was largely due to the geographical isolation of Southern California, high mountains and vast deserts discouraging immigration from the East. The relatively few Americans who braved the hardships of the overland trip or the long voyage around the Horn were hardbitten frontiersmen, traders, miners, and the adventurers—types giving little thought to religion. It was during this period, too, when Los Angeles gained the rather unenviable reputation of being anything but the "City of the Angels."

Into this unpromising pasture, itinerant Protestant ministers with hopes of gathering flocks began drifting, early in the fifties. Among them was the Reverend James W. Brier, a survivor of the Jayhawker party, which defied advice of old-timers and took a short cut across what they named Death Valley to reach the coast. Brier in 1850 preached the first Methodist sermon in Los Angeles to a congregation consisting of his own family and Mayor John G. Nichols.

The next assault was made three years later by another Methodist, the Reverend Adam Bland, who at first preached to three persons, including his wife and daughter. After a few months Bland had built up a slightly larger congregation and started a school, but eventually he decided Los Angeles was a hopeless field, and departed.

In the same year (1853) the Reverend John A. Freeman delivered the first Baptist sermon, and left almost immediately for El Monte, where his church became for a time the only meeting place for the Protestants of the Los Angeles area.

In 1854, a Presbyterian minister, the Reverend James Wood, began to conduct services in a carpenter shop on Main Street; after about a year he departed because of failing health. A more successful Presbyterian was the Reverend William E. Boardman, whose arrival in 1859 elicited from the Los Angeles *Star* the wistful comment: "We hope he will be enabled to organize a congregation." Boardman gathered around him a Protestant group of various denominations and had erected the walls and roof of a meetinghouse when subscriptions for the building began to dwindle because of the Civil War currency inflation. After three years he, too, gave up and for a number of years there was not a single Protestant clergyman in the city.

While early non-Catholics long failed to unite, the Jews were holding services within a decade after California became a part of the United States. Joseph P. Newmark, a business man who was also an ordained rabbi, held the first service in the rear room of "Don Juan" Temple's adobe in 1854. The congregation, named B'nai B'rith, was taken over by Rabbi A. W. Edelman in 1862, and regular services have been conducted ever since.

It was 1865 before the first permanent Protestant congregation was organized. This pioneer congregation was of a nature not usually early represented on the western frontier—the Protestant Episcopal. An Episcopal bishop, William Ingraham Kip, had visited Los Angeles ten years earlier, and decided it was useless to attempt to establish a church there. He had observed that the Protestant clergymen were often unpopular with Angelenos because the ministers preached on "Nebraska or Kansas, slavery or antislavery," and other partisan secular issues of the day.

Nevertheless, these earlier Protestant clergymen had helped to pave the way for the Episcopalians. In 1864, a group of Los Angeles citizens, remnants of the earlier congregations, appealed to the Episcopal Diocese in San Francisco, pleading that "The Americans here are left a life of simple heathenism . . . It is pitiable to think that if a Protestant dies here, he must be buried like a dog; that an infant can never be baptized, and that a Justice of the Peace is the only authority to whom a couple can go to be married." In response to this plea, the Reverend Elias Birdsall was sent to Los Angeles to establish, in 1865, St. Athanasius Church.

That the going at first was no easier for Birdsall than for his predecessors is indicated in a newspaper editorial of 1865, referring to the situation among the Protestants: "It is a burning shame . . . that Los Angeles cannot boast of a full and thorough-going congregation who can spend one hour each Sabbath from the 'busy life,' without being 'drummed up' by handbill or some other method-extraordinary to hear an able and eloquent discourse." Nevertheless, Birdsall gradually built up a congregation, and before long other Protestant denominations were established, among them the Congregationalists (1867), the Methodists (1868), and the African Methodists.

With the beginning of the seventies, Los Angeles changed rapidly from a virtually barren Protestant religious field to a luxuriant pasture for any and all beliefs. The construction of the railroads brought thousands of new residents to the West, and scores of new creeds. Churches as well as real-estate subdivisions mushroomed all over town; no less than forty were erected in the booming eighties and many more in the nineties. With Presbyterians, Lutherans, and Baptists came the Christian Scientists and Mormons. The first Scientist church in Los Angeles received its charter in May of 1898, and the first edifice was erected at 1366 South Alvarado Street shortly thereafter. The Mormons (Latter-day Saints) organized in the Los Angeles territory in 1892, following a period of successful missionary work extending over the entire State. However, it was not until 1923 that Stakes (dioceses) were organized; the church has enjoyed a steady growth since that time. The Hollywood Stake by 1930 contained ten organized bishop's Wards with several branches. It was during the latter part of the past century, too, that the Japanese and Chinese built temples, not only for the practice of their native faiths but also for Christian worship under American leadership. In the early 1900's, Los Angeles could boast of 231 church organizations with 220 of them reporting a total membership of 81,371.

Development of the Los Angeles religious field continued all through the first two decades of the twentieth century, but it was during the prosperous period immediately following the World War that, nourished by a steady stream of newcomers, religion burst into full and spectacular bloom. Many of the new settlers had means, leisure, and inclination to indulge in extensive church activities. A great number, transferring their membership from churches in their former homes to those of the same denomination in Los Angeles, bolstered the local fundamentalist movements.

Others joined some of the newer and more sensational organizations such as the Four Square Gospel, founded by Aimee Semple Mc-Pherson in 1923. The establishment of her Angelus Temple and its subsequent growth, coupled with the theatrical nature of her services, furnished Los Angeles with its greatest demonstration of the spectacular in religion. Thousands flocked to her banner, and records indicate that more than 40,000 persons have been immersed in Angelus Temple's baptistry. In addition to the $2,000,000 temple with its radio broadcasting station, a Bible college, some 400 branch churches, and 178 mission stations in other parts of the world are supported.

It was during this post-war period, too, that Los Angeles was overrun by religious fakers of various types. The epidemic spread and assumed such proportions that legislation curbing their practices resulted, and soothsayers, fortune tellers, and swamis were forced to operate under license. The cosmopolitan populace of Los Angeles became known far and wide for its susceptibility to the teachings of sects and cults embracing such philosophies as divine healing, occult science, spiritual and mental phenomena, reincarnation, and astrological revelations. Herbert W. Schneider of Columbia University, New York, declared a few years ago that every existing religion in the world was represented by branches in Los Angles County.

In 1940, the religious scene is a continuation of that of the twenties and thirties. Orthodox creeds prosper side by side with numerous fanatical movements. There are rites and philosophies to suit all tastes. There are esoteric churches lighted with neon signs depicting soul and astral evolutions; schools of astrology, numerology, divine science, and psychic and occult laws conduct classes for members, and ordain their own ministers.

Despite this multiplicity of religious groups, the Roman Catholics, the larger Protestant groups, and the Jewish congregations continue to flourish; their memberships have increased enormously during the past decade. Nearly all the orthodox churches are supported in part by the many transients. With the increase in membership has come the constant erection of new church edifices. Today there are 1,833 houses of worship spread over the city and county, and 81 missions, 134 religious institutions, and 67 reading rooms. In addition to the Roman Catholic Church with its 147 houses of worship, the 10 leading Protestant denominations support 836 churches. With the Methodist Church leading with 189 churches, there are 165 Baptist, 108 Presbyterian, 83 Christian Science, 80 Lutheran, 57 Jewish, 50 Seventh-day Adventist, 40 Protestant Episcopal, 37 Church of Christ and 27 Latter-day Saints houses of worship.

The extent of the current church activities is shown by the social welfare programs that are carried on by virtually all groups and that embrace nearly every department of social work: the Catholic Welfare Bureau maintains a club for transient boys, a maternity home for unmarried mothers, and numerous other agencies; the Methodists operate the large clinic of the Church of All Nations Foundation, and the Goodwill Industries, which supply employment; the Episcopal Church is active in neighborhood group and hospital work and maintains the Episcopal City Mission; Congregationalists, Presbyterians, Baptists, and members of other leading denominations, working individually and also through church organizations, carry on Y.M.C.A. and Y.W.C.A. activities, and "social action" programs to foster principles of racial equality, social security, and so on.

Important social service work among the Negroes has been instituted by the People's Independent Church of Christ.

Angelus Temple, unlike most of the other fundamentalist organizations, has a free commissary for the indigent; the Jews, who in 1854 founded the city's first charitable organization, the Hebrew Benevolent Society, now support the extensive Federation of Jewish Welfare Organizations, whose thirteen agencies include Cedars of Lebanon Hospital, the Jewish Loan Fund, and a modern orphanage.

In Los Angeles today, such religious groups, together with the less eccentric unorthodox groups, form a dignified background against which the fantastic stands out in garish high lights.

Architecture

Viktor von Pribosic

LOS ANGELES COUNTY GENERAL HOSPITAL

LOS ANGELES PUBLIC LIBRARY
Bertram Goodhue, Architect

University of Southern California

MUDD MEMORIAL HALL OF PHILOSOPHY,
UNIVERSITY OF SOUTHERN CALIFORNIA

Julius Schulman

McALMON RESIDENCE, LOS ANGELES
R. M. Schindler, Architect

BLUE AND SILVER HOUSE,"
THE RESIDENCE OF JOBYNA HOWLAND—BEVERLY HILLS

Julius Schulman   *Lloyd Wright, Architect*

Thomas and Kitchel

A PALM SPRINGS RESIDENCE
Honnold and Russell, Architects

V. D. L. RESEARCH HOUSE, LOS ANGELES
HOME OF RICHARD J. NEUTRA, ARCHITECT

Luckhaus Studio

F. E. Dunham: U. S. Forest Service

FEDERAL BUILDING AND POST OFFICE, LOS ANGELES
G. Stanley Underwood, Architect

COLUMBIA BROADCASTING SYSTEM STUDIOS, HOLLYWOOD
William Lescaze, Architect   *Columbia Broadcasting System*

Edison Company

EDISON BUILDING, LOS ANGELES
Allison and Allison, Architects

A SIERRA MADRE RESIDENCE OF BATTEN CONSTRUCTION
Graham Latta, Architect

AN ALTADENA RESIDENCE (MONTEREY STYLE)
H. Roy Kelley, Architect

The Movies

LONG before Hollywood stirred from its pastoral quiet, the slopes of Edendale, a few miles to the east, were loud with the antics of actors who doubled as roustabouts or carpenters and did their own laundry. On the lots facing that part of Alessandro Street later renamed Glendale Boulevard people from the garment trade spouted through megaphones and "made up" stories as they went along, goading themselves and their players to commit artistic felonies. Picture making went on in whirlwind haste, and without formality—cowboys chased Indians, cops chased robbers, and robbers chased misfit cops. Here, between November, 1909, and July, 1910, Director Charles K. French ground out 185 films for the Bison Company, a firm that took its trademark, a rampant buffalo, from the design on the back of a ten dollar bill. ("If it's good enough for Uncle Sam," they said, "it's good enough for us!") G. M. Anderson (Max Aronson billed as "Broncho Billy") blazed his way from one finished film to another with such dispatch that his six-guns never had time to cool. The first actor-author-producer, and the first of the hard-riding western heroes who feared and detested horses, Anderson produced a picture a week for 376 successive weeks, an all-time record.

Edendale lots were dotted with flimsy prop saloons and ranch house interiors, hapazard structures that frequently toppled over while the camera was grinding. When a cave-in occurred, the players scurried from under, or if they were rugged braced themselves and stood firm beneath the falling walls, never ceasing their exaggerated pantomime. The director, eager for action, often included the accidental collapse as part of the plot. It was in Edendale that the Keystone cops came to fame, as did Mabel Normand, Ford Sterling, Fred Mace, and Fatty Arbuckle; and here Mack Sennett, their director-boss, introduced to the movies the bathing beauty and the custard pie smash.

California had been claimed for the movies in the autumn of 1908 when Francis Boggs, star of the stage melodrama, *Why Girls Leave Home,* came to Los Angeles to direct the final scenes of a single-reeler, *The Count of Monte Cristo,* begun in Chicago by William N. Selig, one of the earliest commercial movie makers. Boggs and his cameraman, Thomas Persons, finished the film at Laguna Beach with a cast totally different from the one that appeared in the opening scenes. Months later they built the first motion-picture studio in Los Angeles, a lean-to of frail boards and canvas sets on a lot behind a Chinese laundry on Olive Street near Seventh.

Meanwhile in the East the movies were engaged in a hurly-burly of suits and injunctions, raids and riots. Since 1897 Thomas Alva Edison had been suing the independent producers for patent infringement. As the "flickers" supplanted shooting galleries and penny arcades in popularity, the producers licensed by Edison entered into an alliance to safeguard their claims to film profits. In 1909 they formed the Motion Picture Patents Company, soon widely known as the "movie trust." It included all of the country's more stable movie makers, and a few of the pirates who managed to turn "legitimate": Edison's Vitagraph, Lubin, Selig, Essanay, Kalem, Pathé and Méliés. Biograph, bluffing its way, refused to affiliate until later when it was able to dictate its own terms.

The trust's monopoly was threatened, however, by a group of small producers and exhibitors who, having been excluded from the pact, began to construct or import bootleg equipment to film their pictures in obscure hide-outs. Against these independents the trust waged one of the most vigorous battles in the history of American industrialism. The pirates fled from cellar to garret, to roof; from New York to Florida, to Cuba, and finally to California, where the scenery of any part of the world could be easily simulated, and where the climate permitted outdoor picture making in all seasons.

Trust companies, attracted by the same climate and topography, speedily followed the independents to southern California. They opened studios, pirates and trust alike, in Edendale, and to a lesser extent in Los Angeles, Santa Monica, Culver City, and Glendale. Not until Edendale became overcrowded did producers begin to move westward through the low rolling hills to Hollywood, where David Horsley's Nestor Film Company had paused in 1911 to make Hollywood's first motion picture in a studio at Sunset Boulevard and Gower Street.

The trust, as it settled in California, formed a new battlefront in its war with the independents, but this time the pirates stood their ground and fought back. And as the independents began to get a firmer foothold, the movies started on their slow and painful struggle to grow up. Maurice Costello, one of the screen's first idols, started the actors on the way to a new independence by declaring that he would no longer help carpenters hammer new sets together; presently Mack Sennett had reached such heights that he felt justified in asking his employers for an office bathtub eight feet long, six feet wide, and drawing five feet of water. More and more movie producers were inclined to remove their hats at the dinner table; Biograph began calling its film processing factory a laboratory; Essanay paid $25 in a contest for the term "photoplay" to replace the term "movies," which nevertheless remained the people's choice.

The Selig lot was walled to shield the players from lookers-on who were accustomed to shouting comments and criticisms. Fred Karno's English pantomime company came to town, and left without its headliner, Charlie Chaplin. Famous Players began production in 1912, bringing together Cecil B. De Mille, Jesse Lasky, and Samuel Goldwyn, and a year later Hal Roach made his first film.

In spite of the industry's sudden flair for all things grandiloquent, a new creative craftsmanship began to evolve through the resourcefulness and superior showmanship of the outlaw producers. Carl Laemmle, a onetime clothing dealer, founded the Independent Motion Picture Company—known as the "Imp"—and here the "star" system was introduced. Laemmle invaded the Biograph lot and for $125 a week hired Gladys Smith, "the little girl with the curls," whom he elevated to stardom under the name of Mary Pickford in *Their First Misunderstanding,* directed by Thomas H. Ince, with Owen Moore as leading man. Having lured the trust's greatest potential money maker, Laemmle taunted the licensed producers with a series of blatant advertisements: "Little Mary Is Now An Imp!"

Another of the pirates' innovations was the introduction of the "feature" picture—a film of more than one or two reels. The first of these, *Queen Elizabeth,* made in France by Louis Mercanton with Sarah Bernhardt and Lou Tellegen, had been imported in 1911 by a onetime furrier, Adolph Zukor, who spurred American producers to the development of picture drama in the grand manner. Within a few years came other films that are remembered today with respect: David Wark Griffith's *Intolerance,* which introduced parallel, or "cut-back," story telling, and *Broken Blossoms,* with Richard Barthelmess; *Tillie's Punctured Romance,* directed by Mack Sennett, with Marie Dressler and Charlie Chaplin; Lubitsch's *Carmen,* starring Pola Negri; *The Squawman,* and Chaplin's *A Dog's Life.* In America's first super-feature, *The Birth of a Nation,* Griffith revolutionized screen technique, creating a picture which critics viewed in terms of art. Based on a story by the Reverend Thomas Dixon called *The Clansman,* the picture opened at Clune's Auditorium in Los Angeles, February 8, 1915, and a month later, with greater assurance (and at two dollars a seat), it had its first showing in New York, where it rolled up an astounding box-office record.

Throughout this period, the trust companies languished, dwindling into oblivion because of their persistent mass production of outmoded short films. The pirates, once hounded across the continent, now set the pace in a new direction and began to dominate the industry— though, even as late as 1925, the movie trust maintained a New York office where their agents dictated blistering letters in a vain effort to collect the license fees that had been carried on the books for more than two decades.

As the twentieth century grew into its 'teens, the film-going public began to demand not only feature productions, but stars, stars, stars. Up in marquee lights went such names as John Bunny and Flora Finch, Lottie Brisco, Grace Cunard, Helen Holmes, Arthur Johnson, Marguerite Clark, Blanche Sweet, Tom Mix, Anita Stewart, Earle Williams, William S. Hart, Charles Ray, Norma and Constance Talmadge, Wallace Reid, Ben Lyon and Bebe Daniels, and the Gish sisters. Angelenos, who had loitered in the old days around the Biograph lot, remember the Gishes: how Dorothy wore a pink ribbon and Lillian wore blue, so that Griffith, their director, could tell them apart.

Casting was carried on in the bar of the Alexandria Hotel, downtown, at Fifth and Spring Streets. Five o'clock was the recognized hour for cocktails, baked ham in hot rolls, and the allocation of parts in new productions. Every unemployed actor in town made for the Alexandria and tried to catch a director's eye with a bit of business—they talked and lived pictures, and the world beyond did not exist for the men and women of shadowland.

The years from 1912 to 1920 brought few radical changes in mechanical methods of movie making—though cameramen perfected the dissolve, the fade, the double exposure, and the close-up—but the World War, ending the competition of European film companies, left the huge and growing world market to American producers. Lewis J. Selznick, brimming with good will inspired by new business, could condescend to pleasantries with Nicholas, the recently deposed Little Father of all the Russias. In the fabulous tradition, Selznick in 1917 dispatched a cablegram to the former Czar: "When I was poor boy in Kiev some of your policemen were not kind to me and my people. I came to America and prospered. Now hear with regret you are out of a job there. Feel no ill will what your policemen did, so if you will come New York can give you fine position acting in pictures. Salary no object. Reply my expense. Regards you and family."

Never again could an actress like Mrs. Patrick Campbell, favorite of British Shavian audiences, cross the sea and a continent to go slumming in Hollywood: to hoist an eyebrow, as she did when meeting Harold Lloyd, with the query: "And you, my good man, tell me, are you employed on the films?" Hollywood actors, knee-deep in butlers, had ideas of their own. Just as their forebears had broken away from the studio carpenters, so did Chaplin, Pickford, Fairbanks, and Griffith break with the producers. In 1919 they organized United Artists, assuming complete control of the process of making their own pictures, and prompting Richard Rowland, head of rival Metro films, to lament that the "lunatics have taken charge of the asylum!"

During these years the movies expanded in still another direction: the ownership of theatres. Chains were organized and battles fought for the control of first-run houses. In an effort to eliminate competition, producers bought hundreds of legitimate theatres and either dismantled them or remodeled them for exhibition of their own films. The general extravagance required money. Money required bankers. Bankers demanded a voice in the industry's affairs. And so it happened that such onetime independents as Adolph Zukor, Carl Laemmle, William Fox, and Samuel Goldwyn found themselves taking orders from Wall Street. By 1936 the major film companies—Paramount, Loew's (Metro-Goldwyn-Mayer), Universal, United Artists, Warner Brothers, 20th Century-Fox, Columbia, and R.K.O.—traced their ownership through the Electrical Research Products, Inc., the Western Electric Company, and the American Telephone and Telegraph Company, to the House of Morgan; or, through the Radio Corporation of America and The Chase National Bank, to the Rockefeller interests.

To meet the new order and to better working conditions the cinema workers began extensive organization in trade unions, and the Motion Picture Producers Association fought back. In an industry generally associated with fabulous money and great generosity, wages became unbelievably low. Average annual technicians' earnings, which in 1929 were $2,463, had dropped by 1935 to $1,767, while in 1937 studio painters, carpenters, and plasterers were averaging $1,500 a year. Members of these crafts worked fewer than 65 per cent of the year's working days in 1937, and not more than 20 per cent had steady employment, while five of the film companies (Loew's, Columbia, Paramount, 20th Century-Fox, and Warner's) reported a 25 per cent increase in profits.

Even the "quickie" producers of "Poverty Row" had junked the helter-skelter production in which carpenters doubled as gladiators, leading ladies made their own costumes, and one man might finance, write, direct, cut, and sell a motion picture film. The movies that reach first-run houses today are produced by a streamlined process in which all efforts are highly organized and specialized.

After the successful talkie revolution (it began in 1927 with *The Jazz Singer* when Al Jolson strode to the piano and words came to life on his lips: "Say, Ma, listen to this!"), movie producers undertook to experiment with new possibilities in color pictures, though the use of color remains restricted because of the extremely high cost. The Technicolor Corporation holds a virtual monopoly on patents, and controls use of the color process, (by leasing the $15,000 color cameras and selling), developing, and printing color film. Walt Disney, the most outstanding artist in the development of the animated cartoon, contracted with the corporation in 1934 to make his Mickey Mouse and Silly Symphony cartoons in color, beginning work the same year on his first full-length feature production, *Snow White and the Seven Dwarfs*. The social and artistic significance of motion pictures has increasingly concerned educators, church groups, women's clubs, and critics of American life. Though the average weekly attendance of 75 million gives the movies an influence equalled only by newspapers and radio, the artists whose creative efforts go into picture making have long felt hampered by the fact that, as Walter Wanger expressed it, "any minority, any individual, any rag, any nation could dictate to us." In July, 1938, a distributors' boycott of *Blockade* crystallized their discontent. At a meeting of 300 delegates, representing 150,000 members of motion-picture unions, guilds, and other organizations, these artists demanded that "gag rule" be removed from the industry, so that motion pictures might become "a very important pillar in the democratic structure."

When the producers themselves, back in the early 1920's, feared a nation-wide boycott because of the cycle of sex and crime films, and the public outcry at the scandals unearthed in stars' private lives, the industry forestalled the pressure groups by forming the Motion Picture Producers and Distributors of America, Inc. With Will Hays as its head at a salary of $100,000 a year the industry began a climb toward public confidence.

Realists in business and politics, the major producers balked at a realistic treatment of any theme in films. Some producers, believing that audiences sought only to forget their troubles, gave them farces, ranging from the mild to the screwball, with a standard rotation of boy-meets-girl inanities, followed by a cycle of boy-slaps-girl. Another school of producers became aware of a plea, grown more insistent in American life, for realism, and even the most romantic pictures began to achieve greater fidelity to essential truth and significance of theme. Gradually, out of this approach to truth-telling, came such films as *I Am a Fugitive from a Chain Gang, Of Human Bondage, Dead End, The Informer, The Life of Emile Zola, Stage Coach, Juarez*, and *Confessions of a Nazi Spy*.

MAKING A MOVIE

"If one goes to the root of the matter," the playwright and screen writer Sidney Howard said, "motion pictures are neither written nor acted, but made." A glance around any of the walled towns that are today's major picture lots bears out Howard's statement. They are dominated by massive sound stages with unwavering lines and unornamented surfaces characteristic of modern industrial design. In large administration buildings file clerks, stenographers, and all the other clerical employees of a modern factory's "front office" labor over books and bills. In laboratories scientists experiment with schemes to speed up production, and in other buildings technical experts operate delicate processing machines of baffling intricacy. The major studio lot contains machine and printing shops, a foundry and a metal works. If the picturesque sets and oddly dressed actors are disregarded the studio is a huge manufacturing plant: on a major lot from 1,000 to 3,000 workers representing approximately 275 crafts methodically pursue the business of making motion pictures.

The head of a motion-picture studio is usually called the head producer. But the word producer is a much overworked term. Cecil B. de Mille, Samuel Goldwyn, and Frank Capra are also producers in the highest sense of the word; they have a financial interest in the productions they make and are responsible for their success or failure. Of such bonafide producers as these, Hollywood contains not more than a dozen. In charge of most of the pictures made in Hollywood are so-called associate producers—men of less authority and power who nevertheless are the top supervisors of most Hollywood movie productions.

Though the head producer is the top official in the studio, he is not all powerful. The major studio corporations are controlled by financial interests largely in New York City, and it is to the eastern corporation officials that he must cock an ear for basic instructions. Besides determining how much money will be available in a given year, "New York" takes a hand in apportioning this money among the various proposed productions—and thereby becomes an influence in the shaping of studio policy. In conferences between the production head and the eastern owners, funds are allotted to pictures of four definite types: "A" pictures, based on a current best-selling novel or popular play, the studio's most ambitious undertakings; "A" productions that are not outstanding but that nevertheless contain the studio's stars; "B" pictures which use feature players rather than stars, and a sprinkling of minor contract players and "unknowns"; and short subjects and cartoons, which most of the studios in 1939 had come to consider an important item in their production schedules. The most ambitious "A" pictures are the movies' biggest gamble. Production costs range from $250,000 to $2,000,000 or $3,000,000, but a profit is never certain. The time taken in making such a picture averages between two and three months. "B" pictures are produced on budgets which seldom exceed $250,000 and usually average between $125,000 and $150,000. With fewer stars to offer the box office, "B" pictures depend on catchy, fresh treatments, and plots paralleling events of public interest. These pictures are block-booked, or pre-sold, sometimes a year in advance of production. The time consumed in production ranges from twelve to twenty days. On "Poverty Row," a short section of Sunset Boulevard near Gower Street, "quickies" are produced at the rate of two or three a week, but these hastily concocted dishes are strictly for "grind" houses and the more backward country regions.

Responsible to the head producer and working closely with him are a corps of field generals numbering eight or ten in the larger studios, that includes the story editor, the man in charge of writers, the production manager (in charge of the studio's real properties and all its tangible assets), and a group of individual or associate producers. As a rule, this staff in joint conference fixes production schedules and budgets for specific productions, sets shooting dates, assigns directors insofar as feasible, and, through swaps or new contracts, maintains the studio's star list at the level it considers advisable. The producer's job is part art and part business. He is responsible for the success of the pictures with which his name is bracketed, and is usually compensated on a percentage basis. He passes judgment on stories, selects writers, directors, and actors. He must consult with artists on costumes and sets, and with musicians concerning scores. At the same time, he must watch the clock, and keep costs within previously set limits.

The director's job is, of course, primarily artistic, but he shares with the associate producer the task of co-ordinating talent and temperament, and he must likewise bear in mind the restrictions of time and budget allowance. In most cases, to insure harmony between script and direction, the director works with producer and writers while the script is taking shape. Sometimes, however, a director is not called in until the screen play assumes its final form, in which case in all probability he will want it completely rewritten to fit his ideas. Preparation, shooting, and editing are the three steps in the production of a motion picture, but many studio departments function simultaneously. Some departments are at work only during the preparatory period; others enter and leave, only to re-enter again when their functions are required. Furthermore, there are no set routines in picture making. Every studio has its own production methods and different pictures call for different routines.

Nevertheless, almost all pictures commence with a search for a story. Hunting stories is the continuous business of the story department, and is regarded as difficult. Every story department contains staffs of readers in Hollywood, sometimes numbering as many as a dozen, and in New York. These readers comb books, plays, and magazines for stories with visual interest and plots abundant in situations readily translatable into action. It is the custom now in most story departments to issue a weekly bulletin compiled from synopses of stories read in Hollywood and New York. These bulletins are sent to all associate producers, and when a producer sees a synopsis that appeals to him he puts in a claim for it. If it is okehed by the studio head, it is purchased and he starts to work.

Because of the risk of being involved in plagiarism suits, the studios will not read stories directly submitted by unknown writers, but the synopsized story, or "original," written specifically for the screen and submitted through recognized agents, is an important source of screen fare today. Such stories are often fewer than twenty pages in length, but written with great attention to possible shots and screen-play construction.

Besides novels, plays, and originals, the producer's story may come from an idea of his own, based on the need of some special star, a biographical or historical character, or something from the world of science or invention. If such is the case, an outside writer's fee is usually eliminated: the studio's own writers are put directly to work hatching the producer's egg. Prices paid for stories are of course based on the demand for them: agents frequently send copies of an original story to all major studios simultaneously, hoping the bidding will hike up the price. Nevertheless, it is not unusual for a relatively unknown author to be paid as little as $500 for a story which will be used as the vehicle for an "A" picture packed with stars and feature players. Best-selling novels, successful Broadway plays, and originals from the pens of well-known authors bring prices ranging from $1,000 up.

In making synopses and passing judgment on stories, the story department readers consider many questions. Is the story a suitable vehicle for any of this studio's stars? Will it lend diversification to the studio's production schedule or broaden its scope? Does it belong to a currently popular cycle, or does it have qualities that might make it a forerunner of a new cycle? If one or more of these possibilities exist, the story editor is likely to call it to the attention of one of the producers on his lot. In 1939 the severest problem of producers, as far as stories were concerned, was finding new material for highly specialized and "typed" stars such as Edward Arnold, George Raft, Grace Moore, and Marlene Dietrich.

Checking title rights is an important duty of the story editor. Because good titles are in great demand, unscrupulous producers not connected with the major lots sometimes register titles with the Hays office (Motion Picture Producers and Distributors of America, Inc.) and assign a cheap writer to work out a story to fit it. Because registration entitles the holder to the title rights for a limited period of time, provided the holder can prove intention of using it, this practice has enabled more than one Hollywood entrepreneur to grab a handsome price running into four figures for a two, three, or four word title.

Although there is some talk around Hollywood to the effect that writers should learn to submit stories in scenario form rather than as originals, very few scenarios are purchased. When a producer gets his hands on what he considers a good story idea his first step is the hiring of a writer to make a *treatment*—an intermediary step between the raw material and the shooting script. From the writer's point of view, the treatment is a description on paper of just how the screen writer plans to make the raw material into a product suitable for screening, and he generally writes the treatment after conferring with the producer and the director. Once the treatment has been accepted at a second story conference, the writer does the first draft of the script itself. If the original material is a novel, the writing of the script involves a great deal of condensation; if a play, the process is one of expansion. Because condensation of literary material generally produces more artistic results than does expansion, most writers find novels more congenial to work with than plays.

In subsequent story conferences with his producer, the director, and perhaps the art director, the script begins to take the form of a motion picture. Such things as camera angles and photographic composition are considered and within a few weeks, if all goes well, the script returns to the producer in final form called shooting script. This final version may be the second draft, or the fifteenth—depending on whether or not the producer is willing to accept the ideas of the director and screen writer working for him. Before production can be launched, however, the script is submitted to the Hays office, whose function is to warn the studio against deletions that may be expected by the censorship boards of various states and the objections of civic and religious groups and foreign nations. The script is then taken over by the technicians and converted into a breakdown, which means that some hundred and twenty-odd typewritten pages are transformed to a large board covered with small tickets, each ticket representing a scene. The breakdown reveals with amazing exactitude how many days will be consumed in the shooting of the picture, and because the length of shooting has much to do with ultimate cost of the picture, cutting is frequently necessary at this point. Once this has been done, the writer's contribution has been made.

In choosing a writer the producer has a large field from which to select. There are thousands of writers in Hollywood, and more thousands elsewhere. He may choose a studio writer, or he may choose a free lance. In any case, his aim is to secure someone adept in following the story through its many drafts, and he will of course choose someone familiar with screen technique. "New York writers," a term that embraces all scribes outside of Hollywood, receive weekly wages in the thousands, but the studios' writing shops contain many "junior writers" who receive less than $50 a week because they lack "prestige."

Some producers call in additional writers to work on the story. One may contribute new situations; another, dialogue; and a third, the continuity or final form of the screen play. Producers of this stripe are for the most part unpopular with authors and directors, however, for the latter believe it is impossible to obtain unity in a story when each writer has a different conception of it.

When the writer submitted his first draft of the script he, perhaps unknowingly, launched the studio into a flurry of activity. Copies of his script were sent to all departments, and the production office, which supervises the budgets and co-ordinates the activities of all departments, has assigned a unit manager to supervise the physical problems and finances. The director has chosen his assistant (except in those cases, not rare, where the director is not picked until the story is close to final form). The art department has prepared sketches for the various sets. The music department has been working on a score, and on special songs, if they are called for, and casting is well under way.

Although the stars are customarily chosen for a picture by the producer and the director, the brunt of the casting job falls to the casting director, who has his special classifications of the thousands of players listed in Hollywood, which he consults as soon as he receives his copy of the script. He makes suggestions for the various parts in the script on an assignment sheet, which he sends to the producer and director. If a director is doubtful about a casting director's choices that director will make his own tests. Otherwise, the casting director himself handles the production tests for the actors tentatively chosen, after which the budget for salaries is checked by the production office and the players' contracts drawn up. The average cost of a production test is $600; consequently the selections of the casting director are made with care.

Hollywood measures its actors strictly according to rank. There are stars, feature players, and bit players in the studio's stock company, and from this roster the casting director makes all selections except extras and atmosphere players. A contract player, or star, is an actor or actress who has a term contract for six months. This contains options renewable up to seven years, a guaranteed salary for twenty out of twenty-six weeks whether or not the player works, and a lay-off period of six weeks during which he or she must have at least one consecutive week's lay-off. The contract also provides for a rising salary scale. On theatre marquees the star's name precedes the name of the picture, whereas those of feature and bit players, contracted for on a weekly and daily basis and considered important in bolstering up a picture, follow the picture title on the theatre marquees.

A star borrowed from another studio is engaged at a fixed sum. Borrowed feature players continue to draw their regular salaries from their home studios.   The borrowing studio pays the home studio not less than a month's salary for the feature player's services, plus an "accumulated carrying charge" fixed at three weeks' salary that presumably reimburses the home studio for having carried the actor during idle periods.   Lesser supporting players are never loaned on less than a monthly basis.

Selecting supporting players is a simple matter compared to the task of picking extras and atmosphere players.   In the studios' early days many agencies sprang up to handle the throngs of people hoping for movie careers.   When a studio needed extras a casting director in one of the agencies would inspect the crowd outside his door and select the most likely types, and those selected paid the agency a percentage of their earnings.   This unfair and inefficient system in 1926 was supplanted by the Central Casting Corporation, an office founded by the Association of Motion Picture Producers.   Receiving over 11,000 calls for work each day, it is the largest employment agency in the world.

In 1939 an extra is any actor not required to speak lines who receives $16.50 or less per day and is not under contract to the studio. All wage distinctions depend on appearance, physical type, and wardrobe.   The lowest wage, $5.50, is paid for nondescript mob and atmospheric types.   Extras who portray attendants, porters and the like receive $8.25, and extras who take the parts of policemen, waiters, business men, and people in street clothes are paid $11 a day.   Those receiving the highest wage must provide and maintain their own wardrobes, including complete sports, afternoon, and evening outfits.   Period costumes and uniforms are, however, provided by the studios.

Babies used in films are well paid.   Babies thirty days old or under receive $75 a day; those thirty to ninety days old receive $50 a day; those from three to six months of age receive $25.   But any child under six months of age is permitted by law to remain at a studio only two hours a day and allowed an actual working time not to exceed 20 minutes, with exposure to artificial lights limited to 30 seconds at a time.   Doctors and nurses must be on hand for frequent physical examinations because the studio is by law responsible for the infants they employ—even six months after their performances.

When production begins, the assistant director each day notifies the casting department what extras are required for the following day. The studio casting directors in the major studios send their orders via teletype to Central Casting, where a bell rings, a light shows, and the order is automatically typed out with the date, the time the extras must report, the name of the director, the number of the production, the type of makeup necessary, and other details.   Then follow the number of extras, their ages, costumes, salaries, and other specifications.   Known as call sheets, these orders are placed in the hands of assistant casting directors, who sit before call boards containing the names of thousands of extras not working that day. The name plate of each extra has a number of colored dots indicating his or her wardrobe. As the calls for the extras required come in, they are conveyed by a loudspeaker from the telephone switchboard to the specially constructed desks. Thus an assistant casting director may have any call turned over to him. He rejects some, assigns others, and himself phones those he particularly wants.

The routine in assigning minors for atmosphere or bits is much the same as for adults, except that the California State Board of Education keeps a watchful eye over the procedure. Children registered at Central must renew a permit from the board every three months. Permission to keep their names active at Central is predicated on a physical examination and a satisfactory scholastic record. While on the set the children must attend school under the instruction of a teacher appointed by the board (salary paid by the studio), cannot be on the set more than eight hours, and must be attended by a parent or guardian.

The intricate files of Central Casting classify the 12,000 registered extras according to sex, age, height, and general appearance; and list such physical assets as chinlessness, large feet, buck teeth, and cauliflower ears. Registrants are also classified as to previous occupation and proficiency in the various entertainment fields. A machine called the mechanical casting director may be used to run through the files and selects extras of desired qualifications by the numbers on their cards, but it is used infrequently because the employees of Central Casting carry relatively complete files in their heads. The head casting director alone knows by heart the names, addresses, wardrobes, and qualification of several thousand registrants. Unfortunately, only about five per cent of Hollywood's army of extras get calls. The casting directors themselves freely state that to join the ranks of the extras is the quickest way down. There is almost no hope of advancement, and every chance of slipping. Outside of the studio, however, producers, directors, and talent scouts conduct a continuous hunt for new stars. Little theatres, radio stations, night clubs, and road shows are combed by scouts who work from a central office in New York City.

The art department is one of the first to start work on a motion picture and one of the last to finish. Shortly after the selection of the story, and while it is still in its synopsis form, the art director confers with the producer and gives his general ideas concerning the treatment of scenes, and at the same time submits a rough estimate of the cost and required space for the necessary sets. When the actual shooting is over, the art director is still on the job to receive the final order to demolish the sets, with parts preserved for possible future use.

The department is headed by a supervising art director, and contains several unit art directors and artists of individual style and talent actually in charge of specific productions, a staff of designers and draftsmen. The set dressing department is also under the supervision of the art department, and the construction department and the drapery department are closely connected with the practical work of the art director.

Keeping in mind the mood of the story, the action encompassed by it, and such problems as lighting and color, the supervising director prepares board plans for the set and turns them over to a unit art director. The latter prepares a layout which includes sketches of every set in the picture and elevation drawings drawn to scale. To assist a non-visual minded director, water-color sketches or small models are sometimes also prepared. From the sketches the designers, draftsmen, and artists construct the working plans of the sets. To prepare a set plan for final approval, the unit director, guided by the final script and assisted by the research department, determines how much of each set must be constructed to cover the action of the scenes and how much may be "faked" with the aid of the special-effects department. For many sets only the lower part of buildings are constructed, the illusion of great distance frequently being created by means of construction on a reduced scale.

From the working plans estimates are made which must closely approximate the budget allowance. When the new plans and estimates have been completed and considered in conference by the producer, director, and others involved, the actual set construction commences, under the supervision of the unit art director. Following the art department's plans and sketches, set dressers collect necessary furniture, rugs, and pictures mostly from studio warehouses. When the supervising art director has passed on the finished sets the various other departments with work to do on them are notified, and the sets are then turned over to the director and production begins. In carrying out the ideas of the art department the property department and set dressers bear in mind that a single off-color or misplaced object becomes "busy" or discordant, and takes attention away from the story and the actors.

From twenty-five to thirty sets are required for the average picture, although some require twice as many. Most of them are erected on the sound stages, although some outdoor scenes may send the company on "location," which usually means to the studio "ranch," a studio site perhaps an hour's distance from the lot. Sets are constructed on the massive sound stages whenever possible. Location trips are expensive and studio equipment is more accessible and physical conditions more readily controlled on the lot. The open areas of the studio lot are also used wherever possible, an entire village frequently springing up almost over night beside administration buildings and sound stages. To the eye of the visitor such sets are extremely life-like, although close inspection will show the stones in a massive building are papier-mache and hollow in back, and the palm trees in a native setting consist of a pole or two ingeniously cloaked in burlap and composition plaster with real fronds fastened to a small platform at the top. Leaves are lacquered to give the appearance of freshness, and the water in the river before a cluster of thatched native huts is from the Los Angeles city water mains. In a thousand such ingenious ways the artists and construction workers of the studio obviate the necessity of expensive miles of travel.

Some studios employ special "experts" to work out required optical illusions, but these are usually referred to the special-effects division of the property department, or, if the special effect desired is novel and extremely difficult, it is worked out in collaboration by several departments. Most of the tricks are standardized. The "breakaway" chairs and tables shattered on an actor's head are constructed of light and brittle balsa wood. Breakaway glass, manufactured from confectioners' sugar, is not only difficult to make but requires special iceboxes and chemicals for preservation. But special resin has recently been developed that can be melted and molded into sheets and stored without difficulty. Fog is manufactured by shooting compressed air through crystal oil, and cobwebs are made with rubber cement sprayed from a special airgun. Blood is usually composed of chocolate syrup and glycerine. Especially gruesome effects with this concoction have been produced for consumption in some foreign countries where censorship has been slight. In a recent production containing gory battle scenes the illusion of a spear passed through a man's body was achieved by means of a leather belt around his waist with pieces of spear screwed to it fore and aft. A spear striking a man was in reality hollow and projected along a wire which ran from a point beyond camera range to a wood pad concealed beneath the victim's clothing. Decapitation and disemboweling were accomplished by means of a dummy head and shoulders attached to an unusually short extra player, and a rubber knife swung against an artificial abdomen fitted with a zipper arrangement spilled the warrior's insides when an invisible string was yanked.

Large-scale illusions are more complex and more expensive. The highly dramatic wind storm in a 1937 production required the use of thirteen wind machines—large propellers attached to airplane motors; and the cascading waves that washed away an entire village were produced by simultaneously releasing the water from a series of storage tanks into a concrete basin in which a miniature village had been constructed. Close-up sequences showing crumbling church walls were produced on a sound stage with the aid of water tanks, papier-mache bricks, and soluble mortar.

A property man can quickly acquire almost anything by consulting his files. Malayan badgers, boa constrictors, parrots, and African beetles all may be rented in Hollywood; butterflies may be ordered by the dozen and ants by the quart.

Costume and make-up departments are both active long before a picture is actually shot. Aside from the fact that Hollywood designers must anticipate styles by at least six months, the astute and talented fashioners of clothing give a great deal of attention to the psychological effect of clothing on both actors and audience. They must also closely consider the photographic problems of light and composition. Costumes are invariably designed for the star and usually for the feminine supporting players. The male members of the cast supply their own wardrobes unless it is a period production. Before work is actually begun on costumes, sketches made by the wardrobe artists are okehed by the producer, the director, and the actors concerned. Besides dressing the stars and feature players, the wardrobe department frequently is called upon to supply hundreds of costumes for extras and bit players. These may be rented from several large Hollywood costume companies that function independently of the studios. Often, however, suitable costumes cannot be rented but must be made. If such costumes are needed in great quantities it is sometimes cheaper for the studio to contract for them with outside wholesale tailoring establishments. Nevertheless, the studios' own storage rooms are choked with clothing of all descriptions from all periods of history. The wardrobe shops of the large studios are in themselves a garment industry, containing rows of cutting and ironing boards, sewing machines, and all the other paraphernalia of the garment trade.

The make-up department is busiest during production, but special make-up for stars and character actors is prepared far in advance of the shooting date. Make-up is broadly divided as "corrective" and "character." The former is skillfully applied shade and color to create or enhance attractiveness and charm, and make-up artists work closely with cameramen to achieve desirable results. Many women with blue eyes, for instance, are always lit with a small spotlight fitted with a magenta-colored gelatin screen to increase their eyes' darkness and sparkle, and one star owes much of her glamor to the consistent use of a strong downward-pointed light on her face, which accentuates her high cheekbones and makes the lower part of her face appear less square.

Make-up and the ability to wear it are probably 75 per cent of a successful character portrayal. Character make-up is an artist's job, involving the transmission of a detailed visualization from paper to the screen. Sometimes many tests with different actors and different types of make-up are necessary before a successful characterization is achieved.

During the period preparatory to shooting the production office has been busy. From the picture's early days a unit man from the production office and an assistant director have been on the job co-ordinating activities and watching time schedules and budget allowances. The production office manager exercises broad supervision over the progress of the film, alloting stage space so that production will not be held up on this account. He eliminates, often over the objections of director and writer, scenes he believes are unnecessary. He is careful to see that pictures start on time to meet release dates, and he makes allowance in his schedule for the six to eight weeks required in the cutting and dubbing rooms. Once the shooting schedule has been set and production commenced, he stands by to see that no time is lost, for, as at no other period in the making of a movie, while production is under way, time is important. Millions of dollars flow through his office and all manner of errors and accidents must be eliminated, or tracked down and adjusted by him.

The production manager's representative, the unit man, however, exercises a more immediate and close supervision over the individual picture. With the assistant director, the unit man breaks down the script after it has been finally okehed. The breakdown reveals the amount of time to be used for each set and the number of players needed, and itemizes in minute detail the requirements of every department. This breakdown tells each department exactly what it will have to furnish throughout the production, with full descriptions and quantities enumerated. It is the studio Bible, and guaranteed to give the assistant director and production unit man a headache superseded only by the one they get from making up the preliminary shooting schedule. The latter must be changed repeatedly until every department is satisfied. The preliminary shooting schedule is written up from the breakdown, and specifies the set time, the time each character actually works, the number of days he is idle, and the total number of days needed for the completion of his part.

It is from the preliminary shooting schedule that the various departments work out their budgets, which they send to the production manager. The head of the electrical department, for instance, after receiving the shooting schedule, consults the production department and with the latter works out estimates of the number of electricians, lights, and the amount of electricity that will be necessary. The same general procedure is followed by art, property, and other departments.

When all departments have turned in their budgets, the production manager assembles them and adds the studio overhead expense, which may run as high as 40 per cent of the total. He then prepares a final shooting schedule, in consultation with all department heads. The production manager includes in his budget allowances for the sound and music departments, transportation and location expenses, script clerks, the photographers who will make "stills" each day of the shooting, stand-ins for the stars, and other miscellaneous items. The last days before shooting begins are hectic ones for the assistant director. Although assigned by the production office he is in reality responsible both to production office and director and he frequently has difficulty pleasing the two. With such paper work as the breakdown and the shooting schedule out of the way, he has tasks assigned by the director. He assembles the staff of technicians, selects extras and bit players for the director to approve, and just before shooting actually begins conducts a last minute inspection of schedules, scenes, props, and players. On the morning when the director arrives on the set to conduct his first rehearsals, it is largely due to the labor of his assistant that chaos has given way to a semblance of order.

Directors are for the most part typed as to temperament, a condition no doubt due to the stereotyping of film stories. One director is known for his skill in handling fast-paced comedies; another is known for his handling of subtle psychological drama. Most directors are specialists in particular fields, having been made so by their past experience.

During pre-shooting preparation the director has met a barrage of questions from the various studio departments, because his is the final judgment in determining what interpretation the story is to receive from the camera. He must pass judgment on questions of art, story construction, costumes, actors, music, lighting, and camera technique. When shooting begins, the director would like to concentrate simply on getting a hundred and fifty harmonious and meaningful photographs on a few miles of celluloid ribbon, but no such happy lot is his. Throughout production he must co-ordinate the work of the various technical departments, at the same time attempting to keep technical and mechanical factors subservient to his artistic plan.

He would like extensive rehearsals, for instance, but for most pictures these are economically impossible. As a rule he must be content with brief rehearsals, trusting his performers to have absorbed something of the mood and feeling of the story beforehand. Not infrequently this trust is misplaced. Before shooting, a careful director rehearses the scene for action. Then it is rehearsed for cameras and lighting, and again for the sound department, which checks the levels and position of the actors' voices. When lighting, focus, and sound are satisfactory the actors take their places. A signal light indicates that sight and sound are in focus. The director and cinematographer give last-minute instructions, and the director calls "action," or "speed." A bell then rings, a red light flashes a warning at the stage entrance, and the cameras begin their work. The shot seldom takes more than two minutes. Then come retakes—two or three, or perhaps a dozen if imperfections are noted. Afterwards, camera, light, and sound adjustments are made for close-ups, long shots, dissolves, fade-ins, and other variations which may later be used to add to the picture's interest and action.

Actual shooting generally requires more than a month for an "A" picture, and to an outsider an interminable amount of time seems to be wasted: in an eight-hour day only three to six minutes of film are shot which will be seen in the theatres. But the long waits are a necessary part of production, during which the many technical adjustments of lights, camera, and sound are made. The script girl is an indispensible aid to the director during production. Sitting beside him, she takes detailed notes concerning "business," use of props, and camera angles. Many scenes are shot in violation of the story's chronology, to enable the production office to get the maximum amount of service from stages as well as from actors. But the shooting schedule, with its careful synopses of scenes, makes this a less difficult task than it might seem. Shooting out of continuity is, however, a major reason why directors like to rehearse the entire script before any shooting takes place.

Most stars as well as directors know that their best efforts can be spoiled by an unsympathetic cinematographer. Formerly called the cameraman, this technician is in actual charge of shooting the scenes. He must, besides possessing the technical skill to create consistently first-rate photographs, be artistically sympathetic to both stars and director. Many director-cameraman teams function on a more or less permanent basis, and the contracts of many stars make provision for their favorite cinematographers. The cinematographer rarely touches the camera, other than to view his set-up on the ground-glass foscusing screen. His real work is to direct the photography of the scene—leaving the mechanics of camera operation to his crew, which consists of an operative cinematographer, who actually runs the camera; one or two assistant cameramen who handle details of focusing, checking and caring for the equipment; a still man who makes the hundreds of still photographs during shooting that are used in theatre lobbies and magazines; and a gaffer, or chief electrician, who is not actually a member of the camera department but is nevertheless in charge of the matter of lighting and an invaluable aid to the cinematographer.

Unless busy on other productions, the cinematographer enters active participation in the preparation of a picture during the early conferences of the art department, costumers, directors, and writers. His experience helps in selecting sites for outdoor scenes, for example, as he determines which points can be conveyed successfully by photograph. By the time shooting begins, the cinematographer has made detailed plans concerning camera angles and positions, and with the aid of stand-ins the lighting has been roughed in. During rehearsals he perfects such details as changes of lighting required by movements of the players and unwanted reflections cast by a piece of furniture or a bowl of flowers. Every factor may be photographically correct in the first take, but four or five are generally made, and the cinematographer tries to make each one better than the last. It is a tribute to Hollywood's camera experts that a scene is seldom retaken for photographic shortcomings.

The cinematographer's intricate technique of painting pictures with light beams to create illusions of depth and roundness owes its steady improvement to the development of improved tools. In the movies' early days lighting simply meant illumination by means of floodlights. Today, almost the only survivor among the cinematographer's early tools is the broadside, commonly called the broad, which is a simple lamp housing two 1000-watt globes side by side in a box-shaped reflector which spreads their light in an even flood over an angle of approximately 60 degrees. The fundamental tool today is the spotlight, of which there are two basic types: the older lens-spots, and the reflecting spots which form their beam by means of a parabolic mirror rather than a lens. A new type, combining the features of both, is called the solar spot. It uses a bull's-eye lighthouse type lens in combination with a small spherical mirror to produce a smoother and more controllable beam than either of the older types. Among a number of special-purpose lamps in use today are the Lupe, a long funnel-shaped lamp holding a tubular globe and mounted on a double-jointed standard which permits it to be used in almost any position; the sky pan, a bowl-shaped reflector used against painted sky backings or backdrops; and the relatively obsolescent banks and strips, which are simply big floodlights holding four, six, or more globes. For natural-color photography the standard lamps are replaced by rotaries, sun-arcs, and Hi-arcs, noiseless arc-lighting units that produce light almost identical with natural daylight.

Many tools are used to control the light projected from the various lamps. Because present-day camera lenses frequently pick up objects in too great detail, the diffusing screen is used to soften a picture. Among diffusers in use are nets of fine gauze, screens of frosted gelatin, and glass discs with a spiderwork tracery of fine lines or concentric circles. There are also such other devices to control the lamp rays as flat or adjustable screens, called niggers and bogos; conical hoods, often called snouts; and snouts with adjustable, flat flaps, which are called barndoors.

Out-of-doors light is controlled by means of reflectors, large squares of plywood covered with tin, aluminum, or gold paint that disperse shadows. Booster lights are also frequently used, as are canopies of netting, called scrims, which are stretched over the players' heads to soften or eliminate direct sunlight. Another important outdoor accessory are the color filters the cinematographer uses to accent particular colors.

Films, lenses, and cameras have all advanced apace, as has the technique of using them. The development of film is largely one of progression from color-blind film sensitive only to blue and ultra-violet light, to the super-panchromatic film in use today that sees colors in very much the same relative strengths as the human eye. Lenses have grown more and more accurate in their delineation of scenes, and faster. Cameras have evolved from relatively unsteady and undependable instruments into high-precision machines costing from five to fifteen thousand dollars.

No hard and fast rules concerning cinematographic technique can be laid down, but there are certain fundamental principles that good moving picture photographers always bear in mind. They attempt to keep their lighting in tune with the dramatic mood of the scene, using an ingenious assortment of variations of the accepted rule that tragedy requires lighting in a low key, while comedy calls for a high key. As with the lighting, the technique of camera angles is essentially a series of elaborations using a simple basic vocabulary. Camera angles are based on the long, or establishing, shot; the medium shot, a closer approach to the subject; the two-shot, which is the closest the camera can approach two people and keep them both in the picture; the close-up, and the extreme or big-head close-up. The effect of an oppressed character is heightened by having the camera look slightly down on him; the effect of happiness or lightheartedness portrayed by a player is intensified by having the camera look slightly up to him.

Moving-camera technique is one of the cinematographer's most difficult problems. Such variable factors as speed, timing, and lighting must be considered. Lighting a big moving-camera shot is in itself a problem. Ordinary lighting satisfactory from one viewpoint is unsatisfactory when the camera has moved to another point. The lighting must be such that during every inch of motion the camera sees things as they should be.

Special process shots, also in the cinematographer's sphere, include trick shots of some varieties, but the purpose of most special process photography is to film normal action more effectively or safely than could otherwise be possible. The most common types of special-process shots are scenes in miniature and projected-background or transparency shots, in which a desired back-ground—perhaps in the Swiss Alps or an African jungle—is projected on a translucent screen behind the actors. The making of special-process shots generally requires the services of a group of cinematographic experts of the special-effects department, but when the principal players appear in such scenes the co-operation of the production's cinematographer is imperative.

Natural color photography, the latest development in cinematography, has brought to the fore new problems in lighting and composition, but cinematographers consider them minor ones and are confident that as color photography nears perfection they will be able to carry on with the same standards they have achieved in black and white.

The motion-picture studio sound department owes its existence to inventions in the field of radio amplification. Because the recording of sound on wax discs has given way to recording on film, the essence of sound recording today is the transformation of sound vibrations into light and onto a roll of film from which they may at will be reproduced as sound. The personnel of a studio sound department usually consists of a director of sound recording, whose work is both technical and administrative; a chief engineer responsible for the technical phases of operation; a chief mixer, in charge of the various staff units working on various pictures; several operating transmission engineers in charge of the recording circuits and other equipment; and sound crews assigned to individual pictures, usually composed of a mixer, a number of stage helpers, and a recorder responsible for the operation of the recording machine and its auxiliary equipment.

Preparation for sound recording of a picture starts with study of the final script to determine the special recording problems that the picture advances. When the sound director and chief mixer have determined the nature and scope of the picture's problems, a sound crew and suitable equipment are assigned to the new picture. The microphones, amplifiers, mixer panels, recording machines, and other apparatus required for a single recording constitute a recording channel, which will be of the fixed type for sound-stage recordings, and mobile, usually mounted on a truck, for location scenes.

Sound crew members report to their posts an hour or so before shooting begins in order to connect power lines, suspend microphones, and test their equipment. While the cast is in rehearsal the mixer checks the quality of sound on his instruments and the recorder is simultaneously checking the sound volume delivered to the recording machine. When the director signals the mixer for a take, the latter signals the recorder, who starts his motor system. Camera and recording machines are of course synchronized. After the take is made the mixer again signals the recorder, who stops the motor system and marks the film for the next scene. If the take is satisfactory from all standpoints it is approved or "choiced" for laboratory processing.

Dialogue is nearly always recorded during the actual filming of a scene, but music is frequently pre-scored, and most other sounds are dubbed in later. Most music scoring is done on stages specifically constructed for that purpose. In pre-scoring a soloist with orchestral accompaniment for instance, the orchestra is first rehearsed to check the arrangement; then the soloist and orchestra rehearse together; and finally the orchestra alone is recorded. If the recording is good the orchestra is then dismissed, and the soloist records her song, synchronizing it with the orchestra background which has already been recorded by means of an earphone. Because she is not being photographed she is free to indulge in facial contortions and mannerisms that would not otherwise be allowable. Voice and orchestra are later combined in one record which is played during actual shooting of the scene in which the solo is heard. The reproducing machine is interlocked with the camera; consequently the camera and playback run at identical speeds. During the shooting the soloist makes lip movements only, concentrating her attention on a visual performance.

The regular scores that add so much to a picture's mood are usually dubbed in after it has been filmed and edited. As a rule they are written specifically for each picture by one of the many numerous composers who have been drawn to Hollywood. Other dubbed-in sounds such as the chirp of a cricket or the roar of a train are secured from the extensive files of the sound library.

Although during the making of a picture sound and photographs are recorded on separate films, later to be synchronized and transferred to a single strip of film, today few sounds are faked. Sound engineers believe the actual sounds to be more realistic than imitations, as indeed they are when recorded and reproduced by Hollywood's increasingly precise and delicate recording instruments.

Echoes are a constant torment to sound men. On sets where heavy draperies cannot be used echoes may spring unexpectedly from a water glass on a table or from the corner of a set. On location, rain and wind are likewise problems, which sound men have ingeniously circumvented. Wind gags and rain gags consisting of a wire framework covered by light silk or linen cloth do not completely eliminate such disturbances, but are sufficiently effective to enable recording to be carried on when it would otherwise be impossible.

At the close of each day's work the director, producer, actors and a few chosen others view the previous day's "rushes," or "dailies," which have been received from the laboratory. The most desirable takes are selected and turned over to the film editor. Although a few studio cutters edit films from movietone prints with both pictures and sound on the same film, the majority prefer the more flexible system of working from separate sound and picture prints.

In dealing with these "dailies," or "rushes," the film editor must exercise ingenuity and a strong sense of pictorial story-telling. His job is to condense 30,000 to 300,000 feet of disconnected pictures into a smooth-flowing story seldom exceeding 12,000 feet.

The more important equipment in a cutting room consists of metal rewinding tables, film bins, storage and filing cabinets, splicing and numbering machines, and moviolas. The moviola is similar in appearance to a projection machine, but much smaller. The picture is seen through magnifying lens on one side, and the sound is heard on the other. The editor uses it to make certain his cuts on the sound track are correct. It also enables him to be certain he has not cut into a movement which should be completed.

The film editor or his assistant put the two separate strips of film —sound and pictures—through a machine that automatically numbers them identically, foot-by-foot. This numbering system enables the cutter always to keep his scenes perfectly synchronized. The film strips are next cut into scenes, after which they are assembled according to the script. The editor endeavors to select shots that give variety and add to the emotional tone of the story. When the various shots have been assembled into a "rough cut" it is ready for projection—first by the film editor to catch slips, and later in a projection room before the director and producer. After the latters' suggestions have been incorporated in the film by means of a recutting, various devices such as fades, dissolves, and wipes are inserted at points that had been previously so designated by printed titles. Such devices, formerly produced on the set by the director and cameraman at great expense,.are now made with an optical printer, an intricate machine that holds an illuminated positive in one end and focuses it on unexposed film by means of a lens. Fades, for instance, are made by decreasing the aperture of the lens. Inserts, symbols of thoughts or ideas such as letters, newspapers, and clocks are also added, after which the film is sent to the laboratory again where the negative is cut to match the new working print and a new print made, called the "feeler print." Then, after the addition of sound effects, dubbed-in music and the like, a print is made on which sound track and picture film are combined.

The film is then ready for a sneak preview at a small theatre in some neighboring town where studio executives and some of the technical staff carefully observe its effect on the audience. Because the film is not yet in final form, the studio endeavors to keep the first preview a secret from the press. After a conference among the studio officials and technicians who witnessed the preview, the picture may be altered considerably, and new scenes may even be added. A final preview is usually then held, to which members of the trade press are usually invited. The picture is then released to the public and its success is measured by the degree of the public's interest as registered at the box office.

Before the picture's release, however, the publicity office has done its bit to make the public acquainted with its story, its players, and its excellence. Studio publicity officials estimate that more than 350,000 words are written and distributed daily by the 350 press agents employed by them. A major studio publicity office includes a director; "planters," whose job it is to get the studio's material into desirable newspapers and periodicals; unit men who write stories and interviews concerning the players, theme, and anything else they can think of about the specific productions; artist and photographers.

Hollywood also contains more than 300 correspondents, each representing journals of 40,000 or more circulation; more than 100 part-time correspondents for smaller papers; and approximately 100 out-of-town columnists, feature writers, and magazine writers who appear at the studios with special assignments at least once a year.

Publicity for a picture may begin before the purchase of the story if the latter is a popular play or novel. Short notices may be released "rumoring" that a certain producer is "angling" for the purchase. But the carefully-budgeted "B" pictures generally receive a publicity allowance approximately 15 per cent of the cost of production. The money is divided among newspapers, magazines, press sheets, billboards, pictures, electrotype plates, newspaper mats and the like, but 90 per cent of all paid advertising is placed through eastern advertising agencies. The advertising for "A" pictures is more complex and indeterminable. If the studio is reasonably certain of a hit, money may be spent lavishly and without any relation to production costs. An advertising campaign is of course launched in the larger metropolitan areas in order to stimulate interest, but in addition to this a "world premiere" costing perhaps $25,000 may be held, and percentage arrangements may be made with exhibitors whereby the latter agree to share advertising expenses as well as profits. Miracles have been requested of the publicity departments in the past, but studio officials are learning that publicity cannot make a picture successful or a star permanent. The trend is away from excessive ballyhoo, and toward emphasis on the story and title rather than the stars.

Radio

RADIO broadcasts are as popular in Los Angeles as elsewhere, perhaps more so. Fully 95 per cent of the homes have radio sets, and the proportion of automobiles equipped with radios is also high. Radio listeners in Los Angeles like what all America likes, and their radio programs are the standardized fare of Jersey City or Des Moines. In the political field, however, radio in southern California reflects the peculiarities of the region; prior to elections the airways are heavy with the propaganda of panacea movements. The EPICs, Townsendites, Utopians, and particularly such pension movements as "Ham and Eggs," have broadcast to an extent unknown in the rest of the country.

Radio's early history in Los Angeles was one of hit-and-miss, of trial and error—the identical experience of radio throughout the United States in the days of crystal sets and earphones. Radio broadcasting began in Los Angeles in 1922, when four stations were established. Three of them—KNX, KFI, and KHJ—dominated local broadcasting from the beginning and continue to do so today, each representing a major national chain. As elsewhere in the country, radio was considered merely a novelty in 1922. The development of KNX, the stormy petrel of early radio in Los Angeles prior to its acquisition by the Columbia Broadcasting System, was due to the originality and persistence of Guy C. Earl, promotion manager of the Los Angeles *Express,* who entered the radio field in 1923 by arranging for his newspaper to give away a thousand crystal sets as part of a circulation drive. So successful was this first effort that he decided to use KNX permanently for promotional purposes. By 1924 the station was selling advertising regularly and operating on 500 watts, though there were no definitely scheduled broadcasts. In 1925, however, the station turned in a profit of $25,000, and Earl began to devote more of his energy to radio, courting feuds with other stations and local newspapers, and accepting advertising from patent medicine firms. Always seeking the sensational, he broadcast a local murder trial despite repeated ejections of his operatives from the courtroom, and in 1928 broadcast the Rose Bowl game by telephone though the telephone company had sold the broadcasting rights to KFI.

KFI, founded by Earle C. Anthony to further sales of his automobile agency, avoided KNX's indiscriminate commercial policy. Underwriting losses, Anthony enabled KFI to pioneer in the use of musical and educational features that he thought would appeal to potential buyers of the automobiles he wanted to sell. The station elaborated continuity and program techniques and initiated a policy of co-operation with schools, government agencies, and civic organizations. In 1924 it presented the first broadcast of a symphony orchestra in the West and sponsored the country's first pick-up of a complete opera presentation from the stage. During these formative years, KFI presented many educational talks for government and city departments, and it was the station's boast that every important personage who visited the West coast addressed KFI's listeners. In 1929 Jose Rodriguez, a musician and newspaperman, joined the station and later developed new types of broadcasts. A few years later when KECA had been started to supplement KFI and found itself burdened with unsalable time, Rodriguez purchased several hundred fine phonograph recordings, broadcast from them, and asked for audience reaction. Seeking 10,000 approving votes, he received 70,000 within a week; since then such musical broadcasts have been an important part of KECA's program. In 1924 KFI had joined KPO of San Francisco in the first West coast network, and was the point of origin for the first West-to-East broadcast. KFI also made the first Hollywood Bowl broadcast. Power was increased from the original 100 watts to 500 in 1924 and then in 1931 to the present 50,000 watts.

KHJ was founded in 1922 by Harry Chandler, publisher of the Los Angeles *Times,* and station identification was by singing canaries. Conservative in policy, it specialized in public events and children's programs. Chandler sold the station in 1927 to Don Lee, automobile agency owner. KHJ became the Columbia outlet in Los Angeles until 1936 when Lee joined the Mutual network. As one of the leaders in experimentation, KHJ has done a great deal of work in the field of television.

In 1927 KFI joined the Red network of the National Broadcasting Company and a year later Columbia Broadcasting System took KHJ into its chain. KECA became the local outlet of NBC's new Gold network in 1934, and after this chain died, of NBC's Blue network in 1936. In 1939 KECA absorbed KEHE and assumed its wave length. A small station connected with the Hearst chain, KEHE had specialized in sports and spot news broadcasts. Within the past two years two smaller chains have made their appearance—the Don Lee chain, covering the stations of the Mutual's Western link and the California Radio System, including KFOX and KFWB in Los Angeles.

In 1938 the Columbia Broadcasting System opened its new studios, Columbia Square, on the site of the old Christie brothers' studios. Its local outlet, KNX, is the key station of its Pacific Coast network, and in 1937 broadcast 18,383 programs, approximately half of them sustaining programs. There were 6,214 educational and cultural programs as against 10,352 "popular entertainment" broadcasts. It broadcasts more programs than any other CBS station. In the spring of 1939 a total of sixteen transcontinental programs were originating in Hollywood. NBC also completed a new studio in 1938, at Sunset Boulevard and Vine Street. The Mutual network is third insofar as national commercial broadcasts are concerned (1939), but ranks with the other leaders in children's programs and in talks on public events.

Los Angeles began its climb to national radio importance when the first film talent program was released from Hollywood in 1928. A program called *California Melodies,* featuring Hollywood stars and film news, went on the air in 1930 and by 1936 many national advertising agencies had opened offices here and programs had become star-studded. *Variety* reports that $5,000,000 was paid to 600 film players for radio broadcasts in 1938. More than $18,000,000 is spent yearly by six Hollywood stations. Five hundred producers, script and lyric writers turn out Hollywood radio fare. The city still lags behind New York, however, in the number of national broadcasts, although each year since 1936 has seen a sizeable increase in Hollywood originations. The facilities of both NBC and CBS are already taxed, with CBS planning additions to its present quarters, and Mutual contemplating the building of a radio center of its own. Recently a few film producers, under pressure from exhibitors, have taken several stars off the air, but it is too early to determine what effect their action will have.

In 1938 network programs became almost completely unionized as a result of a strike vote taken by the newly-organized American Federation of Radio Artists (AFL), embracing actors, singers and announcers. The strike vote, supported by film-radio stars and led by Eddie Cantor and others, threatened a breakdown of transcontinental programs. The country's advertising agencies yielded to AFRA demands, which were designed to improve conditions for rank and file performers by controlling or eliminating hours of and pay for rehearsals, "rubber" salary schedules, blacklists, and the practice of using one performer in more than one part in dramatic and commercial scripts. The union in 1939 was negotiating with the networks and smaller stations. Technicians and musicians had been organized for many years.

Of the many smaller stations in Los Angeles, KFWB is in the medium power bracket, while others have a restricted range. KFWB, a 5,000-watt station founded by Warner Brothers in 1925, introduced in 1939 a policy of broadcasting dramatized versions of current as well as historical events in order to stimulate appreciation of America's democratic ideals. Typical of such programs was "America Marches On" which featured motion-picture stars.

Several of the smaller stations owe their audience-appeal to special features. KGFJ broadcasts sixteen full hours of news each week and owns two ultra-high frequency experimental stations for short-wave broadcasts. KMTR once had the experience of being "heterodyned"; during a talk given by its former owner, an oil promoter, another station took the same wave-length and garbled his broadcast. KMPC broadcasts rehearsals of Hollywood Bowl concerts and KRKD specializes in news and in early broadcasts of election results. KFVD centers its programs around political events, and frequently gives free time to liberal causes. KFSG is a noncommercial station owned by the Echo Park Evangelistic Association and broadcasts Aimee Semple McPherson's sermons. Long Beach has two stations: KFOX, which achieved fame for its emergency broadcasts after the 1933 earthquake, and KGER, which broadcasts daily concerts by the Long Beach Municipal Band.

Educational programs sponsored by the local universities have increased rapidly in number since they were begun in 1930. The University of Southern California released 600 programs in 1938. Three 15-minute broadcasts weekly and a daily broadcast on farm problems are given by the University of California, which also presents the *University Explorer* over NBC. Los Angeles City College owns its own studios and broadcasts over KFAC. In all, around seventy-two educational programs are released locally each week over twelve stations.

The United Press, International and Trans-Radio press services provide news to various stations for broadcasting. As elsewhere, the radio-newspaper war has led most newspapers in Los Angeles to abolish radio news columns, although they all list radio programs.

Many civic bodies in Los Angeles use radio in their work. The Major Disaster Emergency Council, a legal body with power to act in time of emergency, operates a short-wave set in preparation for the "unforeseen and the unpredictable catastrophes such as fire, flood, earthquake, tornado, pestilence." The police department uses radio communication in its squad cars and in 1939 asked for money to install two-way communication. The U.S. Weather Bureau broadcasts weather forecasts over KRKD daily and the bureau's Fruit Frost Division broadcasts night weather-warnings to citrus farmers from November 15 to February 15 each year. A simultaneous range station located near Mines field and controlled at the Union Air Terminal is maintained by the U.S. Department of Commerce for the guidance of commercial planes.

The RCA Marine Corporation maintains a station at Torrance for ship-to-shore communication, and RCA Communications, Inc., provide domestic and international radiogram services, as does the Mackay Radio and Telegraph Company. There are about 3,500 licensed short-wave operators in Los Angeles County, and *Radio,* a magazine with national circulation devoted to amateur radio interests, is published in Los Angeles.

In the field of television, Los Angeles ranks next to New York in the amount of research and the number and popularity of its television broadcasts. Television experimentation began at KHJ, chief station of the Don Lee Broadcasting System, and since 1931 television broadcasts have gone to several hundred receiving sets in the vicinity six times a week. One dramatic serial has been running since March 1938. Many developments and patents, particularly the perfection of the cathode ray receiver, have been contributed to the new industry by the Don Lee staff. In 1939 Earle C. Anthony, operator of KECA and KFI, applied for a permit to erect a television broadcasting station.

More than ten million feet of motion-picture film have been televised from KHJ, and motion-picture interests have kept close watch on such experiments. Television is still undergoing a struggle for control by various interests and is beset by the problems of the high cost of receiving sets, inability to transmit farther than a few miles, the expense of broadcasts, and the difficulties of acquiring advertising sponsorship. Eventually, however, there will be probably a close interlocking between television, with its far-reaching social implications, and the films and radio, and on a very large scale. Already in Los Angeles are the talent, musicians, writers, and the advertising agencies; and more talent is still arriving in droves. It is by no means improbable that Hollywood will become a television center of the world.

The Arts

THOUGH from the beginning music, painting, drama, and architectural design had a part in the life and history of the pueblo of Los Angeles, there has been no continuing line of development in any of the arts. The traditional Spanish culture was gradually diluted in the decades after 1840, and about 1875 was abruptly displaced. It was not until the great numbers of new residents had begun to take root that creative artists appeared and began to turn to the history and esthetic traditions of the region.

ARCHITECTURE

The city of Los Angeles has great expanse but little height. It sprawls over the plain in a seemingly interminable series of suburbs from the City Hall, the only building that can be called a skyscraper. Aggressive real-estate promoters, the desire of many new residents from small towns and farms to avoid metropolitan noise and bustle, and the automobile, are responsible for its size. An ordinance, the result of the earthquake possibilities, limits private buildings to the height of 150 feet. This, and the cost of earthquake-proof construction for tall buildings, are responsible for the low sky line.

The downtown commercial buildings are on the whole sedate and commonplace, but elsewhere Los Angeles is architecturally flamboyant, and even discordant. The city contains structures of every style imaginable, a single block often exhibiting half a dozen different treatments.

Los Angeles architecture is characterized by a flare for the eclectic and the unusual. Lacking discipline in the past, this taste has resulted in experiments that frequently were, to say the least, unproductive. But with the growth of local culture and the development of sounder modern designs all over the world, grotesqueries have been giving way to interesting and important innovations. Particularly is this true of domestic architecture. Besides making contributions to the design of the moderately-priced houses that have been adopted in other sections of the country, Los Angeles architects have evolved, through modifications of earlier local styles, certain features that are particularly fitted to the climate and topography of the region. Los Angeles is becoming a center of the modern movement in architectural construction and design.

Early Los Angeles had a simple, almost uniform type of building constructed of the adobe brick the Indians of Mexico had long used for their dwellings. It is doubtful if any formula existed for the making of these bricks, though Donald R. Hannaford and Revel Edwards, in *Spanish Colonial or Adobe Architecture of California,* have published material on the subject gathered from interviews with descendants of old Spanish families. In the process these people had observed that a basin about twenty feet in diameter and two feet deep was dug in the ground near the building site. Into this was put loam, sand, and clay, together with straw, tile chips, or other binder. After the materials had been stirred to a soupy consistency, the mixture was taken out, put into molds, and dried in the sun.

The design evolved for the California missions was the result of ideas brought from Spain and modified by the experience of the Franciscan padres in Mexico, by the Indian workmen who executed the designs, and by the limitations of the region's building materials. The patio, the covered passage, and the dome recall plans used in Spain; the pierced belfry, the buttress, and the absence of ornament were results of adobe construction.

Two missions, San Fernando and San Gabriel, were established in what is now the metropolitan area of Los Angeles. Both suffered from disuse after the secularization in the 1830's. Only the cloister, or living quarters, and church have been preserved at Mission San Fernando; it is evident that the elongated adobe cloister was conceived as a building of majestic proportions, with sweeping horizontal lines accentuated by the archways of a long arcade. The original floor tiles, worn hollow in places, are still in the arcade floor, and hand-wrought ironwork around doors and windows shows the quality of the work of Indian blacksmiths. The original lines of the rear wall of the cloister have been partly obscured by restoration with modern brick, steel, and concrete, and new openings have been cut without apparent plan. The church behind the cloister still contains some of the original hand-hewn rafters. Lying between the church and the living quarters of the fathers are the roofless ruins of other buildings, formerly shops and the like. No attempt has been made to restore them.

The church of Mission San Gabriel appears much as it did when built, although here also old windows have been bricked up and new ones cut. The proportions of the present belfry, which are unsatisfactory in relation to the rest of the church, suggest that the original belfry, which was situated towards the front of the building, was higher. The living quarters of Mission San Gabriel are smaller and less conspicuous than those of San Fernando.

Civil architectural design, springing from the same traditions and using the same materials, repeated the severe, simple lines of the missions. Adobe brick buildings housed the soldiers, officials, and settlers of the pueblos. There seems to have been no effort to complicate their construction or to ornament them. Not all of those that have survived are beautiful, but most of them are characterized by a simplicity of design that comes from straightforward methods of solving problems of construction and planning.

The walls were laid on light foundations of stone, if any, and averaged about three feet in thickness on the ground floor with an offset on the inner face of the wall at the upper story decreasing its thickness a foot. The walls of the better houses were covered with mud plaster; these were heavily whitewashed at least once a year to protect the surface from the effects of rain. The exterior lines were usually broken only by unobtrusive windows, and, in the two-story houses, by a simple balcony. Economy dictated an even greater simplicity for the less elaborate dwellings, producing small houses with flat, pitch-covered roofs and pleasing lines. Usually they were of one, two, or three rooms, built in a row or in the shape of an L, or, less frequently, forming a rectangle with one open side.

The typical plan of the larger houses was well adapted to the simple and hospitable life of the times. On the ground floor were the living room, dining room, kitchen, storage rooms, and the veranda from which stairs led to the balcony. All bedrooms were usually on the second floor and were entered from the balcony, besides being intercommunicating. Doors opened onto the patio, a wholly or semienclosed interior court inherited from southern Spain. Planted with flowers and sometimes having a fountain, the patio was a social center used almost as much for living as was the house. The Pio Pico mansion in Montebello, a rambling structure with a patio, built about 1824, is probably the best example of a large adobe still standing in the Los Angeles area.

During the Mexican period many of the larger houses served a double purpose: they were both residences and government offices. Thus the Abel Stearns' *palacio* was also the prefect's office, and the curate's house of the Church of Our Lady of the Angels was a jail. The only building used entirely for official purposes was the Government House, an adobe built in the early 1830's.

Before 1850 the Yankee traders, drawn to California largely by the trade in hides and tallow, had begun the blending of New England traditions with those native to California, which resulted in an outstanding subdivision of early California design—the Monterey. Essentially a Spanish adobe structure with woodwork from New England, the most distinguishing feature of the Monterey house was the covered frame balcony projecting from the main facade. One- and two-story porches on several sides of the house were also common.

By 1850 clay bricks were being manufactured locally and were soon being used in nonecclesiastical buildings. Usually brick structures followed the lines of the adobes. The two-story buildings, however, differed from those of native design, and followed the design of buildings in the East. Frame construction gained popularity a few years later when Los Angeles began to import quantities of lumber from the Pacific Northwest. The traditional frame house of the East and the equally traditional wooden store of the frontier with its false second-story facade, became common—even fashionable. Board-and-batten construction, in which planks were nailed upright with the intervening cracks covered by thin wood strips, was likewise used extensively at this time.

The wave of building after the Civil War gave Los Angeles many office buildings and hotels two and three stories high. The builders, for the most part being easterners, naturally followed the prevailing eastern vogue for curlicues, gables, and mansard roofs. Some of the buildings of this period still standing in the northern end of the business district indicate the lack of trained architects in Los Angeles in the sixties, seventies, and eighties, and they show that the plague of overornamentation current at the time was not confined to the East. In residential areas, bay windows bulged from almost every fashionable house; pillars supported little or nothing; colored glass ornamented the doors and windows.

In the nineties architects and engineers came to Los Angeles from the East in increasing numbers, bringing new architectural ideas. Buildings grew taller, their height tending to minimize their overornamentation. In 1898 the city's first structural steel building was erected, the Homer Laughlin building, still standing in 1940. The introduction of structural steel helped to terminate a period of garishness that had lasted for nearly thirty years. Around 1900, builders began to modify the harshness of the new type of structure by grouping windows and introducing light wells.

At the turn of the century an innovation, the bungalow, was introduced from the Far East, and adapted to local needs; the California bungalow gained nation-wide popularity. The stuccoed house was also developed and the design was called Mission style. The Mission style house can be studied for the most part only in photographs, but the bungalow still stands in the older sections of the city—a one-story structure of shingles or redwood siding, frequently with pergolas, occasionally with curved roof lines inspired by the Oriental, and often a front porch supported by cobblestone piers. In its heyday, the California bungalow was almost a symbol of southern California.

Adaptations of American Colonial, French, and English styles appeared shortly after 1900, as highly trained Beaux Arts architects came to Los Angeles from the East. A wave of building in the Swiss chalet style began about 1908, followed soon after by "Dutch" Colonial.

Los Angeles was diverted from the eclectic paths being followed in the East largely through the introduction and wide acceptance of traditional Mexican, Spanish, and Italian Mediterranean designs and motifs. For this diversion Bertram G. Goodhue was largely responsible. A New York architect who had revived traditional designs in the East, Goodhue recognized the fitness of traditional Mexican design for the Southwest. He became chief architect of the San Diego Exposition in 1915, which popularized the revival, just as the Chicago World's Fair of 1893 had popularized a revival of Greek and Roman motifs. His adaptations of Mexican ecclesiastical architecture, a combination of plain surfaces and elaborately carved ornament, directed scores of southern California architects to the Spanish-Colonial revival.

Early southern California efforts in the Mexican tradition were for the most part clumsy, and contrasted sharply with the restrained and tasteful work in the Spanish tradition developed a few years later by George Washington Smith. Smith's own house, constructed in Santa Barbara about 1920, influenced other architects and helped establish a new version of design in the Spanish tradition in southern California. Plans for his house were inspired by the rural buildings of Spanish Andalusia; besides establishing the intimate relationship between house and garden by means of the patio, it was notable for its simplicity and proportions. The work of Elmer Grey and Myron Hunt also had an important bearing on the southern California trend toward designs based on old Mediterranean examples.

Italian adaptations were also evolved during this period, more formal and monumental than the Spanish; but interest was growing in early California structures, caused to some degree by the gradual vulgarization of the Mediterranean styles in untrained hands. Among the first architects to turn toward California's earlier buildings were Reginald Johnson and Roland Coate, who about 1925 began to draw inspiration from the old buildings, particularly those in Monterey because the best examples remaining are in that town. The new southern California designers in what became known as the Monterey style added such details as ornamental cast iron on balconies, inspired by the elaborate iron grills of New Orleans.

Eclecticism is still the keynote. Although the Mediterranean tradition has declined, the Monterey-Early California style shows no signs of decreasing. It is particularly evident in the one-story house constructed entirely of wood. Stucco is the most common exterior surfacing, although brick, stone and wood boarding, vertical boarding, and shingles are common. Adapted American Colonial and English Georgian designs are also prevalent. But in nearly all designs and combinations of designs, such local influences as the patio, low pitch of roofs, large window space, and bright colors, have caused modifications.

Adherents of the modern school that emphasizes a restatement of values and a more logical use of materials and accessories have been growing in influence. They have been particularly strong in the field of domestic architecture since the early thirties, and today Los Angeles is becoming internationally known for its many houses exhibiting the modern trend. This is largely the result of the work of two European-trained architects, Richard J. Neutra and R. M. Schindler, and a group of men under their leadership. During the past few years this group has won many prizes in national competitions. The exteriors of their structures display decks stressing the horizontal line and contrasting vertical surfaces of concrete and glass, which are especially striking when the house projects from the side or top of a hill. The interiors are usually based on a floor plan of flowing room spaces, with wide expanses of glass increasing the effect of cool airiness.

Possibly the best example of Neutra's work is the Beard House on Meadowbrook Road in Altadena. It is of steel, glass, and concrete, no wood having been used in its construction. Frank Lloyd Wright, a pioneer in the field of functional design, planned five residences in the Los Angeles area, but his effect upon public taste as evidenced in local houses has not been great. With the exception of the Millard House (La Miniatura) in Pasadena, and possibly the Barnsdall residence on Olive Hill, now occupied by the California Art Club, Wright's local houses are not considered the best examples of his work.

The worst of southern California's stucco bungalows—and there are many acres of them that are ugly—have been the result of speculative builders' efforts to keep abreast of recurrent waves of newcomers. There is a growing tendency, however, for the speculative builder to follow a few standard floor plans and designs that for the most part are imitative of the work of prominent architects. As a consequence, though lagging behind the professionally designed house, the cheaper residences have improved in appearance and utility in recent years. A number of Los Angeles architects, including H. Roy Kelley, are widely recognized for improving small-home architecture.

Commercial building activities were released during the early twenties in a building boom of tremendous impetus that did not subside until after the economic collapse of 1929. Office buildings, factories, and stores sprang up in surrounding areas as well as downtown. This was the period that produced most of Los Angeles' domed and turreted filling stations, wayside hot dog stands designed to resemble unhappy pups, mammoth ice cream cones, Egyptian temples, baskets of fruit, and piebald pigs. But the tendency of that day was for a minimum of ornament; narrower windows, often recessed; vertical lines; concrete surfaces. And in factories and industrial plants prettification and excrescence were kept down to a minimum. One of the most interesting of the modern industrial structures is the Douglas Aircraft Company hangar at Santa Monica, designed by Taylor and Taylor, where the vast swing of the cantilever construction suggests the soaring lines of flight.

Several of Los Angeles' civic buildings constructed in the late twenties and early thirties seek, within the limits imposed by reinforced concrete construction, to maintain the traditional appearance of massivity of structure, the most conspicuous example being the City Hall. The Central Public Library, characteristic of Goodhue's work in the field of civic architecture, is also massive but restrained, and the new Acute Unit of the County Hospital, and the Los Angeles Times building, the latter designed to harmonize with the adjacent Civic Center, are characteristic of recent commercial and public construction.

An unhappy recent trend is the "moderne" facade, which utilizes polished steel, chromium, curved glass, mirrors, glass blocks, and concrete in what the designers believe to be a startling up-to-dateness. Usually, as seen in many renovated stores along Hollywood Boulevard, these superimposed decorations are both garish and unconvincing. Several attractive buildings, however, have been erected in Hollywood recently: notably the Columbia Broadcasting System Center, designed by William Lescaze, and the National Broadcasting Company's new building of sweeping horizontal lines combined with glass and metal trim.

In the Wilshire Boulevard shopping district are several well-designed modern structures, including Bullock's Wilshire department store, which displays an exterior of buff terra cotta and green metal, and I. Magnin's, a lavish structure with a modernized exterior of classic simplicity and restraint.

In the construction of large commercial buildings Los Angeles is notable for its broad and in some ways original use of structural reinforced concrete and exposed concrete as a finished surface. Because of the high cost of importing structural steel, and the low cost of the plentiful cement, many downtown buildings, including the Paramount Theatre building, the Million Dollar Theatre building, and the Philharmonic Auditorium, are of reinforced concrete construction. When the Second Church of Christ, Scientist, was constructed in 1905-6, its massive dome, a single shell of reinforced concrete, was the only reinforced concrete structure with this feature in the United States. The earthquake hazard has decreased the use of brick and increased the use of this type of concrete construction in recent years.

Most of the churches in Los Angeles are of traditional design, for the most part in the Italian Renaissance and Gothic styles. An example is the St. James Episcopal Church in South Pasadena, designed by Goodhue and combining Tuscan Renaissance design with English Gothic detail. Spanish-Colonial influence is, however, discernible in several of the newer churches, among them the Church of St. Vincent de Paul on West Adams Boulevard. One of the city's largest synagogues, the Wilshire Boulevard Temple, is of Romanesque inspiration with a dome bearing bright terra-cotta tile mosaics.

In the field of school architecture, attempts to relate the plans to both climate and material have been highly successful. After southern California was belatedly awakened to the need for more soundly constructed schools by the 1933 earthquake, which damaged scores of brick school buildings, a large building program was at once drawn up. The architects were influenced by progressive ideas in education and by an appreciation of the possibilities for outdoor school activity in the region, as well as by the necessity for safe construction. Today, attractively landscaped playgrounds, flat roofs, and a spreading arrangement of one- and two-story buildings have become standard in local schools.

In recent years civic groups and architects have joined forces in a movement to extend the present Civic Center, the only actual stone-and-steel realization of many nebulous proposals for city planning. A plan for the Center, prepared by John C. Austin in 1938 for the Los Angeles County Development Committee, envisions development of the new Center within the area bounded by First, Alameda, Ord and Olive Streets, and the replacement of many shabby and dilapidated structures by public buildings, broad streets and parkways. The County Board of Supervisors in 1939 petitioned the Public Works Administration for a Federal grant to carry the project to completion.

Some architects, however, have condemned the plan, saying that the irregular topography of the site is incompatible with the massive formality of arrangement and structure, that the governmental buildings forming the present Center are unrelated in bulk, scale, and character, and that the completed Center will present an incongruous collection of architecturally heterogeneous types.

Through the administration of zoning measures, the City Planning Commission has urged adoption of a more comprehensive city plan designed to bring order out of the chaos engendered by industrial expansion, renewed subdivision activity, and the lack of adequate transportation facilities. Four new zone maps compiled by the Commission from 1936 to 1938 raised the total zoned area to 269 square miles, or 59 per cent of the total area of the city. The present-day trend in rezoning is toward a more restrictive classification, a movement which has been given added impetus through the Federal Housing Administration's insistence on zoning protection as a requirement for mortgage insurance.

One of the most pressing problems confronting the city today arises from the need for inexpensive but soundly constructed dwellings. Los

Angeles housing conditions for low-income groups are somewhat better than those in the crowded population centers of the East; the vast area over which the city is spread permits most families to obtain at least air and sunlight. The city has its share of slums, nevertheless, and its problem of ground rents in blighted areas. Such low-cost housing efforts as have so far been undertaken by Los Angeles County are Federal Housing projects in outlying areas. One is planned for the San Pedro area, one on Atlantic Boulevard near Long Beach, and one in Belvedere Gardens in east Los Angeles. Several privately financed housing projects have been planned or are under construction, including one near Boyle Heights and one in San Gabriel.

Well-planned towns are not a novelty in southern California. Beverly Hills was laid out in 1906, and there are half a dozen other beautifully situated communities with building restrictions including San Clemente, and San Marino. A development in connection with these communities of the wealthy is the use of architectural juries—a group of architects, generally engaged by the developers of the area, to pass on the suitability of proposed residences. This custom has since been adopted by promoters of less expensive subdivisions.

The new low-cost housing projects, designed to bring well-planned and esthetically pleasing houses within the reach of low-income families, are of both architectural and social significance. But there are other factors contributing to a promising outlook for Los Angeles architecture. The restless search for the new and different, which during the twenties resulted in such things as lavender stucco houses with Moorish minarets, has also brought about a ready acceptance of new efforts to make architecture a true expression of the life of the community. Los Angeles lacks the strong tendency to cling to traditional paths that in many other parts of the country has partially barred the way to new architectural ideas. It is clear that a large part of Los Angeles' buildings are ill-adapted to their function and their surroundings. It is less obvious but certainly significant that there are new ideas in the air, a steady and intelligent adaptation of old ones, and much architectural enthusiasm. Consequently Los Angeles seems likely to develop a sane, well-related architecture that will benefit the whole population.

MUSICMAKERS

Music played a vital and intimate part in the everyday lives of southern California Indians. Their music was characterized by the use of many unfamiliar scales, resembling in their pattern no recognized tonal system, and their primitive instruments fluctuated in pitch; vocal intonation was uncertain with the result that subtly differing scale successions were achieved that cannot be duplicated by the twelve fixed keys of the piano. Their patterns were more complex than those of many other American tribes, and were at times curiously suggestive of syncopation. Each song was a series of phrases or measure repetitions, often with melodic ornaments and variations of rhythm that suggest the plaintive Oriental music. Their instruments included flutes blown with the mouth or nose, rattles made of shells or dried skins filled with pebbles, crude drums, wooden clappers, and musical bows that the Indians played so expertly that they are said to have been able to "talk" and make love with them.

When the Indians began to come under the influence of the Franciscan missionaries in the late 18th century, they were taught to intone in Latin for church ceremonies and to play bow instruments, and the guitar and mandolin. The Franciscans tried to induce them to give up their tribal ceremonies and heathen music, but these persisted and have been seen in isolated places until such recent times that the Southwest Museum in Los Angeles has been able to preserve many songs by phonograph recording. These records made in 1900 on cylinders are too worn to be used today, but some of the best have been converted into musical scores available in albums collected by Arthur Farwell.

Spanish and Mexican folk songs were the music of Los Angeles for some seventy years after the founding of the city in 1781. Of the lazy, carefree pueblo, Charles F. Lummis, devoted collector of southwestern folklore, wrote: "There was no paying $5 to be seen chattering in satin while some Diva sang her highest. There was no Grand Opera—and no fool songs. There were Songs of the Soil, and songs of poets and of troubadours, in this far, lone, beautiful, happy land; and songs that came over from Mother Spain and up from Stepmother Mexico. But everybody sang; and a great many made their own songs, or verses to other songs. . . . They felt music, and arrived at it."

When the Yankee invaders arrived in 1847, the music-loving Californios as usual celebrated the occasion with a song. The lyric, whose words were Spanish with the exception of the English "Kiss me!" and "Yes!" is translated as follows:

> "Ay! here come the Yankees!
> Ay! they're here, you see.
> Come and let's dispense with
> All formality.
>
> "Already the senoritas
> Speak English with finesse.
> 'Kiss me!' say the Yankees.
> The girls all answer: 'Yes!' "

When at first the Mexicans showed resentment toward their American conquerors, a person familiar with native psychology offered Commodore Jones, the Yankee commander, this bit of advice: "You have a fine band of music; such a thing was never before in this country. Let

it play one hour in the Plaza each day at sunset, and I assure you it will
do more toward reconciling the people than all your written proclama-
tions, which, indeed, but few of them could read." The suggestion was
taken, with satisfactory results.

The Spanish and Mexican songs lived on for a time under American rule. But after the American influx of the seventies the younger
generations of Angelenos adopted Yankee ways and Yankee music and
the traditional melodies were gradually forgotten. Most of them exist
today only on phonograph records made by Lummis, who for the Southwest Museum recorded more than 450 songs that were sung for him by
survivors of the old era.

During the fifties and sixties much of the town's musical entertainment was provided by military and civilian brass bands, with occasional
visits by light opera companies from Mexico and traveling minstrel
shows. Los Angeles also heard its share of gambling house "orchestras"
with Mexican-Indian players, who according to Horace Bell, chronicler
of that boisterous epoch, "sent forth most discordant sound, by no
means in harmony with the eternal jingle of gold." At the same time,
Los Angeles began singing such ballads brought in by the pioneers as
The New Eldorado.

During the seventies Los Angeles gradually shed the crudeness of
its first Yankee days and began to settle down, but it was not until the
boom times of the middle eighties, when thousands of settlers flocked in,
that Los Angeles became an American community and began to develop
the cultural institutions long established in the East. Music made by
the people was supplanted by music given by professionals in concert
halls, theatres, and opera houses. Road shows came in increasing numbers, and virtually all of the world's then famous artists included
southern California in their tours.

The first serious effort toward the appreciation of classical music
began with a series of chamber music concerts given in private homes
by such family groups as the Heines and by the Haydn Quartet, formed
by Harley Hamilton, the city's musical leader during the eighties and
nineties. Shortly after the turn of the century Alice Coleman (active
today as Mrs. Ernest Coleman Balchelden) and Blanche Rogers (now
Mrs. Clifford Lott), two talented young pianists, took the lead in promoting chamber music; Miss Coleman founded Pasadena's Coleman
Concerts and Miss Rogers the Los Angeles Chamber Music Society. In
1910 Albert C. Bilicke, a local music patron, brought Adolph Tandler,
Rudolph Kopp, and Axel Simonson from Vienna; they with Ralph
Wylie, became the Brahms Quartet. The Saint-Saens Quintet was
organized in 1910; the quintet's cellist, William A. Clark, Jr., became
so interested in promoting public appreciation of music that he later
founded and financed the Los Angeles Philharmonic Orchestra.

The early chamber music groups helped to build up support for symphony orchestras though most of the orchestras had brief histories. One—the Woman's Symphony Orchestra, organized in 1895 by Harley Hamilton—has continued to function and is today the oldest orchestral group on the Pacific coast. Two years later Hamilton formed the Los Angeles Symphony Orchestra. This organization, despite early financial troubles, survived twenty-three consecutive seasons, after which its place in the city's musical life was filled by the Los Angeles Philharmonic Orchestra, founded in 1919 by William A. Clark, Jr., with L. E. Behymer as manager. Walter Henry Rothwell was conductor until his death in 1927. The Philharmonic Orchestra has high rank among the orchestras of the country. Under the permanent direction of Otto Klemperer it now (1939) plays at the Philharmonic Auditorium during the winter and at Hollywood Bowl in summer.

The Hollywood Bowl idea had its inception with the presentation of *Julius Caesar* in a natural amphitheater in Beachwood Canyon, Hollywood, May 19, 1916. The production was a charity affair, directed by Raymon Wells and the cast included such notables as Tyrone Power, Sr., W. De Wolf Hopper, William Farnum, Frank Keenan, Theodore Roberts, Douglas Fairbanks, and Mae Murray. Other dramatic ventures followed, and in 1918 the Theater Alliance was organized under the guidance of L. E. Behymer following which the first concert was presented in what is now Hollywood Bowl in 1922. A world-wide campaign was instituted and by 1923 sufficient funds had been received to pay off all obligations against the new institution. Many notable artists have appeared in the Bowl including Lawrence Tibbett, who was reared in Los Angeles. The operatic and concert baritone made his debut there in September, 1923, as Amonasro in *Aida*.

Since the days when music-lovers had to sit on lap robes on the dusty hillsides, down to 1938, attendance at musical events in the Bowl has steadily increased. By 1939 there were seats for an audience of twenty thousand and every modern facility for the presentation and the enjoyment of music. In the Bowl during the summer season are given the Symphonies under the Stars of the Los Angeles Philharmonic Orchestra. The list of operas, concerts, and other musical events given in the Bowl during its seventeen years is impressive. Among the conductors at the Bowl's summer concerts have been Eugene Goossens, Alfred Hertz, Ossip Gabrilowitsch, Bruno Walter, Ernest Bloch, Pierre Monteux, Albert Coates, Leopold Stokowski, Willem van Hoogstraten, Sir Henry Wood, Hans Kindler, Jose Iturbi, Bernardino Molinari, and Otto Klemperer.

Choral groups, both secular and religious, have for years contributed much to the city's cultural life. Among the several choral societies founded before 1900 was the Euterpe Male Quartet, progenitor of the present Orpheus Club. The Women's Lyric Club, organized in 1903, is still in existence. Preeminent today is the Los Angeles Oratorio Society, formed in 1912 as the People's Chorus. John Smallman, who became the conductor in 1918, exerted wide influence on choral organizations throughout the country until his death in 1937. Active in Los Angeles today are many excellent church choirs, including the First Congregational Church chorus of one hundred voices, which in addition to its church work annually presents a two-day Bach festival, including a performance of the *Messiah*.

Musical education in Los Angeles schools and colleges during the last two decades is partly responsible for the growing music-consciousness of the city. Nearly sixty thousand pupils are enrolled in various music courses in Los Angeles junior and senior high schools. Most universities and colleges in the Los Angeles area maintain choirs and glee clubs, and the larger institutions, such as the University of Southern California and the University of California at Los Angeles, have excellent bands and symphony orchestras. U.C.L.A. presents frequent concerts by vocalists and instrumentalists and daily organ recitals that are free to students.

Attracted by opportunities to work in sound motion pictures, singers, instrumentalists, and composers have come to Los Angeles from many parts of the world, many of them to make their homes here. Among the resident musicians who have done screen and radio work in local studios are Lawrence Tibbett, Grace Moore, Marion Talley, Nelson Eddy, Tito Schipa, Amelita Galli-Curci, Gladys Swarthout, and Jascha Heifetz. The composers employed by Hollywood studios have included Jerome Kern, George Antheil, George Gershwin, Robert Russell Bennett, Irving Berlin, Werner Janssen, Richard Hageman, Herbert Stothart, Sigmund Romberg, Deems Taylor, Max Steiner, Alfred Newman, and Victor Young. Today millions of people throughout the world hear a good part of their music in movie theatres, and most of it is produced in Hollywood.

Among composers now living in southern California but not identified with the film studios are Charles Wakefield Cadman, Elinor Remick Warren, Fannie Charles Dillon, Mary Carr Moore, Homer Grunn, Kathleen Lockhart Manning, Joseph Clokey, Oscar Rasbach, Gertrude Ross, William Grant Still, Edgar Varese, noted for his lavish use of percussion; the modernist Ernest Toch; Arnold Schoenberg, and many others. Several of the most prominent figures in the Los Angeles music world, including Schoenberg, Toch, and Klemperer, are Germans and Austrians.

During 1938 and 1939 one of the most active musical organizations in the city was the Federal Music Project, formed in 1935 under Dr.

Bruno David Ussher to assist unemployed musicians. The Los Angeles project, largest in California, has employed more than 900 people at a time and maintained symphony and concert orchestras, a Negro concert band and two white symphonic bands, operatic units, choruses, dance orchestras, teaching units, and operatic production staffs. Operas and symphonies have been presented commercially and music appreciation programs have been given in public schools and city and county recreational departments, and band concerts in public parks.

The grand opera unit, which had an extensive repertoire, presented the world premiere of Felix Borowski's *Fernando del Nonsentsico,* a satire on classical grand opera, and gave the first performance west of the Mississippi of Deems Taylor's *The King's Henchman.* The light opera group notably presented Auber's *Fra Diavolo* (with an all-Negro cast), Gilbert and Sullivan's *Pinafore* and *Mikado,* and world premieres of *Barbecue Isle* by Homer Grunn and *Gay Grenadiers* by C. Warner Van Valkenburg and Vern Elliott.

The project's symphony orchestra presented numerous new American compositions, and introduced to Los Angeles many symphonic compositions, among them Strauss' tone poem *Macbeth* and *Gettysburg,* scored by Arthur Robinson with lyrics by Morris Ruger. An outstanding success of the Los Angeles project, working in conjunction with the Federal Theatre Project, was the presentation of its Negro chorus of eighty voices (Carlyle Scott, founder-director), in Hall Johnson's folk-opera *Run Little Chillun.*

Popular music—ragtime followed by jazz—came to Los Angeles after the turn of the century, when "hot" music from the South started a national craze. The early careers of many band leaders and musicians, and popular singers are associated with the city. Paul Whiteman used to play at the beach resorts with an itinerant band whose members walked about among the crowds with a big can into which dancers tossed coins; Bing Crosby was hired by Whiteman as one of the "Three Rhythm Boys," then went to the East where he gained renown in radio before he was "rediscovered" by Hollywood; Kenny Baker, Abe Lyman, Gus Arnheim, Jimmy Grier, Donald Novis, and Mildred Bailey have also worked here in their earlier days.

Popular song composers from Tin Pan Alley in New York began a trek to Hollywood in the twenties, when studios began making sound pictures. Songs are usually written to order for a particular film. Many of the studios have close tie-ups with large sheet-music houses, whose branch offices in Los Angeles publish songs from motion pictures. Because of the wide circulation of the movies and the incessant "plugging" of hit songs from current films on radio programs, the music produced in Hollywood is probably heard by more people throughout the world than all the music composed in Tin Pan Alley.

Los Angeles ranks second in the nation in the production of popular phonograph records, which are manufactured in local plants maintained by eastern companies. Transcriptions of musical shows for radio programs are also produced in large numbers. These "platters" have replaced many "live talent" programs and find a rapidly growing market in foreign countries as well as at home. *Variety* estimates that between 85 and 90 per cent of the transcriptions exported to English-speaking countries are made in Hollywood.

LITERATURE

In sheer number of writers and quantity of work produced, Los Angeles is today a literary capital of the first magnitude. Scores of well-known authors and hundreds of obscure ones live in and around the city, turning out many millions of words annually for books, pulp and slick magazines, motion pictures, the stage, and radio broadcasts. But as to the quality of its output, and the extent of its truly native literature, Los Angeles has yet to attain the stature of a true literary center. Few of its writers are mentioned in standard histories of American letters; few have identified themselves and their works with the local scene; and of those who have, most have been undistinguished.

The reason for this is that culturally the area is comparatively young. During almost the whole of its first hundred years Los Angeles was a small provincial town in remote country. Communication with the outside world, and especially with the artistic world, was slow and infrequent. The townsfolk, first the Spaniards and Mexicans and then the early American settlers, had neither time nor inclination for literary activities. As a result, the period from the founding of the city in 1781 to the publication of *Ramona,* more than a century later, was almost wholly unproductive of anything that can properly be termed literature.

Travelers' journals, memoirs of early settlers, descriptive accounts of the region, and local newspaper writings were virtually the only fruits of these long years. The first person to describe the Los Angeles area was Father Juan Crespi, whose diary is a valuable record of the Portola expedition of 1769-70. The earliest known description by an American did not appear until almost forty years later, when William Shaler (1773-1833), a Boston sea captain, wrote a report of his visit to the California coast for the *American Register.* At long intervals other accounts of the strange and little-known land followed. Among the most interesting was the description of San Pedro Harbor in Richard Henry Dana's (1815-1882) *Two Years Before the Mast,* first published in 1840. Dana was not at all impressed by his first sight of the region: "We all agreed that it was the worst place we had seen yet." It was while the *Pilgrim* lay at San Pedro that the brutal flogging of two sailors took place as recorded in his book. Other accounts of southern California appeared in Alfred Robinson's (1806-1895) *Life in California* (1846), one of the first books on this region to reach a large audience in the United States; Edwin Bryant's (1805-1869) *What I Saw in California* (1848), an entertaining record of the author's experiences with the American Army of occupation; and *A Flower from the Golden Land* by Ludwig Salvator (1847-1915), an Austrian archduke who visited southern California in 1876 and whose book was the first work on Los Angeles to have wide European circulation.

Outstanding among pre-*Ramona* publications is the uproarious *Reminiscences of a Ranger* (1881) by Major Horace Bell (1830-1918), a fiery, crusading editor with a flair for Gargantuan humor and caricature. Bell's rollicking accounts of events and personalities in the boisterous Los Angeles of the fifties and sixties are generally unorthodox and questionable, but they probably give a truer picture of those incredible times than any sober chronicle can. A further volume of Bell's memoirs, *On the Old West Coast,* was published posthumously in 1930.

The first local newspaper, *La Estrella de Los Angeles* (The Star of Los Angeles), deserves mention not only for having been the town's chief source of reading matter for almost three decades, but also because it contains writing that is peculiarly expressive of the life and times. Founded in 1851, the paper was printed in English and Spanish until 1855, then in English only until its demise in 1879. Local news was often reported with considerable humor and even sarcasm, as in the issue of February 19, 1853, which related: "On Tuesday of last week we had four weddings, two funerals, one street fight with knives, a lynch court, two men flogged, and a serenade by a callithumpian band; also a fist fight and one man tossed in a blanket. If any of the flourishing up-country towns can hold a candle to that, let them do it forthwith or forever hold their peace." Editorials were frequently vigorous and full of vivid vituperation, particularly during the Civil War when the paper, like most of the town, openly favored the South. An issue of 1863 contained the blast: "Abe Lincoln 'honest'! Why his every act, from the hour of his departure from Springfield to Washington to begin his saturnalia of blood, till the prsent day, has been replete with gross and palpable deception. . . . When an obscure, fourth-rate lawyer at the Illinois capitol, pettifogging for a livelihood and retailing stale jokes and anecdotes for pastime, he was, probably, 'Honest Abe.' . . . But association with corruption has changed the man." That the booster spirit was rampant even in those early days is shown in an item of 1873, entitled "What Nature Has Done" (for Los Angeles): "She has given us the love-chanting mockingbird, the canary . . . to sing in our groves, . . . She has given us . . . the lime, the orange, and the olive, and in splendid wedding has blended together all that is good, harmonious or lovely in the earth, the sea and the air."

The *Star* ceased publication in the late 1870's, and soon afterward there appeared the *Porcupine,* a weekly "journalistic scourge" edited by the redoubtable Horace Bell. This paper of the eighties and nineties crusaded for all kinds of civic improvements, muckraked all manner of graft and scandal, and violently attacked various public figures, from the local sheriff to the Prince of Wales. In an era otherwise devoid of any good writing, the *Porcupine* deserves some mention for its masterful invective.

During the eighties and nineties appeared a number of books designed to acquaint the eastern traveler or settler with the wonders of California. Charles Nordhoff (1830-1901), grandfather of the Nordhoff of *Mutiny on the Bounty* fame, wrote five books about California, the most important, *California for Health, Pleasure, and Residence* (1882), giving a detailed account of the colony settlements, the cultivation of the grapes, oranges, and olives of southern California, and the methods of irrigation. *Our Italy* (1892) by Charles Dudley Warner (1829-1900), describes among other things the commercial and climatic assets of southern California, the price of land, and the prospects for laborers and small farmers. In *Old Mexico and Her Lost Provinces* (1883) William Henry Bishop (1847-1928), devotes a chapter to Los Angeles, dismissing it as "only another San Jose." *Between the Gates* (1878), by Benjamin F. Taylor (1819-1887), includes a romantic and florid account of a trip to southern California. Theodore S. Van Dyke (1842-1923) wrote three books on the Los Angeles region: *Rifle, Rod and Gun in California* (1890) includes a technical description of southern California game; *Millionaires of a Day* (1890) is an account of the great southern California boom; and *Southern California* (1896) describes in detail almost every aspect of topography, climate, and game, as well as "hints" on migrating to California.

The publication in 1884 of Helen Hunt Jackson's (1831-1885) novel, *Ramona,* marked the real beginning of Los Angeles literature, making the fiction-reading public conscious for the first time of southern California's life and historical background. It created a demand for works based on this locale, and acquainted writers with the remarkable possibilities of the region. At the same time, however, the city was undergoing a radical change in character, which was soon to change the scene Mrs. Jackson had described but make it far more receptive to cultural development. In place of the uncouth and illiterate small town of Mexican and early American days, there was now a rapidly-growing and comparatively articulate city, connected by rail with the eastern United States and receiving therefrom not only immigrants but also cultural influences.

Mrs. Jackson, a New Englander, came to Los Angeles in the early eighties to investigate the condition of the Mission Indians and to write a series of articles on southern California for *Century Magazine*. Her articles, later published in a book called *Glimpses of California and the Missions* (1883), are a storehouse of the results of original research that has been utilized and even plagiarized. It was her sympathy for the Indians, however, and in fact for the old order as a whole in its conflict with American aggression, that led to the writing of *Ramona*. "I am going to write a novel," Mrs. Jackson is reputed to have said, "in which will be set forth some Indian experiences in a way to move people's hearts." Much of the work was done while she was a guest at the charming old adobe mansion of Don Antonio F. Coronel, which stood on what is now the bustling corner of Alameda and Seventh Streets. In 1885, a few months after the publication of her book, "H.H." died in San Francisco, unaware that she had produced a romance which was to play an incalculable part in attracting people to southern California.

It is perhaps a commentary on the youthfulness of southern California literature that the first novel to come out of this region is still by all odds the best-known and best-loved. Despite its artistic faults, its dated style, and Victorian sentimentality, *Ramona* has gone through more than 130 printings; it has been filmed time and again, in silent, sound, and color motion pictures; it has been played on the stage, and is performed annually in a pageant at Hemet.

Ramona can be said to have inaugurated the "local color" school of writing that dominated Los Angeles literary circles until well into the twentieth century. This is not to say that writers of that so-called middle period followed the *Ramona* formula; on the contrary, they produced few historical romances. But most of their work—whether novels, short stories, poems, or articles—was based on picturesque aspects of the local life and scene, especially old-time ones: legends, Indians, padres, ranchos, animal and plant life, beautiful scenery—all viewed through fond, sentimental eyes in which quaintness and romance loomed large.

The leader of the regional school was Charles Fletcher Lummis (1859-1928), literary oracle of Los Angeles for three decades. A New Englander and a newspaperman, Lummis arrived in southern California in 1884 after walking 3,500 miles on a roundabout route from Cincinnati. He proceeded to steep himself in southwestern life with such energy and devotion that he soon became more "native" than most born Californians. He wrote constantly ("too many hours a day," as Mary Austin put it) about California, Arizona, and New Mexico; he founded and edited a magazine, served as City Librarian for five years, helped found the Southwest Museum, founded the Landmarks Club, collected Indian and Spanish relics and folksongs, laboring for his adopted country with staggering enthusiasm. He became paralyzed for a time and just before the end of his life went blind. Lummis' magazine, *The Land of Sunshine*—later called *Out West*, crystallized and directed western literary trends by encouraging California writers to take advantage of the wealth of inspiration in their own environment. "The local field," he wrote in 1897, "is literally boundless—the longer I look at it the deeplier I feel this. What we do lack is the people to exploit it—and I am now trying to vaccinate a few of the really competent people we have on the Coast and to get them to group." A large number of southern California literary folk, whom he thus "vaccinated," revolved around Lummis, forming a virtual salon at his home, El Alisal, which he built largely with his own hands on the bank of the Arroyo Seco in Highland Park.

Lummis was by no means a first-rate literary artist, but he was a good storyteller and reporter, with a style that was virile though sentimental. Of his numerous books, including *The Spanish Pioneers* (1893), *The Enchanted Burro* (1897), *A Bronco Pegasus* (1928), and *Flowers of Our Lost Romance* (1929), few are read today, but they are likely to retain value through the years as repositories of southwestern lore.

A similar appraisal can be made of the best works of other writers belonging to the regional traditions: Charles Francis Saunders (1859—), George Wharton James (1858-1923), and John Steven McGroarty (1862—), to name a few. Some fiction was produced by this group and also by resident and visiting writers who were not identified with the regional school. Most of such work, however, was run-of-the-mill stuff which has long since been forgotten. Among the few authors who dealt competently with the southern California scene were Gertrude Atherton (1857—), Peter B. Kyne (1880—), and Mary Austin (1868-1934). The latter was a member of the Lummis colony during her early years of writing, and among her first ventures into print were several poems in *The Land of Sunshine*.

Even before Lummis' death in 1928 the local-color school had begun to decline. Its passing was due in some degree to the city's change of character, and even more to the international change in literary values. The boom of the twenties metamorphosed Los Angeles in a few years from a medium-sized city with a fairly stable population to a metropolis peopled by heterogeneous multitudes. Many things dear to the hearts of old-time Angelenos were submerged, among them the physical evidences of the region's past history, as well as many of its distinctive folkways. The national literary taste, moreover, was switching from sentimental romanticism to realism, and this trend naturally affected southern California.

Today, and in fact since the post-war period, Los Angeles has become a huge word factory. Fiction, particularly, is turned out on a mass-production scale. Writers from all over the world have been drawn here by the motion pictures and later by the radio studios, as well as by the climate, the natural scene and the growing cultural activity. The work produced by these comparative newcomers is so varied that most of it can be classed as "Los Angeles" only because it happens to be written here, and most of it as "literature" only by courtesy. The latter is especially true of film and radio fiction, not only because it is ephemeral but also because much of it is rewrite work and hence not original. But the products of the Hollywood writers reach an audience of millions, thus giving them more influence than authors as a group ever had before. Strangely enough, despite their power and the lavish salaries that many of them receive, screen and radio scribes remain virtually anonymous to the general public, their names being overshadowed by those of the stars, producers, and directors.

To give some idea of the varied array of writers who now live or have lived in and about Los Angeles in recent years, it is perhaps sufficient to name outstanding or typical figures in the different fields: Upton Sinclair (1878—), crusading novelist and pamphleteer, whose sixty books have been translated into an average of thirteen foreign languages apiece, making him one of the most widely-read of living authors; Zane Grey (1874-1939), prolific writer of two-gun Western novels; Edgar Rice Burroughs (1875—), creator of Tarzan; Willard Huntington Wright (1888-1939), who signed himself S. S. Van Dine in the detective stories whose hero was Philo Vance; Earl Derr Biggers (1884-1933), whose detective was Charlie Chan; Jim Tully (1891—), hobo author of *Beggars of Life* (1924) and *Jarnegan* (1926); Rupert Hughes (1872—), author of many short stories, novels and a life of George Washington; Hamlin Garland (1860-1940), whose many books, among them *Son of the Middle Border* (1917), have gained him the title "grand old man of American letters"; Will Rogers (1879-1935), cowboy philosopher, columnist, and author of *The Illiterate Digest* (1924) and *Letters of a Self-made Diplomat to His President* (1926); Eric Temple Bell (1883—), of the California Institute of Technology, who has written adventure novels such as *The Purple Sapphire* (1924) under the pseudonym of John Taine, as well as *Men of Mathematics* (1937) and other scientific bestsellers; Paul Jordan Smith (1885—), scholar and critic; June Hildegarde Flanner (1899—), author of *A Tree in Bloom* (1924) and *Time's Profile* (1929); Lewis Browne (1897—), historian and producer of *Stranger Than Fiction* and *The Story of the Jews* (1925-26).

Dozens of other names, equally prominent or deserving of mention, might be included. Harry Carr (1877-1936), former Los Angeles columnist, wrote that "The Big Leaguers began to come in during the latter days of silent motion-pictures and the talkies washed them hither in a flood. A large part of the [country's] literary population now lives in Los Angeles." Obviously, this legion of writers does not constitute a distinctively southern California "group." Not only is the work produced here extremely varied, including as it does virtually every type of writing from pulp fiction to scientific treatises, but also the bulk of it is almost wholly lacking in indigenous quality. It could just as well be written anywhere else.

Along with this great heterogeneous mass of writing that Los Angeles pours out, a certain amount of local color material continues to appear. A few of the stories, novels, and other works of this type possess real merit. Notable examples are the desert stories of Edwin Corle (1906-——) in his volume entitled *Mojave* (1934), and his novel, *Fig Tree John* (1935), which relates with artistry the story of an Indian's futile hostility toward the encroachments of the whites. In recent years the Lummis tradition of regional writing has been revived to some extent in a more realistic form by the magazine *Westways*, published since 1909 by the Automobile Club of Southern California and called *Touring Topics* until 1934. Since the beginning of Phil Townsend Hanna's (1896-——) editorship in 1927, this monthly has included some fiction, and has given special emphasis to material of a regional nature.

The outlook for the emergence of a distinctive regional literature seems favorable. For one thing, southern California offers the writer unusual themes and varied natural settings; a stimulating and romantic history as well as a dynamic contemporary life; and endlessly varied people in process of amalgamation; a wealth of curious customs, peculiar religions, bizarre political movements, and changing social modes. Another and perhaps a more important consideration betokening the eventual development of southern California literature is that the number of native-born Angelenos is rapidly increasing. Of the writers mentioned in this article, almost none are natives of the region; in fact, only a relatively small percentage of Los Angeles residents of middle age were born here. Thus the two or three generations of writers who have made up the city's brief literary history have been essentially outsiders; their "old home" background has inevitably remained a part of them. But for the constantly growing numbers of native sons and daughters, the only background is southern California. It is their country by right of heritage, not adoption, and it seems reasonable to expect that some of them will write about it with a deeper insight than has so far been manifested.

ART AND ARTISTS

In their designs and handicrafts the Indians of the Los Angeles area ranked among the less developed North American tribes. A peaceful and docile people, they moved about indolently on the mild, sunny beaches of the coast, feeding on the rich supplies of shellfish and sheltering themselves by the most primitive means. The occasional pottery and weaving produced in this low-grade paradise achieved little distinction in pattern or craftsmanship.

These natives and others brought from nearby sections were taken by the Spaniards into the missions, where they were taught to labor in the fields and buildings. The Indian neophytes, under the tutelage of the padres, painted decorations upon the walls of the missions and carved church implements, ornaments, and figurines. In this work the indigenous spirit became oddly intermingled with European styles and conceptions: the mixture is perhaps best exemplified in the *Stations of the Cross* series painted on sail-cloth at the San Gabriel Mission before 1779. The mission fathers and neophytes also produced plaques, iron grille work, costumes, tools, textiles, embroideries, and stamped and colored leather work.

In addition to the murals and carvings executed locally, the missions also contained paintings and sculptures from Mexico and Spain; a number of these works are now in Los Angeles institutions.

The dons and senoritas of the great ranchos, which came into existence shortly after the establishment of the missions, had their portraits painted by wandering Spanish and Mexican artists, and purchased silks, embroideries, and household implements from the Spanish homeland and, later, from traders whose ships had touched the ports of China, Russia, and Peru. Silversmiths and harness makers tooled horse trappings and decorated them with silver inlay work in the Mexican style. This influence later made itself felt in the crafts of the early Yankee settlers.

When the expansion of northern California surged forward in the 1850's, a number of eastern landscape painters mounted the great ranges of the Sierras and descended into the vast valleys of Sacramento and San Joaquin, painting enormous canvases which have since come to be known as the work of the "Heroic School." This phase of American painting, however, scarcely touched the Los Angeles region, and it was not until the 1880's, after the coming of the railroads, that local art began its modern development.

William Wachtel arrived in southern California in 1883 and strove to capture the quality of light and color in the neighboring countryside. During the next few years a number of art clubs and organizations sprang up in and about Los Angeles. The Ruskin Art Club was established in 1888; the Los Angeles School of Art opened in 1890; and the Pasadena Academy of Fine Arts in 1897; and in 1903 the Los Angeles Municipal Art Commission was inaugurated.

William Wendt, who settled in California in 1903, painted many landscapes depicting this region in the different seasons of the year. A contemporary of Wendt, J. Bond Francisco, composed notable landscapes of canyons and wooded mountainsides. The influence of these men, especially that of Wendt, survives today among many California landscapists whose favorite study is the play of sunlight in their locality. Among these sound conservatives are Hanson Puthuff, Jack Wilkinson Smith, Edgar Alwin Payne, Benjamin Chambers Brown, and Marion Kavanaugh Wachtel. Other local painters in the traditional style are Alexander Warshawsky, Emile Jean Kosa, Jr., Arthur Millier, Roscoe Schrader, Dana Bartlett, Alson Clark, F. Tolles Chamberlin, Ejnar Hansen, Orrin A. White, Paul Lauritz, the late George K. Brandriff, Clyde Forsythe, Duncan Gleason, the late Gordon Coutts, and Mabel Alvarez.

Before the World War, Guy Rose was doing important work in the impressionist manner, and S. Macdonald Wright had founded a new movement based on his theories of color relations. In these pre-War years the Southwest Museum was organized (1903), with its collection of early California art material, and the Los Angeles Museum of History, Science, and Art, showing permanent groups of European and American paintings and sculptures, was formally opened in 1913. The Huntington Art Gallery, established in 1919, is renowned for its collection of eighteenth century British art.

The most impressive aspect of Los Angeles art history, however, has been the lively flow of experimentation, both in technique and materials, which has reached its highest level during the past five years. Local artists have shown a creative interest in the new forms emanating from New York and Paris, and large public works of art have made their appearance in the parks, streets, and buildings of Los Angeles. Murals in fresco, tempera, and oil, mosaics, inlays, and monumental sculptures have been sponsored by private agencies and by the Federal Art Project and by the Section of Fine Arts of the U. S. Treasury Department. The "synchromism" of S. Macdonald Wright and the "postsurrealism" of Lorser Feitelson, Helen Lundeberg, Grace Clements, and Elizabeth Mills are local vanguard movements which have achieved recognition beyond the borders of the United States.

Modern schools include among the expressionists, Bear Newman, Boris Deutsch, Jerre Murry, Denny Winters, and Herman Cherry; among the abstractionists, Arthur Durston, Helen Klokke, Olinka Hrdy, Kaye Waters, Warren Newcomb, and Elise Armitage; and among the surrealists, Carlos Dyer, Ben Berlin, and Charles Mattox.

Other artists of the modern school are Nicholas Brigante, Rex Slinkard, Fred Sexton, Conrad Buff, Jack Stark, and Peter Krasnow. Al King, Don Totten, and James Redmond are influenced by S. Macdonald Wright. Outstanding among Los Angeles painters of the American scene are Millard Sheets and Barse Miller; Paul Sample, Lee Blair, Fletcher Martin, Tom Craig, Phil Dike, Dan Lutz, and Ruth Miller Fracker also work in this popular genre. The late Frank Tenney Johnson was widely known for his romantic depictions of western range life and his night scenes. Kathryn Leighton has made an important recording of Indian life. Nicolai Fechin is a portraitist and figure painter in the traditional manner. The decorative tendency in modern painting is exemplified in the work of Jean Goodwin, Arthur Ames, Nathalie Newking, Buckley MacGurrin, Althea Ulber, Suzanne Miller, Viktor von Pribosic, and Hideo Date, who shows a Japanese influence.

The Mexican painters Orozco and Rivera have had an important effect upon Los Angeles mural painting. Another stimulating influence has been the Federal Art Project, which has commissioned murals for scores of public buildings. It is impossible to list here the many excellent murals executed in Los Angeles during the past few years. The history of California, the myths of the Aztecs and other tribes, scenes from contemporary life, and symbolic and cultural themes decorate profusely the walls of the city. Among outstanding works are the decorations of Dean Cornwell at the Los Angeles Public Library and of Charles Kassler in the Library patio; S. Macdonald Wright's *Man's Two-fold Development* at the Santa Monica Public Library; Jose Clemente Orozco's *Prometheus* at Pomona College, Claremont; MacGurrin's *Signing of the Magna Carta* at the Hall of Records, Los Angeles; and the panels of Hugo Ballin at B'nai B'rith Temple, Los Angeles. Other local muralists of note are Giovanni Napolitano, Willy Pogany, Leo Katz, Suzanne Miller, Barse Miller, Conrad Buff, Millard Sheets, and Lorser Feitelson.

In sculpture, too, Los Angeles has witnessed a remarkable growth in recent years. The local craftsmen, George Stanley, Archibald Garner, and Roger Noble Burnham participated in designing the 40-foot *Astronomers' Monument* in Griffith Park, and have contributed many other works. Henry Lion, the late David Edstrom, Merrel Gage, Donal Hord, William Atkinson, Eugenia Everett, Julia Bracken Wendt, and Ada May Sharpless are Los Angeles sculptors whose techniques vary from solid conservatism to the most advanced experimental handling.

In conclusion, mention should be made of Los Angeles commercial art and industrial design. In the Hollywood studios and workshops every phase of decorative technique has been thoroughly studied, and many innovations have been introduced there. The animated cartoons of Walt Disney, in whose studios many local artists have been employed, are known throughout the civilized world. Recognized industrial designers include Walter Beermann, Joseph Sinel, and Kem Weber. The intense activity of the Hollywood workshops has been an important factor in making Los Angeles a new art center of the West.

THE THEATRE

The story of the theatre in Los Angeles is largely a record of the appearances of road shows, ephemeral stock companies, and the rise and fall in popularity of playhouses, producers, and performers. Instead of showing continuous native growth, with sustained local traditions, it is for the most part a history of periods and personalities, succeeding one another with little continuity or interdependence.

During the almost seventy years of Spanish and Mexican rule, religious plays were the sole dramatic fare. Introduced by the Franciscan missionaries and presented only at Christmas time, they usually depicted the journey of the shepherds to Bethlehem, their encounter with the devil along the way, Satan's final overthrow by the Arcangel Miguel, and the shepherds proceeding to the Christ child. Typical of this kind of drama were *Los Pastores* (The Shepherds), which was enlivened by songs, guitar music, and comic incidents; and *La Pastorela* (The Pastoral), written by Padre Florencio of Soledad Mission. The actors were amateurs. A nativity drama similar to these is still presented annually at the Old Mission Plaza Church in Los Angeles. In the last performance of *La Pastorela,* given on Christmas Eve of 1861, the role of the Arcangel Miguel was played by Arturo Bandini, a prominent don. Part of his traditional costume, a pair of curled tissue-paper wings, so aroused the curiosity of a nearsighted old lady that she held up a lighted taper to inspect them. The wings caught fire and blazed away on "Miguel's" back until "Satan" rushed to the rescue.

With the influx of Yankees in the middle of the nineteenth century, the religious pageants were soon overshadowed by a different type of stage entertainment. As early as 1847 outdoor performances were given by a company of strolling comedians, the vanguard of countless traveling troupes, whose frequent visits by 1858, warranted the building of a small playhouse, Stearns' Hall, on South Spring Street. Here, in 1859, the California Minstrels and Burlesque Troupe, with "Ethiopian Comedians," performed to enthusiastic audiences. In the same year Don Juan Temple, an enterprising Yankee, constructed a combined market and auditorium, where the Great Star Company of Stark & Ryer of San Francisco presented Shakespearean drama and the plays of

Von Kotzebue, a favorite European playwright of the time. Other troupes appeared occasionally during the sixties, most of them coming by ship from San Francisco, the theatrical metropolis of the West. Schedules of performances were flexible, allowing for the missing of a boat by a star or troupe or for late arrival of the passenger vessel.

Not until 1870 did Los Angeles possess its first real theatre, the Merced at 418 North Main Street, at which were given such plays as *Esmeralda, The Danites,* and *M'Liss.* The theatre was built by William Abbott and named for his Mexican wife, and its opening was advertised in the Los Angeles *Star:*

MERCED THEATRE
GRAND INAUGURATION
The opening of the New [Abbott's] Theatre will take place on Friday, December 30, 1870, when a Grand Vocal and Instrumental Concert will be given by the 21st Regiment (Wilmington) Band, assisted by several well-known amateurs, who have kindly volunteered their services.

But there was still no regular stage entertainment. The arrival of a troupe was an event. The *Daily News* of January 18, 1871, reported that there was a "woeful lack of amusements" in Los Angeles and that "This has prompted some of the fun-loving spirits to offer on Thursday night, at the Merced, a mirth-provoking exhibition wherein the effect of laughing gas upon different persons will be practically illustrated."

Such groups of fun-loving spirits appeared in increasing numbers during the seventies. Since the town was not yet large enough to support regular theatrical groups for more than short engagements, local social clubs gave "readings," amateur minstrel shows, and one-act plays. Outstanding among these community enterprises was the annual series of entertainments directed by George A. Dobinson and called "Unitarian Thursdays," many of the performers being members of the Unitarian Church. These Victorian "amateur hours" were given at Union Hall on Spring Street near Temple, and continued into the next decade.

The spectacular growth in population during the booming eighties changed Los Angeles from a rough-and-ready frontier town with a limited potential audience to an increasingly important theatrical center, visited more and more by traveling troupes. In 1884 the city was ready for its second theatre building, the Grand Opera House on Main Street south of First. Built by Ozro W. Childs, a local business man, and seating 1,200 people, this was the second largest theatre on the Pacific coast. It was opened with Mlle. Rhea in *The School for Scandal.* Handbills warned that children in arms would not be admitted; the mayor addressed the audience, and intermissions were enlivened with such tunes as "O, Fair Dove! O, Fond Dove!," "Chimes of Corneville," and "Sailor's Joy."

Theatre programs collected by George A. Dobinson, and now preserved at the Los Angeles Public Library, furnish a better picture of the period than any other source. They are filled with society and theatre gossip, advertisements, and columns of what at the time may have been risque jokes: "Many of the costumes worn by the ladies at the Grand last night were extremely elegant. . . . The orchestra played several new numbers. Good work, keep it up. . . . The iced water passed through the audience last night was a great accommodation to the ladies, if not to the gentlemen. . . . Delinquent subscribers are hereby warned not to let their daughters wear this paper for a bustle, as there is considerable due on it, and they might take cold."

By the middle eighties Los Angeles had attained a place on the nation's theatrical map as a regular one-week stand, in which shows were billed "direct from New York." Booth and Barrett in Shakespearean repertoire (1887) grossed $17,936 in one week—a take that many a modern road show might envy. Another good-sized theatre, the Los Angeles, on Spring Street between Second and Third Streets, was built in 1888, and here during the next few years, the city saw such stars as Maurice Barrymore, E. H. Sothern, Lillian Russell, and Sarah Bernhardt. Plays included such European standbys as *Camille, Richelieu, Oliver Twist,* and *La Tosca;* and, among American favorites, *Only a Farmer's Daughter, The Wages of Sin,* and *Col. Mulberry Sellers.*

In the early nineties the stream of imported productions was gradually supplemented by the productions of local professional stock companies. The first of these home-town ventures was launched in 1893 at the Park Theatre (formerly Hazard's Pavilion) at Fifth and Olive Streets, where the Philharmonic Auditorium now stands. This company was short-lived. Similar enterprises appeared during the next few years, prospered for a time and collapsed. None attained anything like permanence until after the turn of the century, but their number steadily grew. Vaudeville, too, began to rival the legitimate stage in the nineties, the Orpheum opening as a vaudeville house in 1894. Sarah Bernhardt appeared at the Orpheum in two of her three Los Angeles engagements. It was during the first of these engagements that she was injured in an automobile accident—an accident seemingly trivial at the time, that later caused the amputation of a leg. Road shows continued, however, to provide the city's most substantial dramatic fare. Performances given in Los Angeles around 1900 included *Trilby, The Prisoner of Zenda, Peck's Bad Boy, The Wolves of New York, The Country Girl, Charley's Aunt,* and numerous Shakespearean plays; and among the popular actors of the time were Helena Modjeska, in whose honor a Los Angeles street is named, William Gillette, Trixie Friganza, Harry Langdon, George M. Cohan, William and Dustin Farnum, and Lionel Barrymore. Many of these remained to join local stock companies and later the films.

During this period of lavish road shows, local stock companies began to compete more and more successfully with them. The arrival of Oliver Morosco in Los Angeles in 1899 marked the opening of an era in which stock companies increased in importance until they dominated the local theatrical scene. Though Morosco leased the Burbank Theatre and at first presented the usual Eastern touring companies, he soon formed his own stock company—an organization that was exceedingly popular during the first quarter of the century. Then in 1909 Morosco took over the Belasco Theatre, which had been opened in 1904 by Fred Belasco—brother of David, and came to the fore as a nationally important producer.

The Belasco attracted wide comment with a series of notable revivals, and new plays. "Leading ladies came and went but the pueblo would never consent to the changing of the leading man: he was Lewis Stone. . . ." Outstanding productions included *When Knighthood Was in Flower, The Admirable Crichton, Zaza, Candida, Girl of the Golden West,* and *Undertow.* The last was among the plays first produced here that later became New York hits.

Between 1904 and 1915 the theatre in Los Angeles attained its majority. A dozen playhouses were doing a profitable business. Plays were capably staged and performed, and as a producing center of new dramas the city was surpassed only by New York. Even the religious motif in drama reappeared with the opening in 1912 at San Gabriel of John Steven McGroarty's *Mission Play,* which was destined to remain a favorite for two decades.

The little theatre movement, which swept the country between 1910 and 1918, led to the formation of numerous amateur organizations, most of which were of little significance because they attempted the same kind of drama that was done more expertly by traveling professional troupes and the motion pictures. One exception, however, was the Pasadena Community Playhouse group, founded by Gilmor Brown in 1917. The Playhouse soon began to attract talent from all over the United States and it became one of the outstanding little theatres. Because of its policy of presenting both premieres of the work of leading dramatists as well as new plays by obscure writers, it has been an active force in stimulating local drama.

But in Los Angeles as elsewhere, motion pictures affected the legitimate stage far more drastically than did the little theatre movement. By 1912 film companies were drawing many actors from the ranks of stage and vaudeville performers. During the World War, as movies attracted increasingly large audiences, the local stage entered a decline, and by the end of the war most of the old stock companies had failed and there were virtually no visits by road companies.

This set-back was only temporary. During the prosperous twenties there was room for both films and stage. "The road" revived, little theatres flourished. Two pageant plays were produced: the *Pilgrimage Play*, a presentation of the life of Christ, given annually in an open-air theatre in Hollywood Hills; and the *Ramona Pageant*, based on Helen Hunt Jackson's novel and performed at Hemet each year since 1923.

The biggest event in recent theatrical history was the opening in 1924 of the Biltmore Theatre with a $10 top price, tickets printed in gold leaf, and Will Rogers as master of ceremonies. The production was *Sally, Irene, and Mary*. In the next three years seven theatres were built: the Figueroa Playhouse, El Capitan, the new Belasco, the Mayan, the Hollywood Playhouse, the Hollywood Music Box, and the Vine Street. The opening of these theatres started the greatest theatrical activity Los Angeles has ever known.

One of the most successful ventures of this period was headed by Henry Duffy, whose policy was to present current New York hits. Beginning with the El Capitan in 1927, he soon had a string of theatres along the Pacific coast that included the President in Los Angeles and the Playhouse in Hollywood. Among his actors were Charles Ray, Will Rogers, Reginald Denny, Colleen Moore, Joe E. Brown, Billie Burke, and Francis Lederer. Edward Everett Horton organized another successful stock company, with himself as producer and leading man. Other outstanding producers included Louis Macloon and his wife, Lillian Albertson.

Stock activity was carried on by Morosco's company, which gave the first presentation of Ann Nichols' *Abie's Irish Rose;* it ran thirty-three weeks in Los Angeles before becoming a record-breaker in New York. But with the disbanding of this troupe in 1927 an era was ended, and most of the stock companies that arose thenceforth had a definite link with the film industry. In Hollywood some of the new companies were organized primarily to exploit the name value of motion picture stars. The local stage was so prosperous that in 1927 movie exhibitors began to complain about the competition—"in the very citadel of the cinema." It was believed that this condition was caused in a large degree by the public's slackening interest in silent films, but even after the introduction of talkies, the legitimate theatre continued to flourish. Between 1928 and 1932 were some of the best seasons on record. While the 1931-32 theatrical season was good from the public's viewpoint, producers were hard hit by financial conditions brought on by the general economic depression. During these years some of the best acting talent in the world, drawn here by Hollywood studios, was available for stage work.

Not until the full force of the depression was felt in southern California, beginning about 1932, did local drama commence a marked decline. Stock companies collapsed and road importations dwindled almost to the vanishing point. Even those perennial local performances, the *Pilgrimage Play* and the *Mission Play,* failed to open. But the little theatres, particularly the Pasadena Community Playhouse, the Beverly Hills Theatre, and the Gateway remained active for many months, supplying the bulk of the legitimate drama. Some of the amateur groups were organized to attract students who wished to enter the films, but instead they frequently drew established movie actors who could not get work in the studios. Productions at the Playhouse in Pasadena, for instance, were the best in its history because of the talent available.

An interest in working-class drama was a noteworthy development of the depression years. Emjo Basshe's *Doomsday Circus* was produced in 1933; the next season saw productions of Paul and Claire Sifton's *Blood on the Moon,* Wolfe's *Sailors of Cattaro,* and Peters' and Sklar's *Stevedore.* In the same season, Odets' *Till the Day I Die* and *Waiting for Lefty* were presented in Hollywood. Other developments of the depression period were the Padua Hills Theatre at Claremont, presenting Mexican actors in a present-day approximation of folk drama; and the Theatre Mart's revival of *The Drunkard,* an old-time melodrama that opened in 1933 and that, in December, 1938, broke the world's record for long runs by surpassing the 283 consecutive weeks in New York of *Abie's Irish Rose.* *The Drunkard* had its 350th performance in 1940.

Strangely enough, the lean 1930's saw one of the most lavish stage spectacles ever presented in Los Angeles, Max Reinhardt's production of *Midsummer Night's Dream,* produced at the Hollywood Bowl in 1934. Two years later the Bowl was the scene of another spectacular outdoor drama, *Everyman;* and in 1938 Reinhardt staged an elaborate production of *Faust* in the Pilgrimage Play Theatre.

In 1937-38 the road showed signs of reviving. The Biltmore Theatre presented many outstanding New York successes and had one of the longest and most profitable seasons in its history. There was considerable activity among the little theatres, and several schools were opened to offer drama training to would-be stage, screen, and radio stars.

The Federal Theatre Project was established in 1935, when the professional theatre was at low ebb. The project's actors were soon providing continuous stage entertainment. The Los Angeles project, second in size of personnel only to that of New York City, had radio and music units, a marionette division, vaudeville, colored, and Yiddish units, and a children's theatre. Shakespearean dramas were given in public schools, and at Christmas time morality plays were presented at various theatres and in churches throughout the city. Among the project's noteworthy presentations were Elmer's Rice's *Judgment Day;* Hall Johnson's *Run Little Chillun,* which opened in July 1938 and ran eleven months; *Ready! Aim! Fire!,* by Jean Stone and Jack Robinson; *Two a Day,* and *Pinocchio,* a marionette show. From 1935 to 1938 the project staged more than 150 productions, including many dramas by new and hitherto unknown authors.

The Business of Pleasure

THE golden flow of outside dollars into southern California began in the 1840's, but the first visitors were chiefly hardbitten men whose names appeared on "Wanted" placards throughout the roaring West. They often arrived only a hop and a step ahead of the law or the vigilantes, hell-bent for the Mexican border. Their headquarters in Los Angeles was the Calle de los Negros (Street of the Blacks), locally called Nigger Alley, the early amusement belt. Along this narrow crowded street near the Plaza the click of roulette wheels and the jingle of gold never stopped. The tempo of life was set by gay fandangos danced to the strains of the harp, guitar, and violin. The notes of the flageolet mingled with the shouts of rancheros and the laughter of senoritas. The frequent pistol blasts brought no halt to the merrymaking, and a public hanging had the aspect of a fiesta.

The most serious undertakings of the Angelenos were conducted with abandon. They gambled recklessly, wagering hundreds of head of cattle and vast tracts of land on the speed of a horse or the turn of a card. Even the children staked the buttons on their clothes with supreme contempt for the consequences. Indians wagered not only their clothes but also at times their wives and children. Dancing, hunting, and cockfighting were the business of life rather than its diversions.

This semi-isolated existence of the sleepy pueblo became a memory after the railroads arrived in the eighties. The Southern Pacific began operation in 1883 and less than three years later the Santa Fe brought in its first passengers. Owning extensive lands along its right of way, the Santa Fe opened up the territory immediately and newcomers, inspired by the articles of romanticists and the adroit advertising of the railroads, began arriving in overwhelming numbers. California became the fad, and during the winters from eighty-five to eighty-seven Los Angeles filled with tourists, many of whom decided to remain permanently.

A land boom developed that brought many adventurers, and amusements quickly responded. But when the boom came to a sudden end values fell off and the influx ceased. Los Angeles had not been alive to its new role of impressario in the business of entertainment, and not for ten years were tourists to return in any numbers.

Meanwhile those who stayed were among the wealthier class of

Movies in the Making

Warner Brothers

THE MAIN STUDIO AT BURBANK
OF WARNER BROTHERS FIRST NATIONAL PICTURES

THE SAMUEL GOLDWYN LOT, SMALLEST OF THE MAJOR STUDIOS

Samuel Goldwyn

WHENEVER THERE'S A QUESTION THERE'S A CONFERENCE

SHOOTING A SCENE ON A SOUND STAGE SET

Samuel Goldwyn

COMPLETED SET

SHOOTING A SCENE WITH A TECHNICOLOR CAMERA

Samuel Goldwyn

Samuel Goldwyn

LUNCH TIME ON THE SET

MEN'S WARDROBE DEPARTMENT

Metro-Goldwyn-Mayer

Metro-Goldwyn-Mayer

EXPERT SEAMSTRESSES ARE EMPLOYED

A CORNER OF THE PROPERTY ROOM

Metro-Goldwyn-Mayer

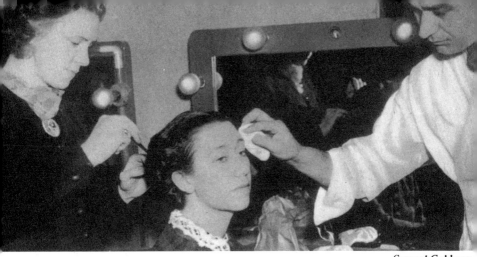

MAKEUP

FOG MADE TO ORDER A HAND-MADE TREE

WAVES ARE MADE BY MOTOR-DRIVEN ECCENTRIC CYLINDERS

VEGETABLES ARE SHELLACKED
TO PREVENT WILTING UNDER HEAT OF LIGHTS

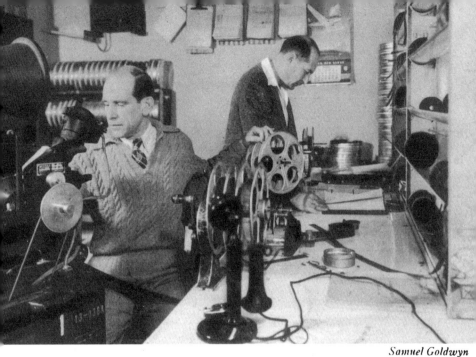

A MODERN MOVIOLA IS USED IN
EDITING, OR "CUTTING," THE FILM

MUSIC IS SYNCHRONIZED ON RECORDS WHICH ARE
PLAYED BACK LATER AND RECORDED ON THE FILM

middle westerners or invalids in search of a health-giving climate. They imposed their traditions upon the pleasure-loving native population. Concerts, opera, and cultural entertainments began to increase and the more disreputable amusements were banished to the outskirts of the city. A weeding-out process was instigated and the adventurous were soon forced to depart, hastened by the dearth of easy money. In 1889 the gambling houses were closed and saloons functioned only on week days.

Then Los Angeles once more took in hand the problem of attracting tourists. A Chamber of Commerce had been created in 1888 to grapple with the wreckage of the boom years. A period of experiment with festivals was inaugurated. Fiestas and pageants of different kinds were designed to hold the remaining population as well as to attract new residents. Answering the taunts of the disillusioned, the Chamber of Commerce in 1890 achieved a triumph of showmanship with its orange carnival at Chicago. On the first day of the same year the Valley Hunt Club of Pasadena had sponsored the first Battle of Flowers in which Pasadenans competed for prizes by decorating their horses and carriages with fresh blossoms. From this festival grew the present annual Tournament of Roses.

La Fiesta de Los Angeles. The Feast of the Angels, as the Merchants Association called it, was conceived in 1894 in hopes of drawing visitors attending the San Francisco Fair. The fiesta, a four-day celebration inspired by the carnivals at Nice and Monte Carlo, consisted in a series of parades, a floral battle, *el dia de las flores,* in Central Park (now Pershing Square), a grand ball, and fireworks displays. After the turn of the century this celebration became known as La Fiesta de Las Flores (The Feast of Flowers) and was held annually for a decade.

Meanwhile the world was bombarded with hundreds of thousands of pamphlets and elaborate exhibitions glorifying southern California. Exhibits and accompanying ballyhoo were seen and heard at fairs and expositions in Germany, France, and Guatemala, as well as in many North American cities. The campaign reached heights of fantasy during the Klondike gold rush when prospectors in Alaska were besieged with propaganda "emphasizing the advantages of southern California climate in a place where they would be most keenly appreciated."

In spite of the change in entertainment the native Angelenos and those of similar temperament continued to enjoy their own amusements. If gambling had been hardpressed, there were still dogfights and cockfights where one could place his bets. "Los Angeles was a great town then," according to James J. Jeffries, former heavyweight boxing champion of the world. "Dog fights? I should say. I had a fighter, a bulldog that weighed about 50 pounds. She cost $600 and whipped everything in sight. They even brought dogs from New York to fight her for big side bets." After 1900, however, a wave of reform swept over the town, reaching such proportions in 1915 that the late Willard Huntington Wright—later known as S. S. Van Dine, author of mystery novels— declared that the tourist in search of urban pleasure would "find himself thwarted by some ordinance, the primary object of which is to force Middle West moralities upon all inhabitants. Puritanism is the inflexible doctrine of Los Angeles." Wright attributed this "frenzy for virtue" to the influx of natives of prairie states. Gambling and Sunday dancing were forbidden in a community that had cut its eye teeth on poker chips. Crusaders became so rampant that Los Angeles voted itself dry two years before prohibition became a part of the Federal Constitution.

Nevertheless recreation was not completely outlawed by the reform movement. During the early 1900's the Chamber of Commerce began to call attention to Los Angeles as an outdoor playground. To its stereotyped advertising of rose-bowered cottages, ideal climate, and conditions suitable for horticulture and manufacturing were added in praise of southern California swimming, boating, fishing, and mountain climbing. Football, baseball, and tennis gained in popularity. By 1920 the Los Angeles area had become a winter playground for approximately 200,000 people a year.

The All-Year Club of Southern California was formed in 1921 to attract visitors during the summer, when the tourist trade annually underwent a decline. This organization strove to analyze the likes and dislikes of the average visitor and decided that eleven cents of every tourist dollar were spent for amusement and recreation. During 1938 in southern California nearly 650,000 winter visitors and one million summer visitors spent approximately two hundred million dollars in Los Angeles.

As early as 1912, when Fred Kelly, a local boy, won the 110-meter hurdle championship at Stockholm, various civic groups dreamed of bringing the Olympic games to Los Angeles. An application for the games was suggested in 1919 at a meeting of the California Fiestas Association. The association immediately launched a campaign to bring the Olympics to Los Angeles. Colonel William May Garland, a local financier, was asked to extend an official invitation. Equipped with abundant figures and facts on the attractions of Los Angeles, plans for a new stadium, and invitations from city, county, state and various civic groups, Garland went to Europe and became a member of the International Olympic Games Committee. He gained the immediate support of a former visitor to California, Baron Pierre de Coubertin, founder of the modern Olympic games and honorary life president of the committee. The VIIIth and IXth Olympiads had already been awarded. The Xth scheduled for 1932, would not be awarded until 1924.

Meanwhile plans progressed for the erection of the new Coliseum. Construction started in Exposition Park in 1921. When completed two years later at a cost of $800,000, the Coliseum had a seating capacity of 76,000. Word was received from Rome in 1924 that the Xth Olympiad had been awarded to Los Angeles and a State Olympiad Bond Act was carried to the polls in the 1928 elections, providing for the enlargement of the Coliseum. This project was authorized and the seating capacity was increased to 105,000.

Unexpected difficulties, however, intervened before the date of the games. European countries discovered that Los Angeles was not "just outside New York." The problem of transportation costs was made serious by world depression. A group of Cuban athletes who landed at Galveston, Texas, were pained to discover that that port is not a suburb of Los Angeles. The Cubans returned home.

The next major development in the southern California sport world was horse racing. Ever since the days of the Spanish dons racing had been popular here. Always dependent upon gambling, it had experienced a severe setback in 1907, however, when pool selling, bookmaking, and wagering were forbidden by state law. For a quarter of a century racing was barred and racing fans were able to wager only through illegal "bookies" and at the Mexican border resorts, Agua Caliente and Tijuana.

The flood of California dollars poured out at Mexican tracks stirred a boundless envy in the hearts of southern California horsemen and promoters, and in 1933 proponents of legal horseracing introduced a bill into the California legislature to "promote horse breeding and thereby benefit agriculture." The measure also provided for the creation of a California Horse Racing Board "for the licensing and supervision of said horse racing and wagering thereon," and contained a number of conciliatory provisions designed to win favor with non-betting voters. The tracks were not to receive more than eight per cent of the pari-mutuel pools plus "breakage," the aggregate nickels and pennies above the pay-off to ten cents. The state's four per cent was to be allocated to county, industrial, and fruit fairs, the State Emergency Relief Administration, the California Polytechnic School, and the University of California. Supporters of the bill emphasized that, even if the source of revenue was not above reproach, the uses to which the money would be put were on such a high moral plane that criticism of the proposed bill seemed all but unpatriotic. On June 27, 1933, the bill became law by a two-to-one majority vote.

The first track licensed in Los Angeles County under the new law was Santa Anita, which opened on Christmas Day, 1934. Its success was so overwhelming that during the final weeks of the first season the promoters voluntarily reduced their "take" from eight to six per cent in order to forestall criticism of a top-heavy financial report. Encouraged by the success of Santa Anita, another group of promoters purchased ground in Inglewood, about twelve miles from downtown Los Angeles, and began construction of Hollywood Park. Civic groups and a militant church bloc, led by the Reverend Robert P. (Bob) Shuler, objected before the racing board, which refused to grant a license to the track. The promoters countered by raising a cry of monopoly, which resulted in a special investigation by the state assembly in 1936. Among other details the Assembly committee discovered that "breakage" at Santa Anita totaled $409,707 for the 1936 season, that unclaimed and forgotten winnings for the same period amounted to $28,451, and that in three seasons the track had paid $1,350,000 in dividends on a million dollar investment.

To offset these profits the track listed large donations to charity. On this subject, however, the investigating committee said: "The committee does not wish to appear unmindful of the generosity of these donations. Neither does the committe wish to appear unmindful of the business judgment used in the manner of their distribution. The committee, however, has been so impressed by the enormous profits in the business that it is clearly of the opinion that the giving has not yet reached the point where it hurts."

Eventually the board reversed itself and issued a license to Hollywood Park. The track held its inaugural meet during the summer of 1938. Its profits were not so large as those of Santa Anita, though the mutuel "handle" for the summer season totaled $16,858,398.

Santa Anita holds a record (1940) for the largest amount of money ($1,707,202) wagered through pari-mutuels in a single day. This record was established March 2, 1940, date of the running of the $100,000 added Santa Anita Handicap. During the 1938-39 season of 52 days at Santa Anita the total mutuel handle was $34,589,051.

Though football is much younger in the annals of Los Angeles than horse racing, the city ranks today as an important football center. Leading teams are the University of Southern California and the University of California at Los Angeles, members of the Pacific Coast Conference. Both engage in intersectional games. Records of the Los Angeles Coliseum show an attendance of 716,000 at football games in 1938, the Southern California-Notre Dame game alone drawing a crowd of 104,000.

One of intercollegiate football's best known events is the annual Rose Bowl game at Pasadena, in which the leader of the Pacific Coast Conference plays an outstanding team from another section of the country. The Rose Bowl game emerged from the desire to provide an attraction to follow the Tournament of Roses parade which is held on New Year's Day morning. In 1902 the University of Michigan's "point a minute" team overwhelmed the hitherto undefeated Stanford University eleven of that year by a score of 49 to 0; a deficit of about $12,000 was incurred and football as a New Year's Day attraction was permitted to lapse until 1916. In that year Brown University was invited to play Washington State and was defeated, 14 to 0. This defeat instituted the modern series of post-season Bowl games.

Less national in character, but nevertheless attracting over a million patrons during 1938, were the boxing and wrestling matches at the Hollywood American Legion Stadium and the Olympic Auditorium. Fight fans know the best place to see movie stars is not on Hollywood Boulevard but in the first six rows of either of these two major fight clubs. Several eastern states, including New York, do not recognize championship bouts held in California where the state law limits all decision fights to 10 rounds. However there is no lack of interest on the part of local fans and Los Angeles is considered a "good fight town." Save in the wrestling industry, with its synthetic and few distinguished titles, championship bouts are rare. Although Henry Armstrong, ex-welterweight champion and former lightweight champion, is a resident of Los Angeles, he has never defended his titles in his home city. Joe Louis, heavyweight title holder, knocked out Jack Roper in the first round of an undistinguished championship bout at Wrigley Field on April 17, 1939.

Prior to 1915 "boxing exhibitions" up to 20 rounds were permitted in Los Angeles. First to bring top-ranking pugilists to town was Tom McCarey, who staged bouts at Hazard's Pavilion at Fifth and Olive Streets. Jim Jeffries, later heavyweight champion, fought his first professional fight in Los Angeles at the old Manitou Club on Main Street in 1892, and Jack Johnson first gained prominence at the Century Club in the early 1900's. In 1903 Johnson persuaded McCarey to promote a title bout between him and Jeffries, the reigning champion, but McCarey was unable to complete arrangements for the match. Seven years later Johnson defeated Jeffries at Reno, Nevada. Many champions and near-champions, among them Stanley Ketchel, Ad Wolgast, Freddie Welsh, and Abe Attell, trained in and around Los Angeles, generally at Jack Doyle's arena in Vernon, then a popular sport center.

In 1915 the legislature banned professional bouts and limited amateur exhibitions to four rounds. In 1924, however, the limit was extended to include professional 10-round decision contests.

Among other sports that attract large audiences are baseball, auto racing, polo, tennis, basketball, and hockey. Baseball ranks as a favorite and Los Angeles has two teams, both members of the Pacific Coast League. Home games of the Los Angeles Angels are played on Wrigley Field. The Hollywood Stars, financed in part by motion-picture people, play their home games at Gilmore Field. The two teams draw over half a million people a year, the introduction of night games having greatly added to the sport's popularity. Army and Navy teams play at Fort MacArthur and Duncan Field in San Pedro, and exhibition games by the Chicago Cubs, the Pittsburgh Pirates, and the Chicago White Sox attract crowds. These teams hold spring training at Santa Catalina Island, San Bernardino, and Pasadena, respectively.

Fast gaining in popularity is the dangerous sport of midget auto racing which originated in Los Angeles. The season opens in April and continues with weekly races to late fall.

Polo is played on week-end afternoons by members of the motion-picture colony and others able to afford the upkeep of polo ponies. There are six clubs, notably the Riviera Country Club, the Will Rogers Memorial Field, and the Midwick Country Club. Within recent years the quality of the western game has greatly improved.

Southern California tennis is outstanding. Championship matches are held on the courts of the Los Angeles Tennis Club the last week of September, and leading professional players appear frequently, usually on the courts of the Ambassador Hotel. There are more than fifty public and semipublic clubs affiliated with the Southern California Lawn Tennis Association, and 90 per cent of all national championships are held by Californians, a majority of them local players.

Collegiate basketball, played at the Pan-Pacific Auditorium, and collegiate hockey at the Tropical Ice Gardens, have consistently outdrawn ventures in the professional and semiprofessional branches of these games.

Those who seek outdoor recreation find the beaches the greatest attraction. Several private clubs provide beach games, and at Santa Monica and Ocean Park there are municipal playgrounds with card and checker tables, basketball, volleyball, ping pong and badminton courts, and the usual assortment of children's swings and slides. There are amusement piers at Ocean Park, Venice, Redondo, and Long Beach.

The warm temperature of the ocean water permits swimming and bathing most of the year. Surfboarding is a specialty at Palos Verdes; aquaplaning at Newport and Balboa, farther down the coast. Though the majority of the people are not yachtsmen or yacht racing fans, sailing and boating have their devotees both at public piers where various types of craft may be hired, and at several yacht clubs situated along the coast. Outstanding races are the annual midwinter national championship and the 2,000-mile Los Angeles to Honolulu biennial race.

Many varieties of deep sea fish are caught in local waters (*see*

Tour 5A). Some limited fishing is possible without a license or other charges from the municipal piers, and hundreds of land-loving fishermen almost continuously line breakwaters and piers. Those seeking game fish take water taxies plying between the beaches and barges anchored offshore, or numerous live bait boats for half or whole day trips. For more extended ocean trips, private boats are chartered in which to stalk the prize tuna or fighting swordfish.

So much emphasis has been devoted in advertising campaigns to southern California's mild winter climate that Angelenos were pleasantly shocked in recent years to discover the presence of frozen assets. Winter sports became popular in Los Angeles about 1927. The initial event was a snow picnic at Lake Arrowhead; since, Los Angeles has achieved a ranking close to Lake Placid and Minneapolis in winter sports. Skiing, ice hockey, skating, tobogganing, and snowshoeing are important features of the winter seasons at Arrowhead, Big Bear Lake, Big Pines, Mount Baldy, and other public and private resorts, the winter carnival at Big Pines attracting ski jumpers from many parts of the world. In town an outdoor rink and several indoor ice rinks operate the year around.

Bowling, which has been an established sport in Los Angeles for a number of years, gained great favor in 1938, and luxurious recreational centers have been installed throughout the county. In 1940, there were 90 such establishments in southern California of which 45 were in metropolitan Los Angeles. The tough atmosphere and glaring lights of the old-time bowling alley are no longer in evidence. Pavilions are air-conditioned and are indirectly lighted; sound is reduced to a minimum by scientific insulation; leather upholstered chairs provide comfort for spectators; cafes and cocktail lounges are a part of the scene. Bowling lanes have a telescore that makes the tally instantly visible to players and spectators, and a photoelectric device registers fouls. Teletalk broadcasters page bowlers with messages or phone calls and subradio is used to broadcast important matches. Included among the largest centers are the Angeles, Arlington, Beverly Hills, Bimini, Hollywood, Luxor, Pico, Southwest, Whittier, and Sunset, the latter reputed to be the largest in the West, with 52 alleys, and seats for 800 spectators.

During the "reformist" early 1900's when bars were closed at midnight and drinking and dancing in the same establishment was banned, Vernon, a small but tolerant town nearby, was the oasis for night-faring Angelenos. They lined six-deep in front of Jack Doyle's bar, "the longest in the world." In 1912 Baron Long opened the Vernon Country Club, patterned after a saloon and dance hall on San Francisco's famous Barbary Coast. Sportsmen, members of society, movie stars, and hordes of unclassified citizens rubbed elbows at Baron Long's.

With the repeal of Prohibition closing time for bars became two a.m., and new laws permitted the mixing of drinking and dancing. Today Los Angeles night clubs range from the raucous honky-tonks of Main Street, to the ultra-elegant restaurants and clubs of Hollywood, the Sunset Strip, and Beverly Hills. Bars selling drinks for ten cents and fifteen cents, with tiny dance floors and electric phonographs, abound in almost all districts, and in the western and southwestern sections of the city there are more elaborate establishments where tariffs are higher and small "hot" bands assiduously stifle conversation.

Among the favorite spots of movie people in 1939 were the Grace Hayes Lodge on Ventura Boulevard (catering to the San Fernando movie colony), such Sunset Strip establishments as Cafe Lamaze, Ciro's and Dave Chasen's restaurant on Beverly Boulevard. Influenced by fan magazine photographs of movie stars amid balloons and confetti, tourists flock to Hollywood night clubs and restaurants. But Los Angeles residents know that many nights and dollars can be spent at better known night spots without a glimpse of a screen star. After a hard day's work most film folk who enjoy night club entertainment prefer small, secluded spots where the management tries to some extent to shield them from autograph seekers and other troubles.

There are exceptions—but that is the tourist's gamble.

PART II

Los Angeles Points of Interest

Downtown Los Angeles

Visible remains and sites important in every period of Los Angeles' history are seen within a radius of a few blocks of the old Plaza. The oldest of these is the site of the Indian village of Yang-Na, settled long before the arrival of the Spanish conquerors. A few relics of the days of Spanish and Mexican rule stand about the Plaza. Evidences of the city's dissimilar periods and cultures create a feeling of confusion in this vicinity; the monumental modern buildings of the new and still uncompleted Civic Center stand side by side with the grimy structures of former years, designed in pseudo-mission and rococo styles, and the aged, crumbling adobes of the pueblo period. There is contrast even in the angles at which the buildings stand, for old structures that are to be razed face streets that have been re-routed, and the modern buildings the modern thoroughfares.

The business section of the city was formerly around the Plaza, but it gradually expanded toward the southwest, and in time a new central district developed and left the Plaza region a backwash. This newer district, although still the focus of much of the commerce and gaiety of the metropolitan district, is already experiencing serious competition from the sections developing along main arteries and in the suburbs of the greater city.

The irregularly bounded CIVIC CENTER spreads north as far as Ord Street, eastward to Avila Street, southward to First Street, and westward to Olive Street. It is still largely in the blueprint stage, although six of the units—the Federal Building, the City Hall, the County Hall of Justice, the County Hall of Records, the State Building, and the Union Passenger Terminal—have been completed. Seven other buildings—the County Courts, Traffic and Safety, Engineering, Consular Offices, Latin-American Hall, Foreign Trade, and State Board of Public Works—are being designed. The Civic Center plans call for the destruction of numerous landmarks, chiefly around Ferguson Alley, in Old Chinatown, and on Court Hill west of the Hall of Records; in their place will be landscaped lawns and parkways. The Plaza, the Church of Our Lady of the Angels, Olvera Street, and possibly a few other landmarks will be preserved.

1. The 32-story LOS ANGELES CITY HALL (*open workdays 8-5; guides*), bounded by Temple, Main, First, and Spring Sts., was designed by Austin, Parkinson and Martin, and is one of the few exceptions to the 150-foot-height limit set by city ordinance upon building in Los Angeles. Its pyramid-capped obelisk tower rises 28 stories

POINTS OF INTEREST
(Downtown)

1. Los Angeles City Hall
2. Federal Building
3. Los Angeles County Hall of Justice
4. Los Angeles County Hall of Records
5. California State Building
6. Los Angeles Times Building
7. Natick Hotel
8. St. Vibiana's Cathedral
9. Baker Building
10. Merced Theatre Building
11. Pico House
12. Plaza
13. Plaza Church
14. Statue of Fray Junipero Serra
15. Lugo House
16. Zanja Madre
17. Avila Adobe
18. Casa La Golondrina
19. El Camino Watering Trough
20. Miniature Landscape and Fish Pool
21. Los Angeles Union Passenger Terminal
22. Kong Chew Chinese Buddhist Temple
23. Yamato Hall
24. Daisha Mission
25. Hongwanji Buddhist Temple
26. Grand Central Market
27. Angel's Flight
28. Philharmonic Auditorium Building
29. Pershing Square
30. Biltmore Hotel
31. Edison Building
32. Sunkist Building
33. Los Angeles Central Public Library
34. Bible Institute of Los Angeles
35. Richfield Building
36. Clifton Cafeteria
37. Los Angeles Stock Exchange Building
38. Alexandria Hotel

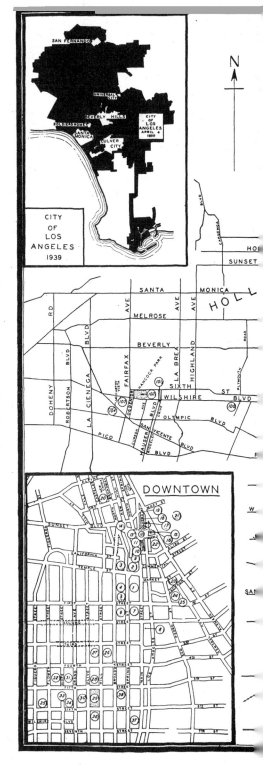

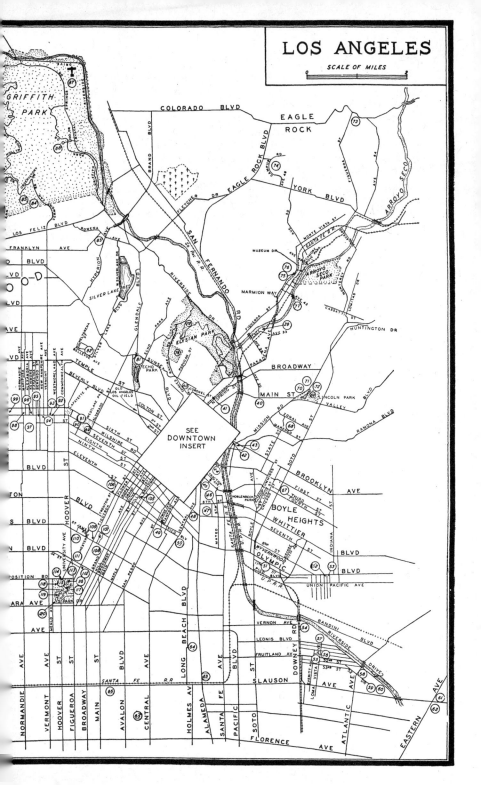

above the four-story base, with the tip 464 feet above the street level. It houses city government offices, including the Police Department and two traffic courts, as well as 31 superior courts.

The base of the building is faced with light-gray California granite; the towering central section and the five-story wings flanking it are of terra cotta. The wings are roofed with dark-hued tiles. Eight heavy buttresses carry the lines of the square central section upward to the 23rd floor, and are duplicated in another series that extends to the balcony of the observation platform. There are sixteen 50-foot columns on the face below the platform and above it rises a stepped pyramid; at the peak of the pyramid is an airplane beacon named in honor of Colonel Charles A. Lindbergh.

The building is entered through a colonnaded and arcaded Forecourt with monolithic columns, tile-and-brick paving, and soft-colored tile panels on the walls. It leads to the Rotunda, in which more than 4,000 pieces of marble are laid in a geometric pattern on the floor. In the Council Chamber are galleries supported by 12 monolithic columns, each of a different kind of marble. Noteworthy are the Board of Public Works Sessions Room, with arcades decorated in green, blue, and gold; the Elevator Lobby, finished in Verona marble, with relief maps showing the city's water system and the projected Civic Center; and the Mayor's Reception Room, which has a floor of East Indian teakwood fastened with dowels.

The ART GALLERY, in Room 351 on the third floor, exhibits paintings by California artists. On clear days the OBSERVATION BALCONY (*open workdays 9:30-4; free*), on the 25th floor, affords a view of the entire city, the mountains, the sea, and the many surrounding communities. The balcony surrounds a large room in which are four large key photographs bearing the names of the principal points seen from the four sides of the platform.

2. The white walls of the FEDERAL BUILDING (*conducted tours by arrangement with postmaster*), in the block between Main, Temple, and Spring Sts., rise 17 stories above Spring Street and 18 stories above Main Street; walls of the sub-story on Main Street are faced with black and gold rainbow granite. The main post office and some sixty United States Government departments and bureaus occupy the greater part of the building. Federal courts are held on the second and the two topmost floors.

The structure, designed by G. Stanley Underwood, is without external embellishment. The central section has a setback at the fourth story. A steel frame makes the building earthquake resistant.

The Spring Street and Main Street entrances are flanked by bronze-based flagpoles and pairs of Doric columns. Between the columns are lacelike aluminum grilles bearing seals of various Federal departments. Ceramic medallions flank the doors. The walls of the lobbies are lined with rose marble and Sienna travertine; the floors are of terrazzo.

3. Oldest of the modern Civic Center buildings, the LOS ANGELES COUNTY HALL OF JUSTICE (*open workdays 8-5*), on

Temple St. between Broadway and Spring St., was completed in 1925 at a cost of $6,000,000. Faced with gray California granite and ornamented with tall polished granite columns—above the balustraded tenth floor level, it represents the last years of the period in which public structures had to have classical embellishments. It is occupied by the County Jail, Criminal Division of the Municipal and Superior Courts, and the offices of the District Attorney, Grand Jury, Sheriff, Tax Collector, Assessor, Health Department, and Coroner.

4. The dusty 12-story LOS ANGELES COUNTY HALL OF RECORDS (*open workdays 9-5*), 220 N. Broadway, is marked for early demolition as the new Civic Center is developed. Its pyramidal gables and fussy ornamentation are typical of the architecture of its time; when it was erected in 1909 it was the million-dollar pride of the city. It stands oblique to Broadway, conforming to old street lines. The offices, which crowd it—those of the County Auditor, Board of Equalization, Civil Service Commission, Board of Supervisors, County Council, Superior Courts, Vital Statistics, and Marriage License Bureau —will eventually be moved to a new County Courts Building.

5. The CALIFORNIA STATE BUILDING (*open workdays 8-5*). First St. between Broadway and Spring St., is the administrative center of state government in southern California. The building, with a broad, 12-story central section and two nine-story wings, was designed by John C. Austin and Frederic M. Ashley. It has simple lines and broad windows, and is faced with light-gray California granite. Although built in 1933, additional quarters are already needed; a supplementary building, to house the State Board of Public Works, has been planned for the northeast corner of First and Olive Streets.

Notable are the lobby, with its columns and pilasters of deep-red Alicante (Spanish) marble, wainscoting of delicate rose marble above a base of green marble, and the floor of black, cream, and red mottled marbles; the Assembly Hall, in which are three brightly colored murals by Lucile Lloyd depicting events in California history; and the California Supreme Court and District Court of Appeals Chambers, completely paneled with oak except behind the seven justices' chairs, where pale-blue tiles have been placed. The ceiling has a similar embellishment.

6. The LOS ANGELES TIMES BUILDING (*conducted tours 3 p.m. weekdays, 2:30 p.m. Sat., reservations 2 days in advance; free*), 202 W. First St., designed by Gordon B. Kaufmann, was built in 1935 at a cost of $4,000,000 for one of the city's three morning newspapers. The structure, with setbacks, has a central section with massive piers and four-story wings. Atop the clock tower is the bronze eagle that survived the dynamiting of the old *Times* plant in 1910 (*see The Historic Background*).

Above the polished black granite base the walls are faced with a pinkish granite to the second floor; above, between the vertical rows of windows separated by dark metal plaques, is cream-colored limestone.

Behind the polished red-granite entrance is the rotunda, with a five and one-half-foot aluminum globe in a bronze base, revolving within a bronze band showing the signs of the zodiac. In the mosaic upon the floor are 13 varieties and colors of marbles in a circular pattern; the base of the walls is faced with reddish marbles, and above are rust-colored murals executed by Hugo Ballin, showing the various phases of newspaper production.

The structure, sound-proofed and air-conditioned, is one of the most modern newspaper plants. A private power plant is the driving force behind the Hoe presses, capable of printing 320,000 papers of 32 pages each in an hour. The auditorium, on the fifth floor, seats 2,000 persons and opens on two roof gardens. The building also contains kitchens, banquet rooms, and remote-control broadcasting rooms.

7. The NATICK HOTEL, 108 W. First St., built in 1880, was once the most fashionable in the city. It boasted of its fireproof construction. The age-discolored marquee over the First Street entrance, the narrow arched windows, and the base of the graceful hardwood staircase—with small, many-globed light standards—represented Victorian elegance. A grilled iron elevator cage rises from the center of the large lobby.

The mile stretch of Main Street, from the Plaza south to about Sixth Street, known as Calle Principal (main street) even in Mexican days, is the principal business street of a district with some 60,000 people of foreign birth or descent—mostly Japanese, Filipinos, Chinese, Mexicans, Negroes, Jews, and Italians. It attracts many and diverse types of derelicts and transients.

Main Street, 25 miles long with its modern extensions, begins north of the city at Mission Road and runs south to the harbor at San Pedro, but only the short section in the city, beginning at the Plaza at Marchessault Street—named for Damien Marchessault, New Orleans gambler and Los Angeles mayor in the 1860's—is a mixture of bars, honkytonks, barber "colleges," tattoo shops, pitchmen, pawn shops, flophouses, and all-night movies serving as dormitories for audiences of derelicts who sleep through continuous reels in spite of the blaring of sound machines.

The frowsiness of most of the buildings is accented by their extravagant and decaying Victorian ornamentation, but the shops and saloons on the street floors are divesting themselves of all ties with the past and growing continually more modern, even junking the lithographs of *Custer's Last Fight,* which once hung in every barroom.

Exodus of the socially elite from the neighborhood of the old Plaza began in the 1870's and was directed south along Main Street. Most of the buildings that remain were erected between 1880 and 1900, when the city's population jumped from 11,000 to 100,000.

8. A rose window and arched niches holding five statues of saints ornament the facade of ST. VIBIANA'S CATHEDRAL (*open 6-8 daily*), 208-216 S. Main St., seat of the Archdiocese of the Province of Southern California. The structure extends from Main Street to

Los Angeles Street, where a low belfry in four stages with a top-heavy dome and tiny lantern strike an incongruous note. The structure itself, with simple walls of gray limestone, a clerestory, buttresses, and severe one-story Doric portico, was designed with much restraint. A relic of St. Vibiana, the child saint, reputedly recovered from the Roman catacombs, is encased in a wax statue, in a gilt-and-plateglass sarcophagus, and reposes in a niche above the high altar. The object is exposed on feast days.

9. The three-story BAKER BUILDING (*open workdays 8:30-12 m.; 1-5 p.m.*), 342 N. Main St., built by Colonel R. S. Baker, was in its day one of the most pretentious structures in town. It shows its Second Empire inspiration in the fluted cast-iron Corinthian pilasters, narrow arched windows, ornate stone cornices, and time-blackened wooden canopy over the street on two sides. Three squat towers are heavily decorated. The Baker block had the first telephone switchboard in Los Angeles and boasted the first elevator, which was raised by Chinese muscle-power.

10. The three-story MERCED THEATRE BUILDING, 418-22 N. Main St., adjoining the Pico House on the south, dates from 1870. It has brick walls covered with discolored gray plaster, and now contains shops and a rooming house.

11. The PICO HOUSE (*always open*), 430 N. Main St., first three-story building in Los Angeles, was built in 1868-69 by Pio Pico, last of the Mexican governors of California, and his brother Andres. The old hotel, its brick walls now stuccoed, is constructed around a large court that formerly held a fountain. In its heyday the hostelry boasted gas lights and extensively advertised its two zinc bathtubs enclosed in wood, one on each of the two upper floors. There are now shops on the street floor, but the hotel is still maintained. Civic Center plans call for the building's demolition.

12. The PLAZA, bounded by N. Main, Marchessault, N. Los Angeles, and Plaza Sts., is a circular plot shaded by rubber trees, palms, and bamboo, and surrounded by a low saw-toothed brick wall with recessed seats. The unbroken rows of wooden benches are continually crowded with loiterers, who doze in the shade or listen to the harangues of economic saviors and religious zealots who hold forth from low concrete platforms that in the 1870's were watering troughs.

In 1781 De Neve platted the Plaza slightly northwest of the present site. Several years after it was ruined by the flood of 1815, it was laid on this slightly higher spot. The life of the pueblo centered about the Plaza from the time of De Neve, though in its early years the place was a treeless, dusty common, in the rainy season a welter of mud. First effort to make the park attractive began in 1859; but wandering goats devoured the shrubs and the natives appropriated the picket fence for firewood.

Though plans for the Civic Center leave the Plaza itself untouched, they threaten the existence of the age-worn buildings around it.

A life-size bronze STATUTE OF FELIPE DE NEVE, founder of Los

Angeles, stands on a boulder in the Plaza pool. The statue was executed by Henry Lion in 1932.

13. The old PLAZA CHURCH (*open 5 a.m.-9 p.m. daily*), 100 Sunset Blvd., faces the Plaza on the west. It is a simple gray-plastered brick building flush with the street and flanked on one side by a bell tower, on the other by a patio entered from the church through a side door and from the street through a gateway in a thick wall. Three date palms in the patio are almost as tall as the two-story edifice itself. The church has undergone many renovations.

The services of La Iglesia de Nuestra Senora la Reina de Los Angeles (the Church of Our Lady the Queen of the Angels), established in 1784, were first held in a small adobe building near what is now Bellevue Street and North Broadway, two blocks to the northwest. Construction of a church was begun in 1814 but when the structure was threatened by the flood of 1815 it was abandoned. Building of the present church, which is on higher ground, was begun in 1818 and it was dedicated on the Feast of the Immaculate Conception of the Virgin Mary, December 8, 1822. Heavy rains in 1859 caused the adobe front to cave in, and in 1861-62 the facade was completely rebuilt and a shingle roof put on. The present *campanario* (bell tower) was built in 1875, and the rectory, a two-story buff-colored stucco building beyond the patio, in 1881. In 1912 the church was enlarged on the west side, and eight memorial windows and a circular sky-light were added. The present tile roof was put in place in 1923.

The "elopement bell," which hangs alone at the pierced left side of the squat companario, is the best toned of the four. It was obtained for the church at the suggestion of the Parish priest, by Henry Fitch, a young American adventurer, as "penance and reparation" for having eloped to Chile with Josefa Carrillo after failing to win her family's consent to marriage. The lower left bell in front was given by Mission San Gabriel in 1821. The other two front bells, the larger of which is used to toll requiem, were made, like the "elopement bell," by G. H. Holbrook of Massachusetts, and were transferred from San Gabriel in 1827.

Over the round arch of the recessed entrance between the two windows, and in medallions on both sides of the arch, are small oblongs with figures incised in cement, all that remains of distemper-murals done by Henri Penelon in 1861. The east end of the present building is the oldest unit of the church and it is believed that removal of the paint in the interior of this section will reveal old murals executed by Indians. The baptistry, directly under the choir loft, contains the original copper baptismal font, used in some 65,000 christenings.

14. A life-size bronze STATUE OF FRAY JUNIPERO SERRA, founder of the California missions, at the intersection of New High St., Bellevue Ave., and Sunset Blvd., faces southeast toward the old Plaza Church. The figure stands on two long concrete islands in the street. The upraised right hand holds a cross; in the palm of the

extended left hand is a miniature mission. The work was executed by E. Cadorin of Santa Barbara.

15. Facing the Plaza on the east is the dormer-windowed LUGO HOUSE (*adm. by permission of occupants*), 516-522 N. Los Angeles St., built by Vicenti Lugo in 1840. It is the only old two-story adobe in the city. Little of it is visible; on the first floor under the balcony are glass-fronted shops, and the rear has been walled with brick. A gable roof with dormers has been added and both ends of the long balcony—which is supported by seven green- and red-painted wooden posts—has been walled in to form rooms. Part of the old balcony, with its balustrades, remains in the center, and the arrow-pointed edging on the eaves shows.

Owing to miscalculations, the house was built obliquely to the curb, two feet nearer at one end than the other. When the front was built, however, it was aligned with the street, but the posts and balcony remain askew.

OLVERA STREET (*concessions open 8 a.m.-2 a.m.*), extending between Marchessault and Macy Sts., is a narrow, block-long alley designed to give tourists a taste of Mexico. Sandwiched between the back walls of old business buildings, the 70-odd stores and booths owned and operated by Mexicans have gay decorations and displays of Mexican foods, pottery, and trinkets.

This old street was named for Augustin Olvera, who fought against Fremont during the American conquest of California. It degenerated into an alley of mud and refuse soon after the American occupation and was not reclaimed until the fall of 1929, when brick and tile paving was laid, trees and shrubbery were planted, and old houses restored. Although the corporation that administers the street has renamed it *El Paseo de Los Angeles* (Walk of the Angels), it is still popularly known by the original name.

Olvera Street's chief festival period, December 16 to 24, is celebrated with *Los Posados* (the lodgings), a pageant re-enacting Mary's journey to Bethlehem in search of a birthplace for Jesus.

16. Near the Marchessault Street entrance to Olvera Street is a three-foot red-brick strip that marks the course of the ZANJA MADRE, or mother ditch. Built in 1782-83, it carried water, raised by a wooden water wheel from the Los Angeles River near Elysian Park, to the pueblo for all purposes—irrigation, bathing, watering stock, and—near its source—for drinking. During the dry season it also served as a reservoir. Meandering along the east side of Los Angeles Street, the mother *zanja* branched into smaller *zanjas*. The white settlers, in the 1850's and 1860's, called the *zanjas* (zan-khas) "sanky ditches." With the introduction of a more modern system in 1863, the ditches were filled in.

17. Adjoining the relic of the Zanja Madre is the renovated AVILA ADOBE (*open 8 a.m.-10 p.m.; adm. 10¢*), 14 Olvera St., the oldest residence in Los Angeles, possibly built as early as 1818 and not later than 1824. It was constructed by Francisco Avila, one-time *alcalde*

(mayor) of the pueblo. Only one seven-room wing remains of the L-shaped 18-room house that was the finest building in town in its day. This remaining wing is a large one-story block with gabled roof, age-darkened walls, and a narrow porch. The walls, two-and-one-half feet thick, show remnants of the cottonwood beams taken from the banks of the nearby Los Angeles River.

Markers, both outside and inside, commemorate various historical events, among them the use of the adobe by Commodore Stockton after the widow Avila's distaste for American occupation caused her to abandon her home. Senora Avila returned after the departure of Stockton and lived in the house until her death in 1855. The earthquake of 1857 destroyed about half of the structure; before restoration began in 1929 a sign "condemned" hung on the roofless, dilapidated walls.

18. One of the city's first brick buildings, CASA LA GOLONDRINA (*open 8 a.m.-10 p.m.; free*), 35 Olvera St., is now occupied by a cafe. It is of disputed age; it was built by an Austrian immigrant after 1850 and before 1865, when it was sold to Antonio Pelanconi. The Pelanconis lived on the second floor and on the first made the wine they sometimes sold, this giving rise to the legend that the house was Los Angeles' first winery. Of interest are the hand-grooved balcony, the low heavily-beamed ceilings, and the fireplace in the first floor.

19. At the Macy Street end of Olvera Street is the stone EL CAMINO WATERING TROUGH, enclosed by a rustic fence and shaded by a small olive tree. The trough, hand-hewn by San Fernando Mission Indians in 1820, is carved from a yellow sandstone boulder. Until its presentation to Olvera Street in 1930 by the Los Angeles Department of Water and Power the trough stood in front of Mission San Fernando (*see Tour 7*) beside El Camino Real. In earlier days it held water for the mounts of travelers and for stock driven to and from Mission San Gabriel.

CHINA CITY (*open 8 a.m-2 a.m.*), bounded by Ord, Main, Macy, and New High Sts., is an American-promoted, Chinese-operated amusement center designed to attract tourists. It was partly destroyed by fire early in 1939, but is now restored. The "city" stands out as an oriental oasis in the midst of Los Angeles' oldest section, which is being reclaimed in the Civic Center new building program. The concessions grouped around a small plaza are visited in a rickshaw (*25¢ per ride*).

Much of the construction material of the "city" was donated: pink sandstone from the old Federal Building was used for the gate, stairs, and walls, and the dedicatory stone of the entrance is from the old *Times* Building. Bamboo poles are from the Los Angeles Park Department, cobblestones from the Street Department.

NEW CHINATOWN (*cafes open 8 a.m.-2 a.m.*), Broadway and College St., is one of two Chinatowns that developed when construction of the Union Passenger Terminal caused demolition of a large part of old Chinatown.

The North Broadway entrance opens into a landscaped court that leads into a narrow arcade lined with shops where bean sprouts, bean curd, herbs, and other Chinese delicacies are sold. The modern though still oriental town consists of a series of separate two-story buildings, of buff, tan, and green stucco, with curved roofs and continuous second-story balconies, and occasional octagonal windows, built around the four sides and in the center of a rectangle.

20. The MINIATURE LANDSCAPE AND FISH POOL, in the center of New Chinatown, was designed and built by Louie Hong Kay and associate artists. Enclosed by a low, square brick wall, a miniature hill, landscaped with dwarf evergreen trees and succulent plants, rises in the center of the pool. Miniature bridges and paths lead up among small figurines of the Chinese Eight Immortals to the hill's summit, where a blue figure of the goddess Quan Yin, guarded on either side by small blue lions, is protected by the arch of a miniature shrine. A small Chinese flag is mounted above the summit.

Visible on the floor of the pool, beneath the gold and silver flashing bodies of fish, are hundreds of coins cast into the water by Chinatown visitors who hope thereby to make wishes come true; the coins are periodically collected by the Chinese merchants who built and maintain the pool, and are applied to the fund for Chinese War Refugees.

21. The huge LOS ANGELES UNION PASSENGER TERMINAL, Alameda St. between Aliso and Macy Sts., designed by a group of architects headed by Donald B. Parkinson, is a T-shaped group of 30 low stuccoed, tile-roofed buildings dominated by a 135-foot observation tower with a clock. The transcontinental and north-south trains of the Southern Pacific, Union Pacific, and Atchison, Topeka and Santa Fe railroads use the terminal.

The large main structure and the smaller buildings are separated by narrow air spaces in a manner intended to absorb earthquake shock.

In the main building is the information desk; to the left is the Main Concourse, with ticket offices and rest rooms; to the right a large arcade leads to the restaurant and kitchen; in the rear is the waiting room. Flanking the waiting room are two large patios; one, the South Patio, with pepper, palm, and olive trees and trumpet and cup-of-gold vines, is intended to represent California planting and garden design at its best. Immediately east of the south patio is the Reception Hall, which is next to the departure and arrival lobby. East of this lobby is a passenger tunnel with ramps giving access to eight platforms and 16 tracks. In the utility buildings on both sides of the departure and arrival lobby, mail, baggage, and express are handled; in one is the power plant. A basement garage has space for 120 automobiles, and parking islands in front of the buildings hold 400 more cars.

Most of the ramshackle red brick buildings of Old Chinatown which cluttered the section east of the Plaza for more than half a century, were razed in 1933 to make way for the Union Passenger Terminal, and most of the remainder will be demolished to make room for a parkway. The old town developed slowly: there were but two Chinese here in 1850, about 2,000 in 1900 (18 years after passage of the first Exclusion Act), and 3,009 in 1930, giving the city fourth rank in Chinese populations in the United States. The dimly lit narrow alleys of Old Chinatown, reminders of the Cantonese origin of most of the inhabitants, are now virtually gone, but the festivities of Chinese New Year (*usually in Feb. or Mar.*), with exploding 'crackers and dragons writhing through the streets, continue.

22. KONG CHEW CHINESE BUDDHIST TEMPLE (*usually open until 5 p.m.*), 215½ Ferguson Alley, occupies the second floor of a small red brick building. Entrance is through a brick archway, an alley, a courtyard, and up orange-painted stairs. The use of unshaded electric lights over the highly-gilded wooden panels produces a tawdry effect. The air is weighted with the perfumed smoke from joss sticks smouldering in peanut oil, burning to the five small gods in the altar. Among these is the grab-bag god with a pile of straws, each straw with a prescription for some ailment wrapped around it. The health seeker draws a straw from the pile and trusts in the god of chance for a cure.

The JAPANESE QUARTER, locally called Little Tokio, is bounded on the north by Aliso St., on the east by Central Ave., on the south by Fourth St., and on the west by Los Angeles St. About 35,000 persons, by far the largest urban group of Japanese in continental United States, either live or do business here. It is one of the oldest sections of the city, a fact little apparent in the spick-and-span stores, neat window displays, and highly colored banners and signs. First Street is the main business thoroughfare.

Little Tokio is gayest during festivals. The Bon festival, July 13-16, which honors ancestral spirits, is sometimes called the "Feast of the Lanterns" by Americans. The Nisei festival, participated in by second generation American-Japanese, is held in August; features are boys in ancient costume dueling with bamboo swords, and dancing girls. The 900-year-old Hina Matsuri (doll festival) is held on March 3 of each year.

The section supports three daily newspapers and one weekly paper, uses telephone directories in Japanese. Little Tokio was first occupied in large numbers after the earthquake and fire in San Francisco in 1906.

23. In YAMATO HALL, the Japanese Community Center, 321 E. Jackson St., occasional road shows from Japan are presented.

24. Lantern standards and superimposed *torii,* or bird perch, give the only Oriental feeling to the DAISHA MISSION (*open 9 a.m. to midnight*), 133 N. Central Ave., a one-story frame building, where the Shing-on sect of Mahayana Buddhists hold their meetings. The light-green interior is hung with hundreds of white paper strips bearing names of worshipers who have made offerings. The altar, which gives the effect of being deeply recessed, screens a painting of Buddha brought from Mount Koya, near Osaka, Japan, scene of the sect's founding in 804 A.D.

25. The HONGWANJI BUDDHIST TEMPLE (*adm. by application*), 119 N. Central Ave., a three-story brick building erected in 1925, belongs to the Jodo Shinshyu sect of the Buddhists. Except for the cement canopy over the entrance, in the form of a *torii,* the building is occidental in appearance. The auditorium, seating 1,000, is simple and modern, but the main altar is richly Oriental; it holds a small Buddha, and has intricate red and gilt ornamentation softly lighted by small electric bulbs; in front are two black pillars, and incense burners.

26. The GRAND CENTRAL MARKET (*open Mon. to Fri. 8-6; Sat. 8 a.m.-9 p.m.*), extending through the block from 317-323 S. Broadway to 314-320 S. Hill St., is the city's largest retail dispensary of perishable foodstuffs. More than 100 business establishments occupy the space and between 35,000 and 50,000 shoppers pour through it daily.

27. ANGEL'S FLIGHT (*open 6 a.m.-12:15 a.m.; round trip fare 5¢*), 3rd and Hill Sts., is a funicular railway transporting passengers 315 feet up and down the steep slope of Bunker Hill between Hill and Olive Streets. An observation tower, rising 100 feet above the station over the mouth of the 3rd Street Tunnel, commands a view of the distant San Gabriel Mountains. In the years immediately following its construction by Colonel J. W. Eddy in 1901, the "flight" was an outstanding tourist attraction. During the 1920's it carried as high as 12,000 passengers a day; this has now dwindled to about three thousand.

28. The PHILHARMONIC AUDITORIUM BUILDING, 427 W. 5th St., is the home of the Los Angeles Philharmonic Orchestra (*see The Arts*), and the Temple Baptist congregation. The exterior of the nine-story structure was remodeled in 1938 on simple, modern lines. The building was erected in 1906 by Temple Baptist Church on the site of the old Hazard's Pavilion, the city's first large concert hall.

29. PERSHING SQUARE, bounded by 5th, 6th, Hill, and Olive Sts., has brick-paved, palm-shaded walks lined with wooden benches generally crowded until the late hours of night. The large brick-paved central plaza is surrounded by banana trees and backed by taller clumps of bamboo. In its center is a large pool and 16-foot fountain in which water trickles over the sculptured figures of four cherubs. Formerly called Central Park, it was renamed in 1918 to honor General John J. Pershing, World War commander.

At the northeast corner of the park is the SPANISH WAR MEMORIAL, a 20-foot granite statue showing a Spanish War veteran at parade rest. Erected in 1900, it was designed by S. M. Goddard. Nearby is a bronze cannon made in 1751 for the navy of Louis XV of France; it was captured in 1898 at Santiago, Cuba, by the American corps commanded by Major General William R. Shafter, who presented it to the city.

On Fifth Street facing the Philharmonic Auditorium is a heroic STATUE OF BEETHOVEN, given by the personnel of the Philharmonic

Orchestra in 1932 and dedicated to William Andrews Clark, Jr., founder of the orchestra. At the northwest corner is the WORLD WAR MEMORIAL, a life-size bronze figure of a doughboy on an 18-foot granite obelisk base. It was designed by Humberto Pedretti, and placed in 1924. In the grass, to the right of the walk near the northwest entrance, is a plaque dedicated "In the memory of Benny, a squirrel." Time was when Benny achieved wide notice by carrying nuts through the congested streets around Pershing Square to his various caches; many grieved and remembered the day in 1934 when the traffic got him. At the southwest corner is an iron cannon from the *U.S.S. Constitution,* presented to the city by the American Legion in 1935.

30. The E-shaped, 13-story BILTMORE HOTEL, 515 S. Olive St., has modified Spanish Renaissance details; the red brick walls have white terra-cotta facing at the top floor. Balconies project from various floors. Corinthian columns and pilasters ornament the walls of the street fronts. With 1,500 rooms, this is the city's largest hotel. The Olive Street building was completed in 1923, the 500-room Grand Avenue addition in 1928. The wide Fifth Street corridor, the *Galeria Real,* is hung with paintings; opening on it is the BILTMORE ART SALON (*open 10 a.m.-6 p.m., 7-9 p.m. daily; free),* in which are shown oils and water colors, chiefly the work of American—particularly Californian—artists.

31. The EDISON BUILDING (*open 8-5 Mon.-Fri.),* 601 W. 5th St., designed by Allison and Allison, is the 13-story home of the Southern California Edison Company. It has setbacks at the third, fourth, twelfth, and thirteenth floors, and is faced with granite, limestone, and buff terra cotta. At night the three-story tower, crowned by neon lights, is illuminated by colored searchlights. In the marble-trimmed entrance lobby is Hugo Ballin's allegorical mural *Power;* in the elevator lobby are three murals, *Transmission and Distribution* by Barse Miller, and *White Coal* by Conrad Buff.

32. The SUNKIST BUILDING (*open 9-5 weekdays),* 707 W. 5th St., headquarters of the California Fruit Growers Exchange, stands on ground cut away from the flank of steep Bunker Hill. Designed by Walker and Eisen in the modern manner, the U-shaped building, topped by a roof-garden and a one-story tower, has strong vertical lines. Four murals, by Frank Bowers and Arthur Prunier in collaboration, enhance the interior: two near the bronze doors at the entrance, and two in the second floor Board Room. They contrast present orange-growing methods with those of mission days.

33. The LOS ANGELES CENTRAL PUBLIC LIBRARY (*open 9-9 weekdays; only periodical rooms open Sun. and holidays 1-9),* 5th St. between Flower St. and Grand Ave., rises from the asymetrically landscaped five-acre grounds shaded by laurel, acanthus, olive, palm, and cypress trees. The low, buff-colored stuccoed building was designed in a straightforward manner with pylons giving emphasis to the facade. Over the entrance are sculptures; a mosaic of brilliant Spanish

tiles in geometric and solar design ornaments the pyramid upon the central tower. Surmounting the pyramid is a sculptured hand bearing a torch. The structure, erected in 1926, was designed by Bertram Grosvenor Goodhue (Carleton Monroe Winslow, Associate); the sculptures are by Lee Lawrie. The building is the main unit of the municipal library system, which has 48 branches and 69 book stations. In the United States it ranks (1939) second in number of books circulated annually, and fourth in number of books owned.

In the lecture room on the Fifth Street level lectures, forums, concerts, and art exhibits are held. Adjoining it on the east is the Children's Court, a patio graced by undulating trees in ivy-topped tile wells, and an eight-foot fountain of veined sienna marble in lotus design. Wall carvings have Mother Goose subjects and others favored by children. On the east wall is a fresco, *Stampeding Buffalo,* executed by Charles M. Kassler for the Federal Art Project.

The Ivanhoe Room, south of the court, is for children; on its walls are murals of scenes from Scott's *Ivanhoe* by Julian E. Garnsey and A. W. Parsons.

In a niche at the head of the Fifth Street stairs on the second floor is a large, symbolic, expressionless figure of Civilization in Italian marble and bronze. Guarding the stair top are two black marble sphinxes with bronze head-dresses, holding plaques inscribed with excerpts from Plutarch. In the second floor rotunda, with its elaborately stenciled dome and arches, are 12 murals by Dean Cornwell. Pale-colored and thickly peopled, they present a pageant of California history. More pictorial and more deeply colored are the 13 murals of scenes in state history on the walls of the History Room, south of the rotunda. They are by Albert Herter.

34. The BIBLE INSTITUTE OF LOS ANGELES, 558 S. Hope St., a co-educational, nondenominational evangelistic training school, occupies the 13-story south wing of its own building adjoining the Public Library. In this wing are the classrooms, dormitories, and cafeteria of the institute. The 10-story central section of the three-unit structure—like the other sections, ornamented with modified Renaissance details—is an auditorium used by the non-sectarian CHURCH OF THE OPEN DOOR. In the north wing is a privately operated hotel. Atop the building are two large signs stating in neon-lighted letters, "JESUS SAVES," and 11 manually operated bells upon which hymns are played three times daily. The Institute, an outgrowth of a young men's Bible class of 1906, offers day and evening theological instruction, and grants the degrees of Bachelor of Theology, Bachelor of Christian Education, and Bachelor of Sacred Music.

35. The 13-story RICHFIELD BUILDING (*open 8-5 Mon.-Fri.*), 555 S. Flower St., designed by Morgan, Walls and Clements, symbolizes the "black gold" of the oil fields; upon the black terra-cotta walls are strong vertical lines accented by gold strips. At the top of the structure a 130-foot skeleton-steel tower brings the total height above

the city's 150-foot building height limit; special permission was obtained for its erection. Over the main entrance are heroic figures in gold by Haig Patigian, representing Aviation, Postal Service, Industry and Commerce. The vestibule is richly decorated in various marbles.
36. The CLIFTON CAFETERIA (*open 6 a.m.-8 p.m.*), 618 S. Olive St., locally famous as "the Golden Rule cafeteria," serves some 16,000 meals daily for any price the customer wishes to pay. Each check, although bearing the regular price of the meal, urges the patron to pay any sum he thinks fair, or nothing if he wishes. The large dining room is decorated with a fountain, artificial palms, flowers, canaries, wall mottoes, and illuminated pictures, most of which depict Biblical themes. There is organ music, and singing by bus-boys and girls. An information desk provides free rental, travel, and civic-government information; free sightseeing trips are available; free advice in planning food budgets is offered; a weekly publication, *Food 4 Thot,* distributed free to patrons, prints customers' letters and poetic contributions, and inspirational paragraphs clipped from other publications; and a Guests' Exchange finds friends for lonely diners. At a second cafeteria, 648 S. Broadway, with an indoor waterwheel and artificial rocks, caves, and trees, five-cent "subsistence meals" are served in the basement (*2:15-4 daily*) to the needy. The two cafeterias are operated for profit by Clifford E. Clinton, whose civic betterment campaign was largely responsible for the recall of Mayor Frank L. Shaw in 1938 and the election of Superior Court Judge Fletcher E. Bowron as mayor.
37. The LOS ANGELES STOCK EXCHANGE BUILDING (*open weekdays 10-11 a.m.*), 618 S. Spring St., is a five-story structure of simple design with a sturdy granite facade broken at the second story level by two narrow, grilled apertures. High above the entrance are three bas-relief panels separated by large fluted pilasters; the central panel shows *Finance* seated on a throne, the bull and the bear—systole and diastole of exchange—on either side. The left panel is *Research,* and the right *Production.* The entrance is of bronze and the lobby and corridor are lined with Sienna travertine. The trading floor is modeled after that of the New York Exchange. The Stock Exchange Club and the Stock Exchange Institute have their quarters in the building, which was erected in 1930.
38. The ALEXANDRIA HOTEL, SW. corner 5th and Spring Sts., an eight-story building with three griffins on the corners of the third-floor base, was in its heyday the largest and finest hotel in Los Angeles. The city's first fire-proof Class A building, it was opened late in 1906. After more elaborate hotels in the newer business districts were built, the Alexandria's popularity ebbed, and for several years it was closed. Modernized and redecorated, it was reopened in 1938.

The Industrial Section

Although Los Angeles is widely known for its manufacture of motion pictures (*see The Movies*) and aircraft (*see Santa Monica and Tour 7*), and the extensive commercial development around its harbor (*see The Harbor*), relatively few people are aware that it produces such diversified goods as automobiles, clothing, pottery, and canned fish in such quantities as to put it in a high place among the industrial cities of the nation (*see The Historic Background*).

Although the city's industrial plants are widely scattered, its largest industrial district is a fairly compact stretch along the railroad-lined Los Angeles River, plants overflowing the city limits into many small, new, independent communities that wholly depend upon the factories for their livelihood. The industrial plants described in this section of the book are representative.

39. The J. A. BAUER POTTERY CO. PLANT (*visitors 8-2:30, workdays*), 415 W. Ave. 33, occupying two drab brick plants and covering a five-acre site, produces pottery glazed in 14 brilliant hues, as well as the more ordinary red clay pots. Some 25,000 pieces, utilizing more than 15 tons of California clay, are turned out daily for wide distribution.

Guides show visitors the various processes: the washing, filtering, and compressing of the clay; the shaping on wheels turned by foot-treads, or in plaster of Paris molds by jiggermen. An experienced jiggerman with an assistant turns out an average of 2,000 pieces in an eight-hour day. After being shaped, the pottery is dried, sponged, and fired, passing through the hands of some 25 workers. The firing is done in eight kilns of the old-fashioned type, and two of the newer tunnel type. The solutions forming the brilliant glazes are mixed by a secret formula and appear pale and chalk-like when applied to the pottery after its first firing; they turn to deep rich hues during the second firing.

40. The LOS ANGELES BREWERY (*45-minute guided tour, 2-5 workdays*), 1920 N. Main St., housed in red brick buildings of the massive Victorian type dominated by a clock tower, is the largest on the Pacific coast. The plant can daily produce 1,800 barrels of beer, each holding 31 gallons.

After being served with the brewery's product in a luxurious tap-room, visitors are conducted through the plant to view the steaming of hops; the mixing and cooking department; the 300-barrel fermenting tanks; the huge, steel, glass-lined storage tanks; the filtering room, with its great presses and tanks; and the bottling room, where the bottles are automatically sterilized, cooled, filled, pasteurized, capped, and labeled. Another production line handles 260 cans of beer a minute.

41. The CAPITOL MILLING COMPANY FLOUR MILL (*open to groups on request*), 1231 N. Spring St., occupies a large group of brick and cement buildings. Although the exact date of establishment is doubtful, the company, whose plant was called the Eagle Mills until 1853, is believed to be the oldest in Los Angeles. It was the seventh name in the city's first telephone directory, which listed 91 subscribers.

The mill, which can produce 500 to 600 barrels of flour daily, is operated completely by electric power.

42. Huge signs call attention to the 15-acre CUDAHY PACKING COMPANY PLANT (*45-minute guided tour, 9-4 workdays*), 803 E. Macy St., the largest meat packing establishment in the far West. In the 10 large buildings and various smaller structures 2,000,000 pounds of meat is prepared weekly for market. Ten million dollars worth of livestock is slaughtered yearly. On an average the plant daily slaughters 1,200 pigs, 300 to 500 cattle, 1,200 sheep, and 100 to 200 calves.

Visitors are shown the coolers, where beef is kept at 38° Fahrenheit pending shipment; the rooms where ham is boned, rolled, boiled or baked, and wrapped in cellophane; and the rooms where bacon is sliced and lard and oleomargarine are wrapped and packed. The killing, skinning, singeing, washing, and cutting processes can be seen only on request.

43. The OLD MISSION WINERY (*visitors 9-3 workdays*), 330 N. Mission Rd., occupies a brick building erected in 1881 and a newer concrete structure with tile roofs and arched recesses along its walls. It produces 100,000 to 300,000 gallons of sweet wines and 5,000 to 8,000 gallons of brandy annually. Visitors are shown the fermenting room, with rows of 10,000-gallon fermenting tanks; the storage room, with 30,000-gallon tanks; the pot stills, where alcohol for fortifying wines is distilled; and the bottling and barreling departments. Samples of the company's products are offered at the end of the tour.

44. In the rambling old brick LOS ANGELES SOAP COMPANY PLANT (*visited on application; one-hour tour*), 617 E. 1st St., spreading over 20 acres, some 600 employees produce more than 75 brands of soap. The company was established in 1860, when Los Angeles industry was in its infancy. Visitors are shown the mammoth boiling vats, the glycerine-extracting vats, the refining process, and the shaping and wrapping of the soap bars.

45. The COFFEE PRODUCTS OF AMERICA, INCORPORATED, PLANT (*open to groups on application*), 800 Traction Ave., is a five-story building of red brick and reinforced concrete. The company processes coffee, tea, and spices. The coffee is imported from Hawaii, Mexico, Central America, Colombia, Brazil, Java, Arabia, and Africa, blended, roasted for 16 minutes at a 300° temperature,

cut by large circular knives, and packed in tins under 31 inches of vacuum.

46. The NATIONAL BISCUIT COMPANY COOKY BAKERY (*visited on application; 45-minute tour*), 673 Mateo St., occupies a six-story brick-faced building covering nearly half a block. Visitors are conducted through a child's dream of heaven—an inexhaustible cooky factory. The intricate machines mix, roll, and cut 50 varieties of cookies, and feed them through gigantic "tunnel" ovens.

47. The CALIFORNIA WALNUT GROWERS ASSOCIATION PACKING HOUSE (*visited on application*), 1745 E. 7th St., is a seven-story tan reinforced-concrete building containing the main offices and one of the two Los Angeles shelling plants of the co-operative organization. Approximately 650 workers handle 10,000,000 pounds of walnuts annually in this plant. The two shelling plants and a warehouse handle the entire crop of the association, averaging 72,000,000 pounds annually.

The walnuts are graded and branded according to size and quality. Loose, stained, or unshapely nuts are shelled. Visitors see the shelling process by an automatic cracking machine, with 24 pairs of curved vertical jaws; the separation of shells and hand-sorting process; the passage of the meats through a cleaning machine; and the boxing for wholesale use by bakers and confectioners, or sealing in vacuum cans for retail markets.

The state association, a federation of 28 local co-operative walnut packing groups, was incorporated in 1912 as a non-profit organization, wholly owned by its grower members. It now represents 8,000 growers operating 135,000 acres of orchards (*see Tour 3*), and markets 85 per cent of the state's walnut crop. Members of the association receive the actual selling price, less the cost of grading, packing, and selling.

48. The 500 stalls of the LOS ANGELES WHOLESALE TERMINAL MARKET, 7th St. from Central Ave. to Alameda St., occupy a large two-story concrete building with short projecting wings, and two similar buildings without wings—the three forming a long narrow open quadrangle covering more than 21 acres. The terminal is the largest wholesale market in Los Angeles. Some $45,000,000 worth of fruit and vegetables, virtually all of the fresh garden produce consumed in the city, annually passes through it and the smaller markets nearby.

In the terminal are 105 produce stores, offices of produce brokers and marketing associations of the U.S. Department of Agriculture, accountants, lawyers, doctors; there are also bank branches, telegraph and express facilities, and even barber shops, beauty shops, and restaurants. Connected with the market are an enormous cold storage plant, and four warehouses, the largest, seven stories high.

Trading begins at 3 a.m. except on Sunday. Until long after dawn there is much hubbub and confusion in the market place as the trucks of buyers and sellers load and unload their produce.

Most of the market's produce is delivered within a radius of 100 miles of Los Angeles, though other parts of southern California and neighboring states are also served. Refrigerator trucks holding 100 tons take fresh fruits and vegetables to Nevada, Utah, Colorado and Oklahoma, and as far north as Seattle. Train shipments are made to the Atlantic seaboard.

49. The LOS ANGELES PLANT OF THE GOLDEN STATE COMPANY, LTD. (*visitors 8:30-5 workdays*), 1120 Towne Ave., covering more than two blocks, employing more than 800 people, and distributing $25,000,000 worth of milk and butter annually, is the largest establishment of its kind in California. The plant, belonging to an organization that handles a third of the state's milk, is one of seven large milk distributors and processors in Los Angeles.

Although operating several dairy farms of its own, the company buys most of its milk from independent producers, over whose dairies it maintains supervision. The product from the various dairies is blended to produce uniform quality, pasteurized by being held at a temperature of 142° for 30 minutes, rapidly cooled to 35°, and bottled by machines that wash, sterilize, fill, and cap the bottles without manual aid.

50. The PLANT OF THE LOS ANGELES COCA-COLA BOT-TLING COMPANY (*visitors*), 1334 S. Central Ave., somewhat resembles an ocean liner. While its gleaming white walls with their numerous portholes look as though they were constructed of steel plate they are actually of concrete. The lone tower is a stylized ship's bridge, and the interior, continuing the nautical motif, is lined with mahogany and trimmed with stainless steel. The factory is one of 1,200 Coca-Cola plants in the United States.

Viewing the operations from a promenade deck, visitors see the battery of six large washing machines, cleaning and sterilizing more than 50,000 bottles an hour. Other machines fill them with syrup and charged water, and add a cap.

WYVERNWOOD, spreading over seventy-two landscaped acres along E. Olympic Blvd. and E. 8th St. between Soto St. and Grande Vista Dr., is a government-supervised but privately owned and financed low-cost housing project. With a total of 1,102 units, the project comprises 142 two-story buildings, 14 acres of lawns, 54 acres of parks planted to more than 600,000 trees, flowering plants, and shrubs, and a 5-acre children's playground.

Wyvernwood was completed in January 1940 at a cost of $6,200,-000, of which $3,000,000 was a bank loan insured by the Federal Housing Administration, which requires the owners to set aside 25 per cent of all income for maintenance and repair, and dictates the rent schedule. To meet the first requirement a full-time staff of gardeners, painters, carpenters, plumbers, and electricians is maintained. Rents for the three-, five-, and six-room apartments, flats, and studios range from $29.25 to $43.75 a month, unfurnished. Designed for families, preferably with children, of business, trades, and professional people with incomes between $125 to $400 a month, the units are rented on

Art and Education

Index of American Design
A STATION OF THE CROSS, MISSION SAN GABRIEL ARCANGEL

PROMETHEUS, MURAL BY JOSE OROZCO
IN FRAY HALL, POMONA COLLEGE, CLAREMONT

Boyd Cooper

LOGGIA, MISSION SAN JUAN CAPISTRANO

Burton O. Burt

BELFRY, MISSION SAN GABRIEL ARCANGEL

MISSION SAN FERNANDO

F. W. Carter

DETAIL FROM PAINTING, *RANCHO LA BREA PITCH POOLS*

IMPERIAL ELEPHANT, LOS ANGELES
MUSEUM OF HISTORY, SCIENCE, AND ART

Theodore Baron

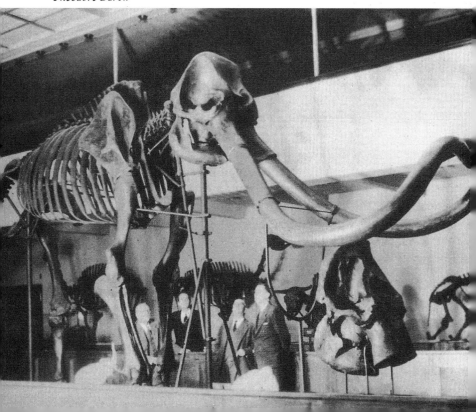

F.W. Carter
IN THE PLANETARIUM, GRIFFITH OBSERVATORY, LOS ANGELES

YOUNG PUBLIC SCHOOL ARTIST

Luckhaus Studio

EXPERIMENTAL PUBLIC SCHOOL, LOS ANGELES
Richard J. Neutra, Architect

THOMAS JEFFERSON HIGH SCHOOL, LOS ANGELES
Stiles O. Clement, Architect   *Board of Education, Los Angeles*

HOLLYWOOD BOWL

MT. WILSON OBSERVATORY

a thirty-day basis with the verbal understanding that the renter will remain at least one year.

The architectural style is eclectic, and the buildings are grouped to avoid monotony through the close proximity of similar designs and colors. Wide lawns and gardens separate the buildings, all of which face upon parkways rather than the street. Designed to be earthquake and fire resistant, exterior walls are of metal-mesh reinforced concrete. Floors are of one-inch hardwood, walls are insulated against heat and sound, and each unit is equipped with electric water heaters, gas or electric room heaters, individual electric refrigerators, and gas or electric ranges.

51. The CALIFORNIA ROTOGRAVURE PLANT (*visited on application*), 2801 E. 11th St., a one-story brick and glass building, does commercial rotogravure work, and prints several weekly and monthly publications.

Visitors see the art department, where pages are designed; the camera room, with cameras capable of making a negative two feet square; the layout department; the plating and polishing room, where the copper cylinders are prepared; the etching room; and the press room. The press has a capacity of 24 full newspaper-size pages, eight of them in color; or 48 tabloid-size pages, with 16 in color.

52. The GENERAL CABLE CORPORATION FACTORY (*visited 8-4 workdays*), 3600 E. Olympic Blvd., manufactures various types of electrical conductors. The company designed and manufactured the 1.4-inch hollow copper cable that carries 287,000 volts of electrical energy from Boulder Dam 271 miles across mountains and desert to Los Angeles. This cable is 1,640 miles long.

Visitors see the conversion of 200-pound copper billets into wire, the spinning of these wires into cables, and the covering of the cables with cotton braid and asphalt, to the accompaniment of a deafening roar of machinery.

53. The low, metal O'KEEFE & MERRITT COMPANY FACTORY (*visited on application*), 3700 E. Olympic Blvd., covering six acres, presents a serrated profile along its sides becaues of its rows of tilted skylights. It annually produces $2,500,000 worth of gas ranges, room and water heaters, electric refrigerators, air coolers for desert homes, and other home appliances, and employs 500 to 600 men. Visitors see the various operations of manufacture: rolling and stamping of sheet metal parts, iron foundry work, and the enameling of stove and refrigerator parts.

54. The LOS ANGELES UNION STOCK YARDS (*visitors admitted*), 4500 Downey Rd., is the largest in the 11 western states, occupying approximately 35 acres, 75 per cent of which holds pens for cattle, sheep, and hogs. It has loading docks, trackage, and six large scales. The trim administration building of modified Spanish type, with towers and tiled roofs, is particularly elegant for such a business.

The rancher ships his stock to the yards, addressed to himself or his commission man; there it is weighed on government scales and run into sales pens for inspection by the buyers. All sales are on an immediate-cash basis. In 1937, 365,037 cattle, 114,405 calves, 90,305 sheep, and 856,000 hogs were sold from the yard.

55. The PACKING HOUSE OF THE CALAVO GROWERS OF CALIFORNIA (*visitors 8-5 workdays*), 4803 Everett Ave., an elongated concrete and glass building, packs and ships 85 per cent of the fruit from southern California's 14,000 acres of avocados. The plant, together with one in San Diego County, both owned by the grower's co-operative association, handles as much as 17,000,000 pounds of avocados a year, direct from the orchards (*see Tour 3*).

The fruit is carried by belt through a cleaner of revolving brushes, then to brightly lighted tables for grading and branding. Fruit that fails to meet the test for branding is sold locally.

Besides avocados, the association handles 85 per cent of the California date crop (*see Tour 2*), much of the California lime crop, and its imported citrons and mangoes.

56. The STUDEBAKER PACIFIC CORPORATION PLANT (*visitors 10-2 workdays*), 4530 Loma Vista Ave., consists of a building of modern lines and an older assembly plant of yellow brick. This is the only branch assembly plant in the United States of the Studebaker Corporation of South Bend, Ind., and serves the far western states. A hundred cars can be turned out daily in an eight-hour shift. Such equipment as tires, batteries, springs, bumpers, paint, and thinner comes from local factories.

Visitors inspect the paint shop, where a coat of paint is applied and dried in five minutes; and the assembly line, where, beginning with a frame, parts are added until the car rolls away under its own power.

57. The massive eight-story WESTLAND TERMINAL BUILDING (*open 8-5 workdays*), 4814 Loma Vista Ave., is topped with an ornate tower. From it are distributed motor cars, radios, and refrigerators.

58. Under the saw-toothed roofs of its four-and-a-half-acre plant, the WOOLWINE-NORRIS CORPORATION (*visitors 8-5 workdays*), 5119 S. Riverside Dr., manufactures electric ranges and water heaters, oil-burning space heaters, and sheet metal products. All parts of the ranges, with the exception of porcelain, are manufactured here. Visitors see 10-foot shears that cut metal of 10-gauge thickness, stamping machines that form metal parts under a pressure of 115 tons, electric spot welding machines, and the range assembly line.

59. The office facade of the U.S. PORCELAIN ENAMEL COMPANY PLANT (*open to groups on request, 8-5 workdays*), 4653 E. 52nd Dr., is ornamented with bright "tiles" of porcelain-enameled iron. Visitors are taken through the metal room, with its 10-foot shears and 115-ton stamping machines; and the rooms where the metal is coated with feldspar and silica, colored with various oxides, and baked in ovens at 1,600°. In the ovens the minerals are melted into glass and fused with the iron, producing a durable glossy coating.

60. The MAYWOOD GLASS FACTORY (*visited on application*),

5615 S. Riverside Dr., a miscellaneous collection of buildings covering ten acres, manufactures an average of 70 to 80 tons of bottles and jars a day. Visitors see the two huge furnaces, each with a capacity of 125 tons of molten glass. Silica, soda ash, and lime are constantly fed at one end of the furnace, while molten glass is measured out at the other, the exact amount required for each article being released automatically into the molding machines, from which the bottles are carried on slow conveyors through long annealing ovens; there they are gradually cooled until ready for packing.

61. The CONSOLIDATED STEEL CORPORATION PLANT (*open to students and technicians*), is entered at the northeast corner Slauson and Eastern Aves. but is scattered over fifty acres of land. The steel-fabricating factory with saw-toothed roofs rises behind sprawling white office buildings of the ranch type. The plant, employing 1,350 in busy seasons, ships steel boilers, bridges, cables, derricks, gates, oil refinery equipment, portable buildings, and towers.

The corporation supplied three ring-seal headgates, costing $120,-000, to the TVA for the Hiwassee Dam in North Carolina, and 40 ring-seal headgates for the Grand Coulee Irrigation Project in Washington; it fabricated the 2,422 steel towers for the Boulder Dam transmission line; and fabricated and installed the huge steel dome for the telescopic lens of the Palomar Mountain Observatory in San Diego County.

62. The administration building of the CHRYSLER MOTORS ASSEMBLY PLANT (*group tours 10 a.m. and 2 p.m. workdays*), SE. corner Slauson and Eastern Aves., is of the modified Mediterranean style, with red-tiled roofs and massive oak doors. In the 30-acre plant behind it all Plymouth motor cars and Dodge trucks sold in California, Nevada, Arizona, and Hawaii are assembled. The plant has a daily capacity of 240 cars and 50 trucks, and receives 64 car loads of material daily.

63. Seen from the air, the 27-acre concrete PLANT OF THE PIONEER-FLINTKOTE COMPANY (*open to adults on application*), 5500 S. Alameda St., forms an intricate pattern, combining curves with the parallels of serrated roofs. It manufactures a wide variety of asphalt roofing and waterproofing materials, chipboard, corrugated cartons, and the like. It is the largest of six factories producing similar products in the Los Angeles area.

Visitors are first shown the storage rooms, where are stacked thousands of tons of baled rags, collected from many parts of the world, and wood pulp from the forests of northwestern America and Sweden. The processing operations are seen next: the shredding and mixing of the raw materials that are then fed from roller to roller of a machine more than 400 feet long, from which they emerge as the finished product. In other rooms paper is impregnated with asphalt—distilled from oil in the plant and cut into strip shingles.

64. In the PLANT OF THE CALIFORNIA SANITARY CANNING COMPANY, LTD. (*visited on application*), 5000 Long

Beach Blvd., many kinds of California fruits and vegetables are processed and canned for a world market. During an average season 7,500 tons of peaches, 5,000 tons of apricots, 7,000 tons of tomatoes, 3,000 tons of spinach, and large quantities of lima beans and ham, pork and beans, baby lima beans, kidney beans, peas, and olives are handled.

65. The FACTORY OF THE GOODYEAR TIRE AND RUBBER COMPANY OF CALIFORNIA (*two-hour guided tours 9:30 a.m. and 1:30 p.m. workdays*), 6701 S. Central Ave., is a group of large brick buildings on a 74-acre tract planted with lawns and trees. This is the largest of four major automobile tire manufacturing plants in the Los Angeles area. This plant, supplying 11 Western states, Alaska, and Hawaii, has a maximum production of 15,000 tires daily, and employs 1,500 to 2,500 workers.

Visitors first see the storage room, where thousands of tons of raw rubber from the company's own plantations in Sumatra and the Philippines are stacked. The raw rubber is cut into small pieces by a machine called a pie-cutter and thoroughly mixed with chemicals. It is then pressed together with fabric (strong cotton cords), between large cylinders. The resulting material is combined with beads of rubber-covered piano wire to produce a raw tire, which is then cured and vulcanized with a tread. In another department, compounded rubber in a long continuous tube is marked off in lengths, fitted with valves, and cut. The ends are then spliced together by an electric weld process, forming inner tubes.

66. A wide expanse of lawn and flower-beds and the brick administration building of the U.S. ELECTRICAL MOTORS, INC., PLANT (*one-hour tour, working hours*), 200 E. Slauson Ave., hide the factory buildings with their saw-toothed roofline. This is the largest producer of electric motors in the western states.

Visitors follow the making of a motor from the rough castings to the completed products in the testing department.

The North and East Sections

Northeast Los Angeles occupies a corner of the original Pueblo of Los Angeles, and the southern part of Rancho San Rafael, oldest land grant in Alta (upper) California, dating from 1784. Eight square leagues—443 square miles—comprised the gift of Pedro Fages, fourth Spanish governor of California, to Jose Maria Verdugo, in token of the friendship of a captain for one of his privates on the Portola expedition of 1769 (*see The Historic Background*). Intervening years have transformed the region into an urban residential section, broken by such metropolitan features as a large county hospital, a zoo, an anthropological museum, a university, and four much-frequented city parks.

Streets crossing at oblique angles in the hilly terrain require a close watch for the markers.

TOUR

S. from City Hall on Main St.; L. from Main on 3rd St.; R. from 3rd on 4th Pl. which becomes E. 4th St.

Crossing the Los Angeles River, East 4th Street traverses BOYLE HEIGHTS, an area roughly bounded by the river, Brooklyn Ave., Indiana St., and 9th St., a section teeming with Jews and Mexicans. It was named for an Irish immigrant, Andrew A. Boyle, who in the early days operated a vineyard and winery in the vicinity. In the late 1880's the section was one of the city's finest residential districts; many of the old houses still stand, dilapidated and subdivided into cramped flats; around them are the newer, smaller houses occupied by the rest of the 200,000-odd residents of the district. On the main business street, Boyle Avenue, which is crossed by 4th Street and lined with large open-air fruit-and-vegetable stands, 5-and-10 cent stores, fish stalls, and kosher markets, an occasional bronze-skinned Mexican boy with shoeshine equipment slung over shoulder darts among gesticulating shoppers, alert for cut-rate street-corner customers. In the district are many small, frame Jewish synagogues, several large homes for the Jewish aged and blind, two city parks, a hospital, and a girls' orphanage.

HOLLENBECK PARK (R), a breathing spot between E. 4th St., S. St. Louis St., S. Boyle Ave., and Cummings St., covers more than 20 acres. Lying in a rough curve below the steep landscaped hills is a five-acre lake (*boating*). Only small sections of the shore are visible from any one spot, and unsuspected vistas open with each turn.

L. from 4th St. on Soto St.; R. from Soto on 3rd St.

67. CHURCH OF OUR LADY OF LOURDES (*open all hours*), 3772 E. 3rd. St., was designed by L. G. Scherer in a highly stylized adaptation of the Spanish mission type of church. The building, dominated by a lofty, metal-capped corner tower, is notable for fine stone and metal grilles. The traditional beamed ceiling of the nave is in sharp contrast with the pointed arches bordering the side aisles and the stepped silhouette of the chancel arch. Over the altar is a slender silk and gold canopy.

Retrace 3rd St.; R. from 3rd on Soto St. passing out of Boyle Heights; L. from Soto on Marengo St.; R. from Marengo on N. State St.

68. The 20-story ACUTE UNIT (*adm. Fri. 2-3 p.m.; guide, free*), 1200 N. State St., largest of the 123 structures on the 56-acre grounds of the LOS ANGELES COUNTY GENERAL HOSPITAL, stands on a knoll and is visible from a large part of the city. The building, of white concrete, is constructed in the wing and set-back style. From both sides of the long, narrow central mass two large wings extend to form the four shafts of an H; front and rear extensions of the central portion carry a smaller wing on either side. The $13,000,000 building, completed in 1933 after five years of research and six years of construction, is the composite work of 60 local architects. It has 75 wards, 16 major surgeries, 4 maternity suites, an acre of kitchen space where 10,500 meals a day are prepared for the staff and patients, and a bed capacity of 2,500.

From the unit an underground passage cuts westward through the grounds to the red-brick and concrete buildings of the OSTEOPATHIC HOSPITAL, which is the second of the two divisions in the hospital administration. Adjacent are the two-story Main Nurses' Home and its cottages, the three-story Laundry, the two-story COMMUNICABLE DISEASES BUILDING, the two-story PSYCHOPATHIC BUILDING, and a heavily-barred two-story building for confinement of ailing county jail prisoners.

The General Hospital is the outgrowth of the Los Angeles Infirmary, opened in an adobe house in the 1850's. The first building on the present site, a two-story frame structure, was erected in 1878. Today (1939) the institution has a bed capacity of 3,600, which can be expanded to 5,000 in an emergency. The average daily ward-patient load is 2,500. Of the 3,500 employees in the institution, 237 are full-time physicians and internes, 784 are registered nurses, and 397 are student nurses; 525 local physicians contribute part-time services free.

The hospital admits indigents able to meet residence requirements who are acutely ill or maternity cases, indigent emergency, communicable disease, and psychopathic cases and county jail prisoners.

L. from N. State on Zonal Ave.; R. from Zonal on Mission Rd.

Forty-six-acre LINCOLN PARK (R), in the angle formed by Mission Rd. and Valley Blvd., with rolling tree-shaded lawns around a six-acre lake (*boating*), is next to Sycamore Grove in popularity for state society picnics.

69. At the extreme eastern edge of the park is a CONSERVATORY (*open workdays 1-5; Sat., Sun. and holidays 10-5; free*), in which is an extensive collection of tropical plants. Other attractions are a picnic ground (*free*), and facilities for outdoor sports.

70. A white one-story stucco house with two-story tower rooms at the ends is the entrance to the LOS ANGELES OSTRICH FARM (*open 9-6; adm. 25¢, children 10¢*), 3609 Mission Rd., lone survivor of several such farms that thrived in southern California in the days of plume-bedecked feminine headgear. The farm was opened in 1906 during the picture-hat vogue. It now breeds ostriches exclusively for exhibition on the grounds, in zoos, circuses, and motion pictures. The birds are sold to foreign markets as well as in America.

71. Behind a white stucco entrance building with a narrow two-story columned portico over a long, one-story columned porch is the CALI-FORNIA ALLIGATOR FARM (*open 9-6; adm. 25¢*), 3627 Mission Rd., home of 1,000 alligators of various sizes and ages, from four-inch newly hatched babies to a 13-foot monster 325 years old. Not counted in the census are the potential 'gators in the incubators, which are also on exhibition. The great cannibalistic lizards are segregated, according to size, in 20 pools on the farm. Some of them perform tricks for visitors, such as sliding down chutes.

L. from Mission Rd. on Huntington Dr. N.; L. from Huntington on Monterey Rd.; L. from Monterey on Ave. 60.

North of the intersection with Monterey Road, Avenue 60 crosses a bridge over ARROYO SECO (dry watercourse), a steep-banked channel that, dry in summer, carries winter rainy-season run-off from the San Gabriel Mountains into the Los Angeles River.

72. ARROYO SECO PARK is that part of the Arroyo Seco extending from the crossing of Pasadena Avenue in Los Angeles to the southern boundary of Brookside Park. In the 276-acre strip, still largely unimproved, are tennis and horseshoe courts, softball diamonds, bowling greens, and a children's playground. Northeastward, the Arroyo Seco forms part of the western boundary of Pasadena (*see Pasadena*).

R. from Ave. 60 on N. Figueroa St. (US 66, State 11).

73. The intersection of North Figueroa St. and Colorado Blvd. affords the best view of grayish, dome-like EAGLE ROCK (R), with a natural formation on its west face which resembles a great spread-winged eagle; the likeness is most pronounced when the shadows fall directly downward at noon. The formation was remarked by the Franciscan explorers and chronicled by many writers of early southern California historical lore. The rock is privately owned.

L. from N. Figueroa St. on Colorado Blvd. (State 134).

Colorado Boulevard is the main business street of EAGLE ROCK (562 alt., 12,349 pop.), a suburban district settled in the 1880's and incorporated in 1911, when it was approximately nine miles from Los Angeles. The metropolis eventually surrounded and in 1923 absorbed Eagle Rock.

L. from Colorado Blvd. on Eagle Rock Blvd.; L. from Eagle Rock Blvd. on Ridgeview Ave.; R. from Ridgeview on Campus Rd.

74. The 14 buildings on the 85-acre campus of OCCIDENTAL COLLEGE, 1600 Campus Rd., describe a rough semicircle in the San Rafael Hills. The buildings, of modified Italian Renaissance type, are of grayish-white stucco with red-tiled roofs. They have often been used as the setting for movies with college scenes.

The college, now nonsectarian and co-educational, was founded by Presbyterian ministers and laymen in Boyle Heights in 1887. The present campus was acquired in 1910. A thousand-acre tract in the foothills of the Santa Monica Mountains has been donated to the college for future expansion.

The college offers courses in liberal arts and natural sciences; a graduate school grants the Master of Arts degree. The student body numbers about 750, the faculty 70. There is an outdoor Hillside Theatre seating 5,000 in addition to the usual college recreational facilities.

Campus Rd. curves southward and becomes Ave. 48; L. from Ave. 48 on York Blvd.; R. from York Blvd. on Ave. 50; R. from Ave. 50 on Figueroa St.

SYCAMORE GROVE PARK, bounded by Figueroa St., Ave. 49, and the Arroyo Seco, covers 15 landscaped acres adjoining a section of Arroyo Seco Park. Sycamore Grove is one of the favorite picnic grounds of state societies. At these affairs thousands of former residents of other states gather annually for speeches, sports, and picnic lunches. The park, purchased by the city in 1905 and increased to its present size by donation in 1907, accommodates 28,000 picnickers. Facilities include a public address system, tables, stoves (*free firewood*), and tennis courts.

75. CASA DE ADOBE (*open 2-5 Wed. and Sun.; free*), 4605 N. Figueroa St., at a corner of the park, is a faithful copy of an early 19th-century southern California house built in 1916 to perpetuate the home setting of the state's Spanish settlers. It is owned by the Southwest Museum.

The one-story yellow-stuccoed, tile-roofed building surrounds a patio, 50 feet square planted with a profusion of trees and flowers. The *casa* is furnished in the manner of the early homes. In the *baño* (bath) is a sunken plunge; in a *dormitorio* (bedroom) is an 18th-century bride's chest with the inscription, *"Dame un beso, Ramoncita"* (give me a kiss, Ramoncita); in another room is a bed once the property of Pio Pico, last Mexican governor of California. On the walls is the Caballeria Collection of paintings, most of them brought from Spain for the missions.

R. from N. Figueroa St. on Ave. 45; R. from Ave. 45 on Marmion Way; L. from Marmion Way on Museum Dr.

76. The SOUTHWEST MUSEUM (*open 1-5 daily except Mon., Christmas, Independence Day, and during Aug.; free*), corner Marmion Way and Museum Dr., stands on a hill overlooking the Arroyo Seco and Sycamore Grove. The long white concrete building has a taller tile-roofed wing at the rear of one end and a high square tower with two rows of narrow openings at the other. The museum contains relics and craft work of the primitive Indians of the Western Hemisphere.

The building can be approached through a long tunnel that penetrates the base of the hill to an elevator under the museum. At the tunnel entrance is a bright MAYAN PORTAL resembling that at the House of Nuns at Chichen Itza in Yucatan. Dioramas in the sides of the tunnel depict the advent of the early Asiatics in America and progress stages of the Indian cultures.

The Hopi Trail, leading from the base of the hill to the Lower Lobby, copied from the stone trails of the Hopi sky cities in northern Arizona, offers an optional approach to the museum.

In the Lower Lobby are general American Indian exhibits. In the north wing of the Southwestern Indians Room are relics and modern handcraft of the Pueblo, Navajo, Apache, and Mohave. The Northwestern Indians Room displays handcraft of Eskimo and of Northwest Coast Indians. Special displays are frequently exhibited in the Members' Room, where the information desk is situated.

A tepee of tanned skins, and clothing and weapons of the Blackfoot, Sioux, Cheyenne, Crow, and Arapahoe, are displayed in the Plains Indians Room. In the Caracol tower is the Prehistoric Southwest Room; here are the relics of prehistory from Southwestern pueblos and cliff dwellers: stone implements, pottery, shell, stone, and turquoise ornaments, fabrics woven from yucca and turkey feathers and colored with brilliant vegetable dyes. In the AUDITORIUM (*lectures on Indians and Southwestern history, travel, and exploration 3 p.m. Sun., Nov. through Mar.; free*), is a large basketry collection. The TORRANCE TOWER contains the museum library, which is devoted largely to works on archeology, ethnology, and primitive art and history of the Southwest and of Spanish-America.

Southwest Museum is the outgrowth of the Southwest Society of the Archeological Institute of America, founded in 1903. The Museum was incorporated in 1907, and the present building opened in 1914.

Retrace Museum Dr., Marmion Way and Ave. 45; R. from Ave. 45 on N. Figueroa St.; L. from N. Figueroa on Ave. 43.

77. EL ALISAL (the sycamore grove) is on the west side of Arroyo Seco at the crossing of Ave. 43. The house (*visited by appointment; free*) was the home of Charles F. Lummis (*see The Arts*), whose efforts were largely responsible for establishment of the Southwest

Museum. The house, which overlooks the tree-lined Arroyo Seco, is built around a patio in which grows a giant sycamore. One of Lummis' colorful yarns was that he built the house himself with the aid of a 12-year-old Indian boy. The walls are made of boulders, and the rafters and girders are hand-hewn. After Lummis' death in 1928 the property passed into the possession of the Southwest Museum. Although a section of it is still occupied by members of the Lummis family, it serves as a repository for a part of the Lummis collections of Indian and Spanish artifacts.

Retrace Ave. 43 to Figueroa St.; L. from Ave. 43 on Figueroa; L. from Figueroa on San Fernando Rd.; R. from San Fernando on Pasadena Ave.; R. from Pasadena on N. Broadway.

ELYSIAN PARK (*open 6 a.m.-8 p.m.*), entrance N. Broadway at the Los Angeles River, is a 600-acre municipal preserve through whose precipitous, heavily wooded hills wind seven miles of paved motor roads and 10 miles of winding foot trails. The park is one of the most rugged and heavily foliaged in southern California; its arroyo-gashed hills and deep canyons are matted with a tangle of creepers, wild roses, blue gum eucalyptus trees, drooping pepper trees, and gnarled live oaks. In shaded areas along the drives are numerous picnic grounds (*tables, stoves, fuel; free*) and children's playgrounds.

Part of Elysian Park, and all of the Plaza and Pershing Square (*see Downtown Los Angeles*), are on lands set aside for public use at the founding of Los Angeles in 1781. Although the original 500-acre Elysian tract has never been privately owned it was not officially made a park until 1886. Since then much land has been added by purchase.

At the main entrance is the FREMONT GATE, which honors General John C. Fremont, volunteer commander of the American forces in the conquest of California. Beyond it is (L) the PORTOLA-CRESPI MONUMENT, a gray granite boulder marking the spot where the Spanish exploring party headed by Gaspar de Portola is supposed to have made camp on its way up the state in 1769 (*see Pueblo to Metropolis*); from this point the party had its first view of the plain to the south on which Los Angeles was to have its beginning a dozen years later.

78. In the park are the LOS ANGELES POLICE DEPARTMENT TRAINING, SOCIAL, AND RECREATIONAL CENTER (*open 8-7 daily*), with a recreational building, an aviary, a small zoo, and a firing range for police pistol practice.

79. A RECREATION LODGE (*open to groups of 25 up; $3-$5 for use of kitchen facilities*), in the southwestern corner of the park, with accommodations for 175; and CHAVEZ RAVINE, which served as the potter's field in pueblo days and as the county "pest farm" during the 1850 and 1880 smallpox epidemics, and which is named for its original owner, Julian Chavez, city councilman in 1850.

80. The NAVAL AND MARINE CORPS RESERVE ARMORY, Chavez Ravine Rd. between Paducah and Coronel Sts., at the SW.

tip of the park, was completed in 1940 at a cost of $1,000,000. It is one of the largest naval armories in the country, having a drill deck on which a thousand-man battalion can be trained. Its dominant structure is a long, white concrete building of modern design.

The Northwest Section

This tour, through the northwestern part of Los Angeles, pauses at Angelus Temple and the former site of Walt Disney Studios, and it passes such less publicized points as the city's first oil field, and Griffith Park, the largest municipal park in the United States.

TOUR

S. from City Hall on Spring St. to 2nd St.; R. from Spring on 2nd St.; R. from 2nd on Glendale Blvd.

The OLD LOS ANGELES OIL FIELD (L), Glendale Blvd. between Beverly Blvd. and Colton St., was the city's first petroleum producing area. Ninety-seven flimsy wooden derricks, survivors of the hundreds that were in the field at the turn of the century, stand on the slope with dwellings encroaching upon them. Developed in 1892 by Edward L. Doheny, the field's production peak has long since passed; as the wells fall below production cost they are abandoned, the derricks removed, and the land is used for stores and dwellings.

ECHO PARK, bounded by Glendale Blvd., Temple St., and Echo Park and Park Aves., a 31-acre municipal park in the heart of a populous residential district, is pleasantly landscaped with many varieties of fine ornamental and shade trees. It has an eight-acre lake (*boating*). On an island in the north end, reached by an arched bridge, is one of the park's three picnic grounds (*tables, gas stoves; free*). Egyptian papyrus and water lilies growing in the shallows at this end afford shelter during the nesting season to numerous waterfowl—swans, ducks, coots, grebes, and geese. In summer a lush growth of lotus springs from the water in the lake's northwest arm, the large pink-and-white flowers attracting many painters and photographers. In the 1870's the lake provided water for adjacent farms, and water power for a woolen mill that stood at Sixth and Pearl (now Figueroa) Streets.

81. ANGELUS TEMPLE (*open to visitors 9 a.m.- 4:30 p.m. daily; guides; contributions received*), 1100 Glendale Blvd., an immense, circular, buff-colored concrete building with a setback and a low-domed roof, is identified by numerous banners and posters, and by electric signs on its facade and upon the broadcasting towers on the roof; on the top of the dome is a revolving cross outlined with neon lights at night, showing red on one side and blue on the other. This is the mother church of the Foursquare Gospel, founded by Aimee Semple McPherson.

Within the auditorium, aisles soft with blood-red carpets lead to an altar under a great proscenium arch. The ceiling of the huge unsupported dome is sky-blue behind fleecy clouds, and light enters through tall stained-glass windows. The temple has four robed choirs, several orchestras, bands, and smaller musical organizations, an expensive costume wardrobe, a vast amount of stage scenery and properties, and a 5,300-glass communion set. Also in the structure are the technical room and studio of Radio Station KFSG—the "Glory Station of the Pacific Coast"—the choir studio, and the Prayer Tower, where alternating shifts of men and women have kept prayer in continuous session night and day since the temple opened in 1923. In the foyer near this tower is a display of X-ray photographs and discarded crutches offered as testimony to the healing power of prayer. Adjoining the auditorium on the east is a rectangular five-story buff concrete building housing the Bible College, the commissary, and the administration offices.

The temple has 57 departments with many subcommittees. The weekly payroll is several thousand dollars though many followers devote time and services free. Much relief work is done through the free employment agency, commissary, and salvage department.

The Foursquare Gospel is preached in 400 branch churches in the United States and Canada, and in 195 missions in foreign countries. In day and night sessions the Bible College has trained more than 3,000 men and women to spread the Gospel of the Foursquare as evangelists, missionaries, and ordained ministers. The creator and guiding light of this institution is Aimee Semple McPherson (*see Religion*). Though appearing in the pulpit less frequently than in former years, she usually conducts the Sunday evening services, which feature sermons profusely illustrated with costumed dramas.

L. from Glendale Blvd. on Park Ave.; L. from Park on Sunset Blvd.; L. from Sunset on Parkman St.; R. from Parkman on Silver Lake Blvd.; R. from Silver Lake on Bellevue Ave.; R. from Bellevue on Micheltorena St.

82. The Russian Orthodox CHURCH OF THE HOLY VIRGIN MARY (*open on application at parish house*), 658 Micheltorena St., is a small white one-story stuccoed building surmounted by a gilded onion-shaped dome; the three-barred Greek-Catholic cross is fixed above the entrance. The white interior walls are heavily decorated with icons of various sizes, most of them with dark, rich, intense colors outlined in gold against a gold background, many with the Greek-Catholic cross at the top. One of the icons is a wood carving of the fifteenth century, and others date from the sixteenth and seventeenth centuries. There is but one short bench for the aged and infirm; all other worshippers stand or kneel during the services, which is in Slavonic. Singing, which forms an unusually large and important part of the services, is unaccompanied by instruments. The choir, usually consisting of eighteen persons, has a high reputation. The music is a

special attraction of the Christmas and Easter celebrations, which
follow the usual dates of these holidays—about two weeks later than
those of the western churches because of the eastern church's use of the
Julian calendar.

More than 20,000 people of Russian birth live in Los Angeles and
include widely diverse elements—Soviet citizens, Russian gypsies, a
group of Molokans (pacifist sectarians who emigrated because of religious persecution in the latter part of the nineteenth century), Jews,
and finally the "whites"—people who fled after the Bolsheviks came
to power in 1917. The Church of the Holy Virgin Mary is one of two
churches supported by the Russian refugees living in and about Los
Angeles.

*Retrace Micheltorena St., Bellevue Ave., and Silver Lake Blvd.; L.
from Silver Lake on W. Silver Lake Dr.*

SILVER LAKE RESERVOIR, bordered on the east by Silver
Lake Blvd. and on the west by Silver Lake Dr., lies in a trough-shaped
fold of the rolling hills. Its earth-fill dam, built in 1907 by the municipal Department of Water and Power, backs up nearly two thousand
acre-feet of water. Eucalyptus trees and weeping willows stand on its
curving shores. The fine homes of the Silver Lake residential district
dot the surrounding hills.

*L. from W. Silver Lake Dr. on Armstrong Ave.; L. from Armstrong
on W. Silver Lake Dr.; L. from W. Silver Lake on Rowena Ave.;
L. from Rowena on Hyperion Ave.*

83. The FORMER WALT DISNEY STUDIOS, 2719 Hyperion
Ave., are a group of cream-colored stucco laboratories and drafting
rooms designed to meet the requirements of making animated films.
They are no longer used since a modern plant has been built at Burbank
(*see Tour 7*).

*Retrace Hyperion Ave.; L. from Hyperion on Rowena Ave.; L. from
Rowena on Los Feliz Blvd.; R. from Los Feliz on Vermont Ave.,
which becomes Vermont Ave. Canyon Rd. at entrance to Griffith Park.*

GRIFFITH PARK (*open 6 a.m.-8 p.m. daily; Vermont canyon
section open 6 a.m.-11 p.m.; free*), into which Vermont Avenue passes
at a point several blocks north of its intersection with Los Feliz Boulevard, is a 3,761-acre tract spreading over five square miles in the eastern
half of the mountains that lie north of Hollywood and Los Angeles.
Its 30 miles of winding, paved drives lead to heights from which sweeping, town-covered expanses of surrounding country are visible; 50 miles
of hiking and bridle trails explore spots still more remote. Picnic
grounds (*tables, stoves; free*) and children's playgrounds are scattered
throughout the lower edges of the park, in canyon mouths and level
roadside areas.

Griffith Park was once part of Rancho Los Feliz, granted to the
widow of Antonio Feliz by the Mexican governor of California in

1841. Colonel Griffith J. Griffith, the last private owner, donated the mountain section to the city in 1896. The flat lands west of the Los Angeles River were purchased by the city from the Griffith estate after his death in 1919.

84. The GREEK THEATRE (*open June to Sept.; hours and adm. prices vary with performances*), Vermont Canyon Rd., presents the Doric facade (L) of its low ivory-colored concrete stage building to the street; behind it, on the open hillside rise tiers of seats. The theatre, built in 1930, with funds for the purpose by Colonel Griffith, seats more than 4,000. It is used for lectures, concerts, ballets, conventions, and civic exercises.

L. from Vermont Canyon Rd. on E. Observatory Dr.

85. The GRIFFITH OBSERVATORY AND PLANETARIUM (*open weekdays 11-11, Sun., holidays 2-11; planetarium demonstration daily 3 and 8:30 p.m.; exhibit halls free, planetarium demonstration 25¢*), designed by John C. Austin, stands at the crest of an elevation separating Western and Vermont Ave. Canyons; it is a long, low grayish concrete structure with a large blackened copper dome in the center and a smaller revolving dome at each end. Before the building is an obelisk, designed by Archibald Garner and Gordon Newell, bearing the stylized figures and names and life dates of the world's great astronomers: Hipparchus, Copernicus, Galileo, Kepler, Newton, and Herschel. Atop the spire is the early astronomical instrument, the astrolabe.

In the center of the floor in the main foyer of the building is a bronze-trimmed marble well in which a 240-pound brass sphere swings, suspended from the ceiling by a 40-foot steel wire. A model of a pendulum invented in 1851 by Jean Foucault, French physicist, it demonstrates the earth's rotation upon its axis.

Halls extending from the foyer contain the museum of physical science divided into four departments: astronomy, physics, chemistry, and geology. The astronomy section contains a large model of the moon as it would appear if only 500 miles away, pale and pitted with craters, its strange mountains casting creeping shadows as a traveling overhead light creates an illusion of sunrise and sunset. The exhibit includes a mechanical model of the solar system and an excellent collection of meteorites. The physics section includes an oscilloscope for graphing visitors' voices, the Wilson Cloud Chamber, spectra of gases, discharge of electricity in vacua, the majority of which may be operated by the observer; a comprehensive exhibit of chemical elements, fluorescent minerals, geological formations and other phenomena. A 12-INCH REFRACTOR TYPE telescope (*open 7 to 10:30 p.m. on weekdays, earlier when objects of special interest are visible in sky; free*) is mounted in the East Dome.

Under the great Central Dome is a circular 500-seat auditorium housing the planetarium. Popular lectures on astronomical subjects are given, accompanied by sky views and other illustrative material projected on the concave ceiling by the Zeiss Planetarium, a large and complex stereopticon machine.

The observatory was built in 1935 with funds set aside for the purpose in the will of Colonel Griffith.

R. from E. Observatory Dr. on W. Observatory Dr.; L. from W. Observatory on Western Ave. Canyon Rd.

86. FERN DELL (*open 6 a.m.-11 p.m., picknicking facilities; free*), in the southwestern end of the park is a heavily wooded ravine with a tumbling brook, rock pools, and bowers of ferns ranging in variety from large tree-ferns to tiny moss-like specimens. They have been growing there from the time when, according to legend, the ravine was used by the Cahuenga Indians for tribal council meetings, and called Mococahuenga (council grounds of the Cahuenga).

Retrace Western Ave. Canyon Rd. to W. Observatory Dr.; L. from Western Ave. Canyon on W. Observatory; L. from W. Observatory on Mt. Hollywood Dr.; L. from Mt. Hollywood on Mineral Wells Dr., which becomes Crystal Springs Dr.

87. In the northeast corner of Griffith Park is (L) the CALIFORNIA NATIONAL GUARD AIRPORT (*open 9-5*), entered from Riverside Dr. east of the intersection with Crystal Springs Dr. This is the home station, Fortieth Aviation Division of the California National Guard. A military radio station (CUS) and two steel hangars are on the field.

R. from Crystal Springs Dr. on Griffith Park Dr.; R. from Griffith Park on Zoo Dr.

88. The ZOO (*open 7-4:30; free*), at the end of Zoo Dr., is in a rugged box-gorge in the eastern face of the Griffith Park Hills. Because of limited maintenance funds, the zoo—although in existence since 1912—is still in a state of development. In 1939 seven cageless moat-fronted pits for lions and bears, and a 10-cage house for monkeys were constructed. The zoo is well-stocked with birds, small animals, herbivores, and lions, but has only one elephant. More large animals are being acquired. Upon the hills above is a high craggy pinnacle called BEE ROCK, reached by hiking trails.

The Wilshire and West Sections

This tour begins in the city's downtown section and ends near the Pacific Ocean; it leads through the Wilshire district just south of Hollywood, filled with fine apartment houses and smart shops; and it passes several beautiful churches and the Brea Pits, the richest source of Pleistocene remains in the world.

TOUR

S. from City Hall on Spring St., R. from Spring on Sixth St., L. from Spring on Figueroa St., R. from Figueroa on Wilshire Blvd.

With the progressive decentralization of the city's business district, which began in the 1920's, Wilshire Boulevard has become the most important of the newer metropolitan arteries. Many of the larger shops and department stores have moved to the five-mile section between Westlake Park and Fairfax Avenue; others have opened branches there, often finer than the parent store.

WESTLAKE PARK, between Alvarado and Parkview Sts., is divided by Wilshire Boulevard. The park, with a large lake (*boating*), is landscaped with a lush growth of trees, shrubs, and grass, and has a children's playground and a picnic ground (*tables, gas stoves; free*), both in the southwest corner.

89. At the eastern Wilshire Boulevard entrance is (L) an eight-foot black cement nude, PROMETHEUS the firebringer, with torch and globe. It was executed by Nina Saemundsson for the Federal Art Project and erected in 1935.

90. At the western Wilshire Boulevard entrance is (L) a STATUE OF HARRISON GRAY OTIS, for 31 years publisher of the Los Angeles *Times*. It was designed by Paul Troubetzkoy.

91. Overlooking Westlake Park is the OTIS ART INSTITUTE (*guides 12-1, 4-5 p.m.; free*), 2401 Wilshire Blvd., a county-maintained school of fine and applied arts housed in three white stucco buildings of the residential type with red-tile roofs, numerous ornamented chimneys, and a columned entrance porch. As The Bivouac, the place was the home of Otis, who bequeathed it to the county for its present use. Facing Park View Street, on the institute grounds, is a 14-foot granite MODEL OF THE OLD TIMES BUILDING.

LAFAYETTE PARK, Wilshire Blvd. between Lafayette Park Pl. and Commonwealth Ave., is a landscaped hollow of winding walks, lawns, and bosky retreats.

92. The STENDAHL GALLERY (*open 9-5:30; free*), 3006 Wilshire Blvd., is one of the oldest commercial art galleries in the city, offering exhibitions by contemporary artists of established reputation and showing, in a rear patio, work in experimental forms.

93. BULLOCK'S WILSHIRE BUILDING, 3050 Wilshire Blvd., a branch of the downtown department store, was designed by John and Donald Parkinson with a striking use of buff terra cotta, green copper, and glass. Above the two-story base, a slender six-story tower with marked vertical lines and irregular set-back for three stories thrusts its blunt, copper-sheathed nose against the sky. A central foyer, a cube with high marble walls, is accented by vertical panels of glass and metal. Each department was planned as a separate unit, with its own design, decoration, and materials.

94. The elaborate new five-story I. MAGNIN CO. BUILDING, SW. corner Wilshire Blvd. and New Hampshire Ave., was designed by Myron Hunt and H. C. Chambers. The first-story base is of black granite, contrasting sharply with the dazzling white Colorado Yule marble of the upper stories. Brilliant nickel-silver trim divides the black from the white. The interior, furnished in shades of apricot, has indirect lighting effects like those achieved by Parisian artists and technicians.

95. IMMANUEL PRESBYTERIAN CHURCH (*adm. by application at office; guides; free*), SW. corner Wilshire Blvd. and S. Berendo St., was designed in a modern adaptation of the Gothic. On one side of the arched entrance is a tall bell tower, on the other a lower and slenderer tower abutted by a secondary entrance. On the boulevard facade five lancet windows rise above the entrance to a rose window of stained glass portraying the nativity; along both sides of the building are stained glass windows depicting events in the life of Christ. Within are Gothic hammer beam trusses, columns and arches, oak furnishings, and huge Gothic chandeliers all harmonizing with the massive exterior. In addition to the two-thousand-seat main auditorium are a chapel, halls, libraries, lounges, and a gymnasium.

96. The BROWN DERBY CAFE NO. 1 (*always open*), 3377 Wilshire Blvd., an incongruous combination of a huge derby hat and a tile-roofed extension to the rear, is typical of the architectural fantasies that dot many of the city's major streets. It lures its customers with the slogan: "Eat in the Hat."

97. The AMBASSADOR HOTEL, 3400 Wilshire Blvd., a vast rambling structure whose spreading tile-roofed wings faintly suggest the buildings of northern Italy, sits far back from the street behind a huge expanse of lawn and is surrounded by its cottages. In the hotel are a bank, brokerage office, post office, library, 35 retail shops, and a motion-picture theatre; on the grounds are a swimming pool with artificial beaches of white sand and an 18-hole miniature golf course.

98. The WILSHIRE BOULEVARD CHRISTIAN CHURCH (*adm. by application at office*) NE. corner Wilshire Blvd., and S. Normandie Ave., is recognized by its tall red-tile-roofed campanile. In the

west wall of the basilica-type auditorium is a rose window copied from that in the Rheims cathedral.

99. Dominating the WILSHIRE BOULEVARD TEMPLE OF B'NAI B'RITH (Children of the Covenant), NE. corner Wilshire and Hobart Blvds. (*open during services, Fri. 7:30 p.m., Sat. 10 a.m.*), largest temple of the Jewish faith in Los Angeles, is a low, immense, mosaic-inlaid dome 135 feet in diameter, surrounded by a base capped with small tapering spires. Broad Kasota stone steps lead to a magnificent triple entrance of Italian marble under a huge rose window. Beyond the massive East Indian teakwood doors is a gold-and-black foyer of Italian marble. Within, Byzantine columns of black Belgian marble rise to the base of the domed ceiling which is finished in dull gold and from which hang eight cast-bronze chandeliers designed in the manner of the ancient prayer spice boxes. The altar, ark, and choir screen are of carved, inlaid mahogany and walnut, framed in black marble and mosaic. Hugo Ballin's Warner Memorial paintings, depicting biblical and post-biblical themes, enrich with glowing color the three lunettes and broad frieze above the mahogany wainscoting. In the rear of the main building is a three-story extension, flanking an open court and housing schoolrooms, halls, and offices.

100. The WILSHIRE METHODIST CHURCH (*adm. daily except Tues. by application at office*), SW. corner Wilshire and Plymouth Blvds., has a very tall clock tower at one corner inspired by the Torracio of Cremona, Italy. The design of the facade is based upon that of the church of St. Francis at Brescia, Italy. The building is an outstanding example of poured concrete construction.

In the ceiling of the nave the dark, profusely-patterned structural members are emphasized, intensifying the beauty of the rose window. The pulpit and lectern are copied from notable Italian pieces.

101. COULTER'S BUILDING, Wilshire Blvd. between Ridgeley Dr. and Hauser Blvd., a four-story commercial structure designed in 1938 by Stiles O. Clements and Irving L. Osgood, is one of the few large buildings of a very modern type in Los Angeles. In the heavy white concrete walls, rounded at the corners, continuous horizontal bands of glass brick serve as windows. A vertical panel of black glass cuts a recess of 32 feet wide into the front face of the building from doorway to roof.

R. from Wilshire Blvd. on Curson Ave.

Thirty-two acre HANCOCK PARK, on the north side of Wilshire Blvd. between W. 6th St., Curson Ave., and Ogden Dr., is notable for La Brea Pits. The park, given to the county in 1916 by Major G. Allan Hancock, an oil magnate, was once part of Rancho La Brea (Tar Ranch), whose square league of territory covered most of the Wilshire district and part of Hollywood.

102. LA BREA PITS, in the eastern end of the park, are ugly black bogs where oil and tar bubble slowly to the surface from subterranean pools. In the rainy season a film of water camouflages the sticky quag-

mire, forming a trap for the unwary, as it did long ago when prehistoric animals, gathering here to drink, were caught and preserved for the enlightenment of modern science.   About one quarter of the asphalt pockets or pits, of which there were formerly more than 100, have yielded specimens that make them the richest source of Pleistocene or Glacial Epoch remains in the world.   The pits are the remnants of small craters formed by the explosion of gas in the oil-bearing strata below.   Asphalt oozed into the basins, creating viscid black lakes. Thousands—perhaps millions—of years ago the region of these craters was an open, well-watered plain, bathed in more fog and rain than descends on southern California today.   Forests of pine, juniper, and spruce shaded the now barren flatlands.   Foraging among the thick grasses and trees were great animals, whose forebears had come to this continent from Asia by way of Bering Straits: the imperial mammoth, 12 to 15 feet high at the shoulder; the mastodon; the giant ground sloth; the flesh-eating short-faced bear, larger than the present-day Kodiak bear; the great lion and saber-toothed tiger; and the Teratornis, a bird that had a wing spread of at least 12 feet.   Sometimes one of these creatures, coming to a pool to drink, tumbled or was pushed in by a thirsty neighbor.   The frantic screams of the animal, trapped in the tar beneath the shallow surface of rainwater, attracted the huge flesh-eaters, who jumped in to enjoy an easy meal, only to meet the same fate as the intended victim.   Through the ages the carcasses sank deeper and deeper into the sticky mass, and the flesh disintegrated, but the bones were preserved by the tar.

The Indians used the tar for waterproofing roofs of huts, as did early Spanish settlers.   In refining the asphalt for commercial use Major Hancock is said to have removed and burned great piles of the prehistoric bones, not realizing their value to science until he found a nine and a half-inch tooth.   This he gave to William Denton, an amateur paleontologist, who identified it as belonging to a saber-toothed cat.   Although Denton published an account of the find the remaining fossils were undisturbed—Hancock's asphalt-refining venture having been a commercial failure—until 1905, when W. W. Orcutt, an oil geologist, sent specimens to the University of California at Berkley. The result was a scramble of paleontological expeditions—by the university, Occidental College, the Los Angeles High School, the Southern California Academy of Sciences, the Los Angeles Museum of History, Science, and Art, and by individuals.   In 1915, when excavation ended, the museum alone had collected some 600,000 specimens.

At Hancock Park the Los Angeles County Park Department has attempted to recreate as nearly as possible the scene as it was in the Pleistocene Age; flora resembling that of the period has been planted, and life-sized groups of representative animals of the time, executed in stone by Herman T. Beck, have been placed among the pits.   To prevent cats, dogs, and even humans from tumbling into the sticky bogs and starting a record of this age for future scientists, stone parapets have been constructed around most of the pits.   Plans have been adopted for the erection of a museum building over one of the pits, a feature of which will be a passageway cut down into the tar where the visitor may view, through plate glass, the interior of the pit as it existed when the animals were trapped.

Retrace Curson Ave.; R. from Curson on Wilshire Blvd.; L. from Wilshire on McCarthy Vista.

103. CARTHAY CENTER PARKWAY, in the middle of Mc-Carthy Vista between Wilshire Blvd. and San Vicente Blvd., is strewn with various memorials—boulders, trees, and statuary. Southwest of San Vicente Boulevard it continues as White Esplanade, a path for pedestrians only.

The JEDEDIAH STRONG SMITH BOULDER is at the corner of Wilshire Blvd. and McCarthy Vista. Smith (1798-1831), that rare creature, a fur trapper who was a praying Methodist, was the first American to reach California by a cross-continental route; he arrived in 1826. At the San Vicente Blvd. intersection is a MEMORIAL SUNDIAL mounted on brick from Mission San Juan Capistrano (*see Tour 4*).

In the trianguler island at McCarthy Vista and San Vicente Blvd. is the FORTY-NINER STATUE, slightly larger than life-size. The figure is booted and long-haired; a small stream of water pours from his gold-pan onto a boulder. The statue, designed by Henry Lion, is dedicated to the men of the first gold rush and to Daniel O. McCarthy (1830-1919), a forty-niner who became a publisher. Carthay Center, a real estate subdivision of the 1920's, was named for him, "Carthay" being a deliberate euphonious corruption of "Carthy."

On White Esplanade, at San Vicente Blvd., is a BUST OF JUAN BAUTISTA DE ANZA, Spanish commander who led colonists across the deserts of Sonora, Arizona, and California in 1775-76 to settle the coast. The bust, by Henry Lion, was placed in 1927. Directly southwest along the esplanade is a small CHINESE PEACH TREE, presented by the Chinese consul in Los Angeles to commemorate the premiere of *The Good Earth* at the Carthay Circle Theatre. On White Esplanade at Commodore Sloat Drive is the *"Snowshoe" Thompson Boulder,* with a bronze plaque showing the bewhiskered face of Thompson, a Norwegian who from 1855 to 1876 carried mail over the Sierras to isolated camps on his homemade skis, rescued the lost, and rendered aid to the needy during the snowbound months. To the rear of the boulder are two young *Sequoia sempervirens* (redwood trees), native to the northern California coast.

104. Renowned as the scene of motion-picture "world premieres," the CARTHAY CIRCLE THEATRE (*open only during perform-ances*) 6316 San Vicente Blvd., is a white concrete building trimmed in bright blue and dominated by a high tower ornamented with multi-colored tiles and equipped with searchlights.

The theatre is something of a repository for Californiana. In the first floor lobby is a painting, *California's First Theatre,* by Frank Tenney Johnson, depicting the Eagle Theatre built in Sacramento in

1849. *Jedediah Smith at San Gabriel*, by Alson Clark, in the main lobby mezzanine, shows the scout's arrival at San Gabriel Mission on November 27, 1826. Painted on the drop curtain is *An Emigrant Train at Donner Lake*, by Frank Tenney Johnson, a tribute to the ill-fated Donner Party.

The Southwest Section

The route of this tour, through the mixed commercial and older residential section of the city, passes the buildings of two large metropolitan newspapers, a hospital devoted exclusively to the treatment of crippled children, and two magnificent churches; and cutting across the campus of the University of Southern California, it ends at Exposition Park, in which are the Los Angeles Coliseum, municipal swimming pools, and the Los Angeles County Museum of History, Science, and Art.

TOUR

S. from City Hall on Main St.; R. from Main on Olympic Blvd.; L. from Olympic on Broadway.

105. The LOS ANGELES EXAMINER BUILDING (*open by arrangement*), 1111 S. Broadway, is a two-story tile-roofed building of buff concrete topped by a large, low tower with a squat, tile-covered dome supporting a slender lantern. This is a reproduction of the California Building at the 1893 World's Columbian Exposition in Chicago. The structure is the plant of the Los Angeles *Examiner,* a morning Hearst-chain newspaper. Visible from the street on the Broadway side are (L) five giant presses, each with a capacity of 32,000 forty-eight-page papers an hour.

R. from Broadway on 12th St.; L. from 12th on Trenton St.

106. The LOS ANGELES EVENING HERALD AND EXPRESS BUILDING (*open weekdays 8:30-5; guides*), 1243 Trenton St., is a three-story cast-cement structure with modified Spanish Renaissance details. Much natural limestone decoration in profusely intricate Churriguerresque (Mexican baroque) design is a remarkable feature of the building, which was designed by Morgan, Walls, and Clements and completed in 1925. It is the plant of the Los Angeles *Evening Herald and Express,* a unit of the Hearst newspaper chain. It has more than three and one-quarter acres of floor space and the 24 press units, set on vibration-proof foundations, have a capacity of 216,000 thirty-two-page papers an hour each.

L. from Trenton St. on Pico St.; R. from Pico on Flower St.

107. The LOS ANGELES ORTHOPAEDIC HOSPITAL (*visited by arrangement 2-4 weekdays, 10-4 Sun.*), 2424 S. Flower St., is a

group of two- and three-story buildings of miscellaneous designs dominated by a buff-concrete Administration Building with a domed cupola. The institution, maintained by the Los Angeles Orthopaedic Foundation, is the only hospital in southern California exclusively for the treatment of crippled children. Some 4,000 children are treated annually, most of them without charge. Occupational therapy and the usual education under teachers provided by the board of education supplement orthopaedic care.

R. from Flower St. on W. Adams Blvd.

108. ST. JOHN'S EPISCOPAL CHURCH (*open 7-5 daily*), 514 W. Adams Blvd., is designed in the manner of an eleventh-century Florentine church. Above the entrance, in the light-gray Tufa-stone facade, is a large rose window set in a carre of bas-reliefs by S. Cartaino Scarpitta. The ceiling in the main auditorium is a copy of that in the Church of San Minato in Florence. The *Corpus* on the rood beam and the *Christus* above the altar were carved from oak by a protege of Anton Lang of Oberammergau.

108a. The headquarters of the AUTOMOBILE CLUB OF SOUTHERN CALIFORNIA (*open 9-5 daily*), 2601 S. Figueroa St., consists of 2 buildings each 3 stories in height, surmounted by a 100-ft. tower. Designed by Hunt & Hunt and Roland E. Coats, architects, it was completed in 1923 at a total cost of $2,052,000. The buildings are of reinforced concrete construction of Spanish design, 80 ft. wide, 267 ft. long on Figueroa St., and 208 ft. on Adams. The membership numbers 126,000, and maintains 34 district and 13 sub-offices, and is the largest independent club of its character in the United States.

109. ST. VINCENT DE PAUL ROMAN CATHOLIC CHURCH (*always open*), 621 W. Adams Blvd., designed by Albert C. Martin, is a buff-colored reinforced concrete edifice in the Spanish baroque style with a tile-inlaid dome at a height of ninety feet over the transept crossing and a tall bell tower with a spire at the left front corner. The building, erected in 1925 as a gift from Edward L. Doheny, oil multimillionaire, is decorated on the outside with statuary and friezes of Indiana limestone.

The interior is embellished with murals, polychromed carving, marble, and bronze. The high marble altar is against a retable of red marble with a high-relief carving of *The Last Supper*. The pulpit is carved from a single block of red marble. Above the altar is a tabernacle of gilded bronze; behind it is a great gilded and polychromed reredos, flanked by elaborately carved French walnut parclose screens.

R. from W. Adams Blvd. on Chester Pl.

Majestically staunch against the general decay of the West Adams residential district are the 10 palatial homes on CHESTER PLACE (*speed limit 10 m. an hour*), a street two blocks long in a twenty-acre residential park, owned (except for one acre) and developed into estates by Edward L. Doheny, oil magnate, whose widow occupies (1939) the grand brick-red plaster house, at No. 8, built about 1898. Arched iron gateways, brick walls surmounted by ornamental iron work, great old trees festooned with bougainvillea and honeysuckle, formal gardens and spacious lawns remain little changed in appearance from the days when much of West Adams district was no less splendid than the estates of Chester Place.

Retrace Chester Pl.; L. from Chester on St. James Park Dr.

West of the mansions of Chester Place are the old-fashioned dwellings of ST. JAMES PARK, another once fine residential section. Although a few of the houses preserve much of the dignity of their past, most of them are ending their years as low-priced boarding and rooming houses.

L. from St. James Park Dr. on Scarff St.; R. from Scarff on W. Adams Blvd.

110. The SECOND CHURCH OF CHRIST, SCIENTIST (*open by arrangement*), 948 W. Adams Blvd., is faced with white glazed brick and has a lofty Corinthian portico. Above the dull-green tile roof is a large dome sheathed in greenish copper.

L. from W. Adams Blvd. on Hoover St.; L. from Hoover St. on W. Jefferson Blvd.

111. The SHRINE CIVIC AUDITORIUM (*open 9-5 workdays, 9-12 m. Sat.*), 665 W. Jefferson Blvd., a very large ochre-colored concrete building with Moorish architectural motifs, has a domed cupola at each end. The meeting place and headquarters of the Al Malaikah Temple, a division of the Ancient Arabic Order of Nobles of the Mystic Shrine, it is also used for grand opera, concerts, conventions, and the like. The cupolas and the loggia along the western facade give it a mosque-like appearance in keeping with the Arabian-Egyptian costumes, symbols, and ceremonies affected by the order. The auditorium, built in 1925-26 at a cost of $2,690,000, seats more than 6,400. Its stage is unusually large. Adjoining the auditorium on the north is the pavilion-ballroom, with floor space for 7,500 dancers, or 5,200 diners; a mezzanine balcony has space for 3,200 more.

R. from Jefferson Blvd. on Figueroa St.

112. Standing well back from the street in a copse is the FIGUEROA ADOBE (*adm. on application*), 3404 S. Figueroa St., built in 1847 by Ramon Figueroa, brother of the Mexican governor (1830) of California whose name was given by the American conquerors to the street on which the house stands. The gabled roof, dormers, and other additions, some of which have been built in later years, are departures from the typical adobe simplicity.

R. from Figueroa St. on 34th St.; L. from 34th on University Ave.
113. The UNIVERSITY OF SOUTHERN CALIFORNIA, University Ave. between 34th St. and Exposition Blvd., is a nonsectarian, co-educational institution spreading over a 45-acre campus. Founded in 1879 by the Southern California Conference of the Methodist Episcopal Church, the university remains under its general control. With a faculty of more than 700, a winter-session student enrollment of 9,000, and with 24 schools and colleges housed in 18 buildings, 10 of which have been erected since 1921, it is the largest and oldest university of continuous existence in southern California.

Named in honor of the university's fourth president, the GEORGE FINLEY BOVARD ADMINISTRATION BUILDING, University Ave. at 36th St. is a red-brick, red-tile-roofed structure with early Italian Renaissance details. The massive central tower, strengthened by eight brick buttresses, bears heroic statues by Caspar Gruenfeld of great educators, statesmen, and philosophers.

At the left front corner, mounted on a 10-foot pedestal, is an eight-foot statue of an armed Trojan warrior, the symbol adopted by the university in 1924; it was designed by Roger Noble Burnham.

Opposite the Administration Building is ALUMNI MEMORIAL PARK, an open lawn planted with sycamores and traversed by walks. Beyond it is the EDWARD L. DOHENY, JR. MEMORIAL LIBRARY, a large, double-winged four-story building of a modified Italian Romanesque style with walls of light-red brick, trimmed with limestone. It was built in 1932 at a cost of $1,105,000 by Edward L. Doheny.

The ALLAN HANCOCK FOUNDATION BUILDING, SE. corner University Ave. and 36th St., is a four-story structure containing more than 100 laboratories furnished with the latest equipment for natural sciences, research, two auditoriums, special stages for scientific demonstrations and equipment for the projection of colored motion pictures, and four drawing rooms for musicales, receptions, and exhibits.

The STUDENT UNION BUILDING, SW. corner University Ave. and 36th St., an ornate three and a half story red-brick and terra cotta structure designed in the manner of an Italian Renaissance palazzo, is the social and recreational headquarters for students and faculty.

SCIENCE HALL, SW. corner University Ave. and 36th Pl., houses the College of Pharmacy and the departments of natural and chemical sciences. The LAW BUILDING, SE. corner 36th Pl. and University Ave., has a two-story-high lobby that serves as a student common room. The library has 47,673 volumes, 3,000 pamphlets, and many current periodicals. Adjoining the Law Building is BRIDGE HALL, in which are the departments of geology, engineering, political science, comparative literature, and languages.

The COLONEL SEELEY WINTERSMITH MUDD MEMORIAL HALL OF PHILOSOPHY (R), University Ave. and 37th St., with a square slender clock tower, was designed in Lombardic Romanesque tradition. It contains the Mudd Collection of 13th, 14th, and 15th century manu-

scripts, and the incunabula of ancient philosophers. It has administration offices, classrooms, incunabula room, and collateral and main
library halls.

L. from University Ave. on Exposition Blvd.

EXPOSITION PARK (*grounds always open; free*), bounded by
Exposition Blvd., Figueroa St., S. Park Dr., and Menlo Ave., is a large
public park operated jointly by the state, county, and city. The park
lands were once part of a tract used by the Southern District Agricultural Society as a fair grounds and race course. Their venture ended
in failure in 1892 and the tract lay unused until the present park
was opened with public funds in 1910.

114. The MEMORIAL GATEWAY, at the central entrance to
Exposition Park from Exposition Boulevard, is flanked by two large
concrete monoliths commemorating the Tenth International Olympiad
whose opening and closing ceremonies were held in the park's coliseum
in 1932.

115. The SUNKEN ROSE GARDEN, beyond the gateway, is a
seven-acre plot planted with 15,000 rose bushes of 118 varieties. The
blooming season begins in March or April and lasts nine months. Four
white stone pergolas and four large sculptures are in a balanced arrangement near the corners of the rectangular plot. A fountain with a lily
pool is in the center.

116. The STATE ARMORY (*open Mon. eve.; free*), east of the
Sunken Rose Garden, a two-story red-brick building, is the headquarters
and training barracks of the 160th Infantry and other detachments of
the National Guard.

117. South of the Sunken Rose Garden is the STATE EXPOSI-
TION BUILDING (*open 10-4 weekdays except Wed. afternoon,
Sun. and holidays 2-5*), an E-shaped two-story structure with walls of
dark-red tapestry brick ornamented with terra cotta, designed by Na-
than Elery. It contains a permanent exhibition showing state resources, industries, and recreational features. A wide hallway lined
with exhibit cases leads from the main entrance to the two-story main
hall, which receives light from the ceiling through four stained-glass
panels showing historical California structures; in the hall is an enormous relief map of the state. In the west wing, decorated with murals
of California fruits and flowers, are the horticultural exhibits, and
models of vineyards and orchards. In the southwest wing is the Hall
of Animal Industries, with model ranches and natural habitat groups
of fish and game found in each county. In the East Hall is the mining
division, with models of oil fields, coal and gold mines, and lumber
camps; on the wall is a large map showing the Bret Harte trail, the
counties mentioned in his stories, and the places incident to Mark
Twain's life in the gold country. In the basement are exhibits of state
park facilities and a model section of a redwood forest with living trees.

118. The LOS ANGELES COUNTY MUSEUM OF HISTORY,
SCIENCE, AND ART (*open weekdays 10-4, Sun. and holidays 2-5*),

originally housed in the tridomed red-brick structure west of the Sunken Rose Gardens, now occupies the concrete addition adjoining the old building in the rear.

In Anthropology Hall is a very large and well-preserved collection of mammal remains, dug from La Brea Pits in Hancock Park (*see the Wilshire and West section*). Grouped about the skeleton of a great-tusked Imperial Elephant, four times the height of a man, are skeletons of the sabre-toothed cat, short-faced bear, dire wolf, giant ground sloth, western horse and camel, and of extinct species of ox and lion. In the collection of bird fossils is that of a giant vulture, the largest bird that ever flew, and a true peacock (*Pavo californicus*), found only in La Brea deposits.

In the Natural History Wing, groups of stuffed animals stand in softly lighted cases against backgrounds reproducing the flora, topography, and sky-tints of their native regions. The bison group, and the water hole group with zebras, giraffes, and many kinds of antelope, are particularly lifelike.

Other exhibits of note are the dioramas modeled to scale, showing California scenes from prehistoric times through the Russian, Spanish, Mexican, and American periods to the present day; the Motion-Picture Exhibit, which includes costumed models of prominent stars of the past and present, make-up boxes, props, Klieg lights, old cinema-house bills, illustrated song slides, and the like; the Harrison Collection of the work of contemporary American artists; the Regan Collection of Rembrandt etchings; the Coronel Collection of early California relics; the Otis Collection of weapons; and the Oriental Collection.

Egyptian mummies, swords, period furniture, snuffboxes, and models and specimens of early airplanes, automobiles, bicycles, and wearing apparel are part of the museum's miscellaneous stock. A Research Library has nearly 20,000 bound volumes and many thousands of unbound pamphlets, magazines and newspapers. The Junior Museum, on a floor below street level with an entrance at the southeast corner of the building, has models, books, and pictures illustrating history, science, travel, and art.

119. The LOS ANGELES MEMORIAL COLISEUM (*open 6-6*), at the end of the long mall, was designed by John and Donald Parkinson. The main entrance is a high, arched peristyle flanked by tall double arcades and topped by the Olympic Torch, which burned, in the tradition of the Olympic games, during the two weeks of the Tenth International Olympiad held in the Coliseum in 1932.

The stadium, with a seating capacity of 105,000, is much larger than that of the Coliseum in Rome. Notwithstanding the size of the stadium's crowds, its 108 portals are capable of discharging the entire attendance within 20 minutes. The coliseum was completed in 1923 after two years of construction, and enlarged to its present size in preparation for the Olympics. It is used for major football games, rodeos, track and field meets, pageants, religious ceremonies, and civic gatherings.

120. In the southwest corner of the park is the LOS ANGELES SWIMMING STADIUM (*open June to Sept. 9:30-5 weekdays, 1-5 Sun. and holidays; children under 16 years of age 10¢, adults 25¢, suits free*), a concrete and steel grandstand, seating 5,000 in view of two pools. One of the pools was designed for the aquatic events of the Tenth International Olympiad upon suggestions made by the swimming-sports leaders of the various participant nations; this pool is rendered extremely "fast" by specially designed sidewalls, splash bunkers, and water-level variations that eliminate ripples and backwash.

PART III

Neighboring Cities

Beverly Hills

Bus Service: Pacific Electric Ry. (2 lines); one from Hollywood-land through Beverly Hills to Westwood, with branch line from Beverly Hills Hotel to Wilshire Blvd. and Camden Dr.; one from Pershing Sq., Los Angeles via Beverly Blvd., Santa Monica Blvd., Canyon Dr., and Sunset Blvd. to Castellammare Beach. Los Angeles Motor Coach Co. (bus No. 82) from Pershing Sq. to Wilshire Blvd. and Beverly Dr.; transfer privileges to No. 88, N. via Beverly Dr. to Santa Monica Blvd., thence S. to Wilshire Blvd., connecting with bus No. 82 to Los Angeles. Fares 6¢ in Beverly Hills; 15¢ to Los Angeles.

Streetcars: Pacific Electric Ry. (2 lines), both from Subway Terminal Bldg., Los Angeles; one through Beverly Hills via Hollywood Junction; one via S. Hill St. and Vineyard. Fares 6¢ in Beverly Hills; 15¢ to Los Angeles.

Taxicabs: Yellow and Red Top stands at Pacific Electric Ry. Station. Fare 20¢ first ¼ mile, 10¢ each ½ mile thereafter.

Information Bureaus: Chamber of Commerce, room 210, 9437 Santa Monica Blvd.; Automobile Club of Southern California, 9344 Wilshire Blvd.

Street Numbers: Numbers N. and S. begin at Wilshire Blvd.; numbers W. on the major thoroughfares begin at San Vicente Blvd. and are continuation of Los Angeles numbers on same streets (with minor exceptions).

Traffic Regulations: Speed limit 15 m. on curves, passing schools, and at obstructed grade crossings; 20 m. in business district; 25 m. in residential district; 45 m. elsewhere. Parking in business district limited to 45 minutes between 8 a.m. and 6 p.m. except Sundays and legal holidays.

Hotels, Apartment Houses: Two internationally known hotels, the Beverly-Wilshire, 9514 Wilshire Blvd., and the Beverly Hills, 1201 Sunset Blvd.; a few others at average rates. Numerous furnished and unfurnished apartments, with greater number of furnished apartments nearer Wilshire Blvd. Rentals vary with the accommodations offered. Higher-priced units in rental area W. of Beverly Dr.

Auto and Trailer Camps: Well-appointed camps on outskirts of the community.

Radio Stations: KMPC (710 kc), 9631 Wilshire Blvd.

Churches: All Saints Episcopal, 504 N. Camden Dr.; Beverly Hills Community Presbyterian, 501 N. Rodeo Dr.; Church of the Good Shepherd, Catholic, Santa Monica Blvd. and Bedford Dr.; First Church of Christ, Scientist, near Charleville Blvd. and Rexford Dr.; Beverly Vista Community, Gregory Way and Elm Dr.

Motion-Picture Houses: Beverly Hills (Warner Bros.), 9404 Wilshire Blvd.; Beverly, 206 N. Beverly Dr.; Elite, 9036 Wilshire Blvd.; Regina, 8556 Wilshire Blvd.; Wilshire, 8440 Wilshire Blvd.

Parks and Playgrounds: Roxbury, Olympic Blvd. and Roxbury Dr.; La Cienega, Gregory Way and La Cienega Blvd.; Coldwater Canyon Park, Beverly Dr. and Coldwater Canyon Rd.; Sunset, Beverly and Canyon Drs.; Reservoir, Beverly Dr. and Coldwater Canyon Alley; Beverly Gardens is a

2-mile parkway, the SW. end of which is marked by an electric fountain, at Wilshire and Santa Monica Blvds.

Sports: Tennis courts at La Cienega and Roxbury Parks; swimming pool in La Cienega Park; eight golf courses within easy reach. Miles of bridle paths in and near Beverly Hills; information and mounts, riding academy at 101 N. San Vicente Blvd.

BEVERLY HILLS (325 alt., 26,823 pop.), a quiet and spotless city, the Gold Coast of the cinema world, is an independent municipality less than five square miles in extent. It lies eight miles west of Los Angeles, into which it fits like a jagged piece in a jigsaw puzzle. Here lawns are required by law; "For Sale" signs must be no more than one foot square, and only one to a lot; none of the 28,000 uniformly-planted pines, acacias, blue-flowering jacarandas, feathery pepper or scarlet-flowering eucalyptus trees that line the thoroughfares can be removed without the consent of 51 per cent of the landowners affected, and then only with a guarantee that they will be replaced by trees of equal age; strict zoning laws forbid business buildings north of Santa Monica Boulevard, which slants southwest across the community; shops are tolerated on few streets outside a small triangle at the junction of Santa Monica and Wilshire Boulevards.

For two miles along the north side of Santa Monica Boulevard runs Beverly Gardens, opposite which, at Crescent Drive, is the imposing City Hall, Spanish Renaissance in design, set in landscaped grounds. South of the parkway, on the level coastal plain, are pleasant streets bordered with attractive and less elaborate houses, although the cost of many ran to five figures. From the other side of the gardens, gently curving streets extend, tendril-like, into cool shaded canyons and up the steep pitches of the Santa Monica foothills, a section of large and often lavish estates, the homes of movie stars whose meteoric careers are currently in the ascendant or at the zenith.

Although Beverly Hills is young, its site was occupied more than a century ago by the 4,500-acre Rancho Rodeo de las Aguas (gathering of the waters), also known as the Rancho San Antonio. In the early 1830's, Senora Rita Villa, nee Valdez, granddaughter of one of the first settlers of Los Angeles and widow of another, maintained a home here and another in Los Angeles. In 1854 the rancho was sold to two Americans, Benjamin (Don Benito) Wilson and Major Henry Hancock, of the adjacent Rancho La Brea. Attempts were made to found a settlement in 1869, and again during the boom of the late 1880's. Both failed, but in 1906, with the organization of the Rodeo Land and Water Company by Burton E. Green, of Beverly Farms, Mass., a new subdivision was laid out on the level ground between Wilshire and Santa Monica Boulevards and recorded as Beverly; the subdivision of Beverly Hills was laid out toward the northwest the next year. The panic of 1907-8 halted development until 1912, when the Beverly Hills Hotel was erected in the middle of a bean field. Two years later the population totaled 500, and Beverly Hills was incorporated as a municipality, governed by five nonsalaried councilmen, one of whom acted as mayor. The 1920 census revealed only 674 residents, but the movement that was to increase the population 2,500 per cent within a decade had already been instituted in 1919 when Douglas Fairbanks, Sr., purchased the hilltop site of Pickfair for $35,000. Other celebrities followed, some to build modest houses, others fired with an ambition to exceed the "magnificent" and the "stupendous," heaping up gigantic establishments that have since become "colossal" stones around their necks. Pickfair has been offered for sale; William Powell's house, with its elaborate gadgets, has been sold; an attempt to auction off John Barrymore's hilltop mansion brought no acceptable bid. "The Chinese Tenement," as Barrymore scornfully refers to it, cost the actor $448,-000. "Frankly," he said, "it was a kind of nightmare, but it might appeal to somebody—maybe some actor . . . Yep, three pools. Incredible, isn't it? In one of them I used to keep rainbow trout . . ."

The real estate boom of the early 1920's inspired considerable bustle and excitement, stimulated in part by the late Will Rogers, who was the city's honorary mayor before his death in 1935, and whose daily syndicated column usually carried a "Beverly Hills" date line. "Lots are sold so quickly and often here," he wrote in August 1923, "that they are put through escrow made out to the twelfth owner. They couldn't possibly make a separate deed for each purchaser; besides he wouldn't have time to read [it] in the ten minutes time he owned the lot. Your having no money don't worry the agents, if they can just get a couple of dollars down, or an old overcoat or shotgun, or anything to act as down payment. Second-hand Fords are considered A-1 collateral."

More than 150 film stars now live in Beverly Hills, as well as such notables as Sigmund Romberg, composer; Freeman Gosden and Charles Correll, the Amos 'n Andy of radio; Grantland Rice, sports writer; Elsie Janis, former musical comedy star; and motor magnates E. L. Cord and C. W. Nash. Some reside south of Sunset Boulevard, between Hillcrest and Walden Drives, but the majority have their houses on Lexington Road, Coldwater Canyon Drive, Tower Road, and Cove Way. For the most part, the mansions are pleasantly situated and unobtrusive, although a few assault the senses and every criterion of good design. None carry neon lights emblazoning the name and fame of the occupants; rather, the eager tourist, usually feminine, chiefly young or of uncertain age, confesses sore disappointment to discover that the lives of those so glamorously portrayed in movie magazines and gossip columns are screened from view by high walls and hedges. Sightseers catch no glimpse of onyx swimming pools, sunken gardens, private golf courses, Borzoi hounds, and elegant tea and cocktail parties on terraced lawns, but they never tire of hearing the guides on the rubberneck wagons shout: "On the right, the home of Jack Benny and Mary Livingstone; also on the right, Eddie Cantor . . . Left, Charlie Chaplin . . . Left, Fred Astaire . . . The vast estate of Harold Lloyd, with its waterfall . . . Right . . . Left . . . Right."

The city continues to grow rapidly. Stars of screen, radio, and stage come in increasing numbers, with financiers and industrialists in their wake, to enjoy Beverly Hills' studied charm and freedom from the smoke, clatter, and conflicts of industry. In recent years many business and professional people of comparatively modest means have come from Los Angeles and other communities to build homes here, with the result that the construction industry has been greatly stimulated locally and in all surrounding territory, but the predominant local "industry," and one that employs thousands, remains that of servicing the manifold, sometimes bizarre, and always expensive needs of those "in the money."

POINTS OF INTEREST

BEVERLY GARDENS is a block-wide parkway extending almost two miles along the north side of Santa Monica Blvd., from Doheny Dr. to Wilshire Blvd. A promenade runs the length of the park under sweeping elms; pergolas, ornamental fountains, flower beds, attractively planted groups of trees, rose and cacti gardens, and a lily pond grace the parkway.

1. The ELECTRIC FOUNTAIN, NW. corner Wilshire and Santa Monica Blvds., can produce more than 60 effects by changes of spray, stream, and color. A kneeling figure on a square column rising from the center of the circular reservoir symbolizes an Indian rain prayer; the frieze around the base pictures incidents in California's early history.

2. The Roman Catholic CHURCH OF THE GOOD SHEPHERD, NW corner Santa Monica Blvd. and N. Bedford Dr., Spanish Colonial in style, with heavy baroque ornamentation, has two massive buttressed towers, with low, black-roofed domes above the open arches of the belfries. Reaching half the height of the facade is an atrium, with three arched doorways, extending from tower to tower. The reinforced concrete building is covered with ivory-tinted stucco. The ivory walls, columns, and ceiling of the interior provide a striking setting for the windows of richly-hued Munich glass that lend the church much of its distinction. The sanctuary extends the full width of the nave, from which it is divided by a marble rail. Shrines with colored figures of the Virgin, angels and various saints, holding staffs that flower into clusters of candles, flank the main altar. Pulpit and altar are of white Italian marble.

The rectory is linked to the church by an arcade, with a screen of similarly designed arches enclosing the formal gardens that surround the rectory.

3. ALL SAINTS EPISCOPAL CHURCH, NW. corner Santa Monica Blvd. and N. Camden Dr., flanked by rose gardens in an expanse of lawn, authentically reproduces the design of the Christian basilicas of ancient Rome. Constructed of concrete, with walls two feet thick, the church has a rough-surfaced facade unadorned except for a line of red tile edging the low-pitched gable. Across the facade, pierced by a small stained-glass rose window, extends a shed-like

atrium, with a tile roof sloping streetward. Leather-covered doors, studded with brass nails, open directly into the plain and simple nave; the brown, hand-hewn timbers of the roof are exposed. Red tiles pave both nave and sanctuary; in the semi-circular apse at the rear of the church, the altar is a flash of gold.

The CIVIC CENTER is developing between Santa Monica Boulevard, Rexford and Crescent Drives.

4. The NEW POST OFFICE, junction N. Crescent Dr. and Santa Monica Blvd., is a California-Mediterranean structure of brick and stone with red-tile roof; the two-story central unit is flanked with one-story wings at either side.

5. The CITY HALL, opposite the Post Office, dominates the Civic Center. Spanish Renaissance in style, it was designed by William J. Gage and built in 1932. From its long, balanced three-story base, a campanile rises eight stories to a finial and small gold cupola, topped with a colorful mosaic hemisphere. From the four corners of the main building project elongated wings—one story in front, two stories in the rear—with ornate window and cornice embellishments. From the Crescent Drive side a wide stairway and promenade leads between the wings through a forecourt to the classical main entrance. The building houses the municipal administrative offices, city jail, public library, and emergency hospital.

6. The FIRST CHURCH OF CHRIST, SCIENTIST, 142 S. Rexford Dr., together with its Sunday School buildings, encloses three sides of an open court paved with square red tiles. The buildings have simple roof lines broken at the center by a small lantern, or fleche. The church has a high pediment supported by slender Corinthian columns; a commodious foyer leads into the 1,250-seat auditorium, with stately windows of white cathedral glass. The pews are luxurious opera chairs, upholstered in soft blue-gray plush. The auditorium is air-conditioned and lighted indirectly by hanging fixtures in delicate patterns of blue and gold.

7. The BEVERLY-WILSHIRE HOTEL, 9514 Wilshire Blvd., has been a rendezvous for wealthy tourists and cinema headliners since its opening in 1928. The U-shaped building, of concrete, with veneer of tan pressed brick, has a flat roof with a wide overhang; the facade reflects strong Italian influence in the arched openings of the first and top floors and in its low-relief baroque ornamentation.

8. The TWENTIETH CENTURY-FOX STUDIOS, 10201 W. Pico Blvd., is in 1939 the largest motion-picture studio in the country. Ivy-covered stucco walls surround the 225-acre lot, where are scattered 20 immense sound stages, one with a plant for freezing ice for winter scenes. There are also wardrobe buildings, containing habiliment for anything from a Roman tyrant to a Salvation Army general; scattered buildings, housing thousands of props; a building that once served as Tom Mix' stables but is now the Arsenal and Sound Effects Department, with equipment for every conceivable noise from a mouse squeak to a volcano rumble; a Norman chateau for writers; and a Hall of

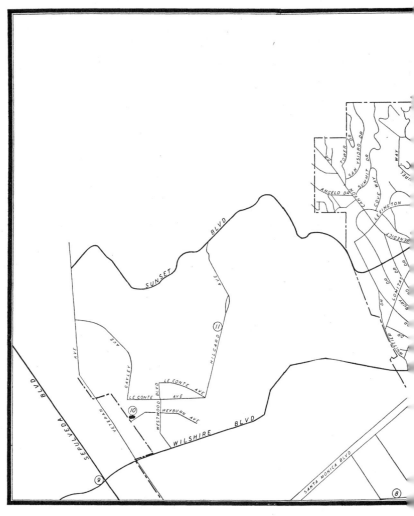

POINTS

1. Electric Fountain
2. Church of the Good Shepherd
3. All Saints Episcopal Church
4. New Post Office

5. City Hall
6. First Church of Christ, Scientist
7. Beverly-Wilshire Hotel

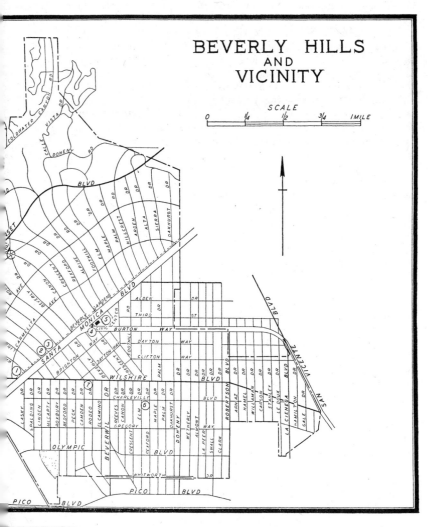

BEVERLY HILLS
AND
VICINITY

SCALE

0   1/4   1/2   3/4   1 MILE

INTEREST

8. 20th Century-Fox Studios
9. Veterans Administration Facility
10. Tropical Ice Gardens
11. University of California at Los Angeles
12. Municipal Park
13. Beverly Hills Hotel

Music with fountained patio, where many successful musical films have been made.

9. The VETERANS ADMINISTRATION FACILITY OF LOS ANGELES (*visited 1:30-3 daily; tubercular wards 3-4:30 daily; psychopathic wards Sun., Tues., and Thurs. 2-4*), Sepulveda and Wilshire Blvds., comprises approximately 175 buildings on 700 acres of land, most of them landscaped with lawns, trees, and flower beds. The institution, locally called the Sawtelle Soldiers' Home, provides free hospitalization for veterans of the Civil, Spanish-American, and World Wars. The largest (1939) soldiers' home in the country, it has facilities to care for 7,700 veterans who are disabled or in need of medical care.

Westwood Boulevard, lined with tall palms and green parkways, is the main thoroughfare of WESTWOOD VILLAGE (388 alt.), a 10-year-old town within the corporate limits of Los Angeles. It is a community resplendent with high-towered filling stations, new, dazzling-white shops under red-tile roofs, and many patios with fountains. It is a shopping center for the very prosperous Westwood and Bel-Air residential districts to the north, and for the students of the University of California at Los Angeles.

10. The TROPICAL ICE GARDENS (*skating, daytime 40¢, evening 55¢, including skates*), just south of the U.C.L.A. campus, at the end of Weyburn Ave., have an outdoor ice floor the year round. A gallery (*occasional exhibitions; adm. 50¢ to $2*) seating 8,000, and a synthetic Alpine village surround the rink.

11. The UNIVERSITY OF CALIFORNIA AT LOS ANGELES, 405 Hilgard Ave., stands in extensive lawns crowning a broad terraced elevation overlooking rolling valleys, plains, and low hills. Behind, the blue-misted Santa Monica Mountains form an irregular sky line. The buildings erected since 1929 stand on grounds thicky bordered with iceplant, but lack the ivy and venerable shade trees of older institutions of learning; the grouping of these buildings has the efficiency and orderliness possible only when a full grown institution is transplanted to a new site.

An integral part of the University of California, the University of California at Los Angeles grew out of the Los Angeles State Normal School, founded in 1881. In 1919 that institution became the University of California, Southern Branch; the present name was adopted in 1927. Two years later it was moved to this campus, which had been presented by the cities of Los Angeles, Santa Monica, Venice, and Beverly Hills.

With a faculty of more than 300, the university offers instruction in the humanities, the sciences, business administration, education, and agriculture to more than 7,000 graduate and undergraduate students.

The four main buildings stand on a low hilltop reached from the Hilgard Ave. entrance by way of a monumental bridge. These central buildings, in the walls and roofs of which is much terra cotta, brick, and tile, are four stories high and display the usual eclectic southern California motifs and architectural features in their decoration. Roman-esque and Italian Renaissance influences are particularly apparent. On the north side of an esplanade is JOSIAH ROYCE HALL, housing the auditorium, classrooms, and faculty offices, and named for the philos-opher who was one of the University of California's notable graduates. With tiled gabled roofs and two massive towers flanking the triple-arched entrance, the facade of the hall to some extent resembles that of the Church of San Ambrogia in Milan. On the south side, across the walk-bordered green, is the vast LIBRARY, housing 322,000 vol-umes. The central unit of the large structure, which has wings and rear extensions, is crowned with an octagonal superstructure with a set-back. Royce Hall was designed by Allison and Allison, the Library by George W. Kelham. Simpler in detail and treatment are the build-ings grouped east and south of Royce Hall and the Library Building: the Chemistry-Geology, the Physics-Biology, the Administration, and Education buildings. At the west end of the esplanade, a broad low brick stairway with terra-cotta balustrades descends to the Men's and Women's Gymnasiums, and their swimming pools. Set apart from the main group, southwest of the Education Building is KERCKHOFF HALL, social center for students and faculty, where the traditional Tudor University note is introduced with a graceful turreted tower and leaded windows. Overlooking the campus from the north is the President's residence. Near the south entrance on Westwood Blvd. is the ME-CHANIC ARTS BUILDING and shops.

12. The MUNICIPAL PARK, Sunset Blvd. and Beverly and Canon Drs., has wide and carefully kept lawns, stately palms, and a central fountain that effectively camouflage the great 8,000,000-gallon water tank beneath, the city's reservoir.

13. The BEVERLY HILLS HOTEL, 1201 Sunset Blvd., set back on a gentle hillside on 10 acres of ornamental shrubbery, lofty fan palms, and spreading date trees, is a diffuse, four-story concrete and stucco structure, with tile roofs and arched entrances reminiscent of the early California missions. Windows are grouped in twos and threes; a spacious second-story balcony overlooks the swimming pool; 20 bun-galows are scattered about the grounds.

Glendale

Railroad Stations: Southern Pacific R.R., Cerritos and Railroad Aves.; Union Pacific R.R., 730 E. Lexington Dr.; Pacific Electric Ry., 106 N. Brand Blvd.

Bus Stations: Motor Transit Lines, 102½ S. Glendale Ave.; Burlington Trailways, 213 E. Broadway; Greyhound and Union Pacific Stages, 202 S. Brand Blvd.

Bus Service: Pasadena-Ocean Park Line to Pasadena, Hollywood, and beaches; Motor Transit Co. to Los Angeles (branch line to Verdugo City); Pacific Electric Motor Coaches, local and interurban (Los Angeles-Burbank) service, local fare 5¢ and 10¢, Los Angeles 15¢, Burbank 10¢.

Streetcars: Pacific Electric Glendale Line, N. on Brand Blvd. to Mountain St.; Burbank Line, N. on Brand Blvd. to Glenoaks Blvd., thence W. to terminus in Burbank; Pacific Electric local line, E. on Broadway from Brand Blvd. to Chevy Chase Dr. (fare 6¢ within city limits).

Airport: Grand Central Air Terminal, 1224 Air Way, 2 *m.* (NE) from center of Glendale, for Pan-American Airways, Palm Springs Air Line, and Mexican Aviation Co. Planes for charter.

Taxicabs: Yellow Cab Co. and Glendale Taxi Service; meter rates.

Traffic Regulations: Uniform traffic ordinances for California cities, as contained in booklet compiled by Automobile Club of Southern California; watch signs for parking rules and one-way streets.

Information Bureaus: Hotel Informant, 709 E. Broadway; Automobile Club of Southern California, 600 S. Central Ave.; Glendale Chamber of Commerce, 116 E. Wilson Ave.; railroad and bus stations.

Street Numbers: Numbered E. and W. from Brand Blvd., and N. and S. from Broadway, 100 to the block.

Accommodations: 11 hotels near Brand and Colorado Blvd.; rates $1-$3.50 per day; 140 apartment houses, 100 bungalow courts.

Auto and Trailer Camps: Auto camp at San Fernando Rd. and Ivy Ave. Trailer camps at Riverside Dr. and San Fernando Rd., at Riverside Dr. and Magnolia Ave.

Radio Station: KIEV, Hotel Glendale, 701 E. Broadway.

Theatres: 8 motion-picture theatres. Occasional performances in Glendale High School Auditorium by Glendale Community Players.

Churches: 42 churches and religious groups, representing most denominations.

Schools: More than 40 public and private institutions.

Newspapers: News-Press, daily, eves. (except Sun.); *Star,* twice-weekly, Thurs. and Sun.

Parks, Playgrounds, Picnic Grounds: Fremont Park, Patterson and Kenilworth Aves.; Glenoaks Park, E. Glenoaks Blvd. and Garden Pl.; Maple

Park, 813 E. Maple and Cedar Sts.; Nibley Park, 1300 E. Mountain St.;
Raymond Park, 1400 block Raymond Ave.; San Rafael Park, 1340 Dorothy
Dr.; Sparr Heights Park, 331 Downing Ave.; Verdugo Recreation Center,'
La Canada Blvd. near Rossmoyne; Wilson Recreation Center, 200 block on
N. Kenwood St.

Golf: Chevy Chase Club, 3067 Chevy Chase Dr., 9 holes (green fees—daily,
weekly, or monthly). Oakmont Country Club, 3005 Country Club Dr., 18
holes; restricted to members and guests.

Tennis: Fremont, Glenoaks, Maple, Nibley, and Raymond Parks.

Swimming: Municipal plunges in Fremont Park and at Verdugo Recreation
Center.

Annual Events: Easter Sunrise Service, Forest Lawn Memorial Park, 1712
S. Glendale Ave. Living Christmas Tree Contest. (Residents vie with each
other in decorating living trees in their yards.)

GLENDALE (650 alt., 82,582 pop.), encircled by wooded hills and
blue-veiled mountains in the narrow southeastern tip of the San Fernando Valley, is an attractive residential city of frame bungalows and
white or pastel-tinted stucco houses with gayly colored roofs, shutters,
and awnings, set off by green lawns and bright gardens. Golden-
tasseled acacia, scarlet-hung pepper, eucalyptus, and palm trees border
many of the city's streets, and thoroughfares frequently present a vista
of green foothills or the Verdugo Mountains, purple in the distance.
Curving roads climb gentle slopes to the newer residential section in the
hills; higher on the hillsides are large mansions, and several health
resorts and sanitariums.

Nine main boulevards intersect the city and connect with transcontinental highways. Modern shops line the business center at Brand
Boulevard and Broadway; most of the buildings are of one or two
stories, but a scattering of seven- and eight-story hotels, clubs, and banks
offer a faint suggestion of a sky line.

Cheap land and power, proximity to oil and gas, extensive local
markets and convenient transportation to larger markets, an open-shop
labor policy and an equable climate have been factors in the city's rise
since 1910 from a drowsy hamlet to a flourishing industrial city, third
in rank among the 44 cities of Los Angeles County. More than 200
plants manufacture such varied products as asbestos roofing, cement,
sprinklers, refrigerators, light posts, sheet metal, motors, incinerators,
automobile accessories, mattresses, beverages, cereals, tents and awnings, musical instruments, and jewelry; most of the kiln products used
in downtown Los Angeles building construction are from Glendale.

Although superseded recently as a transcontinental and international
terminus by the Union Air Terminal at Burbank (*see Tour 7*), Glendale's airport remains one of the finest in the West.

The site of Glendale and several adjoining communities was included in the huge 30,000-acre triangular domain extending from the
Arroyo Seco to the lands of the Mission San Fernando, the first and
largest land grant in the frontier territory of Alta California, which
was given in 1794 to Corporal Jose Maria Verdugo, captain of the

guard at San Gabriel Mission. Here on the Rancho San Rafael, as it was named, Don Jose and his family lived in frontier fashion, turning over the soil with wooden plows, driving cattle over the threshing floor to trample out the grain, throwing grain and chaff against the wind to winnow it. The rancho sheltered priests and soldiers during the troubled years in which Alta California passed from Spain to Mexico and then from Mexico to the United States. Under an oak on the rancho the Cahuenga Capitulation Treaty was signed by General Andres Pico and Lieutenant Colonel John C. Fremont on January 12, 1847.

On Don Jose's death in 1831, the ranch passed to his children, Julio and Catalina. As master of the rancho, Julio continued to live the pleasant life of a caballero; the elite of the countryside were entertained with traditional display and hospitality at Verdugo fandangos and rodeos. Catalina, a blind spinster, made her home with one or another of Julio's many sons, until her favorite nephew Teodoro built for her when she was 60, La Casa de Catalina Verdugo. Division of the property among heirs and relatives, the sale of large parts of the rancho to pay debts, and litigation in the 1870's left the Verdugo family with only 5,000 acres.

Thirteen American families had established homes among fruit orchards and orange groves here by 1883, when the Southern Pacific Railroad was extended through the rancho. Lands were pooled by the farmers, a townsite was laid out, and the community named Glendale for a painting so entitled by an artist whose name has been lost to posterity. Controversy over the name led to the building of another community called Tropico, absorbed by Glendale in 1917. During the booming 1880's a narrow gauge steam line linked the village with Los Angeles; a large hotel was erected, and the Glendale *Encinal* was established by Arthur and Walter Wheeler, enterprising journalists, who made the rounds of adjacent communities twice weekly astride broncos or in mule-drawn carts.

At the termination of the boom in 1888 the settlement had a population of 300, three short blocks of cement sidewalk, the empty Glendale Hotel, and no gas, electricity, or other facilities. But a church, livery stable, blacksmith shop, and a meat market remained to serve the townsfolk.

Renewed cultivation of orchards and farms in the surrounding countryside, brisk marketing of prunes, peaches, apricots, and strawberries, helped to revive the dormant hamlet. By 1904, when the Pacific Electric interurban connection with Los Angeles was completed, the town's population had trebled; commerce had greatly increased, and the Glendale Hotel, acquired by L. C. Brand on a plumber's lien, was leased as a young ladies' seminary and renamed St. Hilda's Hall. The town's population grew from 2,000 in 1906, the year of its incorporation, to 13,000 in 1920. Farms and orchards gave way to business and manufacturing. The city manager form of government was adopted in 1922. The town's own police, fire department, public utilities, school system, and recreational institutions were established.

Today Glendale is a financially sound little city with active civic and business clubs and ambitious cultural and social societies. The suburban residential character of the town is still unthreatened by its expanding industry.

POINTS OF INTEREST

1. The UNITED STATES POST OFFICE AND FEDERAL BUILDING, 313 E. Broadway, Spanish Renaissance in style, designed by George M. Lindsey and completed in 1934 has a two-story central unit and one-story wings surfaced with terra cotta resembling granite.
2. FOREST LAWN MEMORIAL PARK, 1712 Glendale Ave. (*open 8-5*), is 220 elaborate and elegantly groomed burial acres dotted with gleaming white statuary, quaint chapels, ponds with graceful swans and "pure white ducks," a massive mausoleum, and an inspiring Tower of Legends enclosing a 165,000-gallon water tank. This park was the inspiration of Hubert C. Eaton, a banker who on New Year's Day, 1917, stood on a height surveying an old country cemetery here he had just acquired by foreclosure of a mortgage. In the words of the Board of Trustees, "a vision came to the man of what this tiny God's Acre might become; and standing there he made a promise to The Infinite." On returning home he put his promise into words, registering his profound conviction that "the cemeteries of today are wrong because they depict an end, not a beginning," and have consequently become "unsightly stoneyards full of inartistic symbols and depressing customs, places that do nothing for humanity save a practical act and that not well."

Forest Lawn was to correct all this, and it has gone far in its chosen direction. No "unsightly" tombstones are allowed here, merely brass plates on the grass, under which lie with others the remains of Will Rogers and Wallace Reid. Funds were generously invested at home and abroad in sculptured marble and stained glass. Landscape architects were given free rein in laying out dells, nooks, fountains, lanes where "lovers new and old . . . [may] stroll and watch the sunset's glow, planning for the future," and a maze of paved driveways for more modern Romeos. A "lucky" bride's seat was placed in the forecourt of a handsome marriage chapel, modern in conveniences, Old World in atmosphere, where "the only theology is love," a note echoed from cloistered recesses along both sides of the nave where, above masses of greenery and bowers of fragrant blooms, caged canaries "trill the melody of love." The most inspired advertising talent was hired to proclaim far and wide the revolutionary import of this latest conception of the traditional Eternity Acres—to educate the public at large in the builder's credo, based on his belief that Christ "smiles and loves you and me," and to acquaint the world with the artistic, scenic, horticultural, and spiritual beauties of Forest Lawn. Mr. Bruce Barton, public relations counsel, former Congressman from the "Silk Stocking District" of New York City, and author of *The Man Nobody Knows,* has described the place in a signed, framed, testimonial as "a first step up toward Heaven," urging all visitors who come here to go home and establish similar places, for "not until that happens will we be able to call ourselves a truly Christian nation." Prices for burial here start as low as $45, which includes perpetual care, although as much as $100,000 has been spent on a single memorial.

Just within the large wrought-iron entrance gates are (R) the Administration Building, on the lines of a Tudor manor, with a well-stocked flower and art shop, and (R) the mortuary. Southeast of the latter is the LITTLE CHURCH OF THE FLOWERS, a copy of the 14th-century church in the village of Stoke Poges, England, where Thomas Gray was inspired to his "Elegy in a Country Churchyard" by the moldy headstones in the weedy burial ground in the shadow of the church, warning ambition not to mock,

Nor grandeur hear with a disdainful smile
The short and simple annals of the poor.

All but the weeds and the tombstones have been faithfully reproduced here, even the ivy-mantled tower, and in the chapel is the old communion table from the Stoke Poges Church, together with Mr. Barton's tribute, a carved oak contribution box, and other interesting features. The TREE OF LIFE WINDOW, in stained glass, is patterned on a design from an illuminated medieval manuscript.

Eastward on Main Drive is (R) THE FINDING OF MOSES FOUNTAIN, a reproduction of that by Brazza, in the Pincion Gardens in Rome; 22 life-size figures constitute the MYSTERY OF LIFE GROUP, by Ernesto Gazzeri.

Northeast of the Mystery of Life group is the WEE KIRK O' THE HEATHER, of cream-colored sandstone, with slate roof, an exact copy of the little 14th-century church in Glencairn, Scotland, where bonnie Annie Laurie worshiped and was buried in the 18th century. The four double windows in the south wall depict in stained glass her frustrated love. In the forecourt of the church is the ANNIE LAURIE WISHING CHAIR, built of stones from the altar in the Glencairn kirk. "Fairies have blessed these stones," so runs a legend carved in the back of the chair, and luck will attend the bride and groom who sit here, hand in hand, on their wedding day. Adjoining the Wee Kirk is God's Garden, containing a large marble copy of Thorvaldsen's CHRISTUS.

In the southern part of the grounds rises the tower of the $4,500,-000 MAUSOLEUM (*adm. to Memorial Terrace by appointment*), which descends the hillside in six great terraces. In the MEMORIAL COURT OF HONOR, gleaming with rare polished marble and reproductions of Michelangelo's largest sculptures, is the LAST SUPPER WINDOW, a full-sized reproduction in stained glass of Da Vinci's fresco in the Santa Maria delle Grazia convent at Milan. At the entrance to the Me-

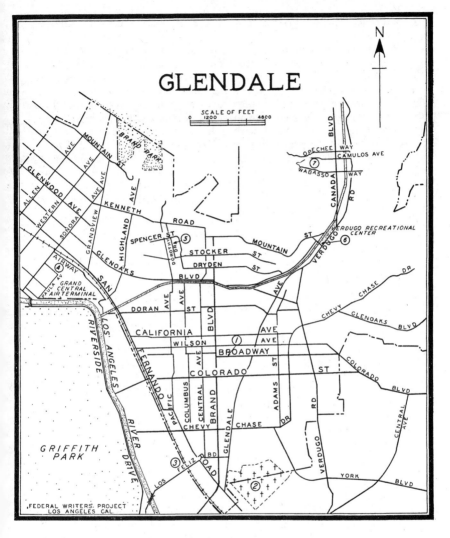

POINTS OF INTEREST

1. U. S. Post Office and Federal Building
2. Forest Lawn Memorial Park
3. Gladding, McBean & Company Plant
4. Curtiss-Wright Technical Institute
5. Casa Adobe de San Rafael
6. Glendale Civic Auditorium
7. Verdugo Adobe

morial Terrace is the FOR SUCH IS THE KINGDOM OF HEAVEN GROUP, by Vicenzo Jerace.

North of the mausoleum, on Sunrise Slope, is the TEMPLE OF SANTA SABINA, brought in 1929 from the Basilica of Santa Sabina in Rome, where it had stood for 400 years, commemorating the martyred wife of the Roman Emperor, Valentinus, and now a memorial to E. L. Doheny, Jr. The baldachino, the work of the 16th-century sculptor, Poscetti, rests on slim marble columns above the sarcophagus-altar of rare marbles, inlaid with gold mosaic. On a high hill on the park's northern boundary rises the TOWER OF LEGENDS, an 87-foot white concrete shaft, bearing Norse figures in relief. Many memorials and other statuary are scattered throughout the several sections—Slumberland, Graceland, Mystery of Life, Vale of Memory, Whispering Pines, and Babyland, in which are many pieces, including *Sleepy Time,* showing two small children asleep in a luxurious tasseled armchair of marble, with even the buttons of the upholstery faithfully represented, and the DUCK BABY, "the Spirit of Forest Lawn."

3. The GLADDING, McBEAN AND COMPANY PLANT, 2901 Los Feliz Blvd. (*display and stockrooms open 8-5*), makes art tiles, pottery, roofing tiles, glazed tile facings, mosaics, and terra cotta ornaments, producing 80 per cent of the kiln products used in the larger downtown buildings of Los Angeles, which uses more terra cotta than any city in the United States. The products of the company have strongly influenced the development of the California version of Spanish mission design. Virtually all raw materials for the kilns come from deposits in Los Angeles County (*see Tour 3*) and neighboring regions.

The GRAND CENTRAL AIR TERMINAL, 1224 Air Way, the Los Angeles terminus of the Pan-American Airways and the Mexican Aviation Company, is a United States Customs port of air entry. The offices and waiting rooms are in the neat tan stucco Terminal Building, on the Air Way side of the 220-acre landing field. The government-approved Grand Central Flying School has headquarters at the field, around which are several private flying schools and many aircraft shops. The air squad of the Los Angeles County Sheriff's office is based here; hangars provide space for private planes.

The "crate" in which Douglas Corrigan "lost his way" on an announced flight from New York City to California in 1938, landing next day in Ireland, was pieced together and tuned up on this field.

The field, established in 1928 by a small group of aviation enthusiasts, passed the following year into the hands of the Curtiss-Wright Corporation which enlarged and developed it. It has recently been superseded in large part as a transcontinental and international airport by the Union Air Terminal at Burbank (*see Tour 7*).

4. The CURTISS-WRIGHT TECHNICAL INSTITUTE (*visited 8-4, free; apply at office in Terminal Bldg.*), which owns and operates Grand Central Air Terminal, is the largest school for aircraft mechanics in the country. There are (1939) approximately 500 students.

BRAND PARK, Mountain St. and Grandview Ave., an irregu-larly-shaped area in the northwest section of Glendale, extends beyond the city limits and embraces 602 acres of natural woodland of the Verdugo Hills. The northern part has been closed to the public since 1934, when floods washed out the main roads. The 82-acre southern section, still open but undeveloped, contains the house and library of Leslie C. Brand, pioneer Glendale subdivider, who willed the park to the city before his death in 1922. Upon the death of his wife the house and library will become the property of the city of Glendale.

5. The CASA ADOBE DE SAN RAFAEL (*open daily except Mon., 1-4; grounds open daily 10-4:30*), 1340 Dorothy Dr., is a rambling whitewashed ranch house, with a splintered wooden porch running along its wide front and across one end. The house, the oldest in Glendale, was built in the 1860's by Tomas Sanchez, first sheriff of Los Angeles County, on a part of the old Rancho San Rafael inherited by his wife Maria Sepulveda, whom he married at the age of 13 and who here bore him 21 children. The bare and crudely finished interior has furniture and other relics of the days when it was built. The grounds, with their original careless charm, have an air of lazy dilapida-tion saved from bleakness only by a scattering of shrubs and a clump of giant shaggy eucalyptus trees, grown from seeds presented to Sanchez by Phineas Banning, developer of Wilmington, who received them from a missionary. The city of Glendale has built a six-foot white-washed wall around the place to protect it as a public monument.

The VERDUGO RECREATIONAL CENTER, 1401 N. Ver-dugo Rd., is a landscaped 7-acre plot in the canyon east of the Verdugo Hills.

6. The center contains the GLENDALE CIVIC AUDITORIUM and an outdoor swimming stadium (*open 10-10 May 15-Sept. 15; rates 10¢-25¢*). The white buildings are of modified Spanish-Colonial design, with blue-green pattern border and red tile roofs. The audi-torium, seating 2,500 persons, has a "floating" dance floor—a floor with an inner layer of resilient material.

7. The VERDUGO ADOBE (*private*), 1517 Camulos Dr., the last of the five houses put up by the Verdugos on Rancho San Rafael, is a plain squat dwelling with thick whitewashed walls and a porch along the front, darkened by a spreading rose vine. Here Dona Catalina Verdugo, who with her brother Julio inherited the valley in which Glendale now lies, lived with her favorite nephew Teodoro, one of Julio's 13 sons.

The Harbor: San Pedro
and Wilmington

Railroad Stations: San Pedro: Pacific Electric Ry. and Southern Pacific R.R., 5th St. and Harbor Blvd. Terminal Island: Union Pacific and Santa Fe R.R. Wilmington: Santa Fe Ry., 711 E. Anaheim St.; Southern Pacific R.R., 331 N. Avalon Blvd.; Pacific Electric Ry., 333 N. Avalon Blvd. 2 Pacific Electric Ry. lines between San Pedro and Los Angeles, one via Dominguez Junction, the other via Gardena. Harbor Belt Line links all rail and steamship lines.

Bus Stations: San Pedro: Union Bus Depot, 240 W. 6th St., Wilmington: Los Angels Motor Coach Corp., 104 E. Anaheim St.; Wilmington Bus Co., 1541 Bay View Ave.

Streetcars: Local service in San Pedro and Wilmington by Pacific Electric Ry., fare 6¢.

Taxis: Several companies; rates under zone system, minimum charge 15¢.

Information Bureaus: San Pedro: Chamber of Commerce, 820 S. Commercial St.; Automobile Club of Southern California, 1432 S. Pacific Ave. Wilmington: Chamber of Commerce, 327 Avalon Blvd.

Streets and Numbers: San Pedro: from 1st St. S. all E.-W. streets are numbered to Paseo del Mar; N. from 1st St. E.-W. streets bear names, as do all N.-S. streets. The principal N.-S. thoroughfare is Pacific Ave. Chief E.-W. route is 6th St., from Waterfront to Pacific Ave., then S. to 9th S. Wilmington: Streets laid out in squares except those skirting the water front. E.-W. streets are lettered from A to R; avenues run N.-S. Exceptions are Pacific Coast Hwy. and Anaheim St. (E.-W.), and Avalon and Wilmington Blvds. (N.-S.).

Hotels and Apartment Houses: San Pedro: 7 first-class hotels. Wilmington: 4 hotels. Numerous small hotels, tourist camps, apartments, and flats.

Churches: San Pedro: 18 churches and 22 miscellaneous religious groups. Wilmington: 11 churches and 8 miscellaneous groups.

Public Schools: San Pedro 13, Wilmington 5.

Motion-Picture Houses: San Pedro 5, Wilmington 2.

Parks, Playgrounds and Picnic Grounds: (*See also Los Angeles General Information.*) San Pedro: Alma, 21st and Meyler Sts,; Averill, Dodson Ave. and Averill Dr.; Leland, Upland and Cabrillo Aves.; Peck, Summerland Ave. and Patton St.; the Plaza, between Beacon St. and Harbor Blvd., from 6th to 16th Sts.; Point Fermin, end of Paseo del Mar and Gaffey St. Wilmington: Banning, bounded by M and O Sts., Eubank and Lakme Aves.

Daily Newspapers: News Pilot (San Pedro); *Journal* and *Press* (Wilmington), daily, except Sun.

Athletic Fields: San Pedro: Navy Field, 34th St. and Pacific Ave., 3 football fields and 8 baseball diamonds; Sports Field, foot of Pacific Ave., football, baseball, tennis, and softball; Daniels Field, 12th and Gaffey Sts., lighted for night baseball and football.

Boating and Yachting: Anchorages in Watchorn Basin, reached by 22nd and Miner Sts. (San Pedro). California Yacht Club, Yacht St. at water front (Wilmington). Other anchorages along West Basin and other points.

Boxing and Wrestling: San Pedro: Army and Navy Y.M.C.A., 921 S. Beacon St. Wilmington: Wilmington Bowl, 909 Mahar St.

Fishing: San Pedro: Shore fishing from breakwater, fishing barges offshore, reached by water taxis, rates $1 including transportation, tackle and bait; charter boats, including live bait and tackle, $35 per trip; two 65-foot launches, equipped for deep-sea fishing, from Pier 124 (May 1 to Oct. 1), fee $2; license for game fishing, residents, $2, nonresidents, $3. Wilmington: live-bait boats from water front for fishing banks off Santa Catalina Island; barges anchored offshore, reached by water taxis; fishing from piers.

Football: San Pedro: High School field, 1221 S. Gaffey St. Wilmington: Phineas Banning High School, 1500 N. Avalon Blvd.

Soccer: San Pedro: 1527 Mesa St., Leland and 22nd St., 3333 Kerckhoff Ave., 1530 W. 7th St. and 1221 S. Gaffey St. Wilmington: 1140 Mahar Ave.

Golf: Royal Palms course (San Pedro), at White Point, 18 holes, open to public. Fees, 35¢ weekdays, 50¢ Sun.

Softball: San Pedro: 828 S. Mesa St., 429 Stephen M. White Dr., 1221 S. Gaffey St. Wilmington: 1331 Eubank St., 1301 Fries Ave., 1196 Gulf St., 1500 N. Avalon Blvd.

Swimming: Cabrillo Beach (San Pedro), landward end of the breakwater, surf and still water. Surf bathing (Wilmington).

Tennis: San Pedro: Peck Park, Summerland Ave. and Patton St., 4 courts, lighted for night playing; Municipal Playground, 828 Mesa St., 2 courts. Wilmington: 2 courts at 1500 N. Avalon Blvd.

Note: Information concerning *Steamship Berths* and *Traffic Regulations,* see Los Angeles General Information.

Unlike many great world cities, Los Angeles is not situated directly on either a navigable river or the sea. Its great modern harbor, with its 25-mile frontage, was created by dredging the mud flats and salt marshes of San Pedro Bay, 25 miles south of the heart of the city. Since 1920 the Federal government and the city of Los Angeles have spent $60,000,000 in deepening channels, building breakwaters, and making other improvements. Today, the harbor is the Pacific base of the U.S. Fleet and one of the nation's five great ports, frequented by thousands of chunky freighters, trim passenger ships, and fishing vessels of many kinds. In 1938 some 5,700 large ships tied up at its piers and wharves to discharge and load cargoes valued at a billion dollars; oil products and manufactures constituted most of the export trade; raw and semi-raw materials for use of industry comprised 75 per cent of the imports.

The two harbor communities of SAN PEDRO (90 alt., 46,685 pop.), and WILMINGTON (25 alt., 13,946 pop.), originally known as New San Pedro, were independent cities until 1909 when they were absorbed by Los Angeles, which organized a Harbor District governed by a board of five commissioners, appointed by the mayor. This board manages the muncipal port facilities, which comprise 95 per cent of those in the harbor. On the west the harbor is protected by the San Pedro Hills and Point Fermin, from which extends a long breakwater, in two sections, protecting it on the south and east. The opening between the two sections, marked by the Breakwater Lighthouse, provides passage into the Outer Harbor. Here the U.S. Battle Fleet (see Long Beach), with tenders and supply, repair, and hospital ships, rides at anchor for many months of the year. Between San Pedro and Terminal Island a deep channel leads into the Inner Harbor, where ships are manoeuvered in the large turning basin and warped into the slips and docks that, like saw teeth, jut out from the water front at Wilmington, four miles inland, the port's chief freight and passenger terminal. On Terminal Island, a man-made improvement, are large docks, boat-building and repair yards, and colorful Fish Harbor. East of the island, Cerritos Channel leads to the Inner Harbor of Long Beach (see Long Beach).

A bustling port, notwithstanding its somewhat somnolent air, San Pedro is the older, larger, and more colorful of the two communities. Along the water front are faded brick buildings of the first decade of the century; the residential district spreads back up the hills known as the Palos Verdes (green woods). Stores along the front streets display nautical gear of every kind—denim jackets, duffle bags, sheath knives, spyglasses, and gargantuan dice. Here are tattoo parlors, "wing-ding joints," semi-secret gambling dives where sailors challenge fortune at cards, roulette, fan-tan, and almost any other game. Everywhere are union halls and posters, for the water front is strongly unionized and thoroughly conscious of its strength. The numerous bars are distinctive in character and name. In an erstwhile bank old salts, and young, straddle stools of steel tube before white marble counters as the "banker" replenishes his stocks from the vaults, where he keeps his liquid assets, often more negotiable than other kinds of bonded stuff. The Silver Dollar saloon has murals by a Chinese who, on completing them, shot himself. Whispering Joe's, Shanghai Red's, and Scuttle Butt Inn are popular. At Goodfellow's huge Scandinavian seamen dance solemnly with one another to wheezy tunes played on an accordion. The maritime workers of San Pedro include Japanese, Jugoslavs, Czechs, Italians, Portuguese, Mexicans, and Scandinavians; the last are the largest group, but these grandsons of the men who sailed the Seven Seas in the days of the old square-riggers have so intermarried with other groups that racially they are now scarcely distinguishable.

South of the Pacific Electric Line's interurban depot, a low gray structure with arcades, through which flows a ceaseless tide of eager tourists and blase wanderers, are fish wharves; beyond are old sun-blistered, pumpkin-yellow buildings, once a station and wharf, at present abandoned to two battered South Sea trading schooners. Nearby, lumberyards occupy a strip of sand known as "Mexican Beach," the hangout of beachcombers and swimmers. Here is "Mexican Hollywood," a collection of shacks, periodically the scene of much nocturnal

revelry, and "Happy Valley," home of seamen between voyages to
distant ports.

San Pedro has long talked of the sea and its lore, and old tars tell
and retell tales of dope-running, rum-running, alien-smuggling, spy
scares, police and gang raids on gambling dens operated on barges
offshore, weird murders on yachts bound for the "isles of somewhere,"
buried treasure, such mysterious vanishings as that of the *Belle Isle*
off the Galapagos in 1935, and many a shipwreck since the day in 1828
when a "Santa Ana" blew the brig *Danube* ashore here, the first to be
piled up in the harbor.

Wilmington, an offshoot of San Pedro, has had a less colorful and
more businesslike career. Established to handle heavy freight, it still
serves that function. Ocean-going ships tie up here to discharge and
take on goods and passengers. Around the wharves and piers are streets
lined with shipping offices and warehouses storing goods from all parts
of the world.

The recorded history of the area dates back to 1542, when Cabrillo
sailed his leaky little craft into the harbor, which he named La Bahia de
los Fumos (bay of smokes), for the Indian fires on the slopes of Palos
Verdes. A map maker years later identified it as La Bahia de San
Pedro to commemorate Vizcaino's arrival on November 26, 1602, the
feast day of St. Peter. During the closing years of the 18th century
Spanish rancheros shipped produce from the bay. In 1808 Captain
William Shaler, a fur trader, sailed in with the first Yankee ship, *Lelia
Byrd,* and although trade with foreigners was forbidden by the authorities, Yankee skippers continued to come, for the rancheros and
even the padres were anxious to trade hides and tallow for manufactured goods.

A description of the harbor in 1838 has been left us by Richard
Henry Dana in his *Two Years Before the Mast:* ". . . there was no
sign of a town. What had brought us into such a place we could not
conceive . . . we lay exposed to every wind that could blow. I
learned to my surprise that the desolate looking place was the best
place on the whole coast . . . and about thirty miles in the interior
. . . was the Pueblo de Los Angeles." San Pedro had developed
somewhat when Major Horace Bell wrote in 1853 that it was a "great
place; it had no streets, for none were necessary. There were two
mud scows, a ship's anchor and a fishing boat . . . broken down Mexican carts, a house, a large haystack and a mule corral." When Dana
returned in 1859 he found a wharf, two or three warehouses, and a
stagecoach, which plied daily between the port and the pueblo.

The early development of the harbor was in large part the work
of Phineas Banning, who came to California in 1851 and soon established freighting service between San Pedro and the pueblo. To gain
an advantage over his one competitor, he bought part of the old Rancho
San Pedro on the inner bay, closer to Los Angeles, and there built a
wharf and warehouse, founding what was known as New San Pedro

in 1858. A gale hastened its development, for it wrecked Banning's wharf at San Pedro and he transferred all his activities to the new port. Every day Banning, wearing red suspenders, labored at the wharf and his booming voice dispatched an increasing number of carts and coaches up the dusty road to the pueblo. For a few years New San Pedro surpassed its parent port both in population and tonnage handled. During the Civil War the United States Army quartered troops in the town, and in 1863, when its population of soldiers and civilians approximated 6,000, the State legislature renamed the town for Wilmington, Del., Banning's birthplace. In 1868 a railroad was built to Los Angeles, but the following year the Southern Pacific purchased the road and extended it to San Pedro. Coastwise vessels thus could load from "ship to car," and San Pedro regained its ascendancy, although the coming of the railroads and the growth of population brought commerce enough to make both ports prosperous. Wilmington was incorporated as a city in 1872; San Pedro, in 1888.

The development of tremendous man-made Los Angeles Harbor from mud flats and salt marshes is a dramatic story. In 1858 small steamers and sailing vessels from San Francisco and South America anchored offshore while their cargo was discharged into lighters. Banning dredged the inner harbor, by a crude system of two boats and rakes, which were dragged along the bottom of the channel, loosening silt, which the tide carried out to sea. But in spite of this work and the dredging of the San Pedro main channel to a depth of 16 feet in 1871, the port remained a shallow basin with little protection from the sea. The Federal government completed a jetty between Terminal Island (then Rattlesnake Island) and Dead Man's Island in 1893, but a bitter controversy developed as to whether a harbor should be constructed here or at Santa Monica (*see Pueblo to Metropolis*). U.S. Senator Stephen M. White, "father" of the harbor, overcame opposition in Washington, and the first rock of the new breakwater was dumped off Point Fermin in 1899. At the turn of the century the port was handling 200,000 tons a year, a four-fold increase since 1871, and two railroads had terminals at the harbor. Increased business and harbor facilities brought the two ports together, and in 1909 they were annexed by Los Angeles and consolidated as the Harbor District. To-day, Los Angeles is one of our five largest seaports.

During recent years the harbor has been involved in the struggle along the Pacific between maritime unions and shipowners. A 100-day strike in 1937 achieved substantial gains for labor and unification of the unions under the leadership of the militant longshoremen's union, which led most of the maritime unions into the Congress of Industrial Organization. Fishermen have likewise unionized themselves both in the CIO and the American Federation of Labor, and a close bond now unites fishermen, longshoremen, seamen, marine engineers, bartenders, and all engaged in wresting a livelihood from their common friend and enemy, the sea.

POINTS OF INTEREST

SAN PEDRO

The CIVIC CENTER, Harbor Blvd. and Beacon, 6th and 9th Sts., lies on the west side of the Main Channel. Its buildings are grouped about the northern end of the tree-studded Plaza, which extends southward to 13th Street. The Plaza offers a good view of the 1,000-foot MAIN CHANNEL between San Pedro and Terminal Island shore lines, which leads from the Outer Harbor to a 1,600-foot turning basin bounded by Smith's, Mormon, and Terminal Islands. At the turning basin the channel branches to the West and East basins of the Inner Harbor.

1. Dominating the Civic Center, at its northeast corner, is the six-story, tan-brick BRANCH CITY HALL, 638 S. Beacon St., built in 1928 to house the Harbor Department offices and various branch units of the Los Angeles municipal government.

2. The new UNITED STATES CUSTOMS HOUSE AND POST OFFICE, Beacon and 9th Sts., a three-story, reinforced-concrete structure completed in 1935, faces the park on the west side. In the lobby is a 40-foot mural by Fletcher Martin, depicting the evolution in the transportation of mail in various parts of the country. The post office and various Federal bureaus are quartered in this building.

3. The UNITED STATES IMMIGRATION STATION (*open 9-4:30*), foot of 22nd St., is a two-story building of gray stucco, with barred windows and an adjoining "bull pen," through which annually pass 15,000 aliens, 60 per cent of whom are Orientals.

4. The MARINE EXCHANGE LOOKOUT STATION (*not open*), on the roof of the six-story Municipal Warehouse No. 1, Pier No. 1, foot of Signal St., is a square glass-enclosed compartment equipped with a powerful telescope by which ships are identified an hour before they arrive at Breakwater Light. Flag signals are used to communicate with ships during the day; a blinker-light system is employed at night.

5. At the tip of Pier No. 1, within full view of Outer Harbor ship traffic, is the two-story cement building of the PILOT STATION (*not open*), headquarters of pilots skilled in navigating the Inner Harbor.

6. At the U.S. NAVY LANDING, 22nd St. at the head of East Channel, officers and men from the warships land in gigs and longboats for shore leave; visitors embark here for the dreadnaughts and cruisers anchored in the Outer Harbor (*Sun. and holidays only, 1-4; transportation free*).

The 450-foot U.S. COAST GUARD PIER, foot of Outer St., in Watchorn Basin, is the headquarters of the local unit of the Coast Guard, which has a force of 150 officers and men, two 165-foot patrol boats, and five smaller craft; the unit patrols the coast from the Mexican border to Point Buchon, north of Santa Barbara. Its gray patrol boats, *Aurora* and *Hermes,* carry three guns each, mounted on the main deck, are equipped with powerful searchlights and radio transmitters, and fly the red-barred Coast Guard flag with its motto, *Semper Paratus* (L., always ready). When planes are needed for an emergency, such as removing a sick or injured person from a vessel at sea, a call is made on the air base at San Diego, also part of the southern California section, for one of its five amphibian planes. Coast Guard activities here, once chiefly concerned with rum-running, now center on the preservation of life and property and the enforcement of customs and navigation laws.

FORT MacARTHUR, LOWER RESERVATION (*open, except during artillery practice*), 244 acres set aside in 1916 and named in honor of General Douglas MacArthur, former military governor of the Philippine Islands, lies on a bluff overlooking West Channel and Outer Harbor. Ranged around three sides of the five-acre parade ground are stucco and frame bungalows occupied by officers of the 63rd Coast Artillery (anti-aircraft) and the Third Coast Artillery. Barracks for enlisted men, the commissary and supply departments, mess halls and garages are massed along the east side. The garrison ranges from 700 to 800 officers and men. In the reservation are two 14-inch guns weighing 365 tons each; mounted on railway carriages, they are 21 feet high, 95 feet long, and fire steel 1,560-pound projectiles at a muzzle velocity of 2,700 feet per second—over 30 miles per minute.

POINTS OF INTEREST

San Pedro

1. Branch City Hall
2. U. S. Customs House and Post Office
3. U. S. Immigration Station
4. Marine Exchange Lookout Station
5. Pilot Station
6. U. S. Navy Landing
7. Statue of Cabrillo
8. Bathhouse
9. Boathouse
10. Government Lighthouse
11. Los Angeles Shipbuilding and Drydock Corp. Plant

Wilmington

12. Old Government Supply Warehouse
13. Santa Catalina Island Terminal
14. Drum Barracks
15. General Banning House
16. Ford Motor Co. Assembly Plant
17. Cerritos Channel Drawbridge Terminal Island
18. Southern California Edison Co. Steam Plant
19. Marine Meteorological Observatory
20. Bethlehem Shipbuilding Corp. Plant
21. Federal Regional Penitentiary

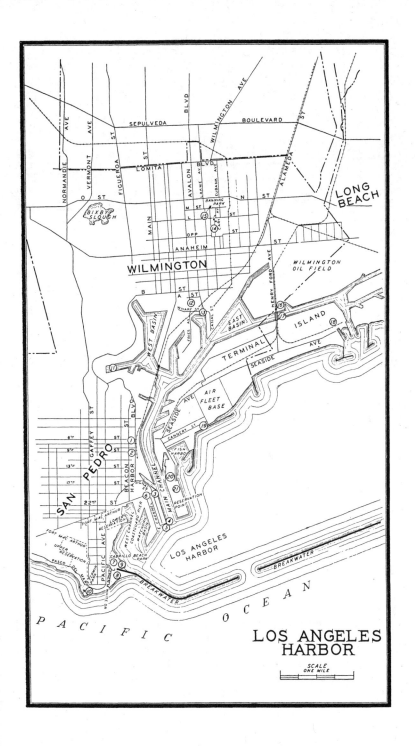

LOS ANGELES
HARBOR

SCALE
ONE MILE

CABRILLO BEACH PARK, foot of Stephen M. White Dr. (*open 6 a.m. to midnight*), named in honor of Juan Rodriguez Cabrillo, is a recreational area with beach, park, and playground facilities.

7. A nine-foot concrete monolithic STATUE OF CABRILLO is the central piece of a circular landscaped plaza in the park.

8. A white stucco BATHHOUSE (*rates, 10¢-25¢*), is at the right of the statue. In the seaward chambers of the building is the CABRILLO BEACH MUSEUM (*open 9-5; free*), a municipal institution exhibiting specimens of marine and shore life along the Pacific coast.

9. A stucco BOATHOUSE left of the bathhouse, with a wooden pier for small craft, maintains boat service to an offshore fishing barge (*rates vary*).

The U. S. GOVERNMENT BREAKWATER extends in two detached sections from the tip of the San Pedro headland at Cabrillo Beach to a point opposite the mouth of the Los Angeles Flood Control Channel, a distance of almost five miles. The curving 11,000-foot section between Cabrillo Beach and Breakwater Light was begun in 1899 and completed in 1912 at a cost of $3,000,000. The second section, a continuation of the first, cost $5,600,000. Both sections consist of rock fill almost 200 feet wide at the base, tapering to a width of 20 feet at the top, which stands 14 feet above the sea at low tide. At the seaward end of the first section is Breakwater Light, built in 1913, having a 110,000 candlepower beam visible 14 miles.

POINT FERMIN PARK, extending (R) along Paseo del Mar (driveway along the sea), a 28-acre expanse of tree-shaded lawns on the rugged bluffs of Point Fermin, has sheltered pergolas, a promenade along the edge of the palisade, and a picnic ground. The park, acquired in 1923, bears the name of Point Fermin, which was so-named in 1784 for Padre Fermin Francisco Lasuen, who succeeded to the presidency of the California missions on the death of Padre Junipero Serra.

10. The old GOVERNMENT LIGHTHOUSE on the point, built in 1874 and still in use, throws a 6,000 candlepower beam visible for 18 miles.

The 176-acre FORT MacARTHUR UPPER RESERVATION (*not open*), on the rolling seaward slopes of the Palos Verdes Hills behind Paseo del Mar, and Gaffey St., was acquired between 1910 and 1921 as a site for modern fortifications in the harbor defense program. Within the enclosing wire fence, concealed behind low hills, are massive guns, their number and caliber guarded as military secrets. Along the Gaffey Street side are barracks, supply houses, and garages.

11. The LOS ANGELES SHIPBUILDING AND DRYDOCK CORPORATION PLANT (*adm. by arrangement*), West Basin north of the San Pedro business district, includes a floating drydock with a lifting capacity of 12,000 tons, shipyards, wharves for ship repair, and facilities for the construction and repair of all types of vessels.

WILMINGTON

12. The OLD GOVERNMENT SUPPLY WAREHOUSE (*not open*), Fries Ave. and A St., the oldest building in Wilmington, is a huge barnlike structure of shiplap construction, held together by square handmade nails; the roof ridge is topped with three square cupolas. Built in 1858, when Drum Barracks was still a tent camp, the warehouse was used to store supplies consigned to Army posts.

13. From the huge concrete and corrugated iron SANTA CATALINA ISLAND TERMINAL, foot of Avalon Blvd., ships annually carry between 500,000 and 650,000 pleasure seekers to Santa Catalina Island (*see Tour 5A*). The landing for hydroplanes to Santa Catalina Island is at the head of Slip 5, west of the ship terminal.

14. At the entrance to DRUM BARRACKS, 1053-55 Cary Ave. (*open by arrangement*), a cypress archway is inscribed "Officers Quarters 1862-68, U.S. Army Supply Depot for Southern California, Arizona and New Mexico, U.S. Department of the Southwest." The white building is covered with vines and surrounded by palms, cypress, and pepper trees. The main building and two rearward wings contain 14 rooms; those in front have high ceilings in the stately manner of the 1860's. The barracks, the second oldest building in Wilmington, was constructed from timbers cut at the Portsmouth, New Hampshire, Navy Yard in 1861, shipped around Cape Horn, and raised by army men in 1862 on a 40-acre site acquired by the Government from Phineas Banning for one dollar. In a rear patio, bright with greenery, is an old ivy-covered well with mossy rope and oaken bucket; the well has been transformed into a shallow goldfish pond.

The barracks, named for General Richard Colton Drum, whose son, General Hugh Drum, planned the military fortifications in Hawaii, were built both as a base for operations against the Indians and to overawe the Secessionist movement in southern California. Here was the terminus of the first telegraph in the Southwest, and of the Government's short-lived camel service (*see Tour 2*), between the barracks and Tucson, Arizona. During the early years of the Civil War, between 200 and 400 soldiers were quartered here. With the subjugation of the Indians in the late 1860's the barracks were abandoned and the land returned to Banning. The remaining building is now a private residence.

BANNING PARK, M and O Sts., Eubank and Lakme Aves., perpetuates the memory of Phineas Banning. The 20-acre tract, acquired in 1927 from the Banning heirs, retains its quiet old-fashioned charm, with its white picket fence and tree-lined walks.

15. The old GENERAL BANNING HOUSE (*not open*), in the park, is a white three-story, 18-room mansion, with a two-story portico. The mansion, still sturdy and well-preserved, has been a landmark in the harbor district for more than half a century. To the rear is a frame stable and carriage house, with a collection of surreys, buggies, and carriages, and a stagecoach that saw service in Banning's California

Stage Company. An old brick reservoir, 50 feet in diameter, west of the mansion, has been converted into a picnic ground. Used for storing water in the Spanish rancho days, its circular brick wall has been fitted with windows and doors, and the interior, open to the sky, has a pergola supporting bougainvillaea and other vines. A stream meanders through the park, widening at places into small lagoons. On the playground to the east are softball, tennis, basketball, and horseshoe courts, a gymnasium, a children's playfield, and an auditorium with a dance floor.

The derricks of the WILMINGTON OIL FIELD, scattered throughout the Wilmington residential district from O Street on the north to Fries Avenue on the west, become a veritable forest of rigs on either side of Henry Ford Avenue, south of Anaheim Street. In July 1938 the field had 483 producing wells, with a combined yield of 95,000 barrels per day. The discovery well was spudded in April 26, 1936.

16. The FORD MOTOR COMPANY ASSEMBLY PLANT (*open by arrangement*), 700 Henry Ford Ave., lies on reclaimed marshland athwart the Los Angeles-Long Beach boundary line, and assembles automobiles and manufactures parts. At capacity production the plant assembles 400 cars daily and employs 2,500 men.

17. The 270-foot CERRITOS CHANNEL DRAWBRIDGE, of the counterpoised or bascule type, foot of Henry Ford Avenue, is the only bridge to Terminal Island.

TERMINAL ISLAND, reached also by ferries from San Pedro, foot of Terminal Way (*5¢; 25¢ per car, 5¢ per passenger*), is largely man-made, representing an investment of $12,000,000. Six miles long, from one-half to three-quarters of a mile wide, the island is lined along the Inner Harbor and part of the Outer Harbor shore with docks, wharves, slips, factories, oil plants, a Federal prison, and offices. Its western two-thirds lie in Los Angeles; the eastern third, in Long Beach.

18. The SOUTHERN CALIFORNIA EDISON COMPANY STEAM PLANT (*open by arrangement weekdays 8-3*), on a 43-acre tract at the east end of Terminal Island, consists of three white concrete buildings with slender concrete stacks, the highest rising 262 feet. Gigantic boilers burning natural gas piped from the Kettleman Hills 215 miles distant convert 20 tons of water into steam every minute. The towers carrying the high voltage cables across Cerritos Channel are 310 feet high, overtopping all structures in the harbor.

The new U.S. FLEET AIR BASE (*adm. by arrangement*), Seaside Avenue to the edge of the Outer Harbor, includes a concrete seaplane haul-out ramp, planes, a landing and tender wharf, a dredged seaplane anchorage protected by an 1,800-foot rock jetty, two runways for land planes, and a corrugated iron hangar, the first of several to be built. There are also men's dormitories, mess halls, officers' quarters, quartermaster and administration buildings.

19. The MARINE METEOROLOGICAL OBSERVATORY (*not open*), at the E. end of Cannery St., operated jointly by the Los Angeles Harbor Department and the California Institute of Technology (*see Pasadena*) on a 24-hour schedule, issues storm warnings and weather data to mariners. Through its associate staff of students and scientists from the California Institute of Technology, it conducts research in meteorology, aerology, climatology, oceanography, modern weather forecasting, and fog studies. The U.S. Navy uses its findings in making weather maps for use of airplane pilots.

FISH HARBOR, an artificial inlet on the south side of Terminal Island, protected by inner and outer moles, is the center of Los Angeles' fishing and canning industry yielding $20,000,000 of products annually. Three sides of the little harbor's quadrangular shore are crowded with canneries, boatyards, fertilizer plants, gasoline filling stations for tuna clippers, and other establishments auxiliary to fishing and canning. The annual pack is valued at $15,000,000; such by-products as fish oil and meal, fertilizer, and pet foods add an additional $5,000,000.

Fish Harbor is the home port of 1,200 fishing boats. Approximately 300 are operated by Japanese, and the remainder by Slavonians, Italians, Portuguese, Norwegians, and Americans. Fleets of Monterey trawlers leave daily and return at dusk with the day's catch. The tuna clippers, equipped with deep wells, live-bait tanks, and Diesel engines, go as far afield as the South Seas.

Ten packing plants, with approximately 3,000 employees, operate in the harbor district. Tuna, albacore, yellowfin, bluefin, skipjack, sardines, mackerel, and other fish are tossed into traveling baskets, which dump them on conveyor belts leading into the canneries. Men of many nations carry on the work in hip boots, sweaters, and knitted caps.

Slavonians, who represent about one-third of the fishermen, live mainly in San Pedro. The Japanese, Italians, Portuguese, and Filipinos, numbering some 2,000, have gathered in a colony of their own on the north shore of Fish Harbor immediately behind the wharves and extending the width of the basin and north from Wharf Street to Terminal Way. The section is criss-crossed with narrow streets bearing such names as Barracuda, Tuna, Shrimp, Bass, and Sardine. On them is heard a babble of many tongues, but seldom English. In the yards of the frame cottages and along the water front, men, women, and sometimes children squat mending fish nets, some of which are 3,000 feet long and valued at $5,000.

The Japanese population numbers approximately 600 fishermen, 150 merchants, about 500 women, and an equal number of children. It forms a closely-knit colony, having its own Fishermen's Association.

20. The 38-acre BETHLEHEM SHIPBUILDING CORPORATION PLANT (*open by arrangement*), 905 S. Seaside Ave., is equipped to recondition and repair all sizes and types of ships. Its floating drydock, with a lifting capacity of 15,000 tons, is the largest in southern California.

21. The new FEDERAL REGIONAL PENITENTIARY (*adm.*

by arrangement), the Government's newest West Coast prison for short-term offenders, occupies the seaward side of the Terminal Island section known as Reservation Point. Completed in May 1938, the $1,380,000 institution is of reinforced concrete, with three cell blocks and nine dormitories, providing quarters for 600 male and 24 female prisoners. The cell blocks, dormitories, machine shops, mess hall, quarantine and administration building, and auditorium surround a quadrangular exercise yard.

Industry and Commerce

Burton O. Burt

UNLOADING TUNA FISH, FISH HARBOR, TERMINAL ISLAND

LOADING SHIP, TERMINAL ISLAND

Burton O. Burt

Bret Weston

GRAIN ELEVATOR

NATURAL GAS TANKS

Bret Weston

F.W. Carter

OIL FIELDS, MONTEBELLO

AIRVIEW OF INDUSTRIAL SECTION, LOS ANGELES

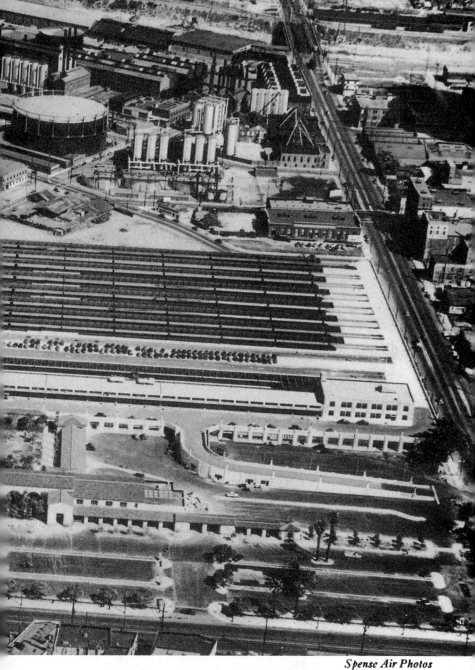

Spense Air Photos

WINE STORAGE VATS

WINE EXPERTS TASTE AND CLASSIFY CALIFORNIA VINTAGES

Art Streib

IN A WALNUT PACKING PLANT

LEMON SIZING MACHINE

California Fruit Growers' Exchange

BODY ASSEMBLY LINE, AUTOMOBILE FACTORY

ASSEMBLY ROOM, AIRCRAFT FACTOR

Hollywood

Bus Stations: Union Bus Terminal, 1629 N. Cahuenga Blvd., for Greyhound Lines, Inland Stages, Pacific Electric Ry. Motor Coach, Pasadena-Ocean Park Stage Line, and busses for Universal City, Warner Bros.-First National Studio, and Burbank; 1646 N. Cahuenga Blvd. for Union Pacific busses to San Francisco; 1735 N. Cahuenga Blvd. for National Trailways, Santa Fe Trailways, and Burlington Trailways.

Streetcars and Busses: Fares: Hollywood zone 5¢ (streetcars only), to downtown Los Angeles 10¢, Santa Monica 20¢.

Taxis: 20¢ first ¼ mile, 10¢ each additional ½ mile.

Information Bureaus: Hollywood Chamber of Commerce, 6520 Sunset Blvd.; Automobile Club of Southern California, 6902 Sunset Blvd.; Randall Motor Club, Inc., 5901 Sunset Blvd.

Accommodations: 24 first-class hotels, numerous apartment houses and bungalow courts (*see Los Angeles General Information*).

Auto and Trailer Camps: Ventura Blvd., 3 miles beyond Hollywood.

Radio Broadcast Theatres: Columbia Square Playhouse, Sunset Blvd. and Gower St., CBS programs; National Broadcasting Co. Studios, Sunset Blvd. and Vine St., NBC programs.

Colleges: Chapman College (Disciples of Christ), 677 N. Vermont Ave.; Immaculate Heart Convent (Catholic), Western and Franklin Aves.

Sightseeing Tours of Motion-Picture Studios: Tanner Gray Line Motor Tours (enter only Warner Bros.-First National Studios, Burbank), leave Biltmore Hotel, 5th and Olive Sts., weekdays only, $4.50 per person; busses pass all other major studios but do not enter. Clifton Motor Tours, Inc., leave from 618 S. Olive St. daily, $1.50 per person; busses pass all major studios but do not enter.

Note: Information concerning *Traffic Regulations, Airports, Street Numbering, Radio Stations, Theatres, Parks and Playgrounds, Sports,* and *Annual Events* in Hollywood may be found in Los Angeles *General Information.*

HOLLYWOOD (385 alt., 184,531 pop.), officially the Hollywood District of Los Angeles, for it is not an independent city, lies on the foothill slopes of the Santa Monica Mountains, eight miles from the center of Los Angeles. Only recently have its boundaries been defined: on the east it is set off from Los Angeles proper by Hyperion Avenue and Riverside Drive; on the south, by Melrose Avenue; the hills and canyons of the Santa Monica Mountains bound it on the north; the city of Beverly Hills adjoins it on the west. Along the base of the mountains runs Hollywood Boulevard, or just "the Boulevard," through the heart of the business district. Midway along it, at Vine Street, is southern California's Times Square, an inexhaustible source of comic and tragic material for columnists, romancers, debunkers, and serious novelists.   Within a few blocks are large and luxurious hotels, Grauman's flamboyant Chinese and Egyptian theatres, elaborate beauty parlors and department stores, offices of booking agents and of *Variety*, expensive shops and 10-cent stores, the Brown Derby and other widely publicized restaurants where the consumption of food and drink is incidental to seeing and being seen by "the right people," such nocturnal "hot spots" as La Conga and The Tropics, Radio City and Columbia Square, from which originate many of the feature programs broadcast throughout the country, and often over five continents, by NBC and CBS.

Along the western section of Sunset Boulevard, known as "the Strip," are other theatrical agencies and expensive night clubs, jewelry and antique shops, plush-carpeted salons of beauticians and couturiers, almost all in gleaming white buildings of modified Georgian Colonial design, flanked here and there with a drive-in Bar-B-Q stand, at which customers are served by hooking trays on the open windows of the old Ford from Iowa or the latest nickel-plated Rolls Royce in lemon and maroon.

In all languages "Hollywood" is synonymous with "movies," yet few film celebrities now live here and most of the studios are in surrounding communities: Culver City, Burbank, and West Los Angeles. Off the main boulevards there is nothing "Hollywoodian" about Hollywood, which is much like any other city, with modest houses along quiet streets, lined with southern California's conventional palm, pepper, and eucalyptus trees.   Most of the houses are stucco or frame bungalows, surrounded with lawns and gardens, although on the slopes of the foothills above Hollywood Boulevard gleam some large and elaborate mansions.

Hollywood, curiously, had a most conservative background.   Unlike Los Angeles, it occupies little space in the early Spanish or Mexican annals.   Only Cahuenga Pass, Hollywood's backdoor through the mountains, receives important mention, for it was the principal route between southern and northern California; through it passed the Portola and the De Anza expeditions, the old Butterfield coaches of the 1850's, and the 10-mule teams that hauled silver ore into Los Angeles. After the Southern Pacific Railroad built its line through San Fernando Valley in 1876, the pass was little used, but in recent years has again come into its own, being one of the two main motor routes to the north. Hollywood's first house, an adobe, was built by Don Tomas Urquidez in 1853, on what is now the northwest corner of Franklin and Sycamore Avenues.   During the next 20 years Yankee homesteaders settled and laid out farms.   Among those who came from the Middle West during the boom of the 1880's were Horace H. Wilcox and his wife, of Topeka, Kansas.   Prohibitionists and active members of the Methodist Church, they bought a large tract of land at the base of the foothills and in 1887 divided it into lots and christened their real estate development Hollywood.   The pious and temperate community grew slowly; as late as 1896 the most exciting event in the daily life of the village was the arrival of the stage, which came crawling and lurching in on the scraggly dirt road that wound across open country to Los Angeles. Hollywood was totally unaware of Thomas Edison's "Living Pictures" then being shown in a Los Angeles theatre. Up to 1900 the population did not exceed 500, and deer often ventured down to Hollywood Boulevard in the early morning. Incorporated as a city in 1903, the community began to grow more rapidly, having some 4,000 people in 1910, but, being in urgent need of additional water supply, it allowed itself to be absorbed by Los Angeles. But it still insisted upon being recognized as a distinct community of sober, serious, church-going people, having no taste for the more cosmopolitan airs of Los Angeles. Within a year, however, its rural quietude was rudely shattered. In 1911 the old Blondeau Tavern, at the corner of Sunset Boulevard and Gower Street, was bought and converted into a makeshift movie studio by the Nestor Company, directed by the Horsley brothers, who had appreciated and decided to capitalize on southern California's almost continuous sunshine, varied scenery, and "Western atmosphere." The respectable and God-fearing were shocked and were themselves soon dancing with rage at seeing baggy-trousered comedians prancing up and down the streets; cowboys paraded the town on their skittish broncos, to the terror and delight of small boys and the fuming exasperation of their elders; cops chased robbers, and cameramen chased both, frantically turning cranks, up one street and down another of the once sedate town, even preempting Hollywood Boulevard on occasion. With the older Hollywood still protesting, other companies built studios, and by 1920 the population had vaulted to 50,000 and the resulting boom in real estate attained fantastic proportions.

The frenzied 1920's, that now almost incredible era of Big Money and still bigger debts, individual and corporate, found full expression here. The movies became a billion dollar industry, and to all the world Hollywood was its home, the fountainhead of the liveliest of the seven lively arts, the great projecting room from which was flashed on screens around the globe an endless series of scenes of genuine heroism and "ham" heroics, of gripping romance and simple "gush," of moving sentiment and unabashed sentimentality, of high artistry and sheer hokum. The current darlings of the screen began to pay income taxes on salaries of six instead of five figures. Writers of reputation were offered contracts that left them breathless and with barely enough strength to sign, only to be left in solitary confinement in magnificent offices, alternately praying and cursing for something to do. Some stars objected, but most did not, as gossip columns and "fan" magazines made public property of the most intimate details of their private lives. Thousands of movie-struck boys and girls, and many a doting parent with a suspected child prodigy in hand, poured into the film capital to live in cheap hotels and rooming houses while they talked shop, read the trade papers, and waited patiently to be "discovered." Periodic scandals rocked the colony, and Hollywood's "morals" became a favorite theme in pulpits from coast to coast. But

Hollywood mores, then as now, did not differ essentially from those of the average American city, although perhaps a bit more frank and cynical in some regards; Hollywood cannot quietly enjoy and smack its lips over a juicy bit of local scandal, as other cities do, for with the spotlight constantly upon it, a local scandal is immediately national news and the inspiration of more censure.

Since 1929, with the advent of the depression and the talkie, a marked change has come over the cinema capital. Ostentatious display of ermines and diamonds, expenditures for gold plumbing fixtures and platinum cocktail shakers, have declined. The talkie has retired the beautiful clotheshorse, whether male or female, and has demanded more accomplished and inspired players, better writers, more imaginative directors, and technicians with higher and more varied skills. These technicians—script writers, assistant directors, still men, score men, costume designers, make-up artists, research workers, electricians, set designers and builders, engineers, cameramen, cutters, and many others—are those who make the wheels go round. Extras and bit players constitute the largest group on the several movie lots and represent virtually all races and nationalities—from Chinese and Egyptians to Russians and Hindus. Here, too, gather men and women of highly diversified talents, all eager to capitalize on them while they may: composers, stage designers, flyers, skaters, baseball and football players, swimmers, novelists, poets, bronco-busters, tumblers and trapeze artists, crooners and swing kings, even symphony conductors.

Although not more than 15,000 Hollywoodians derive their incomes wholly and directly from the movies, three out of four of them are more or less dependent on the industry. Scattered throughout Hollywood are dozens of dance studios and dramatic schools offering training to hopefuls, both children and adults. Two large companies here manufacture endless strips of "celluloid" on which to film miles and miles of dare-devil thrills and "hot" romance. Hundreds of small firms supply the studios with lumber, metal, electrical apparatus, objets d'art, period furniture and costumes, horses, trained animals, wigs, attire of the latest fashion, and thousands of other things required in process of production. Others are employed in the manufacture of movie cameras and in processing film negatives.

Even before the depression it was common knowledge that only a handful of extras earned a living wage and that many an ex-star hungrily accepted any bit part that was offered, but it was not until 1938 that a scientific survey revealed that the average annual wage of technicians was less than $1,500, and that four of every 10 film workers were unemployed. Almost overnight Hollywood, once so individualistic, became unionized—not only technicians and casual workers, but screen writers, directors, top flight actresses and actors. Celebrities gave up their rounds of social activities and their week ends at Palm Springs to attend and often to lead political forums and meetings, organizing an Anti-Nazi League, the Motion Picture Artists Committee, the Motion Picture Democratic Committee, and, more recently,

Associated Film Audiences, designed to marshal public support for artistic films with realistic content and to fight censorship of plays dealing with our current problems. With its high concentration of players, singers, musicians, writers, and other persons of talent, Hollywood has become second only to New York as a radio center. Almost half of the programs broadcast over national hookups originate in the studios here. The city is also an important musical publishing center, making transcriptions of musical revues for radio programs and millions of records of popular songs and dance tunes. One of the more curious businesses is the phonograph recording of snores, sneezes, and thousands of other noises for broadcasting purposes. The manufacture of cosmetics and the creation of styles in women's clothes become more and more important in the local economy, for in certain circles a label bearing the name "Hollywood" has quite as magical an appeal as one reading "Paris."

A new and more serious Hollywood has emerged in recent years. It now has six art galleries, numerous book shops, an art association, and a botanical garden. Plays presented on the legitimate stage at the Hollywood Playhouse and El Capitan do not want for audiences. The "Symphonies under the Stars" presented regularly in the Hollywood Bowl under the direction of conductors of international reputation are known around the world. Sports still preoccupy many: polo and horse racing attract those who can afford them; thousands get their exercise vicariously at boxing matches and baseball games; the Hollywood team in the Pacific Coast League is financed largely by members of the film colony. Although the city is still growing, it is at the same time achieving a new integration as it turns toward the more serious concerns of the world and away from the "Never-never Land" of adolescent romance. Hollywood has settled down to a less fantastic way of living and a more mature view of life, and can no longer be dismissed summarily as "the home of hokum."

POINTS OF INTEREST

BARNSDALL PARK (*picnic facilities*), bounded by Vermont Ave., Edgemont St., Hollywood and Sunset Blvds., a 10-acre park planted with olive trees, was deeded to the city in 1931 by Aline Barnsdall, oil heiress. The former family residence is now an art museum, art library and little theater (*free*). The donor's liberal social and economic views have been for many years given expression on signboards around the encircling strip of land.

1. The CALIFORNIA ART CLUB (*open 2-5; adm. 25¢, free Thurs.*), on the top of Olive Hill in the park, is the former home of Miss Barnsdall. The gray cement structure, designed by Frank Lloyd Wright, recalls the massive temples of the Aztecs. Occasional exhibits of contemporary art and permanent collections of California relics and handcraft are shown here.

2. The names of 20,000 movie extras and bit players, together with detailed information on the appearance, talents, and wardrobe of each,

are on file in the CENTRAL CASTING OFFICE (*see The Movies*), 5504 Hollywood Blvd., maintained by the larger motion-picture studios.

3. COLUMBIA SQUARE (*open 10-10 daily; adm. 40¢; guides*), 6121 Sunset Blvd., is the Hollywood matrix of the Columbia Broadcasting System. The square, opened in 1938, was designed in the modern manner by William Lescaze. Its three units border a patio garden facing Sunset Boulevard. The five-story central structure, of reinforced concrete and glass, houses seven modern studios, an audition room, a transcription studio, and offices. Nationwide CBS broadcasts originate in the 960-seat COLUMBIA SQUARE PLAYHOUSE, which faces the patio garden.

COLUMBIA PICTURES CORPORATION (*no visitors*), 1438 Gower St., was founded by Jack and Harry Cohn, and Joe Brandt, who withdrew from the Universal Pictures Co., Inc., to organize the C-B-C Sales Co. in 1922, renting space in "Poverty Row" near the site of the present studio. The first picture, *The Hall Room Boys,* was followed by their first feature, *More to Be Pitied than Scorned.* In the same year, they purchased the property near Sunset and Gower where the administration building and nine sound stages are situated. In 1924, the name was changed to the Columbia Pictures Corporation, which since has had a sustained comedy production, including such pictures as *It Happened One Night.*

4. EARL CARROLL'S THEATRE RESTAURANT (*open nightly at 7*), 6230 Sunset Blvd., housed in an ultramodern building designed by Gordon B. Kaufmann, and opened in December 1938, has two revolving stages 80 feet in diameter, one within the other; there are three floating stages, disappearing platforms, and a neon lighting system used in musical extravaganzas and revues. The interior, divided into six tiers, accommodates 1,000 persons. Members of the theatre's Inner Circle Club pay $500 to $1,000 to sit in the first tier.

5. The NATIONAL BROADCASTING COMPANY STUDIOS (*open 10-10; adm. 40¢*), Sunset Blvd. and Vine St., are housed in a modern three-story concrete building designed by the Austin Company of Los Angeles. The low horizontal mass is relieved by a higher corner pavilion with vertical fenestration. Its concrete walls are finished in blue green, harmonizing with the sky, lawns, and shrubs. Opened in 1938, the building has eight studios, four of which seat 350 persons each.

6. The HOLLYWOOD POST OFFICE, NW. corner Selma and Wilcox Aves., a white concrete two-story structure designed in the modern manner by Claude Beelman and surrounded by well-kept lawns and shrubbery, is illuminated at night by two large ornamental bronze lanterns, one at each side of the broad front stairway. At the northern end of the main corridor, a decorative relief, *The Pony Express,* by Gordon Newell of the Federal Art Project, depicts two horses and a pioneer stagecoach driver, carved on a piece of mahogany three feet by five feet.

7. DE LONGPRE PARK, bounded by June St., De Longpre and Cherokee Aves., with landscaped lawns, flower beds, clumps of bamboo, and clusters of banana, pepper, and eucalyptus trees, has in the center the RUDOLPH VALENTINO MEMORIAL, designed by Roger Noble Burnham, and erected in 1930 with voluntary contributions from all over the world to commemorate the "great lover" of the 1920's. Entitled *Aspiration,* the monument, a four-foot bronze male nude poised on a globe, rises from a small lily pond. On each Memorial Day since 1930, a "mystery" woman has placed a wreath on the statue.

8. The CROSSROADS OF THE WORLD, 6661-81 Sunset Blvd., extending to Selma Ave., is a block of shops and cafes designed to create an Old World atmosphere. The shops face wide lanes radiating from a spacious central patio; open-air concerts, pageants, and fashion shows are staged in the shady courts. The ATLAS TOWER, above the shops at the entrance, supports a revolving globe of the world, symbolizing the commercial range of the center.

9. The EGYPTIAN THEATRE, 6712 Hollywood Blvd., designed by Meyer and Holler, witnessed the first Hollywood "premiere," with the showing of the silent version of *Robin Hood* in 1922. Now a second-run house, it was the first architectural fantasy of Sid Grauman, Los Angeles movie magnate. Hollywood's first-nighters once promenaded the long narrow forecourt that leads from the boulevard to the four plain white columns at the entrance to the foyer. On the forecourt walls are large colored drawings of ancient Egyptian deities; the south end of the court is adorned with figures in plaster and stucco. A heroic figure of the Egyptian god Osiris, guarding the foyer door, and chattering live monkeys in cages along the court, greet the theatre's patrons.

10. GRAUMAN'S CHINESE THEATRE, 6925 Hollywood Blvd., another bizarre creation by Meyer and Holler, is widely known for the fact that the concrete slabs in its forecourt bear the handprints and footprints of movie stars and their congratulatory messages to Grauman. The pseudo-Chinese facade represents a huge entrance gate to an enclosed temple garden. Around the two gate piers and jutting into the sky are four obelisks with Oriental decoration. At the end of the forecourt, planted with palms and ornamental shrubbery, is a pagoda with

POINTS OF INTEREST

1. California Art Club
2. Central Casting Office
3. Columbia Square
4. Earl Carroll's Theatre Restaurant
5. National Broadcasting Company's Studios
6. Hollywood Post Office
7. De Longpre Park
8. Crossroads of the World
9. Egyptian Theatre
10. Grauman's Chinese Theatre
11. Japanese Gardens
12. Hollywood Bowl
13. Samuel Goldwyn Studios
14. Hollywood Cemetery
15. RKO Studios
16. Paramount Studios

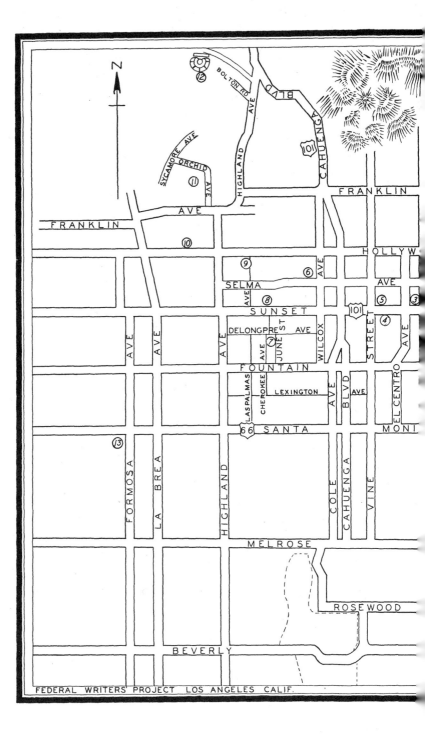

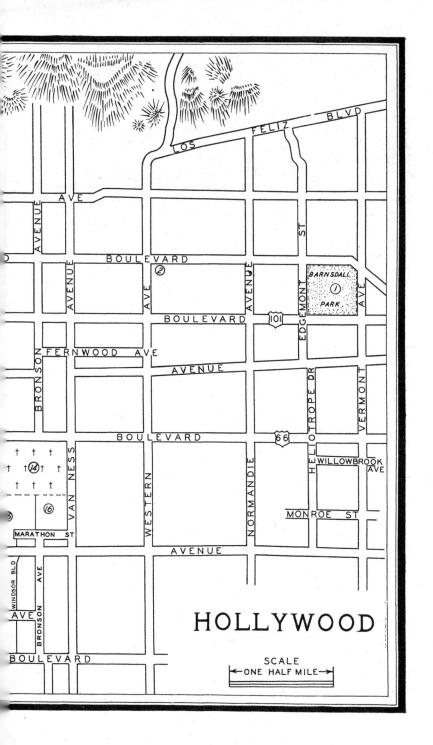

HOLLYWOOD

SCALE
←ONE HALF MILE→

a jade-green bronze roof supported by two coral-red octagonal columns bearing wrought-iron masks; the pagoda shelters a great stone dragon 30 feet high.

11. The JAPANESE GARDENS (*open 10-6; adm. 25¢, children with adults free*), Orchid and N. Sycamore Aves., were created in 1913 by Adolph and Eugene Bernheimer (*see Tour 6*), and enriched with Oriental art objects housed in the 14-room YAMA SHIRO (castle on the hill), designed in the manner of a Buddhist temple. In the eight-acre garden, also known as the California Scenic Gardens and Home, are more than 30,000 trees, including tropic and Arctic shrubs; a pagoda from Japan; and a miniature garden with reproductions of ancient dwellings, dwarf trees, canals, and waterfalls.

12. The HOLLYWOOD BOWL (*open*), end of Bolton Rd., one block south of the Highland Ave. and Cahuenga Blvd. intersection, is a 59-acre natural amphitheatre owned by Los Angeles County. It seats more than 20,000, with sloping runways providing standing room for an additional 10,000. The removable sound shell of the stage, designed by Lloyd Wright and ornamented with shrubbery, supplements the natural acoustics of the surrounding chaparral-covered hills and makes the use of microphones unnecessary, an ordinary voice on the stage being easily heard in the farthest row of seats. In the bowl the "Symphonies under the Stars" series of summer concerts have been presented annually since 1922; the annual Easter Sunrise Service is also held here. Voluntary contributions for the support of the amphitheatre are dropped in a large kettle, or bowl, at the upper end of Pepper Tree Lane, near the entrance.

North of the main entrance a 15-foot figure of a kneeling woman plucking a lyre rises from a fountain and terraced pools. Inside the entrance, on Bolton Road, is an 11-foot male figure, with the traditional tragic and comic masks of the drama; to the north, on Highland Avenue, is the third unit of the group, an 11-foot female figure representing the dance. The granite figures are by George Stanley, in collaboration with the Federal Art Project.

13. The SAMUEL GOLDWYN STUDIOS (*no visitors*), 1041 N. Formosa Ave., formerly the United Artists Studio, affords production and distribution facilities to Alexander Korda, the British producer; Samuel Goldwyn, Mary Pickford, Douglas Fairbanks, Charles Chaplin, Walter Wanger, Selznick-International, and Hal Roach; on its 18½-acre lot, which extends south from the buff-toned, stucco wall and the office buildings along Santa Monica Boulevard, are eight huge sound stages and 59 buildings. Samuel Goldwyn, the film-industry pioneer whose name is now affiliated with the Metro-Goldwyn-Mayer Studio (*see Tour 5*), owns all buildings on the lot; the land is owned by Douglas Fairbanks and Mary Pickford. The burden of the average annual production of 12 pictures at United Artists at present falls upon Samuel Goldwyn and Alexander Korda. The original United Artists Corporation, founded in 1919 purely as a releasing organization, was

the first of the powerful mergers in the motion-picture business, and originated the highly remunerative "block booking" system.

14. HOLLYWOOD CEMETERY, 6076 Santa Monica Blvd., is the resting place of many film notables, including Rudolph Valentino, John Gilbert, William Desmond Taylor, Renee Adoree, Karl Dane, Barbara LaMarr, and Theodore Roberts. Here, too, are the graves of Harrison Gray Otis, long-time publisher of the Los Angeles *Times;* William Andrews Clark, Jr., patron of the Los Angeles Philharmonic Orchestra; and Col. Griffith J. Griffith, who gave Griffith Park (*see The Northwest Section*) to the city.

Every August 23, on the anniversary of the death of Rudolph Valentino in 1926, the VALENTINO CRYPT is a mecca for several hundred men and women, who file through the mausoleum to deposit floral wreaths and bouquets. The unknown "Lady in Black," who for 12 years has come to kneel at the crypt and leave her garland of red roses, is not the Memorial Day pilgrim to the Valentino monument in De Longpre Park.

15. The 13-acre STUDIO OF THE RKO PICTURES CORPO-RATION (*no visitors*), 780 N. Gower St., consists of 19 buildings and nine sound stages. One of the first "big" pictures produced in the studio was *Kismet,* based on the life of Omar the Tentmaker. Between 45 and 50 feature pictures are produced annually at the studio.

16. The PARAMOUNT PICTURE CORPORATION STUDIO (*no visitors*), 5451 Marathon St., occupies an office building, with red-tile roof, and a heterogeneous group of 56 structures on a crowded 26-acre lot. The largest studio in Hollywood, with 20 sound stages, it is the outgrowth of the nickelodeon firm established in 1902 by Marcus Loew and Adolph Zukor, an orphan from Hungary. In 1912 it was reorganized under Zukor as the Famous Players Film Company, which presented such stars of the day as Mrs. Fiske, Ethel Barrymore, and Mary Pickford, "America's Sweetheart."

Long Beach and Signal Hill

LONG BEACH

Railroad Station: Pacific Electric Ry., 156 W. Ocean Blvd.

Bus Stations: Union Bus Depot, 226 E. 1st St., Greyhound Lines, Motor Transit Lines, Motor Coach Lines; Central Bus Depot, 56 American Ave., National Trailways, Santa Fe Trailways; Union Pacific Bus Station, 49 American Ave., Union Pacific Stages, Interstate Transit; All-American Bus Lines, 222 E. 1st St.

Airport: Long Beach Municipal Airport, 3301 E. Spring St.

Piers: Municipal Pier No. 1, Channel No. 3 Inner Harbor (Pico Ave. and Water St.), Los Angeles and San Francisco Navigation Co. ships to San Francisco Tues. 5 p.m. Municipal Navy Landing, between Piers A and B, outer Harbor; visits to warships Sun. and national holidays, by Navy shore boats, 2-4 p.m., free; by water taxi, 50¢ round trip. Charter boats for harbor trips at most piers.

Taxis: Rates by zones and meter; minimum charge, 15¢.

Streetcar and Bus Service: Streetcar, 6¢; bus, 5¢.

Traffic Regulations: Meter parking zone, Ocean Blvd. to 7th St. between and including Pacific and American Aves., 5¢ per hr.; 2-hr. limit in business district outside meter zone. State traffic laws prevail.

Streets and Numbers: Avenues run N. and S., streets E. and W. Numbers E. and W. from Pine Ave., N. and S. from Ocean Blvd.

Shopping District: Between Pacific and Atlantic Aves., from Ocean Blvd. to 7th St.

Information Bureaus: Chamber of Commerce, 109 American Ave.; Travelers' Aid, 156 W. Ocean Blvd.; City Hall, Pacific Ave. and Broadway; Public Library, Lincoln Park, Pacific Ave. and Ocean Blvd.

Newspapers: Press-Telegram, eve. and Sun.; *Sun,* morn. except Sun.

Radio Stations: KFOX, 220 E. Anaheim St., KGER, 435 Pine Ave.

Churches: 98 churches and other places of worship, representing most denominations and creeds.

Accommodations: 88 hotels, 1,375 apartment houses and courts, numerous auto and trailer camps. Wide range of rates.

Theatres: 21 motion-picture houses, principally in downtown business district and amusement zone.

Parks and Playgrounds: 24 public parks and playgrounds totaling more than 980 acres. Almost all types of recreational facilities and equipment available.

Swimming: 8 miles of beaches; still-water swimming at Marine Stadium, Alamitos Bay, and lagoon enclosed by Rainbow Pier at foot of American Ave.;

salt-water plunge, Colorado Lagoon, Recreation Park; adm. free; indoor plunge at foot of Pacific Ave.; adults 40¢, children 30¢.

Golf: Recreation Park (municipal), E. 7th St. and Park Ave., 2 courses, 9 and 18 holes, green fees 50¢ and 75¢ daily, $1 Sun., holidays; $5 per mo.; Lakewood Country Club (*open to public*), Cherry Ave. and E. Carson St., 18 holes, fees 75¢ daily, 50¢ before 8 a.m. and after 3 p.m.; Meadowlark Country Club (*open to public*), Coast Hwy. at Sunset Beach, 18 holes, fees 50¢ daily.

Tennis: 10 municipal courts, 2 lighted. 23 school courts open to public after school hours.

Fishing: Surf and pier fishing permitted. Boats from Pier B, foot of Santa Clara Ave., daily at intervals from 2-7:30 a.m., returning about 3:30 p.m., $2-$3 per day. Barges reached by boat from Belmont Pier, foot of Belmont Pl., daily 8 a.m.-3 p.m. at 1½-hr. intervals, $1. (All prices include bait and tackle.)

Annual Events: See Los Angeles *Calendar of Events.*

SIGNAL HILL

Railroad Station: Pacific Electric Ry., Los Angeles-Newport Beach Line, on private right-of-way, between Walnut and Cherry Aves.

Bus Station: Lang Bus Co., Clearwater-Long Beach line stops on signal at Cherry Ave. interstections.

Taxis: Taxis on call from Long Beach stands. Long Beach zone and meter rates prevail.

Traffic Regulations: State traffic laws prevail.

Streets and Numbers: Avenues and streets in the level area south and west of the hill are continuations of Long Beach thoroughfares. Avenues run N. and S., streets E. and W.

Information Bureau: Signal Hill City Hall and Justice Court, Cherry Ave., between 21st and Hill Sts.

LONG BEACH (47 alt., 164,271 pop.), a seaside resort, a busy harbor, home port for some 40,000 officers and men of the U.S. Navy, and one of the world's great oil centers, stretches for eight miles along San Pedro Bay. The fifth largest of California's cities, it lies 20 miles southeast of Los Angeles. Along the ocean is the long beach for which the city was named—a wide band of white sand, to which come hundreds of thousands every year to bask in the sun, swim, dive into the curving breakers, row or sail boats, and fish from piers or barges anchored offshore. Along the strand, at the foot of Pine Ave., the city's main street, is the Pike, a raucous amusement area, with roller coasters, side shows, hot dog stands, and similar attractions; staid townspeople rather frown upon it as rowdy and noisy, but they overlook this for the sweet music played by tourists' and children's dimes and quarters as they clink at the change booths.

To the west, set off by the Los Angeles River, is the industrial section and the harbor, protected by a breakwater built in 1928. It consists of both an inner and an outer harbor, dredged to accommodate ocean-going ships; marine traffic approximates $50,000,000 a year. Close to the wharves are some 400 industrial plants which produce gasoline and other petroleum products, canned fish, clothing, tools, soap, vegetable oils, and ships. Offshore, for many months of the year, lies the U.S. Battle Fleet, a formidable steel-gray armada by day, at night an eerie line of blinking lights cut by beams of powerful search-lights. The fleet is an important factor in the city's economic life. Almost all of the officers maintain homes in Long Beach, and thousands of blue jackets visit the city regularly on shore leave.

To the east are parks, the newer residential sections, eucalyptus groves, and the lagoons of Alamitos Bay, as the city trails off into open country. On the north, bristling with tall oil derricks, rises Signal Hill, the center of an independent municipality of the same name.

The downtown district of tall office buildings and hotels, shops and theatres, extends northward from the beach along Pine and other streets. Beyond, the city is laid out in rigid rectangular pattern, squared to the main points of the compass; cafes, garages, used-car lots, stores, and markets line the main thoroughfares; along the quiet side streets, shaded by palm and pepper trees, stand frame and stucco bun-galows, for the most part, although there are many larger and more elaborate white stucco houses along East Ocean Blvd., which swings in an arc on the yellow bluffs above the beach, and on the sandy slopes overlooking the ocean, lagoons, and winding canals around Alamitos Bay.

Much of the architecture reflects the origin and the ideals of the elderly Midwesterners, who constitute a large part of the population. The annual Iowa Picnic held in Bixby Park attracts more than 100,000 people. Having come here to spend their declining years, they are conservative, Protestant, church-going, and home-loving, although ven-turing forth frequently to attend Sunday School picnics and Ladies' Aid bazaars. They are inveterate "joiners," supporting some 200 civic and social organizations. Many men play horseshoes daily in Lincoln Park, while others join heated sessions of the "Spit and Argue Club" on the Municipal Pier, to discuss politics and religion. For many years dancing, card playing, drinking, and modern bathing suits were regu-larly and vehemently denounced here, with no appreciable effect on the younger generation, which, unimpressed by jeremiads on fire and brim-stone, went its own light-hearted way and here, as elsewhere, the "shocking" has now become usual. Since the depression the traditional political conservatism of the older generation has broken down, ship-wrecked on the hard rock of reality, for many a retired farmer, trades-man, and country doctor found his savings of a lifetime wiped out in the economic collapse. It is no accident that Dr. Francis E. Townsend, an elderly local doctor from the Middle West, started his old age pen-sion scheme here.

In 1784, three years after the establishment of the pueblo of Los Angeles, Governor Pedro Fages began to distribute land in the name of the King of Spain and to one Manuel Nieto, a soldier, allotted all the land between the Santa Ana and San Gabriel Rivers, a grant of 300,000 acres, extending from the sea to the northeastern foothills; the grant was later split into five ranchos. On Nieto's death, Don Juan José Nieto, his son, succeeded to Rancho Los Alamitos (the little cottonwoods), and Dona Manuela Nieto inherited Rancho Los Cerritos (the little hills); these two ranchos embraced the present site of Long Beach.

In 1840 Abel Stearns (*see The Historical Background*) bought Rancho Los Alamitos, and three years later John Temple, a Los Angeles merchant, became the owner of Rancho Los Cerritos through his marriage with Dona Rafaela Cota, descendant of Don Manuel Nieto. The two Massachusetts Yankees lived as Spanish dons and were the only ranch owners in the entire district. They became friendly rivals, and staged barbecues, rodeos, and bullfights, as well as an annual inter-ranch horse race, the course running from Signal Hill straight to the sea. But the drought years of 1862-64 put an end to the prosperity of the two Yankees; during those years, it is said, 50,000 cattle died on Rancho Los Alamitos alone. Stearns and Temple mortgaged and sold their properties, and by 1878 all of what is now Long Beach had passed into the hands of the Bixby family.

In 1880, W. E. Willmore, an Englishman, secured an option from Jotham Bixby on 4,000 acres, organized the "American Colony," and advertised Willmore City, as he called it, throughout the nation. He offered 5-, 10-, 20-, and 40-acre farms at $12.50, $15, and $20 an acre; and at $100 an acre he offered 3- or 4-year-old orange trees, 70 to the acre. The venture failed, however, and in 1884 Willmore relinquished his option. But the plans of the city remained, for it had been surveyed and laid out in 1882, with its present streets and Pacific Park.

The Long Beach Land and Water Company then took over the settlement, renamed it Long Beach, improved the water system, built a hotel and wharf, instituted a horse-car line, and connected the town with the Wilmington line of the Southern Pacific. Thereafter development was rapid. During the boom of the 1880's Long Beach became a popular seaside resort. With the completion of the Pacific Electric Railway line to Long Beach in 1902 its growth became even more rapid. In 1908 Long Beach adopted its first charter, which provided for a mayor and council form of government. This was succeeded in 1915 by a commission plan; and the present managerial system, under which a city manager is appointed by the council, was adopted in 1921.

In 1906 the Los Angeles Dock and Terminal Company, organized locally, developed the inner harbor by dredging channels and building jetties, and three years later John F. Craig established the first large shipyard in southern California, and dredged a channel from it to the sea. Plans to develop a large port were facilitated in 1911 when the state granted to Long Beach all tidal flats and submerged lands along its boundaries. In 1917 the Los Angeles Dock and Terminal Company deeded all its navigable channels to the city, and the next year

Federal development of the harbor began. Shipping was highly stimulated in 1921 by the discovery of a phenomenally rich oil field on Signal
Hill. A further grant of tidelands along the extended boundaries of
the city was made in 1925, and Long Beach developed into an impor-
tant port and naval base. The Long Beach earthquake of 1933, in which 118 persons lost
their lives and $40,000,000 worth of property was damaged in Long
Beach and the surrounding communities, only momentarily broke
the city's stride. This earthquake, the second most destructive in the
history of the United States, began about dinnertime on March 10 and
continued with lessened violence for several days; it was produced by a
fault slip in the ocean off Newport Beach. Long Beach, like other
communities in the devastated area, had most of its schools leveled by
the shock. Faulty building construction was responsible for much of
the damage; steps have been taken to see that such a condition does
not exist in the future.

SIGNAL Hill (364 alt., 3,184 pop.), a small independent municipality, economically a part of Long Beach, occupies the hill down
which Don Juan Temple and Don Abel Stearns once started their
horses in races to the shore and back again. Streets and roads wind
through a forest of oil derricks, with here and there a cluster of cottages near grimy palm trees.

Here, on June 23, 1921, a discovery or "wildcat" well driven by
the Royal Dutch Shell Company came in, but like many discovery wells,
with a small production. By the end of the year some 500 greasy
derricks spindled skyward; by midyear 1922, 500; by the end of 1923,
more than 1,000 on an area of little more than two square miles,
making the field one of the most intensively developed in the world.
Almost overnight, "million dollar views" became million dollar leases
as production mounted to a daily average of almost 250,000 barrels.
Thousands poured in to work in the field or to speculate in leases;
there was a frenzied boom in surrounding real estate. Within two
years the number of ships using the Panama Canal was doubled by
the increase in tankers carrying California oil. Los Angeles became
one of the great oil ports of the world. Within a decade the population of Long Beach tripled as the flow of "liquid gold" from Signal
Hill was piped to its wharves and refineries. The field reached its peak
production in 1923 with sixty-eight million barrels, the output for the
first ten years being more than four hundred million barrels. Since
discovery it has remained one of the largest producing oil fields in
California.

After the completion in 1859 of the Drake well, the first in the
world, at Titusville, Pa., prospectors sought likely localities around
the oil and tar seepages and natural asphaltum deposits in Humboldt,
Santa Barbara, Los Angeles, and Kern Counties. By 1867 some 50
wells had been drilled but produced only 5,000 barrels of oil, valued
at $10,000. In 1873, C. A. Mentre, a Pennsylvania driller, secured

leases in Pico Canyon (*see Tour 7*), and with primitive equipment drilled a hole 30 feet deep, from which oozed a barrel or two of oil a day. In 1883 the production of crude oil in the State totaled a mere 2,500 barrels a day.

The Brea-Olinda field (*see Tour 4*), the first in the Los Angeles Basin, was opened in 1897; up to 1919 new discoveries in the Los Angeles Basin were confined to the eastern section of Los Angeles County and the northwestern corner of Orange County, consisting of the following fields: Whittier and Coyote, 1912; Montebello, 1917; Richfield-Yorba Linda, 1919; Santa Fe Springs, 1919.

In 1920 development shifted to the coastal strip of Los Angeles and Orange Counties, where 13 new fields were opened prior to 1937. The field at Huntington Beach (*see Tour 5*), discovered in May 1920, followed on June 23, 1921, by Signal Hill, were among the richest ever discovered. The upper sands in the field were soon depleted, but late in 1923 other oil-bearing sands were struck below 5,000 feet, and derricks spread northwest to the Chateau Thierry district and southwest to Reservoir Hill; in 1938 a well was brought in at 10,000 feet. The extraordinary depth of the sands account for the phenomenal aggregate production per acre of the Signal Hill field. The 21 fields in the Los Angeles Basin produced more than half of the State's 250,000,000 barrels of crude in 1938, which represented more than 12 per cent of the national and roughly 8 per cent of the world total. At the same time the fields supplied 267,292,000,000 cubic feet of natural gas.

Refining of crude oil constitutes the greatest single division of industry in Los Angeles County; its 35 refineries had an output in 1937 valued at $228,500,000. In addition, 52 plants produce casing head gasoline from natural gas by a process of evaporation and condensation. This process was discovered in 1911 when it was found that in a gas pipe line laid along the bottom of the Los Angeles River gasoline accumulated in those sections of pipe under water but not at other points on the line. Crude oil is refined by a heating process, which boils out gasoline, kerosene, gas oil, lubricating oil, fuel oil, wax, and asphalt, each of which vaporizes at a different temperature; during the process temperatures range from 200 to 575 degrees. Crude oil is graded by its specific gravity; the higher the gravity, the greater the gasoline, kerosene, and naphtha content. Los Angeles Basin crude oil brought an average price of 99 cents a barrel in 1938.

Drilling was begun on the ocean floor in 1894, and derricks rise in the waters west from Long Beach to Wilmington. Drilling for oil is not the haphazard business it once was. The geologist, paleontologist, and geophysicist have reduced it to a science by a study of the conditions under which oil is likely to be found. It remains for the drill, however, to prove the accuracy of their deductions on the possible presence of oil in untested territory. Many a well driven at their advice has been a "duster," or dry hole.

When a "wildcat" well is to be driven to test a suspected field, a derrick is erected over the chosen spot; most derricks in the Los Angeles Basin are of the combination-rig type, 122 feet high, of wood or steel; steel is frequently required by law in fields lying within incorporated limits of a town or city, to lessen fire hazard. For wells deeper than 6,000 feet—some go down as far as 14,000 feet—huge derricks of 200 feet or more are used. When the derrick has been completely rigged with machinery, boilers, cables, and crown block of wood or metal, fitted with large pulleys, the well is ready to be "spudded," either with a drill that bores into the earth or with a percussion drill that literally pounds its way down. After a depth of 100 to 200 feet has been reached, the drill is withdrawn and a casing is inserted to wall the hole, and this process is repeated at regular intervals.

Operations are interrupted now and again by the necessity of doing a "fishing job" to recover drills or casing lost in the hole. In the coastal area, where subterranean channels of sea water are sometimes encountered, cement is forced down the hole under high pressure; when it hardens, it forms a solid plug, through which the well is then bored. The entire procedure is supervised by a driller, who operates the engine, while "roughnecks" handle pipe, make connections, pull and place slips. A drilling crew works 24 hours a day, in three shifts, called Tours, pronounced "Towers."

When the driller believes that oil sands have been reached, the drill bit and pipe are withdrawn, and an oil string, of "perforated," is inserted. Gas pressure forces oil through the small perforations and up the pipe. As mud and water are bailed out and dumped into the slump hole, the gas gradually lifts the oil toward the surface until it boils out of the casing mouth to be piped to tank farm or refinery. On occasion, however, the gas pressure is such that when the drill is withdrawn, a column of oil spouts into the air to "paint the crown block." These gushers are often difficult to control, but are not to be compared with "outlaw" gas wells. When a drill breaks through the thick "cap rock" over an oil pool, the force of the escaping gas sometimes crumples a derrick as if it were built of matchsticks; it may develop into a burning "gasser" if rocks and pieces of cement strike the casing and throw off a spark. Such "outlaws," which have not destroyed the casing head and control valves, are tamed by the use of long rods attached to the controls. Behind a protective shield, workmen manipulate these bars until the pressure is reduced sufficiently to permit a crane to drop a heavy metal "cap" over the casing. Where valves cannot be worked by remote control but the casing head is still intact, a crane is brought into position and a forty-foot flue is set over it. This elevates the flame to a height where workmen can approach the well and install a control manifold and shut off the flow. In cases where the casing head is destroyed, the modern practice is to drill a vertical hole to a certain depth in the vicinity of the "wild" well and then "whipstock" at an angle until the "outlaw" is tapped. Liquid mud, under heavy pressure, is then pumped into the well until it stops the flow of gas or oil.

The cost of drilling a well varies with geologic conditions, depth, and mechanical difficulties. The average well strikes oil at 4,100 feet and costs approximately $45,000. In fields such as Signal Hill, where properties are numerous and small, many of the wells are uneconomical from any broad point of view. An oil pool is a geologic and economic unit, but is not developed as such. Legally, every producer owns all the oil under his property, but oil is no respecter of property lines and flows toward the nearest well. In self-protection, therefore, producers drill "offset" wells around the edge of their properties to prevent them from being drained by neighboring wells, thus doubling and tripling the number of wells that would be required by any sensible and rational system of exploitation.

Signal Hill, resembling an aroused porcupine, bristles with derricks, in the shadow of which are tanks, engine houses, machine shops, and a few grimy cottages occupied by oil workers. At night the bright lights on the derricks turn the hill, often referred to as "The Pincushion," into a curious, gaunt, illuminated forest.

POINTS OF INTEREST

The CIVIC CENTER includes the City Hall, the Municipal Utilities Building, and the Veterans Memorial Building, which front south toward Lincoln Park on Broadway, between Pacific and Cedar Avenues; the Public Library is in the park itself, facing Ocean Boulevard.

1. The CITY HALL, NW. corner of Broadway and Pacific Ave., facing Lincoln Park, is a modern eight-story building of buff-colored concrete, designed by Horace W. Austin and completed in 1934.

2. The VETERANS MEMORIAL BUILDING, on Broadway west of the Municipal Utilities Building, is a four-story, concrete structure of modern design with a decorative frieze above the entrance. The building, completed in 1938, was designed by George Kahrs; the frieze, by Merrell Gage.

LINCOLN PARK, bounded by Broadway, Ocean Blvd., Pacific, and Cedar Aves., is shaded by 50-year-old pepper and eucalyptus trees. Roque and horseshoe courts contribute to the popularity of this downtown retreat; the Long Beach Tourist Horseshoe Club uses the 10 courts daily. This pioneer playground, originally set off as Pacific Park in the early plats of Willmore City, was donated to the city by the Long Beach Land and Water Company in 1888. Its name was changed to Lincoln Park in 1915, at the unveiling of the Lincoln Monument.

3. Lincoln Park assumes the character of an Old World square on mornings when the MUNICIPAL MARKET (*Tues., Thurs., and Sat., 7-12*), conducted by the city as a public convenience, takes over half the width of both Broadway and Pacific Avenue, on two sides of Lincoln Park. Canvas stalls on the sidewalks display local, state, national, and foreign produce—fruits, nuts, jellies, vegetables, home-

LONG BEACH

SCALE
ONE MILE

N

POINTS

1. City Hall
2. Veterans Memorial Building
3. Municipal Market
4. Public Library
5. Lincoln Monument
6. Million-Dollar Bathhouse
7. Municipal Navy Landing
8. Small Boat Anchorage

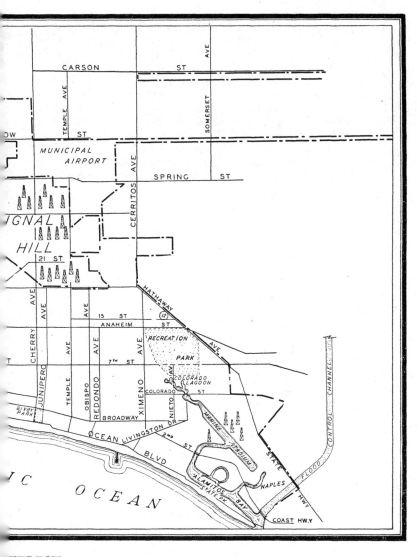

TEREST

9. Procter & Gamble Co. Plant
10. Municipal Auditorium
11. Wayside Art Colony

12. Adobe Los Alamitos
13. Old Long Beach Cemetery
14. Adobe Los Cerritos

made butter, and cottage cheese. Green-tinted duck eggs, chickens and ducks, roasted a rich brown and ready to serve, are sold by the Chinese. Italian fishwives offer filets of yellowtail, sea bass, and barracuda, dressed with olive oil and cured in the sun before smoking. From 15 to 20 different nationalities are represented. Supervised by the City Market Master, who prohibits ballyhoo and barkers, the market and its products are subject to rigid inspection; in general, prices are low, and quality high. The market was established in 1913 and is sponsored by the Woman's City Club.

4. The PUBLIC LIBRARY, in the center of Lincoln Park, built in 1908 with the aid of an Andrew Carnegie grant, was remodeled in 1936-37 by D. E. Herrald on modern lines to harmonize with other Civic Center buildings.

5. To the south of the library is the 15-foot LINCOLN MONU-MENT, a life-size granite figure of the martyred president by Peter Bisson, erected in 1915 by means of private contributions and public funds.

The PIKE, an amusement zone extending almost a mile along the beach west of the intersection of American Ave. and Ocean Blvd., has appropriately been called the "Walk of a Million Lights," and is a major local "industry."

6. Midway along the Pike is the Silver Spray Pier, and the MIL-LION-DOLLAR BATHHOUSE (*rates 30¢ to 40¢*), with an indoor salt-water plunge. Shooting galleries, penny arcades, a roller coaster, side shows, a merry-go-round, miniature automobiles, power scooters, and similar amusements attract children and adults alike. Curio shops offer Mexican hammered silver, pottery, and needlework; Chinese, Japanese, and East Indian brass work; Spanish embroideries and Italian laces; native Indian basketry, shell, and beadwork. Among annual events are the Baby Parade, the Bathing Beauty Contest, the Pet Parade, and the Doll Fiesta. New Year's Eve, Hallowe'en, and Fourth of July are celebrated here by vast crowds of costumed merrymakers.

7. The MUNICIPAL NAVY LANDING, at the foot of Pico Ave. in the Outer Harbor is the clearing station for enlisted men's shore boats, officers' gigs and numerous water taxis, plying between shore and the vessels of the United States BATTLE FLEET (*open to public Sun. and holidays 2-4; transportation on Navy shore boats free*), seen lying at anchor some two to three miles offshore, in the Outer Harbor, much of the year. When the fleet is in 45,000 officers and men swarm ashore at the San Pedro (*see The Harbor*) and Long Beach Navy landings.

Over the waters when the fleet is in, flash burnished launches carrying officers and open shore boats, crowded with sailors and marines. The dock is thronged with the families and friends of officers and men, as they arrive on liberty or leave for their ships. On the wharf of the landing are Roosevelt Post Office, water-taxi ticket offices, Red Cross and Navy Patrol stations, and quarters of the Navy storekeeper.

Los Angeles Harbor is the base of major units of the fleet, including the flagships of the commander-in-chief, and the commanders of the Battle, Base, and Scouting Forces. Regularly stationed here are 14 battleships and two airplane carriers of the Battle Force; 16 heavy cruisers of the Scouting Force; the hospital ship U.S.S. *Relief;* and repair ships, mine sweepers, oilers, and supply vessels of the Base Force. The battleships displace tonnages of 27,000 to 32,500 each, and carry main batteries of 14- to 16-inch guns, supplemented by six-inch secondary and five-inch anti-aircraft batteries. Each carries 60 officers and 1,200 men. The aircraft carriers U.S.S. *Lexington* and U.S.S. *Saratoga* each carry 80 planes of varying types.

The fleet was first based here in 1919, when a portion of the Atlantic Fleet was detached for service in this area in response to insistent demands for more adequate defense on the Pacific coast.

8. The SMALL BOAT ANCHORAGE, head of Slip No. 3, just off Pico Ave., is the home port of numerous yachts and cruisers discarded by wealthy owners, and motorboats of every type. On the shores of the slip are small shipyards.

9. The PROCTER AND GAMBLE COMPANY PLANT (*open workdays 9:30-10:30 and 2-3; guides provided*), 1601 W. 7th St., occupies a group of six-story concrete structures, on a 15-acre site fenced from the street. Visitors can observe the complete process of manufacturing soap from vegetable oils, chiefly cocoanut, cottonseed, and linseed.

10. The MUNICIPAL AUDITORIUM, occupying an eight-acre filled-in area at the foot of American Ave., is a $3,000,000 reinforced concrete structure, with Indiana limestone facing, rising to a height of nine stories. The building, light brown in color, is designed in the Italian Renaissance style with a monumental arched loggia on the front facade and a circular, arcaded bay at the rear. Italian marble has been used in the interior lobbies, and the foyer floors are of terrazzo. A main convention hall, two smaller convention halls, a concert hall, six committee rooms, and an exhibit hall bring the total seating capacity to 8,600. Surrounding gardens contain palm trees, semitropical horticultural specimens, paneled lawns, and spacious flower beds. The building and grounds project into a wide lagoon which in turn is enclosed by an encircling pier. The auditorium, designed by MacDowell and Austin and completed in 1932, is the center for varied activities: Municipal Band concerts, the weekly Sunday morning meetings of the world's largest men's Bible class, the annual Navy Ball, symphony orchestra concerts, and the annual Art Festival; the weekly Community Service Programs include community singing, a stage program, and old-time square dancing.

A tile mosaic, *Recreation in Long Beach,* designed by Nord, King, and Wright, and executed by 40 artists and craftsmen of the Los Angeles Federal Art Project, rises from the fifth story, and is said to be the largest tile mosaic in the world. At night the auditorium is illuminated by powerful floodlights.

Less than a mile west of the Rainbow Pier and the ocean-front amusement zone is the HARBOR DISTRICT. Ocean Boulevard, Broadway, and Seventh Street lead directly to the port from the city's downtown business center, and Pico Avenue penetrates the area from the north.

The inner harbor consists of Cerritos Channel, opening into the East Basin of the Los Angeles Harbor, and two branches, Slips Nos. 2 and 3, extending 3,000 feet eastward. The main channel and the two slips provide nine miles of water frontage. Municipal piers in the inner harbor have 3,600 feet of dockage; those in the outer harbor provide an additional 3,500 feet. Black steamship funnels, swinging cranes, slender factory smokestacks, steel struts carrying power cables, and modern steel oil derricks reveal the mutiplicity of activities in the Long Beach Harbor.

The whole Long Beach Harbor area has been created from half submerged tidelands and low flats at the mouth of the Los Angeles River. Sloughs north of the present Terminal Island formerly carried the main currents to the ocean. In times of flood the river waters washed over the entire flat as far as San Pedro. The deepest of the sloughs have been opened and deepened to form the inner harbors of Los Angeles (*see The Harbor*) and Long Beach.

The first development work followed the establishment of the Craig shipbuilding plant south of the river mouth, now Slip No. 3 of the inner harobr, in 1907. Work was begun on an ocean entrance to the channel and a high tide, in June 1909, finished the work, opening the slough to the sea. Within three months Long Beach voted a bond issue of $245,000 for the purchase of 2,200 feet of water frontage on the channel and the construction of a municipal wharf, and in 1918 Congress provided for the dredging of Cerritos Channel. Construction of the Long Beach jetty, completed in 1928, made possible the development of the outer harbor.

RAINBOW PIER (*open to pedestrian and vehicular traffic*), with entrances at both Pine and Linden Aves. on the shore front, describes a 3,800-foot crescent around the Auditorium's lagoon. The pier, completed in 1931 at a cost of $1,400,000, rests on a rock breakwater and is a vantage point from which to observe water carnivals on the 32-acre lagoon, which also offers ideal still-water bathing. The Long Beach Recreation Commission maintains a supervised recreational program here, including canoeing and various aquatic classes for children.

11. The WAYSIDE ART COLONY, 74 Atlantic Ave., occupies a group of eight brown frame buildings—art shops, studios, and private art schools—in a rustic setting. Activities of the artists, who call themselves "crafters," include wood and metal work, painting, weaving, needlework, music, and dancing.

BIXBY PARK, two city blocks bounded by Ocean Blvd., Broadway, Cherry and Junipero Aves., has wide rolling lawns thickly shaded by live oak, pine, cypress, acacia, sycamore, and palm trees. In the 10-acre park are held many of the state picnics for which Long Beach is renowned. The Iowa picnic on the second Saturday in February is attended by 75,000 to 100,000 former residents of the Hawkeye State. In the park's eastern section are playground apparatus, bandstand, tables and shelters, and a house where food and coffee are heated by attendants (*free*). The park was created in the 1880's when the town-site was laid out, partially under the direction of John W. Bixby, for whom the plot was named, and was deeded to the city in 1903.

ALAMITOS BAY, eastern termination of Ocean Blvd., a popular spot for aquatic sports, covers the old tidal channels through which the San Gabriel River found an outlet to the sea. The bay provides seven miles of landlocked waterways, offering splendid harborage for small craft and still-water bathing. Most of the south and west shores are publicly owned, and contain a number of supervised playgrounds. The 37-acre STATE PARK, one of the bay playgrounds, under lease from the State of California by the Long Beach Recreation Commission, extends to the tip of the peninsula and has 6,000 feet of beach, on both the ocean and bay side of the spit; the bay side is protected from high tides by a 200-foot rubble wall four feet high.

The labyrinth of canals of NAPLES, a section of the Alamitos district lying west of the Vista del Golfo arm of the bay, and reached by way of Second Street, are fed by the tidal currents of the bay. Along the canals are hundreds of attractive houses, set among green lawns and tropical vegetation. Arched bridges, like those of Venice, span the waterways and provide access to the islands.

The OLYMPIC MARINE STADIUM, Colorado St. and Nieto Ave., was constructed for the rowing races in the 1932 Olympiad. The course is 2,000 meters, or 1.31 miles; a boathouse has showers and phy-sican's quarters; grandstand and bleachers seat 20,000 spectators. High school physical education classes in rowing are conducted at the sta-dium, and a model yacht championship regatta is held annually, with some 100 small vessels as entries.

The 81-acre COLORADO LAGOON, south of Recreation Park, affords exceptional facilities for water sports. In the model boatshop, in the clubhouse, many types of miniature craft are constructed under the direction of expert instructors, and an annual exposition is held each April to exhibit the work of amateur shipbuilders.

In RECREATION PARK, 7th St. and Ximeno Ave., is held an annual Twelfth Night celebration at which the city's discarded Christ-mas trees are consumed in a huge bonfire. The park, with a fine ex-panse of lawns and distinctive eucalyptus woodland, contains children's playgrounds, baseball diamonds, bowling greens, clubhouse, barbecue pits, coffee house, and a flycasting pool, a sport rarely provided for.

12. The central and oldest part of the ADOBE LOS ALAMITOS, NW. corner 15th St. and Hathaway Ave., is believed to have been built in 1784 by Manuel Nieto, then 70 years old, as a home for his 16-year-old bride. Set in a semitropical garden on a hilltop, the adobe retains the atmosphere of the Spanish inspiration. The two-story unit and the two wings are finished with offwhite plaster. The left wing is

part of the original adobe, with walls about three feet thick. Clay from the adjacent wet lands was employed in making the large adobe bricks. At the time of construction Nieto had acquired 300,000 acres of land, later known as the Rancho Los Alamitos (ranch of the little poplars), which extended from the Los Angeles River to the Santa Ana River, and as far inland as he could push it without conflict with the prior claims of the Pueblo of Los Angeles and the San Gabriel Mission. In 1840 Abel Stearns (*see Downtown Los Angeles*), a Massachusetts Yankee, purchased the rancho and transformed the old mud hut into a summer home for his bride, Arcadia Bandini, and in 1878 John W. Bixby, who had leased part of the ranch, further restored and enlarged the house. The estate now covers 3,700 acres. Near the house is an ancient Indian kitchen midden, or shell mound.

The LONG BEACH MUNICIPAL AIRPORT, Temple Ave. and Spring St., comprising 588 acres, has two paved runways illuminated at night by floodlights. The revolving beacon is visible from 20 to 80 miles. Buildings include hangars and the administration offices, and both the Army and Navy maintain hangars. The airport, established in 1924, was among the first civic aviation fields in California.

SIGNAL HILL, one of the world's richest oil fields, rises at the northern limits of Long Beach, and is unmistakably identified by the hundreds of oil derricks that encircle and crown it. By 1938, 598,-673,732 barrels of oil and 803,342 million cubic feet of natural gas had been taken from the 1,350 proven acres of the field, a source of wealth to thousands.

13. The four-acre OLD LONG BEACH CEMETERY, NW. corner of Willow St. and Orange Ave., has many headstones, yellow with oil and age, inscribed with the names of many of the pioneer families of Willmore City. Close to the east boundary is an oblong gray granite slab in memory of W. E. Willmore, "founder of Willmore City, later incorporated as Long Beach. Died Jan. 15, 1901. Age 57." Along the north edge of the graveyard, a stone's throw from the rhythmic pumps, is the "million dollar potters' field." The cemetery constitutes an "island" in the oil field, in which derricks are noticeably absent.

14. Don Juan Temple's ADOBE LOS CERRITOS, 4600 Virginia Rd., built in 1844, was one of the first houses of the so-called Monterey type (*see Architecture*) constructed in southern California, and remains the best-preserved example of its type in the Los Angeles region. The white plastered adobe occupies a five-acre estate, the house and garden walls encircling a large patio. The main unit, facing the street, is 100 feet long. Along one end and the full length of the front runs a two-story porch, with the balcony supported by squared timbers and protected by the overhang of the tiled roof. In Temple's day *brea* took the place of the variegated mission tiles that now cover the old mansion. Two wings, 142 feet long, form the patio at the rear of the house. An extensive Spanish garden in the manner of the pastor superior's residence at San Gabriel (*see Tour 3*) surrounds the adobe.

Many of the shrubs and trees planted by Temple still flourish in the parklike grounds. Temple, a pioneer Los Angeles merchant, imported lumber from New England sawmills to build the house; later, it was for many years the home of Jotham Bixby, of the pioneer Long Beach family, who stocked the ranch with sheep. In, 1930 Llewellyn Bixby rehabilitated the house and improved the gardens; authentic restorations preserved the original detail and atmosphere, which recalls the days of bullfights in the adjoining corrals, unquartered beeves hanging ready for the barbecue pits, fandangos in the courtyard, and all the gay color of the fiestas that followed the horse races of the *vaqueros*.

Pasadena

Railroad Stations: Santa Fe R.R., 222 S. Raymond Ave.; Union Pacific R.R., 205 W. Colorado St.; Southern Pacific R.R. ticket office, 148 E. Colorado St.; Pacific Electric Ry., 61 N. Fair Oaks Ave.

Bus Stations: Union Bus Station, 48 S. Marengo Ave. for Greyhound Lines, Union Pacific Trailways, Pasadena-Ocean Park Stage Line to Glendale, Hollywood, the beaches, Motor Transit Line, Mt. Wilson Stage Line. Burlington Trailways, Santa Fe Trailways, 533 E. Colorado St.

Busses and Streetcars: Pacific Electric Ry., fares 6¢ and 10¢; weekly and monthly passes, good on all lines, at reduced rates. Oak Knoll and Short Line cars from Pacific Electric Ry. Station, N. Fair Oaks Ave. and Union St. to 6th and Main St. station in Los Angeles.

Taxis: Yellow Cab and Black and White, 144 W. Colorado St.; White Cab, 235 E. Del Mar St.; Green Cab, 86 N. Fair Oaks Ave.; Red Top, 144 W. Colorado St.; fares 10¢, 1 mile, 5¢ for each additional ½ mile or fraction.

Traffic Regulations: California State statutes are basic. Watch for traffic signs. All parking in streets prohibited between 1 and 6 a.m. Speed zones posted. Left turns permitted in all zones except when prohibited by traffic officer. Right turns permitted against signal, after full stop. U-turns in business zones prohibited from 7 a.m. to 6 p.m.

Streets and Numbers: Colorado St. dividing line for street numbering, N. and S.; Fair Oaks Ave. for E. and W.; avenues run N. and S., streets E. and W. Boulevards and drives are designated.

Information Bureaus: Chamber of Commerce, N. Garfield Ave. and Union St.; Information Booth, City Hall; Union Bus Station, 48 S. Marengo Ave.; Pacific Electric Station, 61 N. Fair Oaks Ave.

Accommodations: More than 100 hotels and apartments with usual range of prices. Well-appointed auto and trailer camps in eastern section of the city.

Churches: 112 churches, representing the leading denominations.

Theatres, Motion-Picture Houses, Amphitheatres: Community Playhouse, 39 S. El Molino Ave., local productions; Civic Auditorium, 300 E. Green St., lectures, opera, orchestral music; 11 motion-picture houses; Gold Shell, N. Raymond Ave. and E. Holly St., civic concerts Sun. afternoons throughout year (transferred indoors in inclement weather), local productions, drama, light opera, pageants.

Radio Station: KPPC, 583 E. Colorado St.

Newspapers: Post, every morn.; *Star-News,* eve. except Sun.

Recreational Areas: Brookside Park, Rosemont Ave., between Scott Pl. and Seco St., 521 acres, with Rose Bowl, municipal golf courses, 3 baseball diamonds, plunges, tennis courts, picnic grounds, children's playground; night lighting.
Tournament Park, 22 acres, SW. cor. E. California St. and S. Wilson Ave.; picnicking, baseball, and football.

Carmelita Park, Colorado St. and Orange Grove Ave. (*open 10-5*), 13 acres of rare plants and shrubs.

Besse Park, 2½ acres, 3203 E. Colorado St., supervised playground; tennis court, swings, baseball diamond, wading pool.

Central Park, 9½ acres, S. Fair Oaks and Del Mar Aves., swings and roque courts lighted at night.

La Pintoresca Park, 3 acres, N. Fair Oaks and Washington Aves., picnic facilities, 4 horseshoe courts.

Lower Arroyo Park, 82½ acres, Linda Vista Bridge, S. to Busch Gardens; large clubhouse, archery green and swings.

MacDonald Park, 1¼ acres, N. Wilson Ave. and Mountain St., 6 swings and 2 horseshoe courts.

Memorial Park, 5½ acres, N. Raymond Ave. and Holly St., gas and wood stoves, picnic tables for 200, amphitheatre seating 1,500.

Oak Grove Park, 334 acres, Oak Grove St. N. to Devil's Gate Dam; picnic facilities for 900, cricket field.

Singer Park, 4 acres, St. John Ave. and California St., rose garden, benches.

Washington Park, 3 acres, N. El Molino Ave. and Washington St., picnic facilities for 78, merry-go-round, 2 tightwires.

Friendship Forum, S. Arroyo Blvd. and La Loma Rd., wading pools, picnic facilities.

La Casita del Arroyo (Sp., the little house of the gorge) (*open; free; $5 for use of parties or meetings, see Pasadena Park Board*), 177 S. Arroyo Blvd.; rustic stone-and-concrete clubhouse, large assembly room with fireplace, kitchen and smaller rooms.

Annual Events: Pasadena Rose Tournament, Jan. 1; Rose Bowl football game between a Pacific coast team of distinction and a Southern or Eastern team of like caliber, Jan. 1; Pasadena Flower Show, Busch Gardens, 3 days in Apr. and Oct. (*adm. 40¢*); Pasadena Kennel Club Show, Civic Auditorium, Feb. and July (*adm. $1*).

PASADENA (alt. 850; 1930 pop. 81,864), a quiet and conservative residential city, lies 10 miles northeast of downtown Los Angeles at the base of the San Gabriel Mountains which stand like a great Spanish comb behind it. To the south and east are southern California's great citrus orchards. The curving Arroyo Seco (dry watercourse) terminates it rather abruptly on the west. In this section is Orange Grove Avenue, "Millionaires' Row," with elaborate mansions of heterogeneous design, a remnant of the 1890's. Colorado Street, the main thoroughfare, cuts across the city from east to west; at its intersection with Fair Oaks Avenue is the small business district, given over largely to smart shops. North of Colorado Street are large and often pretentious houses, extensive estates centering on great mansions, and many massive resort hotels set far back on broad green terraces. Although the per capita income of Pasadena tops that of any other city in the country, shabby houses line dusty streets, many without sidewalks, in a considerable area south of Colorado Street. In the spring of 1939 some 3,100 persons were on relief.

Dignified, reserved Pasadena is a city of many churches. Its well-bred quiet is not broken by the whir of machinery. Indeed, many a retired industrialist with a princely estate here has joined the local Chamber of Commerce for the express purpose of preventing the development of factories in the city or immediate vicinity. What little manufacture is carried on is largely for the satisfaction of local needs. Staid and conservative as it is, it is friendly to labor and allows notable latitude in the exercise of rights of free speech and assembly; Upton Sinclair, veteran advocate of socialism, founder of the Epic movement, has his home here. The Tournament of Roses, inspired by the Carnival of Flowers at Nice, France, breaks into Pasadena's traditional reserve each New Year's Day. Instituted as a village festival to celebrate the midwinter flowering season, the "Battle of Flowers" was first fought in 1890. Celebrants bedecked horses and buggies with blossoms, had their pictures taken and sent to the folks back home, and so publicized the event that Pasadena has been called "the town that roses built." The festival today is marked by a long parade of lavishly-decorated floats, each bearing comely young girls, who pelt the onlookers with flowers. The celebration was climaxed with a thundering chariot race up to 1902; since 1916 the crowning feature has been the football game in the Rose Bowl for the mythical national championship.

The site of Pasadena was once included in the old San Gabriel Mission territory (*see Tour 3*); it was part of the land called Rancho San Pascual, said to have been given by the mission fathers to their aged housekeeper in 1826, but formally granted by Governor Figueroa in 1835 to Juan Marine, a retired officer of the Spanish Army of Mexico, who had meanwhile married the mission housekeeper. Marine's heir squandered the land, and it was neglected by those to whom it passed until in 1843 it became the property of Manuel Garfias, whose title was validated by United States authorities after California's admission to the Union in 1850. Presently the property was sold to Benjamin D. ("Don Benito") Wilson, a Yankee who had come to Los Angeles in 1841 with a party of trappers and was destined to leave his name on many landmarks in the region—a mountain, a lake, a trail, and an avenue. Wilson and his associates passed deeds and options back and forth among themselves with perplexing speed and intricacy. Finally, in 1873, the unsold portion was divided between Wilson and Dr. John S. Griffin, sometime chief medical officer of the U.S. Army in California.

Meantime, the California Colony of Indiana had been organized in Indianapolis by Dr. Thomas B. Elliott and friends, who wished "to get where life is easy." D. M. Berry, their agent, visited the Rancho San Pascual, and finding it suitable, paid Dr. Griffin $25,000 for his 4,000-acre tract. Known first as Indiana Colony, it adopted in 1875 the name of Pasadena, coined from a Chippewa phrase usually translated as "crown of the valley." Although more than half the population spoke only Spanish, and stores closed for a two-hour midday siesta, the community soon felt the invigorating spirit of the pioneers. The schoolhouse became a meeting place and forum; a village literary society was formed and issued a magazine, the *Reservoir,* containing "talent, wit and doggerel in amusing lots." Communication with Los Angeles was established by stage; in 1880 the first citrus fair was held, and the following year a large packing plant was built.

By 1882 the town had a doctor, a photographer, a paper route,

Recreation

TOURNAMENT OF ROSES PARADE, PASADENA

BATHING BEAUTY PARADE, VENICE MARDI GRAS

SURF BOARD RIDING, HERMOSA BEACH

BATHING SCENE AT LONG BEACH

L. A. County Chamber of Commerce
SAILING, ALAMITOS BAY

Santa Catalina Island
MARLIN SWORDFISH
(570 POUNDS), CATALINA

ICE HOCKEY ON JACKSON LAKE, BIG PINES PARK

TOBOGGANING IN BIG PINES PARK

L. A. County Chamber of Commerce

SKIING AT BIG PINES PARK

DOG SLED, ARROWHEAD LAKE

Lake Arrowhead Company

F. W. Carter

FISHING OFF THE PIER, SANTA MONICA

CARD PLAYERS IN THE PARK

Burton O. Burt

BOWLING ON THE GREEN, EXPOSITION PARK, LOS ANGELES

TENNIS COURTS, LA CIENEGA PLAYGROUND, BEVERLY HILLS

HOLLYWOOD PARK RACE TRACK, INGLEWOOD

AIRVIEW, ROSE BOWL, PASADENA

and a community telephone in Barney Williams' general store. A weekly newspaper, the *Chronicle,* appeared in 1883; it was printed on the presses of the *Times-Mirror* in Los Angeles, and each week type-forms were hauled back and forth on horses, which in floodtime almost disappeared in the mud of the Arroyo Seco.

About 1885 many speculators, attracted by the general southern California boom, poured into Pasadena. Brass bands paraded the streets advertising tracts for sale; houses sprang up in orange groves and vineyards; social life was gay and often noisy with the popping of champagne corks and the rattle of poker chips; South Orange Grove Avenue was widened and many mansions built. Pasadena was incorporated in 1886, in which year the Los Angeles and San Gabriel Valley Railroad entered the city, precipitating a clash between Chinese and white workers; the latter attacked and burned a Chinese laundry, to the outrage of most citizens, who assembled in public meeting and resolved that "no mob law be allowed in Pasadena."

By 1888 the boom had subsided. Subdivisions and citrus groves were overrun with weeds. The population dwindled, bank deposits shrank, and everyone appealed to the Board of Trade for aid. Gradually prosperity returned; an irrigation system was extended to surrounding dry lands. The early nineties saw the construction through the city of the Los Angeles and Salt Lake Railroad, the Terminal Railroad, and the beginning of construction of the cable railway up Mount Lowe. The latter was advertised with the slogan "From oranges to the snow." In 1891 Amos G. ("Father") Throop established the polytechnic school that later grew into the California Institute of Technology. By 1900 Pasadena had a population of 10,000.

The Mount Wilson Observatory (*see Tour 1A*) was established in 1904. Civic improvements went steadily forward. Dr. Norman Bridge, who had come to California for his health, remained to bestow $300,000 on "Cal-Tech" for the erection of the Bridge Laboratory of Physics and the Norman Bridge Library of Physics. In 1921 Henry E. Huntington (*see Tour 1*) acquired Gainsborough's *Blue Boy,* the Board of Trade changed its name to the Chamber of Commerce, and building construction amounted to $7,000,000; Pasadena had definitely arrived.

Building continued at a feverish pace throughout the 1920's. During the depression building construction slackened, but the city, for the most part, continued its leisurely and affluent ways, encouraging the arts and sciences, discouraging industry and commerce, still reflecting the spirit of the settlers who came here "to get where life is easy."

POINTS OF INTEREST

The CIVIC CENTER lies along Garfield Ave., between Green St. on the south and Walnut St. on the north. This wide section of Garfield Ave. has broad strips of park along its west side.

1. The buff-colored CITY HALL (*open; apply at Rm. 119 for adm.*

to tower), 100 N. Garfield Ave., designed by Bakewell and Brown, dominates the Civic Center with its tower in four diminishing stages with domes on the third and fourth. Wings project in the rear and are connected by an arcade, forming a large patio. Small cupolas, repeating the lines of the central dome, rise at the corners.

2. The PASADENA PUBLIC LIBRARY (*open weekdays 9-9*), 285 E. Walnut St., designed by Hunt and Chambers in 1925, is a long, two-story, tile-roofed building of modified Spanish Colonial design. Between forward wings is a forecourt surrounded by a loggia. In this court are tall slender fan palms, three on each side of the main entrance. The tile roof of the loggia is supported by frame columns reminiscent of those in old Spanish buildings. Above the magnificent black metal entrance doors are five arched windows. The library contains approximately 200,000 volumes, many rare books and works of art, and a collection of phonograph records for circulation.

3. ALL SAINTS' EPISCOPAL CHURCH (*open*), 132 N. Euclid Ave., is of late English Gothic design with a low, heavy, battlemented tower. A cloister of delicate stone tracery at the rear of a landscaped courtyard leads to parish buildings. The interior is finished in luminous brown oak lighted by windows of richly colored glass.

4. The GRACE NICHOLSON ART GALLERY (*open weekdays 9-4; free*), 30 N. Los Robles Ave., exhibits its collection of modern American and European paintings and art objects in a reproduction of a modern Chinese house, as much an exhibition piece as anything in it. The heavily ornamented roof is of green enameled pantiles from an old temple near Peking, with grotesque terra-cotta dogs and dragons at the points of the roof. On each side of the main entrance—a stone arch with tracery—is a great marble dog of the Ming dynasty, also brought from near Peking.

5. The CIVIC AUDITORIUM (*open Wed. 2-4*), 300 E. Green St., a two-story concrete building with Italian Renaissance decorative motifs designed by Bergstrom, Bennett, and Haskell, has strong horizontal lines emphasized by a low-pitched red tile hip roof with a wide overhang at the eaves. Five upper-story windows in blind arches are decorated at the top with scroll patterns on blue tile.

Inside the auditorium, running entirely around the walls, is a series of panels on mythological Greek subjects adapted from drawings by Raphael, done with cameo effect on a brick-red ground. Frescoes on upper walls and ceiling carry out the theme of the panels. All were done by John B. Smeraldi.

6. The PASADENA COMMUNITY PLAYHOUSE (*open 9-4, except during Sat. matinees*), 37 S. El Molino Ave., is housed in white plaster buildings around a rough-flagged court. Gilmor Brown, manager of the present playhouse, brought a company of professional players to the old Savoy Theatre in 1916, and after an unprofitable season appealed to Pasadena's civic leaders to assist in reviving the drama. An advisory committee of citizens assisted in organizing in 1918 the Pasadena Community Playhouse Association as a non-profit corporation;

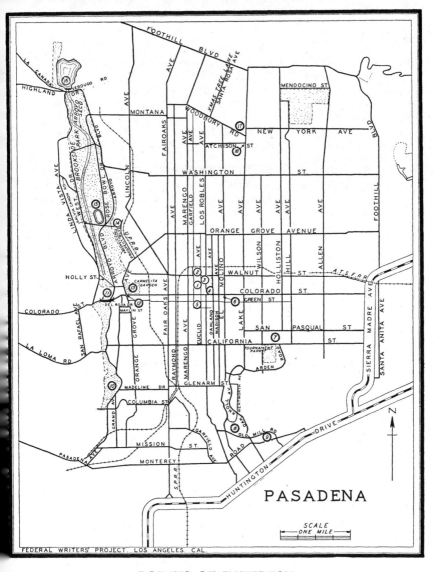

POINTS OF INTEREST

1. City Hall
2. Public Library
3. All Saints' Episcopal Church
4. Grace Nicholson Art Gallery
5. Civic Auditorium
6. Pasadena Community Playhouse
7. California Institute of Technology
8. Huntington Hotel
9. The Old Mill
10. Busch Gardens
11. Colorado Street Bridge
12. Memorial Flagpole
13. California Graduate School of Design
14. La Miniatura
15. Rose Bowl
16. Devil's Gate Dam
17. St. Elizabeth Catholic Church
18. Westminster Presbyterian Church

the present theatre was erected in 1924-25. The playhouse has a wide repertoire and claims the distinction of having produced all of Shakespeare's plays. A Midsummer Dramatic Festival has been an annual event since 1935. More than 80 plays have had national or world premieres here. Casts are chosen from among 1,000 associated players and from the 200 students in the playhouse's School of the Theatre, founded in 1928, which conducts a Laboratory Theatre for the staging of plays by new authors.

7. The CALIFORNIA INSTITUTE OF TECHNOLOGY, 1201 E. California St., had its beginnings in a small vocational training school called Throop Polytechnic Institute, founded in 1891 by Amos G. Throop, onetime mayor of Pasadena. In 1910 it was moved to the present campus and became the Throop College of Technology, the only institution west of the Mississippi devoted exclusively to the training of engineers. During the next decade the school enlisted the interest of several nationally known scientists and educators, and the financial aid of businessmen and philanthropists. In 1920 an executive council was formed, and its chairmanship was assumed by Dr. Robert A. Millikan, who is still president of the institute. In later years the name was changed to the California Institute of Technology. Contributors to the institute's endowment have included the Carnegie, Rockefeller, and Guggenheim foundations. The Carnegie Institution of Washington helps to maintain the Seismological Research Laboratory in the San Rafael Hills, some three miles from the campus. The General Educational Board, an agency of the Rockefeller Foundation, supplied funds for the erection of the institute's great 200-inch telescope and astrophysical observatory on Palomar Mountain in San Diego County.

The enrollment is limited to approximately 800 by scholarship standards. The teaching staff of 200 includes men of national and international reputation in their respective fields who were attracted to "Cal-Tech" principally by the opportunities for research. Dr. Millikan, director of the college's physics laboratory, won the 1923 Nobel award in physics for his discoveries in cosmic ray radiation; Dr. Thomas Hunt Morgan, director of the biological division, won a Nobel prize in 1923 for his studies in genetics; and Dr. Carl David Anderson, a graduate, was awarded the 1936 Nobel prize in physics for his discovery of the positron.

The older buildings on the 32-acre campus are Mediterranean in style; the newer buildings are of functional design with plain geometrical ornamentation, and are connected by loggias. To the left of the main entrance, a wide approach from Wilson Avenue, are the KERCKHOFF BIOLOGICAL LABORATORIES, a long, low, cream-colored concrete unit with an arcaded loggia along the front. The institute's marine station at Corona del Mar supplies specimens for research work and laboratory classes. A 10-acre farm for studies in plant genetics is maintained at Arcadia. Behind the MUDD and the ARMS GEOLOGICAL LABORATORIES (R), which resemble the biological laboratories, is the ASTROPHYSICS LABORATORY, whose staff works closely with those of the Palomar Mountain Observatory and the Mount Wilson Observatory (*see Tour 1A*). Adjoining the Astrophysics Laboratory on the west is CULBERTSON HALL, an auditorium.

Beyond the biological and geological laboratory groups, the approach broadens into a large plaza. The GATES AND CRELLIN CHEMICAL LABORATORY group (L) contains photographic dark-rooms, a glass-blowing room, instrument and carpenter shops, and the chemistry library. The NORMAN BRIDGE LABORATORY OF PHYSICS (R) has many special research laboratories, the general institute library, the engineering library, and the library of physics.

THROOP HALL, in the center of the campus facing west, houses the administration offices and the engineering department. It follows the design of the Carmel Mission near Monterey, having a low central tower, and two lesser towers with open-arched imitation belfries.

DABNEY HALL OF THE HUMANITIES, left of Throop Hall, is a three-story L-shaped building. Right of Throop Hall, in the east wing of another L-shaped building, is the KELLOGG LABORATORY OF RADIATION, equipped for high-potential X-ray work; it contains the famous "atom smasher," Dr. C. C. Lauritsen's high-potential X-ray tube. The HIGH-POTENTIAL RESEARCH LABORATORY is the main unit of this building. A sculpture over the door represents a dynamo tended by two Titans. This laboratory is equipped for the study of problems of electrical transmission at high potentials, and problems in the structure of matter and the nature of radiation. To the east is the ASTROPHYSICS MACHINE SHOP, where new astronomical instruments are being developed for use in the Palomar Mountain Observatory. In this building machines for grinding the 200-inch reflector for the giant telescope were built. The OPTICAL SHOP, east of the Astrophysics Machine Shop, has equipment for grinding the telescope mirror, and its accessory mirrors.

The GUGGENHEIM AERONAUTICAL LABORATORY, a plain three-story building north of the Astrophysics Machine Shop, contains a 10-foot high-speed wind tunnel, an aerodynamics department with several small wind tunnels and auxiliary apparatus, a woodshop large enough for the building of complete airplanes, and the aeronautical library.

TOURNAMENT PARK (*free*), SW corner of E. California St. and S. Wilson Ave., is a large shady common with athletic fields and picnic facilities; here the Tournament of Roses parade ends each New Year's Day. The afternoon sports of the Rose Tournament were held here every year from 1890 to 1923, the year in which the Rose Bowl was completed.

8. The HUNTINGTON HOTEL, intersection of Oak Knoll and Wentworth Aves., from which it is reached by a long driveway, is a rambling six-story building built in 1906 by the late Henry E. Huntington (*see Pueblo to Metropolis*). At the rear of the hotel is the slender, covered PICTURE BRIDGE, hung with wistaria, spanning a garden with lily ponds and a swimming pool; within the bridge are hung paintings of California scenery.

9. The OLD MILL (*private*), 1120 Old Mill Rd., a rough vine-mantled adobe on a hillside under a few lacy shade trees, is a much restored and renovated mill built first under the direction of Father Zalvidea of the San Gabriel Mission in 1812. The upper part of the building housed the two grinding stones; a large lower room on the east side was divided into two wheel chambers, through which water ran, to be discharged through two large arches still seen in the lower east wall. The mill has been twice restored, but the basic construction, much of the old adobe, many of the roof tiles, and parts of the old brick floor remain. The reveals of door and windows still bear the original oxblood coloring. A hitching-block made of two old millstones stands in the front yard.

The ARROYO SECO (dry watercourse) is a wide-spreading gorge choked with blue-green shrubbery, which runs from the San Gabriel Mountains along the base of the San Rafael Hills to the Los Angeles River in Los Angeles. A narrow stream, dry in summer but swollen occasionally to flood proportions in the winter rainy season, twists along the arroyo bottom. Parts of the arroyo have been made into public parks, and it is proposed to improve the entire area. Local laws protect wild life along the arroyo, and birds abound here.

10. The BUSCH GARDENS (*open 9-5; adults 25¢, children 10¢*), 959 S. Arroyo Blvd., lie along the edge of the arroyo and descend its banks to a lake graced by white swans and fed by rills that run down the slope over many miniature waterfalls. Scattered about the gardens are groups of terra-cotta figures representing scenes from such tales as *Hansel and Gretel, Little Red Riding Hood,* and *Cinderella.* The gardens, once part of the grounds surrounding the mansion of Adolphus Busch (1830-1913), St. Louis brewer, are now administered by Pasadena Post No. 13, of the American Legion, which uses admission fees to maintain its disabled veterans' fund.

11. The COLORADO STREET BRIDGE sweeps into Pasadena from the west in a majestic curve over the Arroyo Seco. It was not built on a curve for purely ornamental purposes; at this point no suitable bedrock footings could be found for the construction of a straight bridge. In 1937 the city stretched a fence topped with barbed wire along the balustrade, thus ending the long series of deaths due to jumps from the high parapet into the arroyo that in the 1920's led to the structure's being known as "Suicide Bridge."

12. The MEMORIAL FLAGPOLE, W. Colorado St. and Orange Grove Ave., erected in 1927, commemorates Pasadena's World War dead. The flagstaff, more than 100 feet high, rises from a base bearing bronze World War figures sculptured in high relief.

CARMELITA GARDEN (*free*), 425 W. Colorado St., now a somewhat faded spot with lawn, trees and shrubs, was once the home garden of Dr. Ezra Slocum Carr (1818-1894), author and educator. John Muir brought to the garden many of the trees and shrubs growing here.

13. On the east end of the garden is the CALIFORNIA GRADU-

ATE SCHOOL OF DESIGN (*open Mon. to Fri. 9-4, Sat. 9-12; free lectures and exhibitions at irregular intervals*), which is housed in a two-story multigabled frame building. The school teaches modern industrial design and awards the degree of Master of Arts.

A 4,520-seat grandstand, facing Colorado Street, is set up on the south side of Carmelita Garden every year in preparation for the annual Tournament of Roses parade on New Year's Day. The official reviewing stand and the starting point of the parade are at the nearby intersection of Colorado Street and Orange Grove Avenue. Each year the stands are taken apart after the parade and the pieces stored.

14. LA MINIATURA, 645 Prospect Crescent, a studio-residence built for Mrs. George Madison Millard in 1923, was the first of the concrete-block houses designed by Frank Lloyd Wright. The architect describes the house as a "genuine expression of California in terms of modern industry and American life . . . an interpretation of her [Mrs. Millard's] career as a book collector, something that belongs to the ground on which it stands."

The two-story house, framed by eucalyptus trees, is reflected in a pool in the sunken gardens. The house has double walls to provide insulation against heat, cold, dampness, and fire. The concrete bricks are stamped with a radial cross design which here and there becomes fenestration.

BROOKSIDE PARK, Arroyo Seco between Holly St. and Devil's Gate Dam, is a 521-acre playground containing the Rose Bowl and the municipal golf courses. The recreational section, lighted at night, includes plunges, tennis courts, picnic grounds, baseball fields, and a children's playground, tavern, and bandstand. The grounds are planted to live oak, sycamore, and other native trees and shrubbery. Cut into the canyon walls are many hiking and bridle trails, rock stairways, and secluded nooks with stone benches.

15. The ROSE BOWL (*open free when not in use*), north of the junction of Arroyo Blvd. and Salvia Canyon Rd., is the stadium in which the annual New Year's Day football game is played, the concluding event of the Tournament of Roses. The spacious grounds about the bowl, enclosed within a high steel fence, are planted to a great variety of roses and green shrubbery. The bowl, built in 1922, seats 85,000 and is illuminated with floodlights for night performances. Commencement exercises of the Pasadena city schools, local football and baseball games, political rallies, and other events are held here.

16. DEVIL'S GATE DAM, across the top of which La Canada Verdugo Road passes, is a concrete structure built across the Arroyo Seco channel at Devil's Gate, a narrow gap in a spur of the San Rafael Hills which takes its name from a natural rock sculpture on the canyon wall suggesting a devil's head. The dam, a unit of the Los Angeles County flood control projects, was built in 1920 to control the heavy seasonal run-off from the San Gabriel Mountains.

CHRISTMAS TREE LANE (*lighted 5-10 p.m. Christmas Eve*

to New Year's night), is a double row of deodar trees stretching for more than a mile along Santa Rosa Ave., from Woodbury Rd. north to Foothill Blvd. At night, during the Christmas holidays, the trees are illuminated with colored lights, and draw huge throngs of spectators. While the trees are illuminated, the cars of sightseers proceed three or four abreast with their lights off. Planted about 1888, the tall trees are mature and almost uniform in height.

17. The ST. ELIZABETH CATHOLIC CHURCH (*open*), NW. corner Woodbury Rd. and N. Lake Ave., is a white stucco building of medieval Spanish design with California mission features. A plain square tower rising above the red tile roof is topped with an open-arched belfry. Above the wide arched doorway is a baroque niche with an image of St. Elizabeth.

Inside, at the back of the altar, a screen of baroque design frames a painting of St. Elizabeth, and against the wall at each side of the sanctuary are large statues, one of St. Joseph, and the other of St. Francis of Assisi. The sculptured figure of Jesus stands in front of the sanctuary. These figures and the stations of the cross along the side walls of the nave are by woodcarvers of Oberammergau, Germany.

18. The WESTMINSTER PRESBYTERIAN CHURCH (*adm. by arrangement*), 1757 N. Lake Ave., is of modified French Gothic design. Tall, gray, severe, it towers in strong perpendicular lines above its parish buildings on landscaped grounds that cover a city block. Its single tower, square and buttressed, is surmounted with an octagonal belfry pierced by narrow lancet arches. The church and its buildings are of concrete, with gray stone facing; the roofs are of dark slate. Above the entrance is a rose window 16 feet in diameter.

The vault over the nave, immensely high, long, and narrow, is a rich rust-red with small gold figures. The blue-vaulted apse, also high and narrow, has a tall stained glass window. The brilliant colors of great circular windows, one above the entrance and one at each end of the transept, are best seen from the sanctuary.

Santa Monica

Railroad Stations: Connections by Pacific Electric Ry. interurban, and Los Angeles Motor Coach Co. with trunk railroads. Offices: Union Pacific, 309 Santa Monica Blvd.; Southern Pacific, 416 Santa Monica Blvd. and 3011 Trolleyway; Santa Fe, 312 Santa Monica Blvd.
Interurban Stations: Pacific Electric Ry. Station, 1504 Ocean Ave. Fare within city limits, 6¢; to Los Angeles, 20¢.
Bus Service, Local and Interurban: Santa Monica Municipal Bus Line, terminal at 1613 Lincoln Blvd.; Bay Cities Transit Co., station at 1726 4th St., local and to bay cities. Los Angeles Motor Coach Co., from Wilshire Blvd. and Ocean Ave. to 5th and Hill Sts., Los Angeles, via Wilshire. Pacific Greyhound Lines (through traffic only), station at 1349 4th St. Minimum fare, 6¢.
Airport: Clover Field Municipal Airport, 3300 Ocean Ave., registered with U.S. Government as A.I.A. airport. Sightseeing flights over Bay District. Charter planes available.
Taxis: Mostly privately owned, yellow cabs, 114C Santa Monica Blvd. Rates 25¢ up.
Piers: Municipal Pier, foot of Colorado Ave.; Lick Pier, foot of Marine St.; Dome Pier, foot of Ashland Ave. Water taxis to deep-sea fishing.
Traffic Regulations: Uniform traffic ordinances for California cities, as compiled by the Automobile Club of Southern California, prevail.

Information Bureaus: Chamber of Commerce, Broadway and 4th St.; City Publicity Commission, City Hall, 4th St. and Santa Monica Blvd.; Southern California Automobile Club, 1810 Ocean Ave.

Streets and Numbers: The numbered streets, from 2nd to 26th, and name streets from Princeton to Franklin, run N. and S. Principal avenues and boulevards run E. and W. City boundaries are: N., San Vicente Blvd.; S., Commonwealth Ave.; E., Centinela Ave.; W., Pacific Ocean. Street arrangement somewhat irregular in Ocean Park section, due to number of short streets between shore line and Pacific Electric tracks.

Hotels and Apartment Houses: 43 hotels and 130 apartment houses.

Theatres, Concert Halls, and Amphitheatre: 5 modern movie theatres. Music halls include Convention Hall on Santa Monica Pier, and auditorium of Santa Monica Junior College, 7th St. and Pennsylvania Ave.
Art Galleries: Public Library, Santa Monica Blvd. and 5th St.
Schools: 1 evening school, 1 technical, 1 junior college, 1 high, 2 junior highs, 8 elementary, 8 kindergartens.
Newspapers: Evening Outlook, daily, except Sun.
Parks, Playgrounds, Picnic Grounds: Palisades Park, from Adelaide Dr. to Municipal Pier, 21 acres on bluff overlooking ocean. Lincoln Park, Lincoln and Wilshire Blvds.; Douglas Park, near Wilshire Blvd. and 25th Sts., with fly-casting pool; and Clover Field, 100 acres, largest of community's recreation spots.
Numerous other play centers on sands along ocean front. Parks generously equipped with facilities for outdoor games and picnics.
Boating and Yachting: Stone breakwater in bay provides anchorage for more than 300 boats.

Swimming: City owns and maintains 1 mile of public beach with police and lifeguard service throughout year.
Golf: 18-hole course at Clover Field.
Tennis: Lincoln Park, scene of Dudley Cup annual tennis tournament, Douglas Park, and Clover Field.

SANTA MONICA (79 alt., 53,500 pop.), a city and beach resort independent of Los Angeles on crescent-shaped Santa Monica Bay, lies 15 miles west of downtown Los Angeles on the coastal plain that slopes gently southward from the base of the Santa Monica Mountains. Roughly rectangular in shape, some eight square miles in extent, it is encompassed on three sides by Los Angeles, and on the fourth faces the Pacific Ocean. Santa Monica has an air of small town ease and comfort, combined with the holiday spirit of a shore resort.

Ocean Park, as the southern section of the city is known, is "the Coney Island of the West," with roller coasters, shooting galleries, shoot-the-chutes, and similar appurtenances. Back from the beach are some slum-like streets, but most are lined with the neat small houses of workers in the neighboring industrial plants, the largest of which is the vast Douglas Aircraft Company Plant.

More characteristic of the city is the shore line north from Ocean Park to Santa Monica Canyon. Palisades Park, a narrow attractive strip of greenery, follows the edge of the cliffs and overlooks large beach clubs and elaborate "cottages," some with private swimming pools; in the bay appears the Municipal Pier, with a long breakwater beyond it, providing a sheltered haven for sail and motor craft. Santa Monica's principal residential district stretches back from Palisades Park for several miles, a section of substantial and attractive houses, graced with lawns, shrubs, hedges, and a profusion of flower beds. Except for exotic trees bordering the streets, it might be the comfortable, well-to-do residential section of any medium-sized midwestern city. Farther north, near Santa Monica Canyon, houses and gardens become mansions and estates, spreading along the water-front and into the wooded foothills within and beyond the city.

Santa Monica was so named, according to one story, because Father Juan Crespi, while on a journey in 1769, camped near the present site of the city in a grove of sycamores on May 4, Saint Monica's Day. Another tale has it that Father Crespi, Father Gomez, and two soldiers, searching for a trail up the coast during Portola's stay in Yang-na (Los Angeles), slaked their thirst at two springs they found in a grove of sycamores and named the Pools of Santa Monica. The springs and grove, now gone, were situated close to the eastern edge of the city, near the present Sawtelle Soldiers' Home (*see Beverly Hills*).

Provisional grants were made to "the place called Santa Monica" as early as 1827, but the region was only slightly developed for many years, though the sycamores were a favorite camping spot for parties from Los Angeles. In 1871 a Los Angeles entrepreneur erected a big tent which housed 20 to 30 families during the week and on Saturday nights was turned into a dance hall. Its popularity led in 1872 to the building of a two-story hotel, with eight rooms. "Come and enjoy yourself," the owner advertised, "a week spent at the beach will add 10 years to your life."

In that same year Colonel Robert S. Baker of San Francisco, a forty-niner, paid $54,000 for the Sepulveda ranch, one of the large early land grants; he also acquired two adjoining ranches and stocked all with sheep. Colonel Baker appreciated the value of the water front as a townsite; lacking sufficient capital, he interested English capitalists in 1874 and newspapers announced that a wharf and railroad were to be built and the town was to be called Truxton, but nothing happened. In January 1875 Senator John P. Jones of Nevada purchased a two-thirds interest in the Baker ranch; construction of a wharf and of a railroad to Los Angeles was begun; a town was laid out, and the survey plat of "Santa Monica, Cal." was filed in the office of the county recorder at Los Angeles on July 10, 1875. Home builders and speculators streamed in from San Francisco by boat, from Los Angeles by stage, for a widely advertised auction of lots by Senator Jones's factotum, Thomas Fitch, a Los Angeles newspaperman. The day was hot; there was no shade; horses, wagons, buggies, and stage-coaches raised clouds of dust, but Fitch's eloquence easily vaulted these hurdles.

"At 1 o'clock," Fitch thundered, "we will sell at public outcry to the highest bidder the Pacific Ocean, draped with a western sky of scarlet and gold; we will sell a bay . . . a southern horizon . . . a frostless, bracing, warm yet unlanguid air . . . odored with the breath of flowers. The purchaser of this job lot of climate and scenery will be presented with a deed of land 50 by 150 feet. The title to the ocean and the sunset, the hills and the clouds, the breath of the life-giving ozone, and the song of birds, is guaranteed by the beneficent God. . . ."

The first lot brought $300. Within a few months the Santa Monica *Outlook* began publication, and the first train pulled out of Santa Monica for Los Angeles. On November 24, 1875, the *Outlook* reported, "Santa Monica continues to advance. We now have a wharf where the largest Panama steamers have landed . . . two hotels, one handsome clubhouse . . . two private schools and in a short time we shall have two churches and a public school." Santa Monicans envisaged their town as the great port of southern California, but this hope was blighted in 1876 when the Southern Pacific Railroad was completed to Los Angeles, having been given as a bonus the narrow-gauge railroad that ran from Los Angeles to San Pedro. A rate war began, and within a year Senator Jones was forced to sell his Los Angeles and Independence road to the Southern Pacific, which immediately raised freight rates and diverted business to San Pedro.

Hard times fell on Santa Monica. An epidemic of smallpox followed a severe drought that ruined local sheepmen. The population began to dwindle. Baker and Jones strove to make a resort out of the town during the next two years but were not very successful. The

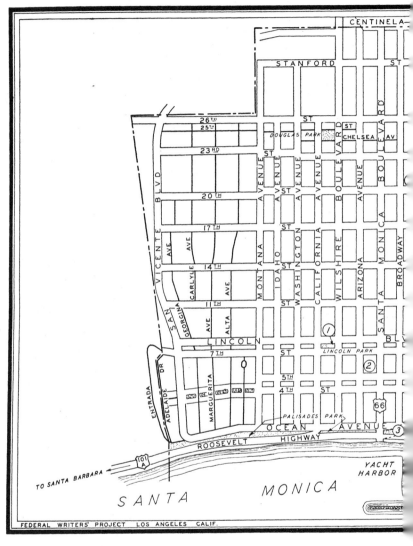

POINTS

1. Miles Memorial Playhouse
2. Public Library
3. Camera Obscura
4. La Monica Building
   Municipal Aquarium
5. City Hall

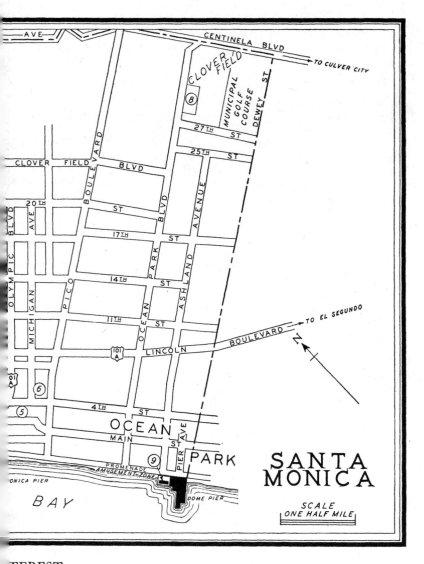

TEREST

5. Memorial Open Air Theatre
7. St. Anne's Chapel

8. Douglas Aircraft Co. Plant
9. Municipal Auditorium

1880 census revealed a population of only 417. Lots bought for hundreds of dollars sold for as little as 10 cents down.

The village revived with the boom in the late 1880's, and on the heels of the boom came a change in the attitude of the Southern Pacific, now headed by Collis P. Huntington, which built a large wharf here in 1891-92 and was soon engaged in a bitter five-year fight with those who favored San Pedro as a harbor (*see Pueblo To Meropolis*). Millions of dollars were spent in the struggle, which finally reached the floor of the Congress, where the Southern Pacific was defeated and Santa Monica's second hope of becoming a large port was blasted.

Almost immediately a campaign was started to advertise Santa Monica as a residential and resort community. In 1892 the Santa Fe and Santa Monica Railroad completed its line from Los Angeles to Ocean Park, then known as South Santa Monica, and built a station, an amusement pavilion, cement promenades along the beach, and advertised excursions to "the Coney Island of the Pacific." Golf links and race tracks were laid out to attract more visitors. Thousands came to watch the Santa Monica automobile road races held between 1909 and 1916. By 1910 the city's population approached 8,000, and during the next decade it grew steadily.

But it was during the booming 1920's that Santa Monica began to assume its present metropolitan proportions. Many of the easterners and middle westerners who poured into California during that period were attracted by the city's quiet residential atmosphere; they built small houses and settled down as year round residents. Movie stars, lured by its sea breezes within commuting distance of Hollywood and Beverly Hills, built elaborate summer houses on the beach. The coming of the Douglas Aircraft Company and its rapid growth freed the city from sole dependency upon its tourist and vacationist trade. Nevertheless, Santa Monica keeps its resort fences in good repair, and even builds new ones: its "Coney Island" is still packing in the nickel-and-dime week-end trade; and the completion of the breakwater in 1932 gave it a fine harbor and a firmer grip on the boat-owning class.

POINTS OF INTEREST

LINCOLN PARK, Wilshire and Lincoln Blvds., a five-acre tract, has a shaded picnic ground and a children's playground.

1. In the park is the MILES MEMORIAL PLAYHOUSE, which stands on the Lincoln Boulevard side of the park among eucalyptus trees and palms. The playhouse is of modernized mission architecture. It was built with funds left to the city in 1925 by James Euclid Miles. It is used for community social, recreational and dramatic events.

2. The SANTA MONICA PUBLIC LIBRARY (*open weekdays, 9-5; limited service Sun., holidays*), 5th St. and Santa Monica Blvd., is a two-story II-shaped concrete building of Spanish Renaissance design. The buff-colored exterior is embellished with dark terra-cotta ornament around the doors and windows. In the main reading room are murals

by S. MacDonald Wright depicting the evolution of literature, art, and science since the dawn of civilization.

PALISADES PARK is a narrow strip of 26 acres along the high bluffs that fringe the ocean between Colorado Ave. and Inspiration Point. Palm and pepper trees line the Ocean Avenue side; trees and shrubbery in the park have been grouped to allow unobstructed views of the sea. A rustic wood and iron fence skirts the face of the precipice, down which narrow stairs with rustic rails wind to the strand.

3. The CAMERA OBSCURA (*open 9:30-5:30; free*), housed in a two-story, shingled structure at the foot of Broadway, was built more than 50 years ago. In summer some 600 persons a day visit the small dark chamber where scenes caught by the revolving lenses, prisms, and mirrors on top of the building are projected in color on a movable, canvas-covered table top.

The YACHT HARBOR, at the foot of Broadway, a municipally operated haven for small pleasure craft, is protected by a 2,000-foot stone Breakwater, completed in 1934 at a cost of $700,000, which parallels the shore 600 feet beyond the end of the pier.

The MUNICIPAL PIER, extending 1,680 feet seaward from the foot of Colorado Ave., is the center of Santa Monica's stillwater angling, and boating and yachting activities. It forms the southeastern boundary of the yacht harbor. From the seaward end of the pier water taxis (*rates vary*) carry passengers to offshore fishing barges.

4. At the end of La Monica Pier, left of the Municipal Pier, is the LA MONICA BUILDING, a concrete and stucco structure housing the Life Guard Service, Municipal Aquarium, and a skating rink. Powerboat agencies, fish stores, restaurants, and miscellaneous amusement concessions wall the north side of the pier.

The MUNICIPAL AQUARIUM (*open 9-5; free*), in the La Monica Building, exhibits mounted and living specimens of sea life peculiar to the waters of southern California. The collection was started as a hobby in 1935 by members of the Santa Monica Lifeguard Service, who have been put in charge of the enlarged aquarium.

5. The new CITY HALL, Main St., between Olympic and Pico Blvds., was begun in March 1939, as the first municipal unit of a proposed Civic Center midway between the northern and southern sections of the city. The H-shaped two-story building is of reinforced concrete construction. Above the Main St. facade a square central section rises in a low set-back beyond the roof line. The dark exterior trim of a squat, square-shaped unit above the central setback is in sharp contrast to the whiteness of the structure as a whole. The building houses all departments of city government.

6. The MEMORIAL OPEN AIR THEATRE, on the grounds of the Santa Monica High School, Pico Blvd. and 4th St., built in 1920, was dedicated the following year to the Santa Monica High School boys who saw service during the World War. The 3,000-seat concrete amphitheatre is used for graduation exercises, fiestas, and various public gatherings.

7. ST. ANNE'S CHAPEL, NW. corner Colorado Ave. and 20th St., a low, gabled cruciform structure with clapboard walls and shingle roof, topped with a small bell tower, is locally famed as the repository of a relic of St. Anne, the mother of the Virgin Mary. The chapel was built in 1908 by Father Patrick Hawe. In 1913 the archbishop of Quebec, Canada, sent an authenticated fingerbone of St. Anne from the shrine of St. Anne de Beaupre, near Quebec, and a rustic rockery for it was built on the chapel grounds. During the annual novena, which precedes St. Anne's Day, July 26, several hundred people daily attend the outdoor services held near the shrine.

DOUGLAS PARK is bounded by Wilshire Blvd. and California Ave., 25th St. and Chelsea Ave. It is a four-acre recreational area of diversified appeal that was named for Donald Wills Douglas, airplane manufacturer, who built the first Douglas planes in an abandoned motion-picture studio that formerly stood on the site. Facilities include one of the few fly-casting pools in southern California, a wading pool, children's playground, and tennis courts.

The CLOVER FIELD AIRPORT, bounded by Ocean Park and Centinela Blvds., 27th and Dewey Sts., one of the first municipal airports in the United States, was established in 1926; the 75-acre airport adjoins the 100-acre MUNICIPAL GOLF COURSE AND RECREATION CENTER, acquired at the same time.

8. The main DOUGLAS AIRCRAFT COMPANY PLANT, 3400 Ocean Park Blvd., a three-story white concrete building, covers 18 acres, with almost 1,000,000 square feet of floor space. Adjoining it on the east is the new hangar-shaped ASSEMBLY BUILDING. Here are built the giant Douglas transport ships—the DC-3, a 21-passenger day and night plane; the DST, a 14-passenger sky sleeper; the huge DC-4 skyliner, weighing 65,000 pounds gross, with a wingspread of 139 feet; bombers and torpedo carriers for the U.S. Army and Navy, and various foreign governments. The Northrop Division plant at El Segundo (see Tour 5) is a subsidiary.

Airplanes were formerly built on a workbench, but manufacturers have adopted the assembly-line methods of the automobile builders. The Douglas company makes most of the parts for its planes in its Santa Monica factory, using a high-speed hydraulic press which weighs 840,000 pounds and is one of the most powerful of its kind. The intricate processes and countless tests involved in the evolution of a new model are revealed in the creation of the Douglas Sky Sleeper DST. In December 1934, engineering projections, based on the designs of previous models, were started. Four hundred engineers and draftsmen made some 3,500 drawings—of each screw and bolt, the detail of every unit. Once the basic design was completed, a model, one-eleventh the size of the proposed ship, was built. Engineers then made 300 tests of the model in a 200-mile-an-hour wind tunnel at the California Institute of Technology (see Pasadena). The construction of the full-size wooden model for determining the most practical seating and storage arrangements required 15,000 work hours, and included tests of the reactions of air passengers to color. The construction and testing of the wooden model cost $400,000. Shaping of steel and duralumin parts on the high-speed hydraulic presses followed, each unit being subjected to load, bending, and torque tests. On December 17, 1935, a year after the first plans had been drawn, the completed DST rolled off the production line, and was given a series of severe air tests before being pronounced ready for production in quantity.

OCEAN PARK, extending along the ocean for several blocks on either side of Ashland Avenue, is Santa Monica's amusement district, "the Coney Island of the West," with roller coasters, shoot-the-chutes, skating rinks, carrousels, hot-dog stands, and carnival booths.

9. The MUNICIPAL AUDITORIUM, foot of Ashland Ave., rests on a pier adjoining Dome Pier. Its arcaded stucco facade overlooks a block-wide, concrete-paved plaza with a bandstand shell in the center. In the plaza, seating 5,000, summer concerts are given by the Santa Monica Municipal Band; the auditorium, seating 1,200, is used for community educational and cultural affairs.

DOME PIER, foot of Pier Ave., the center of Ocean Park's so-called "Fun Zone," is lined almost solidly with concession booths and cafes. Northwest of it stretches the sloping strand of the Santa Monica MUNICIPAL BEACH, which attracts summer holiday crowds of more than 100,000 persons.

Tour 1

TO ARROWHEAD

Los Angeles—San Marino—Arcadia—Monrovia—Azusa—Claremont
—Upland—San Bernardino—Arrowhead Hot Springs—Lake Arrow-
head—Big Bear Lake—Pine Knot Village, 118.5 m.; N. Main St.,
Macy St., Mission Rd., Huntington Dr., N., US 66, State 18.

Concrete or asphalt-concrete paved roadbed throughout; four lanes between
Los Angeles and San Bernardino, two lanes between San Bernardino and Pine
Knot Village.

Pacific Electric Ry. and Santa Fe Ry. parallel route between Los Angeles and San Bernardino.

All types of accommodations; year-round resorts in mountains; summer
and winter sports camps; permission to camp in forest reserve outside
public camping places issued by U.S. Forest Rangers' stations—campers
must have shovel and ax.

This route crosses the San Gabriel Valley, a region of extensive
citrus groves, vineyards, and truck farms cut by rock- and gravel-strewn
washes and containing many attractive little towns. When this valley
was owned by Mission San Gabriel Arcangel (*see Tour 3*), mission-
trained Indians tended great herds of sheep, cattle and horses; tilled
cornfields, and tended orchards here. When the power of the missions
was curtailed (*see Pueblo to Metropolis*), San Gabriel Valley was
broken into Ranchos El Rincón de San Pascual, Santa Anita, and
others. After California had come under American rule, Yankees,
some of them marrying into native families, acquired much of the land
and began developing the country. Most of their heirs dissipated their
wealth, and the great ranchos were divided among small holders.

North of the valley the twisting but well-paved road rapidly ascends
the San Bernardino Mountains, reaching an elevation of more than a
mile and a quarter. High in the pine-and-fir-clothed San Bernardino
National Forest are three popular recreational resorts—luxurious
Arrowhead, popular-priced Big Bear, and undeveloped Baldwin.

From the CITY HALL, 0 *m.,* the route runs north on Main Street
to Macy Street; R. on Macy to Mission Road; L. on Mission Road
to Huntington Drive North; L. on Huntington Drive North.

In SOUTH PASADENA, 7 *m.* (600 alt., 14,356 pop.) (*see Tour
1A*), is a junction with Fair Oaks Ave. (*see Tour 1A*).

SAN MARINO, 9.7 *m.* (557 alt., 8,175 pop.), a residential community with carefully enforced development restrictions, has many
costly mansions and fine bungalows spread over the flat plain of San

Gabriel Valley and along the rolling San Gabriel foothills. Factories are banned here, as are multiple-unit dwellings; municipal supervision extends even to the cost and design of proposed structures.

San Marino, once part of the lands owned by Mission San Gabriel, was included in the 15,000-acre Rancho San Pascual (*see Pasadena*) granted in 1835 by Governor Figueroa to Juan Marine, a retired officer who had served Spain as a lieutenant of artillery in the Department of Mexico. From him it passed through several hands, and in the 1860's was acquired by James DeBarth Shorb as a wedding gift. In 1903 Henry E. Huntington bought the property, razed the old Shorb home, later built the mansion that is now an art gallery, and named the tract for the European Republic of San Marino.

SAN MARINO CITY PARK, between Old Mill and Monterey Rds. and Virginia Ave., west of the middle of town, is a recreational center with a large garden containing several hundred varieties of roses.

HUNTINGTON LIBRARY AND ART GALLERY (*open daily except Mon. 1:15-4:30 p.m., closed in Oct.; free; adm. by card only, obtained by written application stating preferred date of admission, enclosing stamped, addressed envelope; Pacific Electric streetcar service from Los Angeles*), Stratford and Oxford Rds., contains an important collection of rare books and manuscripts, paintings, sculptures, porcelains, tapestries, bronzes, miniatures, and fine old furniture. The library building, a French Renaissance adaptation, is E-shaped; it is of white stone and has a red tile roof. The front is windowless, and the entrances flank a colonnade. In the building are approximately 200,000 books, 4,000 manuscripts, nearly 1,000,000 letters and other holographs, and large numbers of first and early editions and English and American literary manuscripts. These are in Exhibition Hall (R) near the main entrance; among the treasures are the manuscript of Benjamin Franklin's autobiography, a genealogy in the handwriting of George Washington, letters from President Lincoln to General Grant, a rare Gutenberg Bible, the Ellesmere Chaucer, a Shakespeare first folio, a volume of Massachusetts laws of 1648, and other important items. In four rooms of the west wing is the Arabella D. Huntington Memorial Art Collection of Italian and Flemish paintings of the 15th and 16th-centuries, and sculptures, bronzes, porcelains, fine furniture, and other art objects, chiefly from 18th-century France.

The Art Gallery, designed in the Georgian manner and built in 1910 by Henry E. Huntington as his home, faces a lawn-covered court with a trim evergreen hedge, royal palms, and a marble fountain. This building contains an unusually fine collection of 18th-century English portraits, a number of landscapes of the period, and tapestries, miniatures, and French and English furniture. In one room are six Gainsboroughs, including *The Blue Boy;* five paintings by Reynolds, among them his portrait of the English tragedienne, Sarah Siddons, as *The Tragic Muse;* Lawrence's *Pinkie;* a Hoppner; a Raeburn; and a Constable. The favorite room of visitors is the library of the gallery. Here is the tapestry *La Noble Pastorale,* designed by Francois Boucher and woven on the royal looms at Beauvais during the reign of Louis XV. Boucher also designed the chairs and fire screen. The Botanical Gardens has 50 acres of plants and flowers, many of them rare. Notable is a large cactus garden containing an unusually comprehensive collection of desert flora. Henry E. Huntington (1850-1927), founder of the estate, owned large interests in the Los Angeles street railways and the Pacific Electric interurban system. He was a nephew and heir of Collis P. Huntington (*see The Historical Background*), one of the founders of the Central Pacific Railroad. At the age of 60, Henry Huntington, with the advice of experts, began his art collection. At his death in 1927, he gave his estate and treasures to the public by deed of trust and provided maintenance funds under supervision of a self-perpetuating board of trustees. Huntington and his wife are buried on the grounds in a circular white marble mausoleum with a low, column-supported dome.

In SANTA ANITA PARK (*season varies; adm. $1.10, parking 25¢*), 13.2 *m.*, which covers more than 200 acres is held the climactic event of the southern California winter horse races; this is the annual $100,000 Santa Anita Handicap—a mile-and-a-quarter for three-year-olds and up, usually run last week of meet. The light-green concrete grandstand, seating 20,000, with six betting rings and a score of private boxes, faces the one-mile oval track from the southwest. On the roof at the eastern end is the press box, the camera booth—where race finishes are recorded on film—and a radio broadcasting booth.

In the clubhouse, a modern concrete building reached from the grandstand by a footbridge, are a restaurant, lounge, telegraph offices, four betting rings, private-boxes, and a private terraced grandstand with easy chairs. In the grassy infield, reached from the grandstand by a tunnel, are large, carefully-tended flower beds. Fifteen hundred horses can be cared for in the stables.

The track, opened Christmas Day 1934, under the management of the Los Angeles Turf Club, Incorporated, is under the supervision of the State Horse-Racing Board. The average seasonal attendance is 800,000, and during the first four years more than $25,000,000 was wagered through the pari-mutuel betting machines.

The sprawling old frame buildings (R) of the LYON PONY EXPRESS MUSEUM (*open 8-6 daily; adm. adults 25¢, children 10¢*), 14 *m.*, contain a collection of early-day western relics, including a bullet-scarred pioneer barroom and an office equipped with Wells-Fargo Express Company furniture, safes, records and other equipment.

In the barroom is what the owner asserts is the largest known gold scale, "so delicate that it will weigh a pencil mark." In the Indian Room are human scalps, many arrowheads, tomahawks, and other artifacts. Among other relics are a San Francisco vigilante bell that tolled the death of nearly 50 bandits, a shotgun 12 feet long; waxed figures of notable characters of the old West; stagecoaches, including five old Concords; five hand-drawn fire engines; hundreds of revolvers and rifles; an old Spanish cannon; an early printing office with a Washington hand press; an extensive collection of early Western photographs; and a '49 gambling set-up with roulette wheels, lottery, faro tables, loaded dice, and marked cards. The museum, founded in Pasadena in 1922 by W. Parker Lyon, quondam mayor of Fresno, California, was moved to this place in 1935. At 14 m. is the junction with US 66 (Colorado Place), which unites eastward with Huntington Drive North.

Left on Colorado Place 1.5 m. to Old Ranch Road; L. here to the center of the remnant of RANCHO SANTA ANITA, 2 m., where the fabulous E. J. (Lucky) Baldwin held forth between the years 1875-1909, when he died at the age of 81 in comparative poverty. Among fine old palms, eucalyptuses, oaks, pepper trees, and locust trees are the barn, where Baldwin kept his many thoroughbred horses, the coach house topped with Victorian pseudo belfries, the log cabin Baldwin brought here from his father's Hamilton, Ohio farm in the 1880's, the cottage of Queen Anne design that was once the Baldwin guest house and art gallery, and the HUGO REID ADOBE built by the Rancho Santa Anita owner of 1839.

When first granted, the Rancho Santa Anita of more than 13,000 acres, extended from the oak-covered San Gabriel foothills across most of the valley floor, encompassing the sites of the modern cities of Sierra Madre, Arcadia, and Monrovia. Like the rest of the valley, it had belonged to Mission San Gabriel, but in 1841 Governor Alvarado granted it to Hugo Reid, an Englishman who married an Indian woman. Six years later Reid sold it for $33,000. The property was transferred several times subsequently—in 1854 for $33,000 and in 1872 for $85,000; the latter sale was to Harris Newmark, a Los Angeles merchant. In 1875 "Lucky" Baldwin offered Newmark $150,000 cash for this holding. Newmark wanted $175,000; Baldwin hedged. By the time he decided to pay Newmark's price it was $200,000. And for $200,000 "Lucky" took title to the ranch, reduced by that time to 8,000 acres. The mining king immediately invested $100,000 in Kentucky thoroughbreds, built stables, and improved the irrigation system. Until 1883, when he subdivided a large section of the land, Baldwin continued to acquire adjoining property, in time holding some 50,000 acres; he planted walnut, almond, peach, pear, apricot, Japanese persimmon, olive, camphor, and pepper trees, experimented with the growing of coffee and tea plants and maintained a large vineyard and winery. At the height of its prosperity, the ranch was valued at $10,000,000.

Elias Jackson Baldwin was born in Ohio in 1828. At 16 he was already known as a shrewd horse trader, at 18 he was married, and at 20 he owned a general store and three boats transporting grain from Chicago to St. Louis. He arrived in California in 1853; by 1875 he had already amassed between five and eight million dollars, beginning with hotel and livery stable investments, later branching into mining. He was nicknamed "Lucky" because of his fabulous mining success.

But the squire of Santa Anita was even more famed for his love affairs than for his mining luck. Four—and possibly five—times married, he was also the protector of numerous other young women from time to time. In 1883 one of them shot him in the arm, later sued him for the maintenance of her child, and finally went insane. In 1884 shortly after one of his marriages, a 16-year-old inamorata appeared, announced herself a prior fiancee, and won a judgment of $75,000. In 1888 he was again sued by a woman who introduced a child as evidence. Himself 60, Baldwin observed: "The woman is old and homely. Anyone who has seen her would not credit her charge against me." The woman was 31. In court, toward the end of the trial, a sister of the complainant fired a pistol at "Lucky," barely missing his head. "Baldwin's own reputation," said the court, "if not national, was certainly more than local. . . . Wherefore we indulge the not unreasonable hope that this case will prove the last of a malodorous brood."

ARCADIA, 14.4 *m.* (495 alt., 9,122 pop.), a business center for owners of orchards and vegetable farms, is on virtually level valley floor, below occasional large estates, orchards, and vineyards of the foothills. It was founded during a general real-estate boom in 1903 by Lucky Baldwin, on his Rancho Santa Anita.

The SANTA ANITA PLAYGROUND, on the western outskirts of town, contains a large swimming pool, an 18-hole golf course, large shady picnic grounds, eight tennis courts, sand boxes, six horseshoe quoits courts, a baseball field with a concrete grandstand, and other recreational equipment.

The SANTA ANITA STATION of the Santa Fe Railway, built in 1882 on what is now the outskirts of Arcadia, still uses an iron-bellied woodstove, and, as in the past, contains a post office. Although passengers seldom entrain here now, all trains except the *Chief* and the *Super Chief* can be flagged to a stop; this privilege harks back to the days when Baldwin, learning that a certain train had not stopped at Santa Anita, ordered 200 men to tear up the Santa Fe tracks through his ranch. Trains stopped at Santa Anita thereafter.

Left from Arcadia on Santa Anita Avenue to the junction with Foothill Boluevard, 0.8 *m.;* L. on Foothill Boulevard to the junction with Baldwin Avenue, 1.9 *m.;* R. on Baldwin Avenue to SIERRA MADRE (mother range), 2.8 *m.* (835 alt., 3,550 pop.), on a slope of the San Gabriel Mountains, also once part of the extensive Rancho Santa Anita. Sierra Madre was subdivided in 1882 by Nathaniel C. Carter, a New Englander who had gone into business in Los Angeles, but it was not incorporated until 1907. Although partly surrounded by estates, the town is largely supported by the business of growers of oranges, lemons, grapefruit, guavas, avocados, persimmons, and figs.
The WISTERIA VINE (open *9-4 daily; adm. 10¢*), on the Fennel estate, Carter St. and Hermosa Ave., almost engulfs the house of its owner, running over arbors and into trees. The vine, which usually blooms during the last two weeks of March, was planted in 1893. The Wisteria Fete held annually at Blossoming time attracts thousands.

MONROVIA, 15.9 *m.* (560 alt., 12,807 pop.), close to the protecting San Gabriel Mountains, is a modern town with wide, shaded streets, well-kept lawns, flower gardens, and semitropical trees. It has a Carnegie Library, a symphony orchestra, and three municipal parks; it manufactures water heaters, pipe, soap and cemetery monuments. The town was named for W. N. Monroe, a Civil War veteran who was one of three men who established it in 1886 after buying a hundred acres from Lucky Baldwin for $29,855, and another hundred acres from the owner of Rancho Azusa de Duarte (*see below*).

On Gold Hill, at the northern end of Alta Vista Street, is the A. E. CRONENWETT TROPICAL PLANTATION, in which is an orchard with a dozen varieties of papaya trees and experimental plantings of other tropical fruit trees. The papayas were grown from seeds, imported from the Hawaiian and Philippine Islands, Guatemala, Costa Rica, Panama, Nicaragua, southern Mexico, Ceylon, Tahiti, India, and the Malay Peninsula. *Carica papaya,* like the palm, is branchless, its trunk culminating in a crest of palmately lobed leaves about two feet wide. The fruit, which grows in clusters among the stalks of the leaves, attaining a length of eight to ten inches, is shaped like a muskmelon. It matures and blossoms at all seasons, green fruit and ripe are frequently on the tree at the same time. The papaya is used as a breakfast fruit, and is made into marmalade, jelly, pickles, and other delicacies.

DUARTE, 18.4 *m.* (540 alt., 2,197 pop.), is the business center of a district producing citrus fruits and avocados. The town lies on part of the Rancho Azusa de Duarte, a Mexican grant made in 1841 to Andreas Duarte by Governor Alvarado in reward for military services. In 1864-65, after a mortgage on it was foreclosed, it was subdivided.

East of Duarte the highway crosses the San Gabriel River, 19.4 *m.,* dry in summer, often a torrent in winter. Gravel and rock for railroad and highway construction are taken from the river-bed in great quantities.

In AZUSA, 21.2 *m.* (611 alt., 5,209 pop.), at the mouth of San Gabriel Canyon (*see Tour 1B*), are three packing houses that ship approximately 2,000 cars of Valencia oranges a year. Lemons, grapefruit, tangerines, avocados, and walnuts are also shipped, as well as poultry, dairy products, and honey. The town also manufactures chemicals, pipe, and fertilizer.

The origin of the word Azusa is vague. It was the name given to this district by the Spanish settlers, and was doubtless their inaccurate pronunciation of its original Indian name, which was Asuksagua (lodge) according to one source, and Asuksagna (place of skunks) according to another.

Like Duarte, Azusa is on part of the former Rancho Azusa de Duarte. In 1844 Henry Dalton, merchant, shipowner, and importer, bought this ranch from its Mexican owner for $7,000. He fought such a long battle in the courts to evict squatters that he exhausted his capital and had to borrow money from J. S. Slauson, a Los Angeles banker, to carry on. Eventually he lost the property through foreclosure and Slauson and associates founded the town on it in 1898.

Six-acre AZUSA CITY PARK, along Foothill Boulevard, surrounds the CIVIC BUILDING, which houses not only the city offices but also the public library, Chamber of Commerce, and the Civic Auditorium.

Azusa is at the junction with State 39 (*see Tour 1B*).

GLENDORA (L), 23.9 *m.* (776 alt., 2,822 pop.), also near the San Gabriel foothills, calls itself "the Citrus City." It is entirely surrounded by citrus groves and has six large citrus packing plants. The town, founded in 1887 by George Whitcomb, a Chicago manufacturer, was incorporated in 1911.

At 27.1 *m.* is a junction with San Dimas Avenue.

Right on San Dimas Avenue to SAN DIMAS, 1.5 *m.* (955 alt., 3,588 pop.), close to the San Jose Hills on the southern side of San Gabriel Valley. Citrus packing is the chief industry but berries, vegetables, and small fruits are also grown in the environs. There are a number of nurseries here growing ornamental and deciduous trees and tropical and semitropical flowers. Many of the houses have verandas covered with honeysuckle and the lavender-blossoming wisteria.

The town is named for a canyon in the San Gabriel Mountains where Ignacio Palomares (*see below*) is said to have pastured his herds. Because thieving Indians raided his cattle there, so the story goes, Palomares named the canyon for the repentant thief, Dimas, who was crucified with Christ.

Right from San Dimas on San Dimas Ave. 3.5 *m.* to the junction with Mountain Meadows Rd.; L. on Mountain Meadows Rd., to PUDDING-STONE DAM (R), 4.5 *m.*, chief of three in the Puddingstone Creek-Covina Wash flood control project. The main dam, of the earth-fill, concrete-core type, is more than 1,000 feet long and 147 feet high. Two lesser gaps in the hills are closed by the smaller dams. The three dams create Puddingstone Reservoir, with a surface area of nearly 500 acres; it is stocked with black bass, blue-gill perch and catfish (*black bass fishing Dec. 1 to May 29*).

At 27.6 *m.* on US 66 is the junction with San Dimas Canyon Rd.

Left here to SAN DIMAS CANYON PARK (*picnicking facilities; free*), 0.3 *m.*, more than a hundred acres of natural woodland maintained by Los Angeles County.

LA VERNE, 29.4 *m.* (1,050 alt., 3,092 pop.), has four citrus packing plants. The metal-corniced red-brick buildings along San Dimas Avenue, the main business street, date from 1891.

La Verne was founded as Lordsburg, during the boom days of 1888 (*see The Historical Background*); when the boom burst, a three-story $75,000 hotel, stark and empty, remained as a monument. In 1890 the Santa Fe Railway, which had built a station near the settlement, offered: "A free ride from anywhere east of the Rocky Mountains to Lordsburg, California. Anyone purchasing $500 worth of lots in Lordsburg will have his fare paid, and for $750, the fare of two persons." Members of the Church of the German Baptist Brethren Church, sometimes called Dunkers, responded to the offer and by 1895 constituted the majority of the 2,500 population. The present name was adopted in 1917.

LA VERNE COLLEGE, between 1st and 3rd, College and B Sts., now occupies four buildings. FOUNDER'S HALL, deep in the grounds, is a modern white concrete building containing classrooms, an auditorium, and the administration offices. There is one instructor for every 10 students of the 160-170 enrolled annually. The school, founded in 1891 by the Dunkers in the boom-time hotel, was first named Lordsburg College, and opened with nearly as many students as it has today. Room, board, and tuition cost only $137.50 a year. During the lean nineties the school was closed for two years, but in 1903 W. C. Hanawalt, a Philadelphia Dunker, reopened it and enabled the students to earn part of their subsistence; they grew vegetables and raised cattle, milked the cows, churned the butter, and canned food for the winter.

CLAREMONT, 32 *m.* (1,175 alt., 3,057 pop.), surrounded by citrus orchards, is the home of the first California citrus association, formed in 1893. The first oranges shipped from this section—about 2,000 boxes—were packed on the Santa Fe Railway station platform.

Today there are five large packing houses that ship approximately 750,000 boxes annually. Claremont factories produce marmalade, rugs, tree sprayers, and air cleaners for automotive machinery.

In the early days an almost perpetual mire, for some obscure reason called Gospel Swamp, covered much of the district. It was infested with coyotes, wildcats, and rattlesnakes and only a few wagon trails, winding crazily to avoid the morasses, connected Claremont with the rest of southern California.

The town's three colleges, known collectively as Claremont Colleges, Inc., were planned to retain the advantages of small colleges while providing the facilities of a university. The colleges have a common library, laboratories, and equipment, while preserving their individual identities and traditions.

POMONA COLLEGE on a beautiful campus bounded by 1st and 8th Sts., Mills and Harvard Aves., occupies 14 buildings and has approximately 800 students. It was opened by the First District Congregational Association in a small white frame house at 5th and White Aves. in Pomona in 1887. After the real estate boom of the 1880's was over, it was moved to this place and housed in the unfinished and abandoned Claremont Hotel. SUMNER HALL, called Old Sumner, is the remodeled hotel. Other units, some ivy-covered, some ultra-modern, include Holmes—containing the chapel, Pearson Hall of Science, the Library, Crookshank Hall of Zoology, Frary Hall—the dining quarters, the new Memorial Training Building, Harwood Hall of Botany, and Mason Hall of Chemistry.

SCRIPPS COLLEGE FOR WOMEN, bounded by Foothill Blvd., Columbia Ave., 9th St., and Amherst Ave., in 1927 became a part of Claremont Colleges, Inc., through a gift of Miss Ellen Scripps, of the Scripps newspaper-owning family. Rigid scholastic standards keep the enrollment at approximately two hundred.

The seven main buildings, of modified Spanish design, stand among gardens on a lawn shaded by wide-spreading pepper and oak trees and tall eucalyptuses.

CLAREMONT COLLEGE, adjoining the other two colleges, has five main buildings and gives graduate work for about 200 students.

At 32.7 *m.* is a junction with Baldy Road.

Left on Baldy Road to Palmer Canyon Road, 2.8 *m.;* L. here to the PADUA HILLS THEATRE (*performances Wed., Thurs., Fri., Sat., 8:30 p.m., Wed., Sat., 2:30 p.m.; adm. $1*), 3 *m.,* the home of the Mexican Players, who have an extensive repertoire of light comedy and drama in Spanish vernacular. The theatre, seating about 300, is open all the year, with productions running from two to four weeks. The buildings, of modified Spanish design, are on a gentle slope. Adjoining are curio shops, studios, and a restaurant sheltered by a very old olive orchard.

The Padua Hills Theatre, founded in 1930, is a non-profit organization affiliated with the Claremont Colleges, Inc. All student-players and professionals are native Californians.

UPLAND, 35.9 *m.* (1,210 alt., 6,316 pop.), founded in 1882 as a part of Ontario (*see Tour 2*), was first called Magnolia Tract, or

Magnolia Villa. Later it became North Ontario. In 1902 it was given its present name and in 1906 was incorporated. More than 6,000 acres of citrus trees grow in the vicinity, many of the groves more than 45 years old, and there are nine citrus packing plants in the city. Poultry and rabbit raising, production of honey, and tanning are added to local income.

Euclid Avenue, a boulevard of exceptional beauty, extends from the San Gabriel foothills southward 15 miles toward the Chino Hills. It is a wide double-lane road shaded by large pepper and grevillea trees. North of Foothill Boulevard the well-kept center parkway has a bridle path, that leads to the residential section of San Antonio Heights. At the turn of the century a horsecar line ran up the parkway to a terminus in the foothills north of Upland. On return trips the rickety car coasted down grade with the horses riding on the rear platform.

At the intersection of Euclid Ave. and US 66 stands THE MADONNA OF THE TRAILS MONUMENT, a heroic figure of an idealized pioneer woman and children framed by feathery pepper trees. The model of the monument, which is duplicated in many places throughout the country, was selected by popular vote in a contest conducted by E. Marland, Oklahoma oil millionaire. This monument, erected by the Daughters of the American Revolution, commemorates the visit to this region of the first Americans entering California by overland trails—Jedediah Strong Smith and a party of 16 trappers—in 1826.

SAN ANTONIO PARK, near the foothills to the north, is a popular family picnic grounds named for Mount San Antonio—Old Baldy.

CUCAMONGA (R), 39.1 m. (1,220 alt., 4,747 pop.), like all cities dotting this route, is a trade center of ranches. It was named for Cucamonga Peak (8,911 alt.), directly north. Some say that the name means "place of many springs," others "lewd woman." The second translation comes from a legend that an Indian chief sent his wayward daughter to live alone on the peak.

The CUCAMONGA WINERY, 39.3 m., built in 1839 according to a sign on the building, is the oldest winery in California. Within the thick walls are 14 old wine storage tanks. Two 500-gallon vats, no longer used, were brought around Cape Horn. The grape crusher, first operated by hydraulic power, was replaced in 1883 by electrically powered equipment. The annual output of dry and sweet wines, about 150,000 gallons, comes from grapes grown on the 800 acres of land nearby (see Tour 2).

In 1839 Governor Alvarado granted to Tiburcio Tapia, a wealthy Los Angeles merchant, some 20 square miles of land here for grazing purposes. The grant included all of what was then called the Cucamonga Territory, inhabited by Cucamonga, a Shoshone tribe. One of the stipulations of the grant, that Tapia build upon the property immediately, was satisfied by erection of this winery. He also planted 12 rows of grapevines, 12 vines to a row, from San Gabriel Mission stock. The last of these vines were removed in the late 1920's.

In 1858, the property was sold to John Raines, who set out 125,000 more vines. The property eventually fell under control of the Cucamonga Water Company, which established the town.

East of Cucamonga the highway for several miles is bordered on both sides by the vast vineyards of the Italian Vineyard Company (*see Tour 2*).

FONTANA, 47.9 *m.* (1,242 alt., 3,194 pop.), lies amid 5,000 acres of citrus orchards, 3,000 acres of walnuts, and extensive vineyards. Here, too, are large poultry and duck ranches, and a large hog farm. Near the foothills (L) is the UNITED STATES RABBIT EXPERIMENTAL STATION.

RIALTO, 51.5 *m.* (1,203 alt., 1,770 pop.), has seven citrus packing houses, a large cement pipe factory, and a ladder manufacturing plant.

SAN BERNARDINO, 56 *m.* (1,073 alt., 43,646 pop.), a cosmopolitan city that retains an atmosphere of early times missing in most parts of southern California, lies in the flat southwestern corner of sprawling San Bernardino County, of which it is the seat. It is compact and symmetrically-platted, and its residential streets are well shaded. Many of its dwellings and commercial buildings date from the last century. The main business section is east and west along Third Street, and north and south along E Street. It is the chief trading center of a large mining and agricultural district, but the majority of its working population is employed in the extensive shops, yards, and offices of the Santa Fe Railway.

The region around San Bernardino was early known to the padres of San Gabriel Mission (*see Tour 3*) for its fertility. Because of the large Indian population of the region, Father Dumetz established an *asistencia* (chapel) and supply station for the mission in 1810 at the Indian village of Guachama, which was near the present-day city, and named it in honor of St. Bernard of Sienna, patron saint of mountain passes, because of its proximity to Cajon Pass (*see Tour 7*). In 1812 the Indians destroyed the outpost, blaming the numerous earthquakes of that year on the presence of the missionaries. In 1820, however, the station was rebuilt; a large adobe house was constructed for the major-domo and visiting padres, and part of it used as a granary. The chapel was merely an *enramada* (shed). The Indians were enrolled to build the *zanja* (ditch) from Mill Creek Canyon to the station—the first irrigation ditch in the valley. In 1831 the Piute tribes from the desert attacked the station and its Indians. By 1833, when the Mexican Government secularized the church lands (*see Pueblo to Metropolis*), the station had again been rebuilt. In 1834 the Piutes again destroyed it, and the padres left it permanently.

In 1842 a land grant, Rancho de San Bernardino, was presented by the Mexican Government to Diego Sepulveda and the three sons of Antonio Lugo, all of Los Angeles. This grant of 37,000 acres was one of the largest made in California.

In 1851, Captain Jefferson Hunt led 500 Mormons, with their

cattle, horses, and other necessities, from Salt Lake City to this area and a year later the Mormons bought the rancho. Almost immediately they built an elaborate stockade 300 feet wide and 700 feet long for protection against the Indians, where the courthouse now stands. They established a school in 1851 near the foot of Cajon Pass and in the following year another in a tent within the stockade.

In 1853, about 24,000 square miles of land were detached from the eastern part of Los Angeles County and named San Bernardino County; in the following year the town of San Bernardino was incorporated as its seat.

All the town's early structures were of adobe. The Council House, the first public building, was constructed in 1853 inside the stockade. The first postmaster, who worked without pay, distributed the mail— brought in by stages and on horseback—from his hat in front of the fort once a month. Mail service was very irregular until 1858, when a mail stage line between the city and Los Angeles was established.

In 1857 Brigham Young recalled the faithful of all the nation to Salt Lake City and a majority of the Mormons left; enough remained, however, to give the city a present-day Mormon population of about two thousand.

The coming of the railroads through Cajon Pass in 1883 gave the settlement its first real opportunity to grow.

The SAN BERNARDINO COUNTY COURTHOUSE (1926), Arrowhead Ave. between 3rd and 4th Sts., on the site of the Mormon fort, has eight monumental columns on its facade. The County Jail is on the top floor.

In PIONEER PARK, 6th St. between E and F Sts., are the MEMORIAL AUDITORIUM, honoring local World War dead and veterans, a SAILORS' AND SOLDIERS' MONUMENT dedicated to the heroes of the Mexican, Civil and Spanish-American Wars, a PIONEER CABIN containing relics, some from Mormon days, including a cart used by the Mormons in hauling logs from the mountains.

PERRIS HILL PARK, in the northeastern section of the city, has tennis courts, a swimming pool, a baseball and football park, and an outdoor concert bowl used for community sings and concerts.

The NATIONAL ORANGE SHOW BUILDING (*annual show daily for 11 days in March, 10 a.m.-11:30 p.m., adm. 50¢, children 25¢*), Mill and E Sts., is an immense frame structure painted white with blue trim.

The Orange Show has been held every year since 1910, when San Bernardino businessmen inaugurated it. The city goes into carnival attire for the occasion, decorating its streets, store fronts, shop-windows, streetcars and busses with orange-colored banners and other ornaments. A local "queen" leads a parade through the streets on the opening day, and the show grounds are thick with floats, citrus exhibits, Ferris-wheels, and other amusement concessions. Daily programs are presented, with movie and radio stars, acrobats, dancers, orchestras, and bands.

The main building is filled with lighted castles, fans, ships, and diverse other figures made entirely of oranges, grapefruit, and lemons. These exhibits, and those in the industrial section—which show methods and equipment used in the culture and handling of citrus fruits, the manufacture and use of citrus byproducts, and various related matters—are prepared by cities, towns, and counties, growers' organizations, individual orchardists, and sundry organizations.

The citrus industry ranks next to dairying as an income-producer in California. Oranges are the largest single fruit crop; the fruit crops head all others in agriculture, and agriculture ranks second to manufacturing among the state's industries. The annual orange crop is twice as valuable as the gold produced in the state, nearly twice as valuable as the lumber, and nearly five times as valuable as the fish catch. In the production of oranges, California ranks first in the United States, and the United States ranks first in the world.

In California citrus-fruit growing is probably the most highly developed of all crop-cultures, though it is relatively very young. The first orange grove was planted not earlier than 1805, and it was not until the late 1880's that oranges were produced in commercial quantities. The orange is a fruit thriving only under tropical or sub-tropical conditions, and even in southern California great care and skill must be exercised to combat its many natural enemies—heat and dryness in summer, wind and frost in winter, and a plethora of diseases and insect pests. The complicated and scientific nature of the processes involved in producing these fruits in commercially valuable quantities explains the necessity of establishing such an institution as the Citrus Experiment Station of the University of California, at Riverside (see Tour 3).

Today all trees in the important groves of the state are of pedigreed stock; a careful record of each tree's performance is kept from season to season, and when a tree, or even a single limb of a tree, is found to produce fruit of inferior quality or of less than minimum quantity for two or three consecutive seasons, the tree or limb is removed or cut back and re-budded with grafts from selected parent trees—that is, trees known to produce high quality fruit in quantity. Only the best strains of each variety of tree are propagated; great care is taken to prevent the development of abnormal or subnormal strains and also to prevent cross pollenization of the established strains.

The first step in producing a citrus tree is the planting of seed for the root-stock, seed of a strong-rooted, disease-resisting variety of citrus tree—of sour orange for orange trees, of sweet orange for lemon trees. The root-stock tree is removed from the lathhouse beds after a year or more of growth, when it is about 12 inches high, and replanted in an outdoor nursery, where it grows a year or two longer. The next step is grafting. In this operation a twig bearing a healthy bud is cut from a carefully selected parent tree and inserted in a slit in the bark of the young root-stock tree. The little tree's own top is cut off when the graft has developed into a branch, and the branch is then trained to form a new top. After another year, this tree is transplanted to the orchard. It does not begin to bear commercially for another three years, when it is six years old, and will not be in full bearing until about its tenth year. After this, if well cared for, it continues to increase in size and yield for fifty or more years.

In their early years the trees are carefully shaped by pruning of the branches. Citrus trees have a rather dense, brittle, dark-green foliage. Orange trees are commonly trimmed to one of two forms— vase-shaped, with tall up-growing main limbs having framework strength; or bowl-shaped, with the upright limbs cut back and the lateral main limbs encouraged to form a low, round, open-topped tree convenient for picking and spraying.

The war against citrus pests is costly and difficult, and the amount of tree medicines needed varies according to soil, tree, and climatic conditions. Scale insects and citrus red spider, most destructive and hardest to control, are the commonest pests. About once a year the trees are covered with a canvas tarpaulin and fumigated to kill scale. Insecticides of various types are sprayed upon the trees at intervals to eliminate other destructive creatures.

In winter the orchardist keeps a vigil for frost warnings broadcast over the radio and every cold night holds himself ready to light his orchard heaters. Oranges can withstand a low temperature of between 26° and 29.5° and lemons between 27° and 30.5°. The temperature is usually lowest an hour before sunrise. When the mercury is dropping toward the danger point, the waiting crews hurry through the groves lighting the heaters—one to a tree—with long-spouted gasoline torches. Each lighter is followed by a man who regulates the heaters, which are of various types. Those most commonly used are oil-burning stack-pots, slightly smaller than the usual washtub, with a stack two or three feet high. In some districts, however, smudge-pot heating is still widely used; these pots produce a thick blanket of black smoke that hangs low in the air not only over miles of orchards but also over nearby towns.

During the rainless summers the orchards must have irrigation for 48 hours at intervals of three to five weeks according to the climate and soil. Orchard lysimeters are used frequently during irrigation in order to measure the percolation of the water, for the crop is ruined by too much water as well as by too little. Irrigation water is carried to the edge of the orchard by an underground iron or concrete conduit, and brought to the surface by a concrete pipe that empties it into the furrows.

Fertilization is another problem throughly studied by citrus experts. A cover crop, such as vetch or clover, is planted between rows of trees and plowed under in spring to add nitrogen to the soil. Stable manure and various other organic fertilizers are also used. Inorganic fertilizers are used on some soils to counteract acidity. As in combating insect pests, both soil and climate must be studied and correctly diagnosed and the proper materials, quantities, and methods prescribed and used if a crop of commercial value is to be produced. Orchards in windy areas must be protected by tall windbreaks of evergreens; the eucalyptus, Monterey cypress, and the tamarisk are most commonly used.

As fruit matures, a few average oranges from the orchards are tested for their sugar content, which determines the time of picking. Nearly all California citrus orchardites belong to a growers' co-operative—most of them to the giant California Fruit Growers' Exchange. The fruit of the member growers is harvested by trained picking-crews sent out from the association's nearest packing house. Great care is used in handling the crop. The rind of the orange, though a perfect seal for the fruit, is easily harmed by scratches or bruises, causing blue-mold to appear even before the fruit is packed; therefore the picker—who does not pick, but clips the stem close enough to the fruit that no sharp end is left to scratch other oranges—wears soft gloves and places the fruit in a sack with a buttoned flap at the bottom. When full, the sack is placed in a box, the flap is released, and the fruit falls gently into the box. In gathering lemons, the picker cuts only fruit too large to pass through a ring he carries. The lemon orchard is gone over each month, harvesting being determined by size, though the fruit is still dark green in color.

For a day or two after harvest, oranges stand in the packing house until some of the moisture in the rind evaporates, since a drier skin is not so easily injured by handling. The fruit is then washed in warm soapy water, passed through rows of revolving brushes, into cold water, and finally over more brushes under a drying blast of air. The oranges roll on canvas belts to the grading tables where trained workers, usually women, sort according to standards of appearance. Many packing houses now employ a fluoroscope to detect frostbite, granulation, and other internal imperfections of oranges. The size and condition of the skin of an orange has no influence on its quality.

The finest oranges of medium-large size and without blemishes are stamped with the packing house's trademark for best quality. Each association has its own brand-names to designate the various grades. Fruit two or three grades below the best is ripe, has good flavor and perfect inner texture, but differs from the top grade chiefly in appearance.

After it is stamped the fruit is wrapped in tissue paper and packed in a symmetrical pattern, a certain number of a certain size being packed in each box. Oranges are packed in ten principle sizes, ranging from 100 to a box to 344. The boxes are loaded onto freight cars, iced in summer and warmed in the coldest seasons. Fruit trains, especially those carrying citrus fruits, run on express schedule.

The growers' co-operatives have contributed greatly to the reduction of the high cost of orange growing in California by facilitating picking, hauling, packing, and marketing, and by providing these services at cost. The fruit of the grower-members is sold in a pool and the proceeds are divided among the orchardists on the basis of the quality and quantity of fruit each has contributed. The larger organizations have established research laboratories in which methods of putting the citrus fruits to new uses are studied; cull fruits, or those below salable grade, are used in the manufacture of juice concentrates, orange and lemon oils and acids, citrate of lime, citrus pectin, and canned juice.

The chief disadvantages of the co-operatives are their tendency toward monopoly and price fixing. With the development of citrus growing along highly scientific and industrialized lines, and with the large investment (more than $250 an acre) needed to produce an orange crop, only large concerns can operate profitably. Thus the industry is dominated by a comparatively few growers who tend to control markets and prices through the co-operatives. Market reports received regularly from important consumption areas dictate supply. Surplus fruit is sometimes destroyed to maintain prices, although this practice is diminishing since the Surplus Commodity Corporation began functioning.

Most California oranges are of two varieties. The navel, ripening in winter, is grown in the warmer inland regions; it is seedless, of high color, and distinguished from other varieties by the formation of the rind at the blossom-end. The Valencia, ripening in summer, is grown in the cooler coastal regions. It is the Valencia that is usually shown in photographs and paintings as a tinted yellow ball hanging on the tree among new blossoms with a snow-capped peak in the background.

Unlike other oranges the Valencia may be held on the tree for several months after it has attained full color; presently the rind begins to turn green, starting at the stem end. The process does not affect the fruit's flavor; actually it is at complete maturity at this time, though it is commonly mistaken for immature fruit by novices. The ripening seasons of the two varieties overlap, keeping the orange market steady the year round.

The orange, which was introduced into Spain from China by the Portuguese, was brought into this country from Lower California by the Franciscan missionaries. The first orchard was planted at San Gabriel Mission (*see Tour 3*) about 1805. The navel variety was introduced to the United States when two of several small orange trees were sent to Washington from Brazil, where they were developed from sport buds growing on a variety of Portuguese orange tree. In 1873 two of these were received by Mrs. Eliza C. Tibbets of Riverside from a friend in the Department of Agriculture. Mrs. Tibbets sold cuttings, and by the time the first Valencia seedlings arrived from London by way of Spain in 1876 navel orange growing was actually established in California.

Of the other citrus fruits, only two, the lemon and the grapefruit, are produced in important commercial quantities in California. Some tangerines are grown for market, but limes, citrons, and kumquats in only a few places.

In the United States, California alone produces lemons on a large scale, and is third in the production of grapefruit. San Bernardino County leads in lemon growing, Imperial County in grapefruit.

In San Bernardino is the junction with State 18 (Sierra Way), which becomes the main route; L. on this route.

A boundary of SAN BERNARDINO NATIONAL FOREST is at 61 *m*. This reserve of four-fifths of a million acres adjoins Angeles National Forest, of which until 1925 it was a part. The chief purpose of the reserve is water conservation. Most of its timber is too remote for profitable logging but several streams in the area furnish hydro-electric power.

At 62.3 *m*. is the junction with a private, hard-surfaced road.

Right on this road to ARROWHEAD HOT SPRINGS, 1 *m*. (2,000 alt.), on the slope of Arrowhead Peak. The hotel here was constructed in 1939 to replace one destroyed during a forest fire in 1938. There are four main springs—three hot; one used for mud baths. In near-by Waterman Canyon are many natural steam baths—caves heated by more than 100 hot springs; their temperature is frequently as high as 160°. This mile-long hot belt is on the main San Andreas fault (*see Natural Setting*), which is largely responsible for the emergence of the hot springs at this point.

The ARROWHEAD, above the hotel on the southeast side of ARROWHEAD PARK (4,216 alt.), is a natural fissure 1,376 feet long and 449 feet wide. Various Indian tribes who roamed the San Bernardino Mountains before the coming of the white man considered the Arrowhead a sign from the Great Spirit designating a good hunting ground. In this area the Indians hunted *Tukuchu*, the puma; *Tukut*, the wildcat; *Wahilyam*, the coyote; *Wanats*, the wolf, and *Widukut*, the buzzard. Coyotes and buzzards are still abundant and the district below the Arrowhead is now a United States game refuge.

Brigham Young, the Mormon leader, is said to have had a dream in which a heavenly spirit instructed him to send some of his followers toward the Pacific where they would see a strange sign on a mountain. Here, the story goes, Young was ordered to have his followers settle. Whether or not on heavenly instruction, a Mormon caravan came southeast from the Great Salt Lake country, saw the arrowhead, and laid out San Bernardino in 1851.

ARROWHEAD SUMMIT (*gas, cafe*), 74.1 *m*. (5,174 alt.), is merely a wide spot on the highway.

Right from Arrowhead Summit on Crestline Road to CRESTLINE VILLAGE (*ski jumps, toboggan slide*), 4.4 *m*. (4,850 alt., summer pop. 700, winter 100.) This resort town has a compact little business district, with stores, post office, a free county library, an elementary school, and a two-story, many-gabled, rustic lodge.

Large CRESTLINE BOWL is used for pageants and theatrical productions.

The BAYLIS OAK, at the southern end of the village, with a circumference of more than 46 feet, was named for Dr. J. N. Baylis, who promoted the development of the recreational use of the region.

At 4.5 *m*. is the junction of Crestline Road and a remaining stretch of the Mormon Road, a 16-mile stretch built in 1852 by the settlers of San Bernardino in 1,000 days. The cobblestone WAGON WHEEL MONUMENT (L) marks the old road summit. Close by are a pair of cart wheels and a six-foot stone standard holding what is said to be one of the first monitors used in mining in this area.

Right from Crestline Road on the Mormon Road to CAMP SEELEY, 6.4 *m*. (4,700 alt.) (*camping reservations at Los Angeles Municipal Camp head-*

quarters, City Hall, Los Angeles; rates vary with season), a Los Angeles city camp on the floor of the Valley of the Moon. It accommodates 250 people and has an auto camp holding 28 trailers. The camp, among Douglas fir, pine, and cedar, has a large recreation building, many furnished cabins, a cafe, a dance pavilion, swimming pool, tennis, croquet, and volleyball courts, indoor and outdoor sports fields, picnic ground, and a library.

An old circular saw is near the camp entrance, embedded in a monument near the spot where the Mormons built a sawmill in 1853.

The San Bernardino County BAYLIS PARK PICNIC GROUNDS *(tables),* 74.9 *m.* (5,369 alt.), is on a well-shaded promontory.

At 78.4 *m.* is a junction with Arrowhead Road.

Left on Arrowhead Road to LAKE ARROWHEAD VILLAGE *(ski jumps, toboggan slide; adm. $1 a car),* 2 *m.,* a summer and winter resort for the well-to-do on the shore of Lake Arrowhead. The village is a crowded group of buildings with Norman-English embellishments.

Homes, camps, and lodges bordering the lake on all sides are connected by an 18.5-mile road, beginning at the village entrance.

Land not privately owned is leased from the Forest Service by the year. Many Angelenos, attracted by the names of prominent cinema visitors, have cottages along the shores.

LAKE ARROWHEAD is two and one-half miles long and one and a half wide. The earth dam creating it is 1,300 feet thick at the base, tapering to 40 feet at the summit. Construction was begun in 1901 by a private company. After it was completed the state court ruled that the law giving such companies the right to form irrigation districts was unconstitutional; the overflow from Lake Arrowhead is consequently wasted on the Mojave Desert. The lake was formerly called Little Bear. Shortly after the court gave its decision a corporation purchased the land bordering the lake, changed the name and developed the resort.

SKY FOREST POST OFFICE *(gas, general store),* 79.5 *m.* (5,800 alt.), is a small settlement.

East of RUNNING SPRINGS (R), 85.4 *m.* (6,000 alt.), the highway winds easily toward a level stretch, from which are views of the Santa Ana watershed to the south and of the Mojave watershed to the north. On clear days, or clear moon-flooded nights, the two branches of the Mojave River are seen as silver threads in the distance. Many bleached tree trunks are scattered about the plateau, relics of a forest fire. Here, too, is open country profusely carpeted with woodwardia ferns and larkspur.

LAKEVIEW POINT (7,207 alt.), 92.7 *m.,* the highest point on State 18, is a large parking space affording a view of SAN BERNARDINO MOUNTAIN (10,666 alt.) far to the southeast.

East of the summit State 18 is much narrower, and twists and turns along a ledge *(warning, slide areas),* slowly descending into Big Bear Valley. This is the most treacherous stretch of road in southern California.

The 125-foot concrete face of BIG BEAR DAM (R), 98.6 *m.* (6,750 alt.), blocks a narrow canyon at the eastern end of Big Bear Valley. BIG BEAR LAKE, almost eight miles long and four miles wide, is a storage reservoir supplying the cities of San Bernardino and Redlands.

Nearly a hundred privately operated summer and winter resorts (*rates reasonable*) dot the shores of Big Bear Lake (*ski jumps, toboggan slides*). The valley in which it lies is probably the result of glacial action. The name dates from 1845, when a party of settlers visited the area in search of Indians who had been stealing cattle. They reported a dearth of Indians but encountered an abundance of bears, shooting twenty-two.

Gold was discovered in 1859 near the eastern end of Big Bear Valley. Here Fawnskin Village was built. Across the lake, in the general direction of Pine Knot, another gold discovery was made, but both strikes proved to be surface or placer pockets and soon petered out. By 1880 the area was practically deserted.

Lucky Baldwin acquired 6,000 acres of land at the eastern end of the valley in 1870. Finding no gold, he attempted to subdivide his holdings, but his famed luck deserted him. He left the area about 1876.

As early as 1884, construction of a dam was begun in Big Bear Valley. The present dam, built between 1909 and 1912, is now the property of the Bear Valley Mutual Water Company.

BIG BEAR CITY, 108.3 *m.* (6,755 alt., 50 pop.), is distinguished by its white-painted street signs designating streets that do not exist— remains of an ambitious subdivision boom of predepression days. These markers stretch along Big Bear Lake for nearly a mile on both sides of the highway. In the tall pines (L) are a number of small cabins and a few simple summer homes.

In Big Bear City is the junction with Peter Pan Road, which (R) becomes the main route.

Left (straight ahead) on State 18 to BALDWIN LAKE (*duck hunting*), 1 *m.*, a large, shallow body of water fed by springs and mountain streams. It is surrounded by gray, almost treeless hills, infested with rabbits and rattlesnakes.

PINE KNOT (*trailer camps 50¢ a day; cabins $7 to $18 a wk.*), 114.2 *m.* (6,750 alt., 50 pop.), on Peter Pan Rd., is the metropolis of the Big Bear Lake country. It is a rambling community with an array of pine buildings. There are five hotels, several hundred cabins, three dance halls, amusement concessions, a cinema, and the like.

West of Pine Knot, the road winds along the lake, over a rugged ledge cut from the mountain, and across Big Bear Dam rejoins State 18 (*see above*) at 118.5 *m.*

❮❮❯❯❯❯❯❯❯❯❯❯❯❯❯❯❯❯❯❯❯❯❯❯❯❯❯❯❯❯❯❯❯❯❯❯❯❯

Tour 1A

TO MOUNT WILSON

South Pasadena—Pasadena—Flintridge—La Canada—Mount Wilson, 27.9 *m.;* Fair Oaks Ave., Atlanta St., Arroyo Dr., La Canada-Verdugo Rd. (State 118), Foothill Blvd., Haskell St., Angeles Crest Highway (State 2), Mount Wilson Rd.

Asphalt-concrete, two-lane roadbed; drive moderately within five miles of observatory; snow above Red Box Divide in winter and early spring; no gas stations between La Canada and summit of Mount Wilson.
Hotel and cottages on Mount Wilson summit; no camping in cars or trailers permitted on summit.

Cutting through one of the most spectacular areas of the Angeles National Forest, this route winds to mile-high Mount Wilson, which, though chiefly known for its great 100-inch telescope and its many contributions to astronomical research, is also a year-round pleasure resort.

The route branches north from Huntington Drive (*see Tour 1*) 0 *m.,* on Fair Oaks Avenue in South Pasadena.

The limited business center of SOUTH PASADENA, 0.2 *m.* (600 alt., 14,356 pop.), serves a community whose wage earners are for the most part engaged in business or the professions in adjoining Pasadena and Los Angeles. The city is really a southern extension of Pasadena, and many of its residents do their shopping in the mother town.

In the FLORES ADOBE, 1804 Foothill St. (*adm. by request*), Mexican Army leaders met in 1847 for a midnight conference to discuss terms of surrender to Lieutenant Colonel John C. Fremont. They had retreated to this place after their defeat in the Battle of the Mesa, the troops camping among the sycamores at the foot of the hill. The adobe bears the name of General Jose Maria Flores, who fled from it when Fremont accepted the conditions of surrender.

Construction of the one-story, buff-colored adobe structure was begun in 1839 by Jose Perez, a relative of the owner of Rancho San Pascual (*see below*). Perez died in 1840, with the house unfinished. Three years later the grant was withdrawn because of failure to cultivate and stock the land. The next grantee was Lieutenant Colonel Manual Garfias, an impecunious officer on the staff of Governor Micheltorena, who completed the house, but lost the rancho in the 1850's through foreclosure.

The CORNER OAK, a conspicuous California live oak rising at

the intersection of Warwick and St. Albans Avenues, was one of the natural markers used in identifying the southwest corner of Rancho San Pascual and the only corner marker that can now be definitely identified. The grant, made in 1826, covered 13,693 acres, including the present sites of Pasadena, South Pasadena, Altadena, and parts of San Marino (*see Tour 1*).

The CATHEDRAL OAK, also called Portola Oak, on the western side of Arroyo Dr., between Hermosa St. and Paloma Dr., is generally regarded as marking the site of the first Easter services in California, held by Father Juan Crespi, priest-historian of the Gaspar de Portola party, in 1770 (*see The Historical Background*).

PASADENA, 2.5 *m.* (850 alt., 81,864 pop.) (*see Pasadena*).

Points of Interest: California Institute of Technology, Rose Bowl, Brookside Park, Devil's Gate Dam, Colorado Street Bridge, Arroyo Seco, Busch Gardens, and others.

The route continues on Fair Oaks Avenue to Atlanta Street; L. on Atlanta to Arroyo Drive and R. briefly on Arroyo to La Canada-Verdugo Road; L. on La Canada-Verdugo Road (State 118), which at 5.9 *m.* crosses the top of DEVIL'S GATE DAM (*see Pasadena*).

At 7 *m.* is the junction with Foothill Boulevard; L. on Foothill Boulevard (State 118).

The route moves northwest through foothills that billow down from the heights of the San Gabriel Mountains (R), and rise again less steeply into the San Rafael Hills (L), crowned with the white, bowered homes of unincorporated FLINTRIDGE. The San Gabriel Mountains, extending the 75 miles between Newhall Pass and Cajon Pass, are characterized by an inordinately precipitous southern slope and have continuous heights of from 5,000 to 6,000 feet, with occasional sharp upthrusts reaching at some points more than 10,000 feet. A score or more of mile-high peaks are seen at places along this route.

LA CANADA (the valley), 7.8 *m.* (1,563 alt.), a community under county government, spreads over rolling hills at the southern end of Verdugo Valley, with the Verdugo Hills (L) forming a giant back drop. The townsite is a part of the Rancho La Canada, a 5,745-acre grant made in 1843 by the Mexican Governor.

In La Canada is the junction with Haskell Street; R. from Foothill Boulevard on this route to the junction with Angeles Crest Highway, 8.6 *m.;* R. from Haskell Street on Angeles Crest Highway (State 2).

LOOKOUT, 9.6 *m.* (1,750 alt.), provides a view over Pasadena and Altadena, with Devil's Gate Dam and Reservoir prominent in the near distance. Arroyo Seco, a deep narrow valley eroded by flood waters, is seen both above and below the reservoir. The action of water in this canyon in past ages accounts for much of the interest of the scene along this route.

The highway crosses a boundary of ANGELES NATIONAL FOREST (*see General Information*) at 10.8 *m.* The forest covers 643,656 mountainous acres broken by deep canyons, thousand-foot precipices, and scores of peaks ranging from 1,000 to more than 10,000 feet in height. Extending for more than 50 miles along the northern suburban rim of Los Angeles, its proximity to the metropolitan area has made it a recreational district that draws approximately a million visitors annually. Resorts in the Big Pines (*see Tour 7*), and Crystal Lake (*see Tour 1B*) areas attract skiers, tobogganists, bobsledders, and skaters during the winter.

The forest was created primarily for watershed protection, the chaparral-clad slopes soaking up water and helping to prevent heavy run-offs in the rainy season. While most of the preserve growth consists of chaparral, other types of vegetation, from desert cacti to large timber, are numerous. At lower elevations are willows, broad-leaved maples, live and valley oaks, acacias, western sycamores, California laurels, white alders, cottonwoods, eucalyptuses, and pepper trees. In the higher elevations are various kinds of conifer: the big-cone spruce, which occasionally appears as far down as the 2,000-foot level; the Coulter pine, bearing cones weighing up to eight pounds; the western yellow pine, or *Pinus ponderosa,* which forms most of the coniferous growth; Jeffrey, sugar, and one-leaf pine; incense cedar, white fir, and lodgepole pine—also called tamarack. The incense cedar, sugar pine, Jeffrey and tamarack thrive best above 5,000 feet.

Both the chaparral belt and the higher regions contain various beautiful flowering plants, such as Indian paintbrushes, wind poppies, lupines of many kinds and colors, leopard lilies, lemon lilies, and stream and bog orchards.

Deer, the hunting of which is subject to strict state regulation (*see General Information*), abound in the forest. In the rocky crags of Mount San Antonio a few mountain goats survive under federal protection. Among the predatory group are the California cougar, known variously as puma, catamount, or mountain lion; the bobcat, and the desert coyote. Larger birds include hawks and the California vulture, or buzzard. In the interior are a few eagles. The giant condor has vanished from these mountains (*see below*), as have also the black and grizzly bear.

The reservation, created in 1892 as the San Gabriel Timberland Reserve, was the first national forest established in California, and one of the earliest in the United States. In 1908 it was consolidated with the San Bernardino Forest Reserve, but 13 years later was separated.

NINO CANYON LOOKOUT, 11.2 *m.* (2,100 alt.), offers a view (R) across the gorge of Arroyo Seco to BROWN MOUNTAIN (4,485 alt.), a pinnacle named for the two sons of John Brown, the American abolitionist of Harpers Ferry fame, who lived in Pasadena after the Civil War. The big-cone spruce—dark, ragged trees rising from the far slope (R)—are seen here by northbound travelers for the last time on the route.

North of Nino Canyon Lookout the highway ascends the eastern spur of MOUNT LUKENS (5,049 alt.), named for P. T. Lukens, twice mayor of Pasadena and called California's "Father of Reforestation."

It was he who discovered that seeds nurtured first in seedbeds and then replanted produce better and quicker growths than seeds planted directly on mountain slopes.

WOODWARDIA CANYON, 13.8 *m.*, a gorge of primeval beauty, is so-named for the brakes of Woodwardia fern that thrive in its depths. A waterfall tumbles near the highway bridge, and along the contoured walls of the canyon masses of blue lilac bloom in the spring.

GEORGE'S GAP, 18 *m.*, lies around a headland of pink crystalline rock. From this vantage point is a view north (L) across the gap to the gray-granite heights of MOUNT JOSEPHINE (5,558 alt.) and STRAWBERRY PEAK (6,150 alt.). Far to the west is IRON MOUNTAIN (5,637 alt.) and between Iron Mountain and the lookout point is CONDOR PEAK (5,430 alt.), so-named because at one time it was frequented by the California condor, now found only in Santa Barbara County. The condor, with its 11-foot wingspread, is the only North American bird to rival in size the Andean condor of South America.

LADY BUG CANYON, 20.4 *m.*, is a hibernation refuge for the coccinellida, the little red and black beetles commonly called ladybugs. The bugs have been an important factor in the control of citrus pests, since they feed on plant lice and scale insects.

RED BOX DIVIDE, 22.7 *m.* (4,666 alt.), marks the boundary between the watersheds of the Arroyo Seco and the San Gabriel River. It was so-named because of a large red box, still seen (R) above the road, in which forest rangers store fire-fighting equipment.

Here an entirely new panorama opens northeast across the San Gabriel watershed. Almost directly east is Old Baldy, MOUNT SAN ANTONIO (10,080 alt.), the highest peak in Los Angeles County. Between Red Box Divide and Mount San Antonio are a score of lower peaks, ranging in height from 5,800 to 9,000 feet.

At 22.8 *m.* is the junction with Mount Wilson Road; R. here.

The approach to THE SADDLE, 25.1 *m.*, is along a narrow ledge of rock. The range falls away (L) in a series of ridges. Protected by a stout fence (R) is a sheer plunge of 1,000 feet into Upper Eaton Canyon.

Left from The Saddle on Cliff hiking trail to the summit of MOUNT LOWE, 3 *m.* (5,650 alt.).

MOUNT WILSON (5,710 alt.) is topped by a thousand-acre, much-eroded plateau, the grounds of the MOUNT WILSON HOTEL, 27.9 *m.* (*grounds adm. 50¢ a car, refunded to overnight guests; hotel rates reasonable*), and of the Mount Wilson Observatory.

The mountain was named for Benjamin Davis Wilson, who in 1864 blazed a trail to its summit. Although generally credited with having been the first white man to reach the summit, Wilson found two abandoned cabins on the plateau near where the observatory buildings now stand. They are supposed to have been built by marauders who pillaged Missions San Gabriel (*see Tour 3*) and San Luis Obispo, making off with some 3,000 horses during the administration of Governor Alvarado.

Wilson's trail became popular with early hikers. It was used until 1889, when a road was built by the Pasadena and Mount Wilson Toll Road Company. This in turn was replaced by the present route.

The WILSON MONUMENT, erected by the Alhambra and San Gabriel Chapters of the Daughters of the American Revolution, stands on SIGNAL POINT, several hundred feet from the hotel.

The hotel, standing in about the center of the heavily wooded plateau, is a low, simple building with stuccoed walls and with gabled roof steeply pitched to shed the snows; across its front is a wide veranda commanding a view of the vast valley. On foggy days the view is obscured by fleecy, low-hanging clouds (the peak itself is always above the clouds), but on clear days some 60 cities are seen stretching to the distant sea, where offshore Santa Catalina Island (*see Tour 5A*) shimmers in the purple haze. The view is especially notable at night, when the twinkling stars curve down in the bowl of the sky to mingle with a million twinkling lights of the cities.

Scattered about the hotel are small guest cottages; before it is a concrete swimming pool (*adm. 40¢ for transients, free for guests*). Within sight of the veranda is a small, lighthouse-like frame building (R) called, for some obscure reason, the POET'S CABIN. In it is the master stone of the United States Geological Survey from which was made the official survey of the San Gabriel Mountains in 1896. A climb up a steep, winding stairway affords another view of the surrounding peaks and valleys. Footpaths winding among the trees lead to many unusual rock formations, to numerous lookout points, and to a small picnic ground (*free*).

MOUNT WILSON OBSERVATORY, whose white buildings, towers, and domes are scattered among the giant trees (L), is operated by the Carnegie Institution of Washington, D. C. The first telescope was set up on Mount Wilson by the Institution in 1904 under the supervision of George E. Hale, who became the observatory's first director. Mount Wilson was chosen as the site after long search because of its height, freedom from atmospheric disturbance, and proximity to a metropolitan area. The observatory was planned primarily for solar research but "the necessity for seeking, among the stars and nebulae, for evidence as to the past and future stages of solar and stellar life," soon became evident, early resulting in a broadening of the field of the observatory. Today eight telescopes are in use on Mount Wilson. Other facilities include a technical library of more than 13,000 volumes and 10,000 pamphlets, and a large laboratory and optical shop (in Pasadena), where new equipment is perfected and old repaired.

The HOOKER 100-INCH TELESCOPE (*visitors weekdays 2:30-3 p.m.; Sun., holidays 2-3; free*), in a great white metal dome about 300 feet NE. of the hotel, is of the reflector type and has a concave mirror 101 inches in diameter. It has brought into view for study some 2,-000,000 faint extra-galactic nebulae, pushing the boundaries of the known universe out to about 100 million light years. It admits 250,000 times more light than the unaided human eye, and 2,500 times as much light as did the telescope with which Galileo Galilei began the modern era of astronomy on January 7, 1610 at the University of Padua. Images seen by the giant eye are recorded on photographic plates. How the vast mirror weighing four and a half tons is controlled, is explained by a member of the observatory staff during the daily visiting hours. The telescope and dome were installed in 1918 at a cost of about $600,000.

The 60-INCH TELESCOPE (*visitors Fri. 7:30-8:30 p.m.; free*), housed in a white dome near the 100-inch instrument is also an unusually large reflector, though far outstripped by its giant neighbor.

The SNOW TELESCOPE (*no visitors*) is in a 150-foot tower that rises above the pines near the cluster of low, snub-nosed domes. This instrument, the first placed on Mount Wilson, produces an image of the sun 16 inches in diameter. It is elevated to prevent the heat reflected from the ground from interfering with the accurate operation of the delicate mirrors. To increase the steadiness of the lenses and mirrors at so great a height, each steel leg and crosspiece of the tower skeleton is housed within the hollow member of another skeleton tower with sufficient clearance to prevent contact. The inner tower thus carries the instruments, the outer tower carries the dome that carries them.

The two TOWER TELESCOPES (*no visitors*) rise on steel frameworks, one 60, the other 150 feet high. Used like the Snow telescope for solar observation, they represent improvements over that instrument, in that the path of the beam is vertical instead of horizontal, with the mirrors placed high above the ground. In each the spectograph is mounted in a well beneath the tower. The 60-foot tower is equipped with a lens of 60-foot focal length, which is used daily for direct solar photographs and for spectro-heliograms showing the distribution of hydrogen and calcium clouds over the sun. Through its use a continuous photographic record of the sun's surface is maintained, day by day, with a motion-picture camera of a special kind. The 150-foot tower has a lens of 150 feet focal length, and a spectograph 75 feet in length. It is chiefly used for observation of the magnetic fields in sun spots, and for measuring solar rotation.

The 12-INCH TELESCOPE (*visitors 8 p.m.; free*), south of the swimming pool is in a metal dome, some 20 feet high. Planets visible through the telescope are recorded daily on the dome's bulletin board. Visitors are permitted to peer through the lens. Daily at 8 p.m. an astronomical lecture (*free*) is given in the hotel, or at the telescope when the attendance is small.

The AUDITORIUM, a concrete structure with steep sloping roof of iron sheeting, was opened in 1937 to provide a meeting room for scientific lectures. In the building, which seats 272, lectures (*Fri. 7:30 p.m.; adm. free but by card obtainable at office, 813 Santa Barbara St., Pasadena*) are given by members of the staff and demonstrated with slides and instruments.

In the EXHIBIT HALL (*open daily 1:30-2:30 p.m.; free*), opposite the auditorium, are displayed astronomical instruments, charts, graphs, and hundreds of transparencies, mounted in such manner as to illustrate the various types of research undertaken by the observatory. The transparencies are produced from some 70,000 plates made during the course of the observatory's existence.

Behind the maze of mathematical formulae that obscures his activity from the layman, the researcher at Mount Wilson Observatory is participating in a drama a thousand times more thrilling than the tales told by the most imaginative fictionist. Through the silent hours of the night he sits on the mountain peak, alone with the far-flung family of the universe, that man may know a little more of his relation to that universe, and of the beginnings, meaning, and destiny of the earth. Sitting at the eyepiece on the lofty, cramped perch in the shadow of the giant instrument, he knows that he alone in all the world is following the westward movement of some distant star, for no other telescope will reach so far into the outer spaces. On any night he may be as fortunate as Dr. Edwin Powell Hubble was one winter night in 1936, when his photographic plate caught a beam of light, just arrived on earth but created seven million years ago in the distant island universe NGC 4275, when a giant star, 50 times hotter and 10 million times brighter than earth's sun, unaccountably exploded. The light Dr. Hubble saw that night, and which anyone can now see on a photograph in the museum, had been traveling 186,000 miles a second through space since long before man first appeared on earth. Thirty thousand years before it reached earth it passed the outer fringes of the Milky Way; five years before it was inside *Promina Centuri,* earth's nearest star. A month after it struck Mount Wilson's photographic plate it had faded from the view of man, leaving only a photographic record of a mighty celestial cataclysm and the satisfaction for Dr. Hubble of knowing that he had been the first man since 1901 to witness such a spectacle and the second since the telescope was invented.

Tour 1B

TO CRYSTAL LAKE

Azusa—Angeles National Forest—Pine Flats—Crystal Lake; 25.7 *m.;* State 39 and Crystal Lake Rd.

Two-lane asphalt paved highway between Azusa and Pine Flats; one-lane, one-way, graded dirt roads, impassable in wet weather between Pine Flats and Crystal Lake; route sometimes closed for short periods after heavy snows in winter.
Hotels, cottages, and camping facilities.

Crystal Lake, the only natural lake within 50 miles of Los Angeles, lies in a glacier-formed depression among mile-high, pine-rimmed slopes deep in the San Gabriel Mountains. State 39 runs through San Gabriel Canyon by easy gradients, then ascends the sharp rises of North Fork Canyon through forests of pine and spruce.

State 39 branches north from US 66 (*see Tour 1*), 0 *m.,* on Azusa Avenue, a street of tree-shaded homes and flats, in AZUSA (*see Tour 1*).

The highway crosses the rock-strewn alluvial fan of the San Gabriel River, 1.4 *m.,* then follows the river's northwest bank. SAN GABRIEL CANYON, entered at 1.8 *m.,* cleaves the San Gabriel Mountains for 20 miles, between heights rising 5,000 to 9,000 feet. In former years the San Gabriel River, here close to its source, held a constant flood threat for lowland ranches and farms. Today its flow is regulated by three dams.

A boundary of ANGELES NATIONAL FOREST (*see Tour 1A*) is crossed at 3 *m.*

MORRIS DAM, 4 *m.,* is a concrete barrier 245 feet high across a sharp bend in the San Gabriel River in Lower Pine Canyon. The dam, 1,160 feet long at roadway level, is of the concrete-gravity type, capable of impounding 39,300 acre-feet of water. The spillway is in three 70-foot weir sections. The weirs are equipped with automatically operating steel sector gates that rise or drop with the falling or rising water level.

Morris Dam was built by the city of Pasadena to augment its municipal water supply pending completion of the Colorado River Aqueduct System (*see Tour 2*). The Metropolitan Water District, builders of the aqueduct, will eventually take over Morris Dam and use the reservoir for storage of Colorado River waters. The dam and reservoir were named for Samuel B. Morris, chief engineer of the Pasadena Water Department.

North of a headland opposite the dam abutment the road winds along the chaparral-clothed north shore of MORRIS RESERVOIR, which extends northward between narrow canyon walls to the foot of SAN GABRIEL DAM NO. 1, 7.2 *m.,* an unusually large rock-fill dam. An entire mountainside was moved into the gorge, creating a barrier 381 feet high and 1,500 feet long. Facing northwest in a sharp curve in the canyon, it has the appearance of a giant stairway rising from the stream bed in terraces.

To ensure an earthquake-proof structure material for the dam was deposited in six layers. Zone 1, the topmost, consists of quarry material and Zone 2 of compacted loam. Zone 3, considered the backbone or core of the dam, is of quarry material compacted by rolling or tamping and Zones 4 and 5 of fine rock and large rock, respectively. The large rock provides a free drainage mass and protection against erosion. The bottom layer is built chiefly of hard rock. The outlet works are installed in the 30-foot-diameter tunnel that served as a diversion channel during construction of the dam.

The reservoir behind the dam is a catch-basin for a watershed of two hundred square miles and when full forms a lake of 670 acres. San Gabriel Dam No. 1 was built by the Los Angeles County Flood Control District in 1935-37.

At 9.3 *m.* a great scar (R) disfiguring the mountainside is all that remains of the first San Gabriel Dam project. In 1929 millions of dollars were spent here on exploratory work preliminary to the building of a concrete dam that was to have been the highest in the world. Engineers who had been paid $1,000 a day for their work had pronounced the site safe, and months of excavation had been under way when a disastrous landslide revealed geologic fault lines under the foundation. The project on this site was immediately abandoned.

At THE FORKS, 9.4 *m.,* the San Gabriel Canyon branches into the East Fork (R) and the West Fork (L).

On the East Fork, scene of southern California's first major gold boom, is the SITE OF ELDORADOVILLE, a boom town founded in 1855. As early as 1843, five years before the epochal discovery of gold on the American River, Abel Stearns, Los Angeles merchant, bought gold from Indian and Mexican placer miners working in San Gabriel Canyon and shipped it to the Mint in Philadelphia. Widespread development began with the discovery of extremely rich deposits in the gravels of the East Fork in 1855. During the whole period 1855-63 the average daily earnings of each miner panning in the canyon were estimated to be 25 per cent greater than the average of each worker during 1863, the peak year in the northern gold camps. So rich was the dirt, according to one story, that a certain miner recovered an ounce of gold a day by running the sawdust from the Union Saloon through his sluice box.

By 1861 Eldoradoville had a population of 1,600, with saloons, dance halls, and gambling shacks lining its short muddy streets. It was known as "The Downieville of the South," by miners who boasted that in toughness and general iniquity it compared with that Sierra County town, reputedly the hardest-boiled of all the northern camps of the late 1850's.

Floods in 1857 and 1861 severely damaged Eldoradoville and on January 18, 1862, the swollen San Gabriel River swept it into oblivion.

Destruction of the town had little effect on mining production in the canyon, but by the middle 1920's the take had dropped to insignificant proportions.

Right from The Forks on a rough foot trail to HOOVERVILLE, 1 *m.,* now only a scattering of tattered tents and crude log shacks along the banks of the river between Susanna and Graveyard Canyons, but in the depression years 1930-33 a collection of 500-odd shacks, tents, and dugouts occupied by gold-seeking unemployed male transients. Daily the entire population swarmed the near-by canyons to pan for gold with the crudest of equipment—pie plates, old skillets, sieves, screen-wire, discarded granite pots, and the like. The yield per man averaged 50 to 60 cents worth of gold a day—on bonanza days, perhaps a dollar. Through the latter part of 1933 and in 1934 the town waned; by 1935 it had lost two-thirds of its population. In 1938 floods swept away most of the lower-lying shacks, leaving only a handful of indigents still picking the leavings.

At 9.5 *m.* State 39 bears L. into West Fork Canyon.

CAMP RINCON (L), 10.9 *m.,* is a privately operated resort (*rates reasonable*). Near the gable-roofed green frame hotel are a dance hall, a swimming pool, and croquet courts.

At 11.2 *m.* is the junction with a foot trail.

Right on this trail to the PAINTED ROCK, 0.4 *m.,* one of several boulders in the West Fork Canyon bearing pictographs of undetermined origin—two human figures and a mass of geometric designs. The markings are believed to be sign posts of the aborigine along the old Indian trail that descended the North Fork, West Fork, and main San Gabriel Canyons to the valley in the vicinity of modern Duarte (*see Tour 1*).

At 11.6 *m.* the road bears R. into the North Fork Canyon and at 14 *m.* enters a growth of black-barked spruce, always the first conifer encountered in the ascent of southern California mountains. These evergreens grow singly and in groups of five or six along the steep slopes, massing to denser clusters toward the 4,000-foot level. At 16.5 *m.* the grade mounts abruptly, the foothill character of the encircling slopes gives way to mountains of gray and light-brown rock, the acclivities frequently so steep that the spruce and pine find scant foothold. In sun-sheltered gulches patches of snow are seen the year round.

Almost without warning, at 19 *m.,* the highway enters the true forest, its air heavy with the scent of Jeffrey and sugar pines, incense cedar, fir, spruce, and tamarack. The pines are distinguished by their light-red columnar trunks, the firs by their thick, dark needles. In the narrow canyons the trees are thickest.

At 19.9 *m.* is a junction with a private road.

Right on this graded dirt road to HEADLEE'S MOUNTAIN CLUB (*rates reasonable*), 0.1 *m.* (4,000 alt.), a resort with a rustic wood-stone main lodge that crowns a projection overlooking the main highway and the steep drop into the North Fork Canyon. The resort has wading and swimming pools, a nine-hole putting green, and croquet and horseshoe pitching courts.

CRYSTAL LAKE COUNTY RECREATION PARK (*ski runs, toboggan slides*), 22.6 *m.,* is a large 1,350-acre preserve maintained as a public play- and campground by the Los Angeles County Department of Recreation Camps and Playgrounds. A ranger on duty at the ENTRANCE LODGE (5,012 alt.) registers cars and passengers.

Upward from the lodge the road, rising 705 feet in two miles, circles into groves of pines and incense cedars. Many of the trees are more than 150 feet high, with trunks four to five feet in diameter.

State 39 terminates at PINE FLATS, 24.6 *m.* (5,717 alt.), a plateau studded with pines and rimmed by 1,000-foot slopes. A one-story log and stone store (R) faces eastward across the public PICNIC AND CAMPGROUNDS (*camping 25¢ a day each car; season $2.50*). The facilities of an outdoor cook house (*free*) are supplemented by individual grills scattered about the plateau. There are tennis and volleyball courts, a children's playground, outdoor dance floor, and a stone amphitheatre. In summer, before the huge fireplace in the amphitheatre, free entertainment is presented nightly. The park was opened in 1923.

At Pine Flats is the junction with Crystal Lake Road. The route is L. here on a narrow graded dirt road (*one way traffic*) that winds through pine forests to a parking lot (*free*), 25.6 *m.*

CRYSTAL LAKE, 25.7 *m.,* 300 feet from the road's end, is reached by a foot trail down a narrow gorge, and extends along the foot of high ridges on the west side of Pine Flats Basin. Fed only by runoff from the surrounding slopes, the area of the lake varies from a minimum of 11 acres in summer to a maximum of 15 acres in winter. The average depth is 100 feet. Steep pine-clad slopes rim the lake on the eastern and western sides; on the northern shore is a shelving beach. Geologists agree that the Pine Flats area was once occupied by a glacier three and one-half miles high and that the lake basin is of glacial origin. In 1890 the Pacific Light and Power Company, believing the lake to be fed by springs, contracted for the use of the waters for generating electricity. A tunnel driven through the mountain to carry the water to a down-canyon power plant promptly drained the lake, demonstrating the absence of springs.

≪≪≪≪≪≪≪≪≪≪≪≪≪≪≪≪≪≪≪≪≪≪≪≪≪≪≪≪≪≪≪≪≪≪≪≪≪≫≫≫≫≫≫≫≫≫≫≫≫≫≫≫≫≫≫≫≫≫≫≫≫≫≫≫≫≫≫

Tour 2

TO PALM SPRINGS

Los Angeles—Monterey Park—Pomona—Ontario—Colton—Redlands —Beaumont—Banning—Palm Springs—Cathedral City—Indio, 128.4 *m.;* N. Main St., Aliso St., Ramona Blvd., US 99, State 111.

Concrete and asphalt-concrete paved roadbed; three and four lanes wide between Los Angeles and Ontario.
Southern Pacific R.R. roughly parallels route. Greyhound motor coaches between Los Angeles and Palm Springs.
All types of accommodations.

This route runs through the citrus groves of the coastal valley, the wind-swept heights of a mountain pass, and the hot, sandy soil of a below-sea-level basin. In the early spring the orange groves of the San Gabriel and San Bernardino Valleys bloom within sight of snow-capped mountain peaks, and the orchards east of the San Gorgonio Pass are pink and white with blooming almond, pecan, and cherry blossoms. East of the pass, in the desert country, are a luxurious winter resort patronized by film stars, and the date and grapefruit groves that thrive in the hot climate of this lower-than-sea-level desert.

North on Main St. from the LOS ANGELES CITY HALL, 0 *m.*, 1st and Main Sts., to Macy St.; R. on Macy to Mission Rd.; R. on Mission to Ramona Blvd.; and L. on Ramona Blvd. (US 99).

MONTEREY PARK (mountain of the king), 7.5 *m.* (395 alt., 8,531 pop.), a residential community on Los Angeles' northeastern outskirts, has many large estates along the rolling hills (L) of its western section, as well as rows of small, simple cottages and bungalows that extend north and south from the highway in the eastern part of town. It is in an area of rich sandy loam that has been transformed by irrigation into a highly productive walnut, avocado, citrus fruit, berry, truck garden, and poultry district. The city was incorporated in 1916.

EL MONTE (the mountain), 13.2 *m.* (290 alt., 4,746 pop.) (*see Tour 3*), is at the junction with Valley Boulevard (*see Tour 3*).

East of El Monte US 99, traversing an area of small farms and chicken ranches, crosses the SAN GABRIEL RIVER (*see Tour 3*), 14 *m.*

At 15.3 *m.* is the junction with Covina Boulevard.

Left on Covina Boulevard to BALDWIN PARK, 1.5 *m.* (375 alt., 3,910 pop.), an unincorporated community in a fruit- and truck-farming district. Founded in the early 1880's, it is named for E. J. "Lucky" Baldwin (*see Tour 1*). The rock crushers, sand, and gravel plants in the San Gabriel Wash district (northwest) provide employment for many of the residents.

Left from Baldwin Park, 1.3 *m.*, on Ramona Boulevard to the HAGENBECK-WALLACE CIRCUS WINTER QUARTERS (*adm. on application*), W. Ramona Blvd. and Earl Ave. (L). Here, on 35 acres of level land, beside the huge parade wagons, ornate with vivid paint and gold-leaf, and the brightly varnished railroad cars, sidetracked along a spur, are cages of lions and tigers—cats, in circus parlance—camel corrals, elephant sheds, kennels of trained dogs, and pastures of ring horses and ponies. Elephants—called bulls by the circus men—which during the summer season perform tricks in the big-top rings, serve as beasts of burden here, hauling refuse wagons, shunting railroad cars, and piling baled hay. In a large tent at the eastern edge of the grounds aerialists practice their trapeze and high-wire acts, while lions, tigers, elephants, and horses are being trained in its ring. The circus usually remains here from late November to early spring.

On US 99 east of Covina Boulevard truck farms and chicken ranches diminish as unbroken lines of orange trees (*see Tour 1*) and walnut trees (*see Tour 3*) appear on either side of the highway.

WEST COVINA, 18 *m.* (400 alt., 1,072 pop.), with an area of more than eight square miles, has no concentrated business and residential districts, but consists of large lemon, orange, grapefruit, and walnut groves, each with its rambling frame or stucco home built well back from the pepper and eucalyptus-lined avenues. The town was incorporated in 1923.

At 20.3 *m.* is the junction with Citrus Avenue.

Left on Citrus Avenue to COVINA, 1 *m.* (555 alt., 3,049 pop.), the largest citrus shipping center in Los Angeles County. Its 12 packing houses, representing 900 growers, annually ship from 2,500 to 3,000 carloads of fruit.

Between West Covina and the SAN JOSE HILLS, 22 *m.*, are continuous citrus fruit groves. BUZZARD'S PEAK (1,380 alt.), rises (R) at 23.5 *m.*

At 24.8 *m.* is the junction with a private road.

Right on this road into the 750-acre grounds of the UNIVERSITY OF CALIFORNIA INSTITUTE OF ANIMAL HUSBANDRY, 0.3 *m.* (*open daily except Mon. 9-5; free; exhibitions Sun. 2:00-3:30; adm. 10¢, children free*). The main building is of white concrete surrounded with lawns and ornamental flower plantings. Driveways leading to it have hedges of gardenias backed by apricot, prune, and orange trees. The stalls face a rectangular patio. Here purebred Arabian stallions and mares are bred. In Sunday exhibitions, the horses are shown at various gaits and in different types of saddle work, jumping, drilling, and trick performances. The exhibitions are climaxed by a chariot race between two teams of Shetland ponies.

Established in 1925 by William K. Kellogg, Battle Creek, Michigan, cereal manufacturer, the ranch was presented by him in 1932 to the University of California, which now operates it. The gift included the estate, stables and laboratory facilities, 87 registered Arabian horses, and an endowment of $600,000.

POMONA, 28.3 *m.* (859 alt., 23,539 pop.), at the eastern edge of Los Angeles County, lies along the eastern base of the San Jose Hills, which separate Pomona Valley from the rest of San Gabriel Valley.

The city is a shipping point for 30,000 acres of citrus groves and additional acres producing walnuts, hay, grain, and vegetables. Manufactures include brick and tile, paper fruit wrappers, and canned and packed fruits and vegetables.

The site of Pomona was part of Rancho San Jose de Arriba (San Jose the upper), which fell to Ricardo Vejar during a division of the original Rancho San Jose in 1846 (*see Tour 3*). In 1866 the land came into possession of Louis Phillips, whose home, still standing on Valley Boulevard (*see Tour 3*), was the first brick house in this region. Phillips granted a right-of-way to the Southern Pacific Railroad in 1873. A year later the Los Angeles Immigration and Land Co-operative Association was organized to promote a fruit colony and found a town. In a contest to decide the name of the city, Solomon Gates, nurseryman, submitted the winning suggestion "Pomona, Goddess of Fruit," and won a free lot.

In the STANTON CACTUS GARDENS (*free*), 877 W. Grand Ave., are more than a thousand varieties of cacti and succulents gathered by the owner, S. F. Stanton, in the southwestern parts of the United States and northern Mexico. A specimen of saguaro (tree cactus) is 11 feet high.

The 56-year-old CAMPHOR TREE on the front lawn of the Pomona Ebell Club, Holt Ave. and Caswell St., is 50 feet high, has a trunk eight feet in circumference, and branches that divide near the ground and spread 50 feet in all directions. It is considered the oldest camphor tree in California.

The first Christian religious service in Pomona Valley was held under the CHRISTIAN OAK, South Kenoak Dr. near the corner of

Wisconsin St. March 9, 1837. Padre Zalvidea, father-superior of San Gabriel Mission (*see Tour 3*), pronounced a benediction here upon the families and retainers of Rancho San Jose (*see Tour 3*).

The ALVARADO ADOBE (*private*), 1475 N. Park Ave.; in an orange grove about 100 feet back from Park Ave., is a one-story, shingle-roofed structure, built in 1840. Its adobe walls are almost completely hidden by later additions.

The PALOMARES ADOBE (*private*), 1569 Park Avenue, was built in 1837 by Ygnacio Palomares as the first hacienda of his Rancho San Jose (*see Tour 3*). This one-story, thick-walled house, surrounded by oleanders, peach, and orange trees, served as Palomares' home until the completion of the Tavern Adobe (*see below*).

The ruin of the PALOMARES TAVERN ADOBE (L), hidden in an orange grove near the corner of Cucamonga Rd. and Orange Grove Ave., was built by Ygnacio Palomares in 1850. Its three western rooms are roofless, the mud walls reduced to half their original height. The eastern part is more substantial. Here, two small chambers open into a 15-foot-square *sala* (parlor), with a large fireplace, now in ruins.

GANESHA PARK (*picnic facilities, playground, swimming pool, Greek theatre*), Huntington Blvd., between Loma Vista St. and Walnut Ave., Pomona's 60-acre municipal park, extends over rolling hills in the northwestern residential section. Through it wind several miles of drives, one mounting to Inspiration Point, which affords views of San Gabriel and Pomona Valleys and the San Gabriel Mountains. The land was once owned by P. C. Tonner, lawyer and student of Hindu literature, who had named his estate after Ganesha, Hindu god of rain and rivers.

In the 350-acre LOS ANGELES COUNTY FAIR GROUNDS, Huntington Blvd. and Walnut Ave., the annual Los Angeles County Fair is held (*usually last 2 wks. in Sept.; adm. 25¢-50¢; parking free*). Each season more than a half-million visitors are attracted by the 35,000 exhibits, the attending movie stars, and the daily harness and running races held under pari-mutuel regulations on the half-mile track. The stakes exceed $25,000 for the season and there are accommodations for 25,000 spectators in the grandstand and infield. The plant, valued at $2,500,000, contains 52 exhibit buildings, with a combined floor space of more than 30 acres.

The first Los Angeles County Fair was held in Exposition Park (*see Tour D*), Los Angeles, in 1913. The fair was moved to Pomona in 1922. The main exhibits are of machinery, poultry, art, handwork, domestic arts, and livestock.

In Pomona is the junction with US 60 (*see Tour 7*) which branches south from US 99 and runs parallel to it through Ontario.

ONTARIO, 33.6 *m*. (979 alt., 14,197 pop.), the shipping center for approximately 200 dairies, also has numerous fruit canning and packing houses and by-products plants which manufacture orange juice, oil, and vinegar. A plant of the General Electric Company employs

450 workers here in the manufacture of electric irons, refrigerators, and other electrical appliances.

Tree-bordered EUCLID AVENUE (*see Tour 1*), is distinctive among southern California boulevards.

Ontario was founded in 1891 by George B. and W. B. Chaffey, who named it after their native Canadian province.

East of Ontario the vast tracts of low-cut grape vines growing from the gray sandy loam are part of the Italian Vineyards holdings which extend for 4.5 miles along US 99.

At 37.4 *m.* is the junction with Turner Avenue.

Right on Turner Avenue to GUASTI, 0.7 *m.* (400 alt., 450 est. pop.) a town built by the Italian Vineyard Company in the center of their 5,000-acre Guasti vineyard, which is advertised as the largest in the world. The village has its own post office, school, church, and stores. Along Turner and Guasti Avenues the company has built frame bungalows for its married employees and two-story frame dormitories for the single men and women. On western Guasti Avenue is the principal wine-finishing PLANT OF FRUIT INDUSTRIES LIMITED, a state-wide distributing co-operative. Adjoining, between Turner and Archibald Aves. is (R) the ITALIAN VINEYARD COMPANY WINERY (*open by arrangement*), a two-story brick and concrete structure, flanked by a series of vats, process sheds, laboratories, receiving and distributing houses—all part of an assemblage in which annually some two million gallons of wine are produced. In these laboratories the standard is set for all brands of wine made by the nine members of the co-operative.

About a third of the wine distributed by Fruit Industries Limited is produced by the Italian Vineyard Company; the remaining four or five million gallons from its other affiliates are received here as raw wine.

In the Guasti area, California's third largest grape-producing district, and in northern California's inland valleys, the growing of sweet-wine grapes predominates; the principal dry-wine grape-growing region is around San Francisco Bay, where the climate is cooler. Although the state's grape-growing (the fifth most important division of its agriculture), includes table and raisin grapes, California made 91 million of the 98 million gallons of wine produced in the United States in 1937.

The wine is made only in the fall. In late summer as the grapes are beginning to mature the laboratory makes daily tests of their sugar and acid content so that each variety can be harvested at the proper stage of ripeness for making its particular type of wine.

The grapes, cut from waist-high untrellised rows of vines, are hauled to the winery in trucks, unloaded on two long concrete receiving platforms and carried on conveyors to the two crushing machines. At Guasti certain varieties of grapes are gathered and crushed together, thus eliminating the later blending of finished wines.

Crushed grapes are pumped to tanks in the fermenting room, where by a natural process the grape sugar is transformed into alcohol and carbon dioxide (gas) by the activity of the enzymes and the yeasts present in the crushed mass. Of the various organisms—molds, bacteria, and yeasts—found on grapes, all are undesirable for wine fermentation except the true wine yeast; and since the cells of this yeast that are found on California grapes are usually of inferior strains, modern wine makers kill all organisms on the grapes by sterilization, and start fermentation by adding a pure wine-yeast cultivated in laboratories. The yeast cultures used in the Guasti vats are imported from France.

The excessive heat generated during fermentation is controlled by pumping the fermenting wine into concrete sumps cooled with copper coils.

After active fermentation in the open vat, which takes from a few days to more than a week, depending upon the type of wine being made, the juice is drawn off the crushed grapes and run into storage vats to finish fermenting. These vats are equipped with escape bungs—stoppers regulated to retain a certain pressure of carbon dioxide upon the wine, and to let out excess gas without letting in bacteria-laden air. The presence of the carbon dioxide prevents the growth of vinegar bacteria and other organisms that attack wine in the presence of free oxygen. As soon as the fermentation is complete, the wine is drawn off its first, or crude sediment and run into casks or barrels. This action aerates the wine sufficiently to prevent the development of bacteria; it also releases most of the carbon dioxide with which the wine has been charged while fermenting in the storage vats, and which retards aging.

While the wine is aging in oak or redwood casks in the constant low temperature of a cellar it undergoes two principal changes—development of mellowness and flavor by gradual oxidation in the wood, and precipitation of undissolved matter, and "albumins" (principally cream of tartar). The casks, tightly closed to exclude air, are racked from sediment and aerated two or three times a year.

Sweet wines fortified with brandy, such as Angelica, Muscatel, Tokay, Port, Madeira, Malaga, and Marsala, are not considered fit for drinking under two years, and improve indefinitely with the years. They are used as tonics, as dessert wines, and in cooking. Some wines, such as the Sauternes, are naturally sweet (unfortified); their fermentation is arrested with the addition of sulfite when the proper degree of sugar and alcohol is reached. Dry wines—those in which complete fermentation eliminates all sugar perceptible to the taste—are lighter in body, and lower in alcohol content than the sweet wines. They are ready for use after one or two years and are best under 10 years. Sherry is a white wine fermented as any sweet variety and then put through a special process called cooking, which caramelizes the grape sugar and gives a nut-like flavor. At Guasti it is made in a separate building containing tall slender cooking vats in which the wine is kept at a temperature of 140° for about three months. The vats are not directly heated, but the temperature in the building is maintained by log-burning furnaces. Sherry is fortified with brandy and aged before bottling.

The brandy, made in the winery's own distillery, is made in four types— Fortifying Brandy, Grappa, Muscat, and California Grape (Cognac) Brandy. Grappa is distilled from a wash made by adding water to the crushed grape skins and pulps left after fermented wine has been drawn from them; Muscat has a pronounced flavor and bouquet from the Muscat grapes used in making the distilling stock; California Grape (cognac) is the term used for all commercial brandy which does not come under one of the three other classifications.

The Guasti plant also makes champagne, which is naturally fermented a second time in the bottle, after the primary fermentation in the vat given all dry white wines. A measured quantity of sugar in rock candy form, and a culture of selected champagne yeast is put into the bottle with the champagne stock; the bottle is then tightly stoppered and the cork strapped with steel to prevent its being blown out by the pressure of fermentation within. The rock sugar is entirely used in the fermentation and the champagne is perfectly dry when it goes into the aging room. It is cleared by settling with the bottle standing neck down at a 45° angle. When the sediment has collected on the cork, it is the usual procedure to freeze about an inch of the champagne next to the cork, after which the steel straps are removed, and the pressure within the bottle blows out the cork and the frozen sediment. This is called disgorging. At Guasti disgorging is accomplished by a secret process without freezing. After disgorging, the bottles pass at once into a machine which keeps the champagne under pressure and prevents loss of effervescence; here sweetening syrup and brandy in measured amounts are added.

At Guasti, the wines made in the Italian Vineyard Company winery become the property of the co-operative when they are ready for finishing, which includes refrigeration, pasteurization, clarification, and three filtrations.

Wine making in California began with the Franciscan padres. The first vineyard was planted at the Mission San Diego in 1771, and as the missions advanced to San Francisco, their European wine grape, later called the Mission grape, went with them. Though the vine is vigorous its fruit is only fair for making wine, and the padres, who crushed their grapes by having Indians trample them with their bare feet, achieved a very mediocre drink. Crude methods of wine making continued until Count Augustin Haraszthy, a Hungarian immigrant, began experimenting with the culture of fine European wine-grape varieties in the San Francisco Bay area in the 1860's. A wine-making boom resulted. But the young industry was quickly ruined by the inexperienced and unscrupulous who used inferior grapes and fraudulent methods that gave all California wines a bad reputation. In 1880 the makers of good wines gained passage of a pure-wine law by the state legislature, and by the turn of the century California wines were favorably known in many parts of the world.

In 1920 when the eighteenth amendment outlawed alcoholic beverages, many excellent wine-grape vines were torn up and prunes, apricots, and oranges planted in their places. With the repeal of prohibition in 1933, the California wine industry revived and by 1938 had outstripped preprohibition records.

The highway skirts the northern base (R) of SLOVER MOUNTAIN (1,509 alt.), at 50.4 *m.,* which furnishes raw material for 4,000,000 barrels of cement a year. The mountain is owned and worked by the California-Portland Cement Company.

COLTON, 51.9 *m.* (847 alt., 9,686 pop.), is a manufacturing town on the main lines of the Southern Pacific and Union Pacific Railroads and on a branch line of the Santa Fe Railway. Flour mills, railroad repair shops, ice manufacturing plants, cooling establishments for refrigerating fruit express cars, and the near-by cement and quarrying operations in the Slover Mountain district provide the chief sources of employment.

At 58.2 *m.* is a junction with Nevada Avenue.

Right on Nevada Avenue to a junction with Barton Avenue, 1 *m.;* L. on Barton Avenue to the SAN BERNARDINO ASISTENCIA (branch mission), 1.1 *m.* (*open 8-6*). The present tile-roofed, low white buildings (L) ranged about a walled patio, are a restoration built on the old cobblestone foundations of the asistencia that was erected here in 1821 as the San Bernardino Valley headquarters of Mission San Gabriel (*see Tour 3*).

REDLANDS, 60.2 *m.* (1,350 alt., 14,324 pop.), is a college town, and fruit-packing center surrounded by more than 15 thousand acres of citrus groves. In the 1937-38 season this area produced approximately 4,200 cars of navel oranges and 1,300 cars of Valencia oranges, worth six million dollars. Near the business area the palm-lined streets are bordered with small houses and flower gardens. Wealthy easterners, attracted by the winter climate and the setting of snow-capped mountains rising above green orange groves, have built palatial winter homes surrounded by acres of landscaped grounds on the hills in the southern part of town.

Before 1881 when E. G. Judson and F. E. Brown sponsored the digging of a canal, six miles long, from the Santa Ana River to a reservoir in the mouth of Yucaipa Valley, to the east, the region was a semibarren mesa called Redlands for the color of its soil. A year after the canal's completion, 1,500 acres of orange groves were planted here

and 120,000 grapevines were set out by Dr. J. D. B. Stillman on a
100-acre area at Lugonia, then several miles to the north. In four
years these produced so heavily that a winery was built. Redlands,
Lugonia, and other small settlements near by were incorporated as one
community in 1881 and given the name of Redlands.

The 17 buildings of the UNIVERSITY OF REDLANDS, E. Colton Ave.
and University St., are distributed over 100 acres of rolling foothills
that once were a part of Dr. Stillman's vineyard. The ADMINISTRA-
TION BUILDING occupies the site of Dr. Stillman's first home (*see below*), and BEKINS HALL, the site of the Stillman barn. Many of the
buildings have porticos and other Greek Revival motifs. The foundation stones of the PRESIDENT'S RESIDENCE, adjoining the administration building, are from the old winery. The classic, two-story Library
contains over 30,000 books; the Department of Music has a $40,000
four-manual Casavant organ. Through the university grounds runs
the old Judson-Brown Canal, which carries water to Mentone Reservoir, the school's privately-owned, four-million-gallon storage basin. In
a Greek Theatre on the bank of the canal the annual Zanja Fiesta
(Ditch Celebration) is held. The university has an endowment of
more than $5,000,000 and a student enrollment of 700.

SMILEY PARK, between 4th and San Gorgonio Sts., Olive Ave., and
Glenwood Dr., contains a bronze BUST OF WILLIAM McKINLEY,
commemorating his visit to Redlands in 1901. Both the park and the
A. K. SMILEY PUBLIC LIBRARY (*open 9-9; Sun. and holidays 2-4*),
were gifts to the city in 1898 by A. K. Smiley, Redland's pioneer subdivider and philanthropist. The building, cruciform in plan, of red
brick with stone trim, contains more than 110,000 books and manuscripts.

In the REDLANDS BOWL, a palm-rimmed, open-air theatre in the
center of Smiley Park, community concerts are held (*Tues. and Fri.
nights*) during the summer.

The WATCHORN LINCOLN SHRINE (*open weekdays except Fri.,
10-12 and 1-5:30*), at the Eureka St. and Olive Ave. corner of Smiley
Park, was established in 1932 by Mr. and Mrs. Robert Watchorn in
memory of a son killed in the World War. A Carrara marble BUST
OF LINCOLN, by George Grey Barnard, faces the entrance. The building, a hexagonal tower-like structure of white granite rising to a two-
story height, contains approximately 200 original documents, letters,
and manuscripts pertaining to Lincoln and his contemporaries, as well
as relics including carnelian cameo cuff links, used by Lincoln during
his stay in the White House; a packet Bible carried by General T. J.
(Stonewall) Jackson throughout the Civil War, and General U. S.
Grant's field Bible.

Southeast of Redlands US 99 steadily mounts rolling green hills
and intensively farmed valleys. The citrus groves of Redlands, eastern
outpost of southern California's navel orange belt, soon give way to
large apple orchards, interspersed with occasional pecan, almond, and
cherry groves, forerunners of the thousands of similar plantings to the

east. From 71.2 *m.,* Cherry Valley (L) and the ascending foothills beyond appear as a solid mass of cherry orchards, aglow with blooms in early spring.

On the L. above the dark mass of the SAN BERNARDINO MOUNTAINS, rises snow-capped SAN GORGONIO (11,485 alt.), and 20 miles south of it is the wind-beaten summit (R) of SAN JACINTO (10,800 alt.) towering above the San Jacinto Range. These two peaks are the highest in southern California.

SAN GORGONIO PASS, 72.7 *m.,* is a wide, gradually narrowing valley, which reveals itself as a pass on the eastern grade. The strong wind that always blows through the pass seldom changes its west-to-east direction, but when the infrequent east wind does blow, Los Angeles, 80 miles to the west, feels the sting of the so-called "Santa Anas" (*see Tour 3*). Though this is one of the best routes to and from the desert, it was seldom used by white men until the middle of the 19th century, because of the hostility of the Cahuilla tribes. In 1862 a stage line from Ehrenberg, on the Colorado River, to Los Angeles began operations through the pass. Extensive settlement, however, awaited the building of the Southern Pacific in 1875. The railroad company won the good will of the Indians by promising them free train rides, and in 1876 the first train through was greeted with enthusiasm.

BEAUMONT, 74.8 *m.* (2,559 alt., 2,208 pop.), in a mountainous setting near the summit of San Gorgonio Pass, is surrounded by small cultivated valleys having decided pastoral charm. Beaumont is the center of some 4,000 acres of cherry orchards, the principal varieties being Black Tartarians, Bings, Royal Anns, and Lamberts.

Since 1931 the blossoming of the trees has been celebrated with the Beaumont Japanese Cherry Festival (*April*) suggested by the cherry blossom fetes in Japan. Long lines of motor cars drive along the blooming orchards of cherries, almonds, apples, peaches, and plums.

East of the SUMMIT OF SAN GORGONIO PASS (2,600 alt.), 75 *m.,* the highway gradually descends a narrow depression between the mountains.

At 77.2 *m.* is the junction with a paved road.

Left on this road to HIGHLAND SPRINGS, 2 *m.* (2,700 alt.), a private resort and recreation and health center on 400 acres in the foothills of the San Bernardino Mountains. This, the first white settlement in San Gorgonio Pass, was founded in the 1870's on the old stage route from Ehrenberg (later from Yuma) to Los Angeles that crossed the present resort grounds; stage-coaches stopped here for meals and to change horses at the stage station, a one-story adobe structure, placed in service in 1871, and abandoned a few years later when the railroad was put through. Now used as a tool shed this weathered and crumbling building, with its leaking corrugated iron roof, and with only about one-third of the original structure standing, is the only remaining station along this old route.

BANNING, 80.9 *m.* (2,314 alt., 3,874 pop.), the center of southern California's almond-growing area, is the usual approach to the San Jacinto mountain resorts to the south, and is also the site of several sanatoriums. Surrounding the town, in addition to more than a thousand acres of almonds, are several hundred acres each of peaches, pears, apples, and plums; groves of walnuts and olives; and a few truck farms. In the town are a fruit cannery, several fruit-packing, shipping, and drying establishments, and a prune and apricot warehouse. The foothills north of Banning offer the best view of the almond orchards, which are covered in February with creamy white blossoms.

The town was laid out in 1883, and named for General Phineas Banning (*see The Harbor*). In the early 1860's, this site was a stop on the government's camel caravan route from the harbor at Wilmington to Tucson, Arizona. This, the last of the government's attempts to use camels for desert transportation, was discontinued after a year. The idea originated with Lieutenant Edward F. Beale (1822-93) who served with Stockton in California and traveled overland from the Pacific coast to Washington. Beale persuaded Jefferson Davis, then Secretary of War, to try the experiment. The 77 camels, purchased in Egypt and Arabia in 1856 and 1857, were accompanied by four Arab drivers. They were taken to Camp Verde in Texas, and there separated into two divisions. One operated between bases and outposts in Texas, New Mexico, and Arizona. The other was put in charge of Lieutenant Beale who employed them on his survey of a wagon route from Fort Defiance in northeastern Arizona to Fort Tejon (near Bakersfield) in Kern County, California. The charting was completed in 48 days. A few of the camels were taken on a little expedition south over Cajon Pass from Fort Tejon to Los Angeles, where they were met by the mayor and many curious citizens. After his retirement from the service and before his appointment in 1876 as minister to Austria-Hungary, Beale lived on his ranch near Bakersfield and frequently drove a team of camels to town.

The caravan continued to be employed in road construction and route-laying expeditions until the early 1860's, when it was quartered in Wilmington and used in transport between Los Angeles and the harbor, and between the harbor and points in Arizona. During the Civil War those interested in the camels were transferred to other parts, the animals were neglected, and the protests of mule breeders and drivers heeded. The camels were placed on auction and many were purchased by Samul McLeneghan of Sacramento, who took them through Los Angeles and raised $100 by racing them in Agricultural Park, now Exposition Park (*see Tour D*), before he sent them to Nevada mine owners. Within three years the herd was dispersed, some of the beasts escaping into the desert and others being turned loose as unmanageable nuisances. They wandered about the Mojave and Colorado desert regions, harried by plains wolves and shot at by startled prospectors, who told strange tales of the abandoned beasts. An Arizona cave was said to contain several mummified camels' bodies, well preserved in the rare desert air. Even as late as the 1920's a camel lived on the outskirts of Banning, pillaging feed supplies, nipping domestic plantings, frightening farm stock, demolishing camp tents, and doing whatever other damage occurred to his perverse camel mind. Finally a citizens' posse hunted him down and shot him.

East of Banning the green of the mountain slopes gradually fades to the dun-gray of sage and the bronze-green of mesquite and Spanish daggers (*see Tour 7*) grow in the rocky declivities.

In CABAZON, 85.7 *m.* (1,791 alt., 100 pop.), a Southern Pacific Railroad town, sandblasted and weatherworn by the almost continuous winds through the San Gorgonio Pass, is a roundhouse for auxiliary engines that help push freight and passenger trains over the grade. Most of the population is employed by the railroad. The name is a corruption of the Spanish word *cabezon* (big head), believed to have been used by early Spaniards in describing a big-headed Indian chief of the district.

The highway crosses the COLORADO RIVER AQUEDUCT, 87.7 *m.*, of the Metropolitan Water District of Southern California (*see The Historical Background*).

As the route continues its long descent to the desert floor, the velocity of the west wind becomes more pronounced in the restricted channel between the mountains. Cactus increases in number and variety; in the semiarid stretches immediately beside the road, is the deer-head, in the rocky slopes are the low, flat-leaved beavertail, and the Engelmann cactus, with its clusters of cylindrical-shaped leaves.

Sandy wastes stretching to the Indio Hills on the eastern horizon constitute a part of Coachella Valley. Straight ahead, beyond the eastern mouth of the pass, a queer, funnel-shaped apparatus is silhouetted against a background of rock-littered slopes. It is all that remains of the OLIVER POWER GENERATOR, a tube-shaped device resembling the barrel of a giant blunderbuss. This contrivance, removed far enough from the channel of greatest wind velocity to escape most of the drifting sand, was designed to transform the wind into electrical power by means of propellers within the tube. Although it worked, financial difficulties overwhelmed the inventor, and the machine was abandoned.

At 93.6 *m.* is the junction with State 111; R. on this route.

COACHELLA (Ind., small shells) VALLEY, 93.7 *m.,* is a great arid trough 50 miles long and 15 miles wide, bounded by the Little San Bernardino and the Cottonwood Mountains on the northeast and the San Jacinto and the Santa Rosa Mountains on the southwest. Part of it that reaches to the shore of Salton Sea is below sea level. Some millions of years ago Coachella Valley was the head of the Gulf of California, with a beach line still clearly seen, and on which agates, moonstones, and fossilized remains of aquatic life are found. The Colorado River eventually dammed the narrow gulf with silt, thus cutting off the upper end, and creating an immense lake. For a long time the lake was dried up—but an overflow of the Colorado in 1905-7 again filled it, creating the Salton Sea. This change is mentioned in legends of the near-by Cahuilla.

A quarter of a century of irrigation has transformed much of the valley into an agricultural region, producing dates, grapefruit, tangerines, early figs, winter vegetables, alfalfa, and cotton. Approximately 15,000 acres were in cultivation in 1938.

Extending south from the junction with US 99 is a series of sand dunes (L), known as ELEPHANT HEAD DUNES because of their shape. They vary in height from 3 to 12 feet, and are formed in rows, as if marching with the wind. The windward surface usually is covered with squaw tea, a short gray broomlike plant, about 30 inches high. The Indians believed a brew from this plant had medicinal value.

Southeast of the dunes is a billowing sand plain covered with squat honey mesquite (*see Tour 7*), creosotebush, and burroweed. Creosotebush is dark green, sticky to the touch, has a pungent smell and is covered with small yellow flowers in the spring. Burroweed is a small gray bush with a bitter taste that burros relish. From the bronze-green depths of a mesquite clump a roadrunner darts and races across the sand, his characteristic little red feather flashing from behind his head; lizards streak about, and everywhere the sand is marked with the tracks of rabbits, coyotes, pack rats, and occasionally the sinister S-shaped trails of sidewinders, a deadly type of rattlesnake. Rattlesnakes, however, shun man and are seldom seen along the highway. The San Jacinto Mountains (R) make an abrupt rise of almost two miles above the desert floor. In winter and spring the crests of the snowy peaks seem to float in the air, as the base is concealed by mists.

PALM SPRINGS, 104.2 *m*. (455 alt., 4,000 est. winter pop.), is an outpost of Hollywood and Park Avenue in the desert waste at the eastern foot of Mount San Jacinto. Where the copper-hued Agua Caliente Indians formerly trod, is a winter resort metropolis of swank shops, luxuriously-appointed inns, baths, theatres, and private estates, designed in the Spanish-Monterey style. During the winter season in the palm-shaded patios of hotels, liveried servants minister to the loungers and the sidewalks, bridle-paths, tennis courts, and golf greens are thronged with patrons. At night neon signs above the fashionable shops and the myriad lights of the settlement make a desert "white way." From December till May the resort houses a colony of affluent actors, writers, playwrights, and figures prominent in the nation's financial and industrial circles.

For many years before the movies spread glamor and luxury over its desert sands, Palm Springs was a small health resort chiefly dependent on tuberculous patients who lived in the screened porches of its few frame buildings.

Right from Palm Springs on Tahquitz Road to TAHQUITZ BOWL, 1 *m*., scene of a periodically presented desert play, *Tahquitz*, based on Indian legends of an evil spirit of that name who haunts Mount San Jacinto. The motor road ends at a parking place near the bowl, from which a short walk or horseback ride leads to TAHQUITZ FALLS, where the waters of Tahquitz Creek fall in a bridal veil drop over a rocky ledge. Queer rumblings, intensified by the sheer mountain walls, are heard in the canyon. These sounds terrified the Indians, who refused to enter the gorge, and embroidered their timidity with the legend of Tahquitz. According to the story the spirit of Tahquitz, who had been killed for abducting Amutat, the most beautiful girl in the tribe, returns here seeking Amutat or any other beautiful maiden and makes the canyon rumble with his calls.

At 106.2 *m.* is the junction with Palm Canyon Road.

Right on Palm Canyon Road to the PALM SPRINGS INDIAN RESERVA-TION (*adm. 25¢ a car*), 1.5 *m.* Usually the only Indian near the entrance is the extremely aged and profusely wrinkled watchman at the gate, who thrusts forth a copper-hued hand and mumbles something intended to convey the idea of "Two bits." The reservation consists of every other section of land in the Palm Springs district. Some of the tribesmen and their families live in the mountain canyons far from the highway; but others are the white man's land-lords, drive automobiles, and in general follow the white man's way of living. At 2.7 *m.* on Palm Canyon Road is the junction with Andreas Canyon Road; R. here 1 *m.* to the INDIAN CAVES (L), a series of small caverns in the foothill wall in which obsidian knives, ollas and other articles indicating early Indian occupation have been found. On a small plateau overlooking a mountain stream that flows past the caverns is a tree-shaded PICNIC GROUND (*free*). At 2.8 *m.* in Andreas Canyon is the so-called COUNCIL CHAMBER, an irregular circle about 100 feet in diameter rimmed by Washingtonia filifera palms.

In PALM CANYON, 4.5 *m.*, are 4,000 Washingtonia filifera palms, a species never found outside of the Colorado Desert. Some of these trees are 90 feet tall and are believed to be between 1,500 and 2,000 years old.

East of the Palm Canyon Road junction State 111 descends an outthrust spur of the SANTA ROSA MOUNTAINS (R) through the southern section of Coachella Valley.

The SMOKE TREE FOREST (R), 107.3 *m.*, is the largest grouping of the dead-looking indigo bush (*Dalea Spinosa*), sometimes called the smoke tree, in the Colorado Desert. Its lacework of leafless twigs from a distance resemble puffs of white smoke. At blooming time (*mid-June*) the trees are covered with clusters of pealike blossoms of a rare ultramarine color tinged with white.

CATHEDRAL CITY, 110.9 *m.* (315 alt., 250 est. pop.), is a settlement of neat white stucco auto camps, garages, and roadside cafes, so-named for a rock formation in Cathedral Canyon (R), the outline of which suggests a domed cathedral.

Commercial date gardens, for which the southeastern section of Coachella Valley is renowned, appear (L) at 112.2 *m.,* alternating with grapefruit orchards. The graceful palms border the highway and cast dark lacy shadows on its surface. Grapefruit growing, introduced here in the early 1920's, has been very successful and the fruit is noted for its high sugar content. In some areas grapefruit trees are planted between rows of date palms.

From INDIAN WELLS, 121.7 *m.* (97 alt., 75 pop.), a roadside village in the Coachella Valley date region, five million pounds of dates are shipped annually; the estimated crop for 1939-40 is 12 million pounds. Coachella Valley has 70 per cent of the 275,000 date palms growing in the United States. These domestic palms produce more than a tenth of the 65,000,000 pounds of dates annually consumed in this country though as late as 1920 all dates were imported from the Near East.

The Arabic requirement that "a date palm must have its feet in water and its head in the fires of heaven," is fulfilled in the Coachella Valley where the summer heat ranges from 110 to 140° in the shade, and the gardens are irrigated from deep wells every 10 days in summer and every three weeks during the rest of the year. This systematic irrigation regulates the amount of moisture in the fruit and combined with improved methods of culture produces a superior quality. King Feisal of Iraq, Mesopotamia, the world's largest production center for dates, acknowledged a gift from the Coachella Valley thus: "We, who have been growing dates for centuries, have never seen such fine dates in our own country."

Fruit growing in the old world was largely governed by superstition. Because date palms developed from seed are seldom true to the parent, the Arabs recommended that the seed be placed horizontally, then covered with a salt-manure mixture. They believed that the successful planter should possess a merry, philanthropic temperament, but that simulation of joy on the part of a badly dispositioned grower would immediately be obvious to the seed itself, resulting in its failure to grow. In old-world groves, several offshoots are left with the mother palm, as the Arabs maintained that a palm denuded of all its shoots would send forth no more. Roots were irrigated with date syrup or wine lees to insure sweet fruit. When the fruit prematurely fell from the tree as the result of bad weather, or from some other cause, the Arabian planter concluded that his enemy had tied a crab's leg to one of his trees and as a counter-charm erected in his date gardens a pole topped with a sheep's skull.

Pollination, the very essence of date growing, was to old-world growers a vaguely appreciated process. The prophet Mahomet once prohibited his followers from engaging in what he considered to be the unnatural practice of artificially impregnating the date palm. Upon the subsequent failure of the date crop, Mahomet expediently removed his ban.

About 1890, the Department of Agriculture was seeking new food crops for the millions of idle desert acres in America, and sent horticulturists to search the date regions of the Sahara, Algeria, Arabia, and the Nile Valley of Egypt. They brought back numerous varieties of date palm offshoots for testing in the desert regions of California, Arizona, and New Mexico. Success brought the importation of some of the choicest varieties from the Algerian Sahara and between 1912 and 1922 approximately 40,000 offshoots were planted. Mortality of the importations was high, since American growers knew little of date culture, but from those that survived the date growers of California and Arizona have developed their gardens.

Coachella growers have experimented with each of the three general classes of dates: the soft date; the semisoft date; and the dry or bread date. But as Americans prefer the soft or semisoft varieties, which have a high sugar and low moisture content, the valley planters have concentrated on the Deglet Noor variety, a richly flavored semisoft

Street Scenes

Burton O. Burt

IN THE OLD PLAZA

DEBATE IN PERSHING SQUARE

Burton O. Burt

Viroque Baker

**UNPACKING "HUACALES" (MEXICAN PACKING CASES),
OLVERA STREET**

**"LA VIEJA"
(THE OLD LADY),
OLVERA STREET**

Viroque Baker

MEXICAN BLACKSMITH, OLVERA STREET

**MEXICAN POTTER'S
"PRIESTO,"
OLVERA STREET**

Burton O. Burt

CHINESE MARKET

MEXICAN MARKET

Burton O. Burt

Burton O. Burt

MEXICAN NEWS STAND, NORTH MAIN STREET

JAPANESE NEWS STAND, EAST FIRST STREET

Burton O. Burt

ANGELUS TEMPLE

FLOP HOUSE AND "NICKEL SHOW," MAIN STREET

Burton O. Burt

A RUSHING BUSINESS

THE RECORD OF THE STARS, GRAUMAN'S CHINESE THEATER
Burton O. Burt

F. W. Carter

THE BROWN DERBY (WILSHIRE BOULEVARD)

PARASOL LIBRARY IN PERSHING SQUARE

F. W. Carter

date which has a small seed and is very successfully stored. When its ripe fruit is held to the light, the form of the seed is revealed through the translucent flesh; hence the name, which is properly transliterated Deglet Al-Nur (Arabic, date of light).

The only dependable method of propagating any specific variety is by means of the suckers or shoots that spring from the lower base of the tree and which, unlike the seed, are always true to the parent. A healthy female palm produces from 10 to 20 female offshoots. Male palms bear only male shoots. Carefully removed from the parent tree by means of wide, specially designed chisels, the offshoots are planted in rows about 50 to the acre. As young date gardens do not require full use of the soil, most growers plant onions, beans, and other vegetables between rows of young palms, in order to secure some profit during the six years before the date trees produce. Date culture is no poor man's enterprise; to carry one acre of dates to profitable fruition costs from $2,000 to $3,000.

Although the date requires abundant irrigation, rain is its greatest enemy; it breaks the fruit's delicate skin, causing a mold which readily destroys the entire crop. Consequently, during ripening season, date clusters are protected with heavy paper bags.

The date palm belongs to the dioecious group of plants that produce male and female flowers on separate trees. Occasionally, date palms produce male and female flowers on the same tree (monoecious), or even in the same cluster of blossoms (monoclinus); these freaks may revert annually to either sex.

Coachella Valley date palms bloom from about February 15 to May 1. The stalk or "paddle" of both sexes appears with its flowers encased in the sheathlike wrapping, or spathe. Sex of the trees is determined by their flowers; the male's white flowers are predominantly bunched toward the end of the "paddle," while female flowers are yellowish in color, have longer stems, and are more evenly distributed over the stalk. A slight rustling sound signifies maturity in the male blossom, and when cut, the spathe or leafy covering exudes a peculiar odor. The female bloom, anticipating impregnation, produces a drop of moisture which resembles a dewdrop.

Artificial pollination is necessary to secure satisfactory fruit; unpollinated dates are seedless, pale yellow, and contain no sugar. Experiments have proved that the clusters of dates on a single palm will differ in sugar content, size of seed, and ripening time if fertilized with pollen from different types of males. The ripening time can be altered as much as 30 days in this manner. Usually the gardens contain only three or four male trees for every three hundred females. As recently as 1913, growers used only the traditional Oriental method of pollination which consisted of tying sprigs of male flowers to the female flower clusters. Contemporary methods are more complicated, but also more effective. On the spring morning of their opening, the male blossoms are severed and dried. Their pollen or "dust" is transferred to the female blooms either by shaking the pollen on cotton puffs, which are then tied among the female blooms; by dusting it on with a brush, or by means of a spraying machine called the knapsack duster. This inexpensive machine is prodigal in the expenditure of pollen, but is a valuable time-saving device. Unless the female bloom receives the pollen within three or four days after its opening it is unreceptive.

The dates mature in about seven months and are harvested from early September to late December. The female tree produces from 10 to 20 fruit clusters that hang in curving garlands between the palm leaves. Certain clusters attain an individual weight of 30 pounds, and each tree bears from 200 to 350 pounds of fruit. The palm annually grows a new ring of fronds, or branches, and will reach a height of about a hundred feet. But because the cost of pruning, pollinating, and harvesting increases with the height of the tree most growers pull out and replace palms that are more than 50 feet tall. The dates on a cluster do not ripen simultaneously and must be picked one at a time. Fruit pickers reach the dates from square wooden platforms that are fastened to the tree, or from ladders which can be moved about the trees on circular tracks. Ripe dates are transferred from the pickers' small baskets to lug boxes and transported by truck to the packing plant.

There the dates are weighed and put through the first cleaning process, which consists of removing dust and sand with long, soft-bristle brushes. A sample of about 10 per cent is marked and forwarded to experts for grading, and the entire lot is judged by the per cent of each grade found in the sample.

Following compulsory fumigation, all fruit, including the sample, is placed in a second cleansing apparatus, which frequently consists of cylindrical drums lined with turkish toweling and equipped with revolving brushes. This polishing also removes the bloom.

As the dates pass on a moving belt over the grading tables experienced women sort them into fancy, choice, hydrated, and by-product. Graded dates are packed in 15-pound display bulk flats, three-pound fancy tins, and 14-ounce cellophane-wrapped boxes called the grocer's pack. They are placed in freezing storage to await shipment in refrigerated cars to midwestern and eastern cities, where they are stored in cold storage warehouses. The California date can remain in freezing storage for two years without deterioration.

The principal American by-product uses of dates are in candy, ice cream, and soft drink concoctions, and as an ingredient of cakes, cookies, and puddings. A government-sponsored program annually diverts from regular commercial channels more than a million pounds of fallen or second-grade dates for cattle, horse and hog food.

The SHIELDS DATE GARDENS (*open daylight hours*), 124.3 m., include one of America's oldest date groves, grown from seeds imported by the government in the 1880's. They also contain more than a hundred date varieties, each of which develops an individual flavor, color, shape, and size.

East of the SEA LEVEL MARKER, 125.4 *m*. (0 alt.), the descent is imperceptible; about seven feet to the mile.

INDIO, 128.4 *m*. (22 alt.; 2,296 pop.), is the commercial center of the Coachella Valley date, grapefruit, alfalfa, and cotton district. The highway winds through the town between rows of service stations, garages, cafes, and other appurtenances of tourist trade, backed on the west (L) by a scattered residential district merging into date gardens.

Indio originated in 1876 as a freight distributing point on the Southern Pacific Railroad and for almost 50 years slumbered in the desert heat, its railroad vagrants generally outnumbering its permanent population. It was not until US Highways 60, 70, and 99—which use the same route here, and State 111 began to bring motor traffic to the town, that it began to grow. This tourist travel has somewhat polished and subdued Indio, for once it was known as one of the lustiest and toughest of desert settlements. Today it has a circulating library, a theatre, and several churches.

Indio is at the junction of US 99, which provides an optional return route to the north junction with State 111.

Tour 3

TO SAN GABRIEL MISSION AND VALLEY

Los Angeles—Alhambra—El Monte—Puente—Pomona—Ontario—Riverside — Perris — Elsinore — Corona — Anaheim — Norwalk — Downey—Southgate—Los Angeles, 163.5 m.; Valley Blvd., US 60, US 395, State 71, State 18, State 10, Alameda St.

Concrete or asphaltic concrete roadbed throughout; three lanes between Los Angeles and Pomona; two lanes between Pomona and Southgate; three and four lanes between Southgate and Los Angeles.
Route paralleled between El Monte and Ontario by Southern Pacific R.R.; between Puente and Riverside by Union Pacific R.R.; between Riverside and Perris, and between Elsinore and Santa Fe Springs, by Santa Fe Ry.
All types of accommodations.

This route follows a roughly triangular course through the mountain-encircled plain which comprises the so-called Citrus Empire of southern California. The region has two divisions—the navel orange district around Riverside, and the Valencia district around Anaheim.

Scattered along the route are many reminders of California's more leisurely past. The De Anza Trail, the old road from Sonora, Mexico to Monterey, laid out by Captain Juan Bautista de Anza in the 1770's, is crossed at several points. Mission San Gabriel represents the period of early Spanish settlement, when the church dominated not only the cultural life of the region, but the economic life as well.

Here and there among the citrus groves, oil fields, and suburban real estate developments, gray-walled adobe ruins recall California's easygoing rancho days, when vast land grants—gifts of the Spanish Crown and later of the Mexican Government—were surveyed with carefree inexactitude by dons on horseback trailing 100-vara measuring cords behind them. These were the days when the land-owning, cattle-raising dons gradually usurped the power of the padres, reducing the missions to comparative impotence in the economic life of the region.

At the end of the route, below the San Jacinto Mountains, lies the country where Helen Hunt Jackson drew inspiration for her novel, *Ramona,* a work that has probably done as much as anything else to perpetuate California's romantic past.

From the LOS ANGELES CITY HALL, 0 *m.,* 1st and Main Sts., the route goes north on Main St. to Macy St.; R. on Macy St. to Mission Rd.; L. on Mission Rd. to Valley Blvd.; and R. on Valley Blvd.

ALHAMBRA, 6.1 *m.* (450 alt., 38,935 pop.), a residential and industrial community and a distributing point for an important fruit and vegetable growing district, lies at the western entrance to the San Gabriel Valley (*see Tour 1*). It has 50 factories, manufacturing products that range from oil refining equipment, to apiary supplies, yet is primarily a residential city. Amid towering old trees, wide lawns, and landscaped squares are more than 10,000 homes, most of them typical southern California stucco bungalows. Many of its residents are retired easterners and middle westerners; others commute daily to Los Angeles offices and factories.

The site of Alhambra is part of the 13,000-acre San Pascual Rancho (Holy Easter Ranch) of Manuel Garfias, Los Angeles County's first treasurer under American rule. The Garfias rancho was cut from the San Gabriel Mission lands during the Mexican period. It was acquired by J. D. Shorb and Benjamin D. Wilson, whose name is closely linked with the history of Mount Wilson (*see Tour 1A*). In 1874 they laid out a subdivision and called it the Alhambra Tract, so-called because someone in the Shorb family was reading Washington Irving's *The Alhambra* at the time, and convinced the subdividers that the Spanish countryside described by Irving (". . . a stern, melancholy country, with rugged mountains and long, sweeping plains, destitute of trees") was similar to the surroundings of the tract.

At 9.8 *m.* is a junction with Del Mar Ave.

Left on Del Mar Ave. 1.1 *m.* to a junction with Mission Dr.; L. on Mission Dr. is SAN GABRIEL, 1.4 *m.* (375 alt., 11,867 pop.), the first site settled by white men in Los Angeles County. Named for the fourth of the Spanish Franciscan Missions in California, the town grew up around the second Mission San Gabriel, built in 1776, and the third mission church, built in 1794. It was from the settlement of San Gabriel that Governor Felipe de Neve (*see The Historical Background*) led a small party of soldiers and colonists in 1781 to found El Pueblo de Nuestra Senora La Reina de Los Angeles (The Town of

Our Lady the Queen of the Angels). In 1848 when Mexico ceded California to the United States, San Gabriel had but 200 white inhabitants; even in 1913, when it was incorporated as a sixth-class city, the population was less than 2,000.

MISSION SAN GABRIEL ARCANGEL (*open 8-6; adm. 25¢*), 314 Mission Dr., founded in 1771 (consists of the church built in 1794, the former mission dormitories, a modern school, and a chapel. The church, rising above palm and pepper trees, is a long rectangular building 30 feet high, with yellow plastered adobe brick walls supported by massive buttresses that terminate in conical capitals, and broken by small deeply recessed windows. Here and there the surface has crumbled away, revealing aged brick. A brick outer stairway (R) leads to the dormitories, entered through a small wooden door. A simple arched door of wood at the entrance has replaced the original redwood portal, now preserved as a relic. Above the entrance in an ornamented niche stands a statue of a Franciscan and a small kneeling boy. In a belfry of the Spanish type, forming the left end of the building, hang four bells in arches of graduated size. The bell from the fifth arch was stolen many decades ago. Two of the bells were cast in 1795, two in 1828, and the largest in 1830.

The interior of the church has been redecorated and reconstructed. The beautifully colored statues above the altar are all of Spanish origin, and one was a gift, in 1773, from Queen Maria of Spain. Remains of eight priests who served the mission lie beneath the altar. On a stone base in the baptistry, under a curved, ornamented ceiling—called half an orange by the Indians—is a copper baptismal font older than the mission itself.

A white, shingle-roofed adobe, one story high, the former MISSION LIVING QUARTERS, adjoins the campanario on the left. A hedge-bordered walk, garden, and wooden columned portico relieve the simplicity of the expanses of plain wall. It now houses mission relics, among the most noted of which are an old unadorned confessional and several Indian paintings. The Stations of the Cross, painted on sailcloth, the colors made from flowers and berries, bears a resemblance to the art of modern Mexico.

West of the quarters stands the more modern COLEGIO DE SAN GABRIEL. Designed in the familiar mission style—its red-tile roof rising as high as that of the church—the school stands behind a long arcade. The BLESSED SACRAMENT CHAPEL, a modern, flat, tile-roofed building with dark-brown stuccoed walls and amber windowpanes, adjoins the church. Beyond this stretches a long cement wall, enclosing the ruins of a soap factory, and terminating in the cypress-guarded SAN GABRIEL CEMETERY, with its many old polished marble gravestones. It holds the graves of about 5,000 Indians buried one on top of another. From the yard the ruins of the old tower, destroyed in the earthquake of 1812, are seen.

San Gabriel was fourth in the chain of 21 California missions that extended from San Diego to Sonoma, north of San Francisco. Mission San Gabriel Arcangel was founded by the Franciscans, Angel Somera and Pedro Cambon, with the celebration of Mass on September 8, 1771, on a slight rise beside the river called Rio de San Miguel (river of Saint Michael). Subsequently the name was changed to San Gabriel River, after the mission, and later still, to Rio Hondo (deep river). Floods threatened the first chapel in 1776 (*see Tour 4*), and the mission was moved to a site four miles north, where one of adobe was built. The present church, 200 yards south of the site of the second chapel, was built between 1794 and 1806. For a time it was called San Gabriel de los Temblores (Saint Gabriel of the earthquakes). The name was fully justified in 1812 when a quake wrecked the tower at the southeast corner and damaged the roof.

San Gabriel Mission once owned a million and a half acres, extending from the Sierra Madre (mother mountain) to the sea. Between 1806 and 1830 its population was 1,700, and 40,000 cattle roamed its widespread ranges. After the secularization of the missions in 1833 its land deteriorated and in 1846 most of it was given by the Mexican Government to Hugo Reid and

William Workman "in payment for past services"—a transaction that was rescinded two months later.

Division of the lands among many people followed. In 1874 the United States Government granted a patent to the present 13-acre mission property to the Catholic Diocese of Los Angeles. Since 1908 the pastorate has been administered by the Claretian Fathers, who restored the chapel, converted the monastery into the museum, and built the parochial school.

The MISSION PLAYHOUSE, 320 Mission Dr., now a motion-picture theater, has a facade designed in the manner of Mission San Antonio de Padua in Monterey County, with curvalinear gable and flanking belfries. Until 1932 John Steven McGroarty's *Mission Play* was given here.

The GRAPEVINE ADOBE (*open 8-8; free*), Mission Dr. and Santa Anita Ave., adjoins the Mission Playhouse. Across the yellow-tinted adobe front a sign advertises it as the Birthplace of Ramona, vying for attention with a neon dine-and-dance sign set incongruously over the deeply recessed door in the adobe wall. A giant grapevine growing in the patio, sometimes erroneously referred to as the Mother Grapevine in California, was brought here from a canyon in the San Gabriel Mountains in 1861.

LAS TUNAS ADOBE (the cactus house), 308 Mission Dr., an L-shaped 10-room structure (*private*) standing among luxuriant vegetation on a remnant of the once-vast Rancho Las Tunas, was built early in 1776 as living quarters for the padres while the mission building was under construction. In 1805, 400 orange seedlings brought from Mexico were planted in the garden—the first in California. None of them remains. After the adobe passed out of mission control in 1846, various private owner-occupants enlarged it and modernized the interior.

The MAY PLACE (*private*), 725 W. Carmelita St., a gray one-story house with a red tar-paper roof and purple chimney, is the only one of the 19th-century group of San Gabriel adobe houses that was built by an Easterner. It was erected in 1851 by J. R. Everton, Los Angeles' first census taker.

The VIGARE ADOBE (*private*), 616 S. Ramona St., a long, generously proportioned one-story building, with walls higher than those of the mission period, is approached through an old-fashioned garden of orange trees, rose bushes, and jasmine. A modern porch has replaced the old ground-level corridor. The house was built by a soldier of the mission guard.

LA CASA VIEJA DE LOPEZ (the old house of Lopez), 330 Santa Anita Ave., a low, one-story white structure (*private*), was one of the early auxiliary buildings of the mission.

ROSEMEAD, 11.2 *m.* (287 alt., 8,121 pop.), a shopping and distributing center for a poultry and rabbit raising, citrus and vegetable growing district, was named for Leonard J. Rose, a cattleman and vineyardist of the 1860's, upon part of whose ranch the unincorporated town stands.

EL MONTE (the mountain), 13.3 *m.* (290 alt., 4,746 pop.), is the oldest American settlement in Los Angeles County. It grew up around a trading post established in 1849 by Ira Thompson on the Spanish Trail, which was an unofficial extension of the Santa Fe Trail. The post did a thriving business since it was one of the few well-watered camping grounds along this section of the route. The Spanish Trail, sometimes erroneously called the Santa Fe Trail, surveyed in the early 1820's for the benefit of American traders who wanted to tap the rich Santa Fe market after it was freed from Spanish monopoly by the Mexican Revolution, ran from the banks of the Missouri, in the neighborhood of Independence, to Santa Fe, New Mexico. It developed slowly; because of the nature of the terrain between Santa Fe and

Los Angeles, southern California could be reached with much less difficulty by sea. A few hardy traders and trappers followed the route in the 1830's. The first immigrants to use it were the 25 members of the Rowland-Workman party, which set out from Independence in 1841. Few others followed their example until the gold rush began and even then the route was not particularly popular. Traders and immigrants alike often celebrated the end of the difficult journey here and El Monte was known as a tough frontier town until completion of the first transcontinental railroad in 1869 diverted overland traffic to central California.

Resembling an African stockade with its spiked-pole fence and bamboo thickets, GAY'S LION FARM, 14.3 m. (open daily except Mon. 10-5; adm. 25¢), is the breeding farm and home of more than 200 African lions. Many of the animals raised here are trained for circuses, zoos, amusement parks, and motion-picture studios.

The route crosses the SAN GABRIEL RIVER, 15.5 m., beside which, the Gaspar de Portola Expedition camped on July 30, 1769 (see The Historical Background).

BASSETT, 15.9 m. (296 alt., 216 pop.), is a Puente Valley shipping point for oranges, lemons, walnuts, and vegetables.

Southeast of Bassett walnut and citrus groves stretch along the highway (L) in an almost unbroken wall of green foliage. The two-mile-wide plain (R) extending from the highway at 16 m. to the PUENTE HILLS is prairie, broken here and there by small tracts planted with vegetables.

At 18.9 m. is the junction with Central Ave.

Right on Central Ave. 0.2 m. to a private road; L. here to the WORKMAN HOMESTEAD, 0.4 m. (adm. by arrangement with caretaker), a two-story building whose first story was built in 1844 by William Workman, joint owner with John Rowland of the 48,000-acre Rancho de la Puente (ranch of the bridge). Workman, a keen-eyed, thin-lipped Englishman who has been described as "hard-boiled and stern," was a member of a wagon-train party led by John Rowland over the Spanish Trail in 1841. Rowland immediately secured the vast land grant from the Mexican Government and, eager to have a white neighbor near by, offered Workman, his former business associate, half the rancho land if he would build a home and settle here. Each built an adobe house near San Jose Creek, about a quarter-mile apart; only Workman's remains, crowning a knoll within the shadow of his grandson's baronial mansion. The addition of a second floor to the original one-story adobe was made in 1871 by Francisco P. F. Temple, Workman's son-in-law, called Templito (little Temple). In the California financial panic of 1875 his investments crashed and E. J. "Lucky" Baldwin foreclosed on all of Temple's ranches and town property, as well as the ranches of Workman, who had mortgaged them to assist his son-in-law. In 1876 Workman died in the old homestead, a broken man. In 1916, after he had rehabilitated the family prosperity by the discovery of oil in the Montebello Hills, Walter Temple, son of Templito, regained the ancestral adobe and the 92 acres on which it stands —all that remained undivided of the original grant. After restoring the adobe young Temple built TEMPLE MANSION in 1924. It has sixteen rooms and three-foot-thick walls of adobe made on the grounds by Mexicans imported especially for the job. Temple occupied the estate for six years. In 1931, paralleling the experience of his grandfather a half-century before, he lost it through foreclosure.

The WORKMAN FAMILY CEMETERY, an iron-fenced, old-fashioned plot established by William Workman in 1858, lies 300 yards southeast of the mansion. Simple headstones identify the graves of members of the Workman, Rowland, and Temple families; between them are the unmarked graves of many an Indian and Mexican retainer of the rancho's heyday. In the TEMPLE MAUSOLEUM, built in 1923 by Walter Temple in memory of his wife and grandfather, is the unmarked CRYPT OF PIO PICO, one-time wealthy southern California ranchero and last Mexican Governor of California (*see Tour 4*).

Pico died in greatly reduced circumstances in his Los Angeles home on September 11, 1894, at the age of 93. He was buried beside the body of his wife in old Calvary Catholic Cemetery on Buena Vista Street (now North Broadway). A quarter of a century later when the old cemetery was about to give way to Los Angeles' building boom, no one claimed the remains of the former governor and his wife, so Walter Temple volunteered.

PUENTE, 19.8 *m.* (329 alt., 2,200 pop.), is the shipping and packing center for walnut and citrus growers in the southern end of San Gabriel Valley, known locally as La Puente Valley. In Puente are two citrus packing plants, a bean-cleaning establishment, and one of the largest walnut packing plants in the United States.

The eastern end of SAN JOSE VALLEY is at 21 *m.* This narrow, natural corridor of rolling land bounded by the Puente Hills (R) and the San Jose Hills (L) produces lemons, walnuts, and oranges. Considerable acreage in the northwest part is devoted to floriculture, particularly roses.

WALNUT, 23.7 *m.* (400 alt., 275 pop.), is a rail shipping point for the San Jose Valley's walnut crop.

California produces 60 or 70 million merchantable pounds of walnuts annually, or 97 per cent of the total United States crop.

The Persian walnut, known to Americans as the English walnut, was cultivated by the Romans; as Jupiter's acorn it was used by the Persians as a medium of barter. From there, in more recent times, it spread to China and southern Europe, and was brought to California in 1769 by the Franciscan Fathers. Commercial walnut culture in California began in 1867 when Joseph Sexton planted a sack of the nuts near Santa Barbara.

The average walnut grove consists of about 20 acres, planted with 400 trees that yield 1,305 pounds to the acre.

Commercially all California-produced English walnuts fall in three classes: soft shells, budded, and fancy varieties. The soft shells are descendants of the trees planted by Sexton in 1867 and are produced from seedling trees grown from soft-shell nuts. The budded walnut is produced by grafting the bud of a bearing English walnut tree on a California black walnut seedling. The fancy varieties are produced by five kinds of trees: Concord, Eureka, Franquette, Mayette and Payne, the stocks of which are imported from France.

Both blooms, the staminate (male) and the pistillate (female), occur on the same tree. The male bloom is on a long catkin and is about the size of the average man's forefinger. It carries an abundance of light dusty yellow pollen. The female or fruiting blossom is in reality an immature nut; it is about the size of a fingernail, is a waxen white color, and has two feathery branched stigmas that catch the pollen carried from the male blooms by the breeze. After pollinization the male withers away. A majority of the walnut trees in California blossom in April and May.

Harvesting season begins in September and ends in November. As a rule the grower harrows the ground around the trees and runs a drag over it, leaving a smooth soft surface to receive the crop. At maturity the nuts drop of their own accord. Some growers gather the walnuts from the ground day by day; others at intervals of two or three days. Nuts which do not fall are knocked down by shaking the limbs with long hooked poles, or by men and boys who climb the trees and shake the limbs.

After removal of the crop to a field house the few nuts which have failed to rid themselves of the husks are cleaned by machine, then washed in a large cylindrical drum to remove the juice of the crushed hulls. After an ethylene gas treatment to hasten maturity of the hull, the crop is placed in large trays in the sun, or in dehydrating machines for drying.

The nuts are now ready for processing in the packing plants of the marketing organization. Here they are weighed-in, sized, separated as to quality, and placed in large bleaching drums, where stains left in husking are removed. Again the product is sized and dried, then crack-tested and branded with the trade name of the packing organization. Printing machines stamp the trade mark on 30,000 pounds of nuts in an eight-hour day.

The white stucco, red-tile-roofed buildings (R) of PACIFIC COL-ONY, 28.5 m. (*open 9-11 and 1-4 Tues., Thurs. and Sun.*), a state home for the feeble-minded, are surrounded by more than 200 acres of fruit orchards, vegetable gardens, and hayfields that are worked by the inmates.

SPADRA, 28.7 m. (705 alt., 306 pop.), is a cluster of one-story buildings around a general store. Here in the 1860's William (Uncle Billy) Rubottom opened a tavern that soon became a station on the Butterfield Stage Line. The settlement that developed about the tavern was named for Spadra Bluffs, Arkansas, Uncle Billy's home town.

In Spadra is a junction with a private road.

Right here across Diamond Bar Ranch to CASA VEJAR, 1 m. (*private*). Considered in its time the finest adobe in the entire region, this two-story structure was built in 1855 by Ramon Vejar.

The PHILLIPS HOUSE (*private*), 31 m., a two-story mansard-roofed, red-brick structure of 13 rooms, was built by Louis Phillips in 1866 when he acquired title to Rancho San Jose de Abajo. This was the first brick house in Pomona Valley.

Rancho San Jose was granted in 1837 by Governor Alvarado to Ygnacio Palomares and Ricardo Vejar of Los Angeles. By 1846 the rancho was split into northern and southern sections. North Pomona, La Verne, and parts of Pomona and Claremont (*see Tour 2*) were founded on lands of the upper rancho. The lower rancho spread over San Jose and Puente Valleys, including the sites of Puente, Spadra, and the western section of Pomona (*see Tour 2*).

At 31.1 *m.* is a junction with 2nd St.; R. on 2nd St., now the main route.

POMONA, 32.5 *m.* (859 alt., 23,539 pop.) (*see Tour 2*).

Points of Interest: Christian Oak, Ganesha Park, Palomares Adobe, Camphor Tree, Alvarado Adobe, Los Angeles County Fairgrounds, and others.

East (straight ahead) on 2nd St. to Garey Ave.; R. on Garey Ave. to 5th Ave.; L. on 5th Ave. (US 60).

At 36.3 *m.* is a junction with Central Ave.

Right here to CHINO, 3 *m.* (713 alt., 4,204 pop.), trade center for a fruit and sugar beet-growing district in southwestern San Bernardino County. The town was founded in 1887 when part of the Rancho del Chino was subdivided into 10-acre farms around a mile-square townsite. The vaqueros herded the cattle of Antonio Lugo here in the early 1840's, when the old Rancho Santa Ana del Chino was granted. In 1843 Colonel Isaac Williams, a son-in-law, bought Lugo's place and added it to his own holdings to form a ranch of more than 35,000 acres, at that time the largest single Yankee holding in southern California.

One of the skirmishes of the American conquest of California was fought here in September 1846, when a company of American riflemen barricaded themselves in the ranch house, but having exhausted their ammunition, were forced to surrender. The more important Americans were held prisoners of war until Los Angeles was retaken in 1847.

The Spanish word *chino* is loosely translated as Chinese, but in provincial Spanish may also mean curly-headed. According to one story Don Antonio added del Chino to the ranch's name because his major-domo, a half-breed Indian, had curly hair.

The CALIFORNIA STATE PRISON FOR FIRST OFFENDERS (L), 5.4 *m.,* on a tract of more than 2,000 acres between Edison St., Central, Euclid, and N. Robles Aves., was begun in June 1938. Expected to be completed in the summer of 1941, it is designed to hold 2,100 first offenders and milder law violators, who will be segregated here from the more hardened criminals at Folsom and San Quentin Prisons. The completed plant, of 21 buildings, will have 14 dormitories of 52-bed capacity each, with one block of 400 cells for confinement of the more difficult prisoners. An innovation is a proposed psychiatric hospital for the care of prisoners who have been convicted after a plea of not guilty by reason of insanity.

ONTARIO, 38.5 *m.* (979 alt., 14,197 pop.) (*see Tour 2*).

Points of Interest: Armstrong Nurseries, lemon and orange packing plants, and others.

In Ontario is the junction with US 60 which follows California Blvd. East (straight ahead) on California Blvd. (US 60).

In the eastern outskirts of Ontario, US 60 turns southeast through the vineyards of San Bernardino County's grape and wine district (*see Tour 2*).

MIRA LOMA, 46.8 *m.* (787 alt., 250 est. pop.), lies in the northwest corner of Riverside County's most important grape-growing district. The town, first named Wineville, assumed its present name in 1930.

Mission Boulevard (US 60) crosses the SANTA ANA RIVER, 54.7 *m.*, on a graceful concrete viaduct, flanked by pylons. Below the level of the road is green FAIRMOUNT PARK (L), with its 40-acre Lake Evans; Mount Rubidoux (R) rises above the broken volcanic masses that litter its flanks.

At 55.4 *m.* is a junction with Rubidoux Mountain Dr.

Right here (*up-traffic only; road closed at 8 p.m.*) up MOUNT RUBIDOUX (1,364 alt.), a volcanic formation rising 500 feet above the surrounding country at Riverside's western entrance. The road, barely the width of an automobile, winds through thickets of pine and oak, with prickly-pear cactus forming a roadside border for much of the way.

The WORLD PEACE TOWER (*always open*), 2.1 *m.*, was erected in 1925 by neighbors and friends of Frank A. Miller (*see below*).

The summit of Mount Rubidoux, 2.3 *m.*, is a narrow plateau, rimmed with a natural parapet of boulders, with two slightly higher knolls terraced into great stairways to seat worshippers during the annual Easter Sunrise Services. On the highest crag is the SERRA CROSS, unveiled in 1907 by William Howard Taft in honor of Junipero Serra, founder of the California missions. The Serrano and Cahuilla Indians considered Rubidoux a sacred mountain and used its summit as a meeting place for religious ceremonies. In 1909 the first civic Easter sunrise service in southern California was held here, and the services that followed annually thereafter soon became a model for those of numerous other cities. Every Easter, hours before dawn, thousands of persons climb the various footpaths, and motor cars inch slowly upward, discharging passengers at the summit and descending the one-way road on the opposite side. Mount Rubidoux was named for Louis Rubidoux, onetime owner of Jurupa Rancho (*see below*).

RIVERSIDE, 56.6 *m.* (851 alt., 34,696 pop.), is the seat and largest city of Riverside County, and second largest commercial center of the southern California navel orange belt. A city of tree-shaded boulevards, in its residential districts are some of the finest examples of Spanish colonial and mission architecture in the state.

The site of Riverside was a part of the Jurupa Rancho, and belonged to San Gabriel Mission until 1833. Louis Rubidoux came to California in the early 1840's, and in 1847 bought more than 11,000 acres of Jurupa Rancho. A year before his death in 1869 Rubidoux sold a large part of the rancho to Louis Prevost, a French nurseryman and silk expert, who planted mulberry trees and attempted to found a silk industry. Some of these trees are in Fairmount Park. The silk venture expired with Prevost's death in 1869, and the rancho passed to John W. North, of Knoxville, Tennessee, and his associates in the Southern California Colony Association, who in 1870 laid out the townsite of Jurupa—later renamed Riverside for its site near the Santa Ana River.

The architecture of the post office, city hall, public library, municipal auditorium, and other buildings grouped about the civic center, at 7th and Orange Sts., reveals Spanish influences.

The RUMSEY INDIAN MUSEUM, in the basement of the City Hall, 7th and Orange Sts. (*open daily except Sun. 12-4; free*), contains an Aztec calendar stone and other Indian artifacts and relics gathered by the museum's founder and donor, Cornelius Earle Rumsey, local philanthropist.

The MISSION INN (*organ concerts*), bounded by 6th and 7th, Main and Orange Sts., is a luxury hotel noted for its atmosphere, and its collection of Spanish historical objects. The inn's several buildings have numerous Spanish and Mexican features and are connected by loggias, corridors, and solariums that enclose tropical patios. An ivy-clad wall along 7th Street gives access to a courtyard lush with semitropical trees and shrubs. Colored tile flower boxes line the edges of the courtyard, a fountain from Cordoba, Spain, ornaments the center, and every angle reveals arches, iron gates and grilled windows, statuary, clock towers and belfries. In the courtyard is an adobe house, built in 1875 by Captain C. C. Miller and used by his wife to "take in boarders."

In an addition to the inn completed in 1932, are the SAINT FRANCIS CHAPEL with a golden Mexican altar and Tiffany windows; the Rotonda Internacional, meeting place of the Institute of World Affairs; the Galeria; and the Oriental Court. Autographs of noted flyers are inscribed on the wing-shaped copper plaques of the Aviators' Shrine in St. Francis courtyard.

Right from Riverside on State 18, a shorter alternate route to Corona that follows Market St. and Magnolia Ave. The large eucalyptus and pepper trees along the center strip of the double driveway were planted in 1876 by John W. North, who named the street for the magnolias he had intended to plant before he learned that they would cost $2 each and pepper or eucalyptus trees only five cents apiece.

Low PARK (R) 2.6 *m.*, bounded by Magnolia, Palm, and Luther Aves., contains a Friendship Grove symbolizing world friendship and peace.

In a small park area enclosed by an ornamental iron fence, stands the PARENT NAVEL ORANGE TREE (R), 2.7 *m.*, one of two planted in 1873 by Mrs. Eliza Tibbets in her front yard at what is now 4374 Central Avenue. After buds from the trees had been successfully planted the demand soon exceeded the supply and a high barbed-wire fence was placed around the trees to prevent buds being stolen. The first navel orange grove of record was that of B. B. Barney, Brockton and Central Aves., across the street from the Tibbets homestead. In the settlement of the Tibbets estate, one of the original trees was given to Frank A. Miller, who transplanted it to the courtyard of the Mission Inn in 1903. It died early in 1939. The other, presented to the city of Riverside, and placed here in 1902, is some 12 feet tall and still produces a normal orange crop. The State Experimental Citrus Station cares for the tree and protects it with windbreaks and smudge pots.

On a 40-acre campus, (L) between Jackson and Irving Sts., are the mission-style buildings of the SHERMAN INDIAN INSTITUTE (*open 8-4 during school term*). The institution, established in Perris Valley in 1892 and moved here in 1901, is named for James S. Sherman, Vice President of the United States during the Taft administration.

The school is coeducational, and admits only students between the ages of 14 and 21 who are at least one-fourth Indian and are ready to enter the eighth grade or high school. During 1931-32, there were more than a thousand students belonging to 84 tribes, from 16 different states. Courses include academic instruction, and training in 27 trades for the boys and in seven for the girls. The students landscaped the grounds, built all but 12 of the buildings and work on the school's 200-acre farm.

At 13.9 *m.* is the junction with State 71 in Corona (*see below*).

US 60 follows 7th St. to Lemon St.; R. on Lemon to 8th St.
At 60.7 *m.* is a junction uniting US 60 with US 395.

The white stucco Spanish-type buildings of the STATE EXPERIMEN-
TAL CITRUS STATION (*open 9-5; guides*), 61.1 *m.*, which conducts
the only (1940) school of orange culture, occupies more than 700 acres
on the foothill slopes of the Box Springs Mountains. The station,
established by special legislative act in 1913, is operated in connection
with the College of Agriculture of the University of California at Los
Angeles, and provides information and advice to citrus growers. Facilities include a research library, laboratories, insectary, and glass and
lath culture houses. Students and investigators come here from many
parts of the world to study subtropical agriculture.

At 61.2 *m.* is the foot of the Box Springs Grade. A broad view
extends from the summit west over Riverside County and its checker-
board of navel orange groves, and south across the flat mesa land of
Alessandro Valley, which distantly merges into the broken plain of
Perris Valley.

At 62.1 *m.* US 60 branches L. from US 395; R. on US 395.

MARCH FIELD (*adm. by advance arrangement*), 67 *m.,* spreading
over more than 600 acres in Alessandro Valley, has been the headquarters of the First Wing, G.H.A. Air Force, United States Army Air
Corps, since 1935 and center of the Air Defense Zone of 11 Western
States. Complementing the active flying units are a station force, photographic section, and ordnance, quartermaster, medical, finance, and wing
headquarters detachments.

March Field, established in 1918 as a flying school, was named for
Lieutenant Peyton C. March, Jr., a casualty of the World War.
From 1921 to 1927 it was on inactive status, and since 1931 when all
school activities were concentrated in Texas, it has been manned by
tactical units of the Army Air Corps.

South of March Field are Alessandro and Perris Valleys, dun-gray
prairie lands, relieved at intervals by chicken and turkey ranches. In
the San Jacinto Mountains (L) the highest peak is MOUNT SAN
JACINTO (10,805 alt.); on the R. the mesa is broken by isolated buttes,
rising successively higher to the SANTA ANA MOUNTAINS on the western horizon.

PERRIS, 76.1 *m.* (1,500 alt., 1,011 pop.), is the trade center for
Perris Valley, and a shipping point for forage crops, potatoes, deciduous
fruits, and dairy and poultry products. The town also draws considerable trade from the Good Hope mining district (*see below*).

Left from Perris on State 74 to HEMET, 16.9 *m.* (1,600 alt., 2,595 pop.),
in the country that formed the setting for Helen Hunt Jackson's *Ramona.*
The town is surrounded by the orchards, grain fields, and poultry ranches of
the San Jacinto Valley. Every spring (*about May 1*) the towns of Hemet and
San Jacinto dramatize the story of Ramona in the Ramona Bowl (*see below*).
In the afternoon and early evening of the three Saturdays preceding the play,
Hemet stages a municipal fiesta with costume dancing and community singing,
in the Santa Fe Station Square. Turkey raising is an important industry
here, and the Hemet Turkey and State District Fair has been held here

annually (*Nov.*) since 1936. Hemet is a variation of Hemica, name of a Soboba Indian woman.

At 17.7 *m.* on the main side road is a junction with San Jacinto Rd. (State 83); L. here 2.6 *m.* to SAN JACINTO (1,550 alt., 1,356 pop.), hub of a small agricultural district having many mineral springs. The town was founded in 1872 by Procco Akimo, a Russian exile, who erected the first store in what is now Old Town. Russians have other connections with the area; three of them ended the longest (1939) nonstop flight in the history of aviation—Moscow to San Jacinto Valley—on July 8, 1937, in a cow pasture three miles west of the town. The townsite was laid out by H. T. Hewitt, for whom Hewitt Street was named. On this street formerly stood the Palma House, with its hitching rack from which Juan Diego took the horse of Sam Temple, who retaliated by shooting the Indian. Mrs. Jackson calls Diego, Alessandro, and Temple, Jim Farrar, and makes the shooting the climax of her story.

Across the street from the Palma House was the brick house of Mrs. J. C. Jordan, with whom Mrs. Jackson lived while gathering material for *Ramona*. All that remains of the place today, which was referred to in the book as Aunt Ri's Cabin, is the milkhouse. In answer to other California areas, claiming to be the *Ramona* setting, people of this section point to the docket of the San Jacinto justice court, recording the shooting of Juan Diego, the Indian, under circumstances that are little changed in the book; a letter from Dr. H. G. Hewitt, of Santa Rosa, Calif., to the publisher of the Hemet *News*, relating how Temple rode out one day with Hewitt's shotgun, and returned with the tale of having shot the Indian who had stolen his horse; and an interview given to the Hemet *News* by Mrs. Jordan a few years before her death in which she substantiated many of the incidents of the book.

In the foothills rising at San Jacinto's eastern boundary is the SOBOBA (Ind., warm place) INDIAN RESERVATION, last refuge of the 127 survivors of the Soboba, a branch of the Cahuilla that once inhabited this region in large numbers. Many of the reservation Indians work in neighboring towns, and as seasonal harvest hands on ranches and farms. The women weave baskets for sale to tourists. In SOBOBA VILLAGE is the Indian school, to which the first Indian teacher employed by the United States was assigned in 1880. According to Indian legend, MASSACRE CANYON, in the mountains southwest of the village, was the scene of a savage battle in pre-Spanish days. The fighting, which started over a cache of grain, continued for a day till the Temecula drove the Ivah to the edge of a steep cliff, and slaughtered all who did not jump.

Along the base of the San Jacinto Mountains are several mineral springs, believed to have healing properties.

At 17.9 *m.* on the main side road (State 74) is a junction with Girard St.; R. here 2.4 *m.* to RAMONA BOWL, in the San Jacinto foothills in which the *Ramona Pageant* has been presented annually since 1923 (*2 performances each weekend for 3 weeks; usually in April-May; adm. 50¢ and $1*). The huge, distorted rock masses, on the slopes that form the natural amphitheater, are the result of volcanic action. No actual stage is used, the action taking place on the boulder-strewn mountainside opposite the concrete tiered seating section (6,000 capacity), and on the front porch of a replica of the Camulos ranch house, the hacienda of the Moreno family mentioned in the novel.

At 20.6 *m.* is the site of an ancient INDIAN VILLAGE. A series of flat rocks, punctuated with metate grinding holes, is the only remaining evidence of the prehistoric community. Because Cahuillas lived in this area, it is considered probable that the village site was the home of some related tribe.

Southwest of Perris US 395 proceeds through a region of broken volcanic hills (R) along the base of STEELE PEAK (2,528 alt.).

GOODHOPE, 80.5 *m.* (1,550 alt., 150 est. pop.), is a trade center for a gold-mining district within a radius of four or five miles. The settlement takes its name from the Goodhope Mine, now inactive, which in the 1880's yielded one million dollars' worth of gold ore.

ELSINORE, 88 *m.* (1,300 alt., 1,552 pop.), on the northern shore of Lake Elsinore, is a residential and resort city noted for its mineral springs. Natural hot sulphur water is piped to every home in the city through a municipally operated water system. The medicinal springs are known as the Seven Health Waters and are said to have therapeutic value in the treatment of rheumatism, liver, and kidney ailments.

The contiguous area is a rich fruit district, checkerboarded with orchards, citrus groves, and vineyards.

LAKE ELSINORE, extending from the town's western edge to the foot of the Santa Ana and Elsinore Mountains, is the center of the district's water-sport activities, and the scene of periodic regattas. The lake is fed by waters from the San Jacinto Mountains. A part of this run-off is impounded in Hemet Reservoir, southeast of Hemet, the balance flows down the San Jacinto River and empties here. After heavy rainy seasons, Lake Elsinore is more than a mile wide, four miles long, and 15 feet deep; during protracted periods of meager run-off the lake contracts by evaporation to little more than a smelly pond, with reed-grown marshy borders.

The town and lake are named for the fortified seaport of Elsinore in Zeeland Island, Denmark, scene of Shakespeare's *Hamlet.* Juan Machado, native Californian grantee of the 12,000-acre ranch on which the city was established, died believing that the Americanos had named their town "El Senor" in his honor.

Southwest (straight ahead) on Main St. (US 395) to Graham Ave.; R. on Graham Ave. (State 71-74).

The former SUMMER HOME OF AIMEE SEMPLE McPHERSON (*private*), 88.7 *m.,* the Los Angeles evangelist, is a white Moorish-type building overlooking Lake Elsinore from a knoll in the Clevlin Hills (R).

At 91.2 *m.* State 74 branches L.; the route goes R. on State 71.

ALBERHILL, 94 *m.* (1,320 alt., 200 est. pop.), at the mouth of Temescal (Ind., sweat bath) Canyon, is the trade center for an extensive pottery-clay mining and brick and tile manufacturing district. The best quality and largest variety of clays in California for the manufacture of pottery, brick, tile, and heavy-duty dishes are found here. The workings consist of pits, 50 to 75 feet deep, in the perpendicular walls of which are exposed strata of lignite and vari-colored clays, in vertical beds of blue, white, red, and pink. Between 90,000 and 100,000 tons of clay are mined annually, and about 50 tons of coal a year. Most of the latter is used as fuel by the Mexican pit and kiln workers.

At 11.5 *m.* is a junction with Coldwater Canyon Rd.

Left here to GLEN IVY HOT SPRINGS (*rates nominal*), 0.7 *m.,* a privately operated resort at the mouth of Coldwater Canyon in the Santa Ana Mountains. The waters are basically sulphurous, have a maximum temperature of 103°, and are claimed to have curative properties. For these springs, used by the Indians for bathing purposes, the main canyon was named Temescal (*see above*). Relics of former Indian occupation, found in the hotel grounds, have been assembled into a small INDIAN MUSEUM (*open 8-6; free*), in which stone bowls, metates, and other primitive utensils for preparing food are displayed.

In a copse of pepper trees (L), at 101.7 *m.*, is the SERRANO MEMORIAL, a boulder with bronze plaque marking the site of the first house in Riverside County, built about 1824 by Leandro Serrano, the son of a Spanish soldier.

A weather-worn stretch of adobe wall (R) is all that remains of the TEMESCAL CANYON BUTTERFIELD STAGE STATION, 105.9 *m.*

The smooth concrete of State 71 winding up Temescal Canyon northwest of the Serrano Memorial bears little resemblance to the rutty dusty trail followed by John Butterfield's lumbering stages from 1858 to 1861. The first stage left Tipton, Missouri, on September 15, 1858, and arrived in Los Angeles on October 7. Though overland stage service was moved to a route through Wyoming after operating only three years, the Butterfield stages established the route later used by the Wells Fargo Stage and Express Company.

From its eastern terminus in St. Louis, Missouri, the route ran through Fort Smith, Arkansas; El Paso, Texas; and Tucson and Yuma, Arizona. In California it crossed Imperial County to a station at Warner Hot Springs and another near Temecula, then roughly paralleled today's US 395 and State 71 northwestward, through Temescal Canyon, past the site of Corona, to a junction with the old Los Angeles and San Bernardino Road.

Operation of the line required 100 coaches, 1,000 horses, 500 mules, and 800 men. Advertisements in the East warned of attack from Indians: "Fare $200 in gold. Passengers are advised to provide themselves with a Sharp's rifle and one hundred rounds of ammunition . . . Twenty-four days of travel in our luxurious stages and you will arrive in the 'Land of Gold'."

At 106.3 *m.* is a junction with Cajalco Canyon Rd.

Right here to CAJALCO DAM AND RESERVOIR, 5 *m.*, terminus of the Colorado River Aqueduct (*see Tour 2*). The reservoir contains 225,000 acre-feet of water and is the largest man-made lake in California.

At 13 *m.* is a junction with a dirt road. Left on this is lonely MOCKINGBIRD CANYON, named for one of the most numerous and most interesting songbirds in the West. The mocker is found almost everywhere throughout the southern part of the state, wanders as far north as the San Francisco Bay counties in the winter, and even makes parts of the Mojave Desert his habitat. Under a provision of state fish and game regulations he is protected as a non-game bird, and valued for his destruction of insects.

The western mockingbird is a subspecies of the *Mimus polyglottos* (Lat., mimic of many voices) found throughout the southern half of the United States and south to Panama and the West Indies. He is about the size of a robin, but more slender, leggy, long-tailed, and flashy. He is slate-gray in color, with darker wings and tail that show much white when he flies; a large circular white patch in the middle of each wing resolves itself into two parallel bars and a splotch when the wing is folded. Characteristic of the bird is his odd but graceful habit of pausing at intervals, when running along the ground, to lift his wings in two or three tense little jerks, holding them full-spread for a moment before he folds them back and darts on.

Although the voice of the mockingbird is heard throughout the year, the night-singing for which he is famous occurs only during the full-song season in spring and summer. Some mockers, doing comparatively little mocking, use much of their own song—a loud, brilliant, richly varied series of flute-like trills and whistles. It is unlikely that the mocker can imitate other sounds beside birdcalls, for those commonly heard do not even render the calls of some wild birds well enough to fool the careful listener. The farmer who thinks he hears his young chickens cheeping at night, or the bird student who thinks he hears the song of the oriole or the yellow warbler, need listen only a moment and the bird will give himself away by an interval of his own pure, rollicking song.

When singing at the top of a tree or telegraph pole, the mocker often leaps three or four feet in the air while delivering a volley of liquid notes, settling again on his post in a flurry of wings without interrupting his song. Occasionally a mocker will flutter downward from a high perch like a falling leaf, singing as he goes; near the ground he catches himself and flies off, trailing a floating wisp of song over back yards or orchard treetops. This rarely-seen performance is known to naturalists as his dropping song.

Two birds which occur in the western mockingbird's range—one his close cousin and the other a nestling-killing enemy—are sometimes confused with the mocker, one in voice and the other in appearance. The mocker's relative, the California thrasher—a big brown bush bird with a downward-curving beak—often imitates the calls of jays, woodpeckers and valley quail in a rich, sweet voice sometimes mistaken for that of the mocker. The northern shrike or butcherbird, which the novice can scarcely distinguish from the mocker even at close range, has darker wings and tail, a stockier body, and a sharp hook at the tip of his beak with which he tears at his prey.

Mockingbirds breed in April and again in June. Four or five pale green eggs are laid each time in a nest constructed loosely of coarse grass, twigs, and various kinds of trash. The birds are bold and noisy in guarding their nests, attacking human beings, dogs, and cats as well as other birds who venture near. Cats are particularly good sport: the mocker will sight one crossing an open space in the yard, leave the tree with a bursting, piercing note which slides into a long skurring or chuzzing sound as he sails down and nips the cat's back, sometimes hovering in the air, dodging back and forth like a bucking kite as he delivers repeated blows that send the animal scurrying. Some of the nestlings fall out of the crudely-constructed nest while still naked and die instantly; the young birds have a bad habit of coming off the nest too soon, probably because their legs become long and strong at a very early age. At nine or ten days after hatching, they will be fully feathered, amazingly active on their legs, but unable to fly. They hop out of the nest and tumble to the ground, where they squeal while the parents flutter helplessly about, squalling their excitement, attracting the attention of cats and other enemies.

CORONA, 112 m. (615 alt., 8,764 pop.), is in one of the chief lemon-growing areas of southern California. In the immediate vicinity are 6,000 acres planted with citrus fruit trees, lemons predominating. Eight packing houses in Corona handle the crop.

Corona was founded in 1886 as Queen Colony, a name which was almost immediately changed to South Riverside. A wide circular boulevard shaded with pepper trees was constructed to surround the townsite. In 1913 the three-mile circle, paved by that time, was used for an automobile road race as one of the features of the Admission Day (September 9) celebration. With Barney Oldfield, Ralph de Palma, Earl Cooper, and other noted drivers participating, the first race was such a success that it was repeated the next year before a huge number of spectators. Eddie Rickenbacker was an entry in the 1914 race. The race was a financial failure in 1916 and was not attempted again.

State 71 follows 6th St., west from Corona.

The ASHCROFT RANCH (R), at 114.1 m. has served as the scene for a number of motion pictures, being considered a typical Midwestern-type farm. Scenes for the film *State Fair,* in which Will Rogers starred, were made here.

PRADO 115.7 m. (1,500 alt., 200 pop.), in the eastern mouth of Santa Ana Canyon, is surrounded by a diversified farming district. Its population, mostly Mexican, is employed in the manufacture of pottery, made from Alberhill clays.

At 116.5 m. State 18 branches L. from State 71; the route goes L. on State 18.

SANTA ANA CANYON, 117.8 m., a wide, shallow trough through the Santa Ana Mountains, gave its name to the hot dry Santa Ana winds that occasionally sweep the southern California coastal counties. The winds, originating in the 2,000- and 3,000-foot altitudes of the Mojave Desert, occur only from November to February, and rarely more than five times a year. Fine sand is carried by the wind down Cajon Pass, across San Bernardino and Riverside Valleys, and through Santa Ana Canyon. Velocities vary, but at high speeds sand is blown as far as Los Angeles, and sometimes in such quantity that the sun is dimmed and artificial lights required in midafternoon. The sandstorms occur during periods when the barometer is high over Nevada and the Mojave Desert and low in the coastal regions.

At 127 m. is a junction with State 14.

Right here, crossing the SANTA ANA RIVER at 0.7 m., to a junction with Esperanza Rd., 0.9 m.; R. here to RANCHO SANTA ANA BOTANIC GARDENS, 5.5 m. (*adm. by card, obtained through advance application; free*). Into the 200 acres of the gardens' rolling, ravine-cut hills it is planned eventually to compress specimens of all the growths natural to California, including the redwoods. In 1938, 100,000 of the estimated 200,000 varieties in the state had already been set out.

The gardens are divided into several units: a five-acre wild-flower nursery in which 100 different kinds of wild flowers are grown; a herbarium, containing more than 20,000 pressed plant specimens, and collections of seeds and cones; a propagating nursery; and a cactus and nursery garden. The latest development is a grove of between 75 and 100 ironwood trees, found only on Santa Catalina and Santa Cruz Islands. The trees were grown from seeds gathered on the islands. Projects under way include a fern garden, a swamp area for plants that flourish in soggy ground, and a palm forest with 200 trees of the variety found near Palm Springs (*see Tour 2*).

The Botanic Gardens were created in 1934 under a foundation established by Mrs. Susana Bixby Bryant in memory of her father, John W. Bixby, one-time owner of the Rancho Santa Ana. Mrs. Bryant's former country home on the crest of the ridge is used as the administration building. Property and endowment are administered by a self-perpetuating board of trustees.

OLIVE, 131.3 m. (200 alt., 510 pop.), a citrus packing and processing community in the heart of the Valencia orange belt, occupies the site of Burruel Point, a community founded by sons of Antonio Yorba, grantee of Rancho Canon de Santa Ana (*see Tour 4*).

The modern town was started in the 1880's and called Olive Point, for orchards planted by the Yorbas. An old inn, which served as a stage station on the inland route between San Diego, Capistrano, and Los Angeles, is still standing.

The bank of the Santa Ana River, just north of Olive, was a campground of the Gaspar de Portola Expedition on July 28, 1769. Father Juan Crespi recorded in his diary that the party "came to the banks of a river which has a bed of running water about ten varas wide and a half vara (Sp., 2.8 feet) deep. On its right bank there is a populous village of Indians, who received us with great friendliness. . . . I called this place the sweet name of Jesus de Los Temblores, because we experienced here a horrifying earthquake, which was repeated four times during the day. The river is known to the soldiers as the Santa Ana."

ANAHEIM, 135.1 *m.* (150 alt., 11,031 pop.) (*see Tour 4*).

Points of Interest: Pioneer House, City Park, Madame Helene Modjeska Statue, and others.

At 136.4 *m.* is a junction with Firestone Blvd. (State 10); R. from State 18 on this route.

BUENA PARK, 141 *m.* (76 alt., 1,897 pop.), founded in 1887, is an agricultural community surrounded by truck and berry gardens, dairy, and chicken ranches. In recent years a considerable sugar-beet industry has developed.

NORWALK, 146.5 *m.* (97 alt., 8,690 pop.), is in a general truck garden, hay, and dairy region. Many of the town's residents are employed in the near-by Santa Fe Springs oil field, and in the several small dependent factories.

Right from Norwalk on Norwalk Blvd. (State 35) to NORWALK STATE HOSPITAL, 1.3 *m.* (*open daily except Tues. and Fri., 1-3:30 p.m.*), in which annually are treated between 2,400 and 2,500 insane persons and chronic inebriates.

At 2.4 *m.*, at the intersection of Norwalk Blvd. and Telegraph Rd., is the center of the SANTA FE SPRINGS OIL FIELD (147 alt., 200 est. pop.). From this center, locally called Four Corners, clattering oil derricks radiate in all directions, their heights dwarfing the single row of one-story brick business buildings.

Although by 1938 production had dwindled to 34,000 barrels daily, this field ranks as one of the three leading bonanza pools in California. In the 1920's it produced as high as 345,000 barrels daily, exceeding even the productions of Signal Hill (*see Long Beach and Signal Hill*) and Huntington Beach, the other two most valuable areas. Prospecting for oil was attempted as early as 1865, by the Los Angeles Pioneer Oil Company; explorations with the crude equipment available at the time failed, and the lease was abandoned. Drilling was begun with the spudding in of Meyer No. 1 well by the Union Oil Company of California in 1907. The well was drilled to 1,445 feet and abandoned because of collapsed casing. A second well, Meyer No. 2, drilled in 1908, also was abandoned, this time when a string of tools was dropped after the hole had reached the 350-foot level. No further effort was made until February 1917, at which time the Union Oil Company spudded

Meyer No. 3, which, in October 1919, came in as a 150-barrel producer. Intensive development of the field, however, did not come until after the Union-Bell No. 1 blew in as a 2,500-barrel gusher in November 1921, and incontestably established the productivity of the field. A scramble by all major oil companies, innumerable town-lot drillers, and fly-by-night promoters followed, and within a year the field was established as one of the richest pools in petroleum history.

Before the state legislature limited the amount of stock that could be sold in a well (1923), Santa Fe Springs was a promoters' paradise. Prospects, gathered by salesmen who were known in the vernacular as "bird dogs," were hauled to the field in motor busses, and served free lunch in circus tents while hearing glib stories of the fortunes "made in oil."

After 1923, with its yield of more than 79,000,000 barrels, production gradually declined, and in 1928 had dropped to only 16,000,000 barrels. In midyear 1928 the field entered upon a second phase; 11 new strata were tapped, the deepest at 7,400 feet; seven of these were not even considered possible oil bearers, until the Wilshire Oil Company on July 26, 1928, penetrated the Buckbee sands and brought in a 2,000-barrel producer. A month later 78 new wells were drilling in a race for the deep sand levels, and at the close of 1929, 229 wells were going below the original level. The field's production for 1929 jumped to more than 76,000,000 barrels, an increase of more than 60,000,000 barrels over the 1928 figure. This so glutted the oil market that it brought about prorating and restrictive regulations.

By the middle of 1930 exhaustion of the new sands brought a decline, and production has decreased every year since. Up to June 1, 1938, Santa Fe Springs had yielded a total of more than 440,000,000 barrels.

LOS NIETOS (159 alt., 1,240 pop.), 4 m., a farming community at the northwest edge of the oil field, is named for Rancho Los Nietos. Granted in 1784 by Governor Fages to Jose Manuel Nieto, Rancho Los Nietos embraced all the land between the Santa Ana and the San Gabriel Rivers from the mountains to the sea—some 300,000 acres.

The DOWNEY ADOBE, 1847 Puente Hills Rd., was the summer home of John G. Downey, Civil War Governor of California. The adobe has been modernized and excellently preserved, and is still doing duty as a residence.

DOWNEY, 150.7 m. (116 alt., 12,538 pop.), center of a citrus, orchard, and dairying district, was named for the governor. Many of Downey's residents are employed in the factories of the nearby East Side manufacturing district. The town was platted in 1873.

SOUTHGATE, 155.9 m. (120 alt., 26,945 pop.), lies in the heart of the East Side manufacturing district of suburban Los Angeles (see The Industrial Section). It is built on part of the Rancho San Antonio, granted by the King of Spain in 1810 to Antonio Maria Lugo. This rancho was described in superlatives: ". . . no horses so fast, no cattle so fine, no land more fertile, no rancho more famous than the Rancho San Antonio." For almost half a century the grant was kept intact, but soon after the conquest of California by the United States the lands were detached, bit by bit, through sale, foreclosure, and litigation. The last large-scale holder of Rancho San Antonio acreage was Jonathan S. Slauson (for whom Slauson Avenue is named), who bought it in 1883; his heirs disposed of it in 1910 at $500 an acre. Seventeen years later a part of the former rancho lands was sold to the Firestone Tire and Rubber Company of California (see The Industrial Section) as a factory site at $7,000 an acre.

At 156.5 m. is a junction with Alameda St.; the route goes R. on

Alameda St. to 1st St.; and L. on 1st St. to the Los Angeles Civic
Center, 163.5 *m.*

《《《》》》

Tour 4

TO SAN JUAN CAPISTRANO

Los Angeles—Belvedere—Montebello—Whittier—Fullerton—Anaheim—Santa Ana—Tustin—Irvine—Capistrano—Doheny Park, 65
m.; US 101.

Union Pacific R.R. parallels route between Montebello and La Habra; Santa
Fe Ry. between Fullerton and Doheny Park; Southern Pacific R.R. between
Anaheim and Santa Ana; Pacific Electric Ry. between Los Angeles and
Santa Ana; Pacific Electric Motor between Los Angeles and Fullerton, and
Anaheim and Santa Ana.
Concrete and asphalt-concrete roadbed throughout; three to six lanes between
Los Angeles and Santa Ana; two to four lanes between Santa Ana and
Doheny Park.
All types of accommodations.

For more than 60 miles US 101 roughly parallels the course of El
Camino Real (the royal road) connecting the Spanish missions and
military posts in California. Cutting southeastward through the industrial district, the route bisects five oil fields, traverses the heart of
a Valencia orange belt, and passes the ruins of one of the most impressive old missions—San Juan Capistrano.

From the LOS ANGELES CITY HALL at 1st and Spring Sts.,
0 *m.,* east on 1st St. to San Pedro St.; R. on San Pedro to 6th St.; L.
on 6th St., which becomes Whittier Blvd.

El Camino Real, blazed by the Franciscans as they founded their
21 missions, was only one of the many roads and trails of the Spanish
Empire's road system—Los Caminos Reales (the royal roads). Even
after the Spanish and Mexican periods had passed, the name was applied
to the road connecting the old centers, regardless of re-routings in many
places. The early trail ran between Loreto, at the southern tip of
Baja (Lower) California, and Sonoma in Alta (Upper) California.
The Alta California missions, founded between 1769 and 1824, were
not established in consecutive order northward. When a new mission
was placed between two older ones, either the main road was re-routed
to pass it, or a branch road was built to it.

US 101, connecting modern communities with the assistance of
modern road-building techniques, deviates from the road that developed in more primitive days. Today several missions—notably San

Gabriel and San Fernando—are several miles from US 101. The unofficial revival of US 101 with the old name, a comparatively recent development, was partly the result of a desire to perpetuate the Spanish name, and partly a commercial device to attract visitors.

BELVEDERE GARDENS, 4.6 m. (210 alt.), is an unincorporated residential and commercial area with an estimated population in 1938 of 100,000, between the Los Angeles eastern and the Montebello western limits.

MONTEBELLO, 10.1 m. (195 alt., 8,016 pop.), a town with many flower nurseries, is in an extensive petroleum district. Oil, discovered north of the town in the Montebello Hills in 1916, has been a mixed blessing; it has given the town a substantial new industry, but is destroying the older one.

Left from Montebello on 1st St. one block to Poplar Ave.; R. on Poplar Ave. to the center of the nursery district, 0.5 m. Here are tracts of brilliant red, yellow, and orange zinnias; purple, white and red petunias; and many acres of roses, caleopsis, campanulas, digitalis, carnations, verbenas, dahlias, begonias, delphiniums, anthemums. Asters and dahlia are seen in the fall, sweet peas and chrysanthemums, mignonette and other hardy types during the winter.

The first grower here was Roy F. Wilcox, who came to this so-called "frostless strip" in 1906 and developed a wholesale business in palms, boxwood, and other ornamental plants. Redistricting of the area between Beverly Boulevard and the city limits to permit oil drilling is causing many of the nurserymen to move away.

PICO, 11.7 m. (181 alt.), an unincorporated residential community in a citrus district, was named for Pio Pico (1801-94).

US 101 crosses the San Gabriel River (see Tour 3) at 12 m.

LA CASA DEL GOBERNADOR PIO PICO (the house of Governor Pio Pico), 12.2 m., the adobe country home (open daily except Wed., 1-5; free), of the last Mexican governor of California, is surrounded by pepper, olive, and palm trees and masses of neglected shrubbery. Built in 1834, this house, now covered with a gabled shingle roof, was the center of much political and social activity for many years. It is on a tiny remnant of the former 8,000-acre Rancho Paso de Bartola, which Pico called El Ranchito (the little ranch) in comparison with his other holdings of great size.

Only 16 of the 33 rooms survived the 1870 flood. The remaining section is U-shaped, with the open end of the U facing east. Two short wings enclose the old patio, which is paved with red bricks. The former open well on the north side of the patio has been boxed off, and a palm has replaced Pico's fig tree. The house, now deteriorating, was the first in California with two stories and in its day the largest in the Los Angeles area. In its early period it was richly furnished, having handloomed brocade as window drapes, high canopied beds in fine woods, upholstered chairs, a $12,000 piano, and thick soft carpets. Most of the furnishings were stolen by vandals who sacked the place when Pico lost it to creditors in 1891. A few pieces were saved by friends of the family and eventually came to rest in southern California museums.

Pico was born at San Gabriel Mission May 5, 1801, and before his death 93 years later had gained possession of great sections of the former domain of that mission, as well as those of the missions San Fernando and San Juan Capistrano. With the connivance of his brother-in-law, Jose Antonio Carrillo (1796-1862), a power in native politics, Pico in 1831 fomented a revolt against the arrogant Governor Vittoria. Defeating the governor's "army" of 30 men in the "Battle of Cahunega Pass," Pico, with Carrillo's support, assumed the provisional governorship on January 18, 1832. In 1833 Pico conceived and executed the Secularization Act, by the terms of which the missions and their coveted lands were expropriated. Pico himself acquired his holdings either by open personal purchases, or indirectly, through friends and relatives.

The WHITTIER SCHOOL FOR BOYS (R), 13.3 m., is a state-operated reformatory (visiting hrs. 10-4, 2nd and 4th Sun. of each month) for delinquent youths. Widely spaced red-roofed buildings standing on lawns among farm tracts house 700 boys committed for corrective schooling by juvenile courts throughout California. The institution was established in 1889.

WHITTIER, 13.5 m. (325 alt., 16,115 pop.), trade center of a prosperous agricultural area, was named for John Greenleaf Whittier, the Quaker poet, by Friends from the Middle West who settled here in 1887. Around it are vast citrus groves—5,000 acres of Valencia orange trees, 1,000 acres of navel oranges, and 4,000 of lemons; approximately 2,500 acres bear avocados and 3,500 walnuts.

The FRIENDS CHURCH, Philadelphia St. and Washington Ave., belongs to a society organized in 1887 that now has a membership of 1,800. The present red-brick edifice of eclectic design was built in the early 1920's.

WHITTIER COLLEGE, Painter Ave. between Philadelphia St. and Earlham Dr., was established by the Friends in 1891 as Whittier Academy and was ten years later chartered as a coeducational, nonsectarian college. It has approximately 500 students.

The campus spreads upward over the lower slopes of the Puente Hills at the city's eastern edge. Among large trees are Founders, Naylor, and Mendon Halls, housing laboratories and lecture rooms. The Redwood Building contains the department of home economics, and also the library. In the Music Building are a Carnegie set of 945 phonograph records, 151 bound scores, and a small music library. Ownership and administration are vested in an independent and self-perpetuating board of trustees, the majority of whom are members of the California Yearly Meeting of Friends.

The two WHITTIER OIL FIELDS, on the slopes of the Puente Hills east of the college, are among the oldest petroleum-producing areas in Los Angeles County; the first well was brought in about 1897. Average daily production is slightly less than 1,000 barrels.

Southeast of Whittier US 101 proceeds through orange, lemon, and avocado groves, following the curving outline of the Puente Hills. The southern slopes and valleys of these hills have been found exceptionally suitable for growing avocados, and are extensively planted with varieties that, between them, provide virtually a year-round crop.

Most of California's 14,000 acres of avocados are in this part of the state, chiefly in the coastal belt between San Diego and Santa Barbara, a region with the conditions most favorable to their culture— relative freedom from frost with some humidity. Atmospheric dryness is California's greatest single obstacle in the way of extensive avocado production, and young avocado trees in this coastal belt are protected from sunburn during the dry summer months by shelters.

The trees are evergreens, with spreading branches covered with glossy dark foliage. Most varieties have small pale green or yellowish blossoms. There are three groups of avocados—the West Indian, the Guatemalan, and the Mexican. In the United States the West Indian, most sensitive to frost, has been cultivated principally in Florida. It produces a fruit with smooth, medium-thin skin, and a large seed that is often loose in the seed cavity. The Guatemalan group, cultivated in both California and Florida, produces a large fruit with a seed completely filling its cavity, and with a skin that is often thick and warty. The Mexican varieties are the hardiest. Particularly valuable in regions too cold for the others, it is extensively cultivated in California. Its small fruit has a thin, glossy skin, varying in color from green to deep purple, and the seed is commonly larger in proportion to the fruit than in the Guatemalan types.

The *fuerte,* introduced from Mexico in 1911, is a natural hybrid between the Mexican and Guatemalan types, and furnishes 60 to 70 per cent of California's crop. It is a medium-sized fruit, dull-green, with numerous yellow dots, and its small seed is tight in the cavity.

Avocado culture began in this region early in the 20th century, following numerous importations of the Mexican and Guatemalan fruits that had stimulated interest in the new food stuff. Commercial culture of the fruit has been going on since 1910, when orchards were stocked after surveys of the avocado districts of Mexico and Guatemala. Later the United States Department of Agriculture undertook a more extensive study of avocado plants and culture, calling attention to the world's choice varieties.

In this district, the hillsides planted with avocados have been narrowly terraced. This system though increasing the cost of laying out an orchard and of care, because of need for hand culture, not only protects the trees from frost, but also provides adequate drainage for the sandy loam, a requisite of avocado culture. Other favorable sites in California are on level ground adjacent to a slope, which enables use of the square system of planting.

Abundant irrigation is essential during the first two or three years after the young trees are planted and a system similar to that used for citrus fruits (*see Tour 1*) is used—largely the furrow system with the soil harrowed after each irrigation. The amount of water needed varies considerably with the soils, but during the first few years, a thorough irrigation every ten days during the dry season is considered desirable.

Young trees are pruned in the spring or the fall. The Guatemalan types tend to become long unbranched growths, while the Mexican grow more stiffly erect, with stout rigid branches capable of bearing heavy crops. The object of pruning is to produce a tree having a broad, strong, well-branched crown of good proportions and generous fruiting capacity, preferably with a low head to shade the soil beneath it. Little pruning is required for the mature tree, provided it has been well cared for during development.

Although avocado seedlings reproduce some of the major characteristics of their parents, they do not always reproduce a fruit resembling that of the parent in size, color, shape, and other characteristics. It is therefore necessary to propagate the trees with desirable fruits by budding or grafting, in order to insure a consistently satisfactory yield. Of the several methods of propagation, shield-budding used in the propagation of citrus and deciduous fruits is the method now employed by most nurserymen. Selection of the proper type of budwood requires more experience and judgment than any other feature of avocado propagation, for the character of the buds varies greatly among varieties of the same family. In the dependable *fuerte,* however, it is possible to develop 95 per cent of the buds into fruitful trees. Seeds are planted soon after their removal from fully matured fruit, though they are viable for many weeks if kept cool and dry. The seeds are usually sprouted in seedbeds containing a mixture of sand and loam that is kept moist during germination. This process continues slowly until early spring, when the seedlings are ready for transplanting. At this period careful irrigation and protection from sun and wind are particularly necessary.

Avocado oil, the most valuable part of the fruit, provides the single test of maturity. The fruit never softens on the trees, and attains flavor only when sun-ripened before removal. After more than a decade of experimentation in determining the exact time when avocados should be picked, the rather costly refractometer method was developed. In less than half an hour this reveals the fat content of a sample avocado selected by the inspector as typical of immature specimens in a given lot. In accordance with the California Standardization Act, avocados are sufficiently mature to be harvested when they contain at least eight per cent oil. While this minimum content requirement allows a wider spread of the harvest season, it is deplored by many growers and fanciers, for avocados are less tasty if they do not have an oil content of 12 per cent or more.

Near harvest time a special type of protection is needed for the groves. In former years organized marauders succeeded in stealing such impressive quantities of the fruits that the growers had to take action. Today the trespasser who ignores the posted warning in an avocado grove is very likely to be caught in one of many well-concealed bear traps. Should he escape these he would still have to cope with armed watchmen, police dogs, searchlights, and many other devices. The pickers carefully clip the mature fruit, using a bag and nipper at the end of a pole for the taller trees. Avocados are never removed by pulling, as the separation of a fruit from its pedicel or "button" almost always causes rapid decay. Stems are double cut to prevent the tender fruits from scarring each other in the canvas picking pails. Carefully transported in boxes to the packing house, the fruits are cleaned by soft revolving brushes and cloths until they are glossy. Graded by expert workers, the fruits travel over a moving belt to a machine that stamps on each its trade name. A sizing belt then carries the fruit to an automatic grading and counting apparatus, the movement of the belt causing each avocado to trip the proper counterbalance and drop into the proper padded bin. Packers arrange the fruit evenly in standard flats holding one layer of about 13 pounds, padded with soft wood excelsior. A jumbo container is used for extra-large fruits. As with other fruits, the size designation denotes the number of avocados to a flat. Fruit intended for local markets is stored at room temperature until sufficiently softened for consumption. Fruit to be held for longer periods is stored at a temperature of 40° to 45° F.; avocados have been successfully preserved at these temperatures with proper air circulation for as much as two months. Avocados intended for eastern markets are cooled for 48 hours, then shipped or stored with refrigeration. They are firm when delivered and are held by wholesalers or retailers until softened. Properly handled avocados are now satisfactorily shipped by fast freight to the eastern markets, where the demand is high.

Of avocado by-products the most successful is pure avocado oil, extracted from unsalable fruit and used in the manufacture of cosmetics. So far, neither dehydration nor canning has given satisfactory results.

At 20.2 *m.* is a junction with State 39 (Hacienda Rd.).

Left here to HART CITRON EXPERIMENTAL RANCH (*open to visitors*), 1.4 *m.*, Hacienda and East Rds. Before 1935, when Edward Giles Hart achieved his first profitable citron crop, the 5,000,000 pounds of citron used annually in the United States were imported principally from Sicily and the West Indies. The 1938 yield, from the ranch's 4,000 trees, was approximately a quarter of a million pounds. Buildings, erected in 1937, where the citron is processed by methods Hart has developed, are closed to visitors.

Using buds brought from Mediterranean countries by Dr. H. J. Webber, University of California citron expert, Hart discovered that the fruit would mature here when the seedling was grafted on a rough lemon. Since 1924 several new varieties of citron have been developed on this ranch.

At 21.3 *m.* on US 101 is a junction with Hiatt St.

Right here to LA HABRA, 0.5 *m.* (380 alt., 2,273 pop.), which calls itself the "Gateway to Orange County." The site was once part of a grant made to Mariano Roldan in 1839-40 and acquired at the outset of the Mexican-American War by Andres Pico, brother of Governor Pico (*see above*). The surrounding country, once used almost exclusively for pasturing sheep, has produced citrus fruits since the turn of the century. Shortly before the World

War, oil was discovered in the Coyote Hills to the south; the area has yielded more than 148,000,000 barrels.

At 23.7 *m.,* on US 101, is a junction with Cedar St. (Imperial Hwy.).

Left here to S. Pomona Blvd., 1.9 *m.; L.* on S. Pomona Blvd. to BREA (pitch), 2 *m.* (390 alt., 2,567 pop.), founded after the discovery of oil in 1916, and incorporated a year later. The Brea field is not a new anticline, but merely an extension of the older Olinda area. Average daily production of the Brea-Olinda field in 1939 was approximately 9,000 barrels. Brea was so named because of the asphalt deposits in Brea Canyon in the Puente Hills, from which, as early as 1876, asphaltum was shipped to Los Angeles for the manufacture of gas. The deposits were acquired by the Santa Fe Railway in 1897, but were worked for only a few years.
At 2.2 *m.* on S. Pomona Blvd. is a junction with Brea-Olinda Rd.; R. here to Olinda St.; L. on Olinda St. to Carbon Canyon Rd.; R. on Carbon Canyon Rd. to OLINDA, 4.1 *m.* (450 alt., 408 pop.), on a south slope of the Puente Hills, surrounded by the rigs of the OLINDA OIL FIELD, oldest in Orange County. The first well, the Dan McFarland No. 1, was brought in early in 1896 with a yield of about 10 barrels daily, but was abandoned because of drilling difficulties and the small production. Later that year Edward L. Doheny, discoverer of the Los Angeles Field *(see Tour 3),* began large-scale operations here on contract with the Santa Fe Railway.

South of Imperial Highways, US 101 sweeps through the gently rolling gap of COYOTE PASS, with oil derricks visible on both sides.

The SUNNY HILLS CITRUS RANCH (R), 25.7 *m.,* Spadra Rd. and Maria St. (*adm. by application; free*), is among the largest citrus growing areas under one management. In 1937 the corporation controlled 2,590 acres—1,575 with Valencia oranges and 425 with lemons; on the remaining acreage are packing houses, processing plants, laboratories, and homes for employees. Since the 1890's the ranch has been operated by Domingo J., Joseph, and Maria Bastanchury, descendants of Domingo Bastanchury, a Basque who settled in the area in 1858.

The fields around FULLERTON, 26.7 *m.* (180 alt., 10,442 pop.), third largest city in Orange County, produce oranges, walnuts and vegetables; local packing plants furnish employment for several hundred persons. The bulk of the Coyote Hills oil is piped here for shipment.

Fullerton was founded in 1887, two years before Orange County was created out of the southeastern section of Los Angeles County. The settlement was named for George H. Fuller, president of the Pacific Land Company and one of three persons associated in the town's founding. The site had been part of the San Gabriel Mission domain, but in the 1790's had been granted by the Spanish governor, Diego de Borica, to Manuel Nieto, who called it Rancho Los Coyotes (ranch of the coyotes). Regranted to Nieto's heirs by Governor Figueroa during the secularization period, it passed to the Pico brothers in 1846 while Pio was serving his second term as governor. Still later it became one of the numerous holdings of Abel Stearns (*see Downtown Los Angeles*).

The VAL VITA FOOD PRODUCTS COMPANY PLANT (*visitors 8-5*),

Brockhurst and Raymer Aves., annually ships a hundred million cans of soup, vegetables, and fruit juices.

ANAHEIM, 29.7 *m.* (150 alt., 11,031 pop.), oldest and second largest city in Orange County, packs and ships oranges, lemons, and walnuts, and produces a variety of manufactured goods. In 1857, some 50 San Francisco Germans established a co-operative colony here, buying 1,165 acres of communal land that was divided into 50 farm tracts of 20 acres each. They were worked co-operatively under the supervision of a manager. A five and one-half-mile fence—composed of 40,000 willow cuttings—enclosed the whole tract. The balance of the land was reserved for the village, which was named Anaheim because of its position near the Santa Ana River. Town lots were distributed among the shareholders by lottery in 1859.

Grape growing was one of the earliest experiments undertaken by the colonists, and for nearly 25 years Anaheim was one of the leading grape and wine producers in the state. In 1884-85 the so-called "Anaheim blight" attacked the vines and ruined the industry. The colonists then began to cultivate Valencia oranges, which had been introduced in the 1870's. This was the beginning of Orange County's orange industry. The orchards, covering more than sixty-one thousand acres, are planted almost entirely with Valencias (*see Tour 1*).

In CITY PARK (*picnicking grounds, tennis courts, playfields, baseball diamond*), Sycamore and Lemon Sts., are many semitropical trees and shrubs as well as those of California. An open-air theatre in the park is used for the annual Easter Sunrise Service, and for other meetings and entertainments. In the northeastern corner is a heroic STATUE OF HELENE MODJESKA, the Polish actress whose rancho near Placentia Ave. and North St. was a refuge for Count Henryk Sienkiewicz, author of *Quo Vadis,* and other Polish expatriates in the 1870's. The statue was designed by Eugen Maier-Krieg for the Federal Art Project.

PIONEER HOUSE, Sycamore and West Sts. (*visited on application, telephone 3257; free*), now a civic museum housing city and county relics, was built in 1857 by George Hansen, a leader of the co-operative colony. The one-story white-painted frame cottage, now protected by a picket fence, formerly stood on N. Los Angeles St., between Cypress and Chartres. The house and its present site were donated to the city by descendants of Anaheim's founders.

South of Anaheim along US 101 orange and lemon trees line the roadsides in parallel rows, dipping from view beyond distant knolls. During the heavy March-April blooming season of the Valencia orange, the heavy sweet odor of the blossoms fills the air.

The ORANGE COUNTY HOSPITAL, 33.6 *m.* (R), is a two-story structure surrounded by the institution's farm fields. Construction of the hospital was begun in 1914; it can care for 350 people.

At 33.6 *m.* is a junction with E. Chapman Ave.

Left here, crossing the Santa Ana River, to ORANGE, 1.9 *m.* (197 alt., 7,901 pop.), completely surrounded by the groves that justify its name. Four growers' associations handle the citrus crop of this area. Although the town's chief industry is fruit packing 'it also manufactures hosiery, gold-leaf, cable, and cordage. In the center of town, Glassell St. and Chapman Ave., is the Plaza, a circle of trees and lawns, with promenades radiating from a fountain. The city was founded as Richland in 1870 by A. B. Chapman on land accepted in payment of attorney's fees from Abel Stearns (*see Downtown Los Angeles*). In 1875 Chapman decided to rename the place for one of the four leading agricultural products of the region—oranges, lemons, olives, and almonds. He left the choice to the winner in a poker game and the orange won.

EL MODENA, 4.9 *m.* (250 alt., 510 pop.), lies among orchards along the western foothills of the Santa Ana Mountains. It was founded 1886-87. Though many of its settlers were Quakers its population now is largely Mexicans, who harvest oranges nearby.

At 5 *m.* Chapman Ave. becomes County Park Rd., which rises into cactus-covered foothills.

At 7.8 *m.* is a junction with Santiago Canyon Rd.; L. (straight ahead) 1 *m.* to IRVINE PARK (*free*), a small mountain recreation area maintained by Orange County at the mouth of Los Bueyes (the oxen) Canyon. The heavily wooded, rolling tract was donated by James Irvine, Sr., former owner of the Irvine Ranch (*see below*). Much of the area is in its natural state, with riding and hiking trails penetrating deep into the canyons. The many live oak trees, with gnarled boles and twisted, wide-spreading limbs, are impressive. A small lake for boating, picnic sites, playgrounds, and a small zoo are near the main entrance. SANTIAGO DAM, 3 *m.* (700 alt.), 160 feet high and 1,400 feet long, forms a private reservoir for irrigation.

At 14.3 *m.* on the main side route is the junction with Silverado Canyon Rd.; L. (straight ahead) here 3.5 *m.* to ROME SHADY BROOK (*accommodations, small swimming pool*). Many summer homes line this canyon and trails run back into the CLEVELAND NATIONAL FOREST, an 815,000-acre preserve formed in 1910 for protection of the water piped from its springs and rivers to the surrounding country.

At 18.9 *m.* on the main side route is the junction with Modjeska Grade Rd.; L. here 0.7 *m.* to the FOREST OF ARDEN, formerly the estate of Mme. Helene Modjeska, the Polish actress. The large white house is almost hidden among high trees and other greenery. In 1876 Modjeska came here with a group of refugee Polish artists. The colony failed. Modjeska learned English in a few months, turned to the American stage and began a career that carried her to her greatest triumphs. Shortly before her death in 1909, she moved to Modjeska Island.

On the main side route, surrounded by fields of black-eyed peas, is EL TORO (the bull), 27.8 *m.* (144 alt., 108 pop.), a ranch and farming village founded in 1891 by twelve English families.

At 29 *m.* the main side route (El Toro Rd.) meets US 101 (*see below*).

US 101 crosses the Santa Ana River at 33.8 *m.,* and follows Santa Ana Boulevard on the south bank.

SANTA ANA, 36.5 *m.* (133 alt., 31,921 pop.), is the trading center for much of the Valencia orange-growing district. The city manufactures glass, refines beet sugar, and has canneries and citrus and walnut-packing houses. In the residential areas, the predominating white of the homes sharply contrasts with green of lawns and trees. The business district is new and modern, having been largely rebuilt since the earthquake of 1933.

Santa Ana was founded by William H. Spurgeon in October 1869 on 76 acres of land purchased for $594. Spurgeon was the first settler, first postmaster, and first mayor. Santa Ana and the older Tustin (*see below*) were rivals for several years, but in 1877 the Southern

Pacific Railroad extended its line to Santa Ana and gave this place
the advantage of transportation facilities. It has been the county seat
since 1889 when Orange County was formed.

The BOWERS MEMORIAL MUSEUM (*open Tues., Thurs. and Sat.
10-12 and 2:30-4:30*), Main and 20th Sts., has the usual California
mission motifs—corridors, upper veranda, and red-tiled roof—and is
surrounded by palm and pepper trees. Exhibits in one room show
Indian life before the arrival of the Franciscans. In another are costumes loaned by descendants of Spanish-California families; and yet
another has relics of Helene Modjeska, the Polish actress. The museum
was established under a bequest by Charles W. Bowers on the site of
his former home.

The ORANGE COUNTY COURT HOUSE (*open 9-5; Sat. 9-12*),
Broadway and 6th St., an imposing four-story structure of Arizona red
sandstone, was built in 1898. Before the revision of the state's marriage law in 1927, making a three-day notice of intention to marry
mandatory, Santa Ana was a southern California Gretna Green and
scene of many run-away marriages, clergymen and justices of the peace
co-operating in expeditious services. Several marrying parsons did a
flourishing 24-hour business.

The FINE ARTS PRESS of Santa Ana Junior College, 115 Church
Ave., has won wide recognition for the typography and the illustra-
tions of its publications, as well as for their content since its establishment in 1931. The press was founded by Thomas E. Williams,
director of printing in the Santa Ana High School and Junior College,
chiefly to preserve historical documents of the region; stories of local
pioneer life, legend, and lore; and to publish poems by local writers.
The press is housed in a rectangular stuccoed building designed in a
modified mission style.

TUSTIN, 40.4 *m.* (122 alt., 953 pop.), is a citrus packing community founded in the 1860's by Columbus Tustin.

RED HILL (200 alt.), visible (L) southeast of Tustin, was known
to the Spanish as Cerrito de las Ranas (hill of the frogs). It was a
landmark to Indians, missionaries, and the later rancheros, and served
as a direction finder for early map makers. This section of the highway is shaded by a double row of eucalyptus trees.

At 42 *m.* US 101 crosses the borders of the IRVINE RANCH, founded
in 1867 by James Irvine. The 110,000-acre ranch produces lima
beans, citrus fruits, walnuts, and hay, and raises cattle on a limited
scale. Lima bean shipments reach 10,000,000 pounds a year. The
ranch headquarters is one mile L. of US 101 on Myford Rd.

IRVINE, 46.6 *m.* (100 alt., 510 pop.), a privately-owned town
on land of the Irvine Ranch, is primarily a shipping point for ranch
products and the home of Irvine employees.

The highway leaves the orange groves, walnut orchards, and cultivated fields and crosses gray-brown open prairie, overgrown with
wild oats, with only an occasional tree. Rolling range (R) ascends

into the gray San Joaquin Hills. A mesa (L) merges into foothills and the Santa Ana Mountains.

This section of US 101, between Tustin and San Juan Capistrano, is the route followed northward by the Gaspar de Portola expedition, which broke the trail from San Diego to Monterey Bay in 1769.

SAN JUAN CAPISTRANO, 61.7 *m.* (103 alt., 540 pop.), bears the name of the seventh of the upper California missions. Although the street on which the old mission fronts is now Broadway, and El Camino Real has become Main Street, signs in Spanish are still seen, and in the side streets and lanes branching away from the main road are some venerable houses—thick-walled, low-roofed deeply embrasured.

San Juan Capistrano was the only mission that became an officially designated *pueblo* (town). It was formally founded as San Juan de Arguello, in honor of Don Santiago Arguello, son of a California governor. There were then about 70 adobes, built by the mission and occupied by Indians. After the Mexican War the old mission name gradually came back into use. Today only 17 of the mission adobes remain, some still occupied, others falling into ruin. Capistrano depends chiefly on the citrus, vegetables, and cattle in the environs, but it prizes the tourist traffic attracted by the mission.

MISSION SAN JUAN CAPISTRANO (*open 8-6; adm. 25¢*), Main St. and Broadway (L), is now a ruin, reduced by the earthquakes of 1812 and 1918; few of the subsidiary structures have been restored. Entrance to the mission is through an arched gateway at the southwestern corner of the outer wall. The picturesque mass of the ruined stone church is seen (L) above the pepper trees. It was this church, with its Aztec carvings, domed altar, and semi-Moorish design, that gave San Juan Capistrano its reputation for beauty. The tiny mud nests beneath the stone arches are homes of the Capistrano swallows, which appear in large numbers early on every St. Joseph's Day, March 19. Circling downward, they attack and drive away the swifts that nest under the eaves in winter. The swallows occupy the hornet-shaped nests until St. John's Day, October 23, when they circle upward in the dawn and disappear toward Mexico. The birds' record for unvarying punctuality in the annual arrival and departure was shattered in 1939 when the birds left more than a month early.

The mission buildings were built around the four sides of a one-acre patio. At its edge is a paved *atrio* (terrace) behind square brick columns and arches supporting its roof. This terrace, Serra Chapel on the north side, and the mission house on the south side, are the chief relics of the old establishment. The long SERRA CHAPEL, though much restored, is the oldest part of the mission and the only remaining building in which Father Junipero Serra said mass. Mass is still celebrated in it daily, with altar vessels rescued from the ruins of the stone church. The restoration of Serra Chapel was done with unusual care.

The first attempt to found the mission was made in October 1775, but the founding party was called back to San Diego to aid in repelling an Indian attack. On October 31, 1776, Junipero Serra, *presidente* of the California missions, accompanied by Padres Pablo Magartegui and Gregorio Amurrio and 11 soldiers, returned to the site, finding the cross that had been erected the previous year still standing. The adobe church now called Serra Chapel they erected with the help of Indian neophytes, naming it for St. John of Capistrano, a crusader. The church was used for the first time on December 2, 1776.

Work on the great stone church was inaugurated in 1797. Isidro Aguilar, master builder from Culiacan, Mexico, supervised the construction. Indians brought the stone on two-wheeled *carretas* (carts). No wood, except for window and door frames, was used. The floor plan was that of a Latin cross, with nave and transepts; the interior length was 148 feet. The roof consisted of a series of seven domes, and the *campanario* was so high it could be seen 10 miles away. The great church was dedicated on September 7, 1806, but was used only six years and three months. The 1812 earthquake, which took place during the celebration of the feast of the Immaculate Conception, wrecked the roof, the cloisters, the nave, five of the domes, and leveled the tall *campanario;* it also killed 39 worshippers.

The sanctuary and the transepts were unharmed, and people who rushed to that part of the building survived. The mission fathers made no serious effort to rebuild the church, doing little but prevent complete disintegration.

The inventory at the time of secularization, 1833, placed a value of only $55,000 upon the property, and under the administration of Mexican officials the lands and buildings deteriorated further. When in 1845 Governor Pico had the buildings, furniture, garden, orchard, and vineyard sold at auction they brought only $710. Although a commission appointed by the United States Government to examine property claims found the Pico sale illegal, another decade elapsed before the mission buildings and land were conveyed back to the diocese. The patent was signed by President Lincoln on March 18, 1865, a month before his assassination.

SERRA, 64.4 *m.* (50 alt., 400 pop.), populated largely by Mexicans, was named for Junipero Serra, founder of the California missions.

DOHENY PARK, 64.9 *m.* (50 alt., 300 pop.), is a residential village promoted by and named for Edward Lawrence Doheny, former Los Angeles oil operator. Along the shore to the south is CAPISTRANO BEACH, with a club and modern fishing pier.

At 65 *m.* is a junction with the Coast Highway, US 101-A (*see Tour 5*).

《《《》》》》》》》》》》》》》》》》》》》》》》》》》》》》》》》》

Tour 5

TO THE BEACHES

Los Angeles—Culver City—Venice—Redondo—Wilmington—Long Beach—Seal Beach—Huntington Beach—Newport—Balboa—Laguna Beach—Doheny Park, 81.9 m.; Washington Blvd., Venice Speedway, Vista del Mar, US 101A.

Santa Fe Ry. parallels route between Manhattan Beach and Redondo; Southern Pacific R.R. between Wilmington and Long Beach; Pacific Electric Ry. and motor coaches between Los Angeles and Redondo.
Concrete and asphalt-concrete roadbed throughout; six lanes between Los Angeles and Venice; three-lane stretches between Venice and Doheny Park. All types of accommodations.

Most of this route follows the coast of Los Angeles and Orange counties, where oil and resort towns string out like beads of a giant rosary. From downtown Los Angeles the route runs directly across the thickly built-up coastal plain to the Pacific shore, then turns south, with the sea always in view. The shore route crosses tidal flats and regions of sand dunes, then winds along the edge of the shore palisades in southeastern Orange County. Combers—the delight of paddle-board riders—advance and shatter themselves along miles of white strand near the road, boom against the base of outthrust cliffs, crash on rocks covered with primordial aquatic life forms, and spend themselves among a plexus of tidal lagoons—the habitat of sea gulls, cranes, and pelicans. The tidal oil wells, bathing beaches, and vacation resorts give a highly variegated transient population to the towns along the route.

South from the LOS ANGELES CITY HALL, 1st and Main Sts., 0 *m.,* on Main St. to Washington Blvd., and R. on Washington Blvd.

CULVER CITY (L), 10.5 *m.* (100 alt., 8,976 pop.), is a residential city, but is best known for its motion-picture production, the total output—one-half of the films produced in the United States—exceeding that of the imaginary city of Hollywood (*see Hollywood*). The residential and manufacturing districts spread from the base of the Baldwin Hills along the flat coastal plain south of Washington Boulevard.

The town was laid out in 1913 in the middle of a barley field by Harry Hazel Culver, a real estate promoter. The subdivision was not much of a success until the Triangle Studios were built several years later; soon Kalem, Thomas Ince, and others, attracted by low real-estate costs and taxes, followed. When the Metro-Goldwyn-Mayer organization came into existence in 1923 through the merger of the Goldwyn Pictures Corporation, the Metro Film Company, and the Louis B. Mayer Pictures Corporation (*see The Movies*), the nucleus of the vast studio here was built. This plant and the Hal Roach and Selznick International Studios are the chief local producers. Four thousand studio employees live here and in the adjoining suburb of Palms.

A long, two-story, vine-covered building at 8822 W. Washington Blvd. houses the administrative offices of HAL ROACH STUDIOS, INCORPORATED (*no visitors*). The grayish stucco structure faces Washington Boulevard across a lawn, at the west end of which is the STUDIO CAFE (*open to public 9-5*), a one-story building harmonizing with the main plant. South of the administration building is the 10-acre lot, with five sound stages, reserve-set lots, giant cranes, power plants, costume buildings, make-up quarters, scenario writers' quarters, carpenter shops, and other facilities.

Hal Roach began his motion-picture career in 1912, at the age of 20, in minor cowboy roles at the Universal studios. He rose to assistant director, and in 1914 assisted in starting the Rolin Film Company. The company's difficulties were many until 1915, when Roach met Harold Lloyd and produced the first of the *Lonesome Luke* comedies, starring the bespectacled Lloyd. In 1918 Roach became sole owner of the company, changed the name, and moved the plant to Glendale. In 1920 he established it here. Soon thereafter the *Our Gang* series was inaugurated. The comedy duo, Stan Laurel and Oliver Hardy, was guided to popularity by Hal Roach.

The studio now concentrates on the production of Class-A features.

The headquarters of the SELZNICK-INTERNATIONAL STUDIOS (*no visitors*), 9336 W. Washington Blvd., are in the frame structure with long tall portico built in 1915 by Thomas Ince as the first large producer in Culver City. Behind the administration building are four square blocks of sound stages, a film laboratory, carpenter shops, casting offices, and sets.

Selznick International Studios, Inc., is headed by David O. Selznick, son-in-law of Louis B. Mayer, of Metro-Goldwyn-Mayer. Selznick took over the former Ince Studio after it had housed R.K.O.-Pathe for several years.

The METRO-GOLDWYN-MAYER STUDIO (*no visitors*), 10202 W. Washington Blvd., sprawls over 117 acres in the heart of Culver City. The main lot with its huge sound stages, administration quarters and innumerable dressing rooms, costume and auxiliary buildings, is in the triangle bounded by Washington and Culver Blvds., Overland Ave. and Ince Way. This organization annually produces about 55 major films ranging in cost from $150,000 to $1,000,000 each.

The MGM CASTING OFFICE is on Ince Way. Here the thousands of extras present their credentials from the Central Casting Bureau in Hollywood, which supplies most of the studios with "extra" personnel.

Along the Washington Boulevard front, between Jasmine Avenue and Overland Avenue, is a 25-foot-high white wall, behind which is the beehive MGM MAIN LOT, with 30 sound stages, 16 projection rooms, studio-set park, cartoon department, and some 100 or more buildings housing the administrative offices, make-up departments, actors' dressing rooms, and costume, carpenter, machinery, designing, scenario, storage, laboratory and medical units. Along the Culver Boulevard and Overland Avenue sides are towering permanent sets— huge buildings and whole city blocks composed of flimsy, false fronts.

The studio has a private police force of 100; a telephone system with 1,000 stations; a private fire department; and a commissary serving 1,800 persons daily. The average number of employees is 4,000, exclusive of the extras hired for one day, or run-of-the-picture periods. The Studio Club, an employees' benefit organization, has a membership of 3,000.

The Metro-Goldwyn-Mayer organization had its beginnings in a feud between the late Marcus Loew, multimillionaire theatre owner, and his business associate, Adolph Zukor. When Zukor became head of the Famous-Players Lasky Corporation, he made it difficult for the Loew Theatres to obtain pictures. Loew, determined to control his picture source, acquired the Metro Film Company in 1920 and the Goldwyn Pictures Company in 1924. Later in the same year he purchased the Louis B. Mayer Picture Corporation, which brought Mayer, Irving Thalberg, and J. R. Rubin under the Loew banner. From the consolidation of the three firms the present Metro-Goldwyn-Mayer resulted.

The first production of the new organization was *He Who Gets Slapped,* with Norma Shearer, the late Lon Chaney, and John Gilbert. Subsequent hits were *Ben Hur, The Big Parade, Trader Horn, The Merry Widow, The Student Prince, Broadway Melody, Min and Bill,* co-starring Wallace Beery with the late Marie Dressler, *Strange Interlude,* and others. The studio's current list of stars includes Clark Gable, Myrna Loy, Norma Shearer, Jeanette MacDonald, Nelson Eddy, Lionel Barrymore, Luise Rainer, Robert Donat, Rosalind Russell, Spencer Tracy, Robert Taylor, Joan Crawford, Wallace Beery, Greta Garbo, Robert Montgomery, Mickey Rooney, Freddie Bartholomew, and Judy Garland.

The residential settlement of PALMS (R), 10.9 *m.,* though part of Los Angeles since 1915, is so close to Culver City that it is frequently considered part of that community. The district was platted as The Palms in 1886.

At 13.3 *m.* on Washington Blvd. is a junction with Centinela Ave.

Left on Centinela Avenue to BALLONA CREEK MARINE COURSE, 1 *m.,* a riprapped section of the Ballona Creek Channel, completed in 1937 to provide crew racing facilities for Los Angeles colleges. The course is the seaward end of the Ballona Creek Flood Control Project, extending from the Los Angeles city limits to the Pacific Ocean. The racing course extends from Centinela Avenue to the creek's outlet in the Playa del Rey estuary. It is slightly less than 2.5 miles long at low tide and 200 feet wide at mean tide.

At 14.6 *m.* on Washington Blvd. is the junction with Lincoln Blvd. (US 101A) (*see Tour 6*).

At the end of Washington Boulevard is VENICE, 16 *m.* (15 alt., 28,856 pop.), a residential community, oil-producing town, and beach resort, since 1925 a part of Los Angeles. The business center is at Windward and Pacific Avenues, 0.5 miles north of Washington Boulevard. Venice has five miles of beach, and the largest amusement-concession area on the Pacific coast. In the CHILDREN'S PLEASURE PARK, on the elaborate MUNICIPAL PIER, are miniature merry-go-rounds, chute-the-chutes, Ferris wheels, slides, and other concessions.

Venice was founded in 1904 by Abbott Kinney, who named it for Venice, Italy, which served as his model in laying out the town. Buildings were designed with Italian motifs, artificial waterways served as streets, carrying gondolas poled by singing boatmen. The promoter sponsored improving lectures, Chautauqua meetings, and art exhibits, and provided free transportation from Los Angeles; but such visitors as responded preferred the beach to culture and in 1906 Kinney converted his dream city into an imitation Coney Island, building a pleasure zone and importing freaks and side shows. All but 3 of the former 16 miles of canals were filled in by 1930 on demand of property owners who complained of their stench and inconvenience. The remaining three miles are dry. The Venetian ideal survives in some of the buildings along Windward Avenue, where the upper stories extend over the sidewalk, forming an arcade.

Left from Washington Blvd. in Venice on the Venice Speedway, now the main route.

The Venice Speedway, a 20-foot alley extending for the 2.5 miles between Ocean Park (*see Santa Monica*) and Playa del Rey (*see below*), was laid out in pre-automobile days as a bicycle course; it is now a motor headache on busy days.

Derricks of the VENICE-PLAYA DEL REY OIL FIELD, rising amid beach cottages, are concentrated at Thirty-sixth St. and Speedway, 16.2 *m.* Prospecting was carried on in this field for 10 years before commercial production was attained. The first well, drilled in 1921, was abandoned when no oil or gas showed. Since 1930, when the Ohio Oil Company brought in the first well, more than 400 have been drilled, of which 185 are still producing. The field's average daily yield is about 6,000 barrels. The beach resort character of this section of Venice has been completely subordinated to oil production; bedroom windows open directly upon derrick floors, back porches overlook sump holes, and cottages are dwarfed by tall steel rigs.

At 17.6 *m.* (62nd St.) Venice Speedway becomes Trolley Way.

PLAYA DEL REY (beach of the king), 17.9 *m.* (125 alt.) stretches along a narrow strip of land between the sea and palisades. The town, now almost entirely residential, with fine widely spaced Mediterranean style houses, along broad avenues, was developed as a resort in 1903-4 by Abbott Kinney at the same time he was founding

Venice. In 1911 it was annexed to Venice, and with Venice, was consolidated with Los Angeles in 1925.

The temperature of the ocean water along these beaches varies only about 10° between winter and summer, thus inviting bathers the year round. The winter low here, in January and February, is about 57°, while the summer high, in August, is about 67°.

LOYOLA UNIVERSITY, 7101 W. 80th St., occupies the flat tableland at the crest of the Del Rey Hills. The four gray-brick buildings with California Mission motifs, command a sweeping view. Conducted by the Jesuits, Loyola University is an outgrowth of St. Vincent's College founded in 1865. It has about 500 students.

Left from Playa del Rey on Culver Blvd., 0.2 *m.*, to Pershing Ave.; R. on Pershing Ave. 0.4 *m.* to Manchester Ave. (State 10); L. on Manchester Ave. to INGLEWOOD, 6 *m.* (140 alt., 30,114 pop.), in the Centinela Valley district of the coastal plain. Manufactures include textiles, furniture, enamelware, and airplanes.

Inglewood, incorporated in 1908, was platted in 1888 by Daniel Freeman on parts of Rancho Sausal Redondo (round willow clump), granted by Governor Alvarado to Antonio Avila in 1837; and Rancho Aguaje de la Centinela (spring of the sentinel ranch), granted to Ygnacio Machado by Governor Micheltorena in 1844. The city water supply is still drawn from Aguaje de la Centinela.

Aloof among the clump of willows that gave Rancho Sausal Redondo its name is the CENTINELA ADOBE (*private*), Freeman and Inglewood-Redondo Blvd. The long rambling one-story house now has a wide iron-railed porch, in place of the old clapboard *corredor,* and such improvements as hardwood floors, electric lights, and plumbing. Nevertheless, some of the early-day Mexican atmosphere remains. The adobe was built between 1833 and 1840 by Ygnacio Machado by the old Salt Road, whose course approximated that of today's Inglewood-Redondo Boulevard; it led from the pueblo of Los Angeles to a lick, source of the salt used by early Angelenos. Machado and his large family lived in the adobe until 1845, when it passed to Bruno Avila. In 1856 the adobe and rancho were lost to Avila through foreclosure and during the next 29 years passed through successive ownerships before being bought by Daniel Freeman.

At the CHAPMAN SOUTH AMERICAN CHINCHILLA FARM, 4957 W. 104th St. (*adm. by telephone appointment only; free*), the rare Andean Chinchilla, bearer of the valuable pelt, has been raised for the commercial fur market since 1923. On the farm are 30 units containing 900 pens in all to hold 1,650 animals. The animals sell at $1,600 each.

The chinchilla (*Chinchilla laniger*) is a meek-looking hopping rodent, about the size of a large squirrel. It bears a soft, blue-gray fur, the blue merging into pearl-gray and each hair tipped in black and slate blue. It attains a length of approximately 8 inches and a weight of 20 ounces. A nocturnal animal, it spends most of the day crouched in a box-nest. While working in Chile in 1919, M. F. Chapman, an American engineer, saw one of the rodents that an Indian had captured above snow line in the Andes. He soon conceived the idea of raising the animals in the United States and hired Chilean Indians to capture specimens. It took three years for Chapman to obtain 15 animals, 12 males and 3 females. Four died before Chapman left South America, 2 others succumbed on shipboard and 2 were born aboard. Various experiments led to the building of these seasoned lumber structures with pens of cloth spread over a wooden framework to house the animals. The 11 chinchillas soon increased to 70, and reports of the experiment sped through the fur world. Chapman realized he had a world monopoly when the agent of a Swiss syndicate asked to buy specimens. He refused to sell. The agent then allegedly stole 35 of the animals; he was trailed by detectives to a chinchilla farm that he established in Germany, but Chapman was unable to identify the German specimens as his own.

CENTINELA PARK (*plunge, wading pools; bowling, tennis, and horseshoe courts, baseball field, picnic ground with equipment*), Redondo Blvd. and Prairie Ave., is a sixty-acre beauty spot about Centinela Springs in the ravines and gulches along the banks of Centinela Wash. Part of the area is landscaped; the rest is maintained in a natural state. Fossil remains of Pleistocene animals uncovered in the gravel wash have brought the conclusion that the springs were a prehistoric watering place. In the park are a large outdoor amphitheatre and the VETERANS' MEMORIAL BUILDING, built with WPA aid as a meeting place and recreational center for veterans.

Opposite Centinela Park are (R) the 300 gently rolling acres of INGLEWOOD PARK CEMETERY, bounded by Inglewood-Redondo Blvd., Prairie Ave., Manchester and West Blvds. In the NEW MAUSOLEUM are displayed funeral urns, statuary, and other art objects assembled by George H. Letteau, president of the cemetery association; among them is a Greek sarcophagus dating from 100 B.C., that was uncovered along the Appian Way near Rome.

HOLLYWOOD PARK (*racing daily except Sun. and Mon., 47 days beginning late in May; adm. clubhouse $2.20, grandstand $1.10*), is bounded by Century, Crenshaw, and Manchester Blvds. and Prairie Ave., in the southeastern section of Inglewood. Owned and operated by the Hollywood Turf Club, which in turn is largely owned by motion-picture celebrities, the park is laid out in the grand Hollywood manner. Its biggest event is the $50,000 Hollywood Gold Cup Handicap. The streamlined white concrete-and-steel CLUBHOUSE AND GRANDSTAND is banded with tiers of windows. The grandstand, seating 12,000 is accessible from the clubrooms; it is elaborate with terraces, lounges, and boxes. In the enclosed paddock is an amphitheatre accommodating 3,500. A projection machine flashes pictures of close finishes to the audience; from a circular lounge 500 persons can watch the races while lunching; the parking area holds 22,000 automobiles; in the stable are 1,200 stalls and 300 tack and feed rooms; the infield of the one-mile oval track is elaborately landscaped and contains three artificial lakes where ducks, geese, and swans swim. During the racing season a Goose Girl in Dutch costume drives her feathered flocks among the flora.

Right from Inglewood 1 m. on Inglewood-Redondo Blvd. to the LOS ANGELES MUNICIPAL AIRPORT, Mines Field, in Los Angeles, on Inglewood's southwestern border. In 1939 the field had accommodations for 90 planes. The field is to have five paved runways, allowing landings and take-offs in any direction.

The NORTH AMERICAN AVIATION FACTORY, entered from Imperial Highway, is on municipal airport grounds leased from the city. It builds both military and commercial planes. The company, a subsidiary of General Motors Corporation, opened this plant in 1936.

The EL SEGUNDO PLANT OF THE DOUGLAS AIRCRAFT COMPANY (*see Santa Monica*), east of the North American Aviation factory, also manufactures military and commercial airplanes.

Also along Imperial Highway is the new INTERSTATE AIRCRAFT AND ENGINEERING COMPANY FACTORY, which manufactures equipment and precision instruments, handles sub-assembly contracts for North American and Douglas, and makes aircraft armament.

At 17.9 m. Trolley Way becomes Vista del Mar.

At 21.3 m. is the junction with Grand Ave.

Left on Grand Avenue to EL SEGUNDO, 0.6 m. (35 alt., 3,738 pop.), which grew up around the STANDARD OIL REFINERY. The plant covers more than a thousand acres south of El Segundo Boulevard. Representing an investment of $50,000,000, the refinery has a capacity of 100,000 barrels of crude oil a day. Its chain of 14 sub-surface storage reservoirs will hold some 21 million barrels (the largest reservoir covers 18 acres), and above-ground steel tanks store an additional seven million barrels. The refinery obtains crude oil from nearly every field in California, and is connected by pipe lines with all major fields in the Los Angeles basin. The plant, opened in 1911, was named El Segundo (the second), because it was the company's second plant in the state. The EL SEGUNDO OIL FIELD, on the city's eastern outskirts, has been an active producer since the Republic Petroleum Company made its first strike in 1935. The 51 wells produce about 3,450 barrels of oil daily.

By Vista del Mar at 21.7 *m.* the long, slender STANDARD OIL COMPANY PIER juts from the beach above a web of pipe lines from the refinery. Here Standard Oil tankers load gasoline and fuel oil from the storage tanks at El Segundo. Because of the oil smudge few bathers come to this beach.

At 23.1 *m.* Vista del Mar becomes Highland Ave.

MANHATTAN BEACH, 23.7 *m.* (46 to 100 alt., 6,398 pop.), differs from most southern California beach communities in its prohibition of roller coasters, games of chance, and other concessions of similar nature. It is part of an unbroken four-mile stretch of houses along the beach and crests of the sand dunes. The site, once part of Rancho Sausal Redondo, was developed as a real estate subdivision in 1897, but the town was not incorporated until 1912. Most important assets are the two miles of municipally controlled beach, free of undertow or rip-tides, and the long municipal pier that is very popular among fishermen. There is also a well equipped municipal picnicking pavilion (*free*).

At 24.7 *m.* is the junction with Longfellow Ave.; R. from Highland Ave. on this route to Hermosa Ave., 24.8 *m.;* L. on Hermosa Ave., now the main route.

Hermosa (beautiful) Beach, 25.8 *m.* (12 to 150 alt., 7,197 pop.), founded in 1901, is a larger, less restricted counterpart of Manhattan Beach, with which it merges. Amusement concessions support many of the inhabitants. Two miles of beach, a ballroom built over the sea, a municipal stadium with adjoining bowling greens, tennis courts and a baseball diamond, a large pier for fishermen and barge service for deep-sea fishing are the chief recreational facilities.

At 27.4 *m.* is the junction with Pacific Ave.; L. from Hermosa Ave. on this route.

REDONDO BEACH, 27.6 *m.* (20 to 150 alt., 13,092 pop.), dating from 1887, was a fashionable spot in the 1890's. Although it is now largely a middle-class residential town, water sportsmen, fishermen, and other vacationists still come here. The heart of the amusement and beach-front section is Pacific Avenue between Carnelian Street and Torrance Boulevard.

A long-dreamed-of harbor at last began to materialize in 1938, when construction on the first unit of a breakwater was started. The half-mile breakwater is a rock-fill jetty starting at the foot of Tenth Street and angling southward.

Left from Redondo Beach on Torrance B!vd. to the TORRANCE OIL FIELD, 2.2 *m.*, the rigs of which extend along both sides of the road between Redondo

Beach and Torrance. The field, opened in 1922, daily produces (1939) about 21,500 barrels from 702 wells.

TORRANCE, 4.6 m. (75 alt., 9,950 pop.), was established on a potato and bean patch in 1911 by Jared Sidney Torrance, a Pasadena utilities magnate. Before laying out the town the founder consulted various city planners, finally selecting Frederick Law Olmsted, Jr., to draw up the plans. His design provided for functional efficiency in placing the various units of the community: factories are on the edge of the city, in positions where prevailing winds will carry the smoke away from the city; the retail district, whose center is at Torrance Boulevard and El Prado, lies midway between this outer factory fringe and the residential areas; numerous diagonal streets provide shortcuts between the retail, residential and industrial areas. El Prado (The Promenade), running diagonally through the center of the town, is a wide parkway, three blocks long. About it are grouped the City Hall, the public library, the Chamber of Commerce building, the post office and other service structures.

The Torrance area produces flowers in large quantities for the commercial market, specializing in gardenias and orchids. The T. H. WRIGHT GREENHOUSES, 190th St. and Hawthorne Ave., grows more than five million gardenias a year for West Coast and other markets. It ships to New York City daily by planes. A new method of orchid culture being employed in this area cuts in half the time formerly required for producing the blooms. In the past, from five to ten years were required to bring an orchid plant to its first blooming stage. Sterile soil, from which every bit of organic matter has been removed by heat, is used. The orchid sprouts are fed a preparation containing the chemical elements needed for their growth and development. Temperature and lighting are automatically regulated; the buildings containing the plants are sealed; hydrometers measure the moisture; and rain is produced artificially.

The COLUMBIA STEEL CORPORATION PLANT, Torrance Blvd. and Arlington Ave., operated by a subsidiary of the United States Steel Corporation, is the city's largest industrial establishment, producing about 150,000 tons of iron and steel annually. It has open-hearth and electric furnaces, structural and merchant-bar rolling mills, sheet mills for black and galvanized iron sheets, and a foundry.

In Redondo Beach is the junction with US 101A; south (straight ahead) on US 101A, now the main route.

At 28.9 m. is the junction with Park Way.

Right on Park Way 0.1 m. to Catalina Ave.; L. on Catalina, which becomes Granvia La Costa, to PALOS VERDES (green trees) CIVIC CENTER, 3 m., the landscaped cultural and trading center of the PALOS VERDES ESTATES, a residential area in rolling terrain along the high north and west slopes of the Palos Verdes promontory. The Civic Center, around Malaga Cove Plaza, at Granvia La Costa and Granvia Valmonte, is surrounded by stores and public structures. The white expanse of the Mediterranean style buildings is softened by evergreens.

Right from Granvia La Costa on Palos Verdes West Dr. Emerging from a wooded section, the route runs along steep cliffs, that afford a striking view of the curving, crowded beaches along Santa Monica Bay. Pushing far westward into the sea is the deep blue mass of the Santa Monica Mountains. The beds of kelp seen in the ocean here as great brown patches on the water well beyond the surf line extend almost uninterruptedly along the coast from central California to Mexico. One of the largest plants in the world, sometimes attaining a length of 700 feet or more, this giant alga has no roots; it anchors its tough sleek cables to rocks on the ocean bed by means of a hold-fast, and draws its nourishment entirely from the sea water. The blades—the rubbery, rippled, olive-brown "leaves" of the kelp—spread out on the surface of the water in tangled masses kept afloat by air-filled bulbs, one at the stem end of each blade.

There are three varieties of the giant kelp, but only one, *Macrocystis pyrifera,* which attains its greatest growth in these coastal waters, is harvested for commercial use. It absorbs minerals from the sea water, particularly iodine, calcium, phosphorus, potassium, magnesium, and sulphur. From this kelp are manufactured iodine, acetone, livestock feed, fertilizer, and dietetic preparations.

The several converting plants in the Harbor District have kelp-cutting barges operating between the San Pedro breakwater and Redondo Beach. The typical kelp cutter, which is like an immense mowing machine with vertical blades in addition to the horizontal knives, is operated by a gas engine; it shears off the tops of the plants in a swath 18 feet wide, gathering 200 tons in six hours. A kelp bed can be recut every four months, so the supply is virtually inexhaustible. The harvested kelp is ground coarsely, macerated, and then placed in a drier—a huge revolving steel tube with a gas furnace at one end and a fan at the other. There the pulp is subjected to temperatures decreasing from 1400° to 300° F. The dried pulp is ground again and emerges a coarse powder.

A rise of the road at 6.3 *m.* suddenly opens a view to the southwest. Out across the sea, long, mountainous Santa Catalina Island (*see Tour 5A*), 24 miles offshore, is seen.

POINT VICENTE LIGHTHOUSE, 8.2 *m.,* stands in a three-acre reservation at the cliff's edge, surrounded by the U.S. Coast Guard Administration (*see The Harbor*) buildings and radio antennas.

PORTUGUESE BEND, 11 *m.,* a deep curve in the coast, is one of several points where steep trails zig-zag down to the rocky beach. The waters offshore are a favorite haunt of porpoises, who are often plainly visible from the road. Occasionally a whale is seen, sometimes blowing streams of air and water straight upward.

HARBOR LOOKOUT, 15.8 *m.,* a broad parking place on a promontory, affords a view of the entire harbor, from the breakwater at its entrance to the farthest interior slough (*see The Harbor*). San Pedro is just below the lookout point, and Wilmington (L). On the opposite side of the main channel is elongated Terminal Island, with fishing wharves, canneries, and shipbuilding plants. In the background are the modern buildings of Long Beach, flanked (L) by the derrick-forested heights of Signal Hill (*see Long Beach*), and part of the time, by the gray Pacific Fleet.

East of the Park Way junction, US 101A, the Redondo-Wilmington Boulevard, skirts the northern edge of the Palos Verdes Estates (*see above*).

WILMINGTON, 36.5 *m.* (*see The Harbor*) is the point of embarkation for boats to Santa Catalina Island (*see Tour 5A*).

LONG BEACH, 41.5 *m.* (o to 47 alt., 164,271 pop.) (*see Long Beach*).

Points of Interest: Bixby Park, Municipal Pier, Marine Racing Course, United States Pacific Fleet, Alamitos Bay Yacht Harbor, Cerritos Adobe, Curbstone Market, Los Alamitos Adobe, and others.

The SAN GABRIEL RIVER, 48.1 *m.,* is the boundary between Los Angeles and Orange Counties.

The SEAL BEACH OIL FIELD (L) straddles the county line. In 1938 from its 113 wells its average daily production was 8,118 barrels.

SEAL BEACH, 48.5 *m.* (9 alt., 1,553 pop.), in the southwestern corner of Orange County, lies on a flat projection of the tidal flats, with the Bay of Naples on one side and many-armed Alamitos Bay on the other. The town is dominated by the massive LOS ANGELES

BUREAU OF POWER AND LIGHT GENERATING PLANT (R). Seal Beach was so named because of the numerous seals that in former days played in its offshore waters.

Between the Orange County line and Newport Bay the highway is on an embankment, behind which extend miles of shallow tidal channels. Spongy marshes are dotted with tufted islands of salt-grass. White cranes stand solemnly on long legs in the shallow water, or wing slowly across the waste of marshy islands.

This shore is one of those most frequently visited by schools of grunion, little smelt-like fish of the silversides family that run up on the sand to spawn during spring and summer. It is the only fish that spawns in this extraordinary manner, and it does so only on southern California beaches. Spawning occurs at the bi-weekly high-tide intervals from March to August, always on the second, third, and fourth nights of the maximum tide. For many years the grunion runs have been met by crowds of amateur fishermen who bring picnic suppers and build bonfires on the sand. They used to bring all sorts of improvised equipment—small nets, kitchen sieves, sink strainers, window screens, baskets and what not—but by 1926 the grunion appeared so decimated that state laws were passed forbidding the use of any equipment for taking them; so they can now be taken only with the bare hands.

Although the California State Fisheries Laboratory keeps a grunion timetable and publishes in the newspapers the tide schedules on which they operate and the possible positions of the run, many a grunion-fishing party waits in vain for the fish to appear—not because the grunion have skipped a spawning, but because it is impossible to tell with accuracy just which beach they will choose on a particular night.

Not until 1919 was it established that the grunion run up the beach to deposit eggs, not to dance in the moonlight as unscientific observers had always believed. Male and female fish are swept up the beach together, and the moment the wave leaves them the female digs tail-first half the length of her body into the sand and deposits her eggs, which the male instantly fertilizes. The next wave sweeps the fish back into the ocean. The process takes about 30 seconds, and is repeated by others with each wave that breaks. A run may last more than an hour. Because the fish always wait until after the tide has begun to recede before they begin their run, succeeding waves do not reach the deposited eggs. They remain incubating under the sand for two weeks, when the high tide comes in again and washes them into the ocean, where they hatch at once.

The older females spawn every two weeks from March to August, the younger ones from April to June. No grunion-fishing is permitted during April, May, and June, when all females are spawning.

SURF SIDE, 50.2 m., is a collection of one-story frame beach cottages, some built on the tidal flats, others hugging the shore on the sand strip. Southward, the Surf Side cottages merge with those of SUNSET BEACH COLONY, 50.6 m.

HUNTINGTON BEACH, 57.3 *m.* (20 alt., 3,378 pop.), is the chief oil-producing center of Orange County. This oil field has yielded more than 270,000,000 barrels during 18 years of operation.

Southward US 101A follows the crest of a low bluff bordering the sea. A phalanx of spidery oil derricks walls the beach from the interior and the rank smell of crude petroleum smothers the ocean salt smell. Day and night, grotesque counterweights revolve clumsily on the riding beams as the oil is sucked up. Below a concrete retaining wall is the wide beach; deep beneath this beach and the ocean is an estimated half billion dollars' worth of unrecovered oil. Because drilling on the beach is prohibited a technique has been developed locally— the so-called "whipstocking"—whereby wells are drilled at an acute angle to reach under the beach and sea.

The wide mouth of the Santa Ana River, principal waterway of Orange County, is spanned at 60.8 *m.* The river rises in the San Bernardino Mountains.

At 62.3 *m.* is the junction with a ramp.

Right on this ramp 0.1 *m.* to State 55; R. on State 55, which runs along a narrow sandspit between ocean and bay, to NEWPORT BEACH, 0.8 *m.* (0.15 alt.; 4,438 pop.). This town and Balboa are Orange County's principal seaside resort areas. Newport Beach is on the northern end of a long narrow sandspit, so near sea level that unusually high tides, driven by strong winds, sometimes pound the town's business district. Newport Beach was founded in 1892 simultaneously with Balboa. In 1902 the two communities were incorporated as one city; today the municipality also includes Newport Heights and Corona del Mar on the mainland, and Balboa Island and Lido Isle in the bay. The population of the area multiplies several times on week ends and during the summer.

The frame and stucco dwellings of Newport Beach merge with those of BALBOA (6 alt.), at 3 *m.* LIDO ISLE and BALBOA ISLAND, in the bay, are elaborately developed summer-home districts with stucco villas of the Mediterranean type. A viaduct at the northern end of the peninsula provides access to Lido Isle; a ferry to Balboa Island.

A narrow opening at the southern end of the sandspit connects Newport Bay with the ocean. The dredged harbor is the home port of many pleasure and commercial craft. Development of the bay began in 1920, when Orange County appropriated half a million dollars for the purpose. Further development was completed in 1936.

South of the ramp-junction US 101A runs between tidal flats and the bay in view of Lido Isle, Balboa Island, and the sail-dotted waters of Newport Bay.

At the southern end of the bay are the Mediterranean type residences of CORONA DEL MAR (crown of the sea), 66 *m.,* a part of Newport. They are grouped between the highway and sea below the San Joaquin Hills. The bar east of the harbor entrance is popular with surfboard devotees, having exceptionally favorable combers for the sport. BAY ISLAND, just offshore, was the home of Madame Helene Modjeska, the Polish-born actress, from the spring of 1907 until her death in April 1909 (*see Tour 4*); it is sometimes called Modjeska Island.

US 101A ascends the flank of the San Joaquin Hills, with the surface of the sea shattered by sunbeams. Little rocky coves with small shelving beaches notch the cliffs, the highway descending briefly towards each and climbing as swiftly out again. Huge chunks of rocks, once part of the cliffs, stud the shore. Such beaches are populated by marine fauna and flora in such variety that comparatively few kinds are popularly known, and unestimated hundreds remain to be named and classified by scientists. Pools left by receding tides and rocks uncovered at ebbtide are the best places to observe these fantastic and often exquisite forms of life. Sea lettuce, sea moss, and long thin-bladed surf grass commonly predominate in the matted growths of marine vegetation covering many of the rocks; these tangles are rich in small animal life, particularly the lower invertebrates, such as corals and sponges, and brightly colored marine worms, some flat like leaves and others long and round.

One of the most spectacular seashore sights on the Pacific Coast is the after-dark display of luminescence in the breakers which accompanies the occasional appearance—usually in early autumn—of inconceivably great numbers of protozoa called dinoflagellates, each of which is equipped with two whiplike lashes that beat continually, sending it through the water.

The canals of a living sponge are lined with cells having one lash each; these lashes, continually beating in one direction, circulate sea water through the sponge and carry oxygen and food material to the cells. The sponge is such a primitive form of life that the question whether it was an animal or a plant was not settled among scientists until after the perfection of the microscope. Although there are 13 varieties of sponges on the California coast—which appear mostly as flat patches of red, yellow, or dirty white on rocks, wharf piles, and even on the backs of crabs—none are of use commercially.

The sea anemone, which looks like a flower-head with many small fleshy petals, is quite common on California beaches. Colors range from red to green, sometimes bright, sometimes pale; sizes vary from a fraction of an inch to nearly six inches across the disk. In the middle of the disk is the animal's slit-like mouth, to which prey is brought by sudden forcible closing-in of the petal-like tentacles. Unsqueamish bathers who will poke a toe or finger into the sea anemone can feel the slight sucking sensation caused by the contraction. Stingers in the tentacles, which can stun small creatures swallowed by the anemone, do not harm human flesh.

The only true coral on the California coast looks very much like a small sea anemone, but unlike the anemone, which leaves no skeleton when it dies, the coral leaves behind its shallow, thin-walled, calcareous cup patterned inside with delicate ridges. They are found attached to the rocks at the tide's edge. The relationship between the sea anemone and this type of coral is obvious, but while they are relatives of the true colonial corals of tropical waters, the kinship is not so apparent.

Jellyfish, common all along the coast and often washed up on the beach in gelatinous blobs, range from a fraction of an inch to more than 12 inches in diameter and in color from light brown to rose or purple. They have fleshy lips depending from the mouth on the underside of the umbrella; in some varieties long tentacles hang from the umbrella margin. Surf bathers are sometimes painfully stung by brushing against the tentacles, which have nettle cells. Jellyfish are luminous when disturbed after dark, and a boat cutting through a swarm of them will leave balls of blue-green light bobbing behind it in the water.

A delicate, grayish ball of shell-like material, marked from pole to pole with a pattern of bumps and perforations, is frequently found washed up on shore. It is the test, or "skeleton" of the sea urchin, a baseball-sized animal that looks like a purple chestnut. It is considered edible in some countries and thousands are sold in the fish markets of Marseilles. The sand dollar is a flat variety of sea urchin with spines modified to the fineness of velvet; it leaves a thin white cooky-like shell on the beach after death.

Crabs are perhaps the most readily observed of all water's edge life; rock crevices teem with them, and a dead fish on the beach draws numbers of them to feast and fight. Sand crabs—which are not true crabs and have no claws, but look like large steel-gray beetles—bury themselves in colonies in the wet sand where the water washes over them; their hiding places are marked by little V-shaped ripple marks made by their exposed antennae. Sand crabs are good bait for many kinds of fish, and the corbina and yellow-fin are sometimes caught in the surf as they run in for a sand crab tidbit.

The spiny lobster of the Pacific Coast, which lacks the heavy claws of the Atlantic lobster, was named for the short thorn-like spines upon its carapace (forepart of the back). It is about 12 to 14 inches long, lives in the kelp beds offshore, and is less often seen on the beach than is its neatly cast-off "shell," or exo-skeleton.

Little pink- or brown-shelled acorn-cup barnacles are very common along the coast, thickly encrusting rocks. The gooseneck barnacle, frequently washed up on the beach in clumps of three or more, looks somewhat like the foot and leg of some curious little animal with small, blunt toenails or hoof-plates; the principal parts of the animal's body are contained in the "hoof"-plated end, and the tough reddish-brown stalk, by which it is attached to the others of the clump, is an elongation of the head. These barnacles are edible when boiled and skinned, but there is only one record of their use for food in California: in 1916 a chef of a smart San Francisco hotel ordered several pounds prepared for the delectation of epicures.

The rock oyster, which occurs in hard clumps of four or more, is often found on the southern California coast, but is not exploited commercially. The bean clam, which has smooth little whitish-buff shells usually less than three quarters of an inch long, is found only in southern California waters. Families living near the beach gather them by the dishpanful and cook them shell and all, making a soup, but they are not nearly as numerous as they were several years ago when they were often washed up on the beach in mile-long windrows. Abalones are found at low tide in many places.

More than 21,000 species of shelled mollusks are found on the Pacific Coast; many are notable for the beauty or curiosity of their shells. The California frog-shell, the triton, and the trophon are among the rarest but most interesting finds: they are large spiral shells, usually about four inches long, marked with large noded ridges, flaring longitudinal ridges from spire to base, or spectacular crooked spikes flaring outward from the whorls. The Thais shells are small, but exquisitely sculptured; the purple channeled Thais has close-set, deeply-carved ridges following the whorls. The opal shells and wentle traps are sharp-spired shells with ridges crossing the whorls.

Un-shelled mollusks include the sea slugs, the octopus and the squid; two small shore varieties of octopus are found in the tide pools along the coast, or on the beach. These exhibit brighter colors than the huge devilfish of deep water, but the colors of all octopuses and squids continually change as the animals expand and contract various parts of the body, gray or black flowing into brown, chocolate-red, purple, and other shades.

The moray or conger eel, encountered in rock caverns and tide pools along the coast, has strong, sharp teeth with which it fights savagely when caught. A menace to bathers in quiet water at low tide is the sting ray, a brownish creature with very flat body and a whip-lash tail having a sharp spine at its base. The spine can inflict a serious wound if stepped on.

Most birds of the seashore are best observed on uninhabited beaches about the mouths of streams and run-off channels, but sea-gulls are everywhere numerous. These graceful creatures are always hungry; they hover in flapping swarms about fishing pelicans, with grating screeches and hen-like squawks. In winter they fly far inland for week-long visits, perhaps no more to avoid ocean storms than to search for food. The older birds are clean gray and white, the young, mottled brown and white.

There are two pelicans on this coast—the brown and the white. Both are majestic in flight, and often a small flock sails along in single file close to the wharves and beaches.

Cormorants—brown, long-necked, duck-sized birds—also fly single file low over the water, but their wings beat swiftly like those of game birds. After a morning's fishing they flock on rocks or deserted piers where they sit holding out their wings to dry.

Groups of little gray-and-white sanderlings, members of the sand-piper family, scamper after waves on the beach to snatch up small marine creatures uncovered by the receding water, scampering back again as the following wave rolls in. Sometimes they seem to be play-ing tag with the waves, not stopping to eat.

CRYSTAL COVE CAMP, 68.7 *m.,* a colony of seaside cottages, is in a rocky cove below the highway.

The southern end of crescent-shaped EL MORRO (the headland) BEACH, 70.5 *m.*, bordering El Morro Bay, is ABALONE POINT, which juts into the sea. The large edible mollusk for which the point was named was once found along the coast in great numbers before its depletion because of the demand for abalone-shell jewelry and abalone steaks. It is now seen along this coast only occasionally, clinging to rocks uncovered at ebb tide; commercial abalone fishing is done only in the vicinity of Monterey.

Until the Chinese came to California during the gold-rush days, only the Indians used abalones. They ate the meat and pieces of the shell were a medium of exchange. Although the Chinese began using the meat at once with delight, having known it as a delicacy in their native land, they threw the shells away. The Americans did not appreciate either the meat or the shells at first, but with the settling of the seaboard regions and the growth of industries, the possibilities of popularizing abalone-shell curios and jewelry were seen, and manufacture began. By 1879 the value of the shells was twice that of the meats; by 1913 the meat was on the market for Americans, but the manufacture of jewelry from the shell was still important, and remained so until its popularity faded about 1920.

EMERALD BAY, 71.2 *m.*, is a sheltered curve of white sand and clear green water below steep cliffs. Dark trees and thickets temper the starkness of the white villa walls, which have red-tile roofs. Winding roads lead down to the beach on the southern side of Abalone Point.

Seascapes in the vicinity of LAGUNA BEACH, 73.1 *m.* (17 alt., 4,460 pop.), lying between two rocky, tree-tufted capes along a mile of curving strand, have created an artists' colony here. Above the small business district along the highway are the San Joaquin Hills, where many people live because of the exceptional marine views. Crooked streets leading to hilltops, valleys, coves, and rocky bluffs, are lined with homes and studios of unusual design. Studios are seen at every turn—little ones with shingled roofs, big and pretentious ones with huge skylights, and eccentric ones of whimsical shape.

Artists are seen in the coves or on the bluffs at almost any time of the day, sketching, drawing, painting. Annually the Laguna Beach Artists' Ball attracts visitors who stroll about viewing the shop windows filled with the work of local artists. Since 1932 the Festival of Arts, sponsored by members of the Laguna Beach Art Association, has also been an annual event. Highlight of the festival is the Pageant of Masters, in which well-known paintings and sculptures by the greatest artists of the past are recreated with live figures.

Since 1902, when Conway Griffith, a water colorist, was given a free buggy-ride from Santa Ana and told to help himself to the best room in Laguna Beach's leading hotel, the town has been a gathering place for artists, writers, and sculptors. Griffith eventually rented a cottage here, but the first painter to build his own studio was Gardner Symonds.

The beauty of Laguna Beach's surroundings also attracts many excursionists, but for the most part the village has been kept quiet and uncommercial.

The LAGUNA BEACH ART ASSOCIATION GALLERY (*open 10-5; adm. 10¢*), Aster St. and Coast Hwy., is a concrete building of the modified Spanish type. Bi-monthly displays by members are shown in the upper gallery. The lower gallery is used for one-man shows, loaned groups of paintings, etchings, and photographs, and the work of students and school children. Traveling shows originating here are often sent to various parts of the United States.

ARCH BEACH, 74.4 *m.*, a corporate part of Laguna Beach, lies along the broken cliffs, with studios and homes on the bluff and the mountain slope. Art shops, curio stores, and studios line the highway.

Along the entire section of coast between Laguna Beach and Dana Point the highway runs close to the edge of high cliffs, within sound of the perpetual roar of sea against the rocks far below.

THREE ARCH BAY, 77.6 *m.*, is a seaside settlement named for three rocky arches carved out of the cliffs by the sea.

The town of DANA POINT, 80.6 *m.* (175 alt., 140 pop.), is a group of stuccoed buildings, red-roofed and balconied, on the heights.

The name of DANA POINT, a diamond-shaped headland, commemorates Richard Henry Dana, who mentioned the spot in his *Two Years Before the Mast*. Dana, a Harvard student in ill health, had sailed aboard the four-masted brig *Pilgrim* from Boston around Cape Horn to the western coast of North America in 1834. Of this promontory he wrote: ". . . coasting along the quiet shore we came to anchor . . . abreast of a steep hill which overhung the water and was twice as high as our royal mast. The shore is rocky and directly exposed. . . . How we were to get the hides down or goods up on the tableland on which the Mission was located, was more than we could tell. . . . The only habitation in sight was the small, white mission of San Capistrano with a few Indian huts about. . . . Reaching the brow of the hill we found several piles of hides. The captain told us to begin and throw the hides down . . . a distance of 400 feet. Down this height we pitched the hides, throwing them as far out into the air as we could. . . ." Dana on two occasions scaled the cliff by the path to pitch the hides below. The sailors picked them up and carried them on their heads to the waiting shore boats. Some of the hides failed to clear and were lodged in crevices part way down. To reach these, tackle was hung over the top of the cliff and Dana went down a rope to dislodge them.

DOHENY PARK, 81.6 *m.* (0 to 50 alt., 300 pop.), lies partly on the bluffs, partly along the highway at sea level. Named for Edward Lawrence Doheny (*see Downtown Los Angeles*), the oil operator, Doheny Park is a carefully kept group of seaside homes. At the foot of the bluff is DOHENY STATE PARK (R), a public playground and camp site, presented to the state by Doheny in 1934.

At 81.9 *m.* is the junction with US 101 (*see Tour 4*).

Tour 5A

TO SANTA CATALINA ISLAND

Wilmington to Avalon, Santa Catalina Island, 27 m. by sea.

Communication by plane and boat: steamer leaves Wilmington Harbor for island 9:30, 10 a.m., 4 p.m. in summer, 10 a.m. in winter; $3.50-$4.25 round trip, half fares $1.75-$2.15, trip 2¼ hours one way; private automobiles prohibited; all types of accommodations; open all seasons, summer months most popular.

Santa Catalina, 21 miles long by three-quarters to eight miles wide, is the second largest of the eight Channel Islands off the coast of southern California. A rugged mountain chain, culminating in Mount Orizaba (2,109 alt.) and Mount Black Jack (2,000 alt.), extends the length of the island, with canyons and spurs running down to the sea.

In prehistoric times the island was the habitat of sun-worshipping Indians of the Shoshone tribe. Later it was a haven for early Spanish adventurers, and in the 19th century became a port of call for buccaneers and a base for Yankee smugglers. The aura of adventure and violence that enveloped it for more than three centuries ended with a brief mining boom during the Civil War.

At present the 48,438-acre island is a privately owned and exploited pleasure resort. Its metropolis, Avalon, on the eastern end of the leeward side, is an incorporated city with its own municipal government and public schools, and numerous hotels, apartment houses, bungalow courts and cottages. An elaborate casino and other recreational facilities and means of entertainment are in or near the town. One hundred and thirty miles of graveled and dirt roads and a network of bridle paths and hiking trails penetrate the interior, where are wild boar, goat and buffalo herds, quail, Indian caves and burial grounds. Steamships carry most of the half million people who visit the island annually, although seaplanes bring approximately 25,000 a year.

Santa Catalina was discovered by Juan Rodriguez Cabrillo, the Portuguese navigator, in 1542. On October 8 of that year he anchored the *San Salvadore* and *La Vittoria* in the Bay of the Seven Moons, now called Avalon Bay, and named the island La Vittoria for his flagship. Cabrillo died on the northward voyage, but months later his ships returned and again laid over here for several days. In 1602, 60 years later, another expedition, seeking a port for Spanish galleons returning from Manila, sailed from Acapulco, Mexico, under command of Sebastian Vizcaino. Vizcaino's three caravels dropped anchor at the island November 24, 1602, the eve of the feast of St. Catherine of

Alexandria, and the navigator accordingly named the island Santa Catalina (Saint Catherine). From the departure of Vizcaino until the founding of the first mainland missions in the late 18th century, nearly 200 years, Spain showed no more interest in the island than it did in the mainland.

In 1805 Captain William Shaler, master of the *Leila Byrd,* out of Boston, anchored in Catalina Harbor, the first American shipmaster of record to see the place. Thereafter, and until 1821, when Mexico freed herself from Spain and lifted the Spanish ban on foreign trade in California, Santa Catalina was a base for illegal Yankee trading operations with the mainland missions and ranches, and was also visited by Russian hunters from Alaska, who descended with crews of Alaskan Aleuts and Kodiaks to hunt the sea otter that abounded in the waters around the island.

Santa Catalina remained a Mexican possession until the Treaty of Guadalupe-Hidalgo was ratified in the spring of 1848. Two years previous the private ownership of the island had passed, as the last of the Mexican land grants, to Thomas Robbins, an American of Santa Barbara. Robbins petitioned for the island as a ranch, and Pio Pico, the last Mexican Governor, granted it; according to one story the governor accepted a horse and saddle in return.

After American occupation the first recorded transfer of the island was to Nicolas Covarrubias. In 1863, at the height of a gold boom on the north end of the island Covarrubias sold the property to a man named Parker, who in turn sold it to James Lick of San Francisco for $80,000. In 1887 Lick sold it for $200,000 to George R. Shatto, who first undertook to develop it as a pleasure resort. Shatto platted a town (Avalon) at what was then known as Timm's Landing, named it for himself, and sold optional mining rights in the interior to an English syndicate. Ore was carried by burros from Silver Canyon to the town, but the operations proved unprofitable and the syndicate was dissolved in 1889. Three years later Shatto sold the island to Judge J. B., Captain William, and Hancock Banning, sons of Phineas Banning, founder of Wilmington. The Banning brothers formed the Santa Catalina Island Company for the purpose of developing the place as a pleasure and fisherman's resort, put steamers into service from the mainland, built a hotel, and founded an aquarium on the Avalon water front.

William Wrigley, Jr.'s purchase of the island for $3,000,000 in 1919 resulted in the rebuilding of Avalon and an enormous expansion of the various facilities. Wrigley acquired new steamers for the trip to the mainland, built new piers, erected hotels, developed roads and trails to interior points, and sponsored industries. He solved three of the island's outstanding problems—water, housing, and sanitation; more than one million dollars were spent for water facilities alone. Santa Catalina Island is still largely owned by the second Santa Catalina Island Company founded in 1919 by Wrigley and now controlled by his son, Philip Knight Wrigley.

Pier 185, the CATALINA TERMINAL, 0 *m.*, is at the foot of Avalon Blvd. in Wilmington (*see The Harbor*).

AVALON, 27 *m.* (20 alt., 1,637 winter pop., 15,000 to 25,000 summer pop.), along the crescent-shaped shore of Avalon Bay is the center of resort and sports activities. Its modified-Spanish character was introduced by William Wrigley, Jr., shortly after his purchase of the island in 1919. The streets are laid out for leisurely strolling, free from the worries of vehicular traffic. Crescent Avenue, the main street, follows the curve of bay and beach, widening in the downtown area to a plaza. Stores, hotels, cafes, and waiting rooms facing upon it were designed in a modified early Spanish style and painted light neutral tones that blend into a general color scheme. Palms and silver-leaved olive trees, set in stone boxes in the center of the avenue, shade low settees and stone benches; grassy squares and fountains, strumming troubadours in velvet costumes, and senoritas in spangled skirts, strolling among the throngs of summer visitors on boardwalk and strand, give the atmosphere.

When in 1887 Shatto purchased the island, he set aside 731 acres for the town by the bay, including what was then called Timm's Landing. The founder named the town "Shatto" for himself, but later changed it to Avalon, as suggested by his sister, who imagined a resemblance of the site to the fanciful "island Valley of Avilion" (often spelled Avalon), described in Tennyson's *Idylls of the King*. Avalon's growth as a resort was slow and erratic under the ownership of Shatto and of the Banning brothers later. In 1913 tents outnumbered the frame houses. Ridding "Rag City," as it was sometimes called, of this fire hazard was undertaken by the Wrigley organization soon after the island was purchased.

The BOARDWALK, a one and three-quarter mile promenade, skirts the curving shore between Pebbly Beach at the east end of the bay and the St. Catherine Hotel at the west end. After turning Abalone Point and skirting Lovers' Cove, it becomes Avalon's paved and ornamented Crescent Avenue at a point opposite Playground Park, then continues to the St. Catherine Hotel as a boardwalk. Unspoiled by the usual cheap resort refreshment stands and concession booths, it is nonetheless one of the principal recreational facilities of the island.

The municipally owned PLEASURE PIER, foot of Catalina Avenue, has booths where steamer tickets are sold and arrangements are made for hiring or taking passage on various types of sport and pleasure craft—rowboats, motorboats, excursion boats, and fishing barges. Guides are available for excursions and fishing trips. Bait is for sale, and fishing tackle for sale or rent.

EL ENCANTO (the enchanted), approached from Crescent Avenue on St. Catherine Way, is a collection of small shops and booths around a patio. Indian and Mexican craftsmen display native wares in a glorified version of an early California market place. The arcaded shops are on the gentle slope of a hill and the patio holds a central fountain and tropical trees and shrubs. An open-air dining place, reached by ascending steps at the patio's farther end, serves Spanish and American food.

The TUNA CLUB (*members only*), on the Boardwalk, is a two-story, white frame clubhouse, modern Japanese in appearance, on piles above the shore of Avalon Bay. The walls of the various rooms are hung with mounted fish in glass-paneled frames, each with a brass plate bearing the name of the fisherman and the weight and classification of the specimen caught.

The club awards six different buttons, covering the six classifications, according to weight, for taking tuna, marlin, and broadbill swordfish on light or heavy tackle. The 251-pound tuna landed under heavy tackle specifications by Colonel C. P. Morehouse of Pasadena in 1899 is still the record catch in that division. The record for broadbill swordfish is the 573-pounder (heavy tackle) taken by George C. Thomas of Beverly Hills, in 1927; and for marlin, the 406-pound specimen landed by A. R. Martin of Beverly Hills with heavy tackle in 1932.

The Tuna Club was organized in 1896 and incorporated in 1901. It is affiliated with the British Sea Anglers' Society, the British Tunny and the Fly Fishers' clubs of London, and the Swordfish and Tunny Club of Australia.

Forty years ago the deep waters off Catalina Island abounded with game fish of many varieties—yellowtail, albacore, tuna, marlin, broadbill swordfish, bass, barracuda, and numerous other specimens. Commercial fishing has depleted the yellowtail, rock bass, white sea bass, broadbill swordfish, and tuna, although some varieties—including marlin, barracuda, albacore, and dolphin—have been only partly affected. The decrease in game fish has been caused less by commercial catches of the individual specimens than by depletion of the coast's sardine supply, since game fish of migratory habits follow the sardines for food; thus the depletion of sardines inevitably means the partial disappearance of the big fish. As yet no protective legislation has been enacted to conserve the sardine supply beyond the three-mile limit.

The warm summer weather sees the peak of the return of the sporty yellowtail, tuna, and swordfish to local waters. Fish are divided into two classes according to their gameness: those taken on stillhook—mostly from barges—and those that will take a trolled lure. The largest and most indomitable of the fish are usually caught by trolling, that is, with bait trolled behind a launch moving at speeds varying from two to ten miles an hour, depending on the variety trolled for.

One of the favorites of sportsmen is the yellowfin tuna, a member of the mackerel tribe, a spirited and brilliant fighter, prized both as commercial and game fish. It may reach a weight of 450 pounds, though it seldom exceeds 125 pounds on this coast. It is a warm-water fish with a range extending from Point Concepcion to the Galapagos Islands, and is caught the year-round off the Mexican coast, though the best season in California is from August through October. The yellowfin is taken on lures trolled at speeds up to nine miles an hour; but the bluefin tuna, another hard fighter, is so wary that the bait cannot be trolled in the usual manner, directly behind the boat, but must be run out 150 or 200 feet; it is held at the surface of the water by a box kite. The kite is first sent aloft, and the end of the kite string is tied to a thin thread across a loop in the leader; the line is then run out, care being taken that the boat's wake does not cross the path of the fish and so alarm them. When the tuna strikes the hook, usually baited with a flying fish, the thread breaks, and the kite, which falls into the sea, is retrieved later. Albacore, taken by live-bait fishing, is a small tuna, seldom exceeding 70 pounds, that is an excellent fighter on light tackle; its appearance in these waters is now erratic, the period of greatest abundance being usually in July. It has been taken commercially in tremendous quantities for canning.

Of the swordfish and spearfish tribe, whose upper jaw bones are prolonged into a swordlike structure, five kinds are found on the Pacific coast. The broadbill swordfish, most ferocious and powerful of them all, taken in Catalina waters from May to December, is a dark metallic purple to black in color, weighs between 300 and 500 pounds, and has a flattened, sharp-edge "sword," sometimes four feet long. Unlike tuna and other game fish, swordfish do not travel in schools, but rather singly or in pairs; when they encounter a school of barracuda, mackerel, flying fish, or anchovy, they charge into it, flailing right and left with their swords, and return later to pick up their victims. The broadbill swordfish is harpooned instead of hooked, and will occasionally turn in a rage and charge the fishing boat, driving its sword clear through the planking. A hooked broadbill has been known to fight through a whole day and a whole night before being taken.

Another member of the swordfish tribe, the marlin, so-named because of its short rounded spear suggestive of a marlinspike, is a spectacular fighter, weighing up to 500 pounds or more. Once hooked, this acrobat of the sea may tear off a thousand feet of line; it leaps out of the water, "walks on its tail," and fights to the moment it is gaffed. There are two varieties on the Pacific coast, the black and striped marlin, the latter being reputedly the easier to catch. Both are found around the Channel Islands between late June and October; they are most abundant in September. Also a member of the family is the Pacific sailfish, with a spear and an immense sail-like back fin.

The black sea bass, sometimes called jewfish or giant bass, attains a weight of 500 to 600 pounds, but experienced anglers do not consider it as good a game fish as the tuna or swordfish. Several other members of the bass tribe are found in abundance off southern California and Catalina; some of these, excellent both as game and table fish, are the red spotted rock bass, the kelp bass, and the gray and rose threadfin bass. The California white sea bass, steely blue above with a white belly, running from 20 to 90 pounds, and much taken, both from barges and boats, is not a sea bass at all, but belongs to the croaker family.

Unlike its namesake, the porpoise, or "dolphin," which is a warm-blooded mammal like the whale, the common dolphin is a true fish, beautifully colored and a good fighter, but not frequent north of Baja California. California yellowtails, also known as white salmon, are considered excellent game fish; the yellowtail, occurring in schools along the shores of the mainland and Catalina, averages only 10 to 12 pounds, but is an exceedingly game fish, striking viciously and running fast.

One of the most popular small game fish during the summer months is the long slender California barracuda, an excellent food fish, which can be caught with spoons or feathers trolled at a speed of from two to four miles, though live-bait fishing for them is more common. They are not nearly as fierce as some of their Atlantic cousins; although exceedingly voracious, the barracuda of the Pacific never attack human beings. A dozen or so will attack a school of fish, frightening them into gathering in a compact mass, and then make frequent dashes into the churning victims to grab mouthfuls of the smaller ones. Beginning in March, large schools of California barracuda appear along the Channel Islands, where the largest ones are found, and about the end of September disappear.

The SANTA CATALINA ISLAND YACHT CLUB (*members only*), facing the Boardwalk west of the Tuna Club, is a two-story, white clapboarded structure with an observation tower on the bay side. Active membership is open to owners of yachts used for pleasure purposes only. There is an anchorage in Avalon Bay for a small fleet of pleasure craft. Yachting events and trophy races are sponsored during the season, with special programs held on Labor and Independence Days.

The CASINO (*open 9 p.m. to 1 a.m. May 20-Sept. 10*), on the northwest promontory of Avalon Bay, is of circular cantilever construction, ornamented in a modern adaptation of the Moorish-Spanish manner. Its white walls, in bold relief against the blue of the sky and bay, are among the first island features noticed by incoming steamer passengers. The lower floor is a theatre seating 1,200 persons. Two ramps of five stages each give access to the upper floor, in which is a large circular ballroom, unbroken by pillars, and a 100-foot-long Marine Bar decorated with fantastic murals depicting fish. In the lobby are nine panel murals of the submarine gardens, and ten cone-shaped panel murals circle the inner walls.

The building was completed in 1929; in 1930 the architects, Sumner and Spaulding of Los Angeles, were given the Honor Award of the Southern California Chapter of the American Institute of Architects for its design.

The ST. CATHERINE HOTEL, 0.5 *m.,* northwest of Avalon in the mouth of DESCANSO CANYON, is one of the leading centers of social activity. The rambling, three-story tile-roofed structure is surrounded by lawns and subtropical trees. The hotel faces its private beach on Descanso Bay, and has the usual recreational facilities. The first unit of the St. Catherine was built in 1918 by Captain Hancock Banning on the site of his former home. When William Wrigley, Jr., purchased the island a year later he rebuilt this unit and enlarged the hotel to its present size.

The SANTA CATALINA AIRPORT, at HAMILTON BEACH, 0.3 m., west of the St. Catherine Hotel, is the terminus of the Wilmington-Catalina Airline (*two round-trip flights daily in safe weather, flights more frequent depending upon passenger-volume in season, flight schedule varies according to time of tides; $5 one way, $7 round trip, one way by plane and one way by boat, no half fares, 25-pound free baggage allowance; flight about 16 minutes one way*). Two twin-motored Douglas Dolphin amphibian planes make the round trip between the seaplane landing at the foot of Avalon Boulevard in Wilmington to this airport. The plane lands in the water, the wheels are lowered, and the craft rolled up a ramp under its own power to a turntable, where it is about-faced for the return flight. Commercial air service to the island was begun in April 1919 by Sidney Chaplin, brother of Charles Chaplin. The fare at that time was $42.50 for one or two passengers.

The GLIDDEN INDIAN MUSEUM (*open 9-5; adm. 25¢*), on the hill slope above Avalon, contains a comprehensive collection of Channel Island archaeological relics. The collection includes 500,000 pieces of wampum, as well as Spanish and Venetian beads; unassembled bones of an estimated 3,000 skeletons; and some 10,000 teeth. Forty cases are filled with pestles, mortars, flutes, pipes, arrowheads, cooking stones, bone and stone knives, treasure boxes, war clubs, and fishhooks. One of the most interesting exhibits is a great stone burial urn about 18 inches in diameter, its rim geometrically decorated with wampum. When the urn was discovered it contained the flexed skeleton of a girl four or five years old, probably the daughter of a chief. Many of the recoveries came from the large aboriginal burial grounds at White's Landing, Little Harbor, the Isthmus, Empire Landing, and Johnson's Landing on the island.

The museum was established in 1923 by Ralph Glidden, who prior to that time had collected for the Heye Foundation Museum of the American Indian in New York City.

The Santa Catalina Indians, or Gabrielinos (a Spanish term from the Mission San Gabriel), were a branch of the Shoshone, belonging to the great Uto-Aztecan family. In skin pigmentation they were exceptionally fair, and culturally were definitely superior to many California tribes. The Catalenos, as they were known to the Spaniards, called their island "Pimu" or "Pipimar," or sometimes "Pimugna."

The earliest mention of the Santa Catalina Indians in the records of white man is in an account of the voyage of Cabrillo in 1542. Sixty years later, when Sebastian Vizcaino came, he described the Indians as fine-looking, and dressed in skins; and he mentioned the numerous houses and *rancherias* of the isle, and the canoes capable of holding 20 men. Father Torquemada, historian with Vizcaino, considered the Catalenos far superior to the natives of the mainland. He says that the women were attractive and modest, and the children "white and ruddy and very smiling."

Although the manuscripts of the early Spanish historians have been of great value, they do not include much detail of Indian life, and scientists have deduced what is known of these Indians from their artifacts. Almost every canyon and cove hold the remains of villages rich in relics, sometimes only half-hidden under the tangled brush and cacti. Without doubt the Catalenos lived mostly from the sea; the huge piles of abalone shells indicate the importance of abalone as a food, and the numerous bones of tuna and swordfish, seals and whales and sea-elephants, suggest that the Indians were in all likelihood expert fishermen. There is evidence, too, of other food: bones of birds, coyotes, and rattlesnakes; flat mortars of stone, of the kind used for grinding acorns, and deep ones for holding seeds. Stone scrapers for skins are found in numbers, and grinders and pestles of many sizes. Knives are of quartz or chert, some crude, but others showing evidence of patient and skilled workmanship; many have wooden handles. There are finely polished plummets of green stone, used as sinkers for nets, and fishhooks of pearly abalone and of bone, beautifully fashioned, with a groove for the line, which was made of seaweed.

As sculptors the Santa Catalina Indians reached a degree of skill that was not primitive in any sense. In the deepest burial areas crudely shaped vessels have been found, unpolished and irregular, along with blunt clublike instruments. But in overlying deposits are forms showing progressive development until, in the later ones, appear highly conventionalized carvings of dolphins, whales, sea lions, flying fish, in which the artist caught the essence of the subject with imagination and simplicity. With these are the vessels, also cut with stone from stone, simple in outline but of perfect workmanship.

Flutes, whistles, and fifes are frequently discovered in the old townsites; they are of deer bone, many perforated with holes, the larger end closed by asphaltum, some decorated with abalone and asphaltum mosaic. Most probably they were used in the mourning ceremonies, which were held not so much for the death of an individual as in commemoration of all who had died. In historic times the singing and dancing continued for five days, each song or verse ending with a growl. Burial rather than cremation was prevalent with the Catalenos throughout the whole of their history, a practice differentiating them from Indians of the mainland. However, the possessions of the dead were burned, with protracted rites, and great care was taken to see that nothing was left undestroyed. Very little has been discovered concerning other social customs. Marriage was by purchase, and polygamy common; incest was punished by death; infidelity of the wife was also thus punishable, although the usual solution was for the injured man to take the seducer's mate in exchange. In each village there was a chief, but his particular importance and functions are not known.

The Catalenos were primitive builders: their houses, of tule mats on a framework of poles, soon disintegrated and little is known of their appearance. The diary of the expedition of Miguel Costanso in 1769 says that they lived in villages of dome-shaped houses, up to 55 feet in diameter, each house containing four families. In general a town had one sweat-house, partly underground, with a roof of earth, and heated by fire and smoke; and a circular *yoba* (religious house) walled with willows woven wicker-fashion among stakes. The trading-canoes, which were undoubtedly more important to them than houses, were not dugouts owing to the scarcity of big timber on the island, but were made of planks crudely split with wedges, lashed and asphalted together. The Catalina Indians made no pottery; all their dishes and utensils were cut out of steatite from the great soapstone ledges of Santa Catalina, the best supply of this material in California at the time. Their manufactory can still be seen at Empire Landing (*see below*) where they cut *ollas* (pots) with quartz chisels, and expertly rounded and curved the edges.

The reason for the disappearance of the Indians from Santa Catalina Island is not definitely known. It is believed that they were slaughtered in great numbers by the Alaskan Aleuts and Kodiaks brought south by the Russians to hunt otter; they were a gentle people and would have been no match for the fierce northerners. Those who remained were probably induced by the mission priests, during the first half of the 19th century, to come to the mainland for protection, where their identity became lost among the bewildering massing of the tribes about the missions.

In the CHIMES TOWER, above the Glidden Museum, are the Avalon Westminster Chimes, which automatically sound the time at 15-minute intervals from 7 a.m. to 10 p.m. to welcome the incoming steamer from the mainland.

The SANTA CATALINA ISLAND VISITORS' COUNTRY CLUB (*free; greens fee $1*), on a knoll at the head of Sumner Avenue in Avalon Canyon, is open to all visitors the year round. The rambling clubhouse overlooks the spring training park of the Chicago Cubs. The stuccoed building is roofed with red tile, and surrounds a patio planted with palms and shrubbery. Facilities include an 18-hole golf course, a nine-hole pitch-and-putt course, and tennis courts.

Since 1921, the CATALINA BASEBALL PARK (*exhibition games free; 12 m. daily, Feb. 25 to Mar. 15*), Fremont St. and Avalon Blvd., has been the spring training camp of the Wrigley-owned Chicago Cubs, of the National League. The diamond is between Avalon Boulevard and the foothills, with the fairways of the Visitors' Country Club links encircling the farther end. The park is used by an Avalon team during the summer.

The CATALINA NURSERY, east side of Avalon Boulevard south of the Visitors' Club course, grows flowers, trees, and shrubs. During the various blooming seasons the three-acre tract set aside for the cut flower trade is beautiful with asters, dahlias, gladioli, iris, marigolds, zinnias, daisies, chrysanthemums, delphinium, poinsettias, and other flowers.

The 15-acre orchard—almond, fig, orange, lime, grapefruit—extends from the nursery headquarters to the Wrigley Memorial. Many kinds of trees, shrubs, vines, succulents, and cacti are propagated.

The BIRD PARK (*open 8-6; free; reached by busses leaving corner of Crescent and Metropole Aves. every half hr. 7-7*), in Avalon Canyon, 2 *m.* from Avalon, contains more than 8,000 birds of 650 varieties, principally from foreign countries. Of its 20 acres, 10 are set aside for breeding purposes. The birds are housed in 520 cages, most of them outdoors and in surroundings simulating the birds' native habitats. Among the inhabitants are plumed birds of paradise; an ibis, once sacred to the Pharaohs of Egypt; toucans, with huge beaks shaped like bananas; song birds small enough to fit into a thimble; ostriches, emus, and cassowaries; a "double-billed" rhinoceros hornbill, whose kind are rarely kept alive in captivity; trained macaws and penguins; talking ravens; and scores of weird-looking specimens from India, China, South America, Siam, Australia, New Zealand, Malaya, and the South Sea Islands. Visitors are partial to the talking mynah birds from southeastern Asia, which can be taught to pronounce difficult words. Jimmie, a mynah, is the park's foremost conversationalist.

Many of the park birds have appeared in motion pictures, among them Old Jack, a loquacious, 63-year-old raven of kleptomaniac propensities whose caustic replies to greetings are the delight of children and grown-ups alike. Old Jack entered the movies in early silent films and is still in demand. His actions and postures were photographed by cameramen of the Walt Disney Studio and reproduced in one of the characters of *Snow White and the Seven Dwarfs*. Rivaling Old Jack in favor is Oscar the Penguin, whose most recent movie appearance was in *The Young in Heart*. Other bird actors are Cocky, a New Zealand cockatoo that appeared with Fredric March in *Buccaneer;* and the cassowary, a very vicious and short-tempered bird used in a scene in *Treasure Island*.

The WRIGLEY MEMORIAL, head of Avalon Canyon, 1 *m.* SW. of Bird Park, is a white stone mausoleum containing the remains of William Wrigley, Jr. The repository was erected in 1936 from island stone and sand; the only imported material is the Georgian marble lining the crypts. The land surrounding the memorial is maintained in its primitive state.

EAGLES NEST LODGE, 10 *m.* from Avalon in the interior of the island (*visited on the Isthmus Auto Tour; see below*), is a one-story rustic hunting lodge named for nearby Eagle Mountain. All hunting on Santa Catalina Island, which is a private preserve, is conducted in supervised trips (*$10 a day for each person, including guide service and transportation*). For boars and goats—hunted the year round with a deer rifle and from horseback—no state license is required, but sportsmen must obtain a permit from the Santa Catalina Island Company. Hunting of Catalina quail (*Nov. 15 to Dec. 31*), a large variety found nowhere else, requires a state license as well as a permit from the company.

Between 20,000 and 30,000 wild mountain goats and some 2,000 wild hogs roam the interior. The unsupported legend is that their progenitors were left by Spanish explorers, either by Cabrillo in 1542 or by Father Torquemada of Vizcaino's 1602 expedition. Two herds of bison (*no hunting*), donated to the Santa Catalina Island Company several years ago by a motion-picture company after completion of a film, also roam the island.

The ISTHMUS, in the northwest section of the island (*reached on the 'Round the Island Cruise and Isthmus Auto Tour; see below*), is a narrow neck of land where the island is almost cut in two. The flat mesa between Isthmus Cove on the leeward side and Catalina Harbor on the windward side is only a half mile wide. It was in Catalina Harbor that the *Lelia Byrd* dropped anchor in 1805. Fronting Isthmus Cove is a settlement of one-story, thatched cottages used by the summer population. The Isthmus has been chosen by many motion-picture companies as location for sea pictures; more than 60 silent and talking films have been made here, wholly or in part. Among the most recent were *Hurricane, Ebb Tide, Treasure Island* and *Submarine D-1*.

One mile offshore at Isthmus Cove is uninhabited BIRD ROCK, of about two acres, a nesting place for sea gulls, pelicans, and cormorants. SHIP ROCK, a mile beyond Bird Rock, resembles a ship under full sail.

Midway between Isthmus Cove and Catalina Harbor are the former UNITED STATES GOVERNMENT BARRACKS, built in 1864 to house Union troops sent to the island to prevent seizure of Catalina Harbor by Southern sympathizers, who intended to establish a base for Confederate privateers here. Remodeled in 1930, the buildings are now the quarters of employees of the Santa Catalina Island Company.

CONDUCTED TOURS

(*All boats boarded at Avalon Pier; auto trips from Avalon Plaza; rates vary from season to season.*)

The GLASS BOTTOM BOAT TRIP (*frequent daily departures; 5½ miles; 45 minutes*), visits the marine gardens extending along the protected north shore of the island from Pebbly Beach to Emerald Bay, a distance of 17 miles. The section visited by the boat is near Avalon—between Abalone Point and Pebbly Beach. As the glass-bottomed boat proceeds slowly along the coast, a constantly changing view of life on the floor of the sea is revealed. Brightly-colored fish dart in and out among the shell-encrusted rocks, and strands of waving sea fern, sea grasses, rainbow kelp, and boa-feather moss wave upward from beds of red and lavender algae. Quills of a sea-urchin protrude from among rocks to which live abalone cling; and sea cucumbers lie motionless among masses of bridal veil moss and sea heather. On rare occasions a sinister-appearing, but harmless, sandshark is seen prowling the ocean floor. During the trip divers go over the side and swim beneath the boat in view of the passengers.

The SEAL ROCK TRIP (*frequent daily departures; 11 miles; 1½ hrs.*), is made along the jagged lee shore of the island to the cluster of rocks just off NORTHEAST POINT, the home of several hundred hair "seals," or California sea lions. The color of the animals varies from light brown to deep black; some attain a weight of a ton or more, and have a life span of 50 years. Although a few remain on the rocks the year round, most of them follow the shifting of the warm Japan current, going southward to Mexican waters for the summer. They are most plentiful on Seal Rocks from September to May.

The EVENING FLYING FISH TRIP (*daily, Apr. to Oct., 40 minutes*), follows the north here. A 45-million candlepower searchlight attached to the vessel bores through the night sky, attracting thousands of flying fish and reflecting the iridescent colors of their "wings" (fins). The flight of the fish resembles the glide of an airplane, as its fins remain rigid. The wriggling lower part of the tail provides motive power; the upper part acts as a rudder. The fish can glide from 50 to 100 yards, but must return to the water when its wings dry. The flying fish, which range in length from 12 to 18 inches, keep to deep water during the day but at night seek the shallower shore regions. A migratory species, they prefer warm waters, and are seen off Santa Catalina Island only during the summer.

The AVALON SPEEDBOAT TRIP (*frequent daily departures; 2 miles*), is a 50-mile-an-hour ride in high-powered speedboats.

The ISTHMUS BOAT TRIP (*May to Oct.; 28-mile round trip; 3 hrs.*), is a cruise along the lee coast of the island, from Avalon Bay to Isthmus Cove, with an hour's stop for lunch and sightseeing at the Isthmus. The course follows the curving shore and affords close views of the rock formations, caves, and beaches.

The 'ROUND THE ISLAND CRUISE (*10:30 a.m. Sun. only, Apr. to Oct.; 55 miles; 3 to 3½ hrs.*), is taken in a large double-deck excursion boat. From Avalon to Isthmus Cove the boat follows the same course as on the Isthmus boat trip (*see above*). After a 45-minute stop-over at the Isthmus, the course is northwest, past the mouth of CHERRY VALLEY, honey-combed with tunnels and shafts dating from the Civil War mining boom. Just around Red Point, the island narrows to LAND'S END, and the steamer begins to feel the force of waves from the open sea. Rounding Occidental Point, at Land's End, and heading down the south coast, the wildest of the island's land- and seascapes are seen: steep cliffs rearing skyward, the surf booming at their base. This part of the island is as wild and uncultivated as when the white man first visited it 400 years ago. Between Eagle Rock and Catalina Harbor the coast line is incised with a series of small coves—Ironbound Bay, Lobster Bay, Smugglers' Cove—in which Orientals who had been deported under the 1855 China Boy Laws were hidden until they could be smuggled back to the mainland. South of the wide mouth of Catalina Harbor the island widens again, reaching its greatest width at BEN WESTON POINT. The course veers around CHURCH ROCK, aglow after heavy rains with green, lavender, rose, blue and orange tints, then moves along the narrow northeast headland to Seal Rocks and back to Avalon.

The ISTHMUS AUTO TOUR (*daily*) follows the Old Stage Road from Avalon to the Summit (1,520 alt.), then descends to HAY-PRESS LANDING, site of an Indian town in prehistoric days, and enters Middle Ranch Canyon. In this canyon is Middle Ranch, some of whose buildings date from the Civil War period. Westward the road passes Eagles Nest Lodge (*see above*), then the soapstone ledges from which Indians once cut bowls and mortars, and suddenly swings out upon a high ridge. It descends rapidly to the southwest coast, skirting LITTLE HARBOR, with INDIAN HEAD ROCK (resembling the head on buffalo nickels), a symbolic sentinel for the Indian burial ground and kitchen midden on Little Harbor's shore, jutting from a headland.

From Little Harbor the route cuts diagonally across the island again, ascending gradually to West Summit (1,086 alt.), then drops by easy stages to the flat mesa of the Isthmus, where a stop for lunch and sightseeing is made before the return trip to Avalon over the same route.

The STARLIGHT DRIVE (*Apr. to Oct.; 7 miles; 45 minutes*), is made in open busses through the environs of Avalon and its adjacent scenic points. A costumed guitar or accordion player supplies musical background. Stops are made at UPHAM and INSPIRATION POINTS for views over night-lighted Avalon.

The SKYLINE DRIVE (*daily the year round; 30 minutes; 5 miles*), is a trip by motor bus along the major part of the Starlight Drive course.

Tour 6

TO MALIBU

Los Angeles—Hollywood—Sherman Oaks—Tarzana—Girard—To-panga Canyon—Topanga Beach—Castellammare—Santa Monica; US 101, Sunset Blvd., Cahuenga Ave., Ventura Blvd., Topanga Canyon Rd., Roosevelt Highway (US 101A); 45.4 *m*.

Paved roadbed throughout; six-lane concrete between Hollywood and San Fernando Valley; four-lane concrete between Cahuenga Blvd. and Girard; two-lane asphaltum between Girard, through Topanga Canyon, to Topanga Beach; four and six-lane concrete between Topanga Beach and Santa Monica city limits; concrete or asphaltum, varying widths, to Santa Monica. All accommodations.

This route is through Hollywood and the southern end of the San Fernando Valley, with its broad, flat acres of fruits, grain, and vegetables, its busy little towns, and movie stars' estates; through the low Santa Monica Mountains via Topanga Canyon; and along the Pacific Coast between surf line and mountain palisades, to Santa Monica.

North from the LOS ANGELES CITY HALL, 0 *m.*, at 1st and Spring Sts., on Spring St., L. on Sunset Blvd. (US 101), and R. on Cahuenga Blvd. (US 101).

HOLLYWOOD, 7 *m.* (385 alt., 184,531 pop.) (*see Hollywood*).

Points of Interest: Hollywood Bowl, Pilgrimage Play Theatre, motion-picture studios, and others.

At 10.3 *m.* is the junction with Lankershim Blvd.

Right on Lankershim Blvd. to UNIVERSAL CITY, 0.2 *m.* (550 alt.), a tiny segment of unincorporated county territory, around the UNIVERSAL MOTION PICTURE COMPANY STUDIO (*no visitors*). This is the oldest film studio in San Fernando Valley, dating from 1915 when Carl Laemmle acquired 800 acres of the former La Providencia Rancho through a corporation functioning under the name of the Universal Motion Picture Manufacturing Company. The company has centered all its film production activities at this plant since 1923, though nearly three-quarters of the tract bought by the company has been subdivided into residential plots. Along the front of the lot are the executive offices, 16 sound stages, enclosed sets, warehouses, and other structures. To the rear is the Back Ranch, with the outdoor sets where the "westerns," once a prominent part of the Universal production schedule, were filmed. Most of the great barns that once held 300 horses for use in these pictures have been converted to other uses.

CAMPO DE CAHUENGA (L), 3913 Lankershim Blvd., is the place where the Treaty of Cahuenga was negotiated on January 13, 1847, by Lieutenant Colonel John Charles Fremont, General Andres Pico, and General Jose Maria Flores, who represented the provisional Mexican governor (*see The Historical Background*).

The half-acre plot, with pepper and olive trees, wistaria vines, and trellised roses in its center, is a Los Angeles park. Flanking the boulevard entrance stand two one-story adobes of recent construction, one containing a small collection of historical relics.

NORTH HOLLYWOOD, 1.5 *m.* (625 alt., 38,582 pop.), lies in a fruit-growing area at the base of the Hollywood Hills, but is primarily a residential community. North Hollywood originated as Toluca in 1893, later changing its name to Lankershim, to honor Colonel J. B. Lankershim, one-time owner of vast lands in the valley. Four years after the town was annexed by Los Angeles in 1923, it was given its present name.

REPUBLIC PRODUCTIONS STUDIO (*adm. by special pass only*), 4024 Radford Ave., occupies the former Mack Sennett lot, with 15 buildings, including 10 sound stages and a sound-dubbing stage. Extensive outdoor sets for the "westerns" in which this studio specializes cover much of the lot. Republic Productions was formed by the merger of several smaller studios in 1935.

NORTH HOLLYWOOD PARK, bounded by Riverside Dr. and Chandler Blvd., Tujunga Blvd. and Tujunga Wash, is a Los Angeles city park. It contains a community building, a little theatre, and various playfields. Sections along Tujunga Wash in the western end of the park are preserved in a primitive state.

At 15.3 *m.* is the junction with Van Nuys Blvd.

Right on Van Nuys Blvd. to VAN NUYS, 2 *m.* (710 alt., 9,780 pop.), the largest community in the San Fernando Valley incorporated in Los Angeles.

Along the Highway

NORTH SHORE, SANTA MONICA BAY

PALM CANYON, PALM SPRINGS

JOSHUA TREE

Burton O. Burt

SAN FERNANDO VALLEY FROM MULHOLLAND DRIVE

MOUNT SAN JACINTO

F. W. Carter

California Fruit Growers' Exchange

GRAPEFRUIT GROVE

Theodore Baron

ROPING CATTLE

SHEEP

Horace Bristol

Burton O. Burt

CASA VERDUGO, GLENDALE

SHINTO TEMPLE IN JAPANESE
FISHING VILLAGE, TERMINAL ISLAND

Burton O. Burt

Theodore Baron

**LASKY'S BARN, HOLLYWOOD
—FIRST HOME OF PARAMOUNT PICTURES**

OLD LUGO HOUSE ON THE PLAZA, LOS ANGELES

Viroque Baker

Viroque Baker

PORTUGUESE MENDING NETS, TERMINAL ISLAND

It is the administrative center for city government in the valley. Now a suburban area, it came into existence as a farm-trade center. The town was named for I. N. Van Nuys, an early settler.

The VALLEY MUNICIPAL BUILDING, NW. corner Sylvan St. and Sylmar Ave., houses branch offices and bureaus of the city government. Its eight-story central tower flanked by two-story wings—all of white stone and concrete structure, make it resemble the huge Los Angeles City Hall. It contains branches of all the usual municipal departments.

VICTORY-VAN OWEN PARK, between Whitsett Ave., Laurel Canyon Rd., and Calvert St., a 90-acre irregularly shaped tract, was acquired by the Los Angeles Park Department in 1929. It has picnic facilities for 200 persons.

SHERMAN OAKS, 15.5 *m.* (657 alt.), is a suburban real estate development.

ENCINO (Sp., oak), 18.3 *m.* (790 alt., 1,548 pop.), is a residential suburb in a beautiful area. Because of the numbers of great liveoak trees here in 1769 the Gaspar de Portola expedition named the valley Santa Catalina de Bononia de los Encinos (St. Catherine of Bononia of the Oaks). A number of Hollywood notables have built homes in the near-by Santa Monica foothills.

The AMESTOY ADOBE (*private*), 16801 Ventura Blvd. (R), was built in 1851 by Vicente de la Osa, owner of Rancho El Encino during the first two decades of the American regime. Its site was once considered by the Franciscan padres for San Fernando Mission. Containing nine rooms, the long, rectangular adobe, one room in width, faces a small lake, fed by water piped from natural springs south of Ventura Blvd.

The ADOHR MILK FARMS (*open daily 1-5; large parties by special arrangement*), 18000 Ventura Blvd. (L), spreads over 600 acres of valley and foothills at the western edge of Encino. It has a herd of 3,-800, mostly Guernseys. The annual milk yield is more than 1,500,000 gallons. Adohr bulls and cows have been prize winners at agricultural fairs for a number of years. The establishment has barns, employees' dormitories, garages, stables, warehouses, feed sheds, offices, and bottling plants. The administrative buildings stand among great oaks and sycamores along Ventura Blvd.

TARZANA, 20.4 *m.* (760 alt.), is a business and residential area surrounded by small farms used for alfalfa growing, truck gardening, and horticulture. The town was named for Edgar Rice Burroughs' fictional character Tarzan, the author having bestowed that name on the estate of General Harrison Gray Otis, which he purchased in 1917.

Right from Tarzana on Reseda Blvd. to RESEDA PARK, 1.3 *m.* (R), a 42-acre forested area with an abundance of massive oak trees of great age. The city has planted additional trees, shrubs, and flowering plants. The park contains a pool and community clubhouse, and supervised playgrounds for children.

GIRARD, 24.4 *m.* (892 alt., 889 pop.), is a residential suburb of scattered Spanish and Moorish type homes.

Right from Girard on Topanga Canyon Blvd. to CANOGA PARK, 2.1 *m.* (790 alt., 2,460 pop.). Formerly known as Owensmouth, it was laid out in

1912 by H. J. Whitley. In the neighborhood are small farms growing walnuts, citrus fruits, berries, melons, field crops, sugar beets, and alfalfa.

CHATSWORTH, 6.2 *m.* (965 alt.), lies in a navel orange and fig-growing belt at the entrance to Santa Susana Pass. The name was suggested in 1898 by the Duke of Devonshire, who, during a visit to the valley, saw in this region a resemblance to Chatsworth Park, his ancestral home.

RANCHO SAN ANTONIO, 21004 Plummer St., is a home for under-privileged boys 11 to .15 years of age. Its long, one-story buildings of the ranch-house type are on a small farm that is worked by the 43 boys. The home is operated by the Catholic Big Brothers, Inc.

At 24.4 *m.* is the junction with Topanga Canyon Rd., now the main route; L. from US 101 on this road.

Right (straight ahead) on Ventura Blvd. to CALABASAS, 2 *m.* (929 alt.), a settlement consisting of a store, garage, cafe and a few scattered houses. The origin of the name is conjectural: according to one theory the Spanish named the spot Calabasas (pumpkins), because of the wild gourds, resembling pumpkins, that grew here; according to another the word is a corruption of Calahuasa, the name of a Chumash Indian village near Santa Ines Mission, in Santa Barbara County.

The trails of Spanish explorers crossed here several times: the Gaspar de Portola party, returning to San Diego from Monterey, traveled down Conejo Pass and passed this place on January 15, 1770; Juan Bautista de Anza (*see Tour 1*), blazing an overland trail from Sonora to Monterey, traversed the region on April 10, 1774, and a year later his second expedition camped on February 22, 1776 on the banks of Las Virgines Creek. Following the establishment of San Fernando Mission in 1797 Calabasas became a way station for the padres in their journeys along El Camino Real to Ventura, Santa Barbara, and other northern missions. In the 1860's it was a stop on the stagecoach line operated by Flint, Bixby and Company between Los Angeles and a junction of the Southern Pacific Railroad, which at that time had come no farther south than Soledad, in Monterey County. It was during this period that Calabasas developed its reputation as the "toughest" frontier town in southern California.

The L. J. Kramer general store (L), Ventura Blvd. and El Cajon Dr., is approximately on the SITE OF THE CALABASAS CORNER INN, the six-room plank structure that in the 1860's and 1870's witnessed most of the stage station's lusty social life, since it was the store, town hall, dance hall, and saloon. Here, too, the Vigilantes met to decide the fate of captured bandits and cattle rustlers, many of whom were hanged on the massive live oak west of the store that is called the HANGMAN'S TREE. A noose dangling from the limb that extends over US 101 is merely a "prop." The tree's age is estimated at more than 500 years.

Along the east wall of the Kramer store is an oak post that reputedly marks THE SEALED WELL, the grave of three bandits. Following a gun battle of the 1870's between bartenders of the Corner Inn, ranchers, and members of the Tiburcio Vasquez gang, the bodies of three desperadoes were thrown into the well here whose opening was sealed, according to popular legend.

The MIGUEL LEONIS ADOBE, 23537 Ventura Blvd., built in 1869 by Miguel Leonis, son-in-law of one of the first owners of the surrounding Spanish rancho, is now a roadside cafe. The two-story structure, with a wide two-story veranda along two sides stands in a semitropical garden with a grape arbor. Among the first mission lands in San Fernando Valley allotted to private persons were the 1,100 acres in the west end granted to three Indians, Urbano, Odon, and Manuel, who called it El Escorpion Rancho (the scorpion ranch). In 1869 Leonis, a native of southern France, settled in the valley, became a sheepherder, and married a daughter of Urbano. Becoming manager of his father-in-law's property, he soon owned the land and all its cattle, horses, and sheep, though as one historian describes him, he was ". . . a giant in stature and strength, a perfect savage in nature, besotted in ignorance, so illiterate that he could not read a word in any language."

At 2.6 *m.*, is the junction with a private road.

Right on this road 0.4 *m.* to the LOS ANGELES PET CEMETERY (*open 9-5; free*), on rolling land at the foot of the Simi Hills. The cemetery, in use since 1928, is platted after the modern manner in burial grounds, with the graves marked only by tablets flush with the ground. Some 2,000 animals are buried in graves at the foot of the hill, about 50 more are in a mausoleum or in urns in the columbarium. Dogs predominate among the pets, but there are also cats, parrots, canaries, three monkeys, a horse and alligator, an owl, a duck, and a turtle. Interred here is Kabar, a dog that belonged to Rudolph Valentino and reputedly walked from New York City to Los Angeles after the death of his master; the story is that he died of a broken heart. Other residents are possums, a blue Maltese cat, a movie star which signed its own contract with a paw print; Bubbie and Tagalong, Louise Dresser's dogs, and others that belonged to Winnie Lightner, Cesar Romero, Alice Brady, George Brent, Alice Joyce and other cinema luminaries. In adjoining graves lie Bill, a mallard duck, and Patsy, a Scotty. Bill and Patsy were pals who frequently walked, side by side, down Hollywood Boulevard. After Patsy died in 1937, Bill walked in front of an automobile and was killed.

At NEW CALABASAS, 3 *m.*, are the Calabasas Post Office and Justice Court, a general store, a garage, and a few homes.

West of New Calabasas the highway enters CONEJO PASS (rabbit pass) which leads to the Ventura Coastal Plain. In the Simi Hills (R) SIMI PEAK (alt. 2,400) stands out boldly in the northwest; L. are the more abrupt folds of the Santa Monica foothills, with cattle grazing on their steep sides.

At 5.4 *m.* is the junction with Las Virgines Canyon Rd.

Left on Las Virgines Canyon Rd, 4.5 *m.* to TAPIA COUNTY PARK (*picnicking facilities; baseball diamond*), whose heavily wooded terrain is cut by Malibu Creek Canyon.

At 8.1 *m.* on the main side road is AGOURA (1,000 alt.), which advertises itself as "The Picture City," because of its popularity as a location. It was laid out in two tracts in 1928 by the L'Agoura family, Spanish grant owners. Part of the L'Agoura home ranch, with its old ranch house and auxiliary buildings, are now owned by William Randolph Hearst, the newspaper publisher. The charm of the place has caused many Hollywood writers, directors, actors, and artists to build homes here.

At 8.9 *m.*, is the junction with Cornell Rd.

Left on Cornell Rd. into La Sierra Canyon, 2.3 *m.* to the PARAMOUNT PICTURES' INC., LOCATION RANCH (*adm. by pass only*), which extends for more than a mile along a valley below the road. A variety of false-front, painted-canvas movie sets hug the low foothill knolls (R)—groups of log cabins, stockades and forts representing a frontier outpost, clusters of palm-thatched African huts, a street from a town of the Old West, the weathered stone walls and casement windows around a market square of an 18th-century French town, and middlewestern, European, early American, and cattle-ranch buildings.

At the foot of a sharp defile, at 2.8 *m.* where Media and Triunfo Creeks form Malibu Creek, the canyon floor becomes a wide valley holding MALIBU LAKE, an artificial body of water created in 1926 by the Malibu Lake Mountain Club. Scores of cabins belonging to club members line the five-mile lakeshore or cling to the steep, tree-clad slopes. The MALIBU LAKE MOUNTAIN CLUBHOUSE (*private*), on the west bank (R), is a one-story, white stucco structure, with wide French windows and terraces overlooking the lake. Many motion-picture scenes have been photographed on the lake and along its shores.

The road follows the lake to its western end, then swings R. to climb between abrupt slopes.

SEMINOLE HOT SPRINGS, 5.8 *m.*, is a year-round health and pleasure resort, with springs, cottages, bathhouse, open-air mineral water plunge, and cafe buried in a copse of sycamores (R) below the level of the road.

At 12.8 *m.* is the junction with Protrero Rd.; L. from US 101 on this route. The route bears sharply R. at 14.6 *m.*, and moves through sloping meadows that merge with woods of widely-spaced live oaks. Since 1923 when the silent version of the motion picture *Robin Hood,* starring Douglas Fairbanks, Sr., was made here, this area has been known as Sherwood Forest, in memory of the Sherwood Forest of Nottinghamshire, England, celebrated in the Robin Hood legends.

Ascending gradually through the forest, the road tops a rise at 15.7 *m.* and then winds down along the northern shore of SHERWOOD LAKE (L), an irregular, privately owned, body of water formed by a dam at the eastern end. The area was developed as a summer resort, but in recent years about 250 people have established year-round homes here. Among the estate owners are Will H. Hays, censor and president of the Motion Picture Producers' Association. Maria Jeritza, Winfield Sheehan, Jack Holt, Fredric March, Carleton F. Burke, Robert Stewart, and others.

From the Ventura Blvd.-Topanga Canyon Rd. junction, the main tour route ascends the north slope of the SANTA MONICA MOUNTAINS, rising from the valley level to the summit of the coastal watershed divide in less than three miles.

TOPANGA SUMMIT, 27.3 *m.* (1,560 alt.), at the head of Topanga Canyon, is on the divide between the coastal watershed and the San Fernando Valley. The view (*use of telescopes on railing 10¢*) encompasses the greater part of the valley—to the Santa Susana Mountains on the north, and the San Gabriel Range on the northeast.

From the summit the road descends Topanga Canyon in a long, gradual drop between steeply rising mountain ramparts. The canyon slices seaward through the range in a general southerly direction for nine miles. Scattered through it are the homes of some two or three thousand permanent and part-time residents. Bordering Topanga Creek in the lower part of the canyon are thickets of sycamores and alders, and, on the slopes, California holly.

From the sparsely forested uplands, the canyon gradually descends into heavily wooded areas as it approaches TOPANGA MINERAL SPRINGS (*cabins at varying rates, free picnic grounds*), 29.1 *m.* (L), distributing center for waters of a mineral spring.

TOPANGA POST OFFICE (L), 32.2 *m.* (750 alt.), about midway between the summit and the ocean, is a canyon trading center, with a post office, general store and garage.

CAMP WILDWOOD, 32.7 *m.*, is another canyon trading center, supplying the needs of six to seven hundred cabin dwellers in near-by dells and side canyons; many are year-round residents.

TOPANGA BEACH, 36.4 *m.*, a shore colony at the mouth of Topanga Canyon, is part of the old Malibu Ranch. Residential sites are leased but never sold. Many of the houses were built by motion-picture people, but passed into other hands when the film colony moved to Malibu Beach.

At 36.4 *m.* is the junction with US 101A, now the main route; L. from Topanga Canyon Rd. on this road.

R. from Topanga Canyon Rd. on US 101A, Malibu Road, to LAS TUNAS BEACH (cactus beach), 0.4 *m.*, a compact district of gay, brightly-tinted stucco houses between the highway and the mountains.

A row of less imposing frame cottages is on the other side of the highway. LAS FLORES BEACH, 3.4 *m.*, at the mouth of Las Flores Canyon, was part of Rancho Malibu, acquired from Mrs. Rindge for $6,000,000. The land was repossessed by Mrs. Rindge when the project's developer was imprisoned for promotional peculation. The terms of the trusteeship under which the Rindge property now is being administered provide for the re-establishment of the subdivision.

Northwest of Las Flores Beach are the rolling hills and the miles of strand of RANCHO MALIBU, the lost empire of Mrs. May K. Rindge, a widow who resisted the penetration of public roads into her inherited ranch-barony for more than three decades with firearms, law books, and a large fortune.

High wire fences on both sides of the highway remain as reminders of the dispute. Sheets of cardboard attached to the fence posts carry an announcement that the United States Federal District Court in June 1938 approved removing Mrs. Rindge from control of the estate and placing it in receivership. She retains only a life interest in unfinished Rindge Castle and 60 acres surrounding it, and title to three beach properties and the family homestead in Marblehead, Massachusetts.

In 1804 parts of three Spanish grants, Topanga, Malibu, and Sequit, were awarded to Jose Tapia by Jose Arrillaga, military governor of the Californias; Tapia was a *soldado de cuera* (soldier of leather), one of the leather-jacketed men of the Spanish garrison at Santa Barbara—and the grant was a substitute for "back pay" owed by the Crown. The property passed through successive owners until 1892, when 16,000 acres were purchased by Frederick H. Rindge at $10 an acre. Rindge, of a wealthy Massachusetts manufacturing family, had come to California with his bride in that year and had envisioned a Riviera on this coast. By later purchases Rindge increased his holdings to 24,000 acres. During his lifetime, great herds of long-horns and bands of sheep roamed the hills and valleys. The undivided Malibu (Ind. deer) grant outlived all others of the Spanish-Mexican period and became known as the "last of the ranchos." Rindge died in 1905 before his dream of a Riviera had materialized, leaving an estate valued at $54,000,000 to Mrs. Rindge and his three children. After her husband's death the single passion of Mrs. Rindge, who became somewhat of a recluse, was to keep the great rancho intact. She spent a fortune in the attempt; she sued for libel, trespass, and defamation of character to oust squatters; and to close public roads: she continually sought injunctions to prevent road-building. One trial lasted 120 days; another series of lawsuits lasted 10 years. She in turn was sued by others, once by her own son, Samuel Rindge, who charged she was dissipating the estate at the rate of more than $1,000,000 a year. In the course of her fight on a county-built road (1918-19), Mrs. Rindge sent droves of hogs onto it, and once ordered the roadbed plowed under and planted with alfalfa. In 1925 state employees who were surveying the new right-of-way were driven off by armed guards. Construction could proceed only after court injunctions were obtained against her. In 1925 the Superior Court handed down a decision granting the state authority to construct what is now US 101A through the property. A decade later Mrs. Rindge played an entirely different role in court: unsecured creditors filed a petition in bankruptcy against the Marblehead Land Company—the name that Rindge had applied to his venture. Faced with some $10,000,000 in obligations, Mrs. Rindge countered with a voluntary petition for reorganization. In 1938 the Federal District Court ordered the reorganization, and Mrs. Rindge now lives in her West Adams Boulevard home in Los Angeles.

US 101A spans MALIBU LAGOON, 5.9 *m.*, a multitentacled arm of the sea running a short distance inland. On the spray-washed rocks at the lagoon entrance (L) seals sun themselves.

Crowning a truncated promontory (R), about one mile inland, is the 45-room

RINDGE CASTLE (*private*), the uncompleted stronghold built by Mrs. Rindge. Constructed of reinforced concrete and designed in the Spanish-Mediterranean style, the mansion was never occupied. Mrs. Rindge, more than 60 when she began building the castle, could not complete construction because she ran out of cash.

It has been estimated a quarter of a million dollars would be needed to complete it as designed.

Northwest of Malibu Lagoon US 101A, turning slightly inland, forms the northern border of MALIBU BEACH COLONY, 6.1 *m.* which occupies a sand-spit extending to the sea. It consists of a mile of beach houses belonging to film celebrities, artists, writers, and musicians. The community (unincorporated) is closed to the public. A wire fence, frequent "Private Property" signs, and chains across the motor approach, policed by the uniformed Malibu Seashore Patrol guard the privacy of those who can afford to buy their way into this area of the elect.

From the Malibu Rd.-Topanga Canyon Rd. junction, the main tour route goes southeast (L) on US 101A, between the sea and the precipitously rising mountain scarp.

CASTELLAMMARE, 37.6 *m.,* is a seaside area with a private beach (R) and a residential section (L) on terraces carved from the mountain, which here drops sharply to the highway's edge. The terraced slopes have stone revetments and are planted with Lipia grass.

At 38 *m.* is the junction with Sunset Blvd.

Left on Sunset Blvd. to the BERNHEIMER ORIENTAL GARDENS, 0.8 *m.,* (*open 8-6; adults 10¢, children free; Bernheimer home open on irregular days, adm. 25¢*), an eight-acre estate on the edge of the Pacific Palisades, overlooking the sea, scientifically landscaped and beautified in the Oriental manner. From an Oriental gatehouse (R), a palm-lined private road leads to a hill crowned by a group of small one-room Japanese houses—the home of Adolp Bernheimer, cotton exporter and designer of the gardens, who in 50 years made 17 trips to the Orient collecting the treasures in the house and gardens.

To the left of the gatehouse is a reproduction of the stables in the temple grounds at Nikko, Japan, in the black, mauve, and gold colors characterizing all the buildings. Beside the stables is a rock-lined lily pool with a bronze miniature of Lao-tse, Chinese philosopher of the sixth century B.C., mounted on a horse.

The exceptionally life-like bronze figure of Ten-Jin, ninth-century Japanese religious teacher, mounted on a representation of a sacred ox, watches over the entrance to the flower and bronze-lined path which winds to the Bernheimer home. Each room of the home is a separate house, although the four units are connected by pergolas. Treasures include color paintings on rice paper many hundreds of years old, bridal and temple kimonos, fingernail tapestries—woven by specially-grown fingernails; and two pairs of devil-dogs—traditional protectors from evil spirits, the bitch of each pair represented with suckling pups.

More bronzes enhance the downward path to the Sunken Garden, among them a Burmese Buddha in a "wishing well." At the bottom is a miniature lake, replete with miniature temples and figures of warriors and elephants.

Bernheimer, a native of New York, began collecting Oriental objects in 1887, came to Los Angeles in 1913, and in 1915 created an Oriental garden on a hilltop near Hollywood Blvd. and Franklin Ave. (*see Hollywood*). Work was begun on the present location in 1925 and completed in 1927. Total expenditures came to $3,000,000.

The CALIFORNIA STATE BEACH (*free*), 40.2 *m.,* extending (R) between W. Channel Rd. and Mayberry Ave., at the northern edge of

Santa Monica is only one of several state-owned beach lands lying between Santa Monica and Malibu Beach.

Southeast of the state beach, US 101A skirts the edge of the Santa Monica Palisades (L) and a half-mile-long row of beach homes (R), many of which are the seaside residences of film celebrities.

SANTA MONICA, 42.1 m. (100 alt., 53,500 pop.) (see Santa Monica).

Points of Interest: Clover Field, Douglas Aircraft plant, Yacht Harbor, Palisades Park, Municipal Aquarium, Municipal Pier, and others.

At 45.4 m. is the junction with Washington Blvd. (see Tour 5).

《《《》》

Tour 7

TO BIG PINES

Los Angeles—Burbank—San Fernando—Palmdale—Big Pines—San Bernardino; 146.9 m.; US 6, State 138, Big Pines Rd., US 66.

Southern Pacific R.R. parallels route between Los Angeles and Palmdale; Union Pacific R.R. and Santa Fe Ry. between junction US 66 and San Bernardino.
Concrete and asphaltic roadbed entire route; four lanes between Los Angeles and junction US 99; two wide lanes between junction US 99 and San Bernardino. Snowstorms in winter in Big Pines-Wrightwood area, but highways kept open all year.

This route circles the San Gabriel Mountains, by way of two large valleys—the San Fernando and the Antelope, which is roughly at the edge of the Mojave Desert. Topography and climate change constantly as the road leaves the coastal watershed, skirts the Mojave Desert, and mounts the pine-scented mountain ridges, and runs for 20 miles at an elevation of about 5,000 feet through the Angeles and San Bernardino National Forests.

From the LOS ANGELES CITY HALL, 1st and Main Sts., 0 m., west on 1st St. to Figueroa St. (US 6); R. on Figueroa St. to Riverside Dr.; L. on Riverside Dr. to Dayton Ave.; R. on Dayton Ave. to San Fernando Rd.; L. on San Fernando Rd. (US 6-99).

GLENDALE, 8 m. (1,200 alt., 82,582 pop.) (see Glendale).

.Points of Interest: Forest Lawn Memorial Park, Grand Central Air Terminal, and others.

US 6 proceeds along the eastern edge of the San Fernando Valley, predominantly a fertile agricultural basin that, in spite of its proximity to Los Angeles and increasing industrial activity in its southeastern tip, has maintained a distinctively rural and suburban character. None the less, approximately four-fifths of it became part of Los Angeles between 1915 and 1923, after the completion of the Los Angeles-Owens River Aqueduct (*see Pueblo To Metropolis*) had prepared the valley for its conversion from a parched and arid plain to a wide green expanse of cultivated fields and orchards.

The valley is almost circled by mountains that long isolated it from the boom developments of Los Angeles. Today, however, two broad modern highways carry commuters to and from the city, and 500 miles of paved road gridiron the valley floor.

Clinging to the foothill slopes, attractive residences look down upon a flat valley that, the year round, presents a scene of constant activity in fields and orchards. In the valley are three types of farms: predominant are tracts of one to ten acres where vegetables, flowers, and poultry are produced for the Los Angeles market; next are the large ranches, where alfalfa and foodstuffs are produced by mass-production methods; and last are the farm-estates, where cinema executives and other celebrities in the role of country gentlemen, live in beautiful houses on landscaped grounds and direct the production of vegetables and flowers and the breeding of dogs and horses—sometimes for the commercial market. The generally equable climate and the protection of the mountains that ward off fog and humidity have resulted in the building of many hospitals, health resorts, and sanatoria in the higher foothills.

In the southeastern section, near the city, population is increasing rapidly and new subdivisions appear every year, with broad streets fringed with transplanted palms and acacias.

Early San Fernando Valley settlers were subsistence farmers dependent upon natural springs, uncertain amounts of rainfall, and the capricious Los Angeles River to aid in the production of grain and fruits. Now water from the high Sierras, carried more than 200 miles through mountains and desert, is stored in the San Fernando and Chatsworth reservoirs for even distribution to perennially thirsty areas by conduits and channels.

While poultry, dairy products, flowers, and shrubs are produced in considerable quantities, citrus fruits are the most important valley crop in point of acreage and value. Walnuts, introduced in 1893, form the largest single crop acreage. Olives, berries, and fruits, including apples, peaches, plums, and figs, are also grown in quantities. Approximately a third of the grapes grown in Los Angeles County are produced in the eastern foothills of the valley. Though table and raisin grapes are cultivated, wine grapes of the Zinfandel, Mission, and Eastern Concord varieties predominate. Carrots are the most valuable of the truck crops, though all the others are produced.

BURBANK, 11.2 *m.* (555 alt., 34,337 pop.), has retained its suburban and residential flavor in the face of rapid industrial development. Motion-picture production and the manufacture of airplanes and airplane parts are its leading sources of income, though it also produces soaps, cosmetics, motor trucks, liquor, cement, and processed foods. Both houses and business buildings exhibit the local predilection for adaptations of Spanish and Mexican architectural motifs; there are miles of vari-tinted stucco and imitation adobe houses and courts, blossom-bowered bungalows, and bright-colored apartment houses.

Burbank came into being in May 1887, when the boom period Providencia Land, Water and Development Company subdivided the arid site and named it after Dr. David Burbank, a previous owner of the Rancho La Providencia, from whom the company bought 9,000 acres. Within a year the town had 30 residences, a $30,000 hotel, a Southern Pacific Railroad station, a furniture factory, and a horsecar line one and a half miles long. But the town languished with collapse of the boom and growth did not begin until after the Pacific Electric Railway was extended from Los Angeles in 1911 and anticipation of the arrival of water from Owens Valley shortly afterward. The Moreland Motor Truck plant was established in 1917; First National Pictures, now Warner Brothers-First National, opened a motion-picture studio in town. In time the industrial plants were built, gradually cutting down the town acreage under cultivation.

The LOCKHEED AIRCRAFT CORPORATION PLANT (*adm. by arrangement*), 1705 Victory Blvd., on a 50-acre tract, produces large quantities of commercial and military planes. Incorporated in 1926, the company specialized in the designing and building of single- and twin-motored speed planes, known as the Lockheed Vega. In the early 1930's it entered the commercial transportation field. Among its developments were the twin-motored 10-passenger Electra, a plane in wide use among the smaller air lines, and a 14-passenger transport with a cruising speed of 253 m.p.h. and top speed of 273 miles providing the fastest passenger transportation in the world.

The UNION AIR TERMINAL, 2627 Hollywood Way, in the northwestern section of town, occupies an irregular rectangle with a five-fingered, asphalt-paved runway. It is used by Transcontinental and Western Air., Inc., United Air Lines Transport Corporation, Western Air Express Corporation, American Airlines, and various operators of charter ships. There are repair depots, salesrooms, and airplane accessory manufacturing concerns. The field has the usual Federal airfield services, is a regional U. S. Weather Bureau base, and headquarters of a branch of the Aerial Forest Fire Patrol. The white concrete Administration Building of modern design with arcaded one-story wings branching from a three-story tile-roofed central unit, houses ticket offices, waiting rooms, and a cafe. There are six steel and concrete hangars.

The new WALT DISNEY STUDIO (*no visitors*), 2400 S. Alameda St., which opened in 1940, houses the Disney animated-cartoon film plant. With walls of a new earthquake-resistant brick, reinforced by steel grids, the plant has 14 buildings and elaborate equipment. Largest structure is the three-story Animation Building; others include an orchestra, theatre, cutting, process, and painting buildings. There is a special air-conditioning plant to meet the requirements of the delicate film coloring processes, which demand controlled humidity.

To produce a standard 750-foot "short" a staff of 800 must work about three months. A feature-length film requires a slightly smaller staff for some 18 months (*Snow White* was nearly four years in the making). Production of an animated film involves great cost ($50,000 each for shorts, $1,500,000 for *Snow White*) and much labor (10,000 to 15,000 sketches for a 750-foot film). The dialogue, music, and sound effects are recorded first, each on a separate sound track, and then synchronized on one final sound track from which a careful timing graph is prepared for the guidance of the animators in drawing the sketches for the film; if a character is to speak a word, and the sound graph indicates that the word is recorded on eight frames of film, the animator makes eight drawings in which the lips of the character move to speak the word. Sounds of footsteps, of falling blocks, music, etc., are similarly indicated in the graph and followed in the animation. A staff of 50 senior animators makes the key drawings of each series of sketches, leaving the "in-betweeners" to follow through with intermediate sketches. The last process in the Disney plant is the photographing of each sketch on a continuous film strip with a multiplane camera. This is mounted lens downward on a 14-foot iron framework containing brackets placed one below another; the animation sketches, which have been traced, inked and colored on large transparent celluloid squares, are placed one at a time in the uppermost bracket of the framework to be photographed against intermediate background scenes painted on celluloids set in the lower brackets, and a final background scene set in the lowest rack. This process gives an illusion of depth to the finished film, which then goes to the technicolor plant in Hollywood for coloring.

Walt Disney, the guiding hand of this complicated business, no longer finds time to draw his own pictures, but he still records his voice in the role of Mickey Mouse, his favorite creation. Disney, who was interested in drawing and photography while still a boy, was born in Chicago in 1901. While working at various illustrating jobs, he experimented at home in making animated films. One short reel of home-town incidents he sold to local theatres before he was twenty. In 1923 he went to Hollywood and struggled with various animated film projects until he made a small beginning with Oswald the Rabbit cartoons in 1927. Mickey Mouse came into being as a silent film when the first sound movies were being shown, and was therefore lost in the excitement; the third Mickey strip, made with sound (1928), was the first of the phenomenally popular Disney enterprises.

The ANDREW JERGENS COMPANY PLANT (*no visitors*), 99 S. Verdugo Ave., manufactures approximately 100 varieties of toilet soaps, cosmetics, creams, lotions, and pastes.

The COLUMBIA RANCH (*adm. by special pass only*), 3701 S. Oak St., is the set-lot of the Columbia Pictures Corporation of Hollywood. Permanent sets include American and foreign street scenes, single houses each representative of a different architectural style or period, a complete South American village, and a waterfront. Ocean scenes are filmed in a tank, containing a steamer and pier, effects being achieved by the skillful use of mechanical and photographic devices. WARNER BROTHERS-FIRST NATIONAL STUDIO (*adm. by special pass only*), 4000 South Olive Ave., has some 75 scattered buildings and sound stages in which are annually produced between 60 and 65 feature-length films and approximately 175 short ones. Dominating the buildings on the front lot is the three-story research building, opposite the one-story red-brick writers' building. In the background are rows of great sound stages, miscellaneous utility buildings, and acres of stock and permanent sets. There is an artificial lake for shooting sea scenes. In October 1927 the studio produced *The Jazz Singer,* starring Al Jolson; this was the first all-talking feature picture. Its success inspired an expansion program that led to the absorption of the First National Studios by Warner Brothers, the acquisition of a chain of theatres, and the construction of this plant in 1929-30.

ROSCOE, 16.2 *m.* (850 alt.), is a trade center of poultry raisers and small farmers.

PACOIMA, 20.7 *m.* (1,013 alt.), is a scattered community of ranchers.

SAN FERNANDO, 22.6 *m.* (1,076 alt., 9,094 pop.), in the heart of a prosperous area producing citrus fruits, olives, and vegetables, was founded in 1874 by George K. Porter but, like other communities established at the period, was very small until water arrived. It is primarily a trading center but does fruit packing and canning. The city is modern in appearance, with the usual tree-bordered streets.

The UNITED STATES VETERANS' HOSPITAL (*open daily 3-5:30*), in the foothills at the head of Sayre St., was established as a sanatorium for tubercular ex-service men in 1924. It now provides general medical service for women war workers, as well as veterans. The institution, on a foothill of the Santa Monica Mountains, has beautifully landscaped grounds.

Since 1920 OLIVE VIEW SANATORIUM (*open Wed.-Sun. 3-5*), NE. corner Foothill Blvd. and Olive View Dr., has been operated by Los Angeles County for the treatment of the tubercular, and has approximately 1,000 beds in nearly two hundred one-story bungalows built along narrow avenues that overlook hillside olive groves.

The PICO ADOBE (*adm. by permission of occupant*), 10940 Sepulveda Blvd., entrance from Columbia Ave., is a reconstruction of a building erected by mission Indians in 1834 and acquired by Andres and Romolo Pico, brother and nephew, respectively, of Pio Pico, California's last Mexican governor. The first building was much enlarged through the years, but was in ruins in 1930 when it came into possession of the Southwest Museum. The adobe has been carefully restored along the original lines and forms a two-story U-shaped hacienda with low porch running the full length of the east side. In the patio are climbing vines and burnt-tile walks.

Left from San Fernando on State 118 to the restored MISSION SAN FER-NANDO REY DE ESPANA, 1.6 *m.* (*open 9:30-5:30; adm. 25¢*), NW. corner Mission Blvd. and Columbia Ave., 17th of the chain of 21 Franciscan missions founded in California. It was established September 9, 1797, under the supervision of Padres Fermin Lasuen and Francisco Dumetz and named in honor of the canonized King of Castile, Saint Ferdinand III. The first church, completed in 1806, was so severely damaged by earthquakes that a new one was built in 1818. Of the first only a crumbling adobe wall remains. Of the second structure, the *convento* has survived and has been restored—a picturesque adobe building parallel with Mission Boulevard. Along the facade is a long loggia, with 19 semicircular arches supported on massive square pillars. The old tile floor beneath the archway is worn into deep hollows. The work of the Indian blacksmiths is still seen in the hand-wrought ironwork of mouldings around the doors and windows. The east room, remodeled into a chapel, contains old paintings and relics. Visitors are shown the kitchens and dining room, where they climb a crude open stairway to the huge low guest dormitories under the sloping roof, and descend to the cellars, where are old wine vats and the receptacles in which the Indians tramped out the juice of grapes. Narrow deeply embrasured windows open into dank high-ceilinged chambers, now unfurnished, in which the padres and their assistants lived. Northwest of the *convento* is the ancient graveyard where 2,000 Indians are buried. The *convento* and a few acres of land surrounding it, including the burial ground, the ruins of the first chapel, and the crumbling walls of the Indian quarters now are the property of the Archdiocese of Los Angeles.

BRAND PARK, NE. corner Mission Blvd. and Columbus Ave., was presented to the city of Los Angeles in 1920 by a group of persons headed by Leslie C. Brand. Part of the park has been made a Memorial Garden, modeled after a garden at Santa Barbara Mission. Flanking a STATUE OF FRA JUNIPERO SERRA, founder of California missions, near the main entrance, stands a massive stone fountain, a copy of one in Cordova, Spain. Built in 1812-14, the fountain formerly stood in the courtyard of San Fernando Mission. Another relic of mission days is a stone vat with two great ovens, which are used for roasting meats and rendering fats.

US 6 ascends sharply between the sparsely grown chaparral slopes of the San Gabriel Mountains (R) and the more verdant flanks of the Santa Susana Mountains (L).

Across a deep arroyo (R) paralleling the highway at 29.1 *m.* is a boulder monument at the entrance to narrow FREMONT PASS, named for John C. Fremont, who as a major of the California Battalion led his men and artillery through this gap to support the attack on Los Angeles during the Mexican War. The troops had unopposed passage, since the defenders had fallen back, and Fremont was able to occupy San Fernando Mission.

Antiquated wooden derricks straggling up the slopes on both sides of the road at 29.6 *m.* mark one of the producing districts of the NEWHALL-VENTURA OIL FIELD, birthplace of California's petroleum industry.

The first recorded use of oil from this area was in 1850 when Andres Pico, Mexican general and brother of Pio Pico, the last Mexican Governor of California, collected seepage in Pico Canyon, several miles west of US 6, and distilled it in a copper still and worm to obtain petroleum for the lamps at San Fernando Mission.

Although various attempts were thereafter made to commercialize the deposits, the oil industry as such was not organized until 1875 when a spring-hole was completed in Pico Canyon. This well yielded approximately six barrels of oil a day from a 75-foot depth. Subsequently the California Star Oil Works Company, first West Coast oil concern, took over the well and built a refinery near Newhall.

In 1882 two Pennsylvania oil men began drilling in the area. Occasionally other companies and independent operators did some drilling here. In 1916 the last well was sunk by the Standard Oil Company of California. Between 1875 and 1937 the field yielded a total of 55,669,587 barrels of oil. Of approximately 235 wells that had been drilled, 85 were still daily producing one to five barrels each in July 1938.

Until recently NEWHALL PASS, which US 6 traverses, was a bottle-neck for travelers between the San Joaquin and Antelope valleys, and the Los Angeles area. Here the trails of explorers, trappers, priests, and soldiers converged. Francisco Garces, the Spanish priest-explorer, used the pass in 1776; Fremont in 1847; and the remnants of Captain John Doty's Jayhawker party, which left the main party and took a short cut across the deserts from Salt Lake City to Los Angeles in 1849-50. Suffering great hardships while crossing Death Valley and the Mojave Desert, the 32 survivors of the party of 37 were given beds and food at Rancho San Francisquito, which included the Newhall area.

Through the pass went the early stages, and in 1875 the Southern Pacific engineers selected the route through the pass to carry their rails between San Francisco and Los Angeles. Until 1930, US 99 came through the pass; it now follows easier grades to the west.

At 31.7 m. is a junction with Railroad Canyon Rd.

Left here to NEWHALL REFINERY, 0.3 m. (open; free), the first in California, built in 1876 by D. G. Scofield's California Star Oil Works Company to refine crude petroleum from the Pico Canyon field. In the beginning, the refinery could produce only 20 barrels of oil a day. After seven years of operation it was closed, and thereafter oil from Pico Canyon was shipped in tank cars to a refinery at Alameda. In 1924 the Pioneers Petroleum Society of California acquired the abandoned refinery, and some land around it, to make it a memorial to California's early petroleum producers. The carefully restored stills, retorts, and vats are seen grouped together in a small canyon. The four stills, with a combined capacity of 330 barrels, rest on brick furnaces below a ridge on which the old receiving tank stands.
The towering stills, spidery drip racks, and other units of the Union Oil Company's modern refinery, just east of the antiquated pioneer plant, show the sharp contrast between past and present refining methods.

Crowning a low spur of the Santa Susana Mountains (L) at 32.2 m., is the white castellated MANSION OF WILLIAM S. HART (private), former two-gun motion-picture actor. The turreted structure of medieval appearance is the home of Hart and his invalid sister, Mary, and stands on the Hart Horseshoe Ranch.

NEWHALL, 32.4 m. (1,273 alt., 1,104 pop.), was the first oil boom town in the state. Following the exploitation of petroleum deposits in the Pico Canyon district in 1875, a village with many frame cafes and saloons sprang up. Even after the peak of the boom was over, it was sustained by the automobile traffic. The rerouting of US 99 to the west, the diminished oil output, and the 1939 rerouting of the highway—now transcontinental US 6—to the east, have reduced the town to the position of a trade center for ranchers in near-by canyons. Both town and pass were named for Henry M. Newhall, a native of Massachusetts, who came to California in 1850. Newhall helped to promote various California railroads and was an owner of much land.

At 32.9 *m.* is a junction with Placerita Canyon Rd.

Right here into PLACERITA CANYON to MONOGRAM PICTURES CORPORATION SET LOT, 0.5 *m.* (*no visitors*). False-front buildings of the type needed in frontier town scenes are visible above the trees (L).

Below the level of the road (L) at 3.6 *m.*, is the OAK OF THE GOLDEN LEGEND, supposed to mark the site of the first discovery of gold in the state. The bronze plaque that formerly identified the tree was stolen by a souvenir hunter. The story follows the traditional lines of treasure-discovery legends. It is said that one Don Francisco Lopez, sitting under the tree on March 9, 1842, was pulling up wild onions near him to supplement his noonday lunch. He noted glittering particles adhering to the onion roots, and collected enough to head for the assay office in Los Angeles, where he was informed that the particles were gold. News of the discovery precipitated a stampede of fortune hunters from southern California and Mexico—preceding the gold rush of 1849 in northern California by seven years.

SAUGUS, 34.9 *m.* (1,171 alt., 151 pop.), is a railroad junction town whose railroad station (R) is considered by Hollywood studios so typically the rural American depot that it has been the background in hundreds of pictures.

At 35.8 *m.* US 6 veers sharply east and enters MINT CANYON, so named because of the small mint beds still occasionally found in it during the rainy season. The old Mint Canyon Road was one of the earliest routes into the Mojave Desert.

At 37.7 *m.* the trunk of the LOS ANGELES AQUEDUCT is seen climbing over the ridge (L) from Bouquet Canyon. It crosses the Santa Clara River bottoms, and mounts the opposite range on its way to the San Fernando Reservoirs. The aqueduct (*see Pueblo to Metropolis*) brings water from an intake at Aberdeen, in Inyo County, through Owens Valley along the rough eastern foothills of the Sierra Nevada, bores through mountain barriers, bridges, canyons, and burrows under miles of desert.

US 6 spans the SANTA CLARA RIVER, 40 *m.*, an insignificant trickle of water down a gravelly, rock-strewn bed for much of the year, but a torrent when swollen by mountain waters in winter. The section of the river below the San Francisquito Creek confluence, four miles west of this crossing, was the scene of a flood in 1928 in which 451 people died and which caused $12,000,000 worth of damage. The flood was caused by the breaking of the St. Francis Dam, 15 miles northeast of Saugus in San Francisquito Canyon, which sent a 90-foot wall of water down the narrow canyon.

At 53.2 *m.* is a junction with Agua Dulce (sweet water) Rd.

Right here 2.4 *m.* to Toney Ranch Rd.; L. here crossing the A. R. TONEY RANCH (*adm. 25¢ a car; overnight camping 50¢; camping and picnic grounds, tables and fireplaces*), to the VASQUEZ ROCKS, 3.1 *m.*, towering eroded sandstone crags, volcanic masses, and distorted boulders. The mesa out of which the rocks rise is studded with juniper and yucca. The rugged area has been used for locale shots in many motion pictures.

This tricky maze was a favorite hangout of Tiburcio Vasquez, who is said to have hidden here and in many other spots in southern California while evading in accredited will-o-the-wisp fashion, the punitive efforts of the combined constabulary of five counties. Born at Monterey in 1839 and executed a scant 36 years later, Vasquez, in his short lifetime, carved a career in crime second only to that of Joaquin Murietta in the annals of California outlawry. He first became embroiled with the law at age of 14, stabbing a constable during a quarrel at a Monterey fandango. Escaping into the hills, he joined a band of horse thieves, and eventually graduated to the leadership of his own company of desperados. Mounted on a beautiful cream-white horse, Vasquez performed his acts of cunning as well as daring, and led his marauding bandidos through a succession of rapes, pillages, robberies, and murders. For years posses and vigilantes were unable to capture him, partly because of the sympathy and aid rendered to him by a disgruntled peasantry. According to modern standards, however, Vasquez' monetary rewards were trifling: his brigands never divided more than $2,000 among themselves. A propensity for philandering led to his ultimate downfall. Abadon Leiva, one of his men, discovered Vasquez with Senora Leiva and betrayed him. He impressed spectators at his hanging on March 19, 1875, in San Jose, by his calm and dignity, his manner of dying bearing out his proudest boast—that he was "muy caballero."

At the TONEY RANCH HOUSE, 3.3 *m.*, the motor road ends. From here a foot trail leads 1.3 *m.* through rough canyon country to the VASQUEZ CAVES on the GEORGE SCHAEFER RANCH (*adm. 25¢; camping 50¢*) in ESCONDIDO (hidden) CANYON, at the lower end of Agua Dulce Canyon. The caves in sandstone cliffs in which the Vasquez bandits are alleged to have lived, are simply deep depressions sheltered by overhanging ledges. In the larger ones picnic tables, stoves, and other facilities have been placed.

An arch of unhewn stone (L), at 58.1 *m.* is the entrance to MOUNTAIN HOME, a nonsectarian retreat for needy girls operated by Christ Faith Mission of Los Angeles. Two stone dormitories, built by members of the mission, and a frame tabernacle stand on the treeless mesa about 200 yards from the road.

At 61.5 *m.* is a junction with Governor Mine Rd.

Left here to the GOVERNOR MINE, formerly the Old New York, 1.3 *m.* Although the mine is referred to as the oldest gold working in Los Angeles County, evidence to support the statement is inconclusive since the claim was abandoned in early days. It was relocated in 1889 and was worked sporadically until the early 1920's. The advance of gold prices in 1933 encouraged its owners to reopen.

East of the Governor Mine Road junction, US 6—Mint Canyon Road—runs for several miles between hills scarred with prospect holes, abandoned workings and mining properties with low-grade ore. As the road descends the slopes of the San Gabriel Mountains, vistas of desert appear between low hills. At 72.5 *m.* the highway straightens out on the floor of Antelope Valley and heads north between irrigated orchards and alfalfa fields.

ANTELOPE VALLEY, named for the great herds of antelope

that ranged here in early days, is on the southwestern edge of the Mojave Desert. Low hills—the Lovejoy Buttes—separate it from the desert itself. The valley, in Los Angeles and Kern Counties, covers approximately 2,500 square miles, and was reclaimed through tapping the large natural reservoir of water underlying it—a supply constantly replenished by mountain runoff. In the area including parts of 36 Los Angeles County townships are approximately 100,000 acres under cultivation, more than half of it in producing hay, grain, and fruit. Chicken and turkey ranching has been and is still important in the valley, but cattle ranching, once the valley's mainstay, is disappearing.

On spring weekends thousands visit Antelope Valley, particularly the uncultivated stretches, to view the desert blooms. The colorful show begins in early March, comes to a peak during April and continues through May and even into June.

The best-known and first flower to appear is the California poppy, which after sufficient winter rains floods the valley with gold. Sometimes at the height of bloom, the yellow of a single 20-mile stretch of poppies is visible from a peak 40 miles away. This low-growing satin-textured flower, though predominantly golden, is quite variable in color, ranging from cream-white through lemon and pure canary to a deep orange-red.

With the poppies, and after they are gone, come the blue lupines, more common on the coast, but occasionally covering the floor of the valley with what appear from a distance to be pools of blue water. With these arrive the purple-fringed desert asters, and the coreopsis on wiry stalks in shades of yellow and copper. A high note of color is added by the scarlet Indian paintbrush, the bracts of which seem to have been dipped in a brilliant vermilion.

Mixed with the chaparral on the hills are spikes of larkspur—dark purple-blue, and the rose-pink blossoms of the prickly gilia. The encelia, or bush sunflower, also called brittle-bush, is seen everywhere in the chaparral, lighting the gray-green brush with its silvery leaves and pale-gold flowers. In later spring the scarlet larkspur shoots flame-colored spires to a height of six feet or more, beside tall yellow senecios and rose live-forevers. The feathery pink and white bloom of the wild buckwheat can be identified by the murmur of bees seeking its honey. A summer variant of the buckwheat, turkish rugging, grows close to the ground and covers arid spots with a rough rosy carpet. After most of the early chaparral blooms have disappeared, a low-growing plant appropriately named blazing-star opens flowers looking like enormous buttercups.

The typical flowers of the Mojave Desert—apart from poppies and lupines, which are also common in the chaparral—include the desert abronia, a creeping vine that covers the sand for miles with clusters of fragrant lavender-rose flowers; purple phacelia, or heliotrope; and desert mallow, bearing brick-red or lavender blossoms resembling small hollyhocks. During March and April the desert lily sends up a tall blue-green stem carrying from 4 to 18 white lilies with pale green bands radiating from their center. The short-lived desert evening primrose does not open until sunset, when it quickly unfolds a multitude of luminous white blooms that wither and turn a rose color with the next morning's sun.

The most spectacular of the Mojave Desert flowers is the yucca Mohavensis, or Spanish bayonet. The rather clumsy rough trunk of this yucca, with its clumps of bristling rigid leaves, bears distaff-shaped panicles a foot or two long, of small white waxen bells, intensely fragrant. Like the Joshua tree (*see below*), they are fertilized by a night-flying moth. The fruit ripens in September into a purple-black sugar-laden "date," prized by the Indians, who also use the yucca leaf-fibers for weaving horse-blankets, ropes, and baskets.

All cactus flowers present a curious contrast to the formidable plants that bear them, without exception being delicate and silken-textured. The opuntia Mohavensis, the prickly pear of the Mojave, has a lemon-yellow bloom; the beavertail cactus, also an opuntia, has a purple-rose flower with purple filaments. Still another opuntia, the shaggy grizzly-bear, produces a gold or rose-red bloom, and the spiked long-spine cactus a flower of deep magenta. Even the foxtail cactus, having the appearance of a small bottle-washer, is topped with a circle of silvery-pink blooms.

The desert trees have a brief but vivid blooming season. The inconspicuous mesquite is transformed in spring with tender green foliage and swinging yellow tassels. The fruit of this tree is a bean, spiral-twisted in some varieties, sweet and highly nutritious. The bark, as well as the leaves and branches, of the palo verde is bright green, and the whole tree appears lighted with small golden blooms. In the desert washes is the dead-looking indigo bush, or smoke-tree, which bears, late in the spring, pea-shaped blossoms of rich blue (*see Tour 2*).

Because vandals carried away automobile-loads of dying flowers, most southern California counties have passed strict protective ordinances, making it illegal, under severe penalties, to pluck or harm the desert and mountain flora. Particularly protected are the desert-lily, the Spanish bayonet, the Joshua tree, the indigo bush, the ocotillo, and all varieties of cacti.

PALMDALE, 73.2 m. (2,660 alt., 1,419 pop.), at the southern end of Antelope Valley, is the trading center of poultry and cattle ranchers and fruit growers. Palmdale was one of a dozen socialist colonies founded in Antelope Valley between 1883 and 1914. It was established by German Lutherans in 1886 at a place two miles east of the present town, and named for the Joshua trees surrounding it, in the belief that the trees were a kind of palm. Two years later the colonists moved to this place to be near the Southern Pacific Railroad tracks.

At Palmdale the route turns R. from US 6 on State 138, the Pearblossom Hwy.

State 138 traverses irrigated orchards growing Bartlett pears, then, at 75 m., suddenly moves into the Mojave Desert, a waste broken only to the southeast by an oasis of green foliage that marks the settlement of Little Rock (*see below*).

Isolated Joshua trees appear at 75.1 *m.* among the mesquite and sage, increasing rapidly in number until they form a forest on both sides. At 75.3 *m.* the road bisects the site of old Palmdale, from which the Joshua trees stretch across the mesa beyond the range of vision. This is the JOSHUA TREE NATIONAL MONUMENT—established to preserve them. Not a true tree, the Joshua is a giant yucca and a member of the lily family. It was named by early Mormon settlers who remembered the book of Joshua: "Thou shalt follow the way pointed for thee by the trees."

The Joshua tree is found extensively in the Mojave, and in sections of Arizona, Nevada, and Utah. During the early years of its growth it is a branchless stalk, standing like a pole on the desert, but it gradually puts forth clumsy limbs pointing out and upward and bristling at the ends with bayonet-like leaves of a dark gray-green. As these leaves die, they turn grayish-brown and lie back along the branches, giving the plant an odd shaggy outline. Blossoms appear on the end of each branch, from March to June, depending on the advent of warm weather and the altitude. The trees appear to hold the clusters of waxy cream-white flowers with stiff-armed gestures. Though delicate in contrast to the rough dark trunk, the flowers are rather coarse when viewed closely, having the texture of thin leather and a faint mushroom odor.

For fertilization, the flower of the Joshua depends on a small night-flying moth which lays her eggs in the blossom, at the same time rubbing off the pollen gathered on her body. The period of flowering and seed production is very short in spite of the slow growth of the plant, and by the end of June the large fleshy pods have ripened. To facilitate this process, the Joshua sends out an intricate array of fine roots near the surface, thus making the most of the brief spring rains. Far underneath, however, are powerful roots that tap underground waters and provide anchorage against the hard seasonal winds on the open desert.

The age of the Joshuas is popularly compared to that of the Sequoias. Actually, it is impossible to determine the age of the individual plants, since they have no annual rings, and they grow so slowly that specimens kept under observation for long periods of time have shown practically no change. But undoubtedly some of the largest have been living for hundreds of years. An indication of their age is the number of branches; none of the plants grow taller than 40 feet.

Before the trees had been protected by Federal law, various schemes for commercializing the Antelope Valley Joshuas had been promoted. The Atlantic and Pacific Fiber Company had been organized in England and had contracted to furnish paper pulp from the Joshuas for the London *Daily Telegraph*. The concern had acquired 52,000 acres of land, employed crews of Chinese to cut down the trees, and converted a near-by ore stamp mill for reduction of the trees to pulp.

The scheme failed because the first shipment of pulp spoiled on the way to England; and a cloudburst, in February 1886, routed the Chinese cutting crew.

LITTLE ROCK CREEK, 82.5 *m.,* seasonally brings mountain trout to the desert. Normally these San Gabriel Mountain waters vanish in the sands at the desert's edge. But in the spring, when melting snows at the headwaters swell it to a torrent, the stream extends well into the desert along Little Rock Wash. As the water subsides, the trout are left stranded on the sand and in pools and can be caught by hand.

LITTLE ROCK, 83.5 *m.* (2,888 alt., 150 pop.), is an isolated settlement surrounded by irrigated orchards. Settled by Quakers in the 1890's, it is the trade center of ranchers on 2,000 acres of land producing pears and miscellaneous fruits.

PEARBLOSSOM, 89.3 *m.* (2,910 alt.), consists of a few houses, one store, and a garage. The pear orchards that gave it its name have largely reverted to desert, because of the increased competition from other sections. Pearblossom's general store and garage outfit motoring, hiking, and packing trips into the San Gabriel Mountains, and prospecting trips into the desert.

At 90.1 *m.* is a junction with Big Pines Rd., which becomes the main route.

Left (straight ahead) on State 138 to Lovejoy Springs Rd., 3 *m.,* and L. on this road to the ANTELOPE VALLEY INDIAN MUSEUM, 15 *m.* (*open daily 8-6; adm. 25¢*). Perched on the boulder-strewn south slope of Piute Butte on the site of an ancient Mohave Indian village, the long, rambling frame and stone museum building houses a private collection of Indian relics and artifacts, mostly gathered by Howard Edwards, amateur archeologist, and his wife over a period of 12 years. Exhibits are arranged sequentially to tell the story of Southwestern Indian life. The evolution of the grinding stone, for instance, is illustrated by a carefully arranged and labeled series of metates and mortars, and other items are similarly displayed in series. Paintings depict the life of prehistoric desert dwellers.

The pear orchards and vineyards of the 500-acre DARLING RANCH (R), 91.2 *m.,* testify to the magic effect of water on the semiarid regions. Little Rock Creek, with a year-round flow at this point, winds across the ranch toward the desert.

VALYERMO CAMP (R), 96.2 *m.,* is operated by the Los Angeles Police Department for underprivileged children. Dormitories, a mess hall, and playfields occupy the site of this former CCC Camp in the foothills of the San Gabriel Mountains. Basketball and volleyball courts, a baseball diamond, swimming pool, community hall, and other recreational facilities have been provided.

The inhabitants of VALYERMO, 97.1 *m.* (3,894 alt.), a tree-bowered settlement near the junction of Shoemaker and Big Rock Creek Canyons, are almost all employees of Valyermo Ranch, owned by Dr. Levi Noble, who has spent many years studying the geology of Death Valley.

At 97.4 *m.* is a junction with Big Rock Creek Rd.

Right here to a hiking trail, 0.7 *m.;* R. on the trail to the DEVIL'S PUNCH BOWL, 1.2 *m.,* in a region of upheaval along the line of the San Andreas fault (*see below*). Jumbled masses of fantastically eroded rock litter the floor of the bowl, and in the canyon walls are varying strata, some steeply tilted. The Punch Bowl was probably formed by a subterranean disturbance and subsequently weathered. From the marine fossils in formations near the crest of the ridge, and sedimentary deposits underlying the black shale in the bowl, it is deduced that a sea once covered the area.

East of Valyermo the road rises sharply and winds circuitously up the broken north scarp of the San Gabriels, crossing a boundary of the ANGELES NATIONAL FOREST (*see Tour A*) at 100.1 *m.* (*no smoking except in camps and places of habitation*).

At 105.7 *m.* Big Pines Road mounts a rocky rampart (L), and reveals a wide view over tree-clad foothills and the Mojave Desert. Northwest, appearing deceptively close in the clear air, is the blue bulk of the Tehachapi Mountains, on the northern rim of the desert.

At the WEST GATE RANGER STATION, 106.1 *m.,* the western approach to Big Pines County Camp, drivers must register (*no fee*).

East of the station the route moves into the big-timber country. The scattered spruce of the lower elevations are now replaced by forests of towering yellow, Jeffrey, big-cone Coulter, and sugar pine, and tamarack and incense cedar. Private and public camps are numerous.

JACKSON LAKE (R), 106.4 *m.,* is by the road in a steep-sided, pine-rimmed ravine. On the south shore of the lake, which is 200 yards wide and a quarter of a mile long, is a tiny artificial beach that is gay with umbrellas in summer. The waters are stocked annually with trout.

The lake basin was formed during an upheaval along the line of the San Andreas fault, and is one of a series of natural bodies of water strung out along the fault line in the San Gabriel Mountains—Twin Lakes, Jackson, Una, Elizabeth, and Hughes lakes being the others. In 1927 Los Angeles County cleared the lake of tules and other growths, and deepened and enlarged it for water sports.

At 109.5 *m.* is a junction with Table Mountain Rd.

Left here 1 *m.,* ascending through conifers, to the SMITHSONIAN INSTITUTION'S SOLAR OBSERVATORY (*open 2:30-5 p.m. Thurs.; free*), the only station of the kind in the United States and one of four in the world. The small square building housing the instruments is on an excavated shelf near the summit of Table Mountain. In front of the building are two telescopes and a recording device, examples of the many intricate scientific devices at the station. Chief among these is a delicate spectrum apparatus through which the rays of the sun in their various colors and lengths are studied. Other work involves study of the intensity of the sun's rays beyond the earth's sphere, the energy contained in ultraviolet and infrared rays, and the influence of sunspots on the intensity of the sun's rays. Charts covering the variations of sunspots and the movements of the sun itself have been kept ever since 1925 when the observatory was brought here from Mount Harquahala in Arizona.

BIG PINES CIVIC CENTER, 109.6 *m.* (6,864 alt.), surrounded by pine forests, is the center of recreational and administrative activities of

BIG PINES COUNTY PARK. This park is operated by Los Angeles County as a free public playground under jurisdiction of the Department of Playgrounds and Recreation. It is in two divisions—Big Pines and Prairie Fork (2,700 acres). The county owns 760 acres of the Big Pines division, and holds permanent lease from the Federal government on the other 1,940 acres. Facing the square is (L) the BIG PINES LODGE (*rates reasonable*), a rustic structure with a steeply-pitched roof to shed winter snow. The lodge houses a branch post office, general store, recreation hall, and a county public library (*open daily 9-4; free*).

From the Civic Center run numerous trails into mountains inaccessible by automobile. Within a short distance, along motor roads, are 17 public camp grounds (*picnicking free; camping service charge 25¢ a night, $2.50 a year, restricted to 10 successive days*), and 14 organization camps. Rangers at the information bureau in the administration office map hiking and pack trips, and motor tours to other sections of the Angeles National Forest.

The camp's summer recreational activities include dancing, riding, swimming, boating, hiking, and mountain climbing. The site's average annual snowfall of 101 inches has made it a popular rendezvous for skaters, skiers, tobogganers, and bobsledders. With four ski-tracks of graduated height, the camp has become one of the leading ski centers of southern California. Track No. 1 is 1,500 feet long horizontally with a vertical drop of 400 feet and affords one of the highest and most difficult jumps in the West.

The NATURE THEATRE, a natural, pine-bordered bowl 200 yards south of the Civic Center, is used for group meetings, lectures, nature talks, and campfire programs. It has tables and other picnicking facilities, and seats 200 persons.

At the EAST GATE RANGER STATION, 110.3 m., registration of car number and name of driver is required (*no fee*).

WRIGHTWOOD, 113.1 m. (6,000 alt., 50 permanent pop.), is a summer and winter vacation area whose small permanent population seasonally swells to more than 1,500. A steep-roofed rustic lodge (*rates reasonable*) faces the road (R).

Right from Wrightwood on Pine St., 0.1 m., to Eagle and Oriole Rds.; R. on Eagle Rd., 0.5 m., to ACORN LODGE NATURE MUSEUM (*open daily 8-6; adm. 25¢*), a private museum with a collection of freak tree growths and natural oddities gathered in the vicinity.

East of Wrightwood the highway descends through the big-timber country of the Blue Ridge Range, with forests of pine and incense cedar that shut out the sun and keep the road continually shaded.

At 114 m. is a junction with Lone Pine Canyon Rd.

Right here into LONE PINE CANYON, 3.5 m., through which runs the SAN ANDREAS RIFT (*see Natural Setting*), a geologic fault cutting through the San Gabriel Mountains that has been the cause of several California earthquakes.

East of the Lone Pine Canyon Rd. junction, the elevation steadily decreases. At 117 m. a sign indicates the boundary between Angeles National Forest and SAN BERNARDINO NATIONAL FOREST (*see* *Tour 1*).

At 119.2 m. is the southern junction with State 138, which again becomes the main route; R. on State 138.

A boulder monument (L) at 122.6 m. commemorates the Mormon wagon train that crossed the mountains along this route in 1851 and settled San Bernardino Valley (*see Tour 1*).

An area littered with broken masses of rock and eroded sandstone formations tilted at grotesque angles is seen at 125.4 m. The district is a reminder of an upheaval along the line of the San Andreas Rift.

At 127.2 m. is a junction with US 66-395, which becomes the main tour route and continues southeast. US 66-395 here traverses CAJON (box) PASS, discovered in 1772, three years after the Spanish penetrated Upper California, when Pedro Fages, who 10 years later became the fourth governor, stumbled on it while pursuing army deserters. In 1776 Francisco Garces traveled through the pass from the Mojave Desert to San Bernardino Valley. The first American to trek this way was Jedediah Strong Smith (*see Tour C*), the fur trader, in 1826. The following year Smith retraced his journey and several other traders followed. In 1831 William Wolfskill, who later pioneered in orange growing in Los Angeles, blazed a caravan trail from Santa Fe, New Mexico, to California through the pass and in 1851 it was used by Mormons coming from Salt Lake City to settle in San Bernardino Valley (*see Tour 1*). Government surveys to carry a proposed transcontinental railroad through the pass began in 1854, but it was not until 1885 that the rail link between San Bernardino and Waterman, now Barstow, was completed by the California Southern, later part of the Santa Fe.

CAJON POST OFFICE (L), 127.5 m. (2,960 alt., 50 pop.), is a settlement around a garage and a post office housed in a stone general store.

DEVORE, 136.9 m. (2,025 alt., 138 pop.), has a garage and an auto camp. Here the trails of two divisions of the Mormon pioneers converged in 1851.

Right from Devore 1.5 m. to the SITE OF A MORMON CAMP, the last camp before the settlers reached the valley.

SAN BERNARDINO, 146.9 m. (1,073 alt., 43,646 pop.) *see Tour 1*).

Points of Interest: National Orange Show Grounds, Pioneer Park, Memorial Auditorium, courthouse, and others.

PART V

Appendices

Chronology

1542   Juan Rodriguez Cabrillo discovers San Diego Harbor and islands off southern California Coast. Lands at Santa Monica. Claims land for King of Spain.

1602   Sebastian Vizcaino makes a second trip for Spain and goes as far north as Monterey Bay. Names many California coastal points.

1769   Spanish land expedition under Gaspar de Portola and Father Juan Crespi crosses Los Angeles County.

1771   Sept. 8—First Mission San Gabriel dedicated.

1781   Sept. 4—El Pueblo de Nuestra Senora La Reina de Los Angeles de Porciuncula is founded.

1784   Spanish crown inaugurates the policy of giving huge land grants ("ranchos") to private individuals.

1797   Sept. 8—Mission San Fernando founded.

1800   Population of Los Angeles 315.

1804   Alta (upper) and Baja (lower) California separated.

1805   May—*Lelia Byrd,* American trading vessel, arrives at San Pedro.

1810   Population of Los Angeles 415.
        Sept. 16—Revolution in Mexico to free it from Spain.

1820   Population of Los Angeles 650.

1822   Apr.—Los Angeles citizens pledge allegiance to new Mexican Government.
        Dec. 8—Plaza Church dedicated.

1826   Nov. 27—Jedediah Strong Smith completes first overland trip from the "States" to California, and arrives at Mission San Gabriel.

1830   Population of Los Angeles 730.

1831   Dec.—At battle near Cahuenga Pass, revolution unseats the Mexican governor, Victoria.
        American immigrants begin to come into Los Angeles.

1833   Jan.—Breach, which had persisted between northern and southern Californians since expulsion of Victoria is healed, and Governor Jose Figueroa is recognized by both factions.
        Aug. 17—Mexican Congress decrees secularization of the missions.

1835   May 23—Los Angeles proclaimed capital of California by decree of Mexican Congress.

1836   Apr. 7—First vigilante committee formed in Los Angeles.
        Nov. 3-7—Alvarado unseats Mexican governor and declares California an "independent" republic. Southern Californians refuse to recognize him.

1837–8   Revolution in California continues, but Los Angeles is finally captured by the northerners.

1840   Population of Los Angeles 1,250.

Municipal self-government abolished by decree of Mexican Congress and administration of Los Angeles placed under a semimilitary prefect until 1844, when civil administration is re-established.

1842   Mar. 9—Gold discovered at Placerita Canyon near Saugus.

Oct. 19—Commodore Jones of the U. S. Navy, mistakenly "captures" Monterey.

1844   Revolution begun to rid California of governor sent from Mexico.

1846   Mar.—Ordered out of California, Fremont begins hostilities.

May—War declared between United States and Mexico.

1847   Jan. 10—Los Angeles is taken by the American forces under Kearny and Stockton.

Jan. 13—Gen. Andres Pico, in command of Mexican troops in California, signs Articles of Capitulation at Cahuenga.

1848   Feb. 2—Treaty of Peace between United States and Mexico establishes California as a territory of the United States.

Discovery of gold in northern California. Los Angeles becomes practically depopulated.

1850   First U. S. Census Bureau enumeration of California finds Los Angeles to have 1,610 inhabitants.

Feb. 18—County limits are set. They include the territory between San Diego and Santa Barbara, or 34,000 square miles.

First overland freight wagon arrives.

Apr. 4—Los Angeles is incorporated.

Sept. 9—California admitted to the Union.

1851   May 17—First newspaper, the *Star*, begins publication.

1853   Apr. 26—San Bernardino County created out of part of Los Angeles County.

1854   May 20—First Los Angeles city school superintendent appointed.

1855   First city public school building erected.

1857   Apr. 11—Wells, Fargo & Co. express office established in Los Angeles.

1860   Population of Los Angeles 4,385 (Federal Census).

Ten-day mail service by horseback links Los Angeles with Missouri River.

1863–64   Great drought ends the cattle-raising industry in Los Angeles County.

1865   Mar.—St. Vincent's College (now Loyola University of California) founded as first institution of higher learning in southern California.

1866   Apr. 2—Governor approves legislative act creating Kern County out of part of Los Angeles County.

1868   Los Angeles water system begins use of iron pipes.

Sept. 19—Los Angeles-Wilmington Railway begun.

San Gabriel, Los Angeles, Wilmington, El Monte and Anaheim are the only towns in Los Angeles County.
1869 Railway extended to San Pedro.
Los Angeles city Board of Education organized.
1870 Population of Los Angeles 5,728 (Federal Census).
Dec. 17—Last recorded lynching by Los Angeles vigilante committee.
1871 United States Government begins improvements on Wilmington Harbor.
Mar. 27—The *Evening Express* begins publication.
Oct. 24—Massacre of 19 Chinese gives Los Angeles nationwide notoriety.
1873 Oct. 3—Los Angeles *Herald* begins publication.
1874 May 15—Vasquez, notorious bandit, captured.
1875 Dec. 1—First train of the Los Angeles and Independence Railroad begins running to the wharf at Santa Monica.
1876 Sept. 6—With the completion of the Southern Pacific's Los Angeles-San Francisco (eastern route) line, Los Angeles is linked with the transcontinental railroad.
1877 First oranges shipped to eastern markets.
1878 Southern Pacific buys rail and wharf improvements at Santa Monica and closes port, forcing citizens to use Wilmington Harbor exclusively.
1879 June 29—University of Southern California founded.
Subdivision of large Mexican and Spanish land grants leads to settlement of various communities in Los Angeles County.
1880 Population of Los Angeles 11,183 (Federal Census).
1881 Dec. 4—The *Times,* a daily paper, begins publication.
1882 Telephone and electric lighting introduced into Los Angeles.
Aug. 29—State Normal School opened.
1883 Jan.—Southern Pacific's southern route to East opened.
1884 Feb. 26—Pasadena Public Library opened.
At New Orleans Cotton Exhibit, California citrus products win in competition with Florida fruit.
1885 Nov.—Santa Fe brings second major railroad into Los Angeles.
1886 Many travelers, settlers, and speculators arrive as a result of Southern Pacific-Santa Fe rate war.
Major real-estate boom.
June—Pasadena incorporated.
Santa Monica incorporated.
1887 Peak of Los Angeles' land boom. Many towns laid out. Some buildings hurriedly erected.
Los Angeles Clearing House organized.
Soldiers' Home, Sawtelle, founded.
April 20—Occidental College founded.
First public night school opened in Los Angeles.
Sept. 27—Los Angeles Athletic Club incorporated.
Dec. 31—Pomona incorporated.

1888 Feb. 10—Long Beach first incorporated.

Sept.—Pomona College opened.

Oct. 28—Los Angeles adopts a charter.

Land boom collapses.

Los Angeles Chamber of Commerce begins new policy; encouraging commerce and industry, inducing immigration and settlement of land.

1889 First college football game played in Los Angeles, St. Vincent's College (now Loyola) vs. University of Southern California.

1890 Population of Los Angeles 50,395 (Federal Census).

Jan. 1—First Battle of Flowers, later called Tournament of Roses, held at Pasadena.

Mar. 11—Orange County created out of part of Los Angeles County.

1891 Sept. 23—Whittier Academy (now Whittier College) founded at Whittier.

Nov. 2—Throop Polytechnic Institute (now the California Institute of Technology) opened at Pasadena.

Los Angeles' new courthouse on North Broadway completed.

1892 Feb.—Discovery of oil within the city limits of Los Angeles.

Redondo Beach incorporated.

1893 July 4—Railway at Mt. Lowe opened.

Aug.—Co-operative marketing organization, forerunner of present California Fruit Growers Exchange, formed by citrus growers in southern California.

1894 Mt. Lowe Observatory built.

Apr. 10—First Fiesta de Los Angeles held.

1895 Mar. 4—Los Angeles *Record* begins publication.

Oct. 18—Highland Park annexed to Los Angeles.

1896 May—Congress appropriates $2,900,000 for the building of a deepwater harbor at San Pedro.

1897 Henry E. Huntington establishes himself in Los Angeles and begins a vigorous program for development of local transportation.

1898 Mar. 5—Griffith Park presented to Los Angeles by Colonel G. J. Griffith.

Oct. 3—Los Angeles Country Club (first) incorporated.

1899 Apr. 26—Construction begins on Los Angeles Harbor, San Pedro.

June 12—Garvanza and University districts annexed to Los Angeles.

July 29—Southern California Golf Association founded.

1900 Population of Los Angeles 102,479 (Federal Census).

1902 Los Angeles takes over water system.

1903 Alhambra incorporated.

Mar. 26—Los Angeles joins in formation of Pacific Coast Baseball League.

Dec. 12—Los Angeles *Examiner* begins publication.

1904 Mt. Wilson Observatory founded by Carnegie Institute.

1905 A third major railroad, the Los Angeles, San Pedro and Salt Lake Railway (now the Union Pacific) comes to Los Angeles.
Pleistocene fossils discovered in La Brea (tar) pits.
Vernon incorporated.

1906 Glendale, Huntington Park, and Watts incorporated.
Apr. 2—Hollywood *Citizen* established as weekly publication.
June 11—First California-Honolulu yacht race held.
Dec. 26—"Shoestring strip" area contiguous to Wilmington annexed to Los Angeles.

1907 Santa Monica adopts a charter.

1908 Oct. 1—General construction of the Owens River Aqueduct begins.

1909 Aug. 28—Wilmington and San Pedro annexed to Los Angeles.

1910 Population of Los Angeles 319,198 (Federal Census).
Feb. 7—Hollywood annexed to Los Angeles.
Sept.—Motion-picture production begins in Hollywood.
Oct. 1—*Times* building blown up with loss of 20 lives.

1911 Sept. 1—Eight streetcar companies merged to form the Pacific Electric Railway Company.

1912 Feb. 15—First international polo match held.
Whittier oil fields discovered.
Sept. 5—Los Angeles County free library established.
First performance of *Mission Play* at San Gabriel.

1913 Nov. 5—Water turned into San Fernando Valley from Owens River Aqueduct.
Nov. 6—Museum opened at Exposition Park, Los Angeles.

1914 Aug. 3—Southwest Museum opened.
Aug. 28—First ship via Panama Canal arrives at Los Angeles Harbor.

1915 May 22—Los Angeles annexes most of San Fernando Valley.
June—Los Angeles County Flood Control District created and a program for flood control began.

1916 First unit of Los Angeles municipal power system begins distributing electricity from plant at Garvanza.
Hancock Park presented to county.

1917 Mar.—Hydroelectric power from Owens River Aqueduct development inaugurated.
Culver City incorporated.

1918 Installation of 100-inch telescope at Mt. Wilson.

1919 Santa Fe Springs oil field developed.
Sept.—Legislature transfers facilities of State Normal School, Los Angeles, to University of California, and Southern Branch of the State University is founded.
Oct. 24—First concert of Philharmonic Orchestra, Los Angeles.
Wm. Wrigley, Jr. purchases Santa Catalina Island, and begins its development as a playground.

1920 Population of Los Angeles 576,673 (Federal Census).

Nov. 9—Olive View Sanatorium, Los Angeles County institution for tuberculars, opened.

First performance of Pilgrimage Play.

Huntington Beach oil field discovered.

Douglas Aircraft factory established at Santa Monica.

1921   June 25—Oil discovered at Signal Hill, Long Beach.

Los Angeles purchases distribution system (power and light) of the Edison Company.

Aug. 12—Hollywood Legion Stadium opened.

Oct. 1—Hollywood *Citizen* (evening) begins publication as a daily.

Nov. 1—Hollywood *News* (evening) starts daily publication.

1922   Apr.—Radio broadcasting begun by Stations KHJ and KFI, Los Angeles.

Rose Bowl completed at Pasadena.

Hollywood Bowl organized.

Torrance oil fields discovered.

1923   Jan. 1—Angeles Temple dedicated.

Nov. 11—Memorial Coliseum, Exposition Park, Los Angeles, begun in 1921, opened.

Building boom in Los Angeles and surrounding communities reaches post-war apex.

Twelve annexations add 19,031 acres to area of the city.

Illustrated Daily News founded.

Los Angeles Harbor leads world in crude-oil exports.

Rosecrans and Inglewood oil fields discovered.

1925   Jan. 22—Legislature approves new Los Angeles City Charter.

May 18—Community Playhouse, Pasadena, opened.

Long Beach Harbor, improvement of which began in 1924, opened.

1926   June—Los Angeles Public Library's new building opened.

Santa Monica purchases Clover Field for municipal airport.

New Pasadena City Hall and Library completed.

1927   Los Angeles becomes second largest rubber manufacturing center in the United States.

1928   Henry E. Huntington Library and Art Gallery opened to public.

New City Hall opened.

Jazz Singer, first all-talkie motion picture, made by Warner Brothers.

Motion-picture studios begin expansion into San Fernando Valley.

Mar. 13—St. Francis Dam at San Francisquito Canyon, about 50 miles from Los Angeles, collapses, spilling 12 billion gallons of water, causing loss of 450 lives, and damaging property to an estimated extent of $30,000,000.

Union Air Terminal established at Burbank.

Metropolitan Water District, comprising 13 cities, formed to obtain water from Colorado River.

Sept.—Classes begin in new campus of University of California at Los Angeles (Westwood).

1929 176,000,000 barrels of oil produced in Los Angeles County during year.

1930 Population of Los Angeles 1,238,048 (Federal Census).
Los Angeles becomes the nation's fifth largest city. County population exceeds two millions.
May 1—Metropolitan Water District takes over planning of Colorado River Aqueduct project.

1931 Mar.—Independent oil producers form marketing co-operative.
June—Work begins on Boulder Dam.
Sept. 11—$690,000 bond issue for breakwater carried in Santa Monica election.
Sept. 29—$220,000,000 Colorado River Aqueduct Bond issue passed by 13 cities.
Nov. 1—Hollywood *Citizen* and *News* merge as Hollywood *Citizen-News*.
Dec. 10—Los Angeles *Herald* and *Express* merge as Los Angeles *Evening Herald-Express*.

1932 June—County Relief Budget Committee demands $12,000,000 bond issue for unemployment relief.
July 30—Tenth Olympiad opened at Los Angeles Coliseum.
California State Building, Los Angeles, dedicated.
Dec.—Construction of Colorado River Aqueduct begins.
Issuance of scrip to pay wages held violation of state law.

1933 Feb. 22—Dedication of Valley Municipal Building, Van Nuys, administration center for all the San Fernando Valley area which had been annexed to the city of Los Angeles.
Mar. 10—Earthquake, centering in Long Beach, causes total loss in southern California of more than 100 lives, and property damage estimated at $60,000,000.
Aug.—Relief rolls reach peak of 129,000 families in county.
Dec. 12—New Los Angeles County General Hospital opened.
Los Angeles *Record* becomes *Post-Record*.
Dec. 30 to Jan., 1934—Montrose and Crescenta flood.

1934 Oct.—Colorado River diverted through tunnels, and Parker Dam construction started.

1935 Griffith Park Planetarium, Los Angeles, dedicated.

1936 Jan. 7—Los Angeles *Post-Record* changes name to *Evening News*.
Oct. 9—Power from Boulder Dam electric generators brought to Los Angeles.
Federal $70,000,000 flood control plan for Los Angeles County is authorized.

1937 Los Angeles completes purchase of Mines Field for a municipal airport.
Los Angeles becomes fifth in rank among industrial counties of the United States.
Los Angeles leads the nation in motion-picture production, oil refining, airplane manufacturing and secondary automobile assembly.

1938   Feb.–Mar.—Five-day rain beginning February 28 causes record flood and damage in Los Angeles County. About 100 killed and property damage estimated at $65,000,000.

New Federal Building and Post Office opened, Los Angeles.

Sept. 16—Special recall election ousts Mayor Frank L. Shaw, electing in his stead Fletcher Bowron.

1939   Jan. 2—Culbert L. Olson of Los Angeles inaugurated first Democratic governor of California in 42 years.

May 3–5—Three-day celebration marks opening of new Los Angeles Union Passenger Terminal, to be used by Southern Pacific, Union Pacific, and Santa Fe railroads.

Los Angeles County attains rank of fourth in manufacture of women's apparel and furniture, and second in tires in the United States.

1940   Apr. 1—Los Angeles *Evening News* and *Daily News* merge to constitute *The News*, a 24-hour newspaper.

Selective Bibliography

BIBLIOGRAPHIES

Cowan, Robert Ernest, and Cowan, Robert Granniss. *A Bibliography of the History of California, 1510-1930.* 3 v. San Francisco, J. H. Nash, 1933.

Hanna, Phil Townsend. *Libros Californianos, or Five Feet of California Books.* Los Angeles, Zeitlin Press, 1931.

FIRST AMERICANS

Hodge, Frederick Webb. *Handbook of American Indians, North of Mexico.* 2 v. Washington, D.C., U.S. Government Printing Office, 1907-10. (Smithsonian Institution).

Kroeber, Alfred Louis. *Handbook of the Indians of California.* Washington, D.C., U.S. Government Printing Office, 1925.

Reid, Hugo. *The Indians of Los Angeles County.* Los Angeles, Privately Printed, 1926.

Strong, William Duncan. *Aboriginal Society in Southern California.* Berkeley, Calif., University of California Press, 1929.

NATURAL SETTING

Abrams, LeRoy. *Flora of Los Angeles and Vicinity.* Stanford, Calif., Stanford University Press, 1917.

Arnold, Ralph, and Garfias, Valentine Richard. *Geology and Technology of the California Oil Fields.* New York, American Institute of Mining Engineers, 1914.

Bailey, Liberty Hyde. *Hortus.* New York, Macmillan, 1935.

——— *Manual of Cultivated Plants.* New York, Macmillan, 1924.

Colton, Buel Preston. *Zoology Descriptive and Practical.* 2 v. Boston, D. C. Heath & Co., 1903.

Comstock, John Hendy. *Insect Life.* New York, Appleton, 1917.

Dallimore, William, and Jackson, A. Bruce. *A Handbook of Conifereae Including Ginkgoaceae.* London, E. Arnold & Co., n. d. (2nd ed., 1931).

Dawson, William Leon. *The Birds of California.* Los Angeles, 1921. (4 v., later ed. San Diego, Calif., South Moulton Co., 1923).

Eakle, Arthur Starr. *Minerals of California.* Sacramento, Calif., State Printing Office, 1923.

Eliot, Willard Ayers. *Birds of the Pacific Coast.* New York, S. P. Putnam's Sons, 1923.

Eliot, Willard Ayers. *Forest Trees of the Pacific Coast.* New York, S. P. Putnam's Sons, 1938.

Fultz, Francis Marion. *The Elfin-forest of California.* Los Angeles, Times-Mirror Co., 1927.

Grinnell, Joseph, Dixon, Joseph S., and Linsdale, Jean M. *Fur-bearing Mammals of California.* 2 v. Berkeley, Calif., University of California Press, 1937.

Howes, Paul Griswold. *Backyard Exploration.* Garden City, N.Y., Doubleday, 1927.

Jaeger, Edmund Carroll. *The California Deserts.* Stanford, Calif., Stanford University Press, 1933.

———— *Denizens of the Deserts.* Boston, Houghton, 1922.

Jepson, Willis Linn. *A Manual of the Flowering Plants of California.* 2 v. Berkeley, Calif., Associated Students' Store, 1925.

———— *The Trees of California.* Berkeley, Calif., Associated Students' Store, 1923.

Miller, William John. *Geology of the Western San Gabriel Mountains.* Berkeley, Calif., University of California Press, 1934.

Muir, John. *The Mountains of California.* Boston, Houghton, 1911.

Myers, Harriet Williams. *Western Birds.* New York, Macmillan, 1922.

Parsons, Mary Elizabeth. *Wild Flowers of California.* San Francisco, Cunningham, Curtis & Welch, 1909.

Reed, Ralph Daniel. *Geology of California.* Tulsa, Okla., American Association of Petroleum Geologists, 1933.

Reed, Ralph Daniel, and Hollister, Joseph Steffins. *Structural Evolution of Southern California.* Tulsa, Okla., American Association of Petroleum Geologists, 1936.

Saunders, Charles Francis. *With the Flowers and Trees of California.* New York, McBride, 1914.

Van der Leck, Laurence. *Petroleum Resources of California.* Sacramento, Calif., State Printing Office, 1921.

Wheelock, Irene Grosvenor. *Birds of California.* Chicago, A. C. McClurg & Co., 1904.

Wood, Harry Oscar. *Earthquake Study in Southern California.* Washington, D.C. (Division of Publications, Carnegie Institute of Washington, 1935).

DESCRIPTION AND TRAVEL

Audubon, John Woodhouse. *Audubon's Western Journal, 1849-50.* Cleveland, Ohio, A. H. Clark Co., 1906.

Bartlett, Lanier, and Bartlett, Virginia Stivers. *Los Angeles in 7 Days.* New York, McBride, 1932.

Bogardus, Emory Stephen. *Southern California, A Center of Culture.* Los Angeles, Calif., University of Southern California Press, 1938.

Bryant, Edwin. *What I Saw in California.* Santa Ana, Calif., Fine Arts Press, 1936.

Carr, Harry. *Los Angeles, City of Dreams.* New York, Appleton-Century, 1935.

Chase, Joseph Smeaton. *California Desert Trails.* Boston, Houghton, 1913.

Dana, Richard Henry. *Two Years Before the Mast.* Boston and New York, Houghton Mifflin Co., 1911.

Drury, Aubrey. *California, an Intimate Guide.* New York, Harper, 1939.

Duflot, de Mofras, Eugene. *Travels on the Pacific Coast.* Santa Ana, Calif., Fine Arts Press, 1937.

Holder, Charles Frederick. *The Channel Islands of California.* Chicago, A. C. McClurg & Co., 1910.

——— *Life in the Open; Sport with Rod, Gun, Horse, and Hound in Southern California.* New York, G. P. Putnam's Sons, 1906.

Mackey, Margaret Gilbert. *Los Angeles, Proper and Improper.* Los Angeles, Goodwin Press, 1938.

Saunders, Charles Francis. *Finding the Worth While in California.* New York, R. M. McBride & Co., 1916. (5th ed., 1937).

Van Tulye, Bert. *Know Your California.* Los Angeles, Wallace Press, n. d.

W.P.A., Federal Writers' Project. *California.* American Guide Series. New York, Hastings House, 1939.

HISTORY

Adamic, Louis. *Dynamite.* New York, Viking Press, 1934.

Ayers, James J. *Gold and Sunshine.* Boston, Badger, 1922.

Bancroft, Hubert Howe. *History of California.* 7 v. San Francisco, The History Co., 1884-1890.

——— *California Pastoral.* San Francisco, The History Co., 1888.

Bell, Horace. *On the Old West Coast.* New York, Morrow, 1930.

——— *Reminiscences of a Ranger.* Los Angeles, Yarnell, 1881.

Bolton, Herbert Eugene. *Anza's California Expeditions.* 5 v. Berkeley, Calif., University of California Press, 1930.

——— *Spanish Exploration in the Southwest, 1542-1706.* New York, C. Scribner's Sons, 1916.

——— *Fray Juan Crespi.* Berkeley, Calif., University of California Press, 1927.

Bowman, Mary M. *Bowman Scrap Book.* Compiled 5 v. 1887-1914. Los Angeles Public Library.

Burbank, Luther, with Wilbur Hall. *The Harvest of the Years.* Boston, Houghton, 1927.

Chapman, Charles Edward. *A History of California: The Spanish Period.* New York, Macmillan, 1921.

——— *The Founding of Spanish California.* New York, Macmillan, 1916.

Cleland, Robert Glass. *A History of California: The American Period.* New York, Macmillan, 1922.

Cleland, Robert Glass, and Hardy, Osgood. *March of Industry.* Los Angeles, Powell, 1929.

Coblentz, Stanton Arthur. *Villains and Vigilantes.* New York, Wilson-Erickson, 1936.

Colton, Walter. *Three Years in California.* New York, A. S. Barnes & Co., Cincinnati, H. W. Derby & Co., 1860.

Conner, E. Palmer. *The Romance of the Ranchos.* Los Angeles, Title Insurance and Trust Co., n. d.

Cross, Ira Brown. *A History of the Labor Movement in California.* Berkeley, Calif., University of California Press, 1935.

Davis, William Heath. *Seventy-five Years in California.* San Francisco, Howell, 1929.

Denis, Alberta Johnston. *Spanish Alta California.* New York, Macmillan, 1927.

Eldredge, Zoeth Skinner, ed. *History of California.* 5 v. New York, The Century History Co., 1915.

Engelhardt, Fr. Zephyrin (Charles Anthony). *The Missions and Missionaries of California.* 4 v. San Francisco, Barry, 1908-1916.

────── *San Gabriel Mission and the Beginnings of Los Angeles.* San Gabriel, Calif., Mission San Gabriel, 1927.

Fages, Pedro. *California.* Tr. by Herbert Ingram Priestley. Berkeley, Calif., University of California Press, 1937.

Forbes, Alexander. *A History of Upper and Lower California.* London, Smith Elder & Co., 1839.

Forbes, Harrie Rebecca Piper. *California Missions and Landmarks.* Los Angeles, Official Guide, 1903. (3rd ed. rev., 1915).

Fremont, John Charles. *Memoirs of My Life.* Chicago, Belford, Clark & Co., 1887.

Guinn, James Miller. *Historical and Biographical Record of Los Angeles.* 3 v. Los Angeles, Historic Record Co., 1915.

Hanna, Phil Townsend. *California Through Four Centuries.* New York, Farrar & Rinehart, 1935.

Hittell, Theodore Henry. *History of California.* San Francisco, 4 v: V. I & II, Pacific Press Pub. House and Occidental Pub. Co., 1885. V. III & IV, N. T. Stone & Co., 1897.

Hunt, Rockwell Dennis, and Sanchez, Nellie (Van de Grift). *A Short History of California.* New York, Crowell, 1929.

────── *California and Californians.* 4 v. Chicago and New York, Lewis Pub. Co., 1930.

James, George Wharton. *In and Out of the Old Missions of California.* Boston, Little, Brown & Co., 1911.

Ludwig, Salvator. *Eine blume aus dem goldenen lande; oder, Los Angeles.* Prag, Germany, H. Mercy, 1878.

McGroarty, John Steven. *California, Its History and Romance.* Los Angeles, Grafton Pub. Co., 1911.

Nevins, Allan. *Frémont, the World's Greatest Adventurer.* New York, Harper, 1928.

Newcomb, Rexford. *The Old Mission Churches and Historic Houses of California.* Philadelphia and London, J. B. Lippincott, 1925.

Newmark, Harris. *Sixty Years in Southern California.* New York, The Knickerbocker Press, 1930.
Packman, Anna Begue. *Leather Dollars.* Los Angeles, Times-Mirror Press, 1932.
Palou, Francisco. *Life and Apostolic Labors of the Venerable Father Junipero Serra.* San Francisco, P. E. Dougherty & Co., 1884.
——— *Historical Memoirs of New California.* 4 v. Berkeley, Calif., University of California Press, 1926.
Rensch, Hero Eugene, and Rensch, Ethel Grace. *Historic Spots in California—The Southern Counties.* Stanford, Calif., Stanford University Press, 1932.
Richman, Irving Berdine. *California Under Spain and Mexico, 1535-1847.* Boston and New York, Houghton Mifflin Co., 1911.
Robinson, Alfred. *Life in California Before the Conquest.* San Francisco, Private Press of T. C. Russell, 1925.
Sanchez, Nellie (Van de Grift). *Spanish Arcadia.* San Francisco, Powell Pub. Co., 1929.
——— *Spanish and Indian Place Names of California: Their Meaning and Their Romance.* San Francisco, A. M. Robertson, 1914.
Shinn, Charles Howard. *Mining-camps: A Study in American Frontier Government.* New York, C. Scribner's Sons, 1885.
Sinclair, Upton Beall. *The EPIC Plan for California.* New York, Farrar & Rinehart, 1934.
Spalding, William Andrew. *History and Reminiscences of Los Angeles City and County.* Los Angeles, J. R. Finnell & Sons Pub. Co., 1931.
Talbot, Clare (Ryan). *Historic California in Book-plates.* Los Angeles, Graphic Press, 1936.
Walsh, Marie T. *The Mission Bells of California.* San Francisco, Wagner Pub. Co., 1934.
Willard, Charles Dwight. *The Herald's History of Los Angeles City.* Los Angeles, Kingsley-Barnes & Neuner Co., 1901.
Wilson, John Albert. *History of Los Angeles County, California.* Oakland, Calif., Thompson & West, 1880.

EDUCATION

Ferrier, William Warren. *Ninety Years of Education in California, 1846-1936.* Berkeley, Calif., Sather Gate Book Shop, 1937.
Hill, Laurence L. *Six Collegiate Decades.* Los Angeles, Security-First National Bank, 1929.
——— *Your Children and Their Schools.* Los Angeles City Board of Education, 1937.

RELIGION

Dresser, Horatio Willis. *History of the New Thought Movement.* New York, Crowell, 1919.
Smith, Joseph Fielding. *Essentials in Church History.* Salt Lake City, Utah, Desert News Press, 1922.

THE ARTS

Barr, Alfred Hamilton Jr., and others. *Modern Architects.* New York, Museum of Modern Art, 1932.

Cheney, Sheldon. *The New World Architecture.* New York, Longmans, Green & Co., 1930.

Cronyn, George William. *The Path on the Rainbow.* New York, Boni, 1918.

Davis, Carlyle Channing, and Alderson, William A. *The True Story of Ramona.* New York, Dodge Pub. Co., 1914.

Dobinson, George A. *Theatre Programs* (bound collection, 15 v., 1870-1903). Los Angeles Public Library.

Hague, Eleanor, ed. *Spanish-American Folk Songs.* (In Lancaster, American Folk-lore Society, 1917, V. X.)

Hamlin, Talbot Faulkner. *The American Spirit in Architecture.* New Haven, Conn., Yale University Press, 1926.

Hannaford, Donald R. *Spanish Colonial or Adobe Architecture of California, 1800-1850.* New York, Architectural Book Pub. Co. Inc., 1931.

Hill, Laurence L. *La Reina.* Los Angeles, Security-First National Bank, 1929.

Lummis, Charles Fletcher. "The Making of Los Angeles." (In Los Angeles: *Outwest,* April 1909, V. XXX, No. 4.)

Menken, Henry. *California Bungalow Homes.* Los Angeles, The Bungalowcraft Co., 1910.

Perlman, William Jacob, and Ussher, Bruno David. *Who's Who in Music and Dance in Southern California.* Los Angeles, Bureau of Musical Research, 1933.

Roberts, Helen Heffron. *Form in Primitive Music.* New York, American Library of Musicology, W. W. Norton Co., 1933.

Smith, Caroline Estes. *The Philharmonic Orchestra of Los Angeles.* Los Angeles, Press of United Printing Co., 1930.

THE MOVIES

Hampton, Benjamin Bowles. *A History of the Movies.* New York, Covici, 1931.

Kiesling, Barrett C. *How to Make a Movie.* Richmond, Va., Johnson Pub. Co., 1937.

Naumberg, Nancy, ed. *We Make the Movies.* New York, W. W. Norton & Co. Inc., 1937.

Ramsaye, Terry. *Million and One Nights.* New York, Simon and Schuster Co. Inc., 1936.

FICTION

Allen, Jane. *I Lost My Girlish Laughter.* New York, Random House, 1938.

Baker, Dorothy. *Young Man With a Horn.* Cambridge, Mass., Houghton, 1938.

Baum, Vicki. *Falling Star.* Garden City, N.Y., Doubleday, 1934.

Brinig, Myron. *Flutter of an Eyelid.* New York, Farrar & Rinehart, 1933.

Chester, George Randolph and Chester, Lilian. *On the Lot and Off.* New York, Harper Co., 1924.

Jackson, Helen Hunt. *Ramona.* Boston, Grosset, also McClelland, 1935.

Lee, James. *Hollywood Agent.* New York, Macauley, 1938.

Luther, Mark Lee. *Boosters.* Indianapolis, Bobbs-Merrill Co., 1923.

McCoy, Horace. *I Should Have Stayed Home.* New York, Alfred A. Knopf, 1938.

McEvoy, Joseph Patrick. *Simon and Schuster Present Show Girl.* New York, Simon and Schuster Co. Inc., 1928.

O'Hara, John. *Hope of Heaven.* New York, Harcourt, Brace & Co., 1938.

Ryan, Don. *Angel's Flight.* New York, Boni & Liveright, Inc., 1927.

Stong, Phillip Duffield. *Farmer in the Dell.* New York, Harcourt & McLeod, 1935.

West, Nathanal. *The Day of the Locust.* New York, Random House, 1939.

Wodehouse, Pelham Grenville. *Laughing Gas.* Garden City, N.Y., Doubleday, 1936.

Woon, Basil Dillon. *Incredible Land: A Jaunty Baedeker to Hollywood and the Great Southwest.* New York, Liveright, 1933.

Index

(Where more than one page number is given, the first number is the principal reference.)

Abbott, William, 128
Adohr Milk Farms, 381
Adult Education Program, 64-65
Adult Evening College, 65
Agua Caliente, 137
Aguilar, Isidro, 350
Airports: California National Guard, 180; Clover Field, Santa Monica, 272; Grand Central Air Terminal, Glendale, 212; Long Beach Municipal, 252; Los Angeles Municipal, 356; Union Air Terminal, Burbank, 389, 101, 207; U. S. Airbase, Navy, 224
Alamitos Bay, 251, 11, 240
Alessandro Valley, 331
Alexandria Hotel, 160
Alligator Farm, 171
All-Year Club, 55-56, 3, 136
Alvarado, Governor Juan Bautista, 34, 355
Ambassador Hotel, 182
American Colony, 241
American Federation of Labor, 218
American Federation of Radio Artists, 100
American Legion, 55
American rule, 40-44
Anderson, G. M. (Broncho Billy), 73
Angeles National Forest, 296-99, 19, 302, 402
Angel's Flight, 157
Annie Laurie Wishing Chair, 210
Antelope Valley, 395-96
Anthony, Earle C., 98, 102
Anza, Juan Bautista de, bust of, 185
Aqueducts: Colorado River, 51, 52, 315; Los Angeles, 394, 51-52, 58
Arcadia, 281
Architecture, 103-11; Adobe of California, 104; Churches, 109; Frank Lloyd Wright, 108; Mediterranean Style, 107; Monterey Style, 107; Spanish Colonial Style, 104
Armory, State, 191
Armory, U. S. Naval and Marine Corps Reserve, 174-75

Armstrong, Henry, 139
Army, 220, 222, 54, 55, 204, 331, 391
Army of the Californians, 38
Arrowhead Hot Springs, 292
Arroyo Seco, 262, 171, 296
Art and Artists, 124-27
Art Gallery, Los Angeles City Hall, 148
Assembly Plants: Aircraft, 57; automobile, 47
Astronomers' Monument, 126
Atherton, Gertrude, 121
Austin, John C., 110, 179
Automobile Club of Southern California, 188
Auto Races, midget, 140
Avalon, 369-70
Avila, Antonio, 355
Avila, Bruno, 355
Avocado, 342-44, 166, 23, 57
Ayuntamiento, Los Angeles, 33

Baker Building, 151
Baker, Colonel Robert S., 267
Baldwin, E. J. (Lucky), 280
Baldwin Hills, 12
Baldwin Lake, 294
Ballestros, Carlos, 37
Banning, Hancock, 368
Banning, Phineas, 368, 47, 213, 217, 314
Barnsdall Residence, 108
Baseball, professional, 139-40
Basketball, 140
Battles: Cahuenga Pass, 341; the Mesa, 39; San Gabriel, 39; San Pascual, 38, 39
Battle of Flowers, 135
Baylis, Dr. J, N., 292
Beaches: California State, 386; Capistrano, 350; El Morro, 365; Emerald Bay, 365; Hermosa, 357; Huntington, 361; Laguna, 365; Las Flores, 385; Las Tunas, 385; Long Beach, 238-42, 101; Newport-Balboa, 361, 13, 140; Ocean Park, 266;

Redondo, 357; Santa Monica, 276; 273; Seal, 359; Sunset, 360; Topanga, 384.
Beale, Lieutenant Edward F., 314, 38
Bear Flag Republic, 3
Bear Flag Revolt, 36
Bear Valley Mutual Water Company, 294
Beard House, 108
Bee Rock, 180
Beethoven Statue, 157
Behymer, L. E., 114
Belasco Theatre, 130
Bell, Major Horace, 118, 113, 119, 217
Belvedere Gardens, 340
Bernheimer Oriental Gardens, 386
Bethlehem Shipbuilding, 225
Beverly Hills, 197-205, 6, 11
Beverly Hills Hotel, 205
Beverly Hills Theatre, 132
Beverly-Wilshire Hotel, 201
Bidwell, John, 34
Big Bear City, 294
Big Bear Lake, 293, 141
Big Pines, 401, 141
Biltmore Hotel, 158
Biltmore Theatre, 131
Birdsall, Reverend Elias, 70
Bixby, John W., 251, 52
Bixby, Jotham, 241, 253
Bixby, Llewellyn, 253
Blondeau Tavern, 229
Board of Education, 63-64, 66, 85
Board of Supervisors, 63
Boggs, Francis, 73
Boricia, Diego de, 345
Botanical Gardens, 279
Boulder Canyon Project Act, 52
Boulder Dam, 52, 53
Bouquet Canyon, 394
Bowron, Mayor Fletcher, 160
Boxing, 139
Boyle Heights, 169
Brand, Leslie C., 392, 208
Brea Canyon, 345
Breakwaters: Santa Monica, 266; San Pedro, 216, 222
Brier, Reverend James W., 68
Brown Derby Cafe No. 1, 182
Brown, F. E., 311
Brown, John (Lean John), 36-37
Buena Park, 337
Building code, Los Angeles County, 58
Bullock's-Wilshire, 182
Burbank Theatre, 130
Burroughs, Edgar Rice, 381, 122
Burruel Point, 337
Bustamente, Francisco, 62
Butterfield Stage Line, 334

Caballeria Collection of Paintings, 172
Cabrillo, Juan Rodriguez, 25, 46, 220, 367
Cahuenga Indians, 180
Cahuenga Pass, 228, 11
Cahuenga Treaty, 208
Cajalco Dam and Reservoir, 334
Cajon Post Office, 402
Calabasas, 382
Calavo Growers packing house, 166
California Art Club, 108, 231
California Battalion, 36-39
California current, 15
California Fruit Growers Exchange, 49-50, 46
California Institute of Technology, 260-61, 13, 66
California Walnut Growers Association, 163
Camels, 314
Camera Obscura, Santa Monica, 271
Camp of Crespi-Portola, 26
Camp Rincon, 304
Camp Seeley, 292-93
Camphor Tree, 307
Campo de Cahuenga, 380
Canals, Venice, 354
Canfield, Charles A., 45
Carmelita Garden, 262
Carrillo, Jose Antonio, 36, 39, 341
Carrillo, Ramon, 37
Carrillo's gun, 37
Carson, Christopher (Kit), 38
Carthay Center Parkway, 185
Carthay Circle Theatre, 185
Casa Adobe de San Rafael, 213
Casa la Golondrina, 154
Castellammare, 386
Castro, Jose Maria, 34, 35
Cathedral Canyon, 317
Cathedral Oak marker, 296
Catholic Welfare Bureau, 72
Central Casting, 84-85
Central manufacturing district, 57
Cerritos Channel, 216, 224, 250
Chaffey, George B. and W. B., 309
Chamber of Commerce, Los Angeles, 44-45, 49-50, 55
Chandler, Harry, 99
Channel Islands, 11
Chaparral, 19
Chaplin, Charles, 75, 76
Chapman, A. B., 347
Chapman, Joseph, 34
Charitable organizations, 72
Chavez, Julian, 174
Chavez Ravine, 174
Cherry Festival, Beaumont, 313
Chester Place, 188-89
Chicken ranching, 396

China City, 154
Chinchilla Farm, 355
Chinese, 3, 156; massacre, 41; Pasadena, 257; temples, 70
Christian Oak, 307
Christmas Tree Lane, 263-64
Chrysler Motors plant, 167
Churches: African Methodist, 70; All Saints Episcopal, Beverly Hills, 200; All Saints Episcopal, Pasadena, 258; Angelus Temple, 176-77, 71, 72; B'nai B'rith Temple, 183, 69, 126; Chinese Temple, 70; Christ Faith Mission, 395; Church of Our Lady, the Queen of the Angels, 152, 67; Church of the German Baptist Brethren, 62, 283; Church of the Good Shepherd, Beverly Hills, 200; Church of the Holy Virgin Mary (Russian Orthodox), 177-78; Church of the Open Door, 159; Daisha Mission (Buddhist), 156; First Church of Christ Scientist, Beverly Hills, 201; Friends Church, Whittier, 341; Hongwanji Buddhist Temple (Japanese), 157; Immanuel Presbyterian, 182; Japanese, 70; Kong Chew Buddhist Temple, 156; Little Church of the Flowers, 210; Our Lady of Lourdes, 170; Our Lady of the Angels, 105; Peoples Independent Church of Christ, 72; Plaza Church, 68, 152; Reformed New Testament Church, 68; Saint Francis Chapel, 330; Second Church of Christ Scientist, 189, 109; St. Anne's Chapel, Santa Monica, 272; St. Athanasius (Episcopalian), 70; St. Elizabeth, Pasadena, 264; St. James Episcopal, South Pasadena, 109; St. John's Episcopal, 188; St. Vibiana's Cathedral, 150-51, 68; St. Vincent de Paul, 188; Wee Kirk o' the Heather, 210; Westminster Presbyterian, Pasadena, 264; Wilshire Boulevard Christian, 182; Wilshire Methodist, 183; Wilshire Boulevard Temple Synagogue, 110
Cities, Towns and Villages: Alberhill, 333; Alhambra, 322; Anaheim, 346, 337; Arcadia, 281; Azusa, 282; Baldwin Park, 306; Banning, 313-14; Bassett, 325; Beaumont, 313; Belvedere Gardens, 340; Beverly, 198; Beverly Hills, 197-205, 6, 11; Big Bear City, 294; Brea, 345; Buena Park, 337; Burbank, 388-96; Cabazon, 315; Canoga Park, 381-82; Cathedral City, 317; Chatsworth, 382; Chino, 328; Claremont, 283-84, 66; Colton, 311; Compton,

58-59; Corona, 335; Covina, 306; Crestline Village, 292; Cucamonga, 285; Culver City, 6, 351-53; Dana Point, 366; Devore, 402; Doheny Park, 366, 350; Downey, 338; Duarte, 282; Edendale, 73; El Modena, 347; El Monte, 324-25, 69; El Segundo, 356-57; Elsinore, 333; El Toro, 347; Encino, 381; Flintridge, 296; Fontana, 286; Fullerton, 345; Girard, 381; Glendale, 387; Glendora, 282; Goodhope, 332; Guasti, 309; Hemet, 331-32, 120; Highland Park, 121; Hollywood, 227-37, 10; Huntington Beach, 361; Indian Wells, 317; Indio, 321; Inglewood, 355-56; Irvine, 348; La Canada, 296; Laguna Beach, 365-66; La Habra, 344; Lake Arrowhead Village, 293; La Verne, 283; Little Rock, 399; Long Beach, 238-53, 58, 60; Los Nietos, 338; Manhattan Beach, 357; Mira Loma, 328; Monrovia, 281; Monterey Park, 306; Newhall, 393; Newport Beach, 361; North Hollywood, 380; Norwalk, 337; Ocean Park, 266; Olinda, 345; Olive, 336; Ontario, 308-09, 328; Orange, 346-47; Palmdale, 397, 20; Palms, 353; Palm Springs, 316; Pasadena, 254-64, 6, 138, 139; Pearblossom, 399; Perris, 331; Pico, 340; Pine Knot, 294; Playa del Rey, 354-55; Pomona, 307, 328; Prado, 336; Puente, 326; Redlands, 311-12; Rialto, 286; Riverside, 329-31; Roscoe, 391; Rosemead, 324; San Bernardino, 286-92, 402; San Dimas, 282-83; San Fernando, 391-92, 6, 35; San Gabriel, 322-23, 130; San Jacinto, 332; San Juan Capistrano, 349; San Marino, 277-79, 22; San Pedro, 214-26, 6, 37, 38, 47, 48; Santa Ana, 347-48; Santa Monica, 265-73, 387, 6; Saugus, 394; Seal Beach, 359; Serra, 350; Sherman Oaks, 381; Sierra Madre, 281; Signal mill, 242-45; South Gate, 338; South Pasadena, 295; Spadra, 327; Tarzana, 381; Torrence, 358; Truxton, 267; Tustin, 348; Universal City, 380, 6; Upland, 284-85; Valyermo, 399; Van Nuys, 380-81; Venice, 354-55, 140; Vernon, 57; Vista del Mar, 357; Walnut, 326; West Covina, 306; Westwood Village, 204, 63; Whittier, 341; Wilmington, 223-26, 6, 47-48, 215, 217
City Halls: Beverly Hills, 201, 198; Los Angeles, 145, 103; Pasadena,

258; San Pedro, 219; Santa Monica, 271
City Water Company, 51
Civic Auditorium, Pasadena, 258
Civic Centers: Beverly Hills, 201; Long Beach, 245; Los Angeles, 145, 110; Pasadena, 257-58; San Pedro, 219
Claremont, 283-84, 66
Clark, William A., Jr., 113
Cleveland National Forest, 347
Clifton Cafeteria, 160
Climate, 14
Clinton, Clifford E., 160
Coachella Valley, 315-21
Coast Guard Pier, 219-20
Coca-Cola bottling plant, 164
Coffee products, 162
Coldwater Canyon, 333
Coliseum War Memorial, 55
Colorado Lagoon, Long Beach, 251
Colorado River, 52
Colorado-Street Bridge, 262
Columbia Square, 232
Columbia Steel, 358
Condor, California, 298
Congress of Industrial Organizations, 218
Congress, U.S.S., 38
Consolidated Steel, 167
Corner Oak, 295-96
Coronel Collection, California relics, 192
Coronel, Don Antonio F., 120
Corrigan, Douglas, 212
Cota, Dona Rafaela, 241
Craig shipbuilding plant, Long Beach, 250
Crespi, Fray Juan, 26, 117, 266
Cronenwett Tropical Plantation, 281
Crosby, Bing, 116
Crystal Lake, 304-05, 11, 302
Cucamonga Water Company, 286
Cucamonga Winery, 285
Cudahy Packing, 162
Culver City, 351-53, 6
Curtiss-Wright Technical Institute, 212
Custom House and Post Office, San Pedro, 219
Cyane, U.S.S., 36

Dalton, Henry, 282
Dana, Richard Henry, 366, 46, 117-18
Danube, brig, 217
Date culture, 317-21
Deadman's Island, 37
Deep-sea fishing, 140-41
De Mille, Cecil B., 79, 75
Department of Recreation, Camps and Playgrounds, 304

Devil's Gate Dam, 263
Devil's Punch Bowl, 400
Disney, Walt, 389-90, 77-78, 127, 178
Doheny, Edward L., 45, 176, 188-89, 190, 345, 350
Doheny Memorial, 190, 212
Dominguez Hills, 11
Dominguez, Juan Jose, 28
Doty, Captain John, 393
Douglas Aircraft, 272-73, 109, 266, 356
Downey, John G., 338
Downtown Section, 56
Drum Barracks, 223
Drunkard, 132
Dumetz, Padre Francisco, 392

Earl Carroll Theatre-Restaurant, 232
Earthquakes: Long Beach, 242, 58, 101; Los Angeles, 58, 13; San Juan Capistrano Mission, 350
Easter Sunrise services, 329
Echeandia, Governor, 61
Education: 62-66 (*see* Schools)
Egyptian Theatre, 233
El Camino Real, 26, 339
El Camino Watering Trough, 154
El Capitan Theatre, 131
Eldoradoville, site of, 303
Elizabeth Lake, 11
El Modena, 347
El Monte, 69
"Elopement Bell," 152
El Paseo de los Angeles, 153
Elysian Hills, 11
Emerald Bay, 365
EPIC Movement, 59
Escondido Canyon, 395
Exhibit Hall, 301
Exposition Park, 191-93, 137
Express, Los Angeles, 98

Fages, Governor Pedro, 240, 28, 169, 338, 402
Fairbanks, Douglas, 76
Fauna, 15-19
Feast of the Angels, 135
Federal Art Project (W.P.A.), 181, 236
Federal Building, 148
Federal Housing Projects, 110
Federal Music Project (W.P.A.), 115-16
Federation of Jewish Welfare Organizations, 72
Feliz, Corporal Vincent, 28
Figueroa, Governor Jose, 32, 61, 345
Figueroa Playhouse, 131
Figueroa, Ramon, 189
Firestone, tire and rubber, 57, 338
Fish Harbor, 225, 216
Fishing and canning, 225

Fishing, sport, 370-72
Flaco, Juan, 36
Flora, 19-23
Flores, Captain Jose Maria, 36-39, 295, 380
Football, 138-39
Ford Motor assembly plant, 224
Forest Lawn Memorial Park, 209
Fort Hill, 36
Fortieth U. S. Army Division, 54, 55
Fort MacArthur Reservation, 220, 222
Fort Moore, 39
Fort Moore Place, 36
Forty-niner Statue, 185
Fossils, 13-14, 183-84
Fox, William, 77
Franciscan Fathers, 112
Frank Wiggins Trade School, 65
Fremont Gate, 174
Fremont, Lieutenant - Colonel John Charles, 39, 35-36, 174, 208, 295, 380, 392
Fremont Pass, 392, 11

Gabrielino Indians, 373, 24
Game Conservation, 15
Gant, John, 34
Garces, Francisco, 402
Garland, Hamlin, 122
Gaslight, first in Los Angeles, 41
Geology: Archean Period, 12; Jurassic Period, 12; La Brea Pits, 183-84, 26, 181; Miocene Epoch, 13-14; Pleistocene Epoch, 13; Pliocene Epoch, 13-14; Quarternary Period, 12; Tertiary Period, 12
Georges Gap, 298
Gillespie, Lieutenant Archibald H., 36-37
Gilmore Field, 140
Glendale, 206-13
Glendale Civic Auditorium, 213
Glendale *Encinal,* 208
Glendora, 282
Glen Ivy Hot Springs, 333
Gold, first discovery of, 303
Golden State Dairy, 164
Goldwyn, Samuel, 75, 77, 79
Goodhope Mine, 332
Goodrich, tire and rubber, 57
Goodwill Industries, 72
Goodyear, tire and rubber, 168, 57
Governor Mine, 395
Grand Opera House, 128
Grauman's Chinese Theatre, 233
Greek Theatre, 179
Griffith, Colonel Griffith J., 179
Griffith, David Wark, 75, 76
Griffith Observatory and Planetarium, 179
Griffith Park, 178-79, 126

Grunion, 18-19
Guasti Italian vineyard, 309

Hagenbeck-Wallace Circus Quarters, 306
Haiwee Reservoir, 51
Hall of Justice, Los Angeles, 148-49
Hall of Records, Los Angeles, 149, 126
Hancock, George Alan, 184
Hancock, Major Henry, 198
Hangman's Tree, 382
Haraszthy, Count Augustin, 311
Harbor, The: San Pedro and Wilmington, 214-26
Harrison Art Collection, 192
Hart, William S., 393
Hazard's Pavilion, 139, 129
Headlee's Mountain Club, 304
Hebrew Benevolent Society, 72
Hemet Reservoir, 333
Heroic School, 124
Highland Springs, 313
Historic Houses: Adobe los Alamitos, Long Beach, 251-52; Adobe los Cerritos, Long Beach, 252; Alvarado Adobe, Pomona, 308; Amestoy Adobe, 381; Avila Adobe, 153; Casa Adobe de San Rafael, 213; Casa de Adobe, 172; Casa la Golondrina, 154; Centinela Adobe, 355; Church of Our Lady the Queen of the Angels, 152; Downey Adobe, 338; El Alisal, 173, 121; Figueroa Adobe, 189; Flores Adobe, 295; General Banning House, 223; Government House, 105; Grapevine Adobe, San Gabriel, 324; Hugo Reid Adobe, 280; La Casa del Gobornador Pio Pico, 340-41; La-Casa Vieja de Lopez, San Gabriel, 324; Las Tunas Adobe, San Gabriel, 324; Lugo House, 153; May Place, San Gabriel, 324; Miguel Leonis Adobe, 382; Natick Hotel, 150; Palomares Tavern Adobe, Pomona, 308; Phillips House, 327; Pico Adobe, 391; Pico House, 151, 105; Pioneer House, 346; Plaza Church, 152; Temple Adobe, 69; Verdugo Adobe, Glendale, 213; Vigare Adobe, San Gabriel, 324; Workman Homestead, 325
Hollywood, 227-37, 73
Hollywood American Legion Stadium, 139
Hollywood Bowl, 114, 132, 236
Hollywood Cemetery, 237
Hollywood Hills, 131
Hollywood Park, 138, 356
Hooverville, 303

Horse-Racing Board, 137
Horticulture: Avocados, 342-44; Citrus, 49, 288-92, 355; first navel orange grove, 330; grape growing, 309-12, 346; Hart Citron Experimental Ranch, 344; orange groves, 19, 23, 289-91; parent navel orange tree, 330; State Experimental Citrus Station, 331; Sunny Hills Citrus Ranch, 345
Hospitals: Arrowhead Hot Springs, 292; Cedars of Lebanon, 72; County, 109; Los Angeles General, 170; Los Angeles Orthopaedic, 187-88; Norwalk State, 337; Orange County, 346; Osteopathic, 170
Hughes, Rupert, 122
Hunt, Captain Jefferson, 286
Huntington Beach oil field, 57
Huntington, Collis P., 47, 48
Huntington Gardens, 22
Huntington, Henry E., 278-79
Huntington Hotel, 261
Huntington Library and Art Gallery, San Marino, 278-79

I. Magnin Building, 182
Immigration Station, 219
Independence Day, first celebration, 39
Indiana Colony, 41, 256
Indian Village, 332
Indians, 124, 40, 61; Agua Caliente, 316; artifacts, 373, 174; Cahuenga, 180; Cahuilla, 329; caves, 317; early music, 111-12; exhibits, 173; Gabrielino, 373, 24; Glidden Museum, 373; Guachama Village, 286; Indian Museum, 334; legends, 292; Mococahuenga, 180; Palm Springs Reservation, 317; Piute, 286; Santa Catalina Island, 367; Serrano, 329; Shoshone, 285, 367; Soboba Reservation, 332; Tahquitz Bowl, 316-17; Yang-na, 24-25, 28, 40, 145, 266
Inglewood, 355-56
Inglewood Fault, 13
Inglewood Park Cemetery, 356
Interstate Aircraft factory, 356
Iowa Picnic, Long Beach, 250, 240
Irvine Ranch, 348

Jackson, Helen Hunt, 119-20, 131, 332
Jackson Lake, 400, 11
Japanese Gardens, 236
Japanese Quarter, 156
Jayhawkers, 393, 68
Jedediah Strong Smith boulder, 185
Jeffries, James J., 139, 135
Johnson, Jack, 139
Johnston, General Albert Sidney, 41

Jones, Commodore, 112
Jones, Senator John P., 47, 267
Joshua Tree National Monument, 398
Joshua trees, 397, 398

Kearney, General Stephen W., 38-39
Kellogg Stock Farm, 307
Ketchel, Stanley, 139

La Brea Pits, 183-84, 13, 26, 181, 192
La Canada, 296
La Crescenta Valley, 58
Ladybug Canyon, 298
Laemmle, Carl, 75, 77, 380
Lakes: Arrowhead, 141, 293; Big Bear, 293, 141; Crystal, 304-05, 11, 302; Elizabeth, 11; Elsinore, 333; Jackson, 411, 11; Malibu, 383; Quail, 11
La Miniatura, 263
Last Supper Window, 210
Lasuen, Padre Fermin, 392
Lean John, 36, 37
Lelia Byrd, ship, 46, 217
Libraries: A. K. Smiley, Redlands, 312; Central Public, 158-59, 109, 129; Edward L. Doheny, Jr., 190; Huntington Library and Art Gallery, 278-79; Long Beach, 248, 245; Outdoors, 8; Pasadena, 258; Santa Monica, 270, 126
Lincoln Monument, Long Beach, 248
Lion Farm, 325
Literature, 117-128
Little Rock Creek, 399
Little Theater movement, 130
Little Tokio, 156
Lockheed Aircraft, 389
Long Beach, 238-53, 6, 11, 13, 58, 60, 101, 140; municipal auditorium, 249; municipal market, 245; Navy Landing, 248
Lopez, Don Francisco, 394
Los Angeles: Agricultural wealth, 57; area, 10; assessed valuation, 58; bank debits, 58; boom, (1885-87) 42-45, (1920's) 55, 108; building figures, 55; Bureau of Power and Light, 359-60; capitulation to Fremont, 39; Chamber of Commerce, 54-55, 44, 49-50, 135; City Planning Commission, 110; county building code, 58; County Fair, 308; County Museum, 191; drought, 41; founding, 27-28; Immigration and Land Co-operative Association, 307; incorporation of, 40
Love Joy Buttes, 396
Lower Pine Canyon, 302
Loyola University, 62, 66
Lugo, Antonio, 338, 286

Lugonia settlement, 312
Lummis, Charles F., 120-21, 112-13, 173, 174

MacArthur, General Douglas, 220
MacKay Radio and Telegraph Company, 101
Madonna of the Trails Monument, 285
Mahayana Buddhists, 156
Major Disaster Emergency Council, 101
Malibu Lake, 383
Manitou Club, 139
March Field, 331
Marine Course, Ballona Creek, 353
Marine Exchange, lookout station, 219
Marine Meteorological Observatory, 225
Massacre Canyon, 332
Mausoleum, Forest Lawn, 210
Mayer, Louis B., 352
Maywood Glass factory, 166
McAdoo, William Gibbs, 54
McGroarty, John Steven, 121
McKinley, James, 34
McPherson, Aimee Semple, 176-77, 71, 101, 333
Merced Theatre, 128
Mervine, Captain William, 37
Metropolitan Water District of Southern California, 52, 302, 315
Mexicans, 3, 36-37, 49, 117; Boyle Heights, 169; families, 3; folk songs, 112; participation in war, 54; players, 284
Mexican War, 35
Mexico, 39, 3, 35
Micheltorena, Governor Manuel, 34-35, 61
Miles Memorial Playhouse, 270
Millard House, 108
Millikan, Dr. Robert A., 260
Million-Dollar Bath House, Long Beach, 248
Miniature Landscape and Fish Pool, 155
Mint Canyon, 394, 11
Mission Inn, 330
Mission Play, 130
Missions: San Fernando, 392, 30, 104, 207-08; San Gabriel Arcangel, 322-24, 23, 27, 61, 104, 208, 277; San Juan Capistrano, 349-50; secularization of, 32
Mockingbird Canyon, 334
Modjeska, Helene, 346, 347, 361
Mojave Desert, 396-97, 10
Monrovia, 281
Montebello Hills, 11, 340

Moore, Captain Benjamin D., 39
Mormon legend, 292
Mormons, 286-87
Morris Dam, 302
Motion Pictures, 73-97, 6, 60; Biograph, 74, 75, 76; Bison, 73; Central Casting office, 232; Columbia, 77, 232, 390-91; Disney, Walt, 389-90, 77-78, 127, 178; Edison, Thomas Alva, 74; Essanay, 74; Famous Players, 75, 353; film stars, 199; first motion picture, 74; first studio, 73; first talking film, 77; Goldwyn, 236, 352-53; Horsley brothers, 229; Ince, 351-52; Independent Motion-Picture Company, 75; Kalem, 74, 351; Keystone, 73; Loew, Marcus, 353; Lubin, 74; Making a Movie, 78-97; Malibu Beach colony, 386; Mayer, Louis B., 352-53; Melies, 74; Metro, 77, 352-53; Metro-Goldwyn-Mayer, 352-53, 77; Monogram, 394; Nestor, 229, 74; Paramount, 237, 77, 383; Patents Company, 74, 75; Pathe, 74; Producers Association, 77; Producers and Distributors of America, Inc., 81-82, 78; properties, 87; Republic, 380; RKO, 237, 77; Roach, 352; Rolin, 352; Rubin, J. R., 353; Selig, 74; Selznick, 352; Thalberg, Irving, 353; Triangle, 351; Twentieth-Century Fox, 201-04, 77; United Artists, 76-77; Universal, 77, 352, 380; Vitagraph, 74; Warner Brothers-First National, 77; 391; Zukor, Adolph, 353
Motor vehicles, 59
Mountain Home, 395
Mountains: Baden-Powell, Mount, 10; Black Jack Peak, 367, 11; Box Springs, 331; Brown, 297; Buzzard's Peak, 307; Condor Peak, 298; Elsinore, 333; Iron, 298; Josephine Mount, 298; Lukens, Mount, 297; Orizaba, 367, 11; Rubidoux, Mount, 329; San Antonio, Mount ("Old Baldy"), 298, 10, 297; San Bernardino, 313; Sandstone Peak, 10; San Gabriel, 296, 10-11, 14, 19, 302, 399; San Gorgonio, 313, 13; San Jacinto, 332-33; San Jacinto, Mount, 331; Santa Ana, 331, 333; Santa Monica, 384, 10-11, 14, 172; Santa Rosa, 317; Santa Susana, 392, 10-11; Sierra Nevada, 12-13; Slover, 311; Steele Peak, 332; Strawberry Peak, 298; Table Mountain, 400; Verdugo, 207; Wilson, Mount, 298-301
Mulholland, William, 51, 52

Municipal Art Commission, Los Angeles, 125
Municipal Water Bureau, 51
Museums: Antelope Valley Indian, 399; Anthropology Hall, 192; Bowers Memorial, 348; Coronel Collection, 192; Glidden Indian, 373; Huntington Art Gallery, 278-79, 125; Indian, Alberhill, 334; Los Angeles Museum of History, Science and Art, 191, 92, 13, 125, 184; Lyon Pony Express, 279-80; Pioneer House, 346; Rumsey Indian, 329-30; Southwest, 173, 113, 125, 174
Music, 111-17

Naples, 251
National Broadcasting studios, 232, 99
National Forest, first, 296-97
National Guard, State Armory, 191
Navy: 248-49, 12, 55, 174-75, 215-16, 219, 224, 239, 240
Neve, Governor Felipe de, 27, 50, 151, 152
New Chinatown, 154-55
Newhall Pass, 393
Newmark, Harris, 280
Newmark, Joseph P., 69
Newport Bay, 361
New San Pedro, 217
Nichols, Mayor John G., 69
Nieto, Dona Manuela, 241
Nieto, Don Juan Jose, 241
Nieto, Jose Manuel, 240, 338, 345
Night clubs, 142
Ninety-first Division, U. S. Army, 54-55
Nino Canyon Lookout, 297
Normal school, first, 61
North American Aviation factory, 356
North Fork Canyon, 304, 302

Oak of the Golden Legend, 394
Observation Balcony, Los Angeles City Hall, 148
Occidental College, 172, 62, 66
Ocean Park, 273, 140, 266
Oil: (see Petroleum) 40
Old Chinatown, 155
Old Long Beach Cemetery, 252
Old Salt Road, 355
Olive View Sanitarium, 391
Olvera, Augustine, 153
Olvera Street, 153
Olympic Auditorium, 139
Olympic Games, 136-37, 192
Olympic Marine Stadium, Long Beach, 251
Orange, 346-47

Oranges: (see Citrus)
Orange Carnival, 135
Orange County Courthouse, 348
Orange Show, National, 287-88
Orpheus Club, 115
Ostrich Farm, 171
Otis Art Institute, 181, 65
Otis, General Harrison Gray, 48, 181
Outlook, Santa Monica, 267
Out West, magazine, 121
Owens River, 51

Pacific Coast Conference, 138
Pacific Colony, 327
Pacific Electric Railway, 208, 241
Pacific Land Company, 345
Pacific Light and Power, 305
Palm Canyon, 317
Palmdale, 20
Palomares, Ignacio, 283, 308
Palos Verdes, 358, 140, 216
Palos Verdes Hills, 11, 216
Pan-American Petroleum, 17
Parasol library stations, 8
Parks: Arrowhead, 292; Arroyo Seco, Pasadena, 171, 173; Azusa City, 282; Banning, Wilmington, 223; Barnsdall, 231; Baylis Picnic Grounds, San Bernardino, 293; Beverly Gardens, Beverly Hills, 200; Bixby, Long Beach, 250-51, 240; Brand, Glendale, 213, 392; Brookside, Pasadena, 263, 171; Busch Gardens, Pasadena, 262; Cabrillo Beach, San Pedro, 220-22; Carmelita Garden, 262; Centinela, 356; Children's Pleasure Park, Venice, 354; De Longpre, Hollywood, 233; Doheny State, Laguna Beach, 366; Douglas, Santa Monica, 272; Echo, 176; Elysian, 174, 26; Exposition, 191, 137; Ganesha, Pomona, 308; Griffith, 178; Hancock, 183-84, 26, 192; Hollenbeck, 169; Irvine, Orange, 347; Lafayette, 181; Lincoln, Long Beach, 245; Lincoln, Los Angeles, 171-72; Lincoln, Santa Monica, 270; Municipal, Beverly Hills, 205; North Hollywood, 380; Pacific, Long Beach, 241; Palisades, Santa Monica, 271, 266; Perris Hill, 287; Pershing Square, 157; Pioneers, San Bernardino, 287; Point Fermin, San Pedro, 222; Rancho Santa Ana Botanic Gardens, 336; Recreation, Long Beach, 251; Reseda, 381; San Antonio, Upland, 285; San Dimas Canyon, 283; San Marino City, 278; Smiley, Redlands, 312; State, Long Beach. 251; Sycamore Grove, 171, 173; Tapia

County, 383; Tournament, Pasadena, 261; Victory-Van Owen, Van Nuys, 381; Westlake, 181
Pasadena, 254-64, 138, 139
Pasadena Academy of Fine Arts, 125
Pasadena and Mount Wilson Toll Road, 299
Pasadena Community Playhouse, 258-60, 130, 132
Paso de Bartolo, 39
Pattie, James O., 32
Penitentiary, Federal Regional, 225-26
Perez, Jose, 295
Perris Valley, 331
Pershing Square, 157
Pet Cemetery, 383
Petroleum, 12, 45, 46; Brea Canyon, 345; Brea-Olinda, 243, 345; Coyote Hills, 345; deposits, oil, 14; Doheny, Edward L., 176; drilling in Los Angeles County, 243-45; El Segundo, 357; first oil well, 45; gas, manufacturing of, 345; Huntington Beach, 361; Los Angeles Pioneer Oil Company, 337; Montebello Hills, 340; Newhall-Ventura, 392, 45; ocean drilling, 243; oil discovered in Los Angeles, 45; old Los Angeles, 176; Olinda, 345; Pioneers Petroleum Society of California, 393; production, 243-45, 46, 57; Puente Hills, 345; refinery, Newhall, 57, 393; Republic Petroleum, 357; Santa Fe Springs, 337-38; Seal Beach, 359; Signal Hill discovery, 242-43; Standard Oil pier, Vista Del Mar, 357; Standard Oil refinery, 356; Standard Oil tankers, 357; storage tanks, Vista Del Mar, 357; Union Oil, 337-38; Venice-Playa Del Rey, 354; Wilmington, 224; Wilshire Oil, 338
Philharmonic Auditorium, 157, 129
Philharmonic Orchestra, 113-14
Pickfair, 199
Pickford, Mary, 75, 76, 237
Pico Canyon, 393
Pico, General Andres, 36, 39, 208, 344, 380
Pico, Pio, 34-35, 151, 172, 340-41, 345
Pike, the, Long Beach, 248, 239
Pilgrimage Play, 132
Pine Flats, 304
Pine Knot, 294
Pioneers Petroleum Society of California, 393
Piute Indians, 286
Placerita Canyon, 394
Plaza, 151, 145
Plaza Church, 152
Poet's Cabin, 299

Point Fermin, 11, 216
Pomona College, 284, 62, 66, 126
Pools of Santa Monica, 266
Population: Los Angeles, 3, 29, 31, 33, 40, 41, 45, 49, 51, 55
Porcupine, newspaper, 119
Port of Los Angeles, 48
Portola, Captain Gaspar D., 26, 46, 174
Portola-Crespi Monument, 174
Portola Expedition, 337
"Poverty Row," 80, 77
Production for Use, 59
Prometheus Statue, 181
Providence Land, Water and Development Company, 389
Pryor, Nathaniel, 34
Public Works Administration, 110
Puddingstone Dam, 283
Pueblo of Los Angeles, 169
Puente Hills, 11, 12, 325, 341, 342, 345

Quail Lake, 11
Quest for Water, 50-53

Rabbit Experimental Station, U.S., 286
Radio and Radio Stations, 99-102; KECA, 99, 102; KEHE, 99; KFAC, 101; KFI, 98-99, 102; KFOX, 99, 101; KFSG, 101, 177; KFVD, 101; KFWB, 99-100; KGER, 101; KGFJ, 101; KHJ, 98-99, 102; KMPC, 101; KMTR, 101; KNX, 98, 99; KPPC, 254; KRKD, 101; Aimee Semple McPherson, 101; American Federation of Radio Artists, 100; Blue Network, 99; California Radio System, 99; Columbia Broadcasting System, 99, 109; Don Lee Chain, 99, 102; Mackay Radio and Telegraph Company, 101; Mutual Network, 99, 100; National Broadcasting Company, 232, 99; National Guard, 180; radio-newspaper "war," 101; RCA Communications, Inc., 101; RCA Marine Corporation, 101; Red Network, 99; television, 102; University of California, 101; University of Southern California, 101
Railroads: First in Los Angeles, 41; Los Angeles and Independence, 267; Los Angeles and Salt Lake, 257; Los Angeles and San Gabriel Valley, 257; Los Angeles and San Pedro, 47; Los Angeles-Santa Monica, 47; rate war, 43; Sante Fe (Atchison, Topeka and Santa Fe), 134, 13, 43, 281, 283; Southern Pacific, 42, 43, 50, 134, 208, 218, 347-48; Union Pacific, 155, 311

Rainbow Pier, Long Beach, 249-50
Ramona, 119-20, 332
Ramona Pageant, 332
Ranches: Aguaje de la Centinela, 355; Ashcroft, 336; Azusa de Duarte, 282; Chino, 37, 328; Darling, 399; De la Puente, 325; Dominguez, 28; El Encino, 381; El Escorpion, 382; El Rincon de San Pascual, 277; Garfias, 322; Jurupa, 36, 329; La Brea, 13, 184; La Canada, 296; La Providencia, 380, 389; Las Tunas, 324; Las Virgenes, 36; Los Alamitos, 241, 252; Los Cerritos, 241; Los Coyotes, 345; Los Feliz, 178; Los Nietos, 338; Malibu, 385; Paso de Bartolo, 340; Rodeo de Las Aguas, 198; San Antonio, 338, 198, 382; San Bernardino, 38, 286; San Francisquito, 393; San Jose de Abajo, 327; San Jose de Arriba, 307; San Pascual, 38, 256; Sausal Redondo, 355, 357; Sepulveda, 267; Valyermo, 399
Rattlesnake Island, 47
Rebellion of 1846-47 (Los Angeles), 36-39
Red Box Divide, 298
Red Hill, 348
Redlands Bowl, 312
Redlands Canal, 311
Redondo amusement zone, 140
Redondo Beach, 357
Regan Collection of Rembrandt etchings, 192
Religion, 67-72; Angeles Temple, 72; Baptists, 71, 72; Cathedral of St. Vibiana, 68; Christ Faith Mission, 395; Christian Fundamentals League, 67; Christian Science, 70, 71; Church of Christ, 71; Church of the Nazarene, 67; Congregational, 62, 70, 72; Dunkers, 283, 62; Episcopal, 69, 72; evangelism, 67; Four Square Gospel, 71; Hebrew Evangelization Society, 67; Jewish, 71, 72, 69; Jodo Shinshyu Buddhists, 157; Latter-day Saints, 71; Lutheran, 71; Mahayana Buddhists, 156; Methodists, 70, 71, 72; Mormons, 286, 287; Peoples Independent Church of Christ, 72; Presbyterian, 69, 71, 72, 62; Protestant Episcopal, 69, 72, 71; Protestantism, 68, 69; Reformed New Testament Church of the Faith of Jesus Christ, 68; religious plays, 127; Roman Catholic church, 67, 68, 71, 72; Seventh-Day Adventists, 71; Unitarian, 128
Rivers: Los Angeles, 50-53, 11, 47, 239; Mojave, 293; Owens, 51; San

Gabriel, 11, 19, 47, 359; Santa Ana, 337, 361; Santa Clara, 58
Riviera Country Club, 140
Robbins, Thomas, 368
Rogers, Will, 122, 131, 199, 209; Memorial Field, 140
Rose Bowl, 263, 98, 138-39
Rowland, John, 325
Rubidoux, Louis, 329
Running Springs, 293
Ruskin Art Club, 124

Salton Sea, 315
San Andreas Fault, 13, 400
San Bernardino, 286-88, 402
San Bernardino National Forest, 277, 292, 297, 402
San Clemente Island, 12
San Dimas, 282
San Fernando, 391
San Fernando Reservoir, 51
San Fernando Valley, 10, 11, 51, 56, 58, 207
San Francisquito Canyon, 52
San Francisquito Creek, 394
San Gabriel Canyon, 11, 302, 303
San Gabriel Timberland Reserve, 297
San Gabriel Valley, 277
San Gorgonio Pass, 313
San Jose Hills, 11, 12, 307
San Jose Valley, 326
San Marino, 22, 277-79
San Nicolas Island, 12
San Pedro, 214-22, 6, 47
San Pedro Hills, 11, 216
San Pedro Naval Base, 55
San Rafael Hills, 11, 172
Santa Ana, 347-48
Santa Ana Canyon, 336
Santa Anita Park, 297, 137-38
Santa Catalina Island, 367, 223, 11
Santa Fe railway, (Atchison, Topeka and Santa Fe), 134, 13, 43, 281, 283
Santa Monica, 265-73; municipal auditorium, 273; municipal pier, 266, 271
Santa Monica Bay, 266, 10, 11
Santa Monica Canyon, 266
Santiago Dam, 347
Savannah, U.S.S., 37
Schools, Colleges, and Universities, 62-66; Adult Evening College, 65; Berkeley Hall School, 65; Board of Education, 63-64; California Graduate School of Design, Pasadena, 262-63; California Institute of Technology, 260-61, 13, 66; Catholic Girls' School, 66; Chouinard Art Institute, 65; City College, 65; Claremont College, 66, 284; College of Agriculture, U.C.L.A., 331;

County Board of Education, 63; Curtiss-Wright Technical Institute, 212; elementary, 63; enrollment, 63, 65, 66; Federal aid, 64; first normal school, 61; Frank Wiggins Trade School, 65; Harvard School, 65; Immaculate Heart College, 62; John Dewey School, 65; La Verne College, 283, 62; Los Angeles Branch, University of California, 62; Loyola University, 355, 66; Methodist University of Southern California, 62; Occidental College, 172, 62, 66; Otis Art Institute, 181, 65; Pasadena College, 65; Pomona College, 284, 62, 66, 126; private, 63-65; Quaker, 62; Redlands College, 66; school system, 63; Scripps College for Women, 284, 66; Sherman Indian Institute, 330; State Normal School, 204; State Superintendent of Education, 63; St. Vincent's College, 355, 62; teachers, 63; University of California at Los Angeles, 204-05, 63, 66, 101, 138; University of California, Institute of Animal Husbandry, 307; University of Redlands, 312; University of Southern California, 190-91, 62, 66, 101, 138; Whittier College, 341, 62, 65, 66
Sealed Well, the, 382
Sea-level marker, 321
Sea Life, 362-64, 378, 358-59
Sea lions, 378
Sea shells, 365
Secularization of the Missions, 32, 277, 323, 341, 350
Self-help movement, 59
Selig, William, N., 73
Selznick, Lewis J., 76
Seminole Hot Springs, 383-84
Sennett, Mack, 75
Sepulveda, Diego, 37, 286
Serra Chapel, 349
Serra Cross, 329
Serra, Fray Junipero, 349-50; statue, 152
Serano Memorial, 334
Seven Health Waters, 333
Shaler, Captain William, 217, 30, 46, 117
Sherwood Lake, 384
Shipyard, first, 241
Shoestring District, 6, 48
Shrine Civic Auditorium, 189
Sierra Madre, 281
Signal Hill, 238-47
Signal Point, 299
Silver Lake Reservoir, 178
Sinclair, Upton, 59, 122

Sisters of the Immaculate Heart, 62
Slauson, J. S., 338
Small-boat Anchorage, Long Beach, 249
Smith, Jedediah Strong, 285, 402
Smithsonian Institute's solar observatory, 400
Smoke Tree Forest, 317
Smuggling, 30
Snow, 15, 141
Soldiers home, Sawtelle, 266
Southern California Colony Association, 329
Southern California Edison steam plant, 224
Southern Pacific railroad, 42, 43, 50, 134, 208, 218, 347-48
Southwest Museum, 173, 125
Spanish-American War, 48
Spanish and Mexican folk songs, 112
Spanish Artifacts, 174
Spanish War Memorial, 157
Speedway, Venice, 354
Stage Line, Los Angeles-San Pedro, 46-47
Stanton Cactus Gardens, 307
State Armory, 191
State Building, California, 149
State Experimental Citrus Station, 331
State Exposition Building, 191
State Militia, 48-49
State Olympiad Bond Act, 137
State Prison for First Offenders, 328
Stearns, Don Abel, 241, 252, 345
Stendahl Gallery, 182
Stock Exchange, 59; Institute, 160
Stockton, Commodore Robert, 36, 154
St. Bernardine of Sienna, 286
St. James Park, 189
Sunken Rose Garden, 191
Supply Warehouse, 223
Supreme Court, California, 149
Sutter, John, 35
Swallows, San Juan Capistrano, 349
Swimming Stadium, Los Angeles, 193

Tahquitz Bowl, 316-17
Technocrats, 59-60
Tejon Pass, 11
Telescopes, 299-300
Television, 102
Temescal Canyon, 333-34
Temple, John, (Don Juan), 34, 69, 241, 242, 252, 253
Temple Mansion, 325
Tennis, 140
Terminal Island, 224, 216
Theater Alliance, 114
Theater, the, 127
"The Strip," 228

Tibbett, Lawrence, 114
Tijuana, 137
Tile manufacturing, 333
Times, Los Angeles, 149, 99
Toluca, 380
Topanga Canyon, 384, 11, 14, 382
Torrance Tower, 173
Tournament of Roses, 256, 135, 139
Townsend, Dr. Francis E., 240, 60
Townsend Old Age Pension Plan, 240
Triunfo Pass, 11
Tropical Ice Gardens, 204, 140
Tropico, 208
Tully, Jim, 122
Turkey ranching, 396
Tustin, 348
Two Years Before the Mast, 117, 217, 366

Union Air Terminal, 389, 101, 207
Union Hall, 128
Union Oil Company of California, 337-38
Union Pacific railroad, 155, 311
Union Passenger Terminal, Los Angeles, 155
Union Stockyards, Los Angeles, 165
United States Government: Arcadia
Balloon School, 55; Armory, Naval
and Marine Corps Reserve, 174-75;
Breakwater, Los Angeles Harbor,
216, 47, 48, 222; Coast Guard Pier,
219; Customs House and Post Office, San Pedro, 219; Drum Barracks, 223; Federal Building, Los
Angeles, 148; Federal Housing
Projects, 110-11; Federal Regional
Penitentiary, 225-26; First Wing,
G.H.A., Air Force, 331; Fleet Air
Base, 224; Fortieth Army Division,
54-55; Immigration Station, 219;
Lighthouse, 22; Long Beach, 239-
41; March Field, 331; Naval Base,
San Pedro, 55; Navy Landing, 219;
Navy, 248-49, 12, 215-16, 239-40;
Ninety-first Army Division, 54-55;
Palm Springs Indian Reservation,
317; Public Works Administration,
110; Rabbit Experimental Station,
286; Reclamation Service, 52; Reservation, Fort MacArthur, 220,
222; Soboba Indian Reservation,
332; supply warehouse, 223; Veterans' Administrative Facility, 204;
Veterans' Hospital, 391; Weather
Bureau broadcasts, 101
Universal City, 6
University of California at Los Angeles, 204-05, 63, 66, 101, 138
University of Southern California,
190-91, 62, 66, 101, 138

Upland, 284-85
U. S. Army, Pacific Department, 41
Utopian Society, 59

Valentino, Rudolph, 233, 237
Valley Hunt Club, Pasadena, 135
Val Vita Food Products plant, 345-46
Valyermo Camp, 399
Vancouver, Captain George, 46
Vandalia, 37
Van Dine, S. S., 136, 122
Varela, Serbulo, 36-37
Vasquez Rocks, 395
Vasquez, Tiburcio, 395
Venice, 354-55, 140
Verdugo, Corporal Jose, 207-08
Verdugo, Dona Catalina, 213
Verdugo Hills, 11
Verdugo, Jose Maria, 169
Verdugo Recreational Center, 213
Vernon, 57
Veterans' Administrative Facility, 204
Veterans of Foreign Wars, 55
Veterans' Hospital, U. S., 391
Veterans' Memorial Building, Inglewood, 356; Long Beach, 245
Vigilantes, 134, 382
Villa, Senora Rita, 198
Vineyards, Los Angeles, 31, 40; largest in the world, 309
Vittoria, Governor, 341
Vizcaino, Sebastian, 25, 46, 217

Wagon Wheel Monument, 292
Walker Board, 48
Walnuts, 326-27, 23, 57, 163
Wanger, Walter, 78
Warehouse, first in San Pedro, 46
Warner, Jonathan (Don Juan Jose),
34
Watchorn Lincoln Shrine, Redlands,
312
Waterman Canyon, 292
Water Supply, 41, 50-53; Aguaje de
la Centinela, Inglewood, 355; Bear
Valley Mutual Water Company,
294; Big Bear Lake and Dam, 293;
bond issue, first, 51; Boulder Canyon Project Act, 52; Boulder Dam,
52, 53; Cajalco Dam and Reservoir,
334; City Water Company, 51;
Colorado River, 52; Colorado River
Aqueduct, 315; Cucamonga Water
Company, 286; Haiwee Reservoir,
51; irrigation ditches, 19; La Verne
softening plant, 53; Long Beach
Land and Water Company, 241;
Los Angeles Aqueduct, 51-52, 58,
315, 394; Los Angeles River, 51;
Metropolitan Water District of
Southern California, 52-53, 302,

315; Morris Reservoir, 302; Mulholland, William, 51-52; Municipal Water Bureau, 51; Owens River Valley, 51; Parker Dam, 53; Puddingstone Reservoir, 283; Saint Francis Dam, 52, 394; San Fernando Mission, 50; San Fernando Reservoir, 51; San Gabriel Dam, No. 1, 302-03; San Gabriel River, 19; San Jacinto Mountains, 53; Silver Lake Reservoir, 178; water-distributing system, 51; water wheel, 50
Wayside Art Colony, Long Beach, 250
Weapons, Otis collection, 192
Wee Kirk o' the Heather, 210
West Fork Canyon, 304
Westways, magazine, 123
Westwood Village, 204
White, Senator Stephen M., 218, 48
Whiteman, Paul, 116
Whittier College, 341, 62, 65, 66
Williams, Colonel Isaac, 37, 328
Willmore City, 241
Willmore, W. E., 241, 252
Wilmington, 214-26, 6, 47, 48, 314
Wilson, Benjamin D. (Don Benito), 256, 34, 37, 47, 198, 298
Wilson Monument, 299
Wilson (Mount) Observatory, 298-301
Wine making, 309-11, 40
Wineville, 328
Winter Sports, 141
Wisteria Fete, 281
Wolfskill, William, 402
Woman's Symphony Orchestra, 114
Woodwardia Canyon, 298
Workman Family Cemetery, 326

Workman Homestead, 325
Workman, William, 34
Work Projects Administration: Adult Education, 64-65; Art Project, Anaheim, 346; Art Project, Hollywood Bowl, 236; Art Project, Long Beach, 249; Art Project, Los Angeles, 126, 159, 232; Flood-Control Project, Ballona Creek, 353; Music Project, 115-16; *Run Little Chillun,* 116; Symphony Orchestra, 116; Theatre Project, 132; Veterans' Memorial Building, 356
Work Relief, Federal, 59
World Peace Tower, 329
World War, 54
World War Memorial, 158
Wrestling, 139
Wright, Frank Lloyd, 108, 236
Wrightwood, 401
Wrigley Field, 139
Wrigley, William, Jr., 368
Wyvernwood, 164

Yamato Hall, 156
Yang-na, 24-25, 28, 40, 145, 266
Yankee immigrants, 35
Young Men's Christian Association, 72
Young Women's Christian Association, 72

Zalvidea, Padre, 308
Zanja, Madre, 153
Zeiss Planetarium, 180
Zoo, 180
Zukor, Adolph, 75, 77

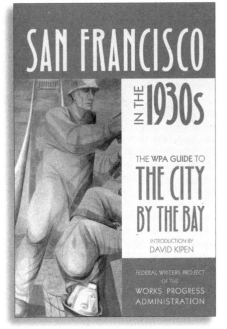

THE FEDERAL WRITERS PROJECT (FWP) of the Works Progress Administration (WPA) not only provided jobs and income to writers during the Depression, it created for America an astounding series of detailed and richly evocative guides, recounting the stories and histories of the 48 states (plus Alaska Territory and Puerto Rico) and many of the country's major cities.

SAN FRANCISCO IN THE 1930S

The WPA Guide to the City by the Bay
Introduction by David Kipen

"San Francisco has no single landmark by which the world may identify it," according to San Francisco in the 1930s, originally published in 1940. This would surely come as a surprise to the millions who know and love the Golden Gate Bridge or the Transamerica Building's pyramid. This invaluable Depression-era guide to San Francisco relates the city's history from the vantage point of the 1930s, describing its culture, and highlighting the important tourist attractions of the time. David Kipen's lively introduction revisits the city's literary heritage—from Bret Harte to Kenneth Rexroth, Jade Snow Wong, and Allen Ginsberg—as well as its most famous landmarks and historic buildings. This rich and evocative volume, resonant with portraits of neighborhoods and districts, allows us to travel back in time and savor the City by the Bay as it used to be.

DAVID KIPEN, former *San Francisco Chronicle* book editor, was for five years Director of Literature at the National Endowment for the Arts.
$24.95 paper   978-0-520-26880-7 (W)

www.ucpress.edu